Burma's Armed Forces

Burma's Armed Forces
Power Without Glory

by
Andrew Selth

Published by Eastbridge Books, an imprint of Camphor Press Ltd
83 Ducie Street, Manchester, M1 2JQ
United Kingdom

www.eastbridgebooks.com

Copyright © 2001 Andrew Selth.
All rights reserved. First edition 2001.
This edition 2017.
23 22 21 20 19 18 17   1 2 3 4 5

ISBN   978-1-910736-77-7 (pbk)
        978-1-910736-78-4 (cloth)

The moral right of the author has been asserted.

Except in the United States of America, this book is sold subject to the condition that it shall not, by way of trade or otherwise, be lent, re-sold, hired out, or otherwise circulated without the publisher's prior consent in any form if binding or cover other than that in which it is published and without a similar condition including this condition being imposed on the subsequent purchaser.

How superior
The tactics of war,
How potent
The weapons!
Without gathering in
The hearts of the people,
Without relying on
The strength of the people,
The sword edge
Will shatter,
The spear
Will bend.

Let-We Thondara (c. 1723-99)

Quoted by Aung San Suu Kyi, in
Freedom From Fear and other writings (1995)

for Pattie

ANDREW SELTH holds degrees in History and International Relations from the Australian National University (ANU), and a Graduate Diploma in Strategic Studies from the Australian Joint Services Staff College. Between 1973 and 1985 he was a member of the Australian Department of Foreign Affairs, and served as a diplomatic officer in Burma, the Republic of Korea and New Zealand. Since 1986 he has been a strategic analyst with the Australian Defence Intelligence Organisation, for the last five years serving as a member of the Senior Executive Service.

In a private academic capacity, Andrew Selth has conducted postgraduate research at ANU and St Antony's College, Oxford. He has twice been granted a Visiting Fellowship at the ANU's Strategic and Defence Studies Centre. He has also published widely on strategic issues and Asian affairs, including two books on international terrorism. His major publications on Burma include *Death of a Hero: The U Thant Disturbances in Burma, December 1974* (Brisbane 1989), *Transforming the Tatmadaw: The Burmese Armed Forces Since 1988* (Canberra, 1996) and *Burma's Secret Military Partners* (Canberra 2000).

Contents

Acknowledgements	ix
Acronyms and Abbreviations	xii
Tables, Figures and Maps	xviii
Glossary	xvix
Foreword	xxii
Introduction	xxv

1. Historical And Strategic Setting   3
    1.1 Burma's Geostrategic Position / 3
    1.2 The Historical Framework / 7
    1.3 International Rivalries Before 1988 / 13
    1.4 The Modern Strategic Environment / 15

2. Defence Policies and Threat Perceptions   28
    2.1 Burma's Defence Policies / 28
    2.2 Domestic Imperatives / 33
    2.3 External Threat Perceptions / 38

3. Tatmadaw Structure and Organisation   48
    3.1 Command and Control / 48
    3.2 Communications / 60
    3.3 Military Computers / 67

4. Recruitment, Training and Doctrine   76
    4.1 Recruitment and Personnel / 76
    4.2 Training and Indoctrination / 82
    4.3 Doctrine and Strategic Concepts / 88

5. Military Intelligence   100
    5.1 Intelligence Before 1988 / 100
    5.2 Intelligence After 1988 / 112
    5.3 Intelligence and Security / 121

6. The Economic Dimension	130
6.1 Burma's Defence Expenditure / 131	
6.2 Burma's Defence Industries / 140	
6.3 The Tatmadaw and the Economy / 145	
7. The Burma Army	155
7.1 The Burma Army Before 1988 / 155	
7.2 The Burma Army After 1988 / 165	
7.3 The New Burma Army / 172	
8. The Burma Navy	184
8.1 The Burma Navy Before 1988 / 184	
8.2 The Burma Navy After 1988 / 191	
8.3 The New Burma Navy / 197	
9. The Burma Air Force	205
9.1 The Burma Air Force Before 1988 / 205	
9.2 The Burma Air Force After 1988 / 212	
9.3 The New Burma Air Force / 221	
10. Burma and Exotic Weapons	233
10.1 Chemical Weapons / 233	
10.2 Biological Weapons / 241	
10.3 Nuclear Weapons / 244	
10.4 Rangoon and Exotic Weapons / 246	
11. The Tatmadaw Today	253
11.1 The Tatmadaw Transformed / 254	
11.2 Challenges to Tatmadaw Unity / 259	
11.3 Burma and Military Rule / 268	
12. The Tatmadaw in a Democracy	275
12.1 Burma's Uncertain Future / 275	
12.2 The Theory / 277	
12.3 The Practice / 284	
12.4 Conclusion / 290	
Appendices	294
1. Burma's Order of Battle / 294	
2. Burma's Defence Expenditure / 313	
Select Bibliography	317
Index	334

Acknowledgements

In one sense, this book has been 25 years in the making. It has its origins in a posting to the Australian Embassy in Rangoon as Third Secretary, between January 1974 and August 1976. This posting was itself prompted in part by descriptions of Burma provided by Geoffrey Fairbairn, a Senior Lecturer in History at the Australian National University (ANU), and himself a Burma-watcher of some note. My time as a diplomatic officer in Rangoon was both professionally stimulating and personally very enjoyable. Unlike most other visitors to the country, who at that time were only granted tourist visas valid for seven days, I had two and a half years in which to explore Burma at my leisure. Through persistent applications to the Foreign Ministry (and a liberal interpretation of the Ministry's strict travel rules), I was able to go to a number of places rarely visited by foreigners. I also made several close Burmese friends, whose guidance and insights would not have been available to the average tourist.

These experiences and personal relationships confirmed in me an abiding interest in Burma which initially focused on its history, society and culture, but later extended to its domestic politics, international relations and strategic affairs. This interest has been manifested in numerous articles and research papers over the years. Some have been published under my own name but, because of various professional constraints, many have appeared under pseudonyms. It was always a matter of regret for me, however, that I did not have the opportunity to follow up these relatively short studies with any in-depth treatment of the subjects which first attracted my attention so long ago. This book is, finally, an exception to that rule.

The genesis of this particular project was a lengthy monograph on the Burmese armed forces written in 1995, while on leave from the Australian Public Service (APS).[1] I am grateful to the ANU's Strategic and Defence Studies Centre (SDSC), and the Australian Defence Department, for the grant of a Visiting Fellowship to undertake that work, and for the opportunity to make a field trip to Southeast Asia to conduct primary research. The SDSC kindly granted me a second Visiting Fellowship in 2000 to continue my studies. Through their invitations to participate in conferences held in Chiang Rai, Washington and Cambridge (Massachusetts) in 1995 and 1996, the Asia Foundation, Open Society Institute and World Peace Foundation made it possible for me to gather additional material. Other conferences, arranged in Washington by the US government in 1998, and a group led by Georgetown University in early 2001, gave me further opportunities to conduct interviews and discuss relevant issues with other members of the Burma studies community. I was also able to make three visits to Burma itself.

I am indebted to all those people, both in Australia and overseas, who have contributed in any way to this study. They are far too numerous to list here, and for various reasons many would prefer not to be cited in person. It is a sad reflection on the state of affairs in Burma today that my friends there, and other Burmese who have helped me with different aspects of this book, do not feel it safe to be mentioned by name. There are some people, however, who I can identify and to whom special consideration is due. David Steinberg, Bertil Lintner, Martin Smith and Mary Callahan all shared their considerable knowledge of Burma with characteristic generosity. David Steinberg in particular was a pillar of support throughout the writing of this book. Over the years, other Burma-watchers have been helpful in different ways, among them Phillip Stonehouse and John Brandon. My visits to Burma in 1995, 1996 and 1999 were made infinitely more productive and enjoyable than they might have been, thanks to Stuart Hume, Lyndall Mclean, Jon Philp and Simeon Gilding. All members of the small Burma studies circle at ANU, myself included, have benefited from the encouragement and support of Desmond Ball.

As far as their official positions have allowed, my colleagues and friends in the Australian Department of Foreign Affairs and Trade, and the Department of Defence, have been very supportive. Their knowledge, experience and advice have been invaluable. Over the years I have also been blessed with a number of sympathetic supervisors in the APS. *Sayagyi* Garry Woodard has been a steadfast friend and source of wise council on matters pertaining to Burma, ever since he was my ambassador in Rangoon 25 years ago. Without John Hartley's far-sighted generosity, and support for my ANU Visiting Fellowship in 1995, this project could not have reached even the first stage. Frank Lewincamp kindly tolerated my extra-curricular enthusiasms and gave me leave to accept a second Visiting Fellowship in 2000. Special thanks are due to Doug Kean for his encouragement and sound common sense, as I have attempted to pursue two separate and potentially conflicting career paths.

Throughout the course of researching and writing this book, I received constant support from my old mates Kim Jackson and Paul Feldman, my parents Betty and Don Selth, and from my parents-in-law Peg and Al Koorey. Over the past five years, all six have probably learned more about the Burmese armed forces than they ever really cared to know. As always, my greatest debt is to my wife Pattie Collins, without whom this study could not have been written.

It goes without saying that, while I gratefully acknowledge the help given by all of the above, I take full responsibility for what I have written. For the record, it should also be noted that this book is based entirely on open sources. While I have no doubt benefited along the way from my professional training as a diplomat and strategic analyst, this study represents my views alone and has no official status or endorsement.

Some aspects of this study have already been explored in conference papers, and subsequently appeared as chapters in books. A number of draft chapters have been published as Working Papers by the SDSC or Asia Foundation. Also, edited extracts, and early versions of some chapters, have appeared as articles in professional magazines and academic journals, some under my own name and some under the pseudonym of "William Ashton". All these publications have been listed separately in the bibliography for ease of reference.

Canberra
June 2001

Acronyms and Abbreviations

AAG	anti-aircraft gun
AAM	air-to-air missile
AAP	Australian Associated Press
ABC	Australian Broadcasting Corporation
ABC	atomic, bacteriological and chemical (warfare, training)
ACDA	Arms Control and Disarmament Agency
AFP	Agence France Presse
AI	Amnesty International
AIDS	acquired immune deficiency syndrome
AIR	All India Radio
ANU	Australian National University
AP	anti-personnel (landmine)
AP	Associated Press
APC	armoured personnel carrier
APS	Australian Public Service
ASEAN	Association of Southeast Asian Nations
ASM	air-to-surface missile
ASW	anti-submarine warfare
ATGL	anti-tank grenade launcher
BA	Burma Army
BAAC	Burma Army Armoured Car
BAe	British Aerospace
BAF	Burma Air Force
BBC	British Broadcasting Corporation
BCP	Burma Communist Party ('Red Flags')
BDA	Burma Defence Army
BFM	bouncing fragmentation mine
BIA	Burma Independence Army
BM	blast mine
BMM	British Military Mission
BN	Burma Navy
BNA	Burma National Army
BRIG	Brigadier
BSI	Bureau of Special Investigations
BSO	Bureau of Special Operations
BSPP	Burma Socialist Programme Party
BVC	Bureau of Verification and Compliance
BW	biological weapons/warfare
C^3I	command, control, communications and intelligence

C^{4}I	command, control, communications, computers and intelligence
CD	Conference on Disarmament
CGC	coast guard cutter
CGE	central government expenditures
CGSC	Command and General Staff College
CIA	Central Intelligence Agency
CID	Criminal Investigation Department
CNI	Chief of National Intelligence
CO	Commanding Officer
COL	Colonel
COMSEC	communications security
CPB	Communist Party of Burma ('White Flags')
CRPP	Committee Representing the People's Parliament
CSI	Christian Solidarity International
CW	chemical weapons/warfare
CWC	Chemical Weapons Convention
DDSC	Directorate of Defence Services Computers
DDSI	Director/Directorate of Defence Services Intelligence
DFM	directional fragmentation mine
DIO	Defence Intelligence Organisation
DKBA	Democratic Karen Buddhist Army
DMT	Directorate of Military Training
DNI	Director of Naval Intelligence
DPRK	Democratic People's Republic of Korea (North Korea)
DSA	Defence Services Academy
DSI	Defence Services Institute
DSSES	Defence Services Signals and Electronic School
DVB	Democratic Voice of Burma
ECM	electronic counter measures
EEZ	exclusive economic zone
ELINT	electronic intelligence
ESM	electronic support measures
EU	European Union
EW	electronic warfare
FAS	Federation of American Scientists
FBI	Federal Bureau of Investigation
FEER	Far Eastern Economic Review
FRG	Federal Republic of Germany (West Germany)
FTUB	Federation of Trade Unions — Burma
GAIC	Guizhou Aviation Industry Corporation
GDP	gross domestic product
GDR	German Democratic Republic (East Germany)
GEN	General
GmbH	*Gemeinschaft mit beschraenkter Haftplicht* (limited liability company)
GNP	gross national product
GPMG	general purpose machine gun

GRU	*Glavnoye Razvedyvatelnoye Upravlenie* (Chief Intelligence Directorate of the Soviet General Staff)
GSM	Global System for Mobiles
GTZ	*Gesellschaft fuer Technische Zusammenarbeit* (Agency for Technical Cooperation)
HEAT	high explosive anti-tank (round)
HF	high frequency
HG	hand grenade
HIV	human immuno-deficiency virus
HMG	heavy machine gun
HQ	headquarters
HUMINT	human intelligence
IDF	Israel Defence Force
IFF	identification, friend or foe
IFV	infantry fighting vehicle
IG	Inspector General
IISS	International Institute for Strategic Studies
ILO	International Labour Organisation
IMET	International Military Education and Training
IMF	International Monetary Fund
IMINT	imagery intelligence
INCP	International Narcotics Control Program
INTERFET	International Force East Timor
IR	infra-red
IT	information technology
IW	information warfare
JAG	Judge Advocate General
JDW	Jane's Defence Weekly
KGB	*Komitet Gosudarstvennoi Bezopasnosti* (Soviet) Committee for State Security
KHRG	Karen Human Rights Group
KIA	Kachin Independence Army
KIO	Kachin Independence Organisation
KKY	*Karkweye* (defence) — used to describe certain militia forces in the 1960s
KMT	*Kuomintang* (People's National Party)
KNDO	Karen National Defence Organisation
KNLA	Karen National Liberation Army
KNU	Karen National Union
LCG(M)	Landing Craft, Gun (Medium)
LCM	Landing Craft, Medium
LCU	Landing Craft, Utility
LDC	Least Developed Country
LIC	low intensity conflict
LID	Light Infantry Division
LMG	light machine gun
LORC	Law and Order Restoration Council

LTGEN	Lieutenant General
MA	Myanmar Army
MAG	Military Appointments General
MAJGEN	Major General
MAP	Military Assistance Program
MAPT	Myanmar Agricultural Produce Trading
MBT	main battle tank
MDAP	Mutual Defence Assistance Plan
MI	military intelligence (see MIS)
MI6	Secret Intelligence Service
MIS	Military Intelligence Service
MISIS	Myanmar Institute of Strategic and International Studies
MM	Myanmar mine
MMG	medium machine gun
MOC	Military Operations Command
MP	Member of Parliament
MPF	Myanmar Police Force
MPPE	Myanmar Petroleum Products Enterprise
MPT	Myanmar Posts and Telecommunications
MRL	multiple rocket launcher
MTA	Mong Tai Army
NAM	Non-Aligned Movement
NATO	North Atlantic Treaty Organisation
NBC	nuclear, biological and chemical (warfare)
NCGUB	National Coalition Government of the Union of Burma
NCO	non-commissioned officer
NDC	National Defence College
NGO	non-governmental organisation
NLD	National League for Democracy
NIB	National Intelligence Board
NIB	National Intelligence Bureau
NPT	(Nuclear) Non-Proliferation Treaty
NUP	National Unity Party
ONUC	*Operation Nations Unies du Congo* (United Nations Operation in the Congo)
OSS	Office of Strategic Studies
OTS	Officers' Training School
PBF	Patriotic Burmese Forces
PLA	People's Liberation Army
PLAN	People's Liberation Army Navy
PM	People's Militia
POF	Pakistan Ordnance Factories
PPF	People's Police Force
PPFB	People's Pearl and Fisheries Board
PPFC	People's Pearl and Fisheries Corporation
PRC	People's Republic of China
RAF	Royal Air Force

RC	Revolutionary Council
RCL	recoilless rifle
RMC	Regional Military Command
RN	Royal Navy
ROC	Regional Operations Command
ROK	Republic of Korea (South Korea)
RPG	rocket propelled grenade (launcher)
RTA	Royal Thai Army
RTN	Royal Thai Navy
SAF	Singapore Armed Forces
SAM	surface-to-air missile
SB	Special Branch
SBS	Special Broadcasting Service
SC	scout car
SCUBA	self-contained underwater breathing apparatus
SDSC	Strategic and Defence Studies Centre
SEATO	Southeast Asia Treaty Organisation
SENGEN	Senior General
SFM	stake fragmentation mine
SID	Special Investigation Department
SIGINT	signals intelligence
SIPRI	Stockholm International Peace Research Institute
SLOC	sea line of communications
SLORC	State Law and Order Restoration Council
SNIE	Special National Intelligence Estimate
SOE	state-owned enterprise
SPDC	State Peace and Development Council
SSA	Shan State Army
SSB	single side band
SSM	surface-to-surface missile
STOL	short take-off and landing (aircraft)
TNT	trinitrotoluene
TOC	Tactical Operations Command
UBA	Union of Burma Airways
UBS	Union of Burma Ship
UHF	ultra high frequency
UK	United Kingdom
UMEC	Union of Myanmar Economic Corporation
UMEH	Union of Myanmar Economic Holdings
UN	United Nations
UNCLOS	United Nations Convention on the Law of the Sea
UNDCP	United Nations Drug Control Programme
UNDP	United Nations Development Programme
UNGA	United Nations General Assembly
UNHCR	United Nations High Commissioner for Refugees
UNHRC	United Nations Human Rights Commission
UNIPOM	United Nations India Pakistan Observer Mission

UNOGIL	United Nations Observer Group in Lebanon
UNSC	United Nations Security Council
UNTAET	United Nations Transitional Administration in East Timor
UNTSO	United Nations Truce Supervisory Organisation
US	United States (of America)
USDA	Union Solidarity Development Association
USN	United States Navy
USSR	Union of Soviet Socialist Republics
UWSA	United Wa State Army
VADM	Vice Admiral
VHF	very high frequency
VIP	very important person
VOA	Voice of America
VOPB	Voice of the People of Burma
VSAT	very small aperture terminal
WP	white phosphorous

Tables, Figures and Maps

1.	Burma: Physical Geography and Administrative Divisions	6
2.	Tatmadaw Rank Structure	49
3.	Burma's Defence Ministry, 1988	52-3
4.	Regional Military Commands, 1988	54
5.	Burma's Defence Ministry, 2000	56-7
6.	Regional Military Commands, 2000	58
7.	Burma's Intelligence Apparatus, 1988	107
8.	Burma's Intelligence Apparatus, 2000	110-11
9.	Military Intelligence Structure, 2000	116-17
10.	Burma's Defence Expenditure, 1978-1987	132
11.	Arms Transfers to Burma, 1973-1987	133
12.	Burma's Arms Imports, 1973-1987	133
13.	Burma's Defence Expenditure, 1988-1995	134
14.	Arms Transfers to Burma, 1987-1997	137
15.	Burma's Arms Imports, 1988-1997	138
16.	Infantry Battalion Structure	157
17.	Light Infantry Division Headquarters	158
18.	Burma Navy Strength, 1988	187
19.	Naval Regional Commands and Major Bases, 2000	190
20.	Burma Navy Strength, 2000	195
21.	Burma Air Force Strength, 1988	209
22.	Burma Air Force Strength, 2000	217
23.	Major Air Bases, 2000	218

Glossary

Any glossary of Burmese words and phrases needs to be used with caution. There is no standard method of romanisation, so in compiling such a list there is ample scope for error and confusion. Also, the Burmese language has four distinct tones, which are difficult to render in romanised form. There are not only different views on the way romanised terms are spelt, but how they are written. In the list below, for example, words have been separated where possible, capital letters have been used where necessary, and hyphens have been used where considered appropriate.

Burmese Language

Ah Chet Pya Set Thwe Yae Hta-na   Directorate of Signals
Ah Htoo Sone San Ye   Special Branch
Ah Por Sar Chae Myan Tak Ma   Light Infantry Division
Ahmyotha Di Mok Aka Yay Si Ahpwe Choke   National League for Democracy
Ah Lot Thin Bo   Apprentice Officer
Bamar Ahmyotha Tatmadaw   Burma National Army
Bamar Karkweye Tatmadaw   Burma Defence Army
Bamar Lutlatye Tatmadaw   Burma Independence Army
Bo (also *Sit-bo*)   military officer (usually a lieutenant), hence *Bo-hmu* (Major) and *Bo-hmu-gyi* (Colonel)
Bogyoke   Major General
Byu-ha Kye Ywa   strategic villages
Da Ka Sa   Regional Operations Command (abbreviation)
Daw   literally 'aunt' but commonly used as an honorific for older or more senior Burmese females
daw (or *taw*)   honorific denoting religious sanctity, state power, or outstanding status
Karkweye   militia (literally 'defence')
Karkweye Hta-na   Defence Services
Karkweye Wun-kyi Hta-na   Ministry of Defence
Ka Pa Sa   Directorate of Defence Industries (abbreviation of *Karkweye Pyitsu Setyoun*)
Ka Sa La   Heavy Industries Corporation (abbreviation of *Akyisar Sethmu Loat Ngun*)
Kha La Ya   infantry battalion (abbreviation)
Kha Ma Ya   light infantry battalion (abbreviation)
kyat   Burmese currency
lon htein   riot police — literally 'security control', after *lonchon yay htein thein*

Ma form of address to younger Burman female
Ma Sa La Burma Socialist Programme Party (abbreviation of *Myanmar Socialit Lanzin Parti*)
Maung form of address to younger Burman male
Myanmar Burman literary term used since 18 June 1989 as the name of the country
Na Ba Ha Brigade Headquarters (abbreviation)
Na Sa Kha Frontier Forces (abbreviation)
Na Wa Ta State Law and Order Restoration Council (abbreviation of *Naingngan-daw Nyein Wut Pi Pya Yae*)
naingngan sovereign state
Naingngan-daw Adipati Head of State
Naingngan Arr Ahphwe Strength of the Nation Organisation (USDA militia)
Naingngan-daw Aye Chan Tar Yar Yae Hint Phont Phyo Yae State Peace and Development Council
Naingngan-daw Nyein Wut Pi Pya Yae State Law and Order Restoration Council
pongyi Buddhist monk
pyat lei pyat 'Four Cuts' (counter-insurgency campaign)
Pyidaungsu Kyant Khine Phont Phyo Yae Ah Thin Union Solidarity Development Association
Pyidaungsu Myanmar Naingngan-daw Union of Myanmar
Pyidaungsu Myanmar Naingngan Si Pwa Yae Corporation Union of Myanmar Economic Corporation
Pyidaungsu Myanmar Naingngan Si Pwa Yae U Pai Ahpwe Union of Myanmar Economic Holdings
Pyithu Hluttaw People's Assembly
Pyithu Sit People's Militia
Pyithu Ah Ku Tat People's Auxiliary Forces
Pyithu Yei Tat Pwe People's Police Force
Sa Ba Ha Tactical Operations Command (abbreviation)
Sa Ka Kha Military Operations Command (abbreviation)
Sa Thon Lon Bureau of Special Investigations
saya teacher, also honorific for respected figure or professional, hence *sayagyi* (senior or great teacher)
sit war (also used for 'army')
Sit Byu Ha Yay Hta Na Strategic Naval Command
Sit Byu Ha Yay Yin Su Strategic Naval Flotilla
Sit Mahar Byu Har Lae Lar Yae Hta-na Office of Strategic Studies
Sit Pyan Sit Hmu Tan Haung Ahpwe War Veterans Association
sit-tat army (or 'armed forces')
sit-tha soldier (literally 'son of war')
sit-wundan tat government militia during the late 1940s, also known as 'territorial units' (literally 'servants of war')
Taik Pwe Win Si Yone Ye Thin Dan Kyaung Combat-Related Organisational Activities Training Centres
Taing Sit Htar Na Choke Regional Military Command
tat forces (usually armed)

Tatmadaw   Burmese armed forces
Tatmadaw Htauk Hlan-ye Ahpwe   Military Intelligence Service
Tatmadaw Htauk Hlan-ye Hyun-kyar Yehmu Youn   Directorate of Defence
         Services Intelligence
Tatmadaw Kyi   Burma Army
Tatmadaw Lei   Burma Air Force
Tatmadaw Lei Ou   Air Force Squadron
Tatmadaw Yay   Burma Navy
Tatmadaw Yay Tat Hta Na Choke   Navy Regional Command
tattwin pyinnyapay   in-service orientation course
tattwin swe-nwe pwe   in-service discussion session
taw hlan-ye tha-ma   revolutionary
Teza   course name (literally 'thunder')
Thakin   title used by early nationalists (literally 'Master')
thaung kyan thu   insurgent
thu-pone   rebel
Thura   literally 'bravery', used as a military honorific, awarded for valour
U   literally 'uncle', but commonly used as an honorific for older or
         more senior Burmese males
Yebaw   comrade
Yei Tat Pwe   Police Force

Other Languages

dacoit   bandit belonging to armed gang (hence dacoity)
dwi fungsi   dual function
en clair   in plain language
jihad   holy war
Kempeitai   (Japanese) military police
Kuomintang   (Chinese) People's National Party
mujahideen   holy warrior
Nai   form of address to Mon male
Naw   form of address to Karen female
Rohingya   Muslims of South Asian extraction living in Arakan State
Sai   form of address to young Shan male
Saw   form of address to Karen male

Foreword

David I. Steinberg

In the contemporary world, there is probably no other country of any significant size or regional influence in which the military has as much and as pervasive power, and has held it for such an extended period — four decades, as in Burma/Myanmar. Its influence is comprehensive, pervading the society to a degree essentially unknown even in other countries where the army is a coercive force with a greater total number of troops.

The leadership of the state is under total military control. The bureaucracy is peppered at every level and in every locale with military personnel who control administration. The military intelligence services are ubiquitous, producing a sense of fear and foreboding that permeates society. Mass mobilisation organisations, specifically established for and publicly subservient to the military, are everywhere, encompassing some one-third of the total population of the state. The avenues of social mobility in the society are under its command; education is controlled, the pervasive Buddhist hierarchy has been registered and its organisation under constant scrutiny. The economy has been opened to some private sector activity, but the reach of the military is long and its influence critical, institutionally through military-run conglomerates, an important procurement production network, and through state-owned enterprises, as well as personally through the individual relationships on which power is also built and which is essential for economic success. What is purportedly known as civil society, those non-governmental groups that provide pluralism in many societies, exists under the aegis and authority of the military and thus is virtually an oxymoron. There are no institutions that can compete with the military. This has been essentially true since Independence in 1948, but the military's influence has expanded, and it has eliminated or co-opted any significant group that might be seen as providing alternative authority.

The military has since Independence been an honourable and desirable career, not only for the perquisites of office, but also because of a strong sense of nationalism that has been evident in Burmese society. But the leadership of the military, once ethnically diverse, has been solidified into one ethnically Burman, with important consequences for minority relations — the single most important and enduring issue facing the state.

In an age when the military in general is in retreat from civil authority in Asia, its continuing presence and command in Myanmar seem anomalous. In South Korea, Thailand, Taiwan, and Indonesia, the military have retired to the barracks. In China and Vietnam, the party exerts effective control. Yet, at the start of 2002, the Burmese military forces are the strongest they have been in post-colonial independence. Their numbers have increased, their equipment has been modernized in part, they are actively fighting against far fewer internal enemies because of cease-fires arranged with a wide variety of ethnic rebel organisations, however ephemeral or delicate some of them may be, and any external foes they may perceive to have are largely products of outmoded concerns from an earlier era. The security concerns of the state, in military eyes, are largely internal — to ensure the state's territorial integrity and sovereignty that the military has believed to be threatened by internal forces. As the Vietnamese military continues to demobilise significant numbers of its forces, the Burmese *Tatmadaw* (armed forces) will likely emerge as the largest military in Southeast Asia.

Not only does the position of the military in Myanmar appear to be an anomaly in the modern world, the lack of interest in that country in both international policy and academic circles is even more singular. Myanmar is both significant in population and in area, and is strategically situated between the two most powerful Asian regional forces — China and India — and has been and continues to be the subject of extensive concerns by both states. The predominant position of either state in Myanmar threatens the interests of the other, and indeed regional stability in the area and in the Bay of Bengal. Neither China nor India, to be sure, ignores Burma, and each in its own way has vied for influence there. It is the Western powers that have been less observant and less concerned. The policy of enforced isolation of the Burmese state by the industrialized nations, with the exception of Japan, because of valid concerns over democracy and human rights has resulted in intellectual isolation and strategic or policy ignorance or disinterest counterproductive to understanding the dynamics of that society and its future in the region. The concerns of ASEAN, which has been in a state of disarray since the economic collapse of Indonesia in 1997, the time Myanmar joined, do not substitute for an understanding of the dynamics of Burma/Myanmar in which the military play multiple, pivotal, roles.

There is today only a small coterie of scholars and serious observers on contemporary Burma/Myanmar. Although any writer on the present situation in that country cannot ignore the military and its present, varied roles, there has been little serious scholarship on Burma/Myanmar, and even less on its key institution, the military — its organisation, training, capacities, equipment, and influence. Internal scholarship within Myanmar is severely restricted and often classified, and although there has been one significant attempt to study aspects of the military prior to the coup of 1962, only Andrew Selth has devoted himself to the serious study of the Burmese military in all its aspects and in its present, comprehensive incarnation. Mr. Selth has become the world's premier writer on the military, and his meticulous scholarship, based on what seems to be a myriad of unclassified but most obscure sources, has been evident in the occasional papers and other works he has published from his base at the Australian National University. In this volume Mr.

Selth considers virtually every aspect of the military, from organisational structure to procurement to training and influence.

This study is unique in the literature on Burma/Myanmar, and it is evident that it will be required reading for anyone seriously concerned with Myanmar, the Southeast Asia region, and indeed with the relationships between India and China. It is not only those observers of the Burmese scene who are in Mr. Selth's debt, but those involved in the study of the military in various societies can learn from this important volume. There are lessons from the problems of Burma/Myanmar applicable in relation to policies in other multi-ethnic states, in economic development, and in civil-military relations. Mr. Selth has given us much to muse on beyond the borders of that unfortunate country.

David I. Steinberg, Director, Asian Studies
School of Foreign Service, Georgetown University
Washington, D.C. January 2002

Introduction

Perhaps the only conclusion which a study of previous attempts to estimate the military power of foreign nations reaches, is that a good deal of scepticism is necessary about any assessment which purports to be exact. — Philip Towle, *Estimating Foreign Military Power* (1982)

Since Burma regained its independence from the United Kingdom (UK) on 4 January 1948, its armed forces (or *Tatmadaw*) have claimed a large place in the country's modern history. The central government in Rangoon has continuously been at war with numerous insurgent groups and private armies. It has also faced an invasion by elements of the defeated Nationalist Chinese government, and in the late 1950s and early 1960s almost came to blows with the communist regime which replaced it. Periodic tensions with other neighbours have occasionally spilled over into armed clashes. As a result, the *Tatmadaw* has been on active service for more than 50 years. Not only has it fulfilled this purely military function, but it has also exercised a major influence on the political, economic and social development of the country. This influence has been most evident since General Ne Win's *coup d'etat* on 2 March 1962, when the armed forces overthrew the democratically elected government of Prime Minister U Nu and imposed their will on almost every aspect of Burmese life.[2] The creation of the *Naingngan-daw Nyein Wut Pi Pya Yae* (State Law and Order Restoration Council, or SLORC) in September 1988, and its reincarnation as the *Naingngan-daw Aye Chan Tar Yar Yae Hint Phont Phyo Yae* (State Peace and Development Council, or SPDC) in November 1997, saw the open reassertion of military power over the civilian population. Regardless of the outcome of the current confrontation between the SPDC and the country's opposition forces, the *Tatmadaw* will continue to be a central element in Burma's development for many years to come.

Since the dramatic events of 1988, when widespread pro-democracy demonstrations were crushed by the armed forces, there has been a resurgence of interest in Burma among foreign journalists, scholars and strategic analysts. Several new and important studies have appeared.[3] Researchers have uncovered or revived hitherto forgotten aspects of Burma's history.[4] International conferences have yielded additional works of value.[5] Yet, despite this greater level of public interest, and the *Tatmadaw*'s critical role in modern Burmese history, it is still very difficult to find any scholarly works in the major languages devoted to the armed forces. A few books and articles cover the formation of nationalist military units which appeared during the Second World War and in the period leading up to Independence.[6] There have also been some notable contributions to Burma studies in broader works, covering such subjects as the involvement of armed forces in the politics of Southeast Asia, and the economic development of new states.[7] Since 1988 Burma has also begun to be included in studies of democracy and security in the Asia-Pacific region.[8] A study of the *Tatmadaw*'s early development has been written by a Cornell University researcher, but its coverage stopped at 1962.[9] A more recent doctoral dissertation by a Burmese student in Australia benefited from access to the *Tatmadaw*'s archives, but was restricted in its scope and has not been given wide circulation.[10] Several Working Papers published by the Australian National University's Strategic and Defence Studies Centre throw light on aspects of the *Tatmadaw* and its internal processes. Nowhere, however, is there a comprehensive and definitive study available in English about the development of Burma's armed forces since 1948, and their current status.

This dearth of published material extends to Burmese sources. From the mid-1950s efforts were made to compile an official history of the *Tatmadaw*, but for many years the only concrete results were some newspaper articles and Ba Than's short book entitled *The Roots of the Revolution*.[11] There were subsequently a large number of works produced by official military historians, but naturally they were written in Burmese, and few were made available to the public. Since 1988 this problem has been recognised by the SLORC and SPDC. A *Concise History of Myanmar and the Tatmadaw's Role* was commissioned (in English) by the military regime in 1989, and a more detailed, multi-volume, official history of the *Tatmadaw* is currently in production. While the latter is in Burmese, it may eventually be translated into English.[12] In 1997, to celebrate its 50th anniversary, the Burma Air Force (BAF) published its own history in English, drawing on an earlier study which had been written (in Burmese) in 1984.[13] The Burma Army (BA) followed in 1999 with a short booklet designed for distribution to foreigners.[14] Given the totalitarian nature of Burma's government since the 1962 military coup, however, and the regime's anxiety to recover support for the armed forces after the 1988 massacres, such sources cannot be relied upon for objective description or analysis. All too often, the division between history and propaganda has been blurred beyond recognition.[15] To a greater or lesser degree, the same can be said of the memoirs written by Burmese servicemen which have appeared during the same period.[16]

With few exceptions, none of the available works consider Burma's broader strategic environment, or offer any serious treatment of purely military matters such as the structure and organisation of the armed forces, the size and composition of the three Services, their arms and equipment inventories or their combat capabilities.[17] Nor are such details provided anywhere by the government in Rangoon. Citing 'national security', the regime has consistently refused to reveal any detailed or accurate information about Burma's annual defence expenditure or arms purchases. The *Tatmadaw*'s order of battle and its combat capabilities have also been considered too sensitive for public disclosure. For example, there has never been a Burmese White Paper on Defence, nor does the military regime provide annual returns to the United Nations Register of Conventional Arms. Estimates of Burma's order of battle can be found in *The Military Balance*, published each year by the International Institute for Strategic Studies (IISS), and in *Jane's Sentinel Security Assessment* for Southeast Asia, which is updated periodically.[18] These are the most useful and accessible public guides, but they cannot be considered definitive. The details provided are often out of date or are contradicted by other sources. There are sometimes reports of arms sales and other military developments in regional newspapers, defence journals and current affairs magazines, but these vary considerably in reliability.

This book represents an initial attempt to fill the gaps in Western literature (and knowledge) about the Burmese armed forces. Unfortunately, given the many difficulties noted above, it has still not been possible to provide an authoritative account of the *Tatmadaw*'s origins and development since 1988, or to be completely confident about some of the information provided. It is to be hoped that it will not be too long before the circumstances in Burma permit such a study to be written. Even so, it has been possible to present a framework for future research and analysis. In doing so, a number of themes have consistently emerged. They include the extraordinary growth and modernisation of the Burmese armed forces under the SLORC and SPDC; the need for the *Tatmadaw* to take further steps if it is fully to translate its newly-acquired manpower and weapon systems into increased capabilities; the important role of external powers, like China; and the regime's continuing sense of insecurity, despite all its political power and military strength. Some of these issues are likely to remain a concern even in the event of a transition to a democratically elected civilian government.

Given the *Tatmadaw*'s central political role in Burma, it is very difficult to isolate purely military matters for analysis, but an attempt to do so would serve a number of purposes. It could contribute towards a deeper and more comprehensive understanding of the *Tatmadaw* and its profound influence on modern Burmese history. A study of the military regime's evolving plans for the expansion and modernisation of the armed forces would add a useful perspective to accounts of political events in Burma since 1988, and the consideration of likely future developments in that troubled country. It could help dispel some of the confusion surrounding certain aspects of Burma's arms procurement program, and throw greater light on the many claims made about the involvement of other countries in Burma's defence activities. Such a study could also inform discussions of arms acquisition programs elsewhere in South and Southeast Asia, and complement analyses of broad strategic trends in the wider Asia-Pacific region, of which Burma is gradually becoming a more active and influential member. Its entry to the Association of Southeast Asian Nations (ASEAN) in July 1997, for example, has contributed to increased ties between the *Tatmadaw* and the armed forces of other regional countries. It has also drawn attention to the wider implications of Burma's close defence links with China.[19]

In this study, the creation of the SLORC in 1988 is taken as a critical turning point. Before then, the Ne Win regime's self-imposed isolation and idiosyncratic economic policies ensured that the *Tatmadaw* remained a small, poorly equipped counter-insurgency force, consisting largely of light infantry supported by weak naval and air forces. The SLORC's ambitious program to expand and modernise the *Tatmadaw*, however, has turned it into one of the largest and best equipped armed forces in Southeast Asia. This program was made possible in large part by radical shifts in policy regarding the economic management of the country and Burma's international relations. Socialism was abandoned, the defence sector was accorded the highest priority for government funding and a close military relationship was developed with China. In broad terms, this program has been maintained under the SPDC and, in one form or another, seems likely to continue for the foreseeable future. Despite its continuing poverty and internal tensions, Burma can no longer be dismissed as a weak and isolated country with no capacity to defend itself or affect the security of its neighbours.

Sources

In an effort to provide a comprehensive and accurate coverage of the subject, this book has drawn on a very wide range of open sources, many of which are listed in the bibliography. Because of the lack of primary material (particularly in the English language), I have been obliged to rely on secondary sources to a much greater extent than I would have liked. Over the past five years my research has, however, benefited from several field trips to Southeast Asia and other parts of the Asia-Pacific region. I have also made visits to centres of Burma expertise in the US and UK. During three trips to Burma I was able to conduct interviews, obtain official literature and observe contemporary developments.

During my visits to Burma I encountered the expected difficulties in gathering research material. I was able, however, to speak with a number of serving members of the *Tatmadaw*, including representatives of the Office of Strategic Studies (OSS), Directorate of Defence Services Intelligence (DDSI), and the Defence Services Museum and Historical Research Institute. Officers from these organisations were prepared to provide me with their particular perspectives on Burmese defence issues and, in a few cases, with factual information which might otherwise have been unavailable. Former members of the *Tatmadaw* with whom I spoke tended to be less constrained about expressing their views. With a few exceptions, the members of the Rangoon diplomatic corps were very helpful, as were a number of journalists, and some local and foreign businessmen. On a number of occasions, I had the opportunity to discuss relevant issues with senior pro-democracy figures, including Daw Aung San Suu Kyi and former General Tin Oo. Speaking to private Burmese citizens about developments in Burma since 1988 was sometimes quite difficult, but invariably very rewarding.

While some of the officials I met were prepared to speak on the record, most of the people with whom interviews were conducted, including Burmese exiles now living in Thailand, India, Australia and the US, did not wish to be cited in this book by name. Others did not make such a stipulation, but for professional or other reasons would clearly prefer not to be quoted directly. Accordingly, where information has been obtained through interviews, a footnote simply identifies the place and broad date of the conversation. Where the text reflects a personal observation by the author (most often in Burma), this is acknowledged in a similar fashion.

Terms and Definitions

After the creation of the SLORC in 1988, Burma's name was officially changed from its post-1974 form, the 'Socialist Republic of the Union of Burma', back to the 'Union of Burma', which had been adopted when Burma regained its independence in 1948. In July 1989 the military regime changed the country's name once again, this time to *Pyidaungsu Myanmar Naingngan-daw*, or the 'Union of Myanmar'. (Due to the tonal nature of the Burmese language the country's new name is sometimes spelt without the final 'r', as *Myanma*). At the same time, a number of other titles and place names were changed in an attempt to remove any traces of the colonial era, as follows:

Peoples

Burman	Bamar
Karen	Kayin

States/Divisions/Cities/Towns

Arakan	Rakhine
Rangoon	Yangon
Syriam	Thanlyin
Pegu	Bago
Prome	Pye (or Pyi)
Pagan	Bagan
Maymyo	Pyin Oo-lwin
Pa-an	Hpa-an
Moulmein	Mawlamyine
Mergui	Myeik (or Beik)
Tenasserim	Tanintharyi
Tavoy	Dawei
Bassein	Pathein

Rivers

Irrawaddy	Ayeyarwady
Salween	Thanlwin
Sittang	Sittoung
Chindwin	Chindwinn

These new names were subsequently accepted by the United Nations (UN) and most other major international organisations. Some governments and opposition groups, however, have clung to the old forms as a protest against the SLORC's and SPDC's human rights abuses and their refusal to hand over power to a democratically elected civilian government. To a greater or lesser degree, they view the military regime as an illegitimate government which has no right to make even symbolic changes of any significance. Democratic opposition leader Aung San Suu Kyi, for example, continues to call her country Burma, and has asked all foreign governments to do the same.[20] Other arguments have been put forward to justify the retention of the old colonial name on more technical grounds.[21] In this study the better known names, for example Burma instead of Myanmar, Rangoon instead of Yangon, and Irrawaddy instead of Ayeyarwady, have been retained for ease of recognition. Where there are different names, or different spellings of Anglicised names, in common use before 1988, the alternatives are given in brackets the first time they are mentioned, for example Sittwe (Akyab) and Nyaung Chidauk (Nyaung chi-dauk).

Some confusion has also arisen over the description of various ethnic groups in Burma. In this book the name 'Burmese' is used to describe the entire population of the country, while 'Burman' is used when referring to the dominant ethnic group. The language of the Burman majority, and since 1948 the official language of the country, is also called 'Burmese'. Other major ethnic groups, such as the Chin, Naga, Kachin, Shan, Kayah (Karenni), Karen and Mon, are called by their own names when specifically referred to as minority peoples. Given that there are estimated to be more than 150 different 'tribes' in Burma, and over 240 spoken languages and dialects, such terms are necessarily used in their broadest context.[22]

Such are the passions which have been aroused by events in Burma since 1988, that a number of other terms have also become controversial. Many opposition groups, for example, refuse to use the formal name *Tatmadaw* to describe the armed forces, on the grounds that these forces have betrayed the principles for which they once stood and the people whom they are sworn to protect. Rather, opposition groups tend to use the more descriptive term *sit-tat* (or 'army'), without the honorific suffix *daw*. I have retained the title *Tatmadaw*, however, as this was the name originally given to the armed forces by its founder, and Burma's revered independence leader, General Aung San. It is also the formal title by which the Burmese armed forces are still known. Similarly, the term 'rebel' (in Burmese *thu-pone*) is rejected by most armed opposition groups in Burma as pejorative and misleading, implying as it does that their struggles against the military regime in Rangoon are in some way unjustified or unlawful. Some groups prefer the term *taw hlan-ye tha ma*, or 'revolutionaries', but I have followed Martin Smith's lead in referring to these groups simply as insurgents (*thaung kyan thu*). This more neutral term still accurately conveys the clear intention of these groups to challenge the central government or seize power using armed force.

Burmese Names

The Burmese naming system is very complex and lends itself to many different variations. The Burmese generally have two names, but one or three are not uncommon. Family or surnames do not exist, although children occasionally carry their father's name in addition to their own, like Aung San Suu Kyi. Wives do not take their husband's names and children usually bear different names from those of their parents. Many Burmese use (or are given) additional names, including nicknames and place names, for better identification, added status or for other reasons. Because Burmans are usually named by their parents depending on the day of the week on which they are born, some names are very common, such as Maung Maung, or Tin Oo (also spelt Tin U). Before 1962, many Burmese (including non-Christians) were given English names, including by Christian missionaries or Burmese teachers at Christian missionary schools. After the 1962 military takeover Burmese names became mandatory, but in some cases these Christian names were retained.

In Burma honorifics are also customary, and vary according to the age and sex of the person addressed. *U* (literally meaning 'uncle') is roughly the Burmese equivalent of 'Mr', and *Daw* (literally meaning 'aunt') is the equivalent of either Mrs or Miss, depending on the age and marital status of the woman concerned. These honorifics usually do not change on marriage. Other forms are sometimes still used to address people regarded as inferiors in age or social standing, such as *Maung* (male) and *Ma* (female). At times, Burmese also use these particular forms to refer to themselves, as a gesture of modesty. The customary Burmese forms of address are frequently used by Burma's ethnic minorities, but many have their own forms of address. For example, Karens use *Saw* and *Naw* respectively as honorifics for men and women. A Shan male is usually referred to as *Sai*, and a Mon male as *Nai*. Some Burmese also have civil or military titles like *Bogyoke*, *Thakin*, *Bo*, *Yebaw* or *Thura* which, being unfamiliar to foreigners, are often taken to be a part of the actual name.

In this book I have tried not to use formal titles. In the case of a few individuals, however, I have included their titles when they are first introduced, on the grounds that their titles have become so closely associated with them that they are often taken to be part of the person's name. For example, as David Steinberg has pointed out, it is widely but erroneously believed that the 'U' in (U) Nu and (U) Thant is part of their name.[23]

Notes

1. Andrew Selth, *Transforming the Tatmadaw: The Burmese Armed Forces Since 1988*, Canberra Papers on Strategy and Defence No. 113 (Strategic and Defence Studies Centre, Australian National University, Canberra, 1996).

2. This is not to forget the military 'caretaker' government, known at the time as the *Bogyoke* government after *Bogyoke* (or, in English, General) Ne Win. This government held power, purportedly at the invitation of the Burmese Parliament, from November 1958 until February 1960.

3. Three notable examples are D.I. Steinberg, *Burma: The State of Myanmar* (Georgetown University Press, Washington, 2001); Bertil Lintner, *Burma in Revolt: Opium and Insurgency Since 1948*, second edition (Silkworm Books, Chiang Mai, 1999); and Martin Smith, *Burma: Insurgency and the Politics of Ethnicity*, second edition (Zed Books, London, 1999).

4. See, for example, Kin Oung, *Who Killed Aung San?*, second edition (White Lotus, Bangkok, 1996); and Josef Silverstein (ed), *The Political Legacy of Aung San*, revised edition, Southeast Asia Program Series No. 11 (Cornell University, Ithaca, 1993).

5. See, for example, Morten B. Pedersen, Emily Rudland and R.J. May (eds), *Burma-Myanmar: Strong Regime, Weak State?* (Crawford House, Adelaide, 2000); Robert I. Rotberg (ed), *Burma: Prospects for a Democratic Future* (Brookings Institution, Washington, 1998); and Peter Carey (ed), *Burma: The Challenge of Change in a Divided Society* (Macmillan, London, 1997).

6. See, for example, Maung Maung, *Burmese Nationalist Movements 1940-1948* (Kiscadale, Edinburgh, 1989). A useful early work is J.C. Lebra, *Japanese-Trained Armies in Southeast Asia: Independence and Volunteer Forces in World War II* (Heinemann, Hong Kong, 1977).

7. Included in this category is J.A. Wiant and D.I. Steinberg, 'Burma: The Military and National Development', in J.S. Djiwandono and Yong Mun Cheong (eds), *Soldiers and Stability in Southeast Asia* (Institute of Southeast Asian Studies, Singapore, 1988). Still useful is R.H. Taylor, 'Burma', in Zakaria Haji Ahmad and Harold Crouch (eds), *Military-Civilian Relations in South-East Asia* (Oxford University Press, Singapore, 1985).

8. See, for example, Tin Maung Maung Than, 'Myanmar: Preoccupation with Regime Survival, National Unity, and Stability', in Muthiah Alagappa (ed), *Asian Security Practice: Material and Ideational Influences* (Stanford University Press, Stanford, 1998); Tin Maung Maung Than, 'Myanmar Democratization: Punctuated Equilibrium or Retrograde Motion?', in Anek Laothamatas (ed), *Democratization in Southeast and East Asia* (Institute of Southeast Asian Studies, Singapore, 1997); and Chao-Tzang Yawnghwe, 'Burma: The Depoliticization of the Political', in Muthiah Alagappa (ed), *Political Legitimacy in Southeast Asia: The Quest for Moral Authority* (Stanford University Press, Stanford, 1995).

9. M.P. Callahan, 'The Origins of Military Rule in Burma', unpublished PhD thesis, Cornell University, 1996.

10. Maung Aung Myoe, 'The Counterinsurgency in Myanmar: The Government's Response to the Burma Communist Party', unpublished PhD thesis, Australian National University, 1999.

11. Ba Than, *The Roots of the Revolution: A brief history of the Defence Services of the Union of Burma and the Ideals for which they stand* (Guardian, Rangoon, 1962).

12. A Tatmadaw Researcher, *A Concise History of Myanmar and the Tatmadaw's Role, 1948-1988*, 2 vols. (Ministry of Education, Rangoon, 1989 and 1991). Five volumes of the official *History of the Tatmadaw* have already appeared; Vol. 1, '1824-1945' (News and Periodicals Corporation, Rangoon, 1994); Vol. 2, '1945: The Anti-Fascist Movement' (News and Periodicals Corporation, Rangoon, 1994); Vol. 3, '1945-1948' (News and Periodicals

Corporation, Rangoon, 1995); Vol. 4, '1948-1962' (News and Periodicals Enterprise, Rangoon, 1997); and Vol. 5, '1962-1988' (News and Periodicals Enterprise, Rangoon, 1997).

13. *History of the Myanmar Air Force*, (Committee for Compilation of the History of the Tatmadaw (Air), Rangoon, 1997).

14. *Brief History of the Myanmar Army* (Defence Services Museum and Historical Research Institute, Rangoon, 1999).

15. This is clearly demonstrated in works such as Min Maung Maung, *The Tatmadaw and its leadership role in national politics* (News and Periodicals Enterprise, Rangoon, 1993); and Mya Win, *Tatmadaw's Traditional Role in National Politics* (News and Periodicals Enterprise, Rangoon, 1992).

16. See, for example, Dr Maung Maung, *To a Soldier Son* (Sarpay Beikman, Rangoon, 1974).

17. One exception to this rule is the survey of Burma produced since 1968 by American University for the US Department of the Army, as part of its Foreign Area Studies series. The latest edition, however, is now more than fifteen years old. See F.M. Bunge (ed), *Burma: a country study* (American University, Washington, 1983). A new edition was commissioned in the early 1990s, and was to include a chapter on the armed forces by John B. Haseman. This project has been abandoned, but Haseman's chapter subsequently appeared as *Burma's Myriad National Security Challenges: The Historical Background and Contemporary Events*, Working Paper No. 50 (Australian Defence Studies Centre, Australian Defence Forces Academy, Canberra, 1997). See also Tin Maung Maung Than, 'Burma's National Security and Defence Posture', *Contemporary Southeast Asia*, Vol. 11, No. 1, June 1989, pp. 40-60.

18. *The Military Balance 2000/2001* (Oxford University Press for the International Institute for Strategic Studies, London, 2000). See also *Jane's Sentinel Security Assessment: Southeast Asia* (Jane's Information Systems, Coulsdon, September 2000-February 2001).

19. Some of these relationships are described in Andrew Selth, *Burma's Secret Military Partners*, Canberra Papers on Strategy and Defence No. 136 (Strategic and Defence Studies Centre, Australian National University, Canberra, 2000).

20. The sensitivity of this issue was illustrated in mid-1997 when the Australian Foreign Minister was chided by ASEAN colleages over his continued use of the name 'Burma'. See 'Downer told it's Burma no longer', *Canberra Times*, 30 July 1997.

21. See, for example, William Ashton, 'What's in a Name: Burma', *Quadrant*, Vol. 316/39, No. 5, May 1995, pp. 51-2.

22. The complexity of Burma's ethnic composition, and the dangers of referring to minority groups in such general terms, is discussed in Peter Kunstadter (ed), *Southeast Asian Tribes, Minorities, and Nations* (Princeton University Press, Princeton, 1967), Vol. 1, pp. 75-121. See also Martin Smith, 'A State of Strife: The Indigenous Peoples of Burma', in R.H. Barnes, Andrew Gray and Benedict Kingsbury (eds), *Indigenous Peoples of Asia* (Association for Asian Studies, Ann Arbor, 1995), pp. 221-45; and Robert Taylor, 'Perceptions of Ethnicity in the Politics of Burma', *Southeast Asian Journal of Social Science*, Vol. 10, No. 1, 1982, pp. 7-22. The official view is that there are eight major nationalities and 135 ethnic minorities in Burma. Hla Min, *Political Situation Of Myanmar And Its Role In The Region* (Office of Strategic Studies, Rangoon, 1999), p. 5.

23. D.I. Steinberg, *The Future of Burma: Crisis and Choice in Myanmar* (University Free Press of America, Lanham, 1990), p. xi.

Burma's Armed Forces

1

Historical and Strategic Setting

> More than most countries, Burma is a complex of antitheses. A national unity and a tribalistic disunity; the cult of serenity and withdrawal, and the cult of force and violence; the worship of absolute authority, together with an absence of social barriers; relaxed and easy personal relations, constantly exploding into tension and schizophrenia: these are some of the attributes of this puzzling country. — Hugh Tinker, 'Burma', in *Asia Handbook* (1966)

It is a truism that the armed forces of a particular country are shaped almost as much by that country's geostrategic position and modern history, as by any features of the contemporary strategic environment.[1] In this, Burma is no exception. Indeed, it could be argued that, at least since Independence in 1948, the *Tatmadaw* accords to this rule more than most armed forces in the Asia-Pacific region.[2] Ironically, it is one of the few things on which all sides of Burmese politics agree.

1.1 Burma's Geostrategic Position

For centuries, that part of Southeast Asia which eventually became modern Burma was largely isolated from, and ignorant of, the wider world. While visited by travellers and traders from a very early date, and Europeans from the 14th century, Burma was really only of strategic interest to its immediate neighbours, with which it fought a number of wars. India, China and Thailand have all invaded, and been invaded by, Burma at different times.[3] As the major European empires expanded, however, and geopolitics began to be practised on a global scale, this situation changed and it became more widely recognised that Burma occupied a geostrategic position of some importance. It was, and still is, the place where South, Southeast and East Asia meet, and where the dominant cultures of these three sub-regions compete for influence. In Samuel Huntington's terms, it lies across the fault lines between three major civilisations, those of the Hindus, Buddhists and Confucians.[4] Also, at critical times, Burma has been a cockpit for rivalry between the superpowers and, in the fluid strategic environment of the early

21st century, its important position is once again attracting attention from analysts and officials.[5]

Covering 657,740 square kilometres, Burma is the largest independent state in mainland Southeast Asia.[6] Its 5,876-kilometre land boundary touches five different countries, including two strategic giants. To the west, it shares a 1,463-kilometre border with India, a nuclear power which dominates the South Asian subcontinent and Bay of Bengal. To the northeast, Burma shares a 2,185-kilometre long border with China, now within reach of the great power status which it has long felt was its due. In the east, Burma's frontier runs southwest and south for 1,800 kilometres alongside Thailand, still an influential player in the region despite a number of setbacks in recent years. At its eastern-most point Burma shares a short (235-kilometre) border with Laos, and at its western-most point another with Bangladesh (193 kilometres long). While in most places these borders cross very rugged and heavily forested terrain, they have always been porous to local ethnic communities, traders, drug smugglers, insurgents and invading armies.

Burma's coastline is 1,930 kilometres long, not counting the 852 islands which lie within its waters (most in the Mergui Archipelago). Burma faces the Bay of Bengal west of the capital, Rangoon, and the Andaman Sea to the south. In 1977 the Burmese government declared a territorial sea of 12 nautical miles (22 kilometres) and a contiguous zone of 24 nautical miles (44 kilometres). Since that time, Burma has also laid claim to a continental shelf, and an exclusive economic zone (EEZ), of 200 nautical miles (370 kilometres), thus extending its maritime interests to cover an area of 148,600 square kilometres.[7] While Burma's security concerns have traditionally been land-based, this large expanse of open ocean and coastal waters has long been exploited by local fishermen, traders, smugglers, poachers, pirates and the navies of other countries.[8] While Burma does not dominate any major sea lines of communication (SLOC), it is close to some Indian Ocean shipping lanes and is crossed by a number of important east-west commercial air routes.

A major dispute over the land boundary with China was satisfactorily resolved in 1960, and the land border with Bangladesh was agreed in 1999, but differences over territorial claims still arise with Burma's neighbours.[9] These disputes tend to occur as a result of imprecise agreements, poorly demarcated boundaries and shifting river courses, leading to tensions with Thailand in particular.[10] Maritime disputes are also common. Burma has laid claim to its waters in a number of ways that seem to violate the United Nations Convention on the Law of the Sea (UNCLOS).[11] An agreement was reached with India over some of Burma's claims in 1986, and in 1993 a trilateral agreement was negotiated between Burma, India and Thailand, over the tri-junction point between the three countries in the Andaman Sea.[12] However, Burma has yet to settle a number of maritime disputes with Thailand and Bangladesh, which still cause frictions over fishing rights.[13] Burma has also attracted criticism from the United States (US) for some of its broader claims, including its insistence that foreign warships must obtain permission from Rangoon prior to entering its territorial sea and contiguous zone.[14]

Surrounded by rugged mountains to the west, north and east, and wide seas in the south, Burma is to a large extent geographically self-contained. Communications with the rest of the world are poor. Indeed, before 1938 there were no road or rail routes to any neighbouring countries. The Second World War saw the construction of the Burma Road between Lashio and Kunming in southern China, the Ledo Road from Mogaung to Ledo in north-eastern Assam, and a railway from Ban Pong in Thailand through Three Pagodas Pass to Thanbyuzayat. However, as Charles Fisher has noted, 'all of these were of strategic rather than commercial importance', and none survived as a trunk route after the war.[15] Access to Burma overland is still very restricted, but there are projects under way to restore parts of the old Burma and Ledo Roads, and to upgrade land communications with India and Thailand.[16] There are still no international rail links, but it is possible that the old Japanese line from Thailand may eventually be rebuilt as part of a proposed trans-Asia railway.[17] As a result of all these factors, most legitimate foreign trade over the last few centuries has been sea-borne. After 1962 smuggling across Burma's land borders reached major proportions, but this trade has declined significantly since the advent of the regime's more open economic policies and a 1989 agreement legalising trade with China.[18]

Within Burma, most rivers run north and south, as do the main transport corridors. East-west travel is difficult. Burma boasts 12,800 kilometres of inland waterways, 3,200 kilometres of which are navigable by large commercial vessels. The Irrawaddy River, for example, permits traffic to penetrate from the sea to Bhamo, more than 1,000 kilometres inland and only 50 kilometres from the Chinese border. The Sittang, lower Chindwin and lower Salween rivers are also used extensively by launches and other river boats, as is the maze of distributaries and creeks in the Irrawaddy delta. Indeed, 'the role of river navigation in traditional Burmese life can scarcely be exaggerated', and these waterways remain a fundamental component in the country's transport network.[19] Burma also has 28,200 kilometres of roads, but many follow the rivers and railway corridors. Only 3,440 kilometres of roads are paved and many bridges cannot take heavy traffic. Since Independence, Burma has placed increasing reliance on air transport but the national fleet has always been small. Of the country's 80 airfields, only three have paved runways over 2,400 metres. Most are unpaved.[20]

Burma's rulers have long been fearful of the massive size of their larger neighbours, and the potential threats they pose. Burma's birth rate has been rising, but its population of 50 million is dwarfed by those of China and India, the world's two most populous countries, with 1,262 million and 1,014 million people respectively.[21] At an average of 73.5 people per square kilometre, Burma's population density is still lower than most major Southeast Asian countries.[22] Greatly complicating the demographic question for Burma is the fact that its population is not homogeneous. At present, about 68% is made up of ethnic Burmans, who have traditionally dominated the central lowlands. The remainder of the population is divided between numerous ethnic groups and sub-groups, most of which have tended to be concentrated in separate areas around the country's highland periphery. The most

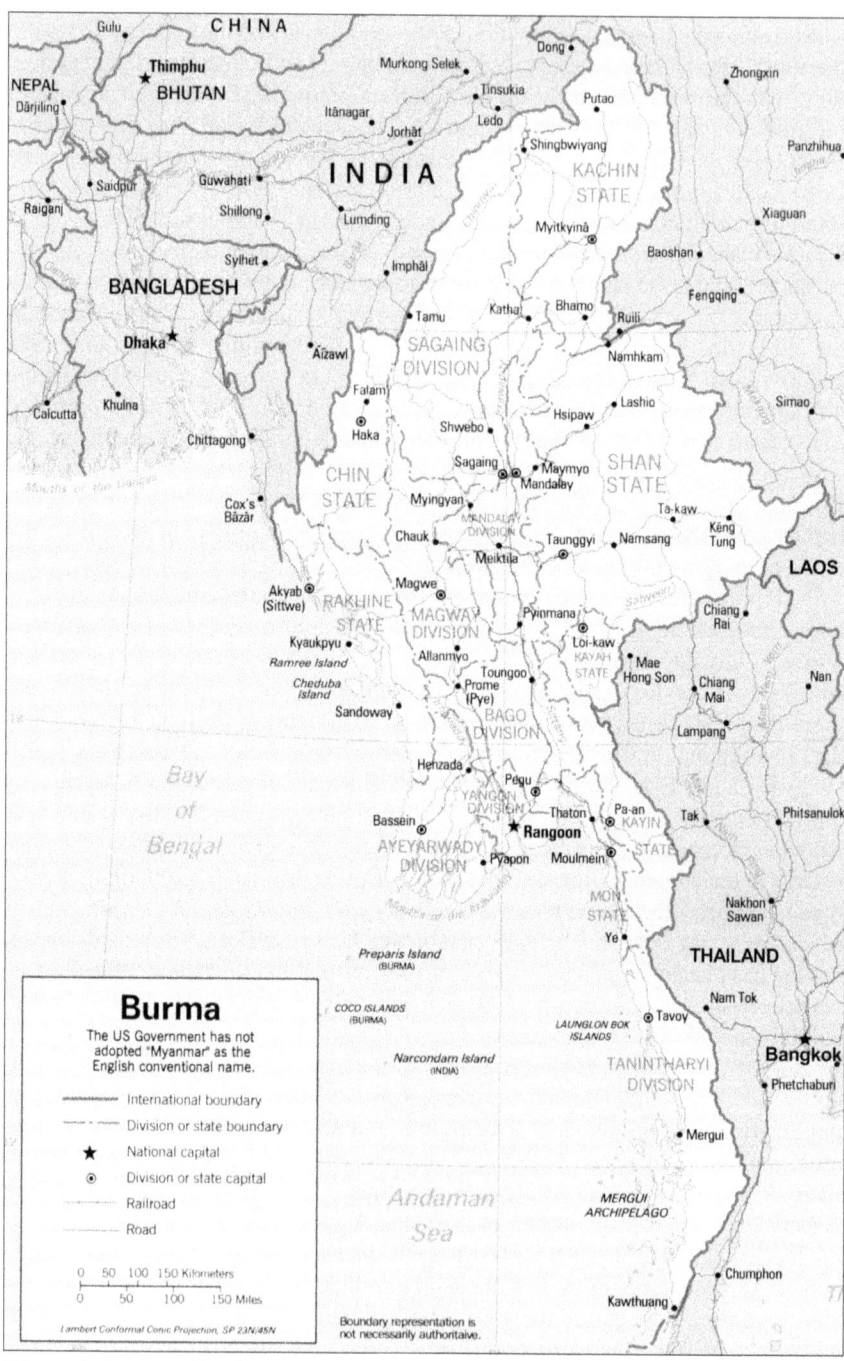

Figure 1: Burma: Physical Geography and Administrative Divisions

important of these groups are the Shan (who constitute 9% of the population), Karen (7%), Arakanese (4%) and Mon (2%). There are significant groups of Chin, Kachin, Kayah (Karenni), PaO, Palaung, Lahu, Wa and Rohingya. There are also sizeable communities of Chinese (3% of the population) and Indians (2%), most of whom are found in the urban areas and along the main transport corridors.[23]

Despite the development of a few cities like Rangoon (with 4 million people), Mandalay (800,000) and Moulmein (300,000), about 70% of Burma's population still lives in small rural towns and villages. Roughly the same proportion is dependent on agriculture as their main means of livelihood, a figure that has held surprisingly constant for the past century.[24] Burma enjoys an abundance of natural resources, and has been described as potentially the richest country in Southeast Asia. Before the Second World War, it was the largest rice producer in the world and a major exporter of oil. Even now, its fishing grounds are relatively unexploited and it has 75% of the world's known reserves of teak. Burma had not recovered from the war, however, before management of the economy fell into the hands of the armed forces, which adopted an ideology known as the Burmese Way to Socialism. Despite some modest growth, this doctrinaire and highly centralised system was a manifest failure, and in 1987 Burma was declared by the UN to be one of the world's least developed countries (LDC).[25] Despite some improvement in the economy since 1988, state-operated enterprises (SOE) remain highly inefficient and privatisation efforts have stalled. There have been attempts to widen the economic base, but the light industrial sector is still small. At US$300, Burma's average annual per capita income is lower than most other Asia-Pacific countries. Nearly 25% of the population is below the official World Bank poverty line.[26]

1.2 The Historical Framework

These geostrategic factors have helped to shape the way Burma views the world, and the way in which its armed forces have developed. Yet domestic political developments have been an even more powerful influence. For, over the past 1000 years, the history of Burma has been punctuated by wars, internecine conflict and social upheaval. It has also been marked by the continued efforts of the Burman majority to gain and maintain control over the other ethnic groups in the country.[27] In all these areas, the role of the armed forces has been critical.

Before the 11th century there were two rival centres of power in Burma, a Mon kingdom in the south and a Burman kingdom based in the central plains.[28] The country was first unified by King Anawrahta in 1044 and remained an independent state until 1287, when an invasion by Kublai Khan's Mongol warriors effectively destroyed political order. There followed five centuries of internal turmoil, compounded from the mid-16th century onwards by intermittent wars with Siam (now Thailand). In the late 18th century the country was reunited by King Alaungpaya. Under him and his successors Burma managed to expand into Thailand, Manipur, Assam and Arakan, while resisting four separate Chinese invasions. During the 19th century, however, Burma became entangled in a competition for regional influence between the British and French. Between 1824 and 1885 Burma fought three unsuccessful wars with the United Kingdom, each of which resulted in the annexation of parts of the country to British India.[29] When the capital of Mandalay finally fell, King Thibaw was exiled to India and the old political system was destroyed. Burma's strong Buddhist culture survived more or less intact, but with the monarchy went many of the country's traditional institutions and social arrangements.

Burma was directly ruled as part of British India from 1886 until 1923, when it was granted a measure of autonomy. This was extended in 1937 when a formal act of separation granted Burma a constitution and limited self-government. Over this 115-year period the British introduced a relatively efficient administrative and legal system. They also oversaw a remarkable development of the Burmese economy, based largely on agriculture and extraction industries. Rangoon, Burma's main port and Britain's headquarters in the delta, came to rival other regional centres as a vibrant, modern city.[30] Yet most of the local population felt disenfranchised, unable to influence events in their own country or benefit from its prosperity. The colonial administration differentiated not only between Europeans and others, but also between the majority Burmans and the ethnic communities in the designated 'Frontier Areas'. Members of the minorities were recruited into the armed forces, and Indians helped run the bureaucracy. Important sectors of the economy were in the hands of British, Chinese or Indian merchants, entrepreneurs and money-lenders. All these factors contributed to a rising sense of nationalism, particularly on the part of the Buddhist Burman majority. In 1930 a rural rebellion broke out in Lower Burma and, as the Second World War approached, there were several major demonstrations and strikes in the cities, protesting against colonial rule.[31]

In December 1941 the Japanese bombed Rangoon, and by May 1942 they had driven the colonial administration out of Burma. With the help of a group of young nationalists led by Aung San, the Japanese established a puppet Burmese government under Dr Ba Maw, as *Naingngan-daw Adipati* (or Head of State). It was overwhelmingly ethnic Burman in character, a factor underlined by the harsh treatment it accorded some Karen communities.[32] Aung San and his followers soon became disillusioned with the Japanese, however, and secretly arranged to throw their support behind the returning Allies. Although a number of the smaller Burmese ethnic groups had remained loyal to the British throughout the war, and helped them conduct a guerrilla campaign against the Japanese, Aung San's widespread popularity and considerable political influence made his nationalist coalition the dominant force in post-war Burma.[33] Recognising these realities, British Prime Minister Clement Attlee agreed to enter into negotiations with Aung San over the question of Burma's independence from the UK. This was granted on 4 January 1948, but not before Aung San himself was assassinated by a jealous rival.[34] The leadership of the nationalist coalition and thus the government of the Union of Burma fell to Aung San's deputy, U Nu.

The new Prime Minister inherited a country devastated by war and riven by political, ideological and ethnic disputes. By 1949 a number of serious insurgencies had broken out and the survival of the fledgling government in Rangoon was in grave doubt. Gradually, however, internal security was restored in the Burman heartland and a measure of economic growth was achieved. Nu's democratic regime was popular, but it was weakened by personality clashes and internal political wrangling which led to a major split in the ruling party in 1958. Faced with the prospect of a military coup, Nu 'invited' the *Tatmadaw*'s Commander-in-Chief, General Ne Win, to form a 'caretaker government' until fresh elections could be held.[35] These took place in 1960 and resulted in a decisive victory for Nu's party. Barely two years later, however, in March 1962, Ne Win seized power. He claimed that the intervention of the armed forces was necessary to restore civil order and to prevent the disintegration of the Union. He set aside the 1948 Constitution and installed a Revolutionary Council (RC) under his own leadership. The Burma Socialist Programme Party (*Ma Sa La*, or BSPP) was declared the sole legal political party and civil society was effectively abolished. Burma's 14-year experiment with democracy had abruptly ended.

In most of these historical events, the armed forces played a critical role. The Burmese monarchs had frequently resorted to military action to settle disputes with their neighbours, enlarge their kingdoms, and to settle local differences. They were not always successful, but over the centuries the nature of these conflicts and the number of their victories gave rise to a certain pride in Burma's military prowess. 'Under the kings the basis of society was not so much the village in which a man lived as the regiment to which he belonged'.[36] This also led to a degree of complacency, however, and as one observer noted 'there was little incentive to spur improvements or modernization of the armed forces, and they remained stagnant, ignoring the progress being made in the world around them'.[37] By the time the British mounted their expedition up the Irrawaddy River in 1885 the Burmese were ill prepared to resist a modern, disciplined military force, equipped with the latest weapons. After Upper Burma was formally annexed the following year, the Burmese armed forces as an institution disappeared. Sporadic guerrilla ambushes against the British continued for another five years or more, but there was no central control over this campaign and often attacks were simple acts of dacoity disguised as patriotism.[38]

Before the formal separation of Burma from India there were no ethnic Burmans in the regular army. A company of sappers and miners had been recruited in 1887, and during the First World War four battalions of Burmese saw active duty in Palestine and Mesopotamia.[39] In 1925, however, a decision was taken by India Army Headquarters to recruit only Chins, Kachins and Karens, whom the British equated with the 'martial races' which they had encountered in India. All Burmans then in the army were discharged on the grounds that it was not only unnecessary and uneconomical to retain them, but also unwise. In general, it was felt, the Burmans had not made good soldiers, and their loyalty had become increasingly suspect as nationalist agitation mounted. The decision was a blow to Burman pride and was bitterly denounced in the Burma Parliament. As defence was an area reserved for the British Governor's direct control, however, there was little the

Burman Members of Parliament (MP) could do. After 1935 the need to open the ranks to Burmans was recognised, but little effort was made to meet it. In any case, young Burmans were not attracted to a career in the armed forces, which tended to be viewed as an instrument of state power through which the minorities helped repress the legitimate aspirations of the Burman majority. As J.S. Furnivall observed, 'the army remained non-Burmese, entirely distinct from the people and an instrument for the maintenance of internal security rather than for defence against aggression'.[40]

When the Imperial Japanese Army marched into Burma in January 1942 many of the Burmans who had been recruited by the British deserted to join the *Bamar Lutlatye Tatmadaw* (Burma Independence Army, or BIA), the force which had been formed in 1941 by Aung San and a group of fellow nationalists, subsequently known as the Thirty Comrades.[41] The BIA was disbanded by the Japanese in mid-1942, largely because of its unruly behaviour but also because they feared that such a large force could constitute a threat to their own position in Burma.[42] In July 1942 a smaller, more disciplined force of some 3,000 BIA men was selected to form the *Bamar Karkweye Tatmadaw* (Burma Defence Army, or BDA) and steps were taken to make this the core of an independent Burmese military force under Japanese control. Aung San was placed in command and Ne Win took charge of one of its three battalions. A military academy was established outside Rangoon, and selected recruits were sent to Japan for advanced training. When Burma was granted its 'independence' by Japan in September 1943, and a Burmese government established under Ba Maw, Aung San was made Minister for Defence. The army was reorganised under Ne Win as the *Bamar Ahmyotha Tatmadaw* (Burma National Army, or BNA).[43] It was this army which Aung San led out of Rangoon in March 1945, ostensibly to fight the Allies, but in fact to join them.

The period between the end of the war in 1945 and Independence in 1948 was one of considerable confusion and tension. The rivalries within both the British and Burmese camps, which had been barely suppressed in the name of defeating the Japanese, quickly re-emerged and multiplied. There were serious disagreements over the country's political future, the place of the ethnic minorities and the fate of those who had fought in various armies. The country was also awash with weapons.[44] Within a few months of Burma regaining its independence, one Communist Party faction had broken away from the coalition government and taken up arms. They were followed by the Muslim *Mujahids* in Arakan State. As described by Ba Than:

> Other insurrections followed one after another until after about a year, there were in all seven insurgent groups totalling over 30,000 in strength, armed and organized, including a considerable number of army deserters, over-running practically two-thirds of the country including strategic towns and keeping the seat of Government virtually under siege.[45]

About one half of the government's own troops mutinied, taking with them 45% of the army's equipment.[46] At the same time, Nationalist Chinese (*Kuomintang*, or

KMT) forces began occupying northeastern Burma, and all around the country small, pocket armies (known as *tats*) were organised by ambitious politicians. By the time that Ne Win assumed the position of Commander-in-Chief in 1949, he had barely 2,000 soldiers under his command. As Mary Callahan has written, 'That the Burmese army emerged from this chaos as the powerful force that after 1962 would dominate state and society for more than 30 years is indeed remarkable'.[47]

In the years that followed, the country's military leadership struggled to organise and develop a force that could meet the many challenges it faced. At first, the *Tatmadaw* was small, poorly trained, under-equipped, and lacking any clear strategy or doctrine. Its organisation was weak, and there were serious differences in the officer corps over how it should be structured and managed.[48] It faced a growing number of insurgencies, as other ethnic and single-interest groups rose against the central government. It also had to manage a plethora of *ad hoc* military forces, including 52 companies of Territorial Forces, or *sit-wundan tats*, which had been raised for local service in the districts.[49] While tackling all these problems, however, the *Tatmadaw* managed to stage a major conventional campaign against the KMT in the 1950s, and followed this in 1961 with a combined operation with the Chinese People's Liberation Army (PLA) against the remaining KMT forces. By the time it seized power in 1962, the *Tatmadaw* had also won back much of central and southern Burma for the government and, by the mid-1970s, most of the remaining insurgent groups had been driven into the country's rugged highland periphery. The armed forces felt that, against enormous odds and at considerable cost, they had saved the Union from disintegration and deserved a major say in its future.

From an early stage, the members of Burma's armed forces saw themselves as having a political role. Many of the young nationalists who helped create the BIA were politicians before they were soldiers, and their ambitions did not disappear with the creation of a regular state army.[50] Aung San took off his uniform in 1945 to pursue a political career, but he remained in close touch with his supporters in the Burma Army and used the threat of renewed violence to win concessions from the UK.[51] As a civilian, Nu was more inclined to view the members of the *Tatmadaw* purely as servants of the state, but the nature of the internal security problems he faced made it inevitable that the armed forces would play a significant role in his government. As Robert Taylor has stated,

> The inclusion of Supreme Commander General Ne Win in the cabinet in April 1949 as Deputy Prime Minister and Minister for Home Affairs as well as for Defence made official for a brief period what was unofficial throughout the first fourteen years of Burma's independence.[52]

Even after Ne Win left the cabinet in 1950, the army remained politically involved. Not only did senior officers keep in touch with key politicians but the complex inter-disciplinary nature of counter-insurgency warfare encouraged field commanders to exercise more than a purely military role. The 18 months of the 'caretaker government' gave the *Tatmadaw* a taste for direct power and convinced many in the military leadership that they could do a better job of running the country than the civilian politicians.[53] This confidence contributed to the decision to seize power in 1962.

During these formative years, the *Tatmadaw* came increasingly to bear the stamp of General Ne Win. Promoting himself as Aung San's heir and successor, Ne Win gradually turned the armed forces into an instrument of immense personal power. He weeded out competitors and dissidents, replacing them with men who owed their positions to him alone. Many were drawn from Ne Win's old battalion, the Fourth Burma Rifles. Signs of disloyalty were ruthlessly crushed. In developing the *Tatmadaw*, as in governing Burma, Ne Win claimed that he was observing the ideals of his assassinated rival, but he introduced many policies and practices which departed significantly from those of Aung San. Even before 1962, but much more so after the coup, the character and tone of the Burmese armed forces were set by Ne Win, who suffered from a deep sense of personal insecurity. Whether this sprang from his mixed Chinese-Burman heritage, modest social origins or failed university career is difficult to say, but he developed a number of marked traits which seemed to be reflected in official policy. His pursuit of a strongly centrist Burman state, economic autarky and strict neutrality in foreign affairs, for example, were allied with a demand for strict political conformity, a distrust of civilian intellectuals, and an abiding suspicion of foreigners.

Even judged against its own standards, the regime's record between 1962 and 1988 was poor. By imposing a single governing philosophy ('The Burmese Way to Socialism') on the entire country for the first time, the *Tatmadaw* affected a profound political, economic and social revolution in Burma. Yet it failed to deliver the results expected. Despite the adoption of a new constitution and the creation of an ostensibly civilian government in 1974, there was widespread resentment against military rule. A pervasive intelligence network helped to keep dissent to a minimum, but from time to time the surface calm in the cities was disrupted by demonstrations against the lack of democratic freedoms, or the regime's economic mismanagement.[54] While there was some growth, the BSPP's doctrinaire socialist policies and lack of professional expertise saw a gradual deterioration in the country's economic fortunes until 1987, when it formally acquired its LDC status.[55] It was really only Burma's natural riches and the ubiquitous black market which permitted most people to survive. The *Tatmadaw* scored some military successes against insurgents, but the regime's harsh policies, particularly towards the ethnic minorities, only encouraged further armed opposition to the central government.

As 1988 dawned, the outlook for Burma was bleak. On all fronts, the military government was struggling to maintain its control. The country was facing severe political, economic and social problems, and Rangoon's writ still did not run in large tracts of territory around the country's periphery. The demonstrations which erupted in August and September that year both resulted from these internal stresses, and greatly exacerbated them, putting more pressure on the old system than it could bear. Some kind of change was inevitable, although few people anticipated the return of military rule and the reinvigoration of the totalitarian system of government which the Burmese had endured since 1962. On 18 September, after weeks of massive public demonstrations in Rangoon and other centres, the *Tatmadaw* created the State Law and Order Restoration Council and took back direct control of the government. The pro-democracy uprising was crushed by the army at the cost of thousands of lives.[56]

The massacres of unarmed demonstrators in Rangoon and other centres was a major turning point. It provoked a strong international reaction, resulting in a series of punitive measures against the military regime. This in turn had a marked effect on the way in which the armed forces saw themselves, and looked at the outside world. Unexpectedly, Burma's position and policies became a focus for renewed international attention.

1.3 International Rivalries Before 1988

Throughout modern history, the importance of Burma's geostrategic position has been recognised by the world's most powerful countries. One of Britain's prime motives for annexing the coastal districts of Arakan and Tenasserim in 1824-6 was to safeguard eastern India and close the gap between Bengal and the Straits Settlements.[57] Sixty years later, both the UK and France were competing for influence at the Burmese court in Mandalay. Indeed, by attempting to balance the rivalry between these two expanding colonial powers, King Thibaw probably helped precipitate his own downfall.[58] The authorities in Delhi subsequently saw Burma as a bulwark against French encroachment west from Indochina. It also promised a possible overland trade route to China. After Japan's invasion of China in 1937, it was quickly realised that Burma offered Chiang Kai-shek's embattled Nationalist government a life-line to Europe. Even before the Burma Road was officially opened in January 1939, vital military supplies were flowing north to Chungking through the port of Rangoon.[59] During the Second World War, Burma was a major theatre of operations. Both Allied and Japanese strategists appreciated that it not only provided China with access to the Indian Ocean, and dominated the Bay of Bengal, but it lay between Japan's conquests in Southeast Asia and the Allied bastion of British India. Lasting from December 1941 until August 1945, the campaign for Burma was to be the longest and one of the most difficult of any during the entire war.[60]

After the war, Burma continued to figure in the security calculations of key Western policy makers. The UK Ministry of Defence, for example, was anxious to retain the rights to use Burmese ports and airfields, and persuaded the Attlee Government to include the question of access in its independence agreement with the Burmese. In the face of rising nationalist sentiment in the Asia-Pacific region, and the danger of communist insurgencies in colonies like Malaya, Mingaladon airfield outside Rangoon became a more important factor in British defence planning. It was considered necesssary 'in connection with His Majesty's Government's air reinforcement route to the Far East, and, in the event of an emergency arising, for the rapid movement of air and land forces, to and through Burma'.[61] Burma was also strategically important in that it was one of the main sources of rice for Britain's Asian dependencies, where food shortages were fuelling anti-colonial sentiment. Burma was inside the Sterling area and rice for places like Malaya could be purchased without the UK using its precious reserves of US dollars.

After 1948, Burma's geostrategic position attracted wider attention. Close to China, India and Vietnam, it was seen as being 'on the periphery of the free world'.[62] During the 1950s, when Rangoon was being threatened by a number of insurgencies, including one led by the powerful Communist Party of Burma (CPB), considerable efforts were made by the British Commonwealth countries to shore up Prime Minister Nu's government.[63] To the members of the Southeast Asia Treaty Organisation (SEATO), Burma at the time was an Asian 'domino' of almost as much strategic importance as Vietnam. The US, for example, firmly believed that 'should Burma come under communist domination, a communist military advance through Thailand might make Indochina, including Tonkin, militarily indefensible'.[64] To the UK, the loss of Burma to the Chinese-sponsored CPB was seen as a threat to the security of Malaya (then including Singapore), and the vital Straits of Malacca.[65] Some other analysts (who clearly had not experienced the terrain) were concerned that China had 'a relatively easy invasion route from Yunnan Province across northern Burma to India's Assam Province'.[66] It has been claimed that India had a tacit understanding with Burma over the joint defence of the Assam-northern Burma area in the event of a Chinese invasion.[67]

Burma may not have been the most important Southeast Asian country facing a communist insurgency at the time, but all these concerns helped to emphasise Burma's strategic role in the ideological struggle then being conducted between the superpowers in the Asia-Pacific region.

The US and its allies were convinced that China was actively supporting communist 'subversion' throughout Southeast Asia, and that this effort was being co-ordinated, or at least encouraged, by the Soviet Union (USSR).[68] While it could not be persuaded to join any military alliances, Burma was identified as an ideal place for the West to establish 'listening posts' and to observe developments inside China. At the height of the Korean War the United States even drew up plans to use Burma as a springboard from which to launch the southern half of a 'double envelopment operation' against China.[69] From 1951 until the mid-1950s the Central Intelligence Agency (CIA) provided covert military support to the *Kuomintang* troops which had fled China after the communist victory in 1949, and established bases in Burma. With additional troops flown in from Taiwan, and supplemented by local insurgents, these forces eventually exceeded 12,000 men. They staged seven unsuccessful 'invasions' of China, before Burmese pressure in the UN forced the US to end its assistance and repatriate some 6,000 KMT troops to Taiwan.[70] Ironically, it was only when Burma sought Chinese help in 1961, and 20,000 PLA soldiers conducted a joint operation with the *Tatmadaw* in northern Burma, that the remnants of the KMT forces were finally driven into Thailand.[71]

The US's secret support for the KMT helped to confirm the reservations felt by Burma's leaders about becoming involved with any foreign power. There was a strong feeling at the time that Burma could, and should, manage its own affairs. In the 1950s Prime Minister Nu was acutely conscious of the need to maintain good relations with Burma's powerful neighbour China, but strove to follow a foreign policy of strict neutrality in international affairs.[72] While Burma was desperately in need of external assistance to recover from the war, he preferred to receive aid from 'independent' countries like Israel and Yugoslavia, and was a major force behind the creation of the Non-Aligned Movement (NAM) in 1961. After 1962 Burma withdrew even further from mainstream global affairs. Fearful of almost all outside influences, the military regime strengthened the former government's neutral foreign policy and shunned most international contacts. In 1979 Burma even withdrew from the NAM on the grounds that the grouping had become unduly influenced by the Eastern bloc.[73] Also, the doctrinaire system introduced by the BSPP permitted little external participation in the country's economy. Foreign aid was still welcomed, particularly after the failure of the regime's socialist policies, but was accepted on a scrupulously even-handed basis. Preference was given to assistance through multilateral bodies like the United Nations and schemes like the Colombo Plan.

After Ne Win's coup, and the country's retreat into xenophobia and isolationism, Burma's geostrategic importance greatly diminished. It rarely figured in published studies of the region's security environment. Yet, to a certain extent, it was still seen as a prize in the global competition between the major power blocs. The United States, Soviet Union and People's Republic of China (PRC) all maintained large missions in Rangoon, which served as bases for active diplomatic and intelligence campaigns.[74] Divided countries, such as the two Koreas, East and West Germany, and North and South Vietnam, also competed for Burma's diplomatic support in forums like the UN General Assembly (UNGA). Burma's success in balancing all these pressures can perhaps be gauged by the fact that, at the height of the Cold War, a Burman, U Thant, was twice unanimously elected Secretary-General of the UN.[75] International interest in Burma's geostrategic position, however, declined even further after the collapse of the USSR and end of the Cold War in 1990. Indeed, had it not done so, it is unlikely that the US (and its friends and allies) would have felt able to maintain such a strong position against the military government after 1988. Ironically, the imposition of economic sanctions and arms embargoes by these countries encouraged the Rangoon regime to develop a much closer relationship with China, a development which has in turn prompted other Asia-Pacific countries to reassess their relations with Burma.

1.4 The Modern Strategic Environment

The Western democracies have all claimed that the strong stance they adopted against Rangoon reflected a principled stand against the massacres of pro-democracy demonstrators, the failure of the regime to recognise the results of the 1990 general elections (which resulted in a landslide victory for the main opposition parties), and the *Tatmadaw*'s continuing record of human rights abuses. This may be so, yet it can be argued that such a strong and sustained policy position would have been less likely if the Cold War had not ended, and Burma's importance in the global competition between the superpowers had not significantly diminished. Lacking any pressing strategic or military reasons to cultivate Burma, and with few direct political or economic interests at stake, countries like the US and UK could afford to isolate the Rangoon regime and accord it pariah status. If this was indeed the calculation made in the late 1980s and early 1990s, then it is possible that the changes which have occurred in the strategic environment since then may prompt a reconsideration of these policies. Already, the development of the *Tatmadaw* and its close relationship with China have served to remind South and Southeast Asian countries at least of Burma's geostrategic importance, and prompted a markedly different policy approach.

The creation of the SLORC in 1988, and subsequent introduction of a range of new policies by the military regime, coincided with some dramatic shifts in the global power balance. The collapse of communism in the USSR and Eastern Europe saw the emergence of the US as the world's sole superpower. In this climate, the agenda of the UN became much more aligned to US interests and values, and more interventionist in nature. Yet this in turn has prompted a backlash by a diverse group of countries united by a desire to deny the US its paramount position in world affairs. Also, with the close of the Cold War came the end of the relative stability and predictability of the old power balance. The proliferation of weapons of mass destruction, and the means to deliver them, has greatly complicated management of the strategic environment. A number of new states and sub-state actors have appeared, and new tensions have arisen. There is now much greater fluidity, and thus greater uncertainty, in international relations. In particular, the last 20 years has seen the rise of China, to the extent that it is now considered a serious competitor for the US's pre-eminent position in the Asia-Pacific region.

Perhaps more than any other factor, it is perceptions of China which are influencing the way in which regional states are responding to changes in the strategic environment. These perceptions may be based, as Robert Tilman has suggested, on a selective reading of history and a number of enduring myths about China's world view, but in international relations perceptions become the reality.[76] Governments make national policy on what they believe to be the case, as much as on the objective truth. For example, China has not, since the 18th century, harboured expansionist ambitions towards, or engaged in open hostilities, with Burma, Thailand or Laos. Although China once included parts of these and other states in a list of 'lost territories', this list has been omitted from Chinese public statements since the 1967 Cultural Revolution. Yet regional perceptions of China's long term strategic intentions are still coloured by the historical evidence of China's support for communist guerrilla movements during the 1950s, 1960s and 1970s, its border war with India in 1962, its (albeit unsuccessful) invasion of Vietnam in 1979, and maps showing China's claims to large tracts of Southeast Asia (including all of Burma and the South China Sea).[77] China's economic growth and military development programs are being watched closely by analysts in the region, and any signs that China is looking to extend its strategic reach are considered causes for concern.

In this regard, Burma's close relationship with China since 1989, in particular its defence links, has attracted considerable attention. Over the past 12 years there have been numerous reports in the international news media and professional journals to the effect that China has provided the Rangoon regime with a wide range of military equipment, arms production facilities and training programs.[78] There has also been a spate of stories stating that China and Burma have an intelligence sharing arrangement, and that Chinese military personnel are helping to operate some of the more specialised electronic surveillance equipment reportedly acquired by the Burmese armed forces.[79] Some commentators have gone even further and claimed that China has already established a permanent military presence in Burma, which includes naval and air bases, and specialised facilities to replenish Chinese naval vessels (including submarines) during regular deployments to the Indian Ocean.[80] Burma has been characterised as a 'pawn' of China, or at least a satellite state.

While some of these reports are true, either in whole or in part, the accuracy of others is highly suspect. Few can be verified from independent sources and a number are clearly based on unsubstantiated rumours or idle speculation. Some of the more outlandish stories may have even been planted deliberately by self-interested parties.[81] Yet, accurate or not, these and similar reports have played on existing suspicions of China's strategic aims, and helped fuel a more immediate concern that Burma's relationship with China could threaten regional stability. These perceptions have in turn prompted a number of specific policy decisions by Southeast Asian governments. For example, while there are clearly strong economic motives, part of their reluctance to join in the West's public condemnation of the Rangoon regime almost certainly stems from a fear of driving Burma further into the arms of China.[82] In addition, there were a number of reasons why Burma was admitted to the Association of Southeast Asian Nations in 1997, against the wishes of its dialogue partners in the West, but a major factor seems to have been a desire on the part of member states to draw Rangoon away from Beijing and prevent Burma from becoming China's stalking horse in the region.[83]

India, at first an outspoken critic of the SLORC, soon reassessed the value of maintaining a hard line against Rangoon. Since 1989 New Delhi has watched anxiously as Chinese capital, aid and military equipment have flowed into Burma. Fears of China's long-term intentions have been heightened by the repeated news reports of Chinese naval bases being constructed on the Burmese coast and intelligence collection stations being developed in and around the Andaman Sea.[84] As one Indian analyst has put it,

> While China professes a policy of peace and friendliness towards India, its deeds are clearly aimed at the strategic encirclement of India in order to marginalise India in Asia and tie it down to the Indian sub-continent.... Pakistan,

Bangladesh, Nepal and Sri Lanka have been assiduously and cleverly cultivated towards this end. Myanmar has been recently added to this list.[85]

These fears prompted a major policy switch in the early 1990s, as India became afraid of pushing Burma further into China's embrace. New Delhi is now engaged in a policy of establishing closer bilateral ties with Rangoon through increased political, trade and even military ties.[86] At the same time, India is trying to develop its economic relations with Southeast Asian states such as Thailand, while offering itself to Singapore, Malaysia and Vietnam as a strategic counter-weight to China.[87]

Other countries in the Asia-Pacific region are also feeling uneasy. For example, Japan is apparently concerned about China's increasing influence in Burma, and the implications for regional stability of its rivalry with India. According to Henry Kissinger, this is one reason why the Japanese government has been keen to restore aid to Burma, despite the opposition of the US and other Western democracies.[88] Japan is also reported to be worried about the security of its SLOCs through the Malacca Strait, which are essential for Japan's Middle East oil imports. The possibility of increased Chinese naval deployments to the Indian Ocean, and the reported construction of Chinese naval and intelligence facilities in the Mergui Archipelago, have added a new factor to Japan's consideration of this issue.[89] The Republic of Korea (ROK, or South Korea) shares some of Japan's concerns. It too is dependent on oil shipments from the Middle East, and hopes to develop its 'textbook-complementary' trade with Burma.[90] While President Kim Dae Jung has been a consistent supporter of the Burmese democratic movement, the ROK too is keen to see international friction avoided in that part of the world.

To date, Burma's foreign policies, and their wider implications, do not appear to have attracted a great deal of interest on the part of Western analysts and officials. Yet this may soon change. Should the Bush Administration continue to see its relationship with Beijing in terms of a 'strategic competition', rather than the 'strategic partnership' once described by President Clinton, then Burma's close relationship with China could assume much greater importance. Rather than being dismissed as a small, isolated and weak player in the region, Rangoon could be seen as an integral part of a much larger and more important security architecture. For example, developing ties between the US and India, including shared interests in a ballistic missile shield, could be viewed as part of a long term move to offset China's strong security relationships with countries like Burma and Pakistan. Similarly, US military aid to Thailand, aimed in the first instance at stemming the flow of narcotics across the Burmese border, could be interpreted as the beginnings of a proxy struggle between the US on the one hand and China on the other, through their Thai and Burmese allies.[91]

For its part, the PRC has much to gain from a close relationship with Burma. China remains anxious about the security of its frontiers, including the long and sensitive border it shares with Burma. A friendly and politically compatible government in Rangoon, looking to China for support against the Western democracies, is very much to Beijing's liking. This is particularly the case, given that the alternative to the military regime may be opposition leader Aung San Suu Kyi, seen by Chinese leaders as being strongly sympathetic to the US. A democratic government in Rangoon would thus add to China's own fears of strategic encirclement by the US and its allies.[92] While regular Chinese naval deployments to the Indian Ocean are a distant prospect, some analysts believe that access to Burmese ports could eventually permit the PLA Navy to 'control and dominate the Indian Ocean's SLOCs', including the Straits of Malacca.[93] Burma's geostrategic position on the Bay of Bengal has reportedly attracted the interest of China's intelligence services.[94] Beijing is also keen to develop the economy of southern China, by exporting goods through a transport corridor stretching from Yunnan to the Irrawaddy River at Bhamo and thence to the Bay of Bengal.[95] Burma is already exporting timber, agricultural and marine products, and precious stones to China, and is receiving light industrial machinery and consumer goods in return.[96]

At a broader diplomatic level, the ASEAN countries are probably correct in judging that China sees Burma as a sympathetic voice in regional councils. In this regard, Beijing would not have to dictate terms to Rangoon, as the Burmese government already shares Beijing's views on such key issues as internal security, human rights and the entitlement of other governments and multilateral organisations to involve themselves in a country's domestic affairs.[97] China no doubt welcomes the addition of Burma to that diverse coalition of countries around the world (including Russia, Iraq, Libya, India and Malaysia) which share a concern about the US's sole superpower status, and global economic influence. These countries also distrust the UN's increased preparedness since 1990 to intervene in global crises, on the grounds of humanitarian sentiment or the need for regional stability. China knows that its position on the UN Security Council (UNSC) is seen by the Rangoon regime as an ultimate guarantee against a UN-sponsored military operation to restore democracy in Burma or to create autonomous ethnic states, along the lines of the multilateral intervention in East Timor.[98] In return, it feels it can count on Burma's support in other UN debates, relating to subjects like human rights.

There are two main schools of thought about China's future relations with Burma.[99] The first harks back to the great power politics and strategic balances of the Cold War era. Its members argue that small, poverty-stricken Burma will inevitably succumb to the pressures of its much larger neighbour, and effectively become a pawn in China's bid to achieve world power status. In addition to China's enormous strategic weight, the members of this school cite China's apparent 'stranglehold' over Burma, as exercised through its loans, arms sales and trade.[100] The second school argues that, throughout history, Burma has always been suspicious of China, and only turned to Beijing in 1989 out of dire necessity after it was ostracized by the West. Proponents of this school claim that China has not been as successful in winning Burma's confidence as sometimes reported. They also believe that the Rangoon government would be prepared to pay a very high price to remain independent, and accept the military regime's repeated assurances that Chinese military bases will never be permitted in Burma.[101] Should the Rangoon government wish to break out of China's embrace, this second school argues, then

India, other regional countries and possibly even the Western democracies would be prepared to assist.[102] The latter school benefits from a deeper understanding of Burmese history but, in any case, the conclusion that Burma has become a satellite of China, and would be a willing ally in any future military confrontation between China and other regional countries, should not go unchallenged.

Indeed, it can be argued that, in many respects, it is not Beijing but Rangoon which has the whip hand. The military regime recognises Burma's considerable debts to China, and its vulnerability to a range of diplomatic, economic and military pressures from its larger neighbour, but it believes it can manage the bilateral relationship in a way that preserves Burma's sovereignty, territorial integrity and freedom of action.[103] The regime may have been encouraged by the way that Chinese officials in Burma have kept a low public profile, and learned to tread warily in contacts with their Burmese counterparts. This seems to be out of concern that they will upset the notoriously volatile and unpredictable Burmese leadership, and lose the gains China has made since 1988. They may even retain memories of the violent anti-Chinese riots in Rangoon in 1967. Also, the SLORC and SPDC have been quick to recognise Burma's growing importance in the more fluid Asia-Pacific strategic environment. Over the past 12 years the military government has become adept at exploiting Burma's geostrategic position and manipulating the concerns of its regional neighbours. For example, it has been quite comfortable about using its close relationship with Beijing, and the possibility that it might become an ally of an expansionist China, to gain attention in important councils like ASEAN, and to attract support from influential countries like India and Singapore.[104]

There are other security issues that have focussed attention on Rangoon since 1988. Thailand and Bangladesh, for example, have both repeatedly expressed concern about the wider implications of Burma's continuing internal problems, particularly the periodic passage of refugees across its borders.[105] Burma has also attracted strong criticism over its failure to stem the flow of narcotics from the Golden Triangle, or to take action to counter Burma's rapidly growing HIV/AIDS problem. Both are seen to have far-reaching strategic implications.[106] The US Secretary of State has even characterised the HIV/AIDS issue as Southeast Asia's greatest threat to health and security.[107] More recently, international attention has been drawn to the problems of forced labour, child soldiers, the indiscriminate use of landmines, and the traffic in small arms. The Rangoon regime has been slow to react to representations about these issues, although it made a rare policy change in 1992 when the Islamic countries in ASEAN expressed concern about the treatment of the Rohingyas in Arakan State. The plight of the Rohingyas also attracted the attention of radical Islamic organisations in Afghanistan and the Middle East. At the time, the United Nations Secretary-General stated that he was 'seriously concerned' that the crisis could threaten the stability of Southeast Asia.[108]

In such an atmosphere of suspicion and distrust, the development of Burma's armed forces, the manner in which this has been achieved, and how they might be used in future, has attracted increased attention. While it still faces a number of problems, the *Tatmadaw* is now capable not only of multiple, large-scale counter-insurgency campaigns against internal security threats, but also more conventional operations in defence of Burma's territory and maritime claims. While it has limited power projection capabilities, neighbouring countries like India and Thailand have already cited Burma's arms acquisition program as justification for costly improvements in their own armed forces. There has also been an increase in the *Tatmadaw*'s international contacts, including in the defence and intelligence fields. In these circumstances, Burma can no longer be dismissed as a weak and isolated player in the region, with little or no impact on the wider strategic environment.

Notes

1. An expanded version of this chapter was published as *Burma: A Strategic Perspective*, The Asia Foundation, Working Paper No. 13 (San Francisco, 2001).

2. For the purposes of this study, the Asia-Pacific region has been taken to mean that part of the world stretching from Afghanistan in the west to Fiji in the east, and from the Russian Far East in the north to New Zealand in the south.

3. For two interpretations of this period, see Maung Htin Aung, *A History of Burma* (Columbia University Press, New York, 1967); and J.F. Cady, *A History of Modern Burma* (Cornell University Press, Ithaca, 1978).

4. Samuel Huntington, *The Clash of Civilizations and the Remaking of World Order* (Simon and Schuster, New York, 1996).

5. As evidence of this trend, an international conference was held in Washington DC on 1 February 2001, to consider 'Strategic Rivalries on the Bay of Bengal: The Burma/Myanmar Nexus'.

6. These and the following statistics are drawn from *The World Factbook 2000*, produced by the Central Intelligence Agency, and found on the internet at http:www.cia.gov/cia/publications/factbook/geos/bm.html

7. *Limits in the Seas, No. 36, National Claims to Maritime Jurisdictions* (Bureau of Oceans and International Environmental and Scientific Affairs, US Department of State, Washington DC, 1995), p. 20. See also George Kent and M.J. Valencia (eds), *Marine Policy in Southeast Asia* (University of California Press, Berkeley, 1985), p. 44.

8. Andrew Selth, 'The Burma Navy Under the SLORC', *Journal of Contemporary Asia*, Vol. 29, No. 2, 1999, p. 234.

9. See *History of Chinese Communist Strategy re Sino-Burmese Border Question: Research Backgrounder* (n.p. , Hong Kong, 1960); and Ralph Pettman, *China in Burma's Foreign Policy*, Contemporary China Papers No. 7 (Australian National University Press, Canberra, 1973), p. 11 and p. 23.

10. See, for example, 'Uncommon ground', *Bangkok Post*, 25 March 2001.

11. Kent and Valencia, *Marine Policy in Southeast Asia*, pp. 242-3. See also J.R. Morgan and M.J. Valencia (eds), *Atlas for Marine Policy in Southeast Asian Seas* (University of California Press, Berkeley, 1983), p. 49.

12. Rahul Roy-Chaudhury, 'Trends in the Delimitation of India's Maritime Boundaries', *Strategic Analysis*, Vol. 22, No. 10, January 1999, pp. 1513-6.

13. See, for example, 'Junta jails more than 300 Bangladesh fishermen', Reuters, 7 December 1999; and 'Burmese boat reportedly fires at Thai fishing trawler in Thai waters', *The Nation*, 15 March 2001.

14. State Department, *Limits in the Seas*, p. 20.

15. C.A. Fisher, *South-east Asia: A Social, Economic and Political Geography* (Methuen, London, 1964), p. 464.

16. Interviews, Rangoon, April 1995. See also Bertil Lintner, 'Burma Road', *Far Eastern Economic Review* (hereafter *FEER*), 6 November 1997, pp. 16-17.
17. Bruce Gilley, 'All Aboard', *FEER*, 14 December 2000, p. 29; and 'New border trade post opened on Sino-Burma border', *Burma News Update*, June 2000, p. 5.
18. It has been estimated by one well-informed embassy in Rangoon that, before 1988, almost half of Burma's actual trade was 'unofficial', ie conducted on the black market. Interview, Rangoon, April 1995.
19. Fisher, *South-east Asia*, pp. 442-3.
20. *The World Factbook 2000*.
21. *The World Factbook 2000*. See also Charles Hirschman, 'Population and Society in Twentieth-Century Southeast Asia', *Journal of Southeast Asian Studies*, Vol. 25, No. 2, September 1994, p. 390; and 'Burma says population passes 50 million', Reuters, 12 July 2000.
22. Those even lower than Burma are Malaysia, Cambodia, Laos and Brunei.
23. *The World Factbook 2000*. See also Kunstadter, *Southeast Asian Tribes, Minorities, and Nations*, Vol. 1, pp. 75-124.
24. Cheng Siok-hwa, *The Rice Industry of Burma, 1852-1940* (University of Malaya Press, Kuala Lumpur, 1968), p. 220. See also *The World Factbook 2000*.
25. Burma only qualified as a LDC, however, by deliberately under-estimating its literacy rate. For a concise summary of this period, see Khin Maung Kyi et al, *Economic Development of Burma: A Vision and A Strategy* (Olof Palme International Centre, Stockholm, 2000), pp. 1-16.
26. *The World Factbook 2000*. See also *Burma: Country Report on Human Rights Practices - 2000* (Bureau of Democracy, Human Rights and Labor, US State Department, Washington DC, 2001).
27. J.W. Henderson et al, *Area Handbook for Burma* (American University and Department of the Army, Washington, 1971) p. 23.
28. In addition to the works by Htin Aung and Cady cited above, see Dorothy Woodman, *The Making of Burma* (Cresset, London, 1962); and F.N. Trager, *Burma: From Kingdom to Independence: A Historical and Political Analysis* (Pall Mall, London, 1966). Details of more specialised studies of Burma's history can be found in P.M. Herbert, *Burma* (Clio, Oxford, 1991).
29. In 1826 the British annexed the Arakan and Tenasserim coastal strips. In 1852 they added Lower Burma, including Rangoon. Mandalay fell in 1885, and with it most of what is now modern Burma.
30. See, for example, F.S.V. Donnison, *Public Administration in Burma: A Study of Development During the British Connexion* (Royal Institute of International Affairs, London, 1953); and J.R. Andrus, *Burmese Economic Life* (Stanford University Press, Stanford, 1953). A more critical interpretation of British rule can be found in Maung Tin Aung, *A History of Burma*. Also relevant is Manuel Sarkisyanz, *Peacocks, Pagodas and Professor Hall*, Papers in International Studies, Southeast Asia Series No. 24 (Ohio University Centre for International Studies, Southeast Asia Program, Athens, 1972).
31. See, for example, A.D. Moscotti, *British Policy and the Nationalist Movement in Burma, 1917-1937* (University Press of Hawaii, Honolulu, 1974); Maung Maung, *From Sangha to Laity: Nationalist Movements of Burma, 1920-1940*, Australian National University Monographs on South Asia No. 4 (Manohar, Delhi, 1980); and Patricia Herbert, *The Hsaya San Rebellion (1930-1932) Reappraised*, Working Paper No. 27 (Centre of Southeast Asian Studies, Monash University, Melbourne, 1982).
32. Andrew Selth, 'Race and Resistance in Burma, 1942-1945', *Modern Asian Studies*, Vol. 20, No. 3, July 1986, pp. 483-507.

33. See Hugh Tinker (ed), *Burma: The Struggle for Independence, 1944-1948*, 2 vols, (Her Majesty's Stationery Office, London, 1983).
34. For details, see Kin Oung, *Who Killed Aung San?*.
35. Callahan, 'The Origins of Military Rule in Burma', pp. 468-80.
36. Hugh Tinker, *The Union of Burma: A Study of the First Years of Independence* (Oxford University Press, London, 1957), p. 312.
37. Henderson, *Area Handbook for Burma*, p. 275.
38. The British lost more men to guerrillas and *dacoits* in the following four years than were killed during the advance on Mandalay. See A.T.Q. Stewart, *The Pagoda War: Lord Dufferin and the Fall of the Kingdom of Ava, 1885-6* (Faber and Faber, London, 1972), p. 108; and Charles Crosthwaite, *The Pacification of Burma* (Frank Cass, London, 1968), pp. 1-3.
39. Tinker, *The Union of Burma*, p. 314.
40. J.S. Furnivall, *Colonial Policy and Practice: A Comparative Study of Burma and Netherlands India* (New York University Press, New York, 1956), p. 184. At the outbreak of the Second World War only 472 Burmans (including here Mons and Shans) were members of the regular armed forces, although together the three ethnic groups constituted over 75% of the country's population. By contrast, there were 1448 Karens (then 9.3% of the population), 868 Chins (2.3%), 881 Kachins (1.05%) and 168 members of other ethnic groups. Of the officers, only four were Burman while 75 came from the minority ethnic groups. See Dr Maung Maung, *Burma in the Family of Nations* (Djambatan, Amsterdam, 1956), p. 90.
41. The 30 men had secretly left Burma in early 1941 to be trained by the Japanese. See Dr Maung Maung (ed), *Aung San of Burma* (Martinus Nijhoff, The Hague, 1962); and Izumiya Tatsuro, *The Minami Organ*, (Higher Education Department, Rangoon, 1985).
42. Joyce Lebra believes BIA numbers reached 200,000, but this is too high. Yoon Won-zoon claims there were only 10,000 in the BIA. Ba Than is likely to be closer to the mark with an estimate of 23,000. See Lebra, *Japanese Trained Armies*, p. 65; Ba Than, *Roots of the Revolution*, p. 33; and Yoon Won-zoon, 'Japan's Occupation of Burma, 1941-1945', unpublished PhD thesis, New York University, 1971, p. 173.
43. By 1944 the BNA consisted of six battalions of infantry, two of anti-aircraft personnel and one of sappers and miners. It was overwhelmingly Burman in character, despite the late inclusion of one battalion of Karens. Tinker, *The Union of Burma*, p. 319. See also Selth, 'Race and Resistance in Burma', p. 493.
44. Two personal perspectives on this period can be found in Balwant Singh, *Independence and Democracy in Burma, 1945-1952: The Turbulent Years*, Michigan Papers on South and Southeast Asia, No. 40 (Centre for South and Southeast Asian Studies, University of Michigan, Ann Arbor, 1993); and J.H. McEnery, *Epilogue in Burma, 1945-48: The military dimension of British withdrawal* (Spellmount, Tunbridge Wells, 1990).
45. Ba Than, *The Roots of the Revolution*, p. 67.
46. *Ibid*. See also *Burma and the Insurrections* (Government of the Union of Burma, Rangoon, 1949).
47. Callahan, 'The Origins of Military Rule in Burma', p. 6.
48. This period is examined in detail by Callahan, 'The Origins of Military Rule in Burma'.
49. Tinker, *The Union of Burma*, p. 323.
50. R.H. Taylor, *The State in Burma* (Hurst, London, 1987), p. 237.
51. Aung San could also use the threat of trouble from the People's Volunteer Organisation, a militia established in December 1945 from Burmese war veterans who had not been taken into the regular army.
52. Taylor, *The State in Burma*, p. 237.

53. For the caretaker government's own record of its achievements, see *Is Trust Vindicated? A chronicle of the various accomplishments of the Government headed by General Ne Win during the period of tenure from November, 1958 to February 6, 1960* (Director of Information, Government of the Union of Burma, Rangoon, 1960). See also Callahan, 'The Origins of Military Rule in Burma', pp. 491-7.

54. See, for example, Andrew Selth, *Death of a Hero: The U Thant Disturbances in Burma, December 1974*, Australia-Asia Paper No. 49 (Centre for the Study of Australia-Asia Relations, Griffith University, Brisbane, 1989).

55. See, for example, Tin Maung Maung Than, 'Burma in 1987: Twenty-Five Years after the Revolution', in *Southeast Asian Affairs 1988* (Institute for Southeast Asian Studies, Singapore, 1988), pp. 73-93. Also useful is a series of articles by Bertil Lintner in the *FEER*, including 'Poor amid plenty' (6 October 1988, p. 65), 'Searching for a new road' (20 October 1988, p. 111) and 'All the wrong moves' (27 October 1988, p. 83).

56. The best source for these events is Bertil Lintner, *Outrage: Burma's Struggle for Democracy* (White Lotus, Bangkok, 1990). A different perspective is given by Dr Maung Maung, *The 1988 Uprising in Burma*, Monograph No. 49 (Yale University Southeast Asia Studies, New Haven, 2000).

57. Fisher, *South-east Asia*, p. 435, note 15.

58. Woodman, *The Making of Burma*, pp. 222-30; and Cady, *A History of Modern Burma*, pp. 117-21. See also O.B. Pollak, *Empires in Collision: Anglo-Burmese Relations in the Mid-Nineteenth Century* (Greenwood Press, Westport, 1979), pp. 153-72.

59. A useful account of the birth of the Burma Road can be found in J.L. Christian, *Burma and the Japanese Invader* (Thacker and Company, Bombay, 1945), pp. 210-36.

60. The best one-volume history is Louis Allen, *Burma: The Longest War, 1941-1945* (Dent and Sons, London, 1984).

61. Tinker, *Burma: The Struggle for Independence*, Vol. 2, p. 693 and p. 736.

62. T.D. Roberts *et al*, *Area Handbook for Burma* (American University, Washington DC, 1968), p. v.

63. For the thinking behind this policy, see Andrew Selth, 'Australian Defence Contacts With Burma, 1945-1987', *Modern Asian Studies*, Vol. 26, No. 3, July 1992, pp. 451-68.

64. '1952 Policy Statement by US on Goals in Southeast Asia', Key Document No. 2, *The Pentagon Papers* (Bantam Books, Toronto, 1971), p. 28. See also Henry Kissinger, *Diplomacy* (Touchstone, New York, 1995), p. 624 and p. 632.

65. A.J. Levine, *The United States and the Struggle for Southeast Asia* (Praeger, Westport, 1995), pp. 12-13. See also Andrew Selth, 'Burma: "Hidden Paradise" or Paradise Lost?', *Current Affairs Bulletin*, Vol. 68, No. 6, November 1991, pp. 4-5.

66. *Union of Burma: Background Notes*, (US Department of State, Washington DC, 1971). Anyone who believes that an invasion of India through this part of Burma would be 'relatively easy' is advised to read Bertil Lintner, *Land of Jade: A Journey Through Insurgent Burma* (Kiscadale, Edinburgh, 1990); and Shelby Tucker, *Among Insurgents: Walking Through Burma* (Radcliffe Press, London, 2000).

67. T.N. Dupuy (ed), *The Almanac of World Military Power* (Dupuy Associates, Dunn Loring, 1970), p. 252.

68. See, for example, Robert Thompson, *Revolutionary War in World Strategy, 1945-1969* (Secker and Warburg, London, 1970), pp. 62-3.

69. Bertil Lintner, 'The CIA's First Secret War', *FEER*, 16 September 1993, pp. 56-8.

70. *Kuomintang Aggression Against Burma* (Ministry of Information, Rangoon, 1953). See also R.H. Taylor, *Foreign and Domestic Consequences of the KMT Intervention in Burma*, Data Paper No. 93 (Southeast Asia Program, Cornell University, Ithaca, 1973).

71. According to Bertil Lintner, KMT activities in Burma did not end here. Until forced out by the CPB in the late 1960s and early 1970s, KMT intelligence networks in northern Burma provided Taiwan and the US with regular reports on developments in China and Chinese arms shipments to neighbouring countries. Lintner, 'The CIA's First Secret War', p. 58.

72. This brief reference does not do justice to the complexity of Burma's foreign policy during the post-war era which, as David Steinberg has pointed out, 'within the overall neutralist position, has shifted markedly in response to both internal and external stimuli'. D.I. Steinberg, *Burma: A Socialist Nation of Southeast Asia* (Westview, Boulder, 1982), p. 122.

73. K.P. Misra, 'Burma's Farewell to the Nonaligned Movement', *Asian Affairs*, Vol. 12, No. 1, February 1981, pp. 49-56.

74. See, for example, Aleksandr Kaznacheev, *Inside a Soviet Embassy: Experiences of a Russian Diplomat in Burma* (Lippincott, Philadelphia, 1962). Edgar O'Ballance has suggested that Russia was looking for access to Burma's naval facilities, but this is unlikely. See 'Burma: Back Water or Black Sheep?', *Asian Defence Journal*, April 1986, pp. 28-35.

75. Thant served as UN Secretary General from 1961-1971. See June Bingham, *U Thant: The Search for Peace* (Victor Gollancz, London, 1966), pp. 211-21.

76. R.O. Tilman, *The Enemy Beyond: External Threat Perceptions in the ASEAN Region* (Institute for Southeast Asian Studies, Singapore, 1984).

77. For example, a Chinese textbook entitled *A Brief History of Modern China*, published in Beijing in 1954, includes a map which shows all of mainland Southeast Asia and the South China Sea falling within China's borders before the Opium War in 1840.

78. See, for example, Bertil Lintner, 'Myanmar's Chinese connection', *International Defense Review*, Vol. 27, No. 11, November 1994, p. 23-6; and Andrew Selth, *Burma's Arms Procurement Programme*, Working Paper No. 289 (Strategic and Defence Studies Centre, Australian National University, Canberra, 1995).

79. See, for example, Bertil Lintner, 'Arms for Eyes', *FEER*, 16 December 1993, p. 26; Bertil Lintner, 'Enter the Dragon', *FEER*, 22 December 1994, pp. 22-4; and Desmond Ball, *Burma's Military Secrets: Signals Intelligence (SIGINT) from the Second World War to Civil War and Cyber Warfare* (White Lotus, Bangkok, 1998), pp. 219.

80. See, for example, 'China and the Indian Ocean: Poised for Chaos', in Jayant Baranwal (ed), *SP's Military Yearbook 1992-93* (Guide Publications, New Delhi, 1992), p. 374; and Poshpinder Singh, 'Concern at Chinese Build-up', *Asian Defence Journal*, February 1993, p. 8.

81. There have been suggestions that certain Indian groups have encouraged fears of a growing Chinese threat in Burma, for both domestic and international political purposes. See, for example, William Ashton, 'Chinese Bases in Burma - Fact or Fiction?', *Jane's Intelligence Review*, Vol. 7, No. 2, February 1995, pp. 84-7; and Sandy Gordon, 'Sino-Indian Relations After the Cold War', *Strategic and Defence Studies Centre Newsletter*, Canberra, March 1993, pp. 1-4.

82. Selth, *Burma's Secret Military Partners*, pp. 38-43.

83. Robert Cribb, 'Burma's Entry Into ASEAN: Background and Implications', *Asian Perspective*, Vol. 22, No. 3, 1998, pp. 49-62.

84. See, for example, Swaran Singh, 'Myanmar: China's Gateway to the Indian Ocean', *Journal of Indian Ocean Studies*, Vol. 3, No. 1, November 1995, pp. 80-7; 'India trying hard to build military ties with Burma', *Asian Age*, 7 July 2000; and Bertil Lintner, 'Arms for Eyes', p. 26.

85. Gurmeet Kanwal, 'Countering China's Strategic Encirclement of India', *Indian Defence Review*, Vol. 15, No. 3, July-September 2000, p. 13.

86. Andrew Selth, 'Burma and the Strategic Competition Between China and India', *Journal of Strategic Studies*, Vol. 19, No. 2, June 1996, pp. 213-30.

87. Michael Vatikiotis, 'A Friend in Need', *FEER*, 10 July 1997, p. 32. See also Ranjan Gupta, 'Singapore buys Indian protection as old friendships cool', *The Australian*, 7 February 1994.

88. 'The new world order, according to Dr Kissinger', *Financial Review*, 17 November 1995; and 'China fears stoke new passions', Reuters, 9 December 2000.

89. Lintner, 'Arms for Eyes', p. 26; and interview, Tokyo, April 2001.

90. See, for example, Than Nyun and Khin Maung Oo, 'Prospects for Myanmar-Korea Economic Cooperation', in Than Nyun and Dalchoong Kim, *Myanmar-Korea Economic Cooperation*, East and West Studies Series No. 22 (Institute of East and West Studies, Yonsei University, Seoul, 1992), pp. 189ff.

91. See, for example, 'US, China Take Sides in Border Skirmish', *Chicago Tribune*, 19 May 2001; and Rodney Tasker and Bertil Lintner, 'Nasty Job For Task Force 399', *FEER*, 19 April 2001, pp. 24-5.

92. Interview, Beijing, October 1999.

93. YB, 'Beijing Consolidates Its Hold on Myanmar', *Defense and Foreign Affairs*, July 1997, p. 3; and Lintner, 'Arms for Eyes', p. 26.

94. Ball, *Burma's Military Secrets*, pp. 219-29.

95. Bertil Lintner, 'Enter the Dragon', pp. 22-4. See also Pan Qi, 'Opening the Southwest: An Expert opinion', *Beijing Review*, Vol. 28, No. 35, 2 September 1985, pp. 22-3.

96. Two-way trade in 1998 was estimated at US$381 million, and growing at 10% per year. Xinhua News Agency, 19 October 1999. See also E.C. Chapman, 'Cross-Border Trade Between Yunnan and Burma, and the Emerging Mekong Corridor', *Thai-Yunnan Newsletter*, No. 19, December 1992, pp. 15-19; and Mya Maung, 'On the Road to Mandalay: A Case Study of the Sinonization of Upper Burma', *Asian Survey*, Vol. 34, No. 5, May 1994, pp. 447-59.

97. Robert Karniol, 'New channels of Asian diplomacy unfold', *Jane's Defence Weekly* (hereafter *JDW*), 24 June 1995, pp. 27-31.

98. Interview, Rangoon, November 1999.

99. These two schools were identified in Kay Merrill, 'Myanmar's China connection: a cause for alarm?', *Asia-Pacific Defence Reporter*, 1998 Annual Reference Edition, Vol. 24, No. 1, January 1998, pp. 20-1.

100. See, for example, J.M. Malik, 'Sino-Indian Rivalry in Myanmar: Implications for Regional Security', *Contemporary Southeast Asia*, Vol. 16, No. 2, September 1994, pp. 137-56; and J.M. Malik, 'Burma slides under China's shadow', *Jane's Intelligence Review*, Vol. 9, No. 7, July 1997, pp. 319-22.

101. See, for example, 'Junta denies it poses threat to region', Reuters, 10 August 1999.

102. See, for example, Selth, 'Burma and the Strategic Competition Between China and India', pp. 213-30; and Kay Merrill, 'A closer look at Sino-Burmese links', *Jane's Intelligence Review*, Vol. 9, No. 7, July 1997, p. 323.

103. Interviews, Rangoon, December 1999; and Washington, February 2001. This interpretation has been questioned by, for example, J.M. Malik, 'Myanmar's Role in Regional Security: Pawn or Pivot?', *Contemporary Southeast Asia*, Vol. 19, No. 1, June 1997, pp. 52-73.

104. See, for example, William Ashton, 'Burma receives advances from its silent suitors in Singapore', *Jane's Intelligence Review*, Vol. 10, No. 3, March 1998, pp. 32-4.

105. One of the best studies on this subject is Hazel J. Lang, *Fear and Sanctuary: Burmese Refugees in Thailand*, (Cornell Southeast Asia Program, Ithaca, forthcoming). See also *Rohingya Refugees in Bangladesh: The Search for a Lasting Solution*, Human Rights Watch/Asia, Vol. 9, No. 7, August 1997.

106. See, for example, Bertil Lintner, *The Drug Trade in Southeast Asia*, Special Report No. 5, *Jane's Intelligence Review*, April 1994; Bertil Lintner, 'Global Reach: Drug Money

in the Asia Pacific', *Current History*, April 1998, pp. 179-82; Sarah Stewart, 'Myanmar facing AIDS catastrophe', Australian Associated Press (AAP), 27 November 2000; and 'Burma continues to present unusual threat', *Burma News Update*, May 1998, p. 8.

107. 'HIV/AIDS Number One Security Threat in SE Asia: Albright', Agence France Presse (AFP), 28 July 2000.

108. Bertil Lintner, 'The secret mover', *FEER*, 7 May 1992, p. 21.

2

Defence Policies and Threat Perceptions

> If a policy is to have the desired impact on its target, it must be perceived as it is intended; if the other's behaviour is to be anticipated and the state's policy is a major influence on it, then the state must try to determine how its actions are being perceived. — Robert Jervis, 'Deterrence and Perception', *International Security* (Winter, 1982-83)

Burma's military government has usually been very reluctant to describe its national defence policies, and to elaborate on the reasons for the remarkable growth and development of the *Tatmadaw* over the past decade. Questioned about Burma's acquisition of a vast array of new weapons and equipment since 1988, for example, spokesmen for the regime have simply stated that 'These arms are for our legitimate defence needs. There hasn't been an excessive amount of buying, just what's adequate for our needs.'[1] Those needs have never been spelt out in detail, but they have usually been related in whole or in part to three 'national causes', or key policy goals, which the SLORC and SPDC have raised to the level of guiding principles.

These broad goals can be interpreted in a number of ways. Indeed, on closer examination, they can be read as codes to disguise a number of persistent fears, the answer to which has invariably been the expansion and modernisation of the country's armed forces. For, despite its obvious political power and military strength, the Rangoon regime still feels insecure. This sense of vulnerability stems mainly from domestic concerns, but is also related to the regime's unique perceptions of external threats.

2.1 Burma's Defence Policies

Burma does not appear ever to have formally promulgated its defence policies — at least, not as a discrete official document of the kind produced by many First

World countries. Nor, despite promises to do so, has it ever published a White Paper on Defence, of the kind increasingly favoured by multilateral organisations like the ASEAN Regional Forum.

There are several reasons for this reticence. Firstly, ever since Independence, the Burmese government has been preoccupied with internal security problems. Clearly, these are not unrelated to defence but, as Robert Taylor has pointed out, internal security has always been seen as 'essentially a matter of domestic politics', and thus not something which required formal expositions to the international community.[2] Also, between 1948 and 1988 the discourse on security in Burma was monopolized by a small elite of the country's political and military leaders.[3] Since the creation of the SLORC this situation has been taken further, with national security affairs now completely dominated by the senior ranks of the *Tatmadaw*. There has thus been no attempt made either by the government or the armed forces (where they have differed) to invite debate on, or even endorsement of, their security policies from members of the public. Indeed, wider discussion of defence issues in Burma has been very restricted, if not actively discouraged. Ever since Ne Win's coup, the defence of the state and the defence of the regime have been viewed as one and the same. Since 1988, there has not even been a distinction between the state, the government and the armed forces, which have all been conflated. In these circumstances, as the opposition National League for Democracy (NLD) has already discovered to its cost, any public discussion of 'defence' or 'security' in Burma is seen as posing a direct challenge to the regime itself.[4]

Generally speaking, external security issues have been less sensitive but, once again, they have attracted little public debate. For the Nu Government, they were 'primarily a problem of diplomacy at the level of state-to-state relations'.[5] As such, a separate defence policy was considered neither necessary nor appropriate. After 1962, the Ne Win regime too was content to rely on official statements of foreign policy to cover broader security issues. These statements emphasised Burma's neutrality and non-alignment in world affairs, its respect for the sovereignty and territorial integrity of other countries, its wish for the abolition of weapons of mass destruction, its faith in the principles of the UN, and its support for 'the ideal of peace, friendly relations and cooperation between all nations based on international justice and morality'.[6] The clear implication of all these statements was that Rangoon subscribed to policies of self-defence and self-reliance, within a strongly nationalist conceptual framework. Unlike some of its regional neighbours, Burma did not see itself as having wider strategic objectives such as fostering the security of its immediate neighbourhood, or maintaining strategic stability in the Asia-Pacific region. Burma's only known contributions to global security during this period were the *Tatmadaw*'s participation in four UN peace-keeping operations during the 1950s and 1960s.[7]

This approach has also been followed by the SLORC and SPDC. Rangoon's non-alignment has been compromised by its strong ties with Beijing, and there has been some criticism of the UN (and its associated agencies), but the main pillars of Burma's external security policy remain much the same as before.

In one area of defence policy formulation, however, there have been some changes. Since 1988 the regime has placed considerable emphasis on the repeated publication of a range of broad goals and political slogans to define its approach to national security issues. In what appears to be a conscious imitation of the numerical ordering system favoured by Theravada Buddhist doctrine, these have been issued as three 'national causes', 12 'national objectives' and three 'people's desires'. The regime's three national causes are:

- The non-disintegration of the Union;
- The non-disintegration of national solidarity; and
- The perpetuation of national sovereignty.[8]

The 12 national objectives are divided equally into political, economic and social objectives, as follows:

- Stability of the state, community peace and tranquillity, and the prevalence of law and order;
- National reconsolidation;
- Emergence of a new enduring State Constitution; and
- Building of a new modern developed nation in accord with the new State Constitution.

- Development of agriculture as the base and all round development of other sectors of the economy as well;
- Proper evolution of the market oriented economic system;
- Development of the economy inviting participation in terms of technical know-how and investments from sources inside the country and abroad; and
- the initiative to shape the national economy must be kept in the hands of the state and the national peoples.

- Uplift the morale and morality of the entire nation;
- Uplift of national prestige and integrity and preservation and safeguarding of cultural heritage and national character;
- Uplift of dynamism of patriotic spirit; and
- Uplift of health, fitness and education standards of the entire nation.[9]

In addition, the regime lists four 'people's desires', as follows:

- Oppose those relying on external elements, acting as stooges, holding negative views;
- Oppose those trying to jeopardise stability of the State and progress of the nation;
- Oppose foreign nations interfering in internal affairs of the State; and
- Crush all internal and external destructive elements as the common enemy.[10]

For several years the regime seemed content to rely on these statements and slogans to explain Burma's national security policy. In July 1997, however, SLORC Chairman Senior General (SENGEN) Than Shwe reportedly made a secret speech to his senior military commanders in which he 'explained Myanmar's defence policy and the missions of the defence forces for the first time'.[11] The text of this speech was not released to the public although, according to Maung Aung Myoe, a 'defence policy' drawn from this speech was published (in English) in early 1999. No Burmese language text was made available. In describing the 'release' of Burma's defence policy, and even in quoting extensively from it, Maung Aung Myoe did not cite any specific document. It appears, however, that he has drawn heavily on a 19-page booklet entitled *Brief History of the Myanmar Army*, which was published by the Defence Services Museum and Historical Research Institute in February 1999. This booklet, which was designed for distribution to foreigners visiting the museum, is largely devoted to a (predictably laudatory) history of the Burmese army, but it concludes with a new and more specific formulation of the military regime's foreign policy and defence goals.

According to the *Brief History*, Burma's national defence policy can only be understood in the light of the country's historical background, geographical location, socio-economic conditions and 'the overall situation of the region'.[12] The salient features of this policy are:

(a) To perpetually safeguard national values concerning independence and sovereignty and prevent all acts detrimental to the three main National Causes which are Non-disintegration of the Union, Non-disintegration of the national solidarity and Perpetuation of national sovereignty.
(b) To build national defence avoiding external dependence as much as possible in striving for stability of the state, community peace and tranquillity and prevalence of law and order based on the strength of national forces within the country and with the Armed Forces as pivot, combining the strength of auxiliary defence forces.
(c) To valiantly and effectively prevent aggression of other nations and external interference in our internal affairs deploying various ways and means while avoiding interference in the internal affairs of other nations.
(d) To employ a defence system that gives priority to world peace, regional tranquillity and friendly relations with neighbours in accord with the Five Principles of Peaceful Coexistence.[13]

Drawing on these broad principles, the regime has also formulated a 'National Defence Mission', as follows:

(a) To build a strong, capable and modern Tatmadaw involving the auxiliary forces in order to dutifully work for the materialization of Our Three Main National causes: Non-disintegration of the Union, Non-disintegration of the National Solidarity and Perpetuation of national sovereignty.
(b) To form a modern people's defence system for national defence and security involving the entire citizenry based on internal forces without depending on foreign elements.
(c) To abide by the provisions of the State Constitution and to safeguard the new nation that will emerge according to that constitution for sustained development.

(d) To train and develop a strong defence force which possesses military, political, economic and administrative outlook in order to participate in the national political leadership role in the future state.

(e) To always carry in the fore and safeguard the 12 objectives of the State in order to see the further burgeoning of the noblest and worthiest of worldly values such as justice, liberty and equality to guarantee security of national economic interests and freedom and security of citizens.[14]

The museum's booklet also spells out a number of key principles of 'non-alignment and peaceful coexistence' which the government states have long been at the core of its national security policy. These are: 'mutual respect for territorial integrity and sovereignty, mutual non-aggression, mutual non-interference in each other's internal affairs, equality and mutual benefit, and peaceful coexistence'.[15] In keeping with these principles, Rangoon claims never to have taken sides with contending parties in any conflict since 1948, but has tried to maintain friendly relations with all, especially its neighbours. Also, the military government 'has never allowed and never will allow the stationing of foreign forces on Myanmar soil against the interest of a neighbouring country'.[16] The *Brief History* goes on to state that Burma has no security cooperation agreements with any country, nor has taken part in any joint military exercises with foreign armies. It claims that Burma's military posture is purely defensive, within a self-reliant defence policy framework. According to the booklet, 'the strength of the nation lies within'.[17]

Most of the regime's causes, objectives and principles were already well known before this booklet appeared. They had been printed in state-controlled newspapers like the *New Light of Myanmar* almost daily, were regularly rehearsed in speeches by government officials and appeared on countless billboards set up around the country. If Maung Aung Myoe's report is accurate, however, and Burma's formal defence policy was only publicly revealed in 1999, then the regime's actions raise a number of obvious questions. The first is why the military leadership left it until 1997 to explain the country's defence policy to those directly responsible for implementing it. The second is why Burma's defence policy should initially be considered secret, particularly given its essentially non-controversial — even predictable — nature. The third is why, at a time when a major campaign was under way to convince the Burmese population of the legitimacy of the armed forces and their political role, a formal statement of the defence policy and mission was not circulated in the Burmese language. The fourth question that might be asked is why the eventual release of this policy was made a 'low key event', when it might normally be expected to attract the kind of national publicity that invariably accompanies even minor decisions by the regime.[18] Also, it is a curious fact that, according to several major diplomatic missions in Rangoon, no foreign governments were advised that this defence policy was being promulgated, nor were they given copies. Indeed, a number are still waiting for the military government to produce a formal statement of Burma's defence policy.[19]

Such a statement would be useful in setting the broad policy parameters for a more detailed consideration of Burma's security concerns and the development of the armed forces. It is unlikely, however, to capture the real thinking behind the military regime's actions since 1988, nor illuminate the peculiar world-view that seems to have prompted the massive expansion and modernisation of the *Tatmadaw* over the past 12 years. An understanding of the regime's motives requires a closer look at its domestic imperatives and external threat perceptions.

2.2 Domestic Imperatives

After 1988, the first and most important priority for the SLORC was to ensure its own survival. The pro-democracy uprising that year was the most significant challenge to military rule since the 1962 coup. The regime was prepared to take whatever measures were required to recover and consolidate its grip on government. As a longer term goal, it was determined to put into place all necessary means to guarantee that the *Tatmadaw* would remain the real arbiter of power in Burma. To achieve these two aims, the armed forces needed to be large enough and strong enough to answer any further challenge to military rule, whether it came from the civilian population in the cities and towns, insurgents and armed dissident groups based around Burma's borders, or even from forces outside the country. It also seems to have been the SLORC's intention that, once these more immediate threats were eliminated or effectively contained, it would relax its grip. The regime could then contemplate general elections and the erection of a new political structure which relieved it of its administrative burden, while disguising the armed forces' continued control of the country's more important processes.[20] In considering these three aims, it can be argued that to date the regime has achieved the first two, but not the third.

Before 1988, the *Tatmadaw* had the capacity to crush sporadic outbreaks of civil unrest in the main population centres, but it lacked sufficient reserves to respond in strength to a large number of demonstrations held concurrently all around the country. Even smaller and more confined protests, like the 1974 U Thant disturbances in Rangoon, had forced the regime to declare martial law and call on troops deployed against ethnic insurgents in the border areas.[21] The enormous and widespread demonstrations in 1988, characterised by Army Chief of Staff General (GEN) Saw Maung as 'an insurrection', severely tested the capacity of the armed forces. Never before in Burma's history had so many people taken to the streets in so many places at the same time. The SLORC was not only faced with the possibility of further demonstrations of this kind, but it even feared that these largely peaceful protests might evolve into an armed uprising against the regime.[22] As a number of observers have noted, the urban-based democracy movement quickly became the SLORC's greatest concern, and the highest priority was given to developing the means to contain and destroy it.[23] This determination to preserve what the regime has called 'national solidarity' has been a major factor behind the expansion of the *Tatmadaw* and the Police Force, and the emphasis on improving the regime's domestic intelligence capabilities. It has also prompted drastic measures to reduce the threat posed by ethnic and other insurgent groups.[24]

Faced with the possibility of further civil unrest in Burma's heartland, the SLORC was particularly anxious to reduce the potential for insurgent groups and narcotics-based armies around the country's periphery to drain its resources and wear down its military strength. There was also a concern after September 1988 that some insurgent groups might try to combine, or at least coordinate, their actions with other anti-government forces in order to bring down the military regime.[25] To help overcome this problem, the regime adopted an approach reminiscent of the discredited policy which saw the creation of the *Karkweye* (also *Kar Kwe Ye*, or KKY) militia groups in 1963.[26] Over the past 12 years the Rangoon government has made a range of sweeping concessions to ethnic insurgents and narcotics-based armies in order to remove them as active opponents of the regime. Cease-fire agreements have been reached with 17 major groups to date, including members of the Kachin, Shan, Kayah, PaO, Palaung, Akha and Wa peoples.[27] In return for undertakings not to fight the central government or disrupt cross-border trade, these groups have been permitted to retain their weapons and exercise control over their old territories (now called 'government special zones'). This has included the freedom to grow opium, refine heroin and manufacture methamphetamines.[28] As an added inducement for them to suspend their armed struggle, the regime has undertaken to help develop the civil infrastructure in border regions controlled by the cooperating groups.[29]

Few of the cease-fire arrangements negotiated to date are likely to become permanent, and the potential remains for Burma's internal security situation to deteriorate again very quickly. These cease-fires, however, have effectively removed many of the most dangerous insurgent groups as immediate security problems. They have permitted the regime to concentrate its military resources against those other forces, like the Karen National Liberation Army (KNLA) and the Shan State Army (SSA), which have so far refused (in the regime's parlance) to 'return to the legal fold'.[30] Some of the compliant insurgent groups, notably the United Wa State Army (UWSA) and Democratic Karen Buddhist Army (DKBA) have even been prepared to undertake combat operations against these forces on the *Tatmadaw*'s behalf. The cease-fire policy has thus given the regime advantages it has not enjoyed before, and contributed indirectly to a number of major military victories.[31] To end the insurgent problem once and for all, however, the regime felt that more manpower and better arms were needed to tip the scales firmly and permanently in the *Tatmadaw*'s favour.

One reason for the failure of the *Tatmadaw*'s counter-insurgency strategy after the mid-1970s was that, once the insurgents had been driven out of Burma's river deltas and central hills into the more rugged border regions, far greater military resources were required to contain and defeat them. Yet the *Tatmadaw* was too small and ill equipped continually to mount large campaigns, sustain lengthy operations or maintain a strong military presence in all areas of operation. Quite apart from the capabilities of the insurgents themselves, their knowledge of the ground and the support they received from sympathetic local populations, the Burma Army was defeated by its lack of size and material strength. Operations were also hampered by weak logistics and communications problems. After taking power in 1988, however, the SLORC resolved that this situation would change. It determined to crush completely any elements of Burma's population which did not come to terms with Rangoon and, in pursuit of this policy, has been prepared to put greatly increased resources into the development of the armed forces.[32] It seems inevitable that, in due course, even those insurgent groups which are currently enjoying truces with the SPDC will come under pressure to acknowledge the authority of the central government. Those which resist can expect to feel the full weight of a very much larger and better equipped *Tatmadaw*.

Most of Burma's insurgent groups have been fighting for independent ethnically based states, or at least greater autonomy from Rangoon under a loose federal system. While some of the current ceasefire arrangements hint at these solutions, the SLORC and the SPDC, like earlier incarnations of Burma's military government, have firmly rejected these options as the answer to Burma's communal problems. Indeed, they are seen as leading to a disastrous fragmentation of the country, with internal unrest and increased vulnerability to external pressures as natural consequences. These fears appear to have been heightened by the political and economic collapse of the former Republic of Yugoslavia, the former Soviet Union and even Indonesia. All three countries have been held up by official spokesmen as examples of what would inevitably happen to Burma, if the centrifugal forces of ethnic, religious and political division in the country were not firmly resisted.[33] Under the rubric of the 'non-disintegration of the Union', the regime has made renewed efforts to exert military control over the country and turn it into a highly centralised, ethnically Burman-dominated state, commanded by the armed forces or its servants. On this basis, any future distribution of power or allocation of civil responsibilities to minority ethnic groups seems bound to be an essentially token gesture. Real power will continue to reside in Rangoon and be exercised through regional military commanders and pliant civilian administrators.

To ensure that this system works effectively, and to guard against any upsurge of irredentism, the Rangoon regime envisages a permanent military presence in almost every part of the country. In the past, Burma's lack of financial and military resources had meant that large tracts of territory were effectively beyond the government's control. Some were ruled by insurgents and drug warlords, or were inhabited only by a few villagers who barely recognised Rangoon's authority. The central government's writ ran when there was a military presence, but the army was spread very thinly. Some places were so remote and difficult to reach that they rarely received more than occasional visits by BSPP officials or army patrols. Foreign intelligence agents, insurgents, black marketeers, narcotics traffickers, adventurers and illegal immigrants all crossed Burma's borders without let or hindrance.[34] Some insurgent bases, like the Karen National Union (KNU) headquarters at Manerplaw, were regularly visited by foreign journalists and tourists, with consequent propaganda gains for the groups based there.[35] Since 1988, the regime has determined to establish a permanent military presence throughout the country to prevent this from occurring. The implementation of such a policy, however, demands much greater manpower and resources.

A permanent presence throughout Burma would give the Rangoon regime a number of direct benefits. It would permit the *Tatmadaw* to monitor political and military developments in the frontier districts more closely, exercise greater administrative control over those areas, better regulate cross-border traffic and improve revenue collection. The armed forces could also help develop the civil infrastructure of the border areas in ways that were conducive to both economic growth and their own strategic mobility. Projects such as roads, bridges and hospitals could be profitably linked to ceasefire agreements made with local ethnic groups. New schools could be used to teach the regime's *weltanschauung* to local children. The *Tatmadaw* already performs these tasks to a certain extent, but this role is likely to increase, possibly along the lines of the Indonesian *dwi fungsi* model which has attracted considerable attention from Burma's new military rulers.[36] This interest in a more formal and comprehensive socio-political role for the armed forces does not seem to have been diminished by the fall of President Suharto in 1998.[37] More importantly, the deployment of soldiers all around the country will help the *Tatmadaw* avoid many of the problems involved in constantly moving large bodies of troops and their equipment from one distant trouble spot to another. Spokesmen for the regime have admitted that the plan is for any outbreaks of civil unrest or ethnic insurgency to be met first with the forces *in situ*, with reinforcements only being sent from other areas when necessary.[38] Such a scheme may make good military sense but, once again, it will require a much larger number of soldiers than were available before 1988.

The expansion of the *Tatmadaw* is also linked to the regime's economic ambitions. Without the means to crush future political unrest, it cannot establish and maintain the kind of internal stability which it believes is necessary to encourage foreign investment and economic growth. Also, without a much larger army, the regime does not feel confident that it can protect the newly restored overland trade routes through the troubled border regions to China, Thailand and India.[39] Nor can it prevent the large-scale smuggling of foodstuffs, livestock, forest products and precious stones to neighbouring countries, or the illegal import of weapons, machine parts and consumer goods. The navy is being expanded in large part to police Burma's EEZ and to guard against the poaching of Burma's rich marine resources. The government has long wanted to enforce its jurisdiction in the Andaman Sea and Bay of Bengal, but has lacked the means to do so. With the new patrol boats and corvettes it has acquired, the Burma Navy (BN) can be in more places at once and act more vigorously against poachers and smugglers.[40] It will also be able to patrol at greater distances offshore and better protect gas and oil exploration ventures and extraction operations, on which the regime is banking to underpin Burma's future economic growth.[41] This growth is sought not only for its own rewards (including the revenue to pay for a larger *Tatmadaw*), but also in the hope that a higher standard of living will help defuse popular demands for a change of government.

Another reason sometimes offered for the expansion and modernisation of the *Tatmadaw* is to ensure the continuing loyalty and cohesion of the armed forces. For, unless the military government can depend on its own troops, then its survival would be gravely threatened. A number of commentators have suggested that the regime has undertaken its massive arms purchasing campaign in order 'to improve the morale of its officers and men...all but estranged from the population at large'.[42] The members of the armed forces have always been promoted as the guardians of the people and protectors of the Union. Since the 1988 massacres, however, the *Tatmadaw* has been faced with a resentful and alienated population which sees it as the blunt instrument of military oppression. Many members of the armed forces clearly shared the broad sentiments being expressed by the pro-democracy movement and some even joined in the demonstrations.[43] To help counter the consequent confusion and low morale in the ranks, the *Tatmadaw* is being encouraged to take greater pride in its historical achievements and its new-found material strength. The opening of a large Defence Services Museum in Rangoon, to mark the *Tatmadaw*'s golden jubilee in 1995, and the publication of a multi-volume official history of the armed forces, can be seen as part of the same plan. Both portray the armed forces in a manner designed to reassure its members (and if possible the general public) about the *Tatmadaw*'s military capabilities and its special place in Burmese society.[44]

The regime's third broad aim after it took power (and abolished the BSPP) was to re-establish a political and administrative structure which would permit the armed forces to exercise real power, without actually having to run the country. In 1990, a relatively free and fair election was held, in the expectation either that the *Tatmadaw*'s own National Unity Party (NUP) would win a majority of seats, or else that so many other parties would have elected representatives that the NUP could still effectively dominate the resulting parliament. Yet to the regime's astonishment and dismay, the NLD and other opposition parties won the election by a landslide.[45] Despite earlier promises to hand over power to the country's elected representatives, the SLORC refused to do so, and since 1990 the regime has made a concerted effort to undermine the election result. It has also maintained that, before parliament can be called, a new state constitution is required. A National Constitution Convention was opened in January 1993, attended by representatives of all the major ethnic groups, political parties and community organisations. Despite being completely dominated by the regime, the convention has still not finalised its proceedings. The expected outcome, however, is already clear.

From all available indications, the Constitutional Convention will eventually deliver a document that safeguards the *Tatmadaw*'s core interests and ensures that it retains real power in Burma. The new constitution may be subject to a national referendum but, as occurred in 1973, the result will be pre-ordained. There will then be another general election (doubtless managed more carefully than in 1990), which will produce an ostensibly civilian government. It may exercise certain administrative and ceremonial functions but will be effectively controlled by the armed forces, which is guaranteed a major role in its operations. As described by Josef Silverstein, under the regime's current draft constitution,

> 25% of the seats in each house of the future legislature must be reserved for the armed forces; the future president must have long military experience as a major qualification for office; the Minister for Defence must be a member of the military and in times of emergency the head of the armed forces will have power to declare a state emergency and take power; the military budget will not be subject to approval by the elected/appointed legislature.[46]

According to Maung Aung Myoe, 'the reservation of defence, internal affairs and border areas portfolios for the *Tatmadaw* is based on their past experience of politicians and civilians meddling in security-related affairs'.[47] Despite its lack of genuine popular support, the regime anticipates that such a government will gradually win the acceptance of the Burmese population and the international community.

Since first setting out along this path, the regime seems to have lost some of the enthusiasm it once felt for a political structure of this kind. Some senior *Tatmadaw* officers may feel that they can run the country better if they retain direct control, as at present. Another reason for the very slow progress made in the convention to date, however, seems to be the practical difficulties of engineering a satisfactory outcome. The NLD, for example, publicly repudiated the constitution drafting process in 1995, 'perceiving both its composition and agenda to be highly controlled by the junta'.[48] The party also pointed out that it failed to reflect the results of the 1990 elections. Later attempts by the NLD to rejoin the conference were rebuffed by the regime. The complex problem of how to manage the demands of the ethnic minorities has still not been resolved, and has been complicated by the more recent demands of various cease-fire groups for a greater say in the constitution drafting process.[49] The likely rejection of the new constitution, and resulting parliament, by influential members of the international community could also be a reason for the delay.

There is another factor that figures in the regime's thinking, however, and that is its continuing sense of threat from external forces supporting the pro-democracy movement.

2.3 External Threat Perceptions

Ever since a large segment of the international community condemned the SLORC for its massacre of pro-democracy demonstrators, the regime has attempted to capitalise on Burma's traditional chauvinism by encouraging suspicion of foreigners, and anything deemed to be tainted by foreign ideas. In this regard, Aung San Suu Kyi has been the most obvious target, with a series of highly personal attacks levelled against her and her (now deceased) British husband in the state-controlled news media. She is clearly meant to be one of those 'relying on external elements, acting as stooges', referred to in the billboards erected around the country. Yet the regime's concerns about foreign influences range more widely than the charismatic NLD General Secretary. For example, in 1997 intelligence chief Lieutenant General (LTGEN) Khin Nyunt stated:

> It has become especially necessary to contain the undisciplined import of foreign beliefs under the pretext of democracy and human rights, unfettered freedom, and Western-style behaviour, such as individualism, which undermines the family or Union spirit which the Myanmar people cherish.[50]

While statements of this kind are reminiscent of Ne Win's diatribes against 'alien cultural influences' during the 1970s, they now have a greater import. Criticism of foreign attitudes and beliefs is seen as a way of strengthening 'national solidarity', and thus the regime itself. Another rationale behind this campaign seems to be that, faced with a range of external threats, there will be less inclination for members of the armed forces (and members of the public) to question domestic political developments. Some of these threats have been deliberately fabricated with this aim in mind, but a number are of genuine concern.

Ever since 1948, Burma's government has been preoccupied with its multifarious internal security problems, but it has never lost sight of external threats. As noted earlier, Burma occupies a critical geostrategic position between the regional giants of India and China, and it has always been acutely conscious of the military and political pressures these countries can bring to bear. It also fears the massive populations and economic potential of its larger neighbours, which to some Burmese threaten eventually to engulf them.[51] Burma's difficult colonial experience, developments during the Second World War and the KMT invasion of Burma in the 1950s have all served to remind the country's leaders of the dangers of becoming caught up in foreign power struggles. After Independence, both the Nu and Ne Win Governments resisted attempts to draw Burma into the strategic competition between the US and USSR. While critical of US policy, the Rangoon government also tried hard to keep out of the conflicts in Korea and Indochina. Within the ambit of the United Nations, Burma adopted a strongly neutral foreign policy, seeking in scrupulous even-handedness and virtual isolation to avoid inviting attention from any hostile power. Such policies also drew on the historical traditions of a country which (with some notable exceptions) has always tended to look inward, rather than towards the outside world.

When it took power, the SLORC adjusted some of these policies. It weakened Burma's neutrality in international affairs by welcoming increased foreign contacts, particularly with China. The regime also abandoned the BSPP's autarkic socialist economic system. Albeit within defined limits, Burma's economy was opened to the outside world and foreign investment was actively encouraged. The regime did not lose its deep suspicion of foreigners, however, and was continually reminded of the pressures that they could bring to bear. Since September 1988 the regime has suffered widespread condemnation for its violations of human rights. Almost all bilateral aid donors have suspended development assistance and support for Burmese loans in international financial institutions has been withdrawn. Even multilateral aid agencies like the United Nations Development Programme (UNDP) have taken steps to deny direct assistance to the military regime.[52] The country's traditional arms suppliers are maintaining their embargo, and there are calls for stronger economic sanctions (from Aung San Suu Kyi and her supporters overseas, among others). Strong criticisms of the regime can still be heard in the UN and other international fora, like the European Parliament. This criticism increased after the arrest of Aung San Suu Kyi in July 1989, and the SLORC's repudiation of the 1990 elections. Despite the support of China and the ASEAN countries, Burma has been consigned to virtual pariah status in international diplomatic circles.

These political and economic measures against Burma were bitterly denounced by the regime as interference in Burma's internal affairs, and firmly rejected as the basis for any significant policy changes. Senior spokesmen for the regime accused the Western democracies of neocolonialism, by attempting to cripple Burma's economy and dictate how it should solve its own problems.[53] International news reports critical of events in Burma during and after the *Tatmadaw*'s takeover were vigorously refuted. Some pro-democracy activists and lobby groups outside Burma have since claimed that economic sanctions and public criticisms of the military government have had a beneficial effect. Yet a direct causal link between sanctions and shifts in regime policy is very difficult to determine. Indeed, it can be argued that such measures have strengthened the military government's nationalistic and isolationist tendencies, and hardened its resolve to pursue its own policies, in its own time, regardless of the consequences for the Burmese population. There is some evidence, however, to suggest that in one respect at least the SLORC was affected by the strong international response to the 1988 massacres, and even feared that it might extend to military action. Since then this fear has abated to a certain extent, but can still be detected in certain SPDC policies.

During the 1988 uprising, there were repeated calls to the international community by pro-democracy activists for help in ending military rule in Burma. In themselves, these calls were not unusual. They had also been made in 1974, for example, when students and *pongyis* (Buddhist monks) appealed to the UN to help them honour the memory of former Secretary-General U Thant, and to restore democratic rule.[54] In 1988, however, the demonstrations were much larger, received far greater publicity and prompted a higher level of international interest. Reports that the US was sending a naval task force to evacuate American nationals from Burma sparked fears in the *Tatmadaw* that an invasion fleet was being sent to help topple the military regime. These fears grew after US naval vessels were unexpectedly detected in Burmese waters.[55] There were stories circulating in Rangoon at the time that US paratroopers had already landed in Burma, prompting some people to begin digging air raid shelters.[56] Despite official US denials of any hostile intent, these rumours appear to have had a major impact on the regime. It remembered the pressure brought to bear against India in 1971 when a US naval task force was sent to the region during Bangladesh's war of independence.[57] SLORC Chairman SENGEN Saw Maung was later quoted as saying that 'a superpower country' had sent an aircraft carrier into Burmese waters at the height of Burma's crisis 'causing fears in Rangoon that the city would be attacked'.[58] These fears help account for the fact that the regime's earliest arms imports included search radars and air defence weapons, neither of which were relevant to any of Burma's internal security problems.[59]

These fears may now appear ridiculous but they were genuinely held at the time and, to a surprising extent, have persisted. In 1991, for example, the *Tatmadaw* was reportedly placed on alert against an invasion when the US landed troops in Bangladesh to assist in flood relief. The regime also took careful note of the multilateral military operation against Iraq in 1990-91, and even placed anti-aircraft guns around Rangoon in case a similar effort was made against Burma.[60] The regime's fears were heightened in April 1992 by remarks made by Prince Khaled Bin Sultan Bin Abdul Aziz, the commander of the Saudi Arabian forces during the Gulf War. This was at the height of the Rohingya refugee crisis, when over 250,000 Muslims of South Asian extraction fled into Bangladesh to escape the depredations of the Burma Army.[61] During a visit to Bangladesh, the Prince called on the UN to do for the Rohingyas 'just what it did to liberate Kuwait'.[62] Most observers interpreted this to be a call for another 'Operation Desert Storm' against the military regime in Rangoon. Once again, following the UN-sponsored landings of US troops in Haiti in 1994, there were rumours in Rangoon that an attempt might be made by the UN or a coalition of UN members to force the SLORC's hand, and make it accept the results of the 1990 general election.[63] Reports that China has pledged support for Burma in the event of any international intervention remain unconfirmed but, for all its defiant rhetoric, the regime clearly felt insecure and vulnerable.[64]

Also during the 1990s, there were concerns that Burma might become a target for Islamic countries angered by the regime's harsh treatment of the country's Muslim minority. After the 1988 massacres Pakistan was quick to support the SLORC (profiting from India's strong stand in favour of the pro-democracy movement).[65] Islamic countries elsewhere in the region, like Malaysia, Indonesia and Brunei, did not initially appear to be troubled by internal developments in Burma, despite the regime's poor human rights record. This situation changed in 1991, however, when there was a strong international reaction to *Tatmadaw* operations against the Rohingya community in Arakan State. In New York, lobbying began for UN intervention.[66] Among the most outspoken critics of Burma at that time were the Islamic countries, including a number in Southeast Asia. Later, there were reports that Rohingya insurgent groups were being provided with funds from the Middle East to buy arms from the Cambodia-Thailand and Afghanistan-Pakistan borders.[67] There were also rumours that Burmese Muslims had declared a *jihad* or 'holy war' against the Rangoon regime and were being assisted by Islamic fundamentalists from abroad, some of whom had been trained by the US for service against the USSR in Afghanistan.[68] These developments prompted a rare policy reversal by the SLORC, which curbed its military operations in the west and reluctantly accepted the return of the Rohingya refugees to Burma under the supervision of the United Nations High Commissioner for Refugees (UNHCR).

More recently, the SPDC has been deeply unsettled by developments in Indonesia. Not only has an apparently strong and successful Asian military government been toppled by a failing economy and popular unrest, but a foreign military force (INTERFET) intervened in one province, prompted by the international community's humanitarian concerns. Even more worrying for the Rangoon regime was the fact that East Timor's demands for independence from Indonesia were supported by the UN, which despatched an armed peace-keeping force (UNTAET) to guard against Indonesian retaliation.[69] This UN force included contingents from a number of regional countries, such as the ROK, Singapore and Thailand. To the generals in Rangoon, this was yet another example of the international community interfering in matters that did not concern it, and imposing Western notions of human rights on Asian countries. It was also an example of external powers using their diplomatic, economic and military strength to support breakaway minority groups. In these circumstances, it did not require too great a leap of imagination for the members of Burma's military hierarchy to foresee Burma becoming subject to similar pressures. Messages of mutual support between Aung San Suu Kyi and East Timorese leader Xanana Gusmão have exacerbated these fears.[70] It is unlikely to be a coincidence that, following the East Timor operation, the *Tatmadaw* took steps to increase its air defence capabilities, the area in which it felt most vulnerable to Western military power.[71]

All these events took place against a background of considerable strategic uncertainty and change. In many parts of the world the collapse of the Soviet Union and the end of the Cold War did not usher in the expected 'new world order' of peace and stability. Rather, it heralded a return to the disorder and tribal rivalries of the old world. With a few notable exceptions, like the confrontation on the Korean peninsula, the problems faced by the Asia-Pacific region tended to be more manageable than those found elsewhere, but the possible withdrawal of US forces aroused fears among many countries that the relative stability and predictability which they had enjoyed for so long would be a thing of the past.[72] China's rise to the status of an economic superpower, coupled with its military modernisation program and claims to the South China Sea, added to nervousness about what the future might hold.[73] Before the Asian financial crisis curbed defence spending, these concerns had already prompted military modernisation programs in countries like Thailand, Malaysia and Singapore.

Faced with persistent criticisms from many influential countries and international organisations, Rangoon viewed these strategic developments with considerable unease. While internal issues remained uppermost in the regime's mind, the 'overall situation in the region' was not a comforting one and could not be ignored. Nor could Rangoon lose sight of the potential for increased frictions with its neighbours. In his 1995 Armed Forces Day speech, new SLORC Chairman SENGEN Than Shwe referred to 'the changing situation in the international arena today' which made it necessary 'to build up the *Tatmadaw* to be modern and strong'.[74] It may be true, as Tin Maung Maung Than has pointed out, that

> Myanmar does not perceive external threats in the form of hostile states bent on conflict and conquest. Yangon's primary concern is with external actors who seek to intervene in the internal affairs of the state to influence the way in which Yangon deals with its domestic problems.[75]

Yet in the back of the regime's mind there remains the lurking fear that such intervention may take the form of military action, or at the least military pressure, of the kind exerted by the US and UN in several other parts of the world. This fear has contributed to measures over the past 12 years to increase Burma's military preparedness.

For all its apparent power and confidence, the picture that emerges from an examination of the regime's defence policies and threat perceptions is that of a persistent sense of vulnerability. Despite some major gains over the past 12 years in terms of internal security and international relations, the SPDC remains concerned about renewed civil unrest in the cities, continuing ethnic insurgencies in the countryside and armed intervention by foreign powers. Even now, after more than a decade, the SPDC remains convinced that a larger, more capable *Tatmadaw* is essential for regime survival and Burma's continued independence. Only with such a massive military machine at its disposal does it feel that it can retain political power (or, in its terms, ensure the 'non-disintegration of national solidarity'), to answer the insurgent threat (ensure the 'non-disintegration of the Union') and to deter, if not defeat, external military pressures (thus securing 'the perpetuation of national sovereignty').

Notes

1. U Aye, Director-General of the Foreign Ministry's Political Division, cited in Charles Wallace, 'Burmese junta buys arms for big push', *Sydney Morning Herald*, 6 October 1992. See also Khin Nyunt, 'The Tatmadaw as Preserver of the Union', *Business Times*, 4 August 1995.

2. R. H. Taylor, 'Burma: Political Leadership, Security Perceptions and Policies', in Mohammed Ayoob and Chai-Anan Samudavanija (eds), *Leadership Perceptions and National Security: The Southeast Asian Experience* (Institute of Southeast Asian Studies, Singapore, 1989), p. 206.

3. Tin Maung Maung Than, 'Myanmar: Preoccupation with Regime Survival, National Unity, and Stability', p. 391.

4. Interview, Rangoon, November 1999.

5. Taylor, 'Burma: Political Leadership, Security Perceptions and Policies', p. 206.

6. *Foreign Policy of the Revolutionary Government of the Union of Burma* (Burma Socialist Programme Party, Rangoon, 1968), p. 5.

7. Burma sent a small staff detachment to the UN Operation in the Congo (ONUC) from 1960-64. Burmese military observers also took part in the UN Observation Group in Lebanon (UNOGIL) in 1958, the UN India-Pakistan Observation Mission (UNIPOM) in 1965-66, and the UN Truce Supervision Organisation (UNTSO) in the Middle East from

1967-69. *The Blue Helmets: A Review of United Nations Peace-Keeping* (United Nations Department of Public Information, New York, 1996), Appendix.

8. Interviews, Rangoon, April 1995. See also Address delivered by SENGEN Saw Maung, Commander-in-Chief of the Defence Services, at the 45th Anniversary of the Armed Forces Day, Rangoon, 27 March 1990.

9. See, for example, *New Light of Myanmar*, 4 January 2001.

10. *Ibid*; and personal observations, Rangoon, Mandalay, Taunggyi and Kalaw, April 1995, November 1996 and December 1999.

11. Maung Aung Myoe, *Military Doctrine and Strategy in Myanmar: A Historical Perspective*, Working Paper No. 339 (Strategic and Defence Studies Centre, Australian National University, Canberra, 1999), p. 18.

12. *Brief History of the Myanmar Army*, p. 16. See also Maung Aung Myoe, *Military Doctrine and Strategy in Myanmar*, pp. 18-19.

13. *Brief History of the Myanmar Army*, pp. 16-17.

14. *Brief History of the Myanmar Army*, pp. 17-18.

15. *Brief History of the Myanmar Army*, p. 16.

16. *Brief History of the Myanmar Army*, p. 18.

17. *Brief History of the Myanmar Army*, pp. 18-19.

18. Maung Aung Myoe, *Military Doctrine and Strategy in Myanmar*, p. 18.

19. Interviews, Rangoon, November and December 1999.

20. See, for example, the statement issued by the SLORC Information Committee at the press conference held in the Ministry of Defence, Rangoon, on 17 November 1989, and reprinted as 'Tatmadaw Will Yield Power to New Gov't', *Diplomacy*, Vol. 15, No. 12, December 1989, pp. 19-21.

21. Selth, *Death of a Hero*, p. 23.

22. These fears were encouraged by the seizure of military weapons from a suburban police station and a Burma Army unit in the Ministry of Trade which was overwhelmed by demonstrators. See Dr Maung Maung, *The 1988 Uprising in Burma*, p. 167 and pp. 225-6.

23. Interviews, Bangkok and Rangoon, April 1995. See also Bertil Lintner, 'Conflict of Interests', *FEER*, 19 May 1994, p. 28.

24. The CPB still posed a threat when the SLORC took power, but collapsed from internal differences in 1989. See Bertil Lintner, *The Rise and Fall of the Communist Party of Burma (CPB)* (Cornell University, Ithaca, 1990).

25. This was never really in prospect, despite efforts by the SLORC to link the pro-democracy movement with the CPB. See *Burma Communist Party's Conspiracy to take over State Power* (SLORC, Rangoon, 1989).

26. During the 1960s about 50 small insurgent groups and private armies were designated *Ka Kwe Ye*, or militias, in return for carrying out anti-communist operations in Shan State. Most, however, simply used their official status to continue their drug smuggling activities. By 1973 all KKYs were declared illegal. Bunge, *Burma*, p. 231; and Smith, *Burma: Insurgency and the Politics of Ethnicity*, pp. 95-6.

27. These groups are listed in a large display mounted in the Defence Services Museum. Personal observation, Rangoon, December 1999. See also *Endeavours of the Myanmar Armed Forces Government for National Reconsolidation* (SPDC, Rangoon, 2000).

28. See, for example, Bertil Lintner, 'Divide and Rule', *FEER*, 27 January 1994, p. 20; and 'Buying Off the Enemy', *Asiaweek*, 9 March 1993, p. 27.

29. See, for example, *Measures Taken for Border Areas and National Races Development*, 2 vols, (Central Committee for Border Areas and National Races Development, Rangoon, 1991?).

30. Interview, Canberra, June 1995. The regime lists more than 30 armed groups which have opposed the central government since 1988, but several others have been eliminated since 1948.

31. See, for example, Bertil Lintner, 'Centrifugal forces', *FEER*, 27 February 1992, p. 16.

32. Ron Corben, 'Beijing arms back Burma's ethnic purge', *The Australian*, 3 March 1992.

33. Interviews, Rangoon, April 1995. See also 'Burma's Path to Democracy', Reuters, 24 November 1992.

34. This is well illustrated, for example, in Lintner, *Land of Jade*; Tucker, *Among Insurgents*; and Edith Mirante, *Burmese Looking Glass: A Human Rights Adventure and a Jungle Revolution* (Grove Press, New York, 1993).

35. See, for example, Christian Gooden, *Three Pagodas: A Journey Down the Thai-Burmese Border* (Jungle Books, Halesworth, 1966), pp. 127-54.

36. Ulf Sundhaussen, 'Indonesia's New Order: A Model for Myanmar', *Asian Survey*, Vol. 35, No. 8, August 1995, pp. 768-80. See also John McBeth and Bertil Lintner, 'Model State', *FEER*, 17 August 1995, p. 27; Bertil Lintner, 'Bristling Border', *FEER*, 13 July 1995, pp. 19-22; and 'Not quite Indonesia', *Economist*, 28 January 1995, pp. 28-9.

37. Kay Merrill, 'Burma looks set to reject the lessons of history', *Jane's Intelligence Review*, Vol. 11, No. 8, August 1999, pp. 51-3.

38. Interview, Rangoon, April 1995.

39. In 1988 Burma officially recognised trade with China through a number of northern border towns (like Muse/Ruili and Panghsai). A bridge was later built across the Moei River at Myawaddy/Mae Sot to facilitate trade with Thailand. Burma has also opened two new Customs posts on the Indian border, at Moreh/Tamu and Champhai/Hri. See, for example, Bertil Lintner, 'Make Way For Trade' *FEER*, 3 November 1994, p. 16; Bertil Lintner, 'The Volatile Yunnan Frontier', *Jane's Intelligence Review*, Vol. 6, No. 2, February 1994, pp. 84-92; and John Zubrycki, 'Burma, India seal border trade pact', *The Australian*, 21 April 1995.

40. When it was proposed that Burma purchase two or three Chinese frigates, one senior military intelligence officer described them to the author as 'poacher chasers'. The same role is envisaged for the three new corvettes which are being built instead. Interviews, Rangoon, April 1995 and November 1999.

41. According to recent calculations of regional demand for Burmese natural gas, this confidence seems to be misplaced.

42. Bertil Lintner, 'Burma — the army's role in politics', *JDW*, 7 October 1989, pp. 715-6; Bertil Lintner, 'Oiling the iron fist', *FEER*, 6 December 1990, p. 28; and Bertil Lintner, 'Lock and load', *FEER*, 13 September 1990, p. 28.

43. In August and September 1988 about 1000 men and women from all three Services joined in the pro-democracy demonstrations. See, for example, Bertil Lintner, 'Backdown or bloodbath', *FEER*, 22 September 1988, p. 14; Lintner, 'Oiling the iron fist', p. 28; and William Stewart, 'Now a Coup', *Time*, 26 September 1988, p. 14.

44. Interviews and personal observations, Rangoon, April 1995 and December 1999. See also M. P. Callahan, 'Cracks in the Edifice? Military-Society Relations in Burma Since 1988', in Pedersen, Rudland and May, *Burma-Myanmar*, p. 33; and M. P. Callahan, 'Junta Dreams or Nightmares? Observations of Burma's Military since 1988', *Bulletin of Concerned Asian Scholars*, Vol. 31, No. 3, 1999, pp. 52-8.

45. Out of 492 constituencies, 485 were contested. A total of 2209 candidates from 93 parties and 87 independent candidates participated. A total of 479 candidates from 27 parties and six independents were elected. Although the NLD polled only about 60% of the valid votes, it secured almost 81% of the seats. The NUP won only 10 seats. 'Statement on

votes gained by candidates who represent parties, seats won by the respective parties and percentages', *Working People's Daily*, 2 July 1990.

46. Statement by Josef Silverstein, Professor Emeritus, Rutgers University, before the US House of Representatives Committee on International Relations, Subcommittee on Asia and the Pacific, hearing on 'Recent Developments in Burma', Washington, 7 September 1995.

47. Maung Aung Myoe, *The Tatmadaw in Myanmar Since 1988: An Interim Assessment*, Working Paper No. 342 (Strategic and Defence Studies Centre, Australian National University, Canberra, 1998), p. 6.

48. US State Department, *Burma: Country Report*.

49. Interview, Rangoon, December 1999.

50. Cited by TV Myanmar (in Burmese), 31 May 1997.

51. For example, Ne Win's strong opposition to birth control reportedly stems from a fear that Burma may eventually be swallowed up by its more populous neighbours. See David Steinberg, 'Myanmar as Nexus: Sino-Indian Rivalries on the Frontier', *Studies in Conflict and Terrorism*, Vol. 16, No. 1, 1993, pp. 1-8.

52. Almost all the UNDP's infrastructure programs in Burma were stopped or significantly curtailed after May 1992, when the 39th UNDP Governing Council decided that UNDP funds to Burma should be de-committed. The funds released by this action were to be used instead for projects likely to have a greater impact at the 'grass roots' level. Minority groups and the poor in Burma were singled out for special attention.

53. See, for example, *The Conspiracy of Treasonous Minions Within the Myanmar Naing-ngan and Traitorous Cohorts Abroad* (Ministry of Information, Rangoon, 1989); and 'West accused of plot', *South China Morning Post*, 17 August 1991.

54. Selth, *Death of a Hero*, p. 12.

55. The US fleet was detected in the Andaman Sea, some 90 nautical miles south of Rangoon, on 12 September, when a local vessel happened to pass through the area and reported the sighting. Interview, Washington, October 1995. See also Tin Maung Maung Than, 'Myanmar: Preoccupation with Regime Survival', p. 730, note 27.

56. 'Washington denies interfering in Burmese Affairs', AFP, 13 September 1988. See also Dr Maung Maung, *The 1988 Uprising in Burma*, p. 226.

57. Interview, New Delhi, May 1995. The US sent Task Force 74, consisting of the nuclear aircraft carrier 'Enterprise' and supporting ships, into the Indian Ocean to show its support for Pakistan in the war over East Bengal (later Bangladesh). The official reason for the deployment was to cover the evacuation of American civilians from Bangladesh. See also E. R. Zumwalt, *On Watch: A Memoir* (New York Times, New York, 1976), pp. 361-9.

58. Yindee Lertcharoenchok, 'Burmese leader calls Thailand a "true friend" ', *The Nation*, 13 April 1989.

59. Lintner, 'Myanmar's Chinese connection', p. 12.

60. Terry McCarthy, 'Paranoia time for Burma's generals', *Canberra Times*, 4 April 1991.

61. See, for example, Amnesty International (AI), *Human rights violations against Muslims in the Rhakine (Arakan) State* (Amnesty International, London, 1992).

62. John Bray, 'Ethnic minorities and the future of Burma', *The World Today*, (August/September 1992), p. 147. See also Bertil Lintner, 'The secret mover', *FEER*, 7 May 1992, p. 21.

63. Interview, Rangoon, April 1995.

64. Philip Smyth, 'Burma grabs tiger's tail of democracy', *The Australian*, 29 September 1994. See also 'Buddy to a Pariah', *Asiaweek*, 3 July 1992, p. 31.

65. See, for example, Selth, *Burma's Secret Military Partners*, pp. 61-9.

66. Lintner, 'The secret mover', p. 21.

67. *SIPRI Yearbook 1992: World Armaments and Disarmament* (Oxford University Press, Oxford, 1992), p. 414. See also Bertil Lintner, 'Distant exile', *FEER*, 28 January 1993, p. 23; and 'Anti-Rangoon forces eyeing Afghan arms', *Bangkok Post*, 17 October 1994.

68. Interview, Rangoon, April 1995. See also 'Muslims in Myanmar Plan "Jihad" ', *Asian Defence Journal*, June 1995, p. 69; and 'Afghans Training Burmese Freedom Fighters', *Asian Defence Journal*, May 1993, p. 85.

69. INTERFET was the International Force East Timor. UNTAET is the UN Transitional Administration in East Timor.

70. See, for example, 'Aung San Suu Kyi: Burma-East Timor', *Burma News Update*, November 1999, p. 32.

71. William Ashton, 'Myanmar: Invasion fears prompt search for air defences', *Asia-Pacific Defence Reporter*, Vol. 27, No. 2, March 2001, pp. 32-4.

72. See, for example, Andrew Selth, 'Strategic Change in the Asia-Pacific Region', *The RUSI Journal*, Vol. 139, No. 5, October 1994, pp. 30-4.

73. See, for example, William Branigin, 'As China Builds Arsenal and Bases, Asians Fear a "Rogue in the Region"', *Washington Post*, 31 March 1993; and Don Pathan, 'The China Threat: empty legacy or legitimate fear', *The Nation*, 24 February 1995.

74. 'Burma: Than Shwe gives Armed Forces Day Address', Reuters, 29 March 1995.

75. Tin Maung Maung Than, 'Myanmar: Preoccupation with Regime Survival', p. 404.

3

Tatmadaw Structure and Organisation

Every deliberate act in war requires a fixed time for its commencement, and a fixed period, and an appointed place, and also requires secrecy, definite signals, proper persons through whom and with whom to act, and the proper means. — Polybius, *The Histories* (2nd Century BC)

As much as any other factor, the *Tatmadaw*'s ability to perform its military roles depends on the efficiency of its command structure and the means by which the military leadership communicates its orders to subordinate units. In some respects these capabilities are still limited, but even the Rangoon regime's strongest critics acknowledge that the Burmese armed forces have undergone a remarkable transformation from the small, weak and divided organisation which characterised the early years of Independence. Since the SLORC took over government in 1988, the pace of development has greatly accelerated. The last 12 years have seen considerable advances in the *Tatmadaw*'s command and control system, and its communications networks are now much more sophisticated and reliable. The way in which the armed forces have assimilated computer technology has surprised many observers.

3.1 Command and Control

Since 1948, the *Tatmadaw*'s command structure has undergone numerous changes. These have been in response to many factors, including the growth and development of the armed forces, the level of resources made available to them, the changing nature of the military challenges they have faced, the evolution of military doctrine and strategy, and the nature of the military leadership itself. At times, even individual officers have had an impact on the way in which the armed forces were organised. After 1962, the higher command's structure and role were directly affected by the demands of government. While the Revolutionary Council existed, the political leadership of the country and the military leadership of the *Tatmadaw* were the same. There was a nominal reversion to civilian rule after a new constitution was introduced in 1974, and elections were held for a People's Assembly (*Pyitthu Hluttaw*). This arrangement collapsed in 1988, however, after the armed forces took back direct control of the country (albeit with the agreement of the 'civilian' government).[1] Since then, in both name and practice, Burma's national political leadership and armed forces leadership have been the same.

Before the SLORC's takeover, overall command of the Burmese armed forces rested with the country's highest ranking military officer (always a full General drawn from the army), who acted concurrently as Defence Minister and *Tatmadaw*

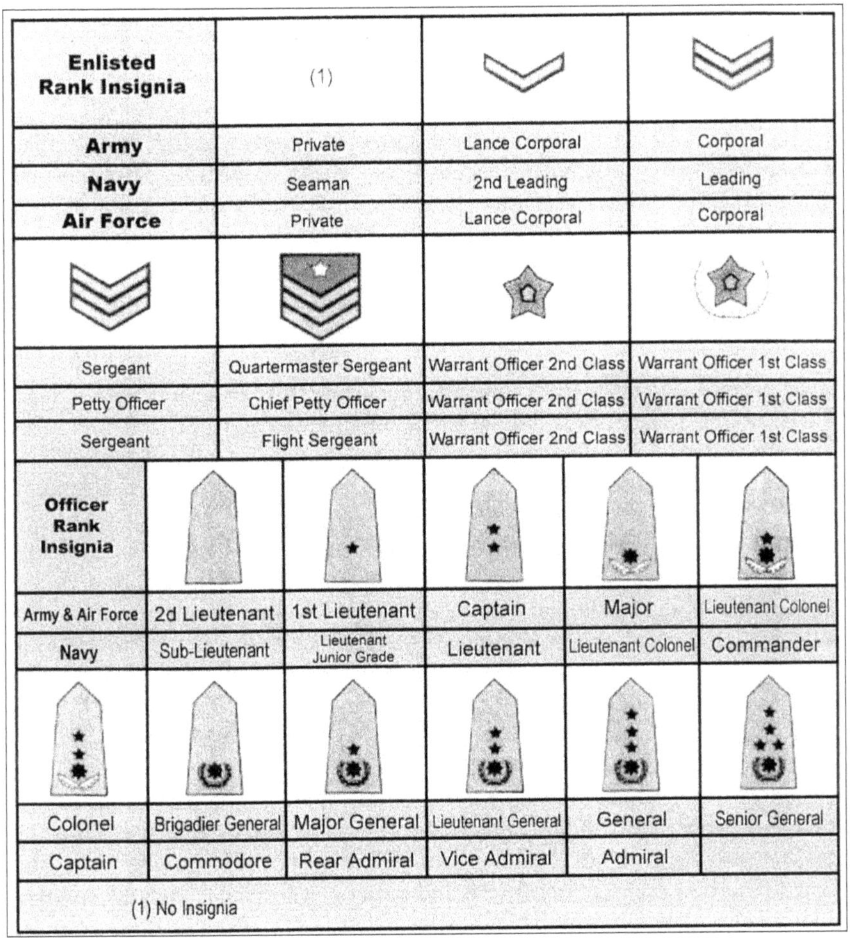

Enlisted Rank Insignia	(1)	∨	∨∨
Army	Private	Lance Corporal	Corporal
Navy	Seaman	2nd Leading	Leading
Air Force	Private	Lance Corporal	Corporal

Sergeant	Quartermaster Sergeant	Warrant Officer 2nd Class	Warrant Officer 1st Class
Petty Officer	Chief Petty Officer	Warrant Officer 2nd Class	Warrant Officer 1st Class
Sergeant	Flight Sergeant	Warrant Officer 2nd Class	Warrant Officer 1st Class

Officer Rank Insignia					
Army & Air Force	2d Lieutenant	1st Lieutenant	Captain	Major	Lieutenant Colonel
Navy	Sub-Lieutenant	Lieutenant Junior Grade	Lieutenant	Lieutenant Colonel	Commander

Colonel	Brigadier General	Major General	Lieutenant General	General	Senior General
Captain	Commodore	Rear Admiral	Vice Admiral	Admiral	

(1) No Insignia

Figure 2: Tatmadaw Rank Structure

Chief of Staff.[2] He thus exercised supreme operational control over all three Services, albeit under the direction of the President, State Council and Council of Ministers. There was also a National Security Council which, in theory at least, acted in an advisory capacity. Ne Win and his immediate circle were quick to become involved in detailed defence matters if they felt the circumstances warranted it but, generally speaking, the Defence Minister exercised day-to-day control over the armed forces. He was assisted by three Vice-Chiefs of Staff, one each for the army, navy and air force. In March 1981 the Vice Chief of Staff (Army) position was upgraded to Lieutenant General. The Vice-Chiefs of the other two Services remained at Major General (MAJGEN) rank. These officers also acted as Deputy Ministers of Defence and commanders of their respective Services. They were all based at the Ministry of Defence (*Karkweye Wun-kyi Hta-na*) in central Rangoon, which operated as both a government ministry and an integrated joint military headquarters.[3]

The joint staff in Rangoon consisted of three major offices, one each for the army, navy and air force. There was also an independent department.[4]

The Army Office had three major departments; the General (or 'G') Staff to oversee operations, the Adjutant General's (or 'A') Department for non-supply administration, and the Quartermaster General's (or 'Q') Department to handle logistics.[5] The General Staff consisted primarily of two Bureaus of Special Operations (BSO), which were created in April 1978 and June 1979. These Bureaus were high-level staff units formed to manage different theatres of operations. They were thus responsible for the overall direction and coordination of the activities of the Regional Military Commands (in Burmese *Taing Sit Htar Na Choke*, or RMC).[6] In broad terms, BSO One covered Upper Burma, while BSO Two was responsible for Lower Burma.[7] The army's mobile Light Infantry Divisions (*Ah Por Sar Chae Myan Tak Ma*, or LID) were managed separately, under a Staff Colonel. Also in 'G' Department were a number of directorates which corresponded to the army's functional corps, such as Intelligence, Signals, Training, Armour and Artillery, and Military (field) Engineering. For reasons which are not clear, 'G' Department also included directorates responsible for Defence Industries, Security Printing, and for the People's Militia and Public Relations. The 'A' Department was responsible for the Adjutant General, the Directorate of Medical Services and the Provost Marshall's Office. The 'Q' Department included the Directorates of Supply and Transport, Ordnance Services, Electrical and Mechanical Engineering, and Military (civil) Engineers.[8]

The Navy and Air Force Offices in the Ministry were headed by the Vice Chiefs of Staff for those Services. Each was supported by a staff officer at full Colonel (COL) level. All these officers were responsible for the overall management of the various naval and air bases around the country, and for broader administrative and personnel issues such as recruitment and training. The Independent Department included the Military Appointments General (MAG), Inspector General (IG), Judge Advocate General (JAG), Director of Procurement and Central Military Accounts Department.

Operational command in the field was exercised through a framework of nine Regional Military Commands, the boundaries of which usually corresponded with those of the country's seven States and Divisions. These RMC were Northern Command (based at Myitkyina), North Western Command (Mandalay), North Eastern Command (Lashio), Eastern Command (Taunggyi), South Eastern Command (Moulmein), Central Command (Toungoo), South Western Command (Bassein) and Western Command (Sittwe). There was also a Rangoon Command, with its headquarters in the capital.[9] Under the Ministry's guidance, the Regional Commanders (all senior army officers, usually at Brigadier [BRIG] level) were responsible for the conduct of military operations in their command areas. Depending on the size of the RMC and its operational requirements, Regional Commanders had at their disposal up to 10 infantry battalions (*Kha La Ya*) in garrisons. Some were managed through smaller Tactical Operations Commands (*Sa Ba Ha*, or TOC), under a Brigadier or Colonel.[10] Five RMCs had two TOCs, and four RMCs had three TOCs each. There were also eight Light Infantry Divisions distributed around the country, each with 10 light infantry battalions (*Kha Ma Ya*) under three TOCs.

Regional Commanders also held senior positions in the ruling Burma Socialist Programme Party, the organisational structure of which closely reflected that of the armed forces.[11] After 1974 there was a formal distinction between the military command structure and the country's political apparatus, but through the BSPP machinery the Regional Commanders were still able to exercise considerable personal influence over the administration of their command areas.

When the SLORC was created in September 1988, the structures of both the government and the defence command system changed dramatically. Initially consisting of 21 senior military officers, the Council was Burma's supreme governing body. In addition, a Cabinet was appointed, with Ministers drawn entirely from the armed forces. Most SLORC members also held Cabinet portfolios.[12] The size of the SLORC remained constant but, by 1997, the Cabinet had swollen to 38 members, with an additional 32 Deputy Ministers. There was also a National Security and Management Committee chaired by the Home Affairs Minister (a Lieutenant General). One astute observer has speculated that this committee was 'the focal point for dealing with security matters at the state level'.[13] It is a matter for debate whether this unwieldy structure was prompted by the failure of Ministries to perform efficiently, or by the need to give prestigious and often lucrative positions to ambitious *Tatmadaw* officers, as a way of bolstering their loyalty to the regime. In a remarkable admission of the failure of the regime's domestic policies since 1962, the BSPP's massive nationwide organisation was abolished and replaced with a hierarchical structure of Law and Order Restoration Councils (LORC), run directly by serving military officers.

To manage the rapid expansion and modernisation of the *Tatmadaw*, the SLORC also made a number of significant adjustments to Burma's military command structure. The country's most senior army officer, by 1990 a Senior General, concurrently held the positions of SLORC Chairman, Prime Minister and Defence Minister, as well as being appointed Commander-in-Chief of the Defence Ser-

52 Burma's Armed Forces

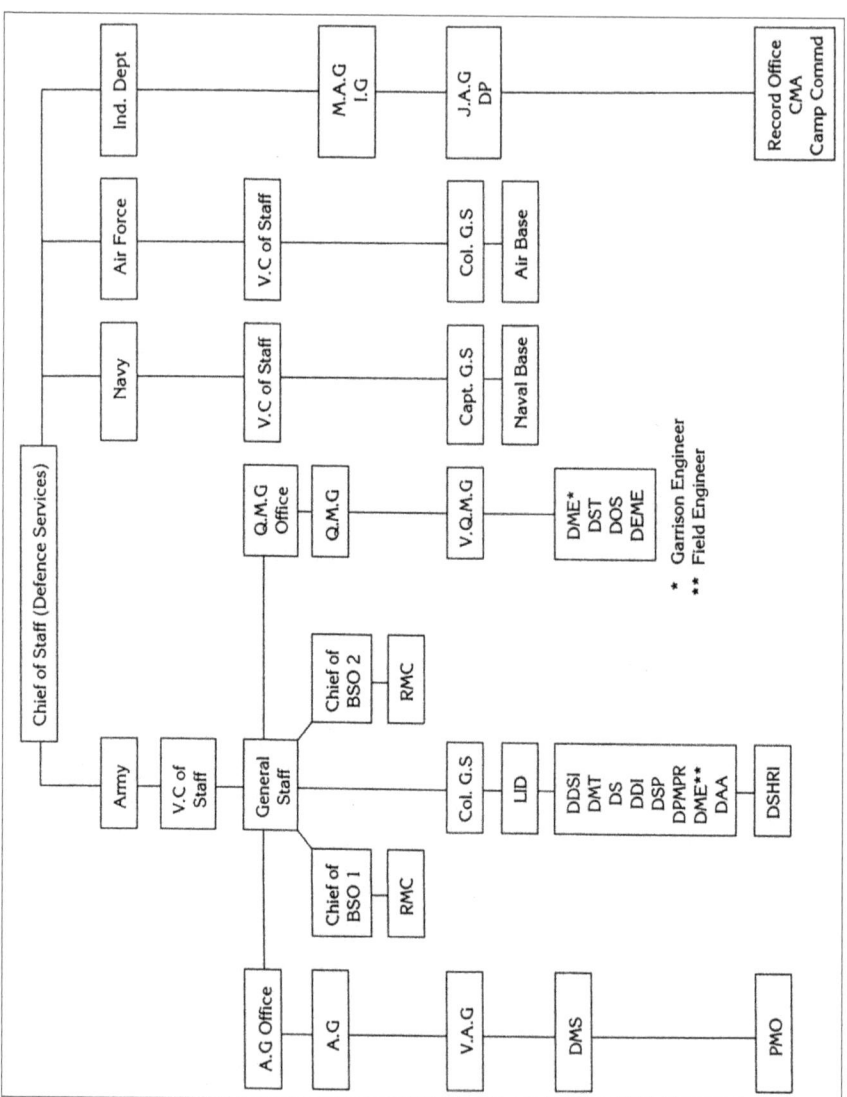

Figure 3: Burma's Defence Ministry, 1988.
Source: Maung Aung Myoe, *Building the Tatmadaw: The Organisational Development of the Armed Forces, 1948-98,* Working Paper number 327 (Strategic and Defence Studies Centre, Australian National University, Canberra, 1998).

V.C of Staff = Vice Chief of Staff
A.G = Adjutant General
Q.M.G = Quartermaster General
V.A.G = Vice Adjutant General
V.Q.M.G = Vice Quartermaster General
BSO = Bureau of Special Operation
RMC = Regional Military Command
Col. G.S = Colonel General Staff
LID = Light Infantry Division
M.A.G = Military Appointment General
I.G = Inspector General
J.A.G = Judge Advocate General
DMS = Directorate of Medical Services
DDSI = Directorate of Defence Services Intelligence
DMT = Directorate of Military Training

DS = Directorate of Signals
DDI = Directorate of Defence Industries
DSP = Directorate of Security Printing
DPMPR = Directorate of People's Militias and Public Relations
DME = Directorate of Military Engineers
DAA = Directorate of Armour and Artillery
DST = Directorate of Supply and Transport
DOS = Directorate of Ordnance Services
DEME = Directorate of Electrical and Mechanical Engineers
DP = Directorate of Procurement
PMO = Provost Marshal's Office
DSHRI = Defence Services Historical Research Institute
CMA = Central Military Account
Camp Commd = Camp Commandant

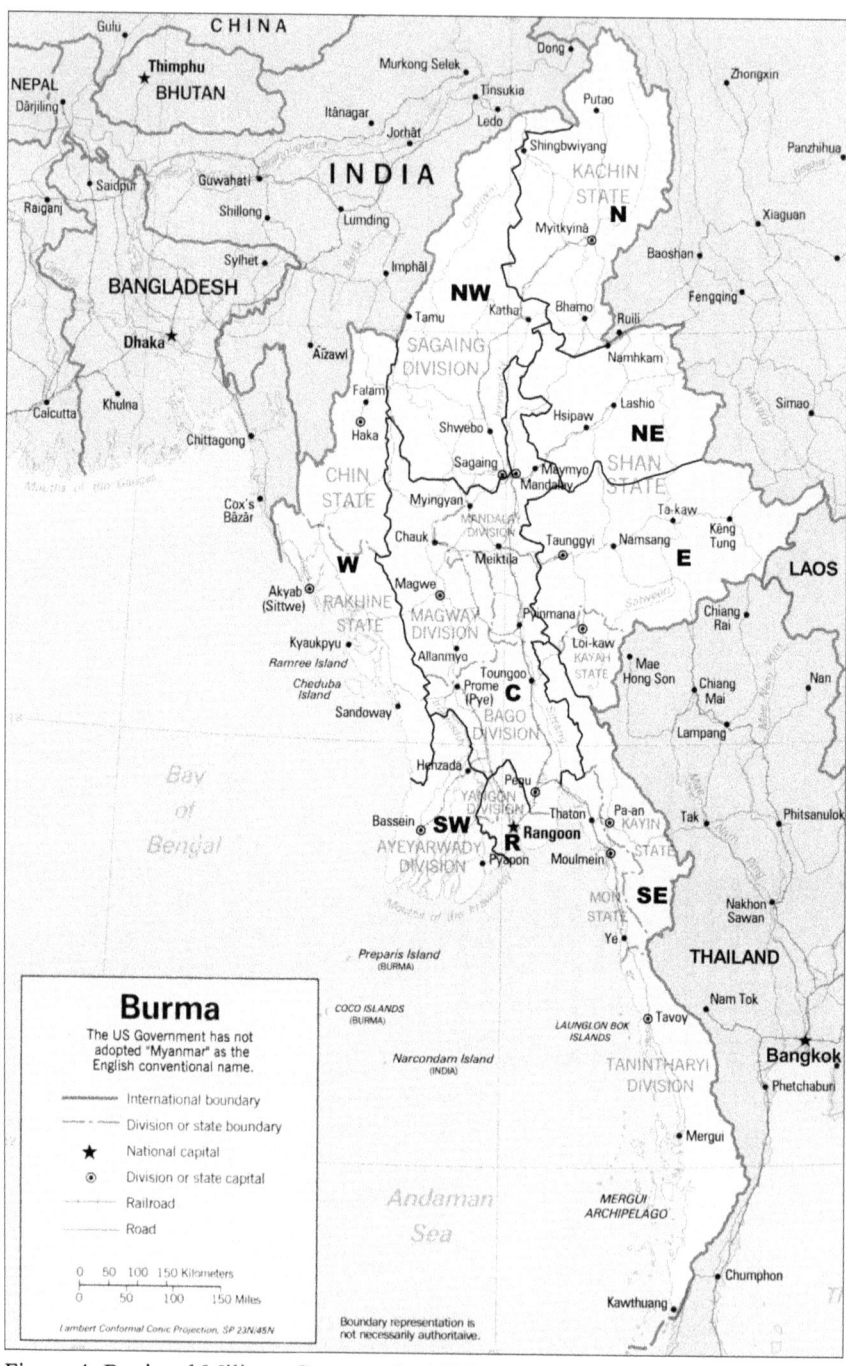

Figure 4: Regional Military Commands, 1988.

vices.[14] He thus formally exercised both political and operational control over the entire armed forces.[15] While military ranks were still closely observed, in practice the SLORC tended to act as a collegiate body and major decisions were often reached by consensus. Also, given the Chairman's many political duties, it is likely that his more routine Defence responsibilities were shared with, or even delegated to, his subordinates. Since May 1989 each Service has had its own Commander-in-Chief, and Chief of Staff. The Army Commander-in-Chief, now elevated to full General rank, also acted as Deputy Commander-in-Chief of the Defence Services. The Commanders-in-Chief of the air force and navy hold the equivalent of Lieutenant General rank, while all three Service Chiefs of Staff were raised to Major General level. At the Defence Ministry the bureaucratic structure remained essentially the same as before, except that the Chiefs of the two Bureaus of Special Operations, the heads of Q and A Departments, and the Director of Defence Services Intelligence, were all elevated to Lieutenant General rank.[16] Thus, the reorganisation of the armed forces hierarchy after 1988 'resulted in an upgrading by two ranks for most of the senior positions'.[17]

Following these and a number of other adjustments, the organisation of the Defence Ministry changed. There remained separate offices for the army, navy and air force, and an independent department for the MAG, JAG, IG and Director of Procurement. The Army Office, however, was significantly restructured and expanded. One Bureau of Special Operations was abolished around 1994. Its place was taken by the Office of Strategic Studies (*Sit Mahar Byu Har Lae Lar Yae Hta-na*), a policy and planning organisation currently commanded by LTGEN Khin Nyunt, who is also the Director of Defence Services Intelligence. The remaining BSO took over the oversight of the Regional Military Commands, and management of all military operations, including control of the LIDs. A number of new subordinate command headquarters (HQ), known as *Da Ka Sa* (Regional Operational Commands, or ROC) and *Sa Ka Kha* (Military Operational Commands, or MOC), were also formally placed under the Chief of the BSO. The Chief of Staff (Army) retained responsibility for the Directorates of Signals, Armour and Artillery, Defence Industries, Security Printing, People's Militias and Psychological Warfare, and Military Engineering.[18] Around the same time as these changes were being made, a Colonel General Staff position was created in the G Staff to manage a new Directorate of Public Relations and Border Troops, the Directorate of Defence Services Computers (DDSC), and the Defence Services Museum and Historical Research Institute. In addition, a Directorate of Resettlement was added to the 'A' Department.[19]

Outside Rangoon, all Regional Commander positions were raised to the level of Major General. With the formal demise of the BSPP, these officers were also appointed Chairmen of State and Division-level LORCs. They were thus formally vested with both military and administrative responsibility for their command areas. Also, three additional regional military commands have been created. In early 1990 a new RMC was formed in Burma's northwest, facing India. In 1996, further changes were made, with the division of Eastern Command (in Shan State) into

56 Burma's Armed Forces

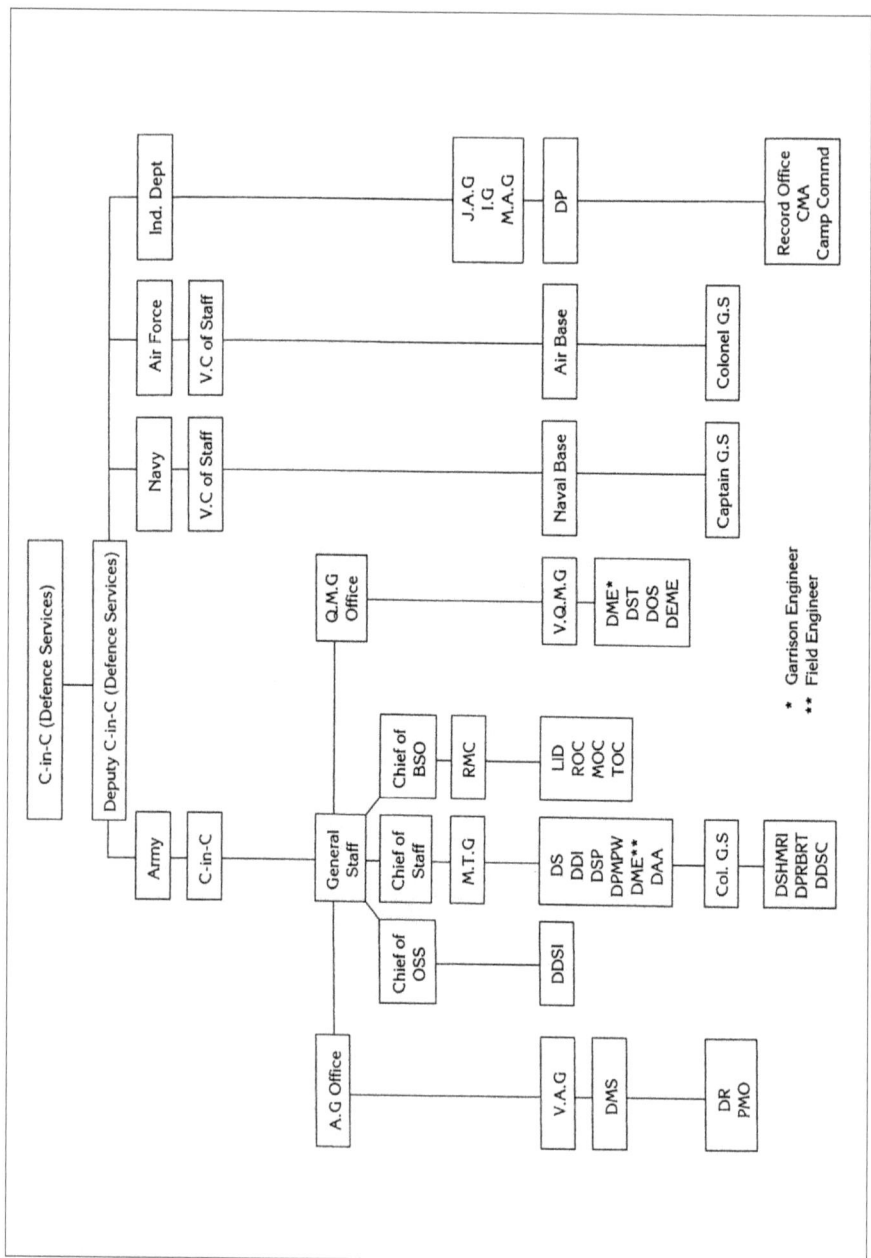

Figure 5: Burma's Defence Ministry, 2000.
Source: Maung Aung Myoe, *Building the Tatmadaw: The Organisational Development of the Armed Force in Myanmar, 1948-98,* Working Paper number 327 (Strategic and Defence Studies Centre, Australian National University, Canberra, 1998).

C-in-C = Commander-in-Chief
OSS = Office of Strategic Studies
A.G = Adjutant General
Q.M.G = Quartermaster General
V.A.G = Vice Adjutant General
V.Q.M.G = Vice Quartermaster General
BSO = Bureau of Special Operations
RMC = Regional Military Command
G.S = General Staff
LID = Light Infantry Division
ROC = Regional Operations Command
MOC = Military Operations Command
M.A.G = Military Appointment General
T.O.C = Tactical Operations Command
I.G = Inspector General
J.A.G = Judge Advocate General
MTG = Military Training General
DMS = Directorate of Medical Services
DDSI = Directorate of Defence Services Intelligence
DS = Directorate of Signals
DDI = Directorate of Defence Industries
DSP = Directorate of Security Printing
DPMPW = Directorate of People's Militias and Psychological Warfare
DME = Directorate of Military Engineers
DAA = Directorate of Armour and Artillery
DST = Directorate of Supply and Transport
DOS = Directorate of Ordnance Services
DEME = Directorate of Electrical and Mechanical Engineers
DP = Directorate of Procurement
PMO = Provost Marshal's Office
DR = Directorate of Resettlement
DPRBRT = Directorate of Public Relations and Border Troops
DDSC = Directorate of Defence Services Computers
DSHMRI = Defence Services Historical Museum and Research Institute
CMA = Central Military Account
Camp Commd = Camp Commandant

58 Burma's Armed Forces

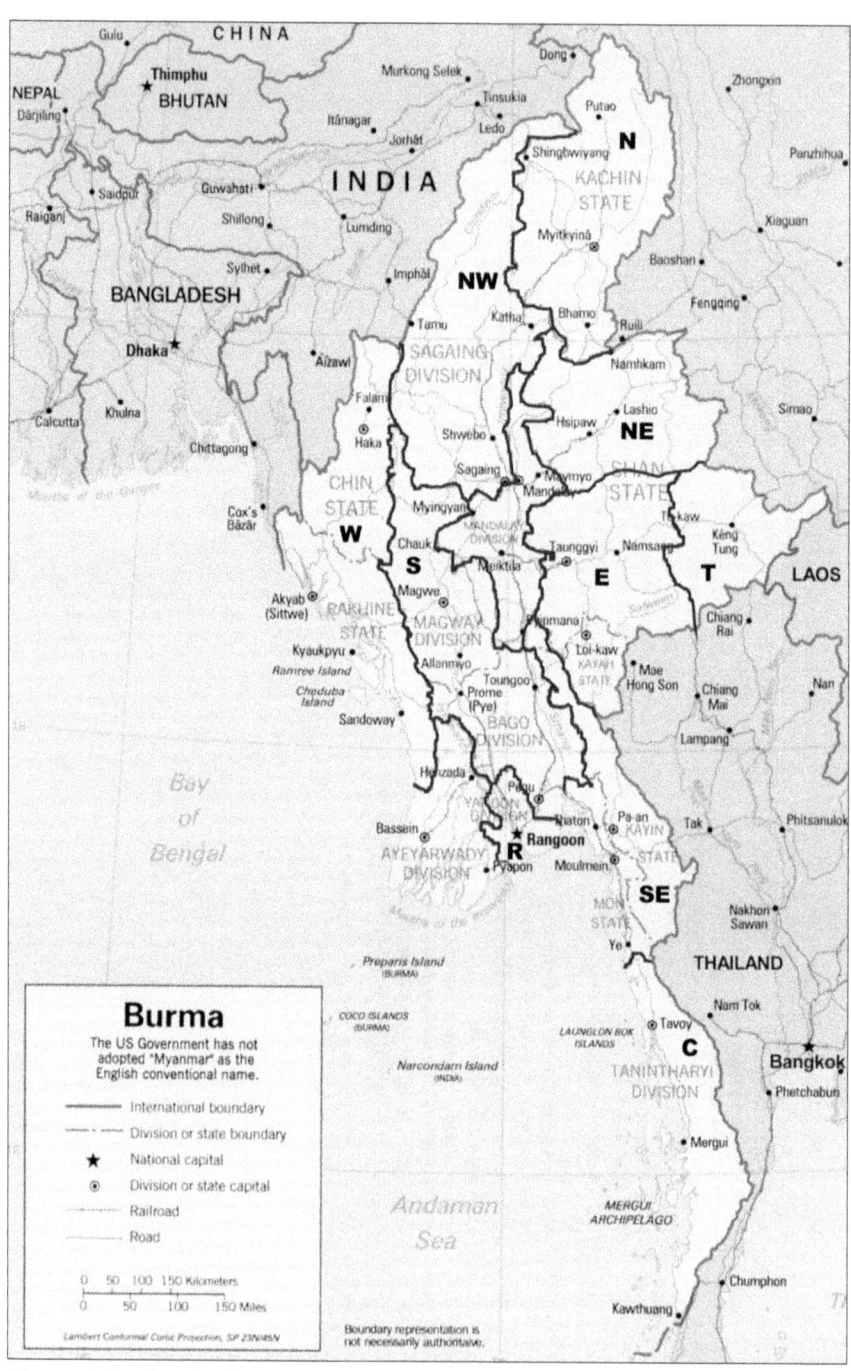

Figure 6: Regional Military Commands, 2000.

two RMCs, and the division of South Eastern Command to create a new RMC in Burma's far south.[20] Burma's 12 RMCs are now Northern Command (covering Kachin State, with its HQ in Myitkyina), North Western Command (Sagaing Division, Monywa), North Eastern Command (northern Shan State, Lashio), Central Command (Mandalay Division, Mandalay), Eastern Command (southern Shan State, Taunggyi), Triangle Command (eastern Shan State, Kengtung), Western Command (Arakan and Chin States, Sittwe), South Western Command (Irrawaddy Division, Bassein), Southern Command (Pegu and Magwe Divisions, Toungoo), Rangoon Command (covering Rangoon Division, Mingaladon), South Eastern Command (Mon and Karen States, Moulmein) and Coastal Command (Tenasserim Division, Mergui).[21]

In general, the LIDs, and certain combat arms like the armour and artillery, were considered strategic assets and were controlled by the Defence Ministry. Through the directorates, the Ministry also administered to the needs of the various corps on issues like personnel, equipment and training. Operational control over other army units, however, was largely left to the Regional Commanders, who since 1988 have been accorded much greater independence. The air force and the navy had their own separate command structures, emanating from their offices in the Defence Ministry. While permitted a fair degree of autonomy, these two Services were always subject to Ministry oversight. They were also considered subordinate to the army, and were occasionally handed over to Regional Commanders for specific operations. More often, however, if the infantry wanted air or naval support, a formal request had to go through the Regional Commander to the Ministry, where it would be passed to the relevant Chief of Staff for action. This process could take half a day.[22] It is not clear whether the Ministry's wish to maintain control of strategic assets like the LIDs, and air and naval forces, was prompted by a concern to efficiently manage and conserve scarce resources, or out of fear that they could be used by mutinous officers in an attempt to overthrow the military government.[23]

In November 1997 the Rangoon regime gave itself a new political face, by abolishing the SLORC and creating the State Peace and Development Council. The SPDC is slightly smaller than the SLORC, with 19 officers.[24] This number includes the Chairman and Commander-in-Chief of the Defence Services, a Senior General, who also holds the positions of Prime Minister and Defence Minister. The SPDC Vice-Chairman is the Deputy Commander-in-Chief of Defence Services and Commander-in-Chief of the Army. There are three SPDC Secretaries (all of Lieutenant-General rank). The Commander-in-Chief of the Navy and the Commander-in-Chief of the Air Force are both members of the SPDC, and act concurrently as Deputy Prime Ministers. An army Lieutenant General (currently the Quartermaster General) acts as a third Deputy Prime Minister. The Council also includes the commanders of the 12 Regional Military Commands, half of whom were themselves newly-appointed. A 40-member Cabinet has been appointed, consisting mainly of military officers drawn from the RMCs and LIDs.[25] At the same time, a new Ministry of Military Affairs has been established, headed by a

Lieutenant General.²⁶ Unlike the SLORC, in which a dozen or more Council Members concurrently served as Cabinet Ministers, only the SPDC's Chairman serves in both capacities.²⁷ There are 33 Deputy Ministers, including a Deputy Minister of Defence at Brigadier level.²⁸

When the SPDC was established a 14-member Advisory Group was created, consisting mainly of the displaced members of the SLORC.²⁹ It was a token body, however, designed largely to soothe the feelings of the ousted SLORC members and to preserve the image of armed forces unity. It was quietly abolished in June 1998. All its members were forced to relinquish their military commissions and a committee of enquiry was established under the National Intelligence Bureau (NIB) to investigate charges of corruption.

The SPDC has been promoted as a new structure with a new set of policies, namely 'to ensure the emergence of an orderly and democratic system and to establish a peaceful and modern state'.³⁰ The name change also subtly opens the door to a longer-term institutional function for the *Tatmadaw*, rather than supposedly 'temporary' law and order duties. Yet the SPDC does not denote any real change in Burma's government or military hierarchy. The most senior personnel have remained the same, and there have been no genuine policy changes. Yet the creation of the SPDC achieves several aims. It permits the regime's power brokers to rid themselves of the more obviously corrupt and incompetent members of the SLORC, and to allow younger officers from lower down the military command chain to play a greater role in running the country. This helps satisfy their ambitions for advancement, always a key factor in the management of the Burmese armed forces, and brings fresh blood into senior circles. By locking them into business in the capital, it also reduces the likelihood that these officers will attempt to carve out independent fiefdoms for themselves in the RMCs, as their predecessors had done. At the same time, however, the heavy responsibilities of the Regional Commanders will leave a small number of key individuals in Rangoon to continue wielding power on a day-to-day basis, through a large and compliant Cabinet.

Like the SLORC, the SPDC rules by decree, without a constitution or legislature of any kind.

3.2 Communications

There are a number of difficulties in describing the development and current status of Burma's military communications. Like everything else in Burma deemed to be related to 'national security', such details are considered highly sensitive and guarded closely. Also, while there is clearly a separate military communications network, devoted largely to operational matters, there appears to be a parallel (and often overlapping) system which is used to gather and disseminate intelligence, including signals intelligence (SIGINT). The armed forces also rely heavily on the civil communications system to carry a great deal of traffic which is of less importance, or less sensitivity. In any case, it can be expected that in a country like Burma where little distinction is made between the military and civil spheres, all these networks would be used in a contingency. This is in addition to any use the military government might make of the country's national radio and television systems to broadcast political messages to a wider audience.

In the national crisis which arose immediately after Independence, communications were critical to the *Tatmadaw*'s efforts to establish itself as a coherent, effective organisation, and to fight the numerous insurgencies which it faced. Yet, from the very beginning, the Signal Corps encountered major difficulties. Almost half of the new army's signallers were ethnic Karens, who had served in this role and acquired considerable combat experience during the guerrilla resistance against the Japanese. This initially augured well for the Burma Army but most defected in 1949 to join the Karen National Defence Organisation (KNDO) revolt against the Rangoon government. This left the Burma Army with barely half of its trained signallers, and at a critical time a major effort had to be put into recruiting and training replacements.[31] In this regard, considerable assistance was provided by the British Military Mission (BMM) which, as a result of the 1947 Let Ya-Freeman Agreement, remained in Burma until 1954 to help the *Tatmadaw* become established.[32] The BMM provided basic equipment and training in all important aspects of signals operations, including communications security (COMSEC), interception and elementary cryptography.[33] The defection of the Karens necessitated a number of changes in technique and language, but progress was gradually made.[34] As the *Tatmadaw*'s signals capabilities grew, they made an increasing contribution to the central government's campaign to restore law and order.

From this early period, the structure of the Burma Army Signal Corps was largely geographically based but, subject to available resources, was adapted to meet changing operational requirements. The hub of the network was initially BA headquarters at Mingaladon, but was later moved to the War Office in Rangoon. Outside the capital there were a number of regional command centres and bases, some with specific training or maintenance responsibilities. Signals units were attached to major headquarters and posted out where possible to subordinate commands and operational formations. In September 1948, for example, there was a Signal Company at Burma Army HQ at Mingaladon, a Signal Training Company at Maymyo, a Signal Platoon serving the North Burma Sub-District HQ at Maymyo, another platoon serving the South Burma Sub-District HQ at Mingaladon, and a Signal Platoon at Sittwe.[35] By 1953 the Australian Legation in Rangoon could report:

> There are two signals regiments, one of which is a training regiment [and] the other is split all over Burma handling communications from War Office down to battalions. Equipment is short and in poor condition but plans are in hand for a large expansion of Burma Signals and new equipment is arriving.[36]

A similar hierarchical structure appears to have been adopted by the navy and air force. There were fixed communications links between the War Office in Rangoon, specific commands and major bases. From there subordinate nets were used to communicate with smaller units and individual platforms.

The current *Tatmadaw* communications network is commanded by the Directorate of Signals (*Ah Chet Pya Set Thwe Yae Hta-na*) in the Ministry of Defence, with the army's Signals Corps headquarters at Maymyo. There are about 16 individual signals battalions (or 'regiments' in *Tatmadaw* parlance), distributed around the country to Rangoon, Hmawbi, Meiktila, Maymyo, Myitkyina, Bassein, Toungoo, Monywa, Sittwe, Moulmein, Lashio, Taunggyi and Mandalay. Smaller signals squadrons are based at Monywa, Akyab and Indaing (Indine). A separate LID signals unit is based at Prome. Signals workshops are located at Mingaladon, Hmawbi, Meiktila and Mandalay, and there are stores units in Mandalay and Indaing.[37] In addition to these bases, signals units are attached to all levels of command, from Regional Military Commands down to battalion and company level.[38] Infantry platoons also have their own radios, but it is not known if this capability extends to section level. Major strategic assets like the LIDs, armoured formations and artillery units, have their own direct links with the Ministry of Defence. DDSI intelligence units also appear to have their own facilities and communicate through a separate net. Navy and air force communications have been extended greatly as these Services have expanded. Since 1988 the acquisition of new equipment (both land-based and on individual platforms) has improved communications coverage and performance.

In addition to the regular signals network, there is a Signals Security Battalion based at Mingaladon, under the direction of a Signals Security Department in the Directorate of Signals. This parallel organisation, which also has units posted around the country, is primarily responsible for collecting signals intelligence through the interception and decryption of foreign, insurgent and dissident telecommunications.[39] While formally a separate part of the Defence structure, of necessity it works closely with the Directorate of Defence Services Intelligence.

The training company created in 1948 formally became the Burma Signals Training Regiment in 1951, and the base in Maymyo became the Signals Corps Centre. It has since evolved into the Defence Services Signals and Electronic School (DSSES). The school offers a range of courses designed for both officers and other ranks. Officers in the Signals Corps are required to attend courses on signals operations at both platoon and company level.[40] This instruction appears to be quite comprehensive. According to one Burmese source, 'These courses include radio operation, signals intelligence, interception, cipher making and decoding, electronic warfare and so on.'[41] Some courses are also provided for infantry officers, so that they can 'gain [a] basic knowledge of combat-level signal operations'.[42] Courses in 'signals [electronic] engineering' are also conducted at the DSSES.

Before 1988, the *Tatmadaw* appears to have relied for its communications on a diverse mixture of UK, US and Japanese radio equipment, supplemented by other sources as opportunity presented itself. It can be assumed, for example, that the BNA had been provided with some British and Japanese communications equipment which it retained after 1945.[43] Also, a basic suite of field telephones, transmitters, receivers, direction finders and field exchanges was probably left behind by the departing Allied forces in 1948, (and the BMM in 1954) as part of the UK's commitment to help equip the new Burmese armed forces.[44] Additional items of equipment were supplied, evidently by the UK and US, during the 1950s and 1960s.[45] Given the difficulties under which the *Tatmadaw* was labouring at the time, however, it was prepared to take whatever it could find, and the armed forces' inventory came to include equipment from a wide range of countries. For example, Burma was given (or, out of deference to its neutrality, was permitted to 'purchase') some Eastern bloc communications equipment following the visits of Marshall Tito of Yugoslavia in January 1955, and Soviet Communist Party First Secretary Nikita Khrushchev later the same year. It appears that some Japanese and German radios were also received during this period.

As a result of all these acquisitions, the *Tatmadaw* was required to become familiar with a wide range of equipment. Judging by the Signals Corps display in the Defence Services Museum in Rangoon, the army's inventory included AN-PRC-6, AN-PRC-9 and AN-PRC-10 portable transceivers, and FM-1-CN2 and AN-VRQ-2 sets, all from the US, and Redifon No. 53 and Redifon G-251 transceivers from the UK. The Burmese also acquired some Pye FM-8702, WS-62, HF-15B, HF-15G and TRA-906C sets from the UK. The latter two were either modified or rebuilt in the Burma Army's workshops to produce the *Tayza* and *Thura* radio sets, respectively.[46] The Burma Army also used W/T-18, W/T-19 and W/T-22 sets, SSB-1, SSB-125T and SSB-130 sets, and BRT-400 sets. In addition, the army acquired some Yugoslav TFUGK and TORMFU D-2 radio equipment, and Soviet R-107 HF, R-209 VHF and 10.PT transceivers. At the larger headquarters there were C-12, RA-1772 and AN-GRC-9 transmitters, F&F exchanges and S.50P teleprinters, most from the US. For direction finding, the *Tatmadaw* used British G-2 sets with four pole Adcock antennae, Munston AN PRD-1 and AN-PRD.1.PSU sets from the US, Telefunken PST.396, 286.C DF and P-100 sets from West Germany, and PE.484 sets from Japan.[47]

As late as the 1980s, the Burma Army was using British WS-62 radio transceivers at the battalion level and TRA-309 sets at the company level. Also in use at that time were TRA-906, PCC-30, 156, AN-PRC-9 and AN-PRC-10 radio sets, mainly acquired from the UK and US.[48]

After the creation of the SLORC, and the development of defence relations with China, the PRC provided the *Tatmadaw* with a large quantity of radar and other communications equipment. One initial shipment was estimated to be worth at least US$5 million.[49] In late 1995 the SLORC reportedly ordered a range of additional radio equipment from Russia.[50] Singapore too has probably provided the regime with a range of modern equipment for command, control, communications, computer and intelligence (C^4I) purposes, extending from personal computers and software to radios and radars.[51] Other equipment has been purchased on the open market, either directly or through intermediaries. Also, there is reason to believe that the SLORC may have acquired some equipment to protect Burma's military communications from interception by hostile agencies. China, for example, is reported to have sold the Burma Army some frequency-hopping radios.[52] They have already proven useful in protecting *Tatmadaw* signals from interception by insurgents, and have probably also provided a measure of protection against other countries.[53] Both Thailand and India, for example, are reported to monitor Burmese military and diplomatic radio traffic on a regular basis.[54] Despite Rangoon's closeness to Beijing at present, there would also be traffic which the Burmese would wish to keep from the Chinese.

Details are difficult to obtain, but it appears that the new equipment was gradually distributed to all levels of the Burma Army. While they probably have more powerful fixed sets at their headquarters, the LIDs and RMCs now use small PRM-4051 Squadcal 2 HF/SSB manpack transceivers purchased in the late 1980s. At battalion level, and in communications with the TOCs and MOCs, the army uses XD-D6M-1 5W HF/SSB field radios, acquired from China in 1993 and 1994. A portable transceiver, this radio was first used operationally during the battle for Manerplaw in December 1994.[55] At the company level, the BA uses Chinese XD-D6M sets on fixed channels. TRA-906 Squadcal HF/SSB manpacks are still found at the battalion, company and platoon level. These hardy radios were first produced in the UK in the 1960s, but remain in service in many parts of the world, including Burma. There are unconfirmed reports that AN/PRC-104 HF/SSB manpacks are also used by the BA.[56] It is likely that the highest priority for the more advanced communications equipment in the *Tatmadaw*'s inventory would be given to the major command centres, and strategic assets like the LIDs. The older and less reliable equipment has probably been passed down to garrison forces.

Despite all these improvements, the *Tatmadaw* still has communications problems. For example, there seems to be continuing difficulties with long distance networks, although whether this problem relates to direct links between Rangoon and the more distant Regional Military Commands, or between RMCs and subordinate units in the field, is not clear. The harsh nature of Burma's terrain, particularly in the insurgent-held border areas, and the annual monsoon, must contribute to the difficulties faced by Burma's signallers. Ground-to-air communications are another problem, as the radios fitted in the BAF's aircraft are not able to link up directly with those of the army. This has reportedly contributed to cases of mistaken identity and even some inadvertent attacks by BAF aircraft against BA positions.[57] One solution has been to use small hand-held SE-120 radio telephones from Switzerland to communicate between the pilots and men on the ground. Even then there are difficulties, as these sets operate in the VHF band and can only be used when there is a clear line of sight.[58]

In recent years there has been a number of references in the open literature to Burmese plans to create its own military satellite communications network, as part of its overall armed forces modernisation program. As described by one trade journal,

> The initial requirement is for the construction of a Very Small Aperture Terminal [VSAT] hub station in the capital Yangon, with around 15 remote stations and up to five mobile stations, although the plan calls for a total of around

200 remote stations in time. These would be connected to a leased transponder on a commercial satellite, and operate in the C-band.[59]

The system would be required to provide secure voice and data links, and possibly also encrypted video-conferencing facilities.[60] It was noted in one journal that a possible hurdle which the regime would have to overcome would be problems Rangoon would encounter in attempting to lease a transponder service from a commercial satellite operator. The satellites which this system could use are mainly owned and operated by the US, which has long maintained sanctions against the military government.[61] Even Asiasat, which is owned by a Chinese company, uses a US satellite.

All of the public telecommunications facilities in Burma are state-owned and controlled. There are two AM, three FM and three shortwave radio broadcast stations, and two television stations.[62] The *Tatmadaw* operates the Defence Forces Broadcasting Unit, transmitting in short-wave from Taunggyi in Shan State, and the Myawaddy Radio Station, which broadcasts in both short-wave and medium-wave, probably using the same facilities.[63] Since 1995 the Taunggyi transmitter has also been used to jam broadcasts from foreign radio stations critical of the Rangoon regime, such as the British Broadcasting Corporation (BBC) and Voice of America (VOA).[64] Radio Free Asia has not reported any problems, but attempts have been made to jam the opposition 'Democratic Voice of Burma' (DVB), which is broadcast from Norway.[65] The *Tatmadaw* has had some ability to jam HF broadcasts as early as 1970, when efforts were directed against former Prime Minister Nu's clandestine 'Patriotic Youth Front Radio'.[66] The CPB's 'Voice of the People of Burma' (VOPB), however, with its more powerful transmitter, was able to broadcast for nearly 20 years, despite repeated attempts by the *Tatmadaw* to jam it.[67] BBC and VOA signals are once again getting through to Burma, but the higher level of jamming directed against them may signal the *Tatmadaw*'s receipt of more powerful equipment, perhaps from China. Burma's unpredictable electric power generating capacity may make such activities difficult to sustain.[68]

Since the SLORC took over government, a major effort has been put into improving Burma's civil telecommunications network. In 1992, for example, Myanmar Posts and Telecommunications (MPT) contracted Sumitomo Corporation of Japan to install a 14,000 line exchange/telephone system, and Ericsson (Australia) won a contract to install five microwave radio base stations and one mobile exchange for an analogue cellular phone system covering Rangoon. The latter began operation in December 1993.[69] In 1994 Loxley of Thailand became the effective investing partner in a plan to install a cellular mobile telephone network in Mandalay and to supply 1000 telephones. The first phase was launched in 1995, and a second phase doubling the system's capacity began the following year. Siemens also won a contract to install an international auto exchange and radio telephones in Rangoon, and was made responsible for the extension of international satellite communications lines at Syriam (Thanlyin) Ground Station. Also in 1994, MPT signed a contract with Interdigital Communications Corporation of the

US for the installation of 700 radio telephone links with a wireless digital loop carrier.[70] In 1996 Ericsson won a contract to upgrade the analogue mobile phone system in Rangoon to a digital service. In early 2000 a new US$144 million mobile phone project was announced, which would be centred on the satellite-based Global System for Mobiles (GSM).[71] A joint Thai-Taiwanese-Burmese consortium has undertaken to build a fibre-optic manufacturing plant in Burma for television, cellular networks and fixed line telecommunications systems.

Attention has also been given to Burma's long distance telecommunications. There are now seven analogue microwave systems with a capacity of 960 channels each. Together with UHF-VHF systems, they carry both voice and television transmissions to 60 towns including Rangoon.[72] In an effort to enhance links with strategic border areas, MPT has increased the number of digital microwave routes from five in 1997 to ten. 'The routes stretch all over the country and seek to provide telecommunications to the most remote areas'.[73] In addition, MPT is using domestic satellite earth stations in 12 locations, linked to Thaicom, to serve isolated regions. During 1998, very small aperture terminal systems were introduced, and there are now four in service.[74] International communications between Burma and other countries are gradually improving but the local satellite facilities are still unable to meet the demand. In February 1979 a Standard-B earth station was commissioned, equipped with 60 telephone channels and connected with seven countries. In 1989-90, China installed an Asiasat-linked network to improve Burma's telecommunications links.[75] A Standard-A satellite earth station, capable of handling 306 channels destined for 15 stations in 14 countries was commissioned in 1994 and upgraded in 1998.[76] Both these stations are situated at Syriam. It appears that Burma currently leases three transponders on Inmarsat (although it has in the past used Asiasat, Intelsat and the Indonesian Palapa satellite).[77] Also, when another project is commissioned, a fibre-optic link will connect Burma by submarine cable with the SEA-ME-WE-3 member countries, the Middle East and Europe.

By the beginning of 2000, Burma was described by industry sources as 'fully equipped', with 523 local exchanges, serving over 225,000 fixed line telephones.[78] In addition there are now about 10,000 cellular phones. The current number of phones gives a national telephone density of about 0.50 per 100 people, a dramatic increase in the last 10 years, particularly in the urban areas.[79] The availability of telephone services in the rural districts (where most Burmese live) is much lower.[80] There are about 1750 registered fax machines (and many more unregistered).[81] A high priority for the future is the public switched telephone network which, according to industry observers, must expand to meet the high demand for subscriptions.[82] Also, it will be necessary for the MPT to replace the existing analogue long-distance transmission links with digital systems. National roaming facilities for cellular phones will be available as soon as the Mandalay digital system is connected to the upgraded Ericsson network in Rangoon, and global roaming capabilities should follow the completion of the GSM project. The old manual and cross-bar exchanges will need to be replaced by a greater number of more reliable digital switches, and there is a need for more long-distance transmission links, such as digital microwave radio relay systems. The implementation of new digital microwave routes between Rangoon and Mandalay along the western bank of the Irrawaddy River (where there are several important defence industries) is already under way.[83]

All these projects are being promoted by the regime as part of a wide-ranging scheme to improve the country's domestic communications infrastructure and encourage foreign investment. Given the position of the *Tatmadaw* in Burma, however, it would be extraordinary if it was not fully exploiting the improvements being made to the civil system to improve its own capabilities. It is not a coincidence that government services and long distance trunk lines are being given priority for attention.[84] However, the civil communications system still suffers from major problems. The regime has not been able, or willing, to allocate sufficient funds to conduct a major overhaul of the entire system. Also, the government is reluctant to transfer management of its communications to foreign companies in exchange for investment.[85] This policy derives in part from a deep-seated fear of foreign interests acquiring too large a stake in Burma's economy, but it probably also stems from a wish to retain control over a strategically important part of the country's infrastructure. As a result, the government has been forced to rely on piece-meal measures which have caused numerous problems. For example, MPT now obtains equipment from more than a dozen different suppliers, with resulting inefficiencies and confusion. It is likely that the military communications network suffers from similar problems.

3.3 Military Computers

Before 1988, the armed forces were familiar with certain specialised types of electronic equipment, but there were very few computers in Burma, and few Burmese who could operate them with any real facility. The armed forces relied on more traditional means of communication and data storage. Since then, however, a major effort has been put into upgrading the *Tatmadaw*'s computer inventory, and exploiting new information technologies (IT). A survey in late 2000 even placed Burma among the Asia-Pacific region's 'top ten' exponents of information warfare (IW).[86]

The first step in the *Tatmadaw*'s upgrade program seems to have been a plan to improve the IT systems operated by the Ministry of Defence in Rangoon, and to improve the electronic communication links between the capital and the (then) 10 RMCs. A Singaporean company was hired by the SLORC to install a computer network in the Ministry and to provide basic and advanced training courses.[87] From Rangoon, the use of defence computers seems to have spread quickly to regional commands and designated subordinate units. To oversee this program a Directorate of Defence Services Computers was created in the Ministry's General Staff Office, probably around 1990. By 1995 the DDSC was known in-house as the *Tatmadaw*'s 'Cyber Warfare Department', and reportedly had the largest computer facility in Burma.[88] To assist in the development and use of these facilities, special courses are now conducted at the Signals and Electronic School in Maymyo. According to one insider,

> In order to catch up with developments in electronic and information technology, a number of new courses are offered for infantry officers. According to some sources, this includes a basic course on command, control, communications, computer and intelligence (C^4I) warfare.[89]

In addition, a computer science degree course has been added to the curriculum of Burma's Defence Services Academy (DSA), also at Maymyo.

The pace and extent of the IT changes occurring in Burma's defence sector are difficult to determine, but clearly considerable progress has been made. For example, the BA is now using computer technology to produce more modern maps of the country and other operational aids.[90] Digital photographs are being scanned using Intergraph Image Station software. Also, 22-metre resolution imagery is being merged with five-metre panchromatic data using the same system.[91] Advances in the *Tatmadaw*'s use of IT can be judged by the fact that a number of other Burmese government agencies have also made the transition to computer-based systems. MPT, for example, changed to a personal computer-based system in 1995, for administration, budgeting, supervision and management.[92] It can be assumed that, if such improvements were being made in the civilian sector, then the armed forces (which are given first priority for funds and other resources) would be much further advanced.

The second phase of the *Tatmadaw*'s computer development program, or perhaps a logical consequence of it, seems to have been the improvement of Burma's electronic monitoring capabilities.[93] One of the principal missions of the DDSC is reportedly to help process and analyse intercepted telecommunications, including telephone calls, facsimiles, electronic mail and other types of computer exchanges.[94] According to Desmond Ball, 'One of its particular responsibilities is to monitor the import, possession and use of certain types of computer equipment.'[95] Under the Computer Science Development Law of 27 September 1996, for example, it is an offence (punishable with sentences of 7 to 15 years in prison, and fines of up to US$5,000) for anyone 'who uses computer networks or information technology for undermining State security, law and order, national unity, the national economy or national culture, or who obtains or transmits State secrets [by means of computers and information technology]'.[96] For example, the regime regularly monitors the public internet discussion on Burma, which is dominated by pro-democracy activists around the world.[97] The DDSC, presumably in close collaboration with the Directorate of Defence Services Intelligence, has evidently been able to monitor a large proportion of the country's electronic mail traffic through the MPT, Burma's offical internet service provider. In 1997 MPT signed an agreement with a Singaporean firm to use Singapore as a gateway for Burma's first digital communications link with the rest of the world. Several private e-mail servers later appeared but were closed down by the regime in 1999 after they were used in violation of the Computer Science Development Law.[98]

There have been a number of arrests and convictions under this law. One related to an elderly Burmese democracy activist who was imprisoned for three years (but died in jail after only a few weeks) for possessing nine facsimile machines and two phone lines which were not registered with the government. Anti-regime circles have claimed that his arrest was part of an attempt by the DDSI to close down the NLD's international communications links.[99] In addition, in December 1999 a number of people in Burma (including at least one senior army officer who worked in the DDSC) were arrested and charged for violating the Official Secrets Act, apparently for accessing and distributing reports carried by an opposition internet news service.[100]

In order to combat the increasingly sophisticated electronic lobbying campaign being conducted against the Rangoon regime (and its foreign supporters) over the internet, the *Tatmadaw* has also developed a nascent information warfare capability. For example, the free internet news service known as BurmaNet News, established in 1993, has long been the target of IW attack.[101] In the interests of free speech and full debate, the decision was made by the service's operators to allow known representatives of the SLORC (and later the SPDC) to subscribe to BurmaNet and post messages giving Rangoon's viewpoint. According to a study by the US Institute of Peace,

> a known SLORC representative...regularly transmits the regime's official statements on BurmaNet and the *soc.culture.burma* newsgroup. Others who are believed to be representatives of, or at least sympathetic to, the regime also participate in the debate.[102]

At times, the regime has gone further and, before precautions were taken to prevent it from occurring, BurmaNet was subject to some highly critical messages from *agents provocateurs*. Also, false and malicious reports were posted on the net, clearly designed to confuse or undercut the pro-democracy campaign.[103] It is likely that these activities were either being conducted or controlled by the DDSC, under the guidance of the DDSI.

The Rangoon regime also responded to the rapid spread of BurmaNet by paying a US company to establish its own website, *www.myanmar.com*, which is registered in Laurel, Maryland. This website features pictures of Burma, and information about tourism and business opportunities. It initially did not discuss politics, but simply extolled the virtues of 'Myanmar, the Golden Land'. More recently, however, it has included a journal called 'The Truth', in which the OSS 'interprets' statements by the NLD and other opposition groups. According to a recent UK survey, the website also engages in 'bombarding unsuspecting journalists and others with e-mails on the country'.[104]

In 1997, the SLORC launched a more aggressive attempt to use the internet. In May that year the regime began its own electronic mailing list, MyanmarNet, specifically designed to compete with BurmaNet. Articles were selected or rejected for electronic distribution by an individual known as Okkar, who stated that his policy would be

(a) to accept most of the submitted postings, omitting 'only those junk mails and very rude usages', and (b) to welcome submissions of news, information and comments about political, social and economic affairs in Burma that have 'not been posted elsewhere such as soc.culture.burma and other mailing lists'.[105]

In this way, material which had already appeared on BurmaNet was effectively excluded, although a few critical items were initially allowed through (presumably to give the site some credibility). The MyanmarNet site essentially echoes the regime's point of view. It includes the state-controlled *New Light of Myanmar* newspaper, official government statements and news of business opportunities in the country. It also reprints foreign articles favourable (or at least neutral) to the military regime.[106]

'Okkar' is believed by pro-democracy activists to be a Burma Army officer working for the OSS, who often acts as the regime's public spokesman. Another regular participant in the internet debate, who uses the pseudonym 'Maung Myanmar', is thought to be one of the regime's most senior diplomats, operating from a Burmese embassy overseas.[107]

Also in 1997, the Rangoon regime waged a disinformation campaign against several international non-governmental organisations (NGO), which were accused of supporting terrorism in Burma. These accusations, and the biographical details of several NGO workers, were published by the regime on the internet to ensure the widest possible distribution. Those people and organisations targeted in this way were later obliged to post strong denials on the web that they supported terrorism in Burma.[108] In February 2000, it was revealed that the regime had taken a further step in its IW offensive against its critics overseas. Many pro-democracy activists began receiving e-mail messages from SPDC agents, with attachments containing damaging computer viruses.[109] This campaign too seems to be orchestrated by the DDSI, either through or with the support of the Defence Ministry's 'cyber war department'.

In all these activities, the *Tatmadaw* has shown an ability over the years to modify its structures, change its methods of operation and introduce new ways of thinking, to meet changing circumstances. From 1988 in particular, it has demonstrated a flexibility and readiness to adopt new technology in ways that have surprised many observers. To a certain extent, these changes have probably been prompted by the advent of a younger military leadership more comfortable with modern systems, and the much greater budget allocations made to defence since the SLORC was created. Yet the Rangoon regime seems to be driven, as always, by its instinct for survival. It seems to have realised that it needed to adapt and increase its capabilities if it was not to fail in its determination to retain political power. Even with larger and more modern military forces, it needed to develop asymmetric forms of attack against opponents that were either too strong, or too diffuse, for a frontal assault. To this end, anything was justified, including the embrace of computers and cyber war techniques.

Notes

1. Some observers have described the formation of the SLORC as a 'coup', or at least an assumption of power by the armed forces. This is incorrect. Despite the creation of numerous ostensibly civilian political institutions after 1962, Ne Win and the armed forces were always the real arbiters of power in Burma. All that happened in 1988 was that the retired military officers in public office stepped aside, and permitted serving members of the armed forces hierarchy to assume direct control. For a different perspective, see Dr Maung Maung, *The 1988 Uprising in Burma*, pp. 221-47.

2. If the US star system is used, a Burmese Senior General has five stars, a General has four stars, a Lieutenant General has three, a Major General has two and a Brigadier has one. The equivalent navy and air force officers can be described using the same system.

3. Bunge, *Burma*, p. 252. The Defence Ministry occupies a large compound in central Rangoon, between Shwedagon Pagoda Road and Ahlanpya Pagoda Road (formerly Signal Pagoda Road). Although its location is obvious, and known to most residents of Rangoon, the compound is not shown on any Burmese maps, presumably for security reasons.

4. Selth, *Transforming the Tatmadaw*, pp. 9-10; See also Maung Aung Myoe, *Building the Tatmadaw: The Organisational Development of the Armed Forces in Myanmar, 1948-98*, Working Paper No. 327 (Strategic and Defence Studies Centre, Australian National University, Canberra, 1998), p. 53.

5. It has been suggested that there was once a fourth major department headed by the 'Master General of Ordnance', but this seems unlikely. See *The Military Powers Encyclopedia: Southeast Asia* (Société I^{3}C, Paris, 1991), p. 34.

6. Tin Maung Maung Than, 'Burma's National Security and Defence Posture', p. 45.

7. BSO One was responsible for Northern Command, North Eastern Command, North Western Command and Eastern Command. BSO Two was responsible for South Eastern Command, South Western Command, Western Command and Central Command. Interview, Sydney, October 1996. See also Maung Aung Myoe, *Building the Tatmadaw*, p. 26.

8. The Burma Army has three kinds of engineers. There are the Field Engineers who are responsible, for example, for laying and removing landmines. There are the Construction Engineers who perform civil tasks, such as garrison maintenance and infrastructure development. The third are the Electrical and Mechanical Engineers.

9. Between 1961 and 1972 the country was divided into six RMCs, with independent Brigades based at Mytikyina and Pa'an. In 1972, however, the structure was revised. Northern and North Eastern Commands were created to cope with the increased level of operations in that part of the country, and Western Command was added. Interview, Canberra, October 1997.

10. *The Military Balance 1988-1989* (International Institute for Strategic Studies, London, 1988), p. 159.

11. Bunge, *Burma*, p. 252.

12. The CIA Directorate of Intelligence publishes a list entitled 'Chiefs of State and Cabinet Members of Foreign Governments: Burma'. This can be found on the internet at http://www.cia.gov/publications/chiefs/chiefs29.html. See also *Military Bureaucracy of the SLORC*, All Burma Student Democratic Front, Documentation and Research Centre, Mae Hong Son, 4 September 1995 (copy in author's possession).

13. Tin Maung Maung Than, 'Myanmar: Preoccupation with Regime Survival, National Unity and Stability', p. 392. Others, however, have dismissed this committee as having little weight. Interview, Canberra, September 1997.

14. The rank of Senior General was created for the Commander-in-Chief in May 1990.

15. Faced with a nervous breakdown, SENGEN Saw Maung relinquished his Defence Ministerial responsibilities to his deputy, General Than Shwe, shortly before the latter re-

placed him as Chairman of the SLORC in April 1992. See Tin Maung Maung Than, 'Neither Inheritance nor Legacy: Leading the Myanmar State Since Independence', *Contemporary Southeast Asia*, Vol. 15, No. 1, June 1993, p. 60, note 128.

16. See Bertil Lintner, 'Burma - Struggle for Power', *Jane's Intelligence Review*, Vol. 5, No. 10, October 1993, p. 470; *The Military Powers Encyclopedia*, p. 34; and *Military Bureaucracy of the SLORC*.

17. Tin Maung Maung Than, 'Neither Inheritance nor Legacy', p. 60, note 128. See also Moshe Lissak, *Military Roles in Modernization: Civil-Military Relations in Thailand and Burma* (Sage, Beverly Hills, 1976), p. 179, note 61. There was a feeling in the Rangoon diplomatic community at the time that this was to give senior Burmese officers parity with their Thai counterparts.

18. Before his death in a helicopter crash in February 2000, LTGEN Tin Oo was both Army Chief of Staff and Chief of the BSO.

19. Maung Aung Myoe, *Building the Tatmadaw*, p. 54.

20. Robert Karniol, 'Burma creates improved regional C^2 structure', *JDW*, 29 May 1996, p. 12.

21. Lintner, 'Burma - Struggle for Power', p. 470. See also Tin Maung Maung Than, 'Neither Inheritance nor Legacy', p. 60, note 126; and Maung Aung Myoe, *Building the Tatmadaw*, p. 56.

22. Interview, Sydney, October 1996.

23. The structure of the three Services outside the Defence Ministry is discussed in later chapters.

24. State Peace and Development Council Notification No. 1/97 of 15 November 1997.

25. State Peace and Development Council Notification No. 2/97 of 15 November 1997.

26. Bertil Lintner, 'Cosmetic Changes', *FEER*, 27 November 1997, p. 23; and Bruce Hawke, 'Myanmar seeks fresh look in major reshuffle', *JDW*, 26 November 1997, p. 25.

27. Bertil Lintner, 'Just as Ugly', *FEER*, 27 November 1997, p. 23-4.

28. State Peace and Development Council Notification No. 2/97 of 15 November 1997.

29. State Peace and Development Council Notification No. 3/97 of 15 November 1997.

30. State Peace and Development Council Notification No. 1/97 of 15 November 1997.

31. By March 1949, 288 Karen signals personnel had deserted, while another 55 had been imprisoned. Together this amounted to 44% of the army's signallers. Callahan, 'The Origins of Military Rule in Burma', p. 369.

32. Tinker, *Burma: The Struggle for Independence*, Vol. 2, pp. 734-6.

33. Ball, *Burma's Military Secrets*, p. 53.

34. By 1951 'the military adapted Burmese to code for use in signalling'. Josef Silverstein, *Burmese Politics: The Dilemma of National Unity* (Rutgers University Press, New Brunswick, 1980), p. 221.

35. Ball, *Burma's Military Secrets*, p. 53. In 1950 the two Sub-District headquarters at Maymyo and Mingaladon were reorganised and renamed, becoming Northern Command HQ and Southern Command HQ respectively.

36. Quoted in Ball, *Burma's Military Secrets*, p. 55. The War Office, which was created in 1948, became the Defence Ministry in 1956.

37. Interviews, Chiang Mai, November 1999.

38. Personal correspondence, September 1995. See also Ball, *Burma's Military Secrets*, p. 81.

39. Ball, *Burma's Military Secrets*, pp. 91-123. Burma's signals intelligence activities are discussed in Chapter Five.

40. Maung Aung Myoe, *Officer Education and Leadership Training in the Tatmadaw: A Survey*, Working Paper No. 346 (Strategic and Defence Studies Centre, Australian National University, Canberra, 2000), p. 11.

41. *Ibid.*
42. *Ibid.*
43. During the war the Japanese tended to give their Burmese allies captured British equipment, but it is likely that some Japanese equipment fell into Burmese hands before or after 1945. For details of the latter, see US War Department, *Handbook on Japanese Military Forces*, Technical Manual TM-E 30-480 (United States Government Printing Office, Washington, 1944), pp. 303-21.
44. Tinker, *Burma: The Struggle for Independence*, Vol. 2, pp. 404-5.
45. Stockholm International Peace Research Institute, *The Arms Trade with the Third World* (Paul Elek, London, 1971), p. 319.
46. Personal observation, November 1999.
47. Personal observations, April 1995 and November 1999. The names of specific items of equipment have been taken from displays in the Defence Services Museum in Rangoon, and may reflect local usage.
48. Interview, Sydney, January 1998.
49. Lintner, 'Arms for Eyes', p. 26. See also Lintner, 'Myanmar's Chinese connection', p. 23.
50. 'Malaysia to receive new batch of MiG-29s', Itar-Tass (in English), 3 January 1996.
51. Selth, *Burma's Arms Procurement Programme*, p. 27.
52. Interview, Canberra, September 2000.
53. See, for example, A Resident of Kayin State, *Whither KNU?* (News and Periodicals Enterprise, Rangoon, 1995), p. 41.
54. Desmond Ball, *Signals Intelligence in the Post-Cold War Era: Developments in the Asia-Pacific Region* (Institute of Southeast Asian Studies, Singapore, 1993), p. 59 and p. 73. See also Desmond Ball, 'Signals Intelligence in India', *Intelligence and National Security*, Vol. 10, No. 3, July 1995, pp. 387-407.
55. Interview, Canberra, July 1999.
56. Details are given in *Jane's Military Communications 1996-97* (Jane's Information Systems, Coulsdon, 1996), p. 102.
57. Interview, Mandalay, November 1996.
58. Interview, Mandalay, November 1996.
59. 'Myanmar', *Military Procurement International*, Vol. 9, No. 12, 15 June 1999, p. 4.
60. Robert Karniol, 'Myanmar to set up military satellite network', *JDW*, 19 May 1999, p. 15.
61. 'Myanmar', *Military Procurement International*, 15 June 1999, p. 4.
62. *The World Factbook 2000*. Until the 1980s only a small proportion of the population was reached by the mass media. There was only one radio station and television did not begin regular colour broadcasts until 1980. Most newspapers were printed in Rangoon and movie theatres tended to be confined to the main population centres.
63. *World Radio TV Handbook: The Directory of International Broadcasting*, Vol. 54 (WRTH Publishing, Milton Keynes, 2000), p. 275.
64. 'BBC Burma Jammed', *International Herald Tribune*, 22 August 1995; 'BBC News in Burma Jammed', *Bangkok Post*, 23 August 1995; 'Burma: Radio Jammed', *FEER*, 31 August 1995, p. 13; and 'Burma Joins the Jammers', Voice of America Editorial, 3 September 1995.
65. Personal communication, Martin Smith to the author, 9 November 1995.
66. See L.C. Soley and J.S. Nichols, *Clandestine Radio Broadcasting: A Study of Revolutionary and Counter-revolutionary Electronic Communication* (Praeger, Westport, 1987), pp. 295-6.
67. Ne Win ordered that the VOPB be jammed, but apparently this could not be achieved. It closed down in 1989 when the CPB collapsed. See Lintner, *The Rise and Fall of the Communist Party of Burma*, p. 46; and Ball, *Burma's Military Secrets*, pp. 113-4.

68. Andrew Selth, *Burma's Intelligence Apparatus*, Working Paper No. 308 (Strategic and Defence Studies Centre, Australian National University, Canberra, 1997), pp. 31-2.

69. Over 100 of the first units were vehicle phones for the cars of SLORC members and other senior military officers. Interview, Canberra, November 1995. See also *Country Economic Brief: Myanmar* (Department of Foreign Affairs and Trade, Canberra, 1994), pp. 22-3.

70. *Country Economic Brief: Myanmar* (Department of Foreign Affairs and Trade, Canberra, 1995), pp. 26-7. See also 'Myanmar/Cable', *Asian Communications*, November 1995, p. 3.

71. San Yun Aung, 'US$144 mobile phone network ready in "weeks"', *Myanmar Times and Business Review*, Vol. 1, No. 1, 6-12 March 2000.

72. *The APT Yearbook 1999* (Asia-Pacific Telecommunity, Bangkok, 1999), p. 305.

73. *Ibid.*

74. *Ibid.*

75. *Country Economic Brief: Burma (Myanmar)* (Department of Foreign Affairs and Trade, Canberra, 1992), p. 16.

76. *The APT Yearbook 1999*, pp. 306.

77. See *Jane's Space Directory 1996-97* (Jane's Information Systems, Coulsdon, 1996), p. 320. Also, 'Burma opts for Thaicom-3', *The Nation*, 12 May 1998.

78. *The APT Yearbook 1999*, pp. 304.

79. San Yun Aung, 'US$144 mobile phone network ready in "weeks"'.

80. *The APT Yearbook 1999*, pp. 303-6. Over a quarter of the country's automatic exchanges are in Rangoon, while the rest are in provincial centres. For the increase in the number of telephones, see Teruko Saito and Lee Kin Kiong, *Statistics on the Burmese Economy: The 19th and 20th Centuries* (Institute for Southeast Asian Studies, Singapore, 1999), p. 169.

81. *Country Economic Brief: Burma* (Department of Foreign Affairs and Trade, Canberra, 1998), p. 41.

82. *The APT Yearbook 1999*, p. 304.

83. *Ibid.*

84. Aung Than, 'Rural Telecommunication in Myanmar', paper presented at the Asia-Pacific Telecommunity Seminar on Rural Telecommunications, 6-12 February 1991, Brisbane, Australia.

85. *Country Economic Brief: Burma* (1998), pp. 40-1.

86. 'Asian infowar: the top ten', *Jane's Foreign Report*, No. 2617, 16 November 2000, pp. 5-6.

87. Interview, Singapore, May 1995. See also Selth, *Transforming the Tatmadaw*, p. 26.

88. Robert Karniol, 'Myanmar Spy Centre Can Listen In To Sat-Phones', *JDW*, 17 September 1997, p. 18. See also Clay Hathorn, 'Cyber-war in Burma', *Pretext Magazine*, found on the internet at http://www.pretext.com/nov97/shorts/short1.htm; and Ball, *Burma's Military Secrets*, p. 84.

89. Maung Aung Myoe, *Officer Education and Leadership Training*, p. 11.

90. The Burma Army has long depended on 1:63360 (one inch to the mile) maps produced by the Survey of India in 1944 for the Fourteenth Army's reconquest of Burma. Interview, Mandalay, November 1996. See also *World Mapping Today* (Butterworths, London, 1989), p. 296.

91. Personal observation, Rangoon, November 1999.

92. *The APT Yearbook*, p. 305.

93. 'Listening Post', *FEER*, 18 September 1997, p. 12.

94. Karniol, 'Myanmar Spy Centre Can Listen In To Sat-Phones' p. 18.

95. Ball, *Burma's Military Secrets*, p. 84.

96. *Situation of Human Rights in Myanmar* (United Nations General Assembly, Commission on Human Rights, E/CN.4/1997/64, 6 February 1997), p. 4.

97. See, for example, Nigel Holloway, 'Caught in the Net', *FEER*, 28 November 1996, pp. 28-30; and Swaroopa Iyengar, 'Wired: Myanmar's Tangled Web', *BurmaNet News*, 31 October 2000.

98. 'Junta Cracks Down on Internet: Media Group', AFP, 22 January 2000.

99. See, for example, 'Suu Kyi supporter dies in jail', *The Australian*, 24 June 1996; and 'Death of James Leander Nichols', *BurmaNet News*, 24 June 1996.

100. 'Six Arrested for Reading BurmaNet - Breach of Official Secrets Act', DVB, 24 December 1999 (in *Burma News Update*, January 2000, p. 9). See also 'Regime Silent on Arrests, Closures Said Related to BurmaNet', *BurmaNet News*, 29 December 1999; and US State Department, *Burma: Country Report*.

101. For a detailed examination of this internet campaign, see Tiffany Danitz and Warren P. Strobel, *Networking Dissent: Cyber-Activists Use the Internet to Promote Democracy in Burma*, United States Institute of Peace, Virtual Diplomacy Report, 8 November 1999, found at http://www.usip. org/oc/vd/vdr/vburma/vburma_intro.html

102. Danitz and Strobel, *Networking Dissent*.

103. Interview, Canberra, December 2000. See also Danitz and Strobel, *Networking Dissent*.

104. 'Asian infowar: the top ten', pp. 5-6.

105. Danitz and Strobel, *Networking Dissent*. See also Matthew Pennington, 'Fearing free speech Pandora's box: Myanmar's rulers block internet', Associated Press (AP), 18 April 2000.

106. Danitz and Strobel, *Networking Dissent*.

107. 'Six Arrested for Reading BurmaNet - Breach of Offical Secrets Act',

108. Danitz and Strobel, *Networking Dissent*. See also Khin Nyunt, 'How Some Western Powers Have Been Aiding and Abetting Terrorism Committed by Certain Organisations Operating Under the Guise of Democracy and Human Rights by Giving Them Assistance in Both Cash and Kind', translated typescript, Rangoon, 29 June 1997.

109. 'Burmese Flu', *FEER*, 10 February 2000, p. 8.

4

Recruitment, Training and Doctrine

The process of military training is designed as much to inculcate the group cohesion and solidarity upon which fighting spirit depends, as it is to produce an adequate level of technical or tactical expertise. — John Keegan and Richard Holmes, *Soldiers: A History of Men in Battle* (1985)

As a result of the massive military expansion and modernisation program introduced since 1988, the Burmese armed forces have been obliged to give a high priority to the issues of recruitment and training. The transformation of the *Tatmadaw* into a much larger, better-equipped conventional defence force has also required a significant revision of Burma's military doctrine, and its core strategic concepts. Above all else, the military leadership has been concerned to indoctrinate the members of all the uniformed services with a number of key political messages. For, despite all the rhetoric since 1962 about the 'people's armed forces', 'people's militias' and 'people's war', the government in Rangoon recognises that its survival depends not just on enhanced military capabilities but on a shared commitment by the members of the armed forces to continued military rule.

4.1 Recruitment and Personnel

Before 1988, the *Tatmadaw* consisted almost entirely of volunteers. There was a legal basis for conscription in the National Service Law and People's Militia Act of 1959. If formally promulgated, this law would have permitted the government to conscript all male citizens between the ages of 18 and 35, and females between the ages of 18 and 27, for between six months and two years full-time military service.[1] It also allowed for part-time service (less than 30 days per year). It is not clear whether this law ever formally entered into force, since no official notification appears to have been made, as required by Section 1(2) of the Act. Yet its provisions have long been used by the regime to secure the services of technical specialists such as doctors and engineers, for periods of up to three years. Also, the state constitution introduced by the BSPP in 1974 stipulated that every Burmese citizen had the duty to 'protect and safeguard the independence and sovereignty and territorial integrity' of the country and to 'undergo military training and undertake military service for the defence of the State'.[2] These clauses were never invoked before 1988, however, when the constitution was repudiated by the SLORC.

In any case, with between 200,000 and 250,000 young men reaching military age annually, there were more than enough volunteers during this period to meet the armed forces' requirements.[3] As Moshe Lissak has pointed out,

> Although there is no direct evidence on this issue, it appears that the attitude of the Burmese people toward the military profession changed, from 1948 to 1962, from a negative to a much more positive one. The role played by the army on the battlefield apparently strengthened the soldier's status in Burmese society after independence.[4]

This feeling was naturally strongest among the ethnic Burmans and others who owed their primary loyalty to the central government in Rangoon. After 1962 there was widespread resentment over the lack of democratic freedoms in Burma and the failure of the BSPP government's economic policies. This led to a marked reduction in the *Tatmadaw*'s status and popularity yet, largely for historical reasons, it still managed to retain sufficient prestige to attract more applications to enlist than it needed to fill its ranks.[5] At a more practical level, military service was seen as a way of acquiring privileges and benefits not readily available in Burmese society, and of learning technical skills which could be profitably exploited on return to civilian life.

Most recruits signed on for two years, but periods of four or six years were not uncommon. Standards were kept high, and in the early 1970s it was reported that only one half of the eligible males were usually found fit for military duty.[6] The minimum age for enlistment was 18 years, and recruits had to be in good physical condition.[7] Educational qualifications and mechanical skills were in high demand, to help the Services fill technical positions. In practice, this meant that the navy and air force tended to take more people from the urban areas than the poorer rural districts, which were the main source of army recruits. Indeed, there is evidence to suggest that young men from peasant backgrounds were specifically identified as making the best (and most malleable) foot soldiers.[8] Most recruits were Burman, but members of other ethnic groups (notably the Chins, but also some Mons, Karens, Kayah and Kachins) also joined the ranks. In broad terms, the armed forces were ethnically integrated and were seen by some minority peoples as the most available channel of social mobility in a Burman-dominated state.[9] The large majority of officers, however, were ethnic Burmans, a trend which was given a fillip by the 1962 coup. A small number of females were also recruited. They were primarily assigned to medical and administrative duties, but a few worked in signals, supply or engineering units. None were in combat fields.[10]

Largely by these means, the *Tatmadaw* was able to grow steadily from about 18,000 (reduced to less than 5,000 after the mutinies in 1948 and 1949), to almost

200,000 officers and other ranks by 1988. The army was the strongest service with 184,029 personnel, followed by the navy with 8065 and the air force with 6,587.[11] It has been estimated that another 73,000 men and women served in the paramilitary People's Police Force (*Pyithu Yei Tat Pwe* or PPF) and People's Militia (*Pyithu Sit*, or PM).[12] A large proportion of the PPF had been given basic military training and could be used to support the army in an emergency. The PM was created in the 1960s as part of the regime's national counter-insurgency strategy and, by the mid-1980s, consisted of an estimated 35,000 rural villagers.[13] They tended to be poorly trained and armed, however, and were of limited use in any combat role. They assisted with village defence and served as guides and informers. Burma had no Reserve Forces as such, but personnel who left the *Tatmadaw* were under an obligation to remain in inactive reserve for a specified period on the termination of their enlistment. There was no national mobilisation plan, but rudimentary military training was given to large numbers of BSPP members, civil servants and students, with the idea that the 'people in arms' could assist in any emergency.

Throughout this period, the *Tatmadaw* was a relatively small, professional organisation, able to meet its essential manpower needs from regular recruitment. The set of policies put in train after the SLORC's takeover dramatically increased the size of the *Tatmadaw* but transformed it into an entirely different kind of force.

The most significant expansion occurred in the Burma Army. This was initially achieved through a vigorous recruitment drive, carried out mainly in impoverished rural villages where young men had little chance of regular employment. It was accompanied by a major propaganda campaign in the government-controlled news media to try and attract additional recruits, by appealing to their sense of duty and national pride.[14] Many young men were tempted by promises of a cash payment on enlistment, and later access to the privileges and perquisites which are usually enjoyed by members of the armed forces in Burma. Sometimes, the attractions were as basic as free clothing, rations, accommodation and medical care. Others joined in an attempt to protect their families from harassment by the authorities. Also, recruiting standards appear to have been lowered significantly to boost numbers. Medical standards are no longer as stringent.[15] More importantly, while the regime claims that the official minimum age for joining the armed forces is still 18, recruits accepted by the *Tatmadaw* have been as young as 14 years old, or even younger.[16] There have been reports of the army enlisting orphans, runaways and other homeless children, counting on their gratitude to ensure continuing loyalty to the military regime.[17] There have also been claims that some children have been tricked into enlisting.[18] Burma is now reputed to have one of the highest number of children, including children under 15 years of age, in the armed forces anywhere in the world.[19]

These programs appear to have achieved some initial successes, but the number of volunteers later fell away and other measures had to be introduced. Since 1993, there have been persistent reports that most communities in Burma have been tapped to provide recruits for the army.[20] According to a 1998 International Labour Organisation (ILO) Commission of Inquiry:

Information provided to the Commission indicated that there was regular forced recruitment throughout Myanmar, including of minors, into the *Tatmadaw* and various militia groups. It appeared that this did not occur pursuant to any compulsory military service laws, but was essentially arbitrary.[21]

Most villages in Burma have been required to provide the armed forces with a certain number of recruits, with quotas being given to the local authorities. If these authorities fail to achieve their quota, they can be fined. Conversely, rewards are granted for each recruit provided in excess of the quota. This procedure has resulted in many young men being forcibly recruited into the army, or fleeing to avoid conscription.[22] The ILO Commission report continued:

> In cases where a certain number of recruits was demanded, it was common for the village or ward authorities to hold a 'lottery' to choose those who had to undertake military service. Those chosen were then forcibly conscripted and commonly included minors.[23]

There have also been numerous reports of young men in the cities being rounded up and press-ganged into the army. Such measures are apparently seen by the regime as preferable to invoking the 1959 National Service Law, and formally introducing conscription. Given the strength of feeling which has arisen against the armed forces since 1988, even among Burmans, the regime probably fears having large numbers of resentful men and women in the ranks who could disrupt important military operations. They could even turn their training and weapons against the regime itself.[24]

By these and other means, the SLORC and SPDC have been able to swell the numbers of armed forces personnel to around 400,000. Again, the largest number is in the army, which by the end of 1999 had reached about 370,000. There were about 16,000 in the navy and 15,000 in the air force.[25] The vast majority are Burmans, but the increased demand for recruits has blurred ethnic divisions. Indeed, there have been suggestions that the *Tatmadaw* is actively seeking more recruits from the minority ethnic groups. As Martin Smith has noted, 'Ethnic opposition parties claim that, in the face of continuing opposition in the towns, the SLORC has been recruiting ethnic minority village youngsters to spread *Tatmadaw* influence into new areas...'.[26] There have also been suggestions that the regime is trying to force or persuade village boys to join the army 'in a way guaranteed to bring the *Tatmadaw* presence into every community in the country'.[27] Whether or not these reports are true, there are clear signs that the regime has given recruitment a high priority, and is prepared to cast its net very wide in order to reach the manpower target it has set itself.

In 1995 the SLORC let it be known that it was aiming for a well equipped military machine of 500,000 by the turn of the century.[28] Despite a recent claim in the Thai press that it already has 620,000 men and women in uniform, the *Tatmadaw* appears to be having considerable difficulty in reaching this target.[29] In 1998 a

SPDC spokesman denied that this target ever existed, stating that 'even if we want to, we cannot afford that much'.[30] He added that the armed forces currently stood at 'not over 350,000' and was unlikely to climb any further.[31] While economic factors may have contributed to the reduced number, it seems more likely that, even with a limited form of conscription, the regime has been unable to attract and retain enough suitable recruits to fill all the *Tatmadaw*'s new positions. The figure of 500,000 still appears to stand as the *Tatmadaw*'s official wartime establishment, but is no longer considered a realistic target.

Adding to the regime's problems is the fact that many men who answered the call after 1988 are choosing to leave, rather than sign on for further service. As Christina Fink has pointed out, however, it is very difficult to resign, even after lengthy periods of service.[32] The army in particular is facing personnel retention problems, arising from poor man-management, harsh conditions of service and low morale. Losses through desertion have been greatly exaggerated by some observers, but are certainly a much larger problem than in the past.[33] Illness too is thinning out the ranks. For example, new and more virulent strains of malaria are taking their toll on Burma Army soldiers, particularly in the border areas, and up to 8% of *Tatmadaw* recruits in the higher age groups are believed to be HIV positive.[34] While the other two Services do not seem to be experiencing the same difficulties, there has been a shortage of experienced pilots in the air force and the navy is reportedly finding it difficult to crew all of its new ships.

There is also evidence to suggest that, in some respects, the *Tatmadaw*'s rapid expansion since 1988 has occurred more on paper than in reality. While the number of combat units has increased significantly, the actual fighting strength of the armed forces is not as great as appearances first suggest. For example, few army battalions are up to full strength. Many seem to operate with two-thirds or even half of their formal establishment and in some units, such as those performing garrison duties, troop numbers could be even lower.[35] There are other problems. Recruiting officers have inflated their figures to meet specific targets and there have been reports that in many units payrolls have been padded with non-existent personnel. Poor record-keeping and endemic corruption (up to and including senior officers) have helped disguise these manpower shortfalls.[36] More importantly, the increased demands of government and administration since 1988 seem to have absorbed a much greater proportion of the *Tatmadaw*'s strength than originally anticipated. For example, about 80% of the Director-General-level positions in the government ministries are now held by military officers.[37] These civil commitments detract further from the pool of men and women available for military duties.

The regime's goal becomes closer, and the target of 500,000 a little more realistic, if Burma's various paramilitary forces are also counted. Since the SLORC took power, a major effort has gone into increasing the size and capabilities of the Police Force, and in creating various kinds of 'militias'. Under different names, the latter still feature strongly in the regime's security architecture, and in the development of its formal defence doctrine.

The People's Police Force was formally reorganised in 1995. As the Myanmar Police Force (*Myanmar Yei Tat Pwe*), it has grown to about 72,000 men and women, including 4500 Combat Police organised into nine battalions.[38] These battalions are based at Hlawga, Maungtaw, Shwemyayar, Patheingyi, Hmawbi, Shwepyitha, Kyauktan, Mingaladon and Hlaingthaya.[39] They are reportedly assisted by two support battalions, including signals units. While formally separate from the *Tatmadaw*, these forces are usually commanded by army (or ex-army) officers and effectively act as extensions of the Burma Army. There is also the Frontier Force (*Na Sa Kha*). Although listed as a separate paramilitary organisation, this seems to be another extension of the Burma Army, but with integrated immigration, customs and police officers. It is also closely associated with Burma's intelligence agencies. The Frontier Force seems to be managed by a directorate in the Defence Ministry, but is probably under the day-to-day command of Regional Commanders. As its name would suggest, the Frontier Force is based largely around Burma's periphery. From the Burma-Thai and Burma-Bangladesh borders, *Na Sa Kha* units have gradually spread to key points along the Indian border.[40] Its strength is unknown.

In addition, basic military training has been given to members of the Auxiliary Fire Brigades and the Myanmar Red Cross Society. The former is about 104,000 strong, but there are plans to increase its strength to 300,000. The latter, 'a reserve force for peace and stability in addition to its normal duties', has 250,000 members, including 160,000 'Red Cross Brigade' members.[41] Together with the War Veterans Association (*Sit Pyan Sit Hmu Tan Haung Ahpwe*), these organisations are now considered an integral part of Burma's broader 'Defence Services' (*Karkweye Hta-na*). They even march with the army, navy and air force at the annual Armed Forces Day celebrations.[42] Training in basic military tactics and the use of infantry weapons has also been given to Burma's civil servants and members of the 14 million-strong Union Solidarity and Development Association (*Pyidaungsu Kyant Khine Phont Phyo Yae Ah Thin*, or USDA), a mass organisation created in 1993 to mobilise political support for the military regime.[43] All these trained personnel seem to be classed as 'People's Auxiliary Forces' (*Pyithu Ah Ku Tat*), which are available for military duty when required. Even the Myanmar Maternal and Child Welfare Association and the Myanmar Women's Entrepreneurial Association are considered to be 'under the *Tatmadaw*'s influence', and would probably be mobilised to assist in an emergency.[44]

Some confusion currently surrounds the old People's Militia units, and the status of several other armed organisations In Burma.[45] According to the DDSI, there are no longer active PM units in each village, along the lines seen before 1988. In most rural areas, the arms issued to these units have been collected and placed in army stores. However, villagers are still required to perform certain security functions (particularly in specially-created 'strategic villages'), and to assist the *Tatmadaw* if required. Considerable flexibility is exercised by Regional Commanders in managing these and other kinds of armed groups. For example, in Burma's northeast, semi-official status has been given to the 600-strong 'Kutkai Rangers', who are permitted to carry arms and retain their operational independence, provided they abide by certain rules.[46] A number of the larger insurgent groups which have negotiated cease-fire arrangements with Rangoon since 1988 have been given official cover as *pyithu sit* (or 'people's militias'), and their commanders designated 'government special policemen'.[47] Despite their formal status, however, it is unlikely that such groups would be considered reliable enough to be included in the regime's wider defence plans.

4.2 Training and Indoctrination

Burma's military leaders realised from an early date that they needed to give a high priority to training.[48] The mutinies of 1948 and 1949 deprived the *Tatmadaw* of a large proportion of its most experienced officers and men. Of those remaining, some had undergone formal training at the hands of the British and Japanese, but the armed forces were desperately short of professional skills. Basic courses were offered by fledgling institutions like the Burma Army Regimental Centre, Burma Army Training Depot, Burma Army Central School, Burma Army Officers' Training School, Burma Army School of Education and the Burma Army Staff College, but it was not enough. In addition to the demands of fighting the insurgents then threatening the central government, the development of skills at both the staff and operational levels was severely hampered by a lack of proper courses, insufficient instructors and inadequate training materials. From 1948 the BMM provided instructors and made a major contribution to the *Tatmadaw*'s early development. It was always viewed with suspicion by General Ne Win, however, and in 1953 was asked to leave Burma (which it did in early 1954).[49] Military advice was then sought from a few 'uncommitted' countries like Israel, Yugoslavia and Australia, each of which provided Burma with one or more instructors. This helped meet certain needs, but still fell far short of the *Tatmadaw*'s overall requirements.

As a consequence, a major effort was made to send Burmese military personnel overseas for specialised training and advanced courses. Between 1948 and 1954, 907 officers and 344 other ranks attended foreign training programs.[50] These included courses at the Royal Military College, Sandhurst, the US Army Staff College at Fort Leavenworth and the Australian Army Command and Staff College at Fort Queenscliff. Burmese officers also attended schools in India and Pakistan. Other courses (particularly those for air force and naval personnel) tended to be more technically oriented, or were directly related to arms purchases. For example, Australia trained Burmese ground crew at the Royal Australian Air Force's School of Technical Training at Wagga Wagga, and the Israel Defence Force (IDF) provided training for Burmese pilots after Rangoon's purchase of 30 Spitfire fighters from Israel in 1954. It was initially planned that the officers trained at foreign institutions would take over responsibility for the *Tatmadaw*'s own training programs. However, until the mid-1970s, many senior training positions were still held by older officers who had been trained by the Japanese during the Second World War.[51]

While foreign assistance helped fill some critical gaps, it did not solve the problem of how to meet the needs of Burma's steadily growing and increasingly sophisticated armed forces. A comprehensive training regime was clearly required. To help decide what form this might take, and how best to provide it, a number of delegations were sent overseas to study the military training programs of other countries. Among those places visited were India, Pakistan, Israel, Yugoslavia, the German Democratic Republic (GDR, or East Germany), the UK, US, USSR and Australia.[52] The lessons learned by these delegations were subsequently incorporated into a major plan to overhaul and upgrade Burma's military training regime. In 1953 a Directorate of Military Training (DMT) was created (at Colonel level) in the Defence Ministry and a formal training policy developed.[53] Regional Military Commands and individual units retained important responsibilities for field training, but institutional training was increasingly directed from the Ministry. During the mid- to late-1950s several new centres were opened. These included the Burma Army Non-Commissioned Officers' School, Combat Forces School, Defence Services Academy and National Defence College. Policy directives were issued and training manuals were translated into Burmese, including several British Army publications.[54] By the time of Ne Win's coup the DMT had become responsible for all aspects of the *Tatmadaw*'s training.

After 1962 most foreign military contacts were cut off and, more than ever, the Burmese armed forces were forced to rely on their own resources. These were severely restricted by the country's persistent economic problems, but from the time of the coup until the SLORC's takeover 16 years later, the *Tatmadaw* managed to develop a complex structure of specialised training institutions. It catered for all three Services, at all levels, as well as providing a number of joint schools for the instruction and political education of the officer corps. Since 1988, this structure has been expanded and refined as the SLORC, and later the SPDC, has devoted considerable resources to upgrading the *Tatmadaw*'s military capabilities and strengthening the political reliability of its members.

There are currently two main centres of instruction for prospective officers in the *Tatmadaw*, the Officers' Training School (OTS) and Defence Services Academy. The OTS (recently renamed the Defence Services (Army) Officers' Training School) was established in Maymyo in 1948. It moved to Bahtoo in 1957, transferred to Hmawbi in 1964 and moved back to Bahtoo in 1991. Until 1962 the majority of cadets were Non-Commissioned Officers (NCOs) from the Burma Army, selected for promotion from the ranks. Since the coup, most cadets have had a university education, although some NCOs without degrees (but with appropriate experience) have been permitted to enroll. Training courses usually last for about nine months and 'are designed to provide basic military training and military strategy and tactics for junior levels of command'.[55] Little attention seems to be paid to purely academic subjects. Between 1949 and 1988 there were 75 intakes of officer candidates. Between 1988 and 1999, 5,914 cadets were commissioned in 26 intakes.[56] Almost all officers graduating from the OTS are posted to the Burma Army.

The DSA is considered Burma's equivalent of Sandhurst or West Point.[57] A tri-service school, it opened in Bahtoo in 1955, and later moved to Maymyo where it has remained. The Academy accepts high school leavers between 16 and 19 years of age, for a four year course. Instruction in military science is given a high priority, but academic subjects and political training are also integral parts of the curriculum. Graduating cadets are usually awarded a Bachelor of Arts or a Bachelor of Science degree. On passing out, cadets are commissioned into one of the three Services. Under the SLORC, the DSA was expanded to accommodate 1000 cadets, with annual intakes of about 250 a year.[58] The Academy's facilities were also greatly improved and its curriculum widened. For example, it is now possible to take a degree in computer science. Under the SPDC, the annual intake of cadets has been increased even further, raising the number of cadets to around 1500.[59] The reasons for these dramatic increases are not known, but almost certainly relate to the much higher demand for trained and politically reliable officers to command all the new units created since 1988. For example, in 1996 an additional 240 cadets were recruited exclusively for the air force.[60]

Related to these two institutions is the *Teza* or *Ah Lot Thin Bo* (Apprentice Officer) scheme. The first *Teza* course intake took place in 1971, with 115 cadets. They were high school leavers aged between 16 and 19 years of age. For the first six months of their course they undertook basic military training and college level academic courses at the DSA. They then attended the OTS for 18 months, studying junior officer level subjects. This was followed by a year's assignment to battalions in the field, after which the successful candidates received a commission in the Burma Army. Probably due to the pressures being felt by the DSA and OTS, the first six months of the *Teza* course is currently conducted at the Burma Army Training Depot in Maymyo, with the following 12 months being undertaken at the (renamed) Defence Services (Army) Non-Commissioned Officers' School. The last six months is spent training in military subjects at the OTS. This accelerated training program seems to have been used to boost the numbers of junior officers available to staff new units. Between the SLORC's takeover and the end of 1999, 2,247 *Teza* cadets had received commissions. Most went into the army but seven took up positions in the navy and 28 went into the air force.[61]

Before 1988, specialised training for officers was usually conducted by their respective corps. Since then, however, the *Tatmadaw* has invested enormous resources in a number of new military educational institutions. For example, a Defence Services Institute of Medicine was opened in 1993, to overcome the perennial shortage of professional medical staff in the armed forces. The first intake of 47 cadets was commissioned as Lieutenants in 1999. A large and well-equipped Defence Services Institute of Technology was established at Maymyo in 1994, to offer *Tatmadaw* personnel degrees in most major fields of engineering.[62] The first intake of cadets graduated in 1999. Similarly, the Defence Services Institute of Nursing opened in 2000, offering a Bachelor of Science (Nursing) degree. The first intake, of about 50 young women, will be commissioned as Second Lieutenants.[63] Other schools created or upgraded by the SLORC and SPDC include the

Defence Services (Army) Non-Commissioned Officer School, the Defence Services (Army) Infantry Artillery School, the Defence Services Physical Education and Training School and the Defence Services (Army) Combat Forces School. About 12 training camps have been established and the same number of training battalions formed.

The creation or improvement of all these training facilities after 1988 seems to have been prompted in large part by the rapid expansion of the *Tatmadaw*. There were, however, other reasons. For example, the requirement for specialised skills has increased as the SLORC and SPDC acquired more sophisticated arms and equipment from abroad. It has also been difficult for the armed forces to find enough qualified officers to help staff the civil administration. It is likely too that the repeated and lengthy closures of Burma's civilian higher educational institutions, for fear of student unrest, has seriously degraded the qualifications of Burma's young men and women, on whom the *Tatmadaw* used to depend for its officer recruits. Rather than invest in the education of Burmese society as a whole, the regime has chosen to develop its own specialist military educational institutions. This helps account for the fact that in recent years applications for trainee officer positions have greatly exceeded the number of available places.[64]

Like other developed armed forces, the *Tatmadaw* operates a number of schools to provide officers with post-commission training. Some cater to all three Services, but most are run by specific Corps or Services to provide specialist courses. Of particular importance are the Command and General Staff College (CGSC) and the National Defence College (NDC). The CGSC was established in Maymyo in 1948, but since 1990 has been based in Kalaw. It offers Major and Lieutenant Colonel level officers a nine-month course designed to teach them 'to be able to command infantry divisions and to perform staff duties of regional commands'.[65] Most trainees are from the army, but the air force, navy and police force also participate in courses. The NDC was established in Rangoon in 1958 but did not provide regular courses until 1994. It now provides a 12 month course for Colonel and Brigadier level officers. Foremost among its aims is to train officers to be able 'to research and develop the appropriate military doctrine and public policy for the perpetuation of national independence and sovereignty, national solidarity and development and progress of the Union of Myanmar.'[66] From 1998 the NDC has offered a Masters degree program. Formally, all these schools fall under the guidance of the Directorate of Military Training, the head of which was upgraded to Brigadier level in 1990 and to Major General level in 1995.

Since the SLORC took power, more than 11,304 officers have been commissioned into the three Services of the *Tatmadaw* — 10,391 in the army, 546 in the navy and 368 in the air force.[67] This level of recruitment and training represents a massive commitment by the regime to increasing the size and capabilities of the officer corps. There has also been a much greater interest in acquiring foreign expertise.

Under Ne Win, the number of *Tatmadaw* members sent overseas for training declined. 'Between 1948 and 1962, a total of 1070 officers and 782 other ranks were sent abroad. However, between 1963 and 1989, only 415 officers and 83 other ranks were sent'.[68] While there was clearly an official preference for training in Burma, the regime was prepared to allow selected officers to attend overseas courses which were considered essential. They were usually more advanced or more technically sophisticated than could be offered at home. After 1971 such courses tended to be sought in the UK, US, Federal Republic of Germany (FRG, or West Germany), Israel and Australia.[69] The only foreign military instructors permitted in the country during this time were personnel associated with specific equipment purchases, such as new aircraft for the air force. The high cost of Burma's isolationist policies was becoming apparent to the regime before 1988, and an increased level of overseas training was under consideration by the DMT when the SLORC took power. As soon as that occurred, however, all traditional sources of military instruction were denied to the *Tatmadaw* as the US, UK, Australia and the other Western democracies broke off military relations.

Since then, the SLORC and SPDC have been keen to develop alternative sources of military expertise. Indeed, the policy of seeking more foreign training appears to be an integral part of the regime's military expansion and modernisation program. According to the DMT's records,

> Between 1990 and 1999, 389 army personnel, 98 navy personnel and 455 air force personnel were sent abroad for training. Out of a total of 942 persons, 615 went to the PRC, 53 to India, and 34 to Pakistan. Among 455 air force personnel, 330 went to the PRC, 7 each to India, Pakistan and Singapore, 37 to Russia and 12 to Yugoslavia. Out of 98 naval personnel, 79 were sent to the PRC and 8 to India while the remaining 11 went to Pakistan. 206 army personnel went to the PRC for training, such as staff college, armour and artillery schools.[70]

During 2000, other foreign training places were secured, for example in China, the Philippines and Pakistan. In addition, overseas training courses have been arranged by other Directorates (such as Medical Services and Intelligence), and instructors from a number of countries (including China, Russia and probably Israel) have provided the *Tatmadaw* with military training in Burma itself.

Most of this foreign training appears to be technical in nature, and directly linked to the purchase of new arms and equipment. However, some is aimed at developing new skills and enhancing Burma's conventional defence capabilities.[71] For example, Pakistan is developing into a major source of military expertise for the *Tatmadaw*, and has provided courses in artillery, armour and 'submarine' operations.[72] There were several reports that Pakistani instructors were based in Burma after 1988 to train special forces and airborne personnel, and that Pakistan has helped train members of the *Tatmadaw* in the use of Chinese arms also found in Pakistan's inventory, but none of these stories has yet been confirmed.[73] India too has provided the BA with armour and artillery training. The Singapore Armed Forces (SAF) have provided training in Singapore for a Burma Army parachute team. The

Tatmadaw has also received training in the use of IT systems and communications equipment provided to Burma by Singaporean companies.[74] There have been persistent rumours in Rangoon that the SAF has provided the *Tatmadaw* with artillery training in Burma, but they have never been confirmed. Nor has it been possible to verify claims that Singapore is training members of Burma's police and military intelligence agencies in Singapore.[75] Reports of Israeli military instructors in Burma during the early 1990s were probably fabricated by Rohingya insurgents, to obtain greater support from Islamic countries. Israel may, however, have provided training to Burma's elite counter-terrorist squad, and possibly the SLORC's personal bodyguards. There are persistent rumours of a close connection between Israel's Central Institute for Intelligence and Security (known as Mossad) and DDSI, which has included a training component.[76]

Over the past 12 years a number of other countries have been mentioned in this context. For example, there have been claims that Malaysia has provided Burma Air Force pilots with training on the Lockheed C-130 Hercules transport aircraft.[77] However, there are no C-130s in the BAF's order of battle, which makes such training highly unlikely. Reports in the late 1980s, that military advisers from the USSR were helping the *Tatmadaw* suppress internal unrest in Burma, were probably designed to win support for opposition groups from the US and other Western democracies.[78] French reports around the same time, that specialist military instructors from Vietnam were active in southern Burma before (and possibly even after) the creation of the SLORC, have never been verified and are unlikely to be true.[79]

In a major break from the Ne Win era, a number of *Tatmadaw* officers have attended higher defence or staff colleges in China, India, Pakistan, Malaysia, the Philippines and Singapore. These postings have provided the desired 'foreign exposure and experience', but the courses taken at these institutions appear to have had very wide-ranging curricula.[80] Except in the broadest sense, they do not appear to be related to the development of specific strategies, doctrines, or operational procedures. While they doubtless reflect the host country's particular world view and strategic perspectives, nor do they include any overt political or ideological content. Indeed, any attempts by these countries to influence members of the *Tatmadaw* in this way would be likely to provoke a strong reaction from Rangoon. While it recognises the need to improve its understanding of modern trends in strategic thinking and military planning, the regime still views foreign contacts with considerable suspicion. It is anxious to avoid any 'contamination' of its personnel by foreign political ideas, 'alien' concepts of human rights or incompatible military cultures. It is probably for this reason that, since 1988, relatively few officers posted overseas for lengthy periods have returned to critical line positions which could give them the opportunity to spread dissent, undermine the fighting spirit of the troops, or even mount a military challenge to the regime.[81]

This deep-seated insecurity in the face of different world views, and competing ideas about the role of armed forces in society, helps explain the high priority that has always been given to political education in the *Tatmadaw*. Initially, 'the

Tatmadaw leadership argued that it was necessary to arm itself with ideological weapons not only to defeat communist insurgency but also to prevent the infiltration of communists into the Tatmadaw'.[82] The ideology developed was a curious blend of Buddhism, Marxism and nationalism which, after 1962, was transmogrified and codified as the political doctrine of the ruling Burma Socialist Programme Party. To have 'a correct ideological orientation and clear political outlook', every member of the *Tatmadaw* was required to study BSPP tracts such as *The System of Correlation of Man and His Environment*.[83] Personnel were also sent to in-service ideological orientation courses (known as *tattwin pyinnyapay*) at both Regional Command Training Centres and the BSPP's Central School of Political Science in Rangoon. The orthodox view was reinforced at in-service discussion sessions (*tattwin swe-nwe-pwe*) organised once a month at battalion level and once a week at lower levels. There were no political 'commissar' positions as such, as all officers were expected to become members of the BSPP and to promote its ideals. As the failings of the 'Burmese Way to Socialism' became more apparent, this role increasingly began to be questioned by junior officers, but a complex and subtle system of rewards and punishments ensured that form was usually observed.

Despite the abolition of the BSPP in 1988, the same level of indoctrination has continued under the SLORC and SPDC. However, in place of the party and the state, the focus of ideological commitment has become the *Tatmadaw*. What is good for the *Tatmadaw* is seen *ipso facto* as good for the government, and good for the country.[84] This message is taught at a number of Combat Related Organisational Activities Training Centres (*Taik Pwe Win Si Yone Ye Thin Dan Kyaung*), which were opened in the early 1990s. All armed forces personnel must take a three-month course at these institutions at some stage during their career. In addition, the Directorate of Peoples Militias and Public Relations operates several training centres for 'the political education of the officer corps'.[85] For, despite assertions to the contrary, the military leadership harbours deep-seated fears that the armed forces will once again be riven by serious internal dissension, possibly causing the military government to fall. This profound sense of insecurity is reflected in the curricula of all the *Tatmadaw*'s training institutions, which are seen as critical to the process of bringing all members of the armed forces 'into line with its ideological orientation', the better to 'cement its grip on state and society'.[86]

4.3 Doctrine and Strategic Concepts

Ever since Independence, the development of Burma's military doctrine and strategic concepts has suffered from a number of contradictions.[87] There has been a constant tension between the need to guard against possible external threats, while at the same time facing more immediate insurgent problems. Flowing from this, there has been a tension between the wish to develop conventional military capabilities, in the manner of other countries, and the need to structure the *Tatmadaw* in a way better suited to counter-insurgency and other internal security operations. There has been yet another tension between the perceived need to field very large defence forces, and the lack of resources to do so. On almost every occasion that these issues have been considered by Burma's armed forces leadership, usually at annual Commanding Officers' (CO) conferences, the answer given to these dilemmas seems to have been to 'mobilise the population'. Yet this solution betrays a fundamental flaw in the *Tatmadaw*'s thinking, and may help explain some of the difficulties the regime has had in achieving its core military objectives over the past 50 years.

Before 1948, most Burmese with military experience had either fought the Japanese as part of the guerrilla resistance fomented by the Allies, or had been a member of the more conventional armed forces created by the Japanese. After Aung San's switch of allegiance in March 1945, the BNA gained some experience in unconventional operations, harassing the retreating Japanese and supporting the Allied Fourteenth Army's spectacular 'race to Rangoon'.[88] Yet despite this background in guerrilla warfare, and the rash of insurgencies which it faced after Independence, the *Tatmadaw*'s first impulse was to develop a conventional military force structured for defence against a foreign invasion. In the early 1950s, the War Office drew up plans which envisaged large infantry formations (up to division strength), armoured brigades equipped with tanks, and motorised infantry. An important element was the mass mobilisation of the population to support the war effort. The objective of this plan was to contain any invading forces at the Burmese frontier, if necessary for a couple of months, until an international force could come to Burma's rescue, as had occurred in Korea in 1950.[89]

It could be argued that there were some grounds for thinking in these terms. At the time the plan was written, the insurgent threat to Rangoon had receded a little, (although there was growing apprehension over the growth of KMT forces in northern Burma). More importantly, it was believed in Rangoon that communist China posed an immediate threat, and preparations needed to be made for a possible invasion.[90] The War Office plan, however, was completely unrealistic. The *Tatmadaw* was still weak, divided, and poorly equipped. Its command and control system was poor, and its logistics support structure was inadequate. Even more so, Burma's geography made conventional operations of the kind envisaged extremely difficult, as the Second World War had so vividly demonstrated. Also, Burma was still suffering from the devastation wrought by the war, and the restoration of its economy had been hampered by widespread internal unrest. The Nu Government had no means to raise the forces, or acquire the kind of conventional arms and equipment, needed for large-scale operations of the kind proposed. In addition, mobilising the Burmese population in the political climate of the time would have been very difficult. All this was demonstrated in 1953 when the strategy was tested in an operation against the KMT code-named *Naga Naing*, or 'Victorious Dragon'. The Burmese forces were soundly defeated. Yet, despite this failure, the *Tatmadaw* continued to rely on the broad concepts of positional warfare and strategic denial until the mid-1960s.[91]

These fears of an invasion from a neighbouring country never really went away.[92] From the late 1950s, however, Burma's military leaders increasingly focussed their attention on ways in which the *Tatmadaw* might overcome the country's more immediate internal security problems. Having been unable to prevail with more conventional methods, the larger insurgent groups like the KNDO and CPB had turned to guerrilla warfare, a development which demanded a fresh approach from Rangoon. The *Tatmadaw* had conducted counter-insurgency operations before, but they suffered from a number of key weaknesses, one of which was a lack of understanding about military tactics. To help overcome this problem, an Australian Army counter-insurgency expert was invited to spend three months in Burma, advising the *Tatmadaw* on this subject. He made such an impression that he was later asked to remain for a further two years, during which time he helped establish two jungle warfare schools (one in Upper Burma and another in Lower Burma) modelled after the Land Warfare Training Centre at Canungra in northern Australia.[93] Other problems for the *Tatmadaw* arose from poor intelligence (at all levels), lack of operational security and what was euphemistically described as 'poor public relations'.[94]

At the COs' conference in 1962, it was announced that the General Staff Office in the Defence Ministry had drafted a document outlining the broad principles of anti-guerrilla warfare, and begun teaching it in the country's military training schools. Officers were encouraged to read the literature available on this subject, including Mao Tse-tung's military writings (which had been translated into Burmese), Lin Piao's *People's War* and Che Guevara's *Guerrilla Warfare*. Yet it took some time for these principles to be translated into workable strategies. Also, the demands of government and administration after the coup was a drain on the *Tatmadaw*'s resources, just at the time when they were badly needed to conduct more comprehensive, better coordinated and more mobile counter-insurgency operations. Most importantly, the armed forces were failing to win the support of the rural population, which was becoming increasingly sympathetic to the insurgents. In words that echo other guerrilla wars the world over, a 1963 General Staff Office report stated:

> It is difficult to distinguish insurgents from villagers. If we cannot distinguish insurgents from villagers, we will suffer. We will always face the insurgents having the upper hand in operations. It is necessary to step up organisational activities in villages.[95]

The Defence Ministry began to draw up plans for the transformation of the *Tatmadaw* from a force geared primarily to fighting a conventional war to one better suited to fight a 'people's war'.

The 'people's war' concept was the subject of considerable debate among Burma's senior military officers throughout the 1960s and 1970s. Once the political rhetoric and military jargon is stripped away, it was derived in part from the lessons of other insurgencies, and in part from harsh necessity. There were two key elements. The first was the creation of village self-defence forces, or militias. These were seen as giving the rural population much greater responsibility for its own defence, while permitting the armed forces to focus their scarce resources on military operations directed against the insurgents. In 1964 a delegation was sent to Switzerland, Yugoslavia, Czechoslovakia and the GDR, to study the 'organisational structure, armaments, training, territorial organisation and strategy of people's militias'.[96] The second element of 'people's war' in Burma was the coordination of the so-called 'five columns', namely the political, social, economic, military and public management spheres of government activity. This was meant to ensure a more coordinated approach to winning the hearts and minds of the rural population. The concept was first tested by Central Command in operations against the CPB in 1966. Deemed a success, the concept was subsequently used by other Regional Commands, and the People's Militia plan was formally adopted by the Defence Ministry.

By the late 1960s another important element had been added to the *Tatmadaw*'s counter-insurgency operations, and that was the 'four cuts' (*pyat lei pyat*) program. This strategy drew on the example of the 'new villages' created by the British to defeat communist insurgents in Malaya, and the 'strategic hamlets' which the US later established in Vietnam. Burma's Regional Military Commands were sub-divided into areas designated 'black' (if controlled by insurgents), 'brown' (where both sides exercised some measure of control) and 'white' (which were declared free of insurgents). The idea was to clear one area at a time until the whole country was 'white'.[97] Burmese villagers were forcibly relocated into specially guarded settlements, dubbed 'strategic villages' (*Byu-ha Kye Ywa*), under military control on the plains, or near garrison towns in the hills. The surrounding countryside was then laid waste and 'free fire zones' established in which anyone not specifically authorised to be there was automatically suspected of being an insurgent. The area was then subject to massive 'search and destroy' operations by special units to clear it of insurgents. Soldiers periodically returned to confiscate food, poison wells and destroy crops that might support the insurgents. Those forced to live in the strategic villages were obliged to join the local militia, observe a curfew and report on any suspicious activity. As Martin Smith has noted, 'Every community must fight, flee or join the *Tatmadaw*'.[98]

The aim of this strategy was to deny the insurgents the four essential elements of food, funds, intelligence and recruits.[99] In Maoist parlance, the supporting 'sea' was to be drained away from the guerrilla 'fish'. The strategy enjoyed considerable success in lower and central Burma, where the *Tatmadaw* was able to cordon off specific areas (usually about 50 kilometres square), and flood them with troops. Yet it broke down in the border regions where the distance and terrain made large-scale operations of this kind much more difficult. Also, the proximity of porous international borders often made it possible for the insurgents to escape.[100] In the black and brown areas some attempt was made to win the sympathy of the villagers but, despite the BSPP and *Tatmadaw* rhetoric, the strategy lacked any real commitment to the villagers' social and economic development. Nor was the Rangoon regime prepared to address the broader political concerns raised by the ethnic minorities. The emphasis was overwhelmingly on the military defeat of the insurgents and the intimidation of the local inhabitants, a policy that continues in most border areas today. Forced relocations of villagers are still occurring on a large scale in Shan, Kayah and Karen States, and in areas of Mon State and Pegu Division.[101] International criticism of the four cuts strategy and its associated abuses of human rights have prompted spokesmen for the regime to deny that it ever existed, but its adoption and use have been well documented.[102]

While attempting to devise a comprehensive and workable doctrine for the conduct of counter-insurgency warfare, the Defence Ministry never lost sight of the possibility of external attack. This was seen as coming either from 'an enemy of equal strength' (presumably Thailand) or 'a more powerful enemy' (presumably China). There was also some nervousness that the war in Indochina could spill over its borders and pose a threat to Burma.[103] These different kinds of threat each demanded a different kind of response, and to a certain extent a different kind of *Tatmadaw*. Counter-insurgency operations were seen to require the support of the rural population in many ways, but most obviously through the militias. A war against a country like Thailand required a more conventional defence force, albeit one that rested on the entire resources of the country. Against a more powerful enemy, the Ministry envisaged a 'total people's war', in which the entire population supported a guerrilla war by the *Tatmadaw* to wear down the invader until a counter-offensive could be mounted.[104] To meet the demands of all these strategies, the Defence Ministry recommended a standing army of one million, with another five million in the militias as reserves.[105] In a country (at the time) of only 25 million people, already struggling with major political and economic problems, such a force was clearly not feasible, but the notion that Burma could be saved by mobilising the entire population persisted.

The creation of the SLORC in 1988 ushered in a third phase of doctrinal development. Ironically, it seems to have been prompted in part by fears of the kind of international intervention upon which the *Tatmadaw*'s first military doctrine was premised. Even after it overcame its initial concerns about a multinational force restoring democratic rule to Burma, the regime was still convinced that it needed a much larger, stronger conventional military force. This, they reasoned, could not only exert greater pressure against the insurgents, but also protect Burmese sovereignty and guard against external attack.

A much larger army, better equipped, more mobile and with greater firepower, all enhanced the regime's ability to prosecute its counter-insurgency campaigns. The resource shortages which had so often hampered operations in the past were significantly eased, permitting more vigorous, more sustained and more comprehensive attacks against those insurgent groups which refused to accept cease-fire deals and 'return to the legal fold'. In addition, the *Tatmadaw* has begun to experiment with new approaches to counter-insurgency, which are both permitted by and make the most effective use of, its new weapon systems. For example, 'Junior commanders are more keen to introduce concepts of low-intensity conflict (LIC) than the decades-old "four cuts" and "people's war" in counterinsurgency operations.'[106] Attempts have been made to avoid long, slow deployments by infantry on foot, by creating air-mobile forces of the kind used by the US in Vietnam. To date, this scheme has not worked very well, largely because of insufficient resources, but greater use of the *Tatmadaw*'s new aircraft and vehicles has certainly increased the army's mobility.[107] Efforts have also been made to improve the coordination between the army and air force on counter-insurgency operations, utilising the new technologies and better command and control systems acquired since 1988.

It has been necessary also to devise a more modern conventional warfare doctrine, and new operating procedures. Never before has Burma's military leadership been required to manage such large numbers of troops, or to integrate the supporting arms (mainly artillery and armour) into operations on such a scale. The acquisition of modern fighter-interceptors has made it imperative for the *Tatmadaw* to devise a more sophisticated air defence doctrine, and the navy has been required to work out how best to manage its much larger fleet of new and more capable vessels. The development of improved command, control, communications and computer capabilities has made it possible to coordinate these elements better and to conduct much more complex conventional military operations. Overseas training courses can give some insights into this process, but Burma seems to be relying largely on its own resources to develop the doctrine required for the management of all these assets in the most effective manner.[108]

It would appear that some progress has been made in this field. Over the past five years there have been several reports that the *Tatmadaw* has begun conducting joint military exercises, some on a large scale. Exercises held in 1995, 1996 and 1997, for example, were reported to have involved over 30,000 troops, 100 field artillery pieces, nearly 300 armoured vehicles, about six squadrons of aircraft and around 30 naval vessels.[109] Members of the local militias, auxiliary forces and USDA members have also been mobilised. According to one observer,

> The exercises were designed to introduce strategic denial and counter-offensive capabilities to the existing people's war doctrine....[T]he purpose of such a counter-offensive was to counter low-level foreign invasion and to turn the enemy country into a battlefield....[S]hould the standing conventional force fail to defeat an invading force in the beachheads or landing zones, resistance would be organised at village, regional and national level to sap the will of the invading force. When the enemy's will had been sapped, its capabilities dispersed and exhausted and sufficient force had been mustered, a counter-offensive would be launched to drive the invader from Myanmar.[110]

Other joint exercises have followed, including a large-scale amphibious exercise which was reportedly held in southern Burma, involving infantry, armoured vehicles, artillery and both naval and air force assets.[111] It is not known whether these are still largely scripted exercises, with each Service playing carefully prescribed roles, or whether they have evolved to the extent that the major participating elements have the freedom to use their initiative and act more independently. The experience of other armed forces attempting this doctrinal transition, however, suggests that the process will be a long and difficult one, even if the *Tatmadaw* receives advice from friendly countries like China.[112]

This major overhaul of Burma's defence doctrine has reduced the emphasis on, but not replaced the concept of 'total people's war'. Indeed, it has underpinned a renewed effort by the regime to mobilise the Burmese population in its support, as a kind of strategic reserve to assist the *Tatmadaw* defend the country against both internal and external threats. Just before leading the 1988 takeover, Burma's most senior military officer advised his commanders that the country still needed to 'draw up a nation-wide mobilisation, training and command and control system for people's militias and people's war'.[113] This does not yet seem to have been fully implemented. However, as noted above, basic military training is being given to all members of the 'Defence Services', a term which now embraces most uniformed forces. As Auxiliary Forces, the USDA, civil servants and several other government-sponsored groups are also considered potential sources of personnel. The theory is that, in any emergency, the millions of people in Burma who have been given basic military training can be mobilised to support the *Tatmadaw* resist an invader.

In all the studies written about Burma's defence doctrine and the debates in annual COs' Conferences about the most appropriate military strategies, reference has constantly been made to 'the people'. The need to gain the support of the population, either to isolate insurgent groups or to support a more conventional effort against a foreign invader, has been a recurring theme. As late as 1985, senior *Tatmadaw* officers were giving speeches to the effect that

> [t]herefore what we have to do in the case of foreign invasion is to mobilise people in accordance with the people's war doctrine. For defence of our country, the entire population must be involved in the war effort. So also is the case in counterinsurgency. Remember, the support of the people will dictate the outcome of the war.[114]

Yet in this critical area the theory has consistently failed to reflect the reality. Even an observer close to the *Tatmadaw* has admitted that 'troop discipline and public relations had been a huge problem since the 1950s'.[115] After 1962 the lack of fundamental human rights in Burma, resentment over the regime's inept handling of the economy, the *Tatmadaw*'s harsh treatment of rural villagers, abuses of power and corruption had turned many people against the armed forces. Even before the early 1970s, when the BSPP was changed from a cadre party into a mass organisation, most members' commitment to the BSPP was nominal, at best. Particularly among the ethnic minorities, large segments of the population could not be relied upon to support the central government or respond to any future call to arms by the regime.

Since 1988 the regime's constant references to the 'people's armed forces', the 'people's militia' and 'people's war' ring rather hollow when held up against the bitterness and alienation many Burmese feel towards the SLORC and SPDC. The ethnic communities still have little cause to feel any real loyalty to the central government in Rangoon. While most members of the Police Force and the other uniformed services might be counted upon in an emergency, a large proportion of the USDA have been forced to join, or have joined simply because of the material benefits of doing so. Also, in 1990 a large proportion of the population supported the democratic opposition and probably still do. As patriotic Burmese they would no doubt resist an invasion by a country like China, Thailand or India, but their prime allegiance is to their country, not to the military government. Their support would be less assured in other circumstances, for example in the event that the United Nations endorsed a multinational force to intervene and restore democracy in Burma. Depending on the circumstances, and who they were called upon to fight, the reliability under fire of many Burmese civilians must be open to question.

Notes

1. See *Report of the Commission of Inquiry appointed under Article 26 of the Constitution of the International Labour Organisation to examine the observance by Myanmar of the Forced Labour Convention, 1930 (No. 29)*, Official Bulletin, Vol. 81, Serial B, Geneva, 2 July 1998, para 255. This report is available on the internet at: http://www.ilko.org/public/english/standards/relm/gb/docs/gb273/myanmar.htm

2. Constitution of the Socialist Republic of the Union of Burma, Articles 170 and 171. See A.D. Moscotti, *Burma's Constitution and Elections of 1974* (Institute of South East Asian Studies, Singapore, 1977), p. 117.

3. Henderson, *Area Handbook for Burma*, p. 278. See also issues of *The Military Balance* for this period, and the *World Factbook 2000*.

4. Lissak, *Military Roles in Modernisation*, p. 157.

5. Selth, *Transforming the Tatmadaw*, p. 39.

6. Roberts, *Area Handbook for Burma*, p. 333.

7. Young Burmese could join the Red Cross Brigade at 16 years.

8. Martin Smith (with Annie Allsebrook), *Ethnic Groups in Burma: Development, Democracy and Human Rights* (Anti-Slavery International, London, 1994), p. 118.

9. Lissak, *Military Roles in Modernisation*, p. 157.

10. Bunge, *Burma*, p. 249. See also Maung Aung Myoe, *Building the Tatmadaw*, p. 18.

11. Maung Aung Myoe, *Military Doctrine and Strategy in Myanmar*, p. 13. These figures are a little higher than those published by the IISS. See *The Military Balance 1988-1989*, pp. 159-60.

12. *The Military Balance 1988-1989*, pp. 159-60.

13. *Ibid.* See also Bunge, *Burma*, pp. 259-69.

14. See, for example, Maung Myo Thu, 'The Tatmadaw wants you', *Working People's Daily*, 24 March 1993.

15. *No Childhood At All: A Report About Child Soldiers in Burma* (Images Asia, Chiang Mai, 1997), p. 9.

16. Lintner, 'Consolidating power', p. 23. See also 'Troops freed by Karen army fear government reprisals', *The Nation*, 11 January 1993; and 'Burmese Rebels Await a Foe's Lucky Number', *New York Times*, 22 March 1992. Most insurgent groups in Burma also have children in their ranks.

17. There is an organisation called the 'Ye Nyunt Youth' (Brave Sprouts Organisation), which appears to be designed to cater for such children. Boys as young as 14 are given 'a military-style' education, and politically indoctrinated in special camps before being trans-

ferred to the armed forces. *No Childhood At All*, p. 31; and *Asia Report: Myanmar*, Coalition to Stop the Use of Child Soldiers, London, May 2000. This report can be found on the internet at http://www.child-soldiers.org/reports_asia/myanmar.html

18. National Coalition Government of the Union of Burma (NCGUB), *Human Rights Yearbook 1994: Burma* (NCGUB Human Rights Documentation Unit, Bangkok, 1995), p. 73. See also *Asia Report: Myanmar*; and Ilene Cohn and G.S. Goodwin-Gill, *Child Soldiers: The Role of Children in Armed Conflict* (Clarendon Press, Oxford, 1997), p. 29.

19. *Asia Report: Myanmar*. See also *No Childhood At All*. This includes the child soldiers who are members of Burma's various insurgent groups.

20. Smith, *Ethnic Groups in Burma*, pp. 118-19. See also 'Burmese Army to conscript youths', *Asian Defence Journal*, May 1993, p. 86.

21. *Report of the ILO Commission of Inquiry*.

22. *Asia Report: Myanmar*. See also *No Childhood At All*, pp. 27-31.

23. *Report of the ILO Commission of Inquiry*.

24. While these measures are used to gather recruits for the armed forces, large numbers of men and women in Burma are also forced to serve the *Tatmadaw* as forced labourers and 'porters'. This widespread practice has also been investigated and publicly condemned by the ILO.

25. Andrew Selth, *Burma's Order of Battle: An Interim Assessment*, Working Paper No. 351 (Strategic and Defence Studies Centre, Australian National University, Canberra, 2000).

26. Smith, *Ethnic Groups in Burma*, p. 118.

27. Smith, *Ethnic Groups in Burma*, p. 119.

28. Interview, Rangoon, April 1995. This number was later confirmed in official statements by senior members of the regime.

29. A Thai newspaper has claimed that there are 586,196 in the Burmese army, 17,349 in the navy and 15,892 in the air force, making a total of 619,437. No source was given for these figures, but they seem to be drawn from a document circulating in Rangoon which purports to be a summary of a Tatmadaw payroll. See 'Burma Border Situation: Arms Buildup Noted', *Bangkok Daily News*, 31 May 1999; and 'Strength of Myanmar Armed Forces' (copy in the author's possession).

30. Barry Wain, 'Myanmar Military Growth Worries The Neighbours', *Asian Wall Street Journal*, 22 January 1999.

31. *Ibid.*

32. Christina Fink, *Living Silence: Burma Under Military Rule* (Zed, London, 2001), p. 147.

33. The International Crisis Group's rather credulous claim that desertions have reduced the *Tatmadaw* to 200,000, for example, cannot be sustained. See Peter Alford, 'Generals forced to open a new front', *The Australian*, 24-25 February 2001.

34. 'Supplies shortage, malaria causing death and desertion among soldiers', DVB (in Burmese), 27 July 2000; Union of Myanmar Ministry of Health, HIV Sentinel Surveillance, September-October 1999; and 'Sickening', *Economist*, 11 November 2000, p. 43. Also relevant is Chris Beyrer, *War in the Blood: Sex, Politics and AIDS in Southeast Asia* (Zed Books, London, 1998), pp. 36-52.

35. *No Childhood At All*, p. 26; and interviews, Rangoon and Mandalay, April 1995 and November 1999. See also Bruce Hawke, 'Myanmar academy triples cadet intake', *JDW*, 29 November 2000, p. 17.

36. Interviews, Rangoon and Mandalay, April 1995 and November 1999.

37. Interview, Rangoon, November 1999.

38. *The Myanmar Police Force* (Ministry of Home Affairs, Government of the Union of Myanmar, Rangoon, 2000).

39. Selth, *Burma's Order of Battle*, pp. 23-5. These combat battalions have reportedly absorbed the *lon htein* riot police.
40. See, for example, Mizzima, 'Nasaka on the Indo-Burma border', *BurmaNet News*, 24 January 2001.
41. Figures for these organisations are taken from D.I. Steinberg, *Burma: The State of Myanmar* (Georgetown University Press, Washington, 2001), p. 115.
42. Similar training has been provided to many of their spouses and dependents.
43. See, for example, D.I. Steinberg, 'The Union Solidarity Development Assocation: Mobilization and Orthodoxy', *Burma Debate*, Vol. 4, No. 1 (January-February 1997), pp. 4-11; and *New Light of Myanmar*, 12 March 1996. The USDA militia is called the *Naingngan Arr Ahpwe*, or 'Strength of the Nation'.
44. The head of the Myanmar Maternal and Child Welfare Association is LTGEN Khin Nyunt's wife. It has 340,000 permanent members and 1.1 million ordinary members. Steinberg, *Burma: The State of Myanmar*, p. 115; and Maung Aung Myoe, *The Tatmadaw in Myanmar Since 1988*, p. 10.
45. The figure given for the People's Militia in *The Military Balance* has remained unchanged for several years. See also *Jane's Sentinel Security Assessment: Southeast Asia* (September 2000-February 2001), p. 350.
46. Interview, Washington, February 2001.
47. *Jane's Sentinel Security Assessment*, p. 350.
48. There is very little written on this subject in English. The following section draws mainly on Maung Aung Myoe, *Officer Education and Leadership Training in the Tatmadaw: A Survey*, Working Paper No. 346 (Strategic and Defence Studies Centre, Australian National University, Canberra, 2000). Only statistics and direct quotations from this work have been cited. The training programs of the three individual Services have been covered in later chapters.
49. Tinker, *The Union of Burma*, p. 332.
50. Maung Aung Myoe, *Officer Education and Leadership Training*, p. 3.
51. See, for example, Dr Maung Maung, *To A Soldier Son*, p. iv.
52. Australia is not listed by Maung Aung Myoe among those countries visited as part of this information-gathering exercise. See, however, Selth, 'Australian Defence Contacts with Burma', pp. 451-68. See also Selth, *Burma's Secret Military Partners*, pp. 45-9.
53. Maung Aung Myoe, *Officer Education and Leadership Training*, p. 1.
54. Some British manuals were simply re-badged and issued as Burma Army publications. See, for example, Burma Army Staff College, *Tactics 5: Combined Operations* (War Office, Rangoon, 1953).
55. Engineers and veterinary surgeons are also recruited through this program. Maung Aung Myoe, *Officer Education and Leadership Training*, p. 7.
56. *Ibid.*
57. Interview, Harvard, December 1996.
58. Maung Aung Myoe, *Officer Education and Leadership Training*, p. 7.
59. Bruce Hawke, 'Myanmar academy triples cadet intake', *JDW*, 29 November 2000, p. 17.
60. Maung Aung Myoe, *Officer Education and Leadership Training*, p. 7. See also Maung Aung Myoe, *Building the Tatmadaw*, pp. 16-17.
61. Maung Aung Myoe, *Officer Education and Leadership Training*, p. 6.
62. Interview and personal observation, Maymyo, April 1995.
63. This paragraph is largely drawn from Maung Aung Myoe, *Officer Education and Leadership Training*, pp. 7-8.
64. Interview, Rangoon, November 1999. A survey of the educational qualifications of *Tatmadaw* officers in 1997 showed that 61.1% were university graduates. In the army the

figure was 57.8%, in the navy 96.9% and in the air force 87.9%. See Thein Shwe, 'Human Resource Development in Nation Building: The Role of the Armed Forces', in *Human Resource Development and Nation Building in Myanmar* (Office of Strategic Studies, Rangoon, 1998), p. 156.

65. Maung Aung Myoe, *Officer Education and Leadership Training*, p. 13.
66. Maung Aung Myoe, *Officer Education and Leadership Training*, p. 14.
67. Maung Aung Myoe, *Officer Education and Leadership Training*, p. 15.
68. Maung Aung Myoe, *Officer Education and Leadership Training*, p. 4.
69. *Ibid*. Some Burmese naval officers appear to have attended courses in Denmark during this period. Most of the courses in the US were for air force personnel, although some senior army officers attended courses at Fort Leavenworth and Fort Benning. The FRG tended to offer engineering courses.
70. Maung Aung Myoe, *Officer Education and Leadership Training*, p. 5.
71. William Ashton, 'Myanmar: Foreign military training a mixed blessing', *Asia-Pacific Defence Reporter*, Vol. 24, No. 2, February/March 1998, pp. 10-11.
72. Interviews, Rangoon, November 1999.
73. Selth, *Burma's Secret Military Partners*, pp. 64-6. See also 'Air Forces Survey - Myanmar', *Asian Aviation*, Vol. 14, No. 6, June 1994, p. 34.
74. Interview, Singapore, May 1995; and Lague, 'Evans seeks support for ban on Burma'. No mention of Burma occurs in the *Defence of Singapore,* published annually by Singapore's Ministry of Defence, but nor does this official publication mention the 'navigational' flights regularly made to and from Rangoon by SAF aircraft, including Lockheed C-130 Hercules and Fokker F-50 transports.
75. Ashton, 'Burma receives advances from its silent suitors in Singapore', pp. 32-4. See also Selth, *Burma's Secret Military Partners*, pp. 27-43.
76. Selth, *Burma's Secret Military Partners*, pp. 49-56.
77. Alan Boyd, 'Burma arms itself against rebels in secret', *The Australian*, 18 May 1990; and *Towards Democracy in Burma* (Institute for Asian Democracy, Washington, 1992), p. 58.
78. 'Soviets Deny Sending Arms, Advisors to Burma', AFP, 7 November 1988.
79. *The Military Powers Encyclopedia*, p. 38 and p. 46.
80. Thein Swe, 'Human Resource Development in Nation Building', p. 157.
81. Interview, Canberra, August 1998. See also Maung Aung Myoe, *Building the Tatmadaw*, p. 9.
82. Maung Aung Myoe, *Building the Tatmadaw*, p. 10.
83. *The System of Correlation of Man and His Environment: The Philosophy of the Burma Socialist Programme Party* (Burma Socialist Programme Party, Rangoon, 1963).
84. Tin Maung Maung Than, 'Myanmar: Preoccupation with Regime Survival, National Unity and Stability', pp. 394-5. Since 1999 these courses have had a strong anti-NLD focus. See, for example, 'Junta holding mandatory anti-NLD meetings in the army', *Burma News Update*, June 2000, p. 1.
85. Maung Aung Myoe, *Officer Education and Leadership Training*, p. 9.
86. Maung Aung Myoe, *The Tatmadaw in Myanmar Since 1988*, p. 19.
87. There are very few open sources on this subject. The following section draws mainly on Maung Aung Myoe, *Military Doctrine and Strategy in Myanmar.* Only statistics and quotations from this work have been specifically cited.
88. William Slim, *Defeat Into Victory*, (Cassell, London, 1956), pp. 479-507.
89. See, for example, Callahan, 'The Origins of Military Rule in Burma', pp. 418ff; and Maung Aung Myoe, *Military Doctrine and Strategy in Myanmar,* pp. 1-2.
90. As late as 1958 the Burmese High Command was trying to formulate a plan to resist a Chinese invasion. F.P. Serong, 'Report on Visit to Burma, June-August 1957'. File: 'Burma,

1957-59', Australian Archives A4311/1 Box 579/10. See also Selth, 'Australian Defence Contacts with Burma', pp. 451-68.

91. To a certain extent, the doctrine was vindicated by the *Tatmadaw*'s success against the KMT in the late 1950s, but by then it had been heavily modified.

92. Tin Maung Maung Than, 'Myanmar: Myanmar-ness and Realism in Historical Perspective', in Ken Booth and Russell Trood (eds), *Strategic Cultures in the Asia-Pacific Region* (St Martin's Press, New York, 1999), pp. 165-81.

93. This officer's assignment to Burma may have been extended for a third year, but after the 1962 coup Ne Win asked him to leave the country. Selth, 'Australian Defence Contacts with Burma', pp. 451-68.

94. Maung Aung Myoe, *Military Doctrine and Strategy in Myanmar*, p. 4.

95. Maung Aung Myoe, *Military Doctrine and Strategy in Myanmar*, p. 6.

96. *Ibid.*

97. See Smith, *Burma: Insurgency and the Politics of Ethnicity*, p. 259.

98. Smith, *Burma: Insurgency and the Politics of Ethnicity*, p. 260.

99. Different authors give different names to the four factors which were to be denied to the insurgents, but these are the essential elements. Compare, for example, Maung Aung Myoe, *Military Doctrine and Strategy in Myanmar*, p. 10, with Smith, *Burma: Insurgency and the Politics of Ethnicity*, p. 259.

100. Smith, *Burma: Insurgency and the Politics of Ethnicity*, p. 259.

101. US State Department, *Burma: Country Report*. See also *Dispossessed: Forced Relocation and Extrajudicial Killings in Shan State* (Shan Human Rights Foundation, Chiang Mai, 1998).

102. Smith, *Burma: Insurgency and the Politics of Ethnicity*, p. 259.

103. Maung Aung Myoe, *Military Doctrine and Strategy in Myanmar*, p. 10. When living in Burma during the mid-1970s, the author observed first-hand the nervousness of senior Burmese officials following the communist victories in Vietnam and Cambodia.

104. Consciously drawing on Maoist guerrilla doctrine, this strategy was characterised as 'defence, mobile defence, counter-offensive and the total offensive'. Interview, Sydney, October 1996.

105. Maung Aung Myoe, *Military Doctrine and Strategy in Myanmar*, p. 7.

106. Maung Aung Myoe, *Military Doctrine and Strategy in Myanmar*, p. 16.

107. Interviews, Rangoon, November and December 1999.

108. In this process, the National Defence College in Rangoon seems to be an important testing ground for new strategies and military concepts. Interview, Rangoon, December 1999.

109. Interviews, Rangoon, November and December 1999. See also Maung Aung Myoe, *Military Doctrine and Strategy in Myanmar*, pp. 15-16.

110. Maung Aung Myoe, *Military Doctrine and Strategy in Myanmar*, p. 16.

111. 'Rangoon junta forces hold joint military exercise near Burma-Thai border', DVB (in Burmese), 25 September 2000; and 'Burmese junta troops ready for military exercise in Tenasserim Division', DVB (in Burmese), 23 July 2000.

112. The appearance of PLA observers at some of these exercises has given rise to speculation that they are acting as advisors. See, for example, 'Burma, China to hold joint military exercises in Coastal Region', *Burma News Update*, August 2000, p. 8.

113. Maung Aung Myoe, *Military Doctrine and Strategy in Myanmar*, p. 15.

114. Cited in Maung Aung Myoe, *Military Doctrine and Strategy in Myanmar*, p. 13.

115. Maung Aung Myoe, *Military Doctrine and Strategy in Myanmar*, p. 8.

Chapter 5

Military Intelligence

> Dictatorships are dependent for their survival on good Intelligence and are therefore more generous than democracies to Intelligence organisations. — Peter Gudgin, *Military Intelligence* (1989)

Although there has always been a number of civilian intelligence and security agencies in Burma, they have been completely dominated by the country's vast military intelligence apparatus.[1] Not only has the latter provided the *Tatmadaw* with operational intelligence and assessments of the strategic environment but, after the 1962 coup, it was used as a blatantly political instrument to crush domestic dissent and help perpetuate military rule. Since 1988, the SLORC and SPDC have come to depend even more on the intelligence services to retain political power in the face of widespread domestic and international opposition. An effort has also been made to improve the purely military capabilities of Burma's intelligence apparatus, in order to reap the full benefits of the armed forces' expansion and modernisation program.

5.1 Intelligence Before 1988

Soon after it took office, the Nu Government organised a number of intelligence and specialised security agencies. Their prime functions were to maintain civil order and help defeat the insurgent groups then challenging Rangoon. Given the complex inter-disciplinary nature of counter-insurgent warfare, and the scarce resources then available to the government, it was inevitable that during the civil war period the civilian and military intelligence agencies would work closely together. Their separate roles and responsibilities, however, were never entirely clear and there was considerable overlap and confusion. According to one early study,

> A variety of intelligence-security organizations have come and gone on the national scene; missions and functions frequently have been duplicated, personnel has been arbitrarily transferred from one service to another and ten-

sions and rivalries have developed from time to time that seriously hampered the effectiveness of the entire security apparatus.[2]

The main elements of this apparatus were the *Tatmadaw*'s three military intelligence arms, later combined as the Military Intelligence Service (MIS), which answered to the Minister for Defence; the Bureau of Special Investigations (BSI), which was directly responsible to the Prime Minister; the Ministry of Foreign Affairs; the Criminal Investigation Department (CID), and the Special Investigation Department (SID). As parts of the Burma Police Force, the latter two agencies were responsible to the Minister for Home and Religious Affairs.[3]

The *Tatmadaw*'s military intelligence capabilities appear to have developed slowly and rather haphazardly. In the years immediately following Independence there was little central coordination or control. Internal rivalries and communications problems meant that field units were usually left to set their own collection priorities and meet their own intelligence requirements, without direct support from the War Office in Rangoon. Indeed, as Mary Callahan has pointed out, around this time 'the War Office had almost no idea what was going on upcountry'.[4] As the central government gradually regained control, however, and the armed forces became more unified and better administered, so the *Tatmadaw*'s military intelligence capabilities grew.[5] Few details are available, but it appears that there was an Intelligence Section in the War Office, with links to Military Intelligence Sections in Southern Command Headquarters at Mingaladon, and Northern Command Headquarters at Maymyo. There was also more regular radio contact with Intelligence Officers posted to various Burma Army commands and units in the field.[6] Following the models provided by the Royal Navy (RN) and Royal Air Force (RAF), and promoted until 1954 by the BMM, the Burma Navy and Burma Air Force also established small intelligence cells.

The highest priority of all these intelligence units was to provide operational support to different arms of the *Tatmadaw* in the planning and conduct of its counter-insurgency campaigns. As resources permitted and circumstances demanded, however, they also monitored broad strategic trends and external developments which had a bearing on Burma's security, such as events in China, Thailand and to a lesser extent India.[7] The latter role increased during the early 1950s, after the KMT remnants established their military bases in northern Burma and started mounting operations against the PRC.[8]

By the mid-1950s, Burma's military intelligence apparatus commanded numerous sources, mainly in Burma but also in neighbouring countries. It was capable of performing all basic collection, collation, analysis and dissemination tasks, in support of both military operations and broader political objectives. Indeed, as Mary Callahan has suggested, the establishment of KMT bases in Burma and the consequent threat of an armed response from the PRC, helped provide the necessary impetus for the *Tatmadaw* to graduate from a group of loosely coordinated anti-guerrilla units into a more structured, centrally-administered armed force capable of large-scale operations.[9] That development was necessarily accompanied by an increase in the *Tatmadaw*'s military intelligence capabilities. Even so, progress appears to have been slow. Personal rivalries and continuing antagonisms between War Office staff and field commanders undermined the benefits of organisational changes and doctrinal developments. One commentator has described the country's military intelligence apparatus during the 1950s as 'not particularly effective'.[10]

In addition to increasing their capabilities to support combat operations, the *Tatmadaw*'s intelligence units also became more influential in civil affairs. For, even in the days of Nu's democratic government, military intelligence had a political role. This flowed in large part from the country's parlous security situation and the *Tatmadaw*'s importance in government pacification and reconstruction programs. It also stemmed from the conviction of many senior military officers that the armed forces had saved the Union from disintegration, and were therefore entitled to play a special role in the country's affairs.

This attitude became obvious after November 1958, when Nu was forced to surrender temporary control of the government to General Ne Win, pending a fresh round of elections. One of the first steps undertaken by the military 'caretaker' government was to 'revamp and reorganise' the *Tatmadaw*'s intelligence units, and form a separate Military Intelligence Service (*Tatmadaw Htauk Hlan-ye Ahpwe*). According to Harriet O'Brien, the MIS was Ne Win's 'special creation'.[11] A program was implemented to

> expand and retrain the military intelligence forces....The MI became increasingly powerful and their operations gradually extended beyond merely gathering information to assist troops fighting the insurgent armies. ...They became a network of spies, a powerful secret police force monitoring the activities of ordinary people.[12]

Ne Win's inspiration was reportedly the Japanese *Kempetai* military police, from which he had himself received instruction during the Second World War.[13] MIS officers were also posted to important positions in the government bureaucracy. During the 'caretaker' period, the MIS (or simply 'the MI', as it became widely known) was an integral part of the military administration. It re-assumed this role after the 1962 coup.

The Bureau of Special Investigations (*Sa Thon Lon*) was originally created by the Nu Government in 1951 as the People's Property Protection Police. Described by one scholar as 'Burma's F.B.I.', the BSI had extensive investigative powers.[14] While it was ultimately responsible to the Prime Minister, it operated under the guidance of a Special Investigations Administrative Board. The role of the BSI was mainly to investigate corruption among political leaders and government employees, a task it pursued with considerable vigour. The Criminal Investigation Department was primarily responsible for the investigation of civil crimes. It did not devote significant resources to monitoring domestic dissent but, under the Union's broad criminal code, inevitably found itself drawn into the investigation of some political activities. That particular role, however, belonged to the Special Investigation Department (*Ah Htoo Sone San Ye*), which was designed to be Burma's equivalent to the UK's Special Branch. Indeed, until a reorganisation of Burma's police forces in 1964, the SID was more often known by this name. Like its British counterpart, the SID was formally responsible for internal security and counter-intelligence. It investigated treason, subversion and other anti-government activities, whether perpetrated by Burmese citizens or by foreigners living in Burma.[15]

The Ministry of Foreign Affairs (originally known as the Foreign Office) also exercised certain intelligence functions. These included the traditional diplomatic roles of overt information collection, analysis and reporting on international developments of current interest. The Ministry of Foreign Affairs also provided administrative support for Burma's network of Defence Attachés. These officers (usually Burma Army Colonels and Lieutenant Colonels) were posted to the country's larger and more important diplomatic missions, such as those in London, Washington, Beijing, Tokyo, Bangkok and New Delhi. The Attachés were formally controlled by the Defence Ministry's Military Attachés Office, which answered directly to the *Tatmadaw*'s Chief of Staff.[16]

During this period, Burma's intelligence services established a number of training camps throughout the country including, in 1950, a Military Intelligence Training Centre at Mingaladon. Training assistance was provided by several countries, including the UK and the US. For example, according to Kin Oung,

> Burma sent promising young men to Britain to receive instruction from not only the Criminal Investigation Department of London's Metropolitan Police Force (Scotland Yard) but also MI6, the British Secret Service. Most of this training took place at the Sheffield Police Academy, and a selected few went to a much more secretive intelligence school called Shetmead.[17]

In the 1950s and 1960s, military intelligence officers were trained in the UK, and by the CIA on Okinawa and the Pacific island of Saipan. Until 1987, others were trained in the continental US.[18] Some observers have suggested that Ne Win also turned to countries like Israel, Yugoslavia, the USSR, FRG and GDR to help develop Burma's domestic intelligence apparatus, and to appear even-handed in his international contacts.[19]

After the 1962 coup, the Revolutionary Council took a number of measures to rationalise the country's national security apparatus and to exert greater central control over its operations. In 1964 the RC created the National Intelligence Board (NIB), a small policy-making body that was responsible for 'coordinating the activities of the country's various intelligence and security agencies' at the highest level.[20] The NIB's membership consisted of the heads of the country's four main intelligence and specialised security agencies, the MIS, BSI, CID and SID. (The Foreign Ministry was not represented.) The NIB itself was nominally headed by a Director General and was a component of the Central Security and Administrative Committee of the Office of the Chairman of the Revolutionary Council.

After 1974, when the RC formally transferred power to the 'civilian' BSPP government, a National Intelligence Bureau Law was passed to give the NIB a new name and formal status. The Bureau was attached to the Office of the Prime Minister, who headed a supervisory committee also comprising the Ministers of Foreign Affairs, Planning and Finance, and Home and Religious Affairs. Known as the NIB Control Board, this committee gave 'guidance and advice' to the members of the NIB. The committee's *ex-officio* Secretary was the Director General of the NIB, often referred to as the Chief of National Intelligence (CNI, or simply 'Chief of Intelligence').[21] This position seems always to have been occupied by the Director (or former Director) of the MIS, by then the dominant member of the country's intelligence apparatus. To balance the CNI's power, in 1974 Ne Win also created the position of 'Military Assistant to the President and Council of State', with responsibility for oversight of intelligence matters. For all these bureaucratic mechanisms, however, in practice the NIB Control Board's oversight role was exercised very loosely. As Tin Maung Maung Than has observed, the CNI post 'had sweeping discretionary powers enjoying a form of autonomy that could lead to problems of accountability and abuse of power'.[22]

This arrangement survived until mid-1983, when a major restructuring of the country's intelligence apparatus occurred, purportedly prompted by the misuse of power by a number of senior MIS (and former MIS) officers. In October that year legislation was passed in the *Pyithu Hluttaw* placing all intelligence operations in Burma under the direct control of a new body (also to be known as the National Intelligence Bureau, or NIB), chaired by the Prime Minister.[23] The amended National Intelligence Bureau Law effectively consolidated the intelligence agencies belonging to various government ministries under this single high-level organisation. It enjoyed more supervisory and monitoring powers over the different agencies than its predecessor, 'whose composition, role and functions were not clearly defined'.[24] As one observer has pointed out,

> With reorganization, the new NIB was, in fact, a sub-cabinet chaired by the Prime Minister with Ministers for Defence, Planning and Finance, Home and Religious Affairs, and Foreign Affairs as members.[25]

In contrast to the old NIB, which gave considerable personal power to its Director General, there was no provision for a CNI, or even an *ex-officio* Secretary to the Bureau. This latter post was to be served by different NIB members taking it in turns, 'as a safeguard against a single member being invested with prerogatives accruing to the position'.[26]

The new NIB law gave the Bureau wide-ranging powers to make decisions and to issue orders. It was required to submit reports on 'important matters' to the State Council, the country's highest government body. The Council in turn reported to the President, usually through the National Defence and Security Council. The NIB also had responsibility for summarising reports received from the different intelligence agencies, and for submitting them with appraisals to the Council.[27] Like its earlier namesake, the new NIB exercised oversight of the MIS, BSI, CID, SID and (at least as far as its intelligence functions were concerned) the Foreign Ministry. Through a small staff it also appears to have supervised a number of lesser intelligence and security bodies. These included the Intelligence and Research Section of the Customs Department, the Police Force's Detective Department and the Immigration Department's Intelligence Squads. The 1983 National Intelligence Bureau Law made all these agencies responsible not only to their respective Ministers, but also to the NIB.[28] The NIB's effectiveness at the time can be gauged by the fact that it was rated by outsiders as 'probably the most efficient government agency in Burma'.[29]

Under the RC and BSPP Government a number of other changes were made to Burma's intelligence and security apparatus. The roles of the CID, BSI and SID were expanded, but were still focussed on domestic issues. The Ministry of Foreign Affairs continued to exercise its traditional diplomatic roles, but under the Ne Win regime had an increased intelligence function. Burmese missions abroad assisted the domestic intelligence agencies in monitoring the activities of expatriate Burmese communities, including emigrants and foreign nationals critical of the military government. The Foreign Ministry also provided diplomatic cover and administrative support for Burmese intelligence officers posted abroad in a clandestine role. After 1962, for example, MIS officers appear to have been posted to Burmese diplomatic missions in selected countries, like Thailand, to report on the activities of Burmese exiles and anti-Ne Win insurgent groups based there. They were also sent to consular posts where there was no Defence Attaché, like Hong Kong and Chiang Mai.[30] A number of Burmese ambassadors around this time were former MIS officers. Also, the mission's cipher clerks (often Burma Army NCOs) were trained by the MIS. The Foreign Ministry continued to support Burma's Defence Attaches, who monitored military developments in their assigned countries and changes in the wider strategic environment. They also helped to arrange arms purchases from overseas suppliers. While still formally administered by the Defence Ministry's Military Attachés Office, these officers also had reporting responsibilities to the MIS.

During this period the MIS was greatly expanded. It remained nominally separate from the government and the BSPP, but extended the scope of its operations even further into the civilian sphere (to the extent that 'the MI' soon became a generic term for all Burma's intelligence agencies).[31] Until the NIB was created in 1974, for example, the MIS coordinated the work of all other Burmese intelligence and security agencies.[32] Later, and probably coinciding with another reorganisation of the Defence Ministry, the MIS was formally placed under a Directorate of Defence Services Intelligence (*Tatmadaw Htauk Hlan-ye Hyun-kyar Yehmu Youn*). Operating from the Ministry's General Staff Department, the DDSI commanded more than a dozen MIS units (variously called battalions, companies or detachments) posted throughout the country.[33] These were usually designated numerically, such as MI-1, MI-2 and MI-6. While their primary responsibility continued to be the collection of military intelligence, particularly as it related to the country's persistent insurgent problems, they increasingly focussed their resources on other internal security issues such as the loyalty of the armed forces and the political mood of the civilian population. The DDSI/MIS appears to have had 'almost unrestricted authority to arrest without warrant, detain and investigate anyone suspected of political dissent, violent or non-violent'.[34]

More changes were made to the DDSI/MIS structure in 1983, after a terrorist attack in Rangoon demonstrated severe weaknesses in Burma's intelligence capabilities. Twenty-one people (including four South Korean Cabinet Ministers) were killed when a team from the Democratic People's Republic of Korea (DPRK or North Korea), secretly infiltrated into Burma by Pyongyang, planted a bomb at the Martyrs' Mausoleum in Rangoon. The bomb was intended to explode during a visit to the shrine by the President of the Republic of Korea, but was detonated prematurely.[35] Soon after this incident, the then COL Khin Nyunt, reportedly a close protégé of President Ne Win, was recalled to Rangoon from a posting to 44 LID and instructed to 'rebuild the shattered agency'.[36] It is not known precisely how Khin Nyunt set about this task, but it included a number of important personnel changes. For example, immediately after the DPRK terrorist attack the Director of the MIS and his deputy were relieved of their posts because of the MIS's failure to provide adequate security for the visiting ROK delegation.[37] Khin Nyunt's new MIS Director was a Burma Army officer without any specific intelligence background.[38] Loyalty to the regime, and to Ne Win, was considered more important than any specialised technical knowledge or professional experience.[39]

The individual armed Services within the *Tatmadaw* also continued to develop their own intelligence staffs and capabilities.[40] The Burma Army, for example, had a cadre of soldiers trained to collect, analyse and disseminate combat intelligence to commanders in the field. Each infantry battalion had an Intelligence Section within the Security Platoon of its Headquarters Company.[41] There were also military intelligence staffs within each of the army's TOCs, and in the headquarters of both the mobile LIDs and the RMC. The BN and BAF too maintained intelligence staffs, to provide them with the specialised information and analyses they needed to patrol Burma's extensive air space and maritime claims, and to help direct ships and aircraft against particular targets. These personnel also served as links with Army intelligence during joint counter-insurgency campaigns.

These Service intelligence staffs remained formally under the control of DDSI. In the case of the Burma Army, unit intelligence staffs were simply extensions of the MIS. Suitable army personnel were initially identified and transferred to the MIS from BA units. After a period of instruction at the DDSI's training centre, some were posted to MIS branches or companies to carry out 'political' and counter-intelligence work, while others were sent to particular army commands or units to perform intelligence functions more closely related to combat operations.[42] These military intelligence staffs were given considerable power and independence. For example, until the country's intelligence command arrangements were revised in 1983, they reported directly back to the DDSI in Rangoon, without having to clear their reports through the appropriate BA channels. This was apparently

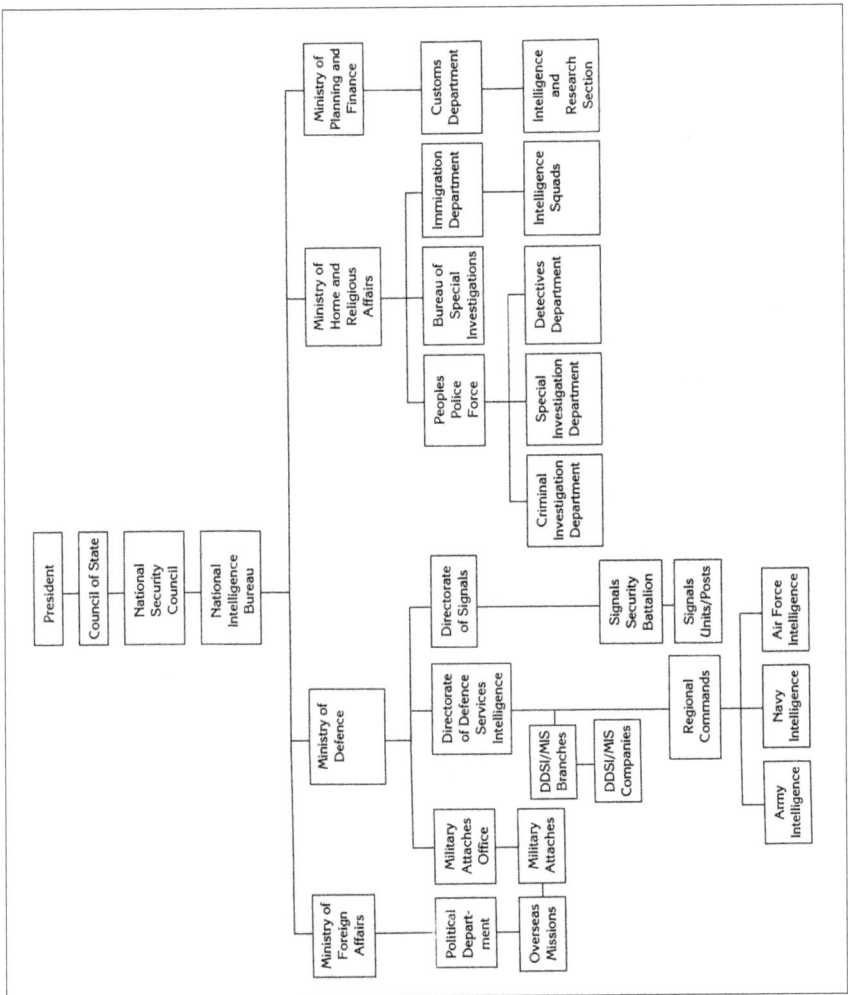

Figure 7: Burma's Intelligence Apparatus, 1988.

a source of some friction between intelligence staffs and the Regional Military Commanders, who felt that their authority was being undermined. There was also a concern that critical information might be denied to field units by the Defence Ministry, or passed on too late to be of value. After 1983, however, all military intelligence reports were directed to Rangoon through the RMCs.[43]

The air force and navy intelligence staffs were also formally responsible to DDSI. They received training from the DDSI and maintained close contacts with DDSI headquarters, even after being posted back to their own Service units.[44] The BAF maintained an intelligence staff at Mingaladon airport and had smaller units at other major air bases, like Meiktila and Myitkyina. The Navy had its main intelligence staff at Fleet Headquarters, or at Irrawaddy Command's Monkey Point base, with smaller units at the other two Regional Naval Commands (Arakan and Tenasserim). Naval Intelligence Officers may have also been stationed at some of the smaller commands scattered around Burma, like Bassein and Coco Island. Until 1983, these intelligence staffs too maintained their own direct links back to DDSI in Rangoon, bypassing the normal chains of command.

Owing largely to the slim resources available to the military regime before 1988, and the nature of the security problems it faced, the country's intelligence apparatus depended heavily on human intelligence (HUMINT). The DDSI in particular controlled large numbers of paid and unpaid informers all around the country, and even overseas. Many were full-time operatives but this core of professionals was supplemented by a much larger number of part-time informers, who were either coerced or bribed to provide information about their friends, neighbours, students, colleagues and others, on a regular or an opportunity basis. In addition to the country's many insurgent groups (including narcotics-based armies), political dissidents and other critics of the regime were high priority targets.[45] After the 1974 U Thant disturbances in Rangoon, for example, a major effort was made to increase the number of informers among the student population, which had a long history of political dissent. According to one senior diplomat posted to Burma at that time, one in four students at tertiary educational institutions around Rangoon were reputed to be in the pay of one or other of the intelligence services. University and College staff members were required to report any unusual activity by their students, on pain of arrest and dismissal.[46] Also, a significant part of the regime's counter-intelligence effort was directed against resident diplomats and the few other foreigners allowed to live in Burma after the military coup.

The purpose of this pervasive surveillance seems to have been to thwart any intelligence operations directed against the regime, as well as other kinds of 'subversive' activities. This concern was well founded. Not only did the military government face serious challenges from numerous insurgent and dissident groups, but it was also the target of a number of foreign intelligence agencies. For example, despite official denials at the time, the CIA and Taiwanese intelligence services actively assisted the KMT remnants based in northern Burma during the 1950s and possibly even later.[47] Around the same time the USSR's embassy in Rangoon harboured representatives of both the KGB (Committee of State Security) and GRU

(Chief Intelligence Directorate of the Soviet General Staff), both of which targeted the Burmese armed forces.[48] The Chinese intelligence services also paid close attention to Burma. They not only monitored developments along the China-Burma border and in Burma itself, but they actively supported the CPB in its long armed struggle against the Rangoon government.[49] Given their proximity to Burma, and the tensions which periodically occurred along their common borders, it is likely that both Thailand and India included Burma among their usual intelligence targets.

Technical intelligence gathering was much more difficult. From an early stage, Burma's intelligence agencies demonstrated that they had the means to plant covert listening devices ('bugs') and listen to private conversations held indoors.[50] It was also taken for granted by diplomatic personnel living in Burma at this time that the regime could tap the telephones of selected targets, including embassies, consulates and the offices of international organisations. This practice was made easier by the obsolete telephone equipment then used and the small number of exchanges. Even then, anecdotal evidence suggests that taps could only be applied to a limited degree, and by using the most basic interception and recording techniques.[51]

Burma appears to have had its own national SIGINT capability during this period (managed by the *Tatmadaw*'s Directorate of Signals) but it was probably quite modest.[52] Burma lacked the foreign exchange to acquire much sophisticated modern communications or computer equipment, nor did it have the indigenous technical expertise to manufacture its own. At the strategic level, Burma's SIGINT effort most likely included attempts to eavesdrop on the official radio traffic of neighbouring countries like China, India and Thailand. The telex and radio transmissions of diplomatic missions and international organisations in Rangoon, Mandalay and Sittwe were probably also targeted by the Burmese intelligence services. Most embassies used coded telexes for communications with their headquarters during this period, utilising lines leased from the Department of Posts and Telecommunications. From the antennae sited on the roofs of the US, PRC, USSR and several other missions, however, it was apparent that some at least made extensive use of radio communications to keep in touch with their headquarters.[53] The success (or otherwise) of the Ne Win regime in intercepting diplomatic transmissions from Burma is not known, but it is unlikely that it would have been able to break the sophisticated communications codes commonly used by the major powers.

Burma also monitored short-wave radio broadcasts from public sources overseas, like the BBC, VOA and All India Radio (AIR). These activities were mainly directed through the *Tatmadaw*'s large communications facilities at Mingaladon and Hmawbi, although smaller listening posts were probably maintained at strategic locations around Burma's borders.[54] These facilities would have also been useful for monitoring clandestine radio stations like the CPB's 'Voice of the People of Burma'. Inaugurated in March 1971 from a station in southern China, VOPB broadcasts provided a valuable guide to doctrinal shifts in the Party and, before the station closed down in 1989, it revealed considerable information about the CPB's military strategy and tactics.[55]

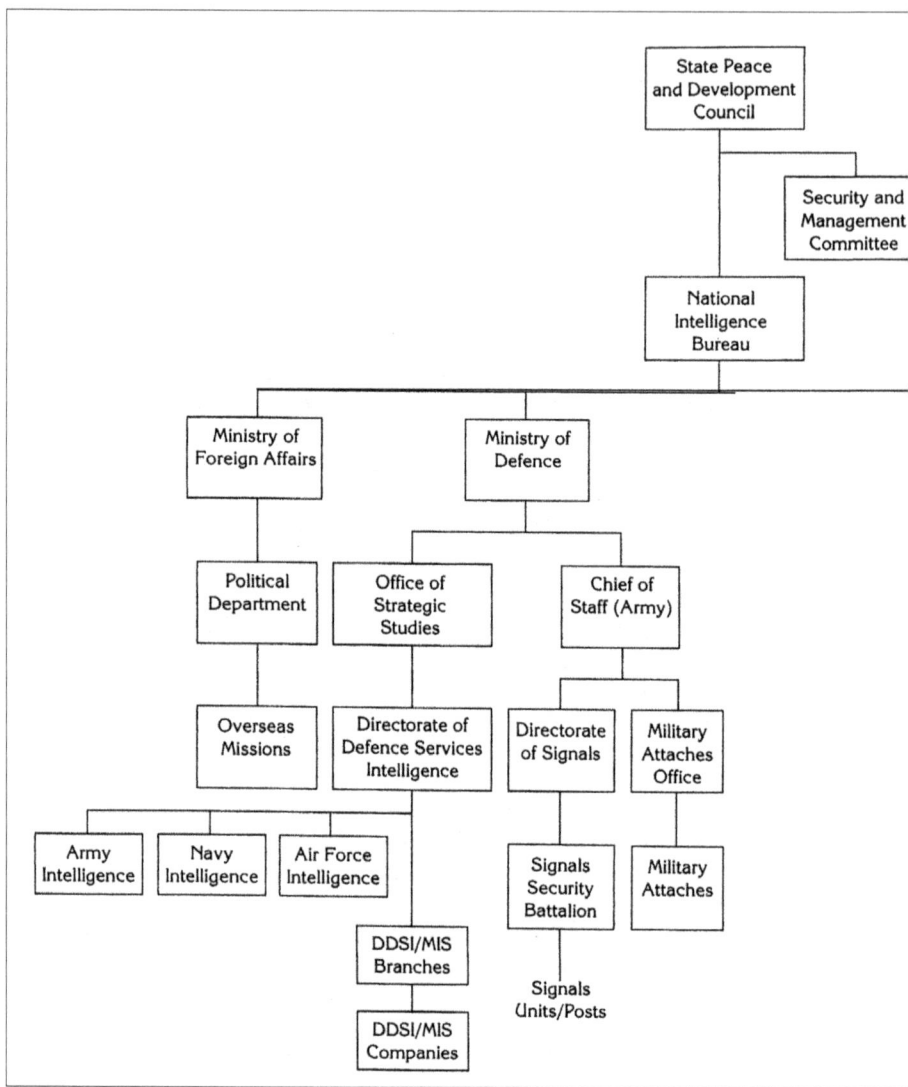

Figure 8: Burma's Intelligence Apparatus, 2000.

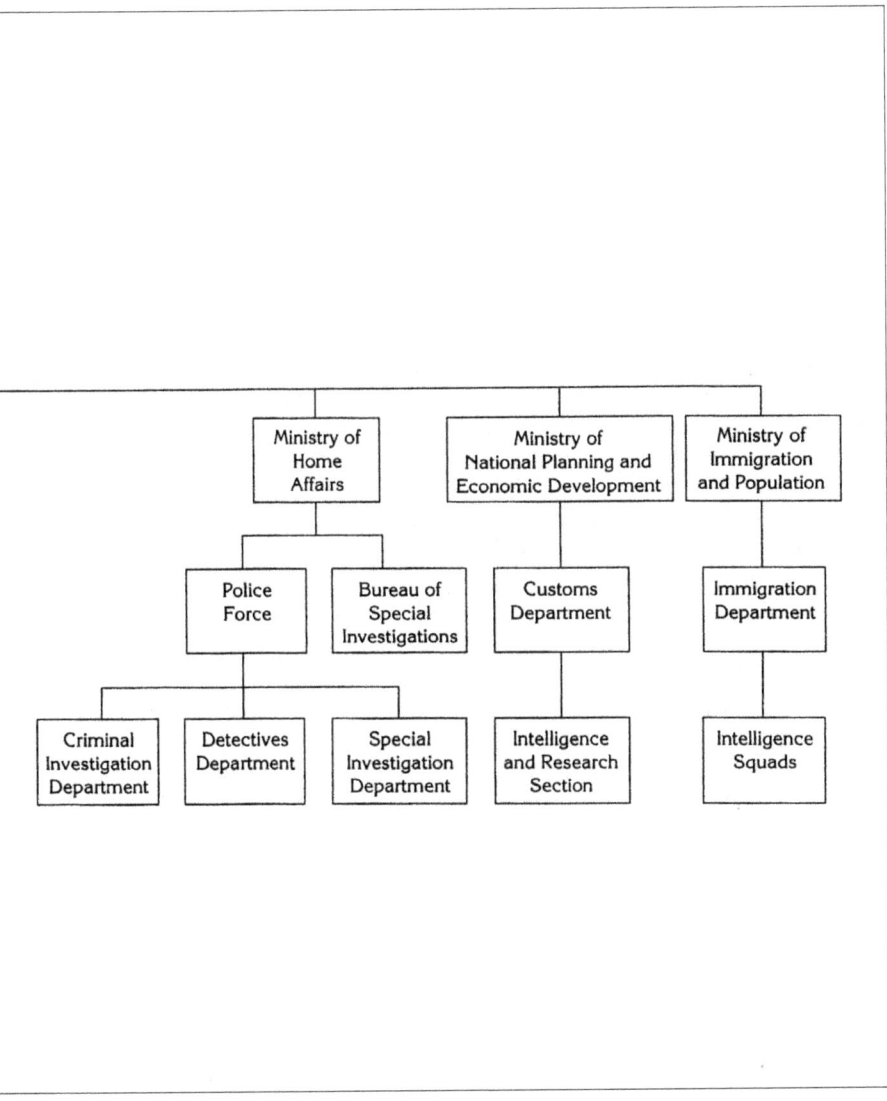

The *Tatmadaw* also had an ability to intercept radio traffic generated by ethnic separatist, ideological and 'economic' insurgent groups. This appears to have been done both at the command level and the operational level. There was a Signals Security Battalion based at Mingaladon, for example, which out-posted personnel to the Regional Military Commands.[56] Tactical level intercepts also occurred, often during counter-insurgency campaigns, using direction finders and standard triangulation techniques. For example, the *Tatmadaw* nearly captured deposed Prime Minister Nu in the early 1970s by tracking his clandestine radio signals.[57] The BA used a range of direction finding equipment, most of it supplied by Western countries. Some Japanese, Yugoslav and Soviet equipment also seems to have been employed.[58] Intercepted radio communications were regularly used by the Burma Army (and the insurgent groups themselves) to secure valuable intelligence about their opponents' positions, strengths, dispositions and plans.[59] Indeed, such was the threat from this quarter that BA units on operations were often obliged to observe radio silence in order to cloak their movements from the insurgents tracking their signals.[60]

Burmese interception of foreign and insurgent radio traffic (and also insurgent interception of *Tatmadaw* communications) was usually made considerably easier by the very poor COMSEC practices employed. From an early stage, both the *Tatmadaw* and the major insurgent groups learned how to encypher local language transmissions, with the Karens leading the way.[61] Given the numerous reports of codes being broken, however, it would appear that on both sides they were relatively unsophisticated.[62] Although Morse Code seems to have been used most often by the armed forces and insurgents alike, voice transmissions were also common, particularly from the 1980s when more sophisticated equipment like small portable 'walkie talkies' were readily available from Thailand. Often, there was little effort made to conceal the content of particular messages, which were sent *en clair* or using barely veiled speech. One well-informed observer has noted that, at times, the two sides even engaged in open banter over the airwaves.[63] There were cases, however, where the decryption of insurgent radio traffic was beyond the *Tatmadaw*'s technical capabilities. According to Martin Smith, for example, the sophisticated Chinese codes used by the CPB in the late 1960s for 'battlefield instructions' could not be broken by the *Tatmadaw*, despite considerable efforts to do so.[64]

5.2 Intelligence After 1988

It was perhaps inevitable that, after the armed forces took back the reins of government in 1988, Burma's intelligence apparatus would be reviewed. Yet, in many respects, its structure appears to have remained the same. The greatest change has been in the size and scope of its operations, and the means by which they are conducted.

Under the SLORC and SPDC, the NIB has been retained (in theory at least) as the country's highest intelligence organ, deciding broad policy and overseeing the activities of the country's other intelligence agencies. The NIB now reports directly to the SPDC, but is also subject to the National Security and Management Committee. If not actually an extension of the DDSI, the NIB once again appears completely dominated by it. The DDSI is still a part of the Defence Ministry, but provides the Bureau's Director General (LTGEN Khin Nyunt) and its staff, all of which are members of the armed forces. The CID, SID and BSI all seem to have been retained and, generally speaking, still appear to exercise their earlier functions. These three agencies are now formally under the jurisdiction of the (renamed) Ministry of Home Affairs. The other intelligence functions exercised by the Ministry of Foreign Affairs and the (renamed) Ministry of National Planning and Economic Development do not seem to have changed significantly. The Ministry of Immigration and National Registration was abolished in 1974, but was recreated as the Ministry of Immigration and Population in 1992. It continues to have certain intelligence functions.

A major new addition to the country's intelligence apparatus is the Office of Strategic Studies.[65] A small body directly answerable to Khin Nyunt, the OSS was initially believed to be a semi-academic institution similar to the strategic studies institutes and 'think tanks' found elsewhere in the region (and further afield). Some commentators have speculated that the OSS was created in part to give Burma a seat at various 'one and a half track' (a mixture of both academics and officials) and 'second track' (academics only) talks on security issues that were then becoming common in the Asia-Pacific region.[66] While the OSS does perform these roles, another explanation for the creation of the OSS was that a new 'Strategic Command' was required within the Defence hierarchy, to justify Khin Nyunt's elevation in 1994 to Lieutenant General rank.[67] This places the OSS higher than the DDSI in the formal Defence Ministry structure, equating to a Bureau of Special Operations in the General Staff Department. Even so, Khin Nyunt has retained the titles of both Chief of the OSS and Director of Defence Services Intelligence (as well as being Director General of the NIB and Secretary (1) of the SPDC).

From small beginnings, the OSS has grown quickly and taken on some weighty responsibilities. It now consists of about 50 people, divided into five main departments.[68] These cover international affairs, narcotics, domestic security and ethnic affairs. There is also an administrative department. Departmental heads are usually full Colonels, but some separate areas, such as science and the environment, are run by general staff officers (GSO1) at the Lieutenant Colonel level. Deputy department heads are also at the GSO1 level. All OSS officers are members of the armed forces and most seem to be drawn from the ranks of the DDSI. Some retain their DDSI roles, even as members of the OSS.[69] Since its creation in the early 1990s, the OSS has taken a strong interest in Burma's expanding international relations, in effect directing the diplomatic activities of the Foreign Ministry. Together with the DDSI, it enjoys cordial relations with numerous foreign intelligence agencies, including those of China, Singapore, Malaysia, Thailand, India, Pakistan and Israel. It has been instrumental in negotiating the cease-fires with various insurgent groups. The OSS has also demonstrated a close interest in the activities of dissidents and opposition politicians, notably Aung San Suu Kyi and the NLD.

Although the DDSI was already the largest and most powerful intelligence agency in Burma before 1988, it has greatly expanded in numbers and is now even more influential than before. It not only runs the MIS apparatus in the field (including, since March 1997, two or three battalions of dedicated troops based in Rangoon), and is a coordinating secretariat for the intelligence staffs of the three armed Services, but it also controls the NIB, and thus the activities of all the other Burmese intelligence agencies. A measure of the DDSI's increased power under the SLORC and SPDC is that, since 1992, DDSI/MIS branches and companies outside the capital have once again been permitted to report directly to Rangoon, without going through the RMCs.

As a directorate in the Ministry of Defence, the DDSI is based at the Ministry's compound in central Rangoon.[70] Under LTGEN Khin Nyunt, it is reportedly managed by a small number of senior officers (at Major-General and Brigadier rank) supported by a group of about 25 loyal army officers at more junior levels. The Directorate is divided into nine bureaus, each of which has responsibility for the oversight of a broad area of interest. For example, Bureau MI-1 oversees combat intelligence, MI-2 covers security, MI-3 covers counter-intelligence, MI-4 covers intelligence from overseas sources, MI-5 is responsible for liaison with the Defence Attache corps, MI-6 manages administration, and MI-9 looks after special issues like counter-terrorism and anti-narcotics operations. MI-7 and MI-8 cover the navy and air force.[71] Although there is a Directorate of Public Relations and Psychological Warfare in the Ministry of Defence, the DDSI and OSS also manage some information warfare and propaganda activities, as evidenced by the more sophisticated public relations campaign being waged by the regime in recent years.[72]

DDSI also has companies at regional command level (again designated numerically). They in turn control smaller MIS detachments scattered around their command areas of responsibility. Confusingly, these units too are usually designated (in English) only by number, such as MI-14, MI-20 etc. In 1989 there were some 14 intelligence companies and 17 units spread throughout the country.[73] By 1991 the number of companies had almost doubled to 23.[74] According to Bertil Lintner, 'The new intelligence units cover some urban centres hit by demonstrations [in 1988]...together with border areas fronting on Bangladesh, China and India.'[75] There are now believed to be about 40 intelligence companies, including three in the navy and four in the air force. They are usually under command of a Major level officer.[76] Some of these MIS companies are specifically responsible for the surveillance of armed forces personnel. The DDSI also continues to rely on thousands of agents and informers who spy on insurgents, dissident groups, students and members of the public. As Amnesty International has stated, 'Surveillance by Military Intelligence officers of critics or people connected with critics of the government is pervasive in Myanmar'.[77]

While the instruction provided to Burma's intelligence operatives in the past may have been quite rudimentary, a greater effort has clearly been made by the SLORC and SPDC to increase the quality and scope of the training given. There have also been reports that several countries have provided training and other assistance to Burma's intelligence services since 1988. China is most often named as the source of technical equipment and training for Burma's intelligence agencies. Singapore too has developed a close military relationship with the regime and is reported to be training large numbers of Burmese 'secret police' at an institution in central Singapore. There have also been persistent rumours that Mossad has provided training for Burma's intelligence agencies. While all these claims are quite plausible, they are very difficult to verify.[78]

The public statements made by LTGEN Khin Nyunt, and the publications issued in connection with the so-called 'communist' and 'right-wing' plots, give a good indication of the DDSI's interests and capabilities.[79] It is clear, for example, that a major effort is put into gathering information about the structure, membership, policies and methods of various 'underground' and 'above ground' organisations deemed a threat by the regime. These range from the CPB, insurgent armies and illegal opposition groups, to dissident student movements and legal political parties. Enormous resources have been put into compiling personal dossiers on known and suspected dissidents in Burma, members of the local diplomatic community and even critics of the regime who live abroad. Much of this material is photographic and documentary, including reports lodged under a range of regulations and martial law decrees.[80] The intelligence agencies still seem heavily dependent on HUMINT, resulting from static and mobile surveillance, *agents provocateurs*, and the use of informers and infiltrators to report from within suspect groups. It would also appear that the DDSI employs the full range of counter-intelligence techniques, including the installation of secret listening devices, telephone taps, mail interception and unauthorised access to local bank accounts.[81] The DDSI may even interfere with diplomatic mail.

Outside Burma, the DDSI tries to maintain a close watch over the many 'politicised Burmese exiles' living in places like the UK, FRG, Thailand, Australia and the US.[82] It is commonly assumed, for example, that such groups are infiltrated by intelligence agents, a belief that is probably welcomed by the regime. As Bertil Lintner has written, 'Among the Burmese community abroad, no one was ever sure who was an informer or not; mutual suspicion neutralised them as a political force'.[83]

Since 1988, DDSI and its MIS units have been responsible for most reported arrests and investigations of political suspects in Burma. It is also the most often accused of brutality and other human rights violations.[84] The US State Department and credible organisations like Amnesty International and Human Rights Watch have documented numerous cases of torture by military intelligence units over the last 12 years. Those units most often identified have been based in and around Rangoon and Mandalay, but their reputation may derive simply from the fact that most public reports have come from political activists and other dissidents captured and interrogated in the main population centres. AI has also identified more than 20 prisons and detention centres across Burma where brutal interrogations have taken place. These include the main DDSI interrogation centre at Ye Kyi

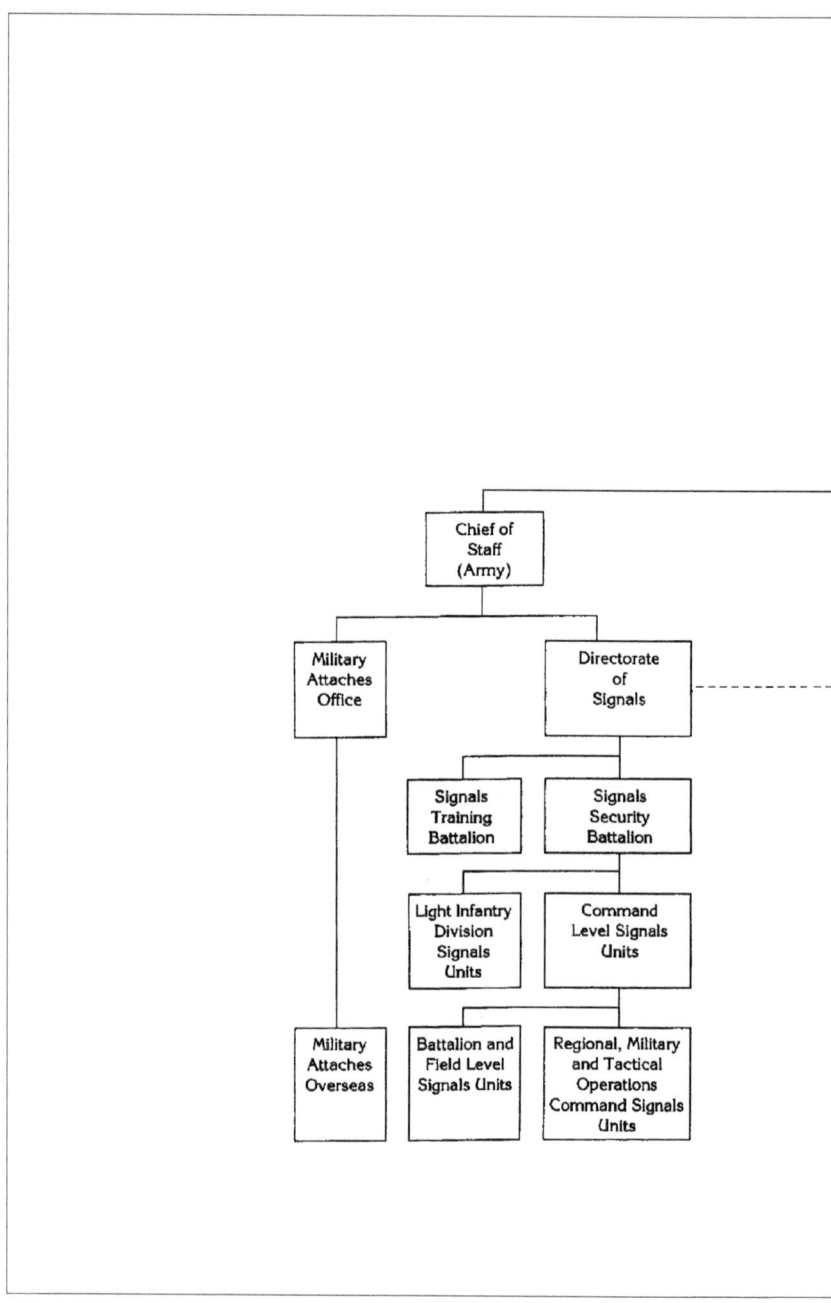

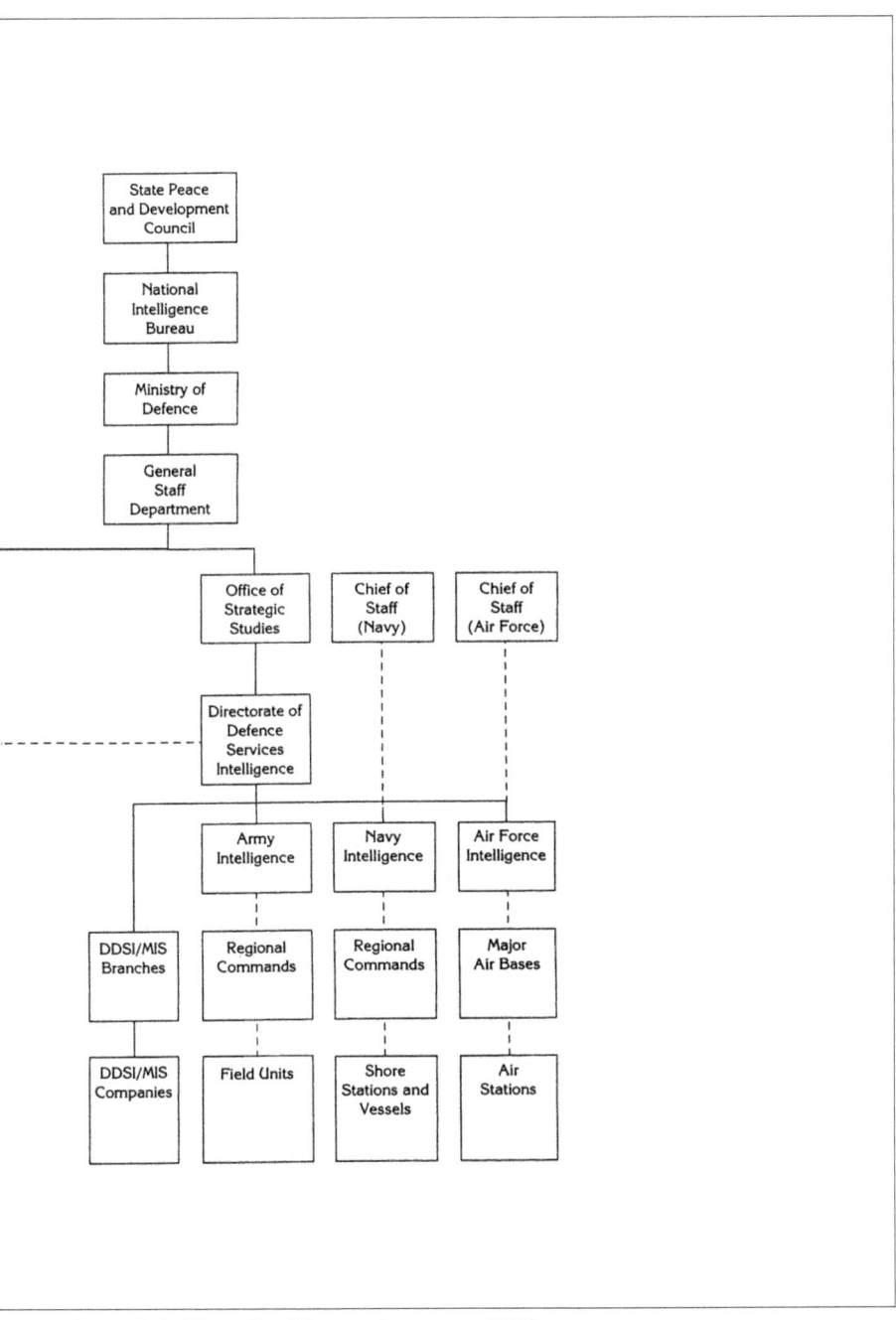

Figure 9: Military Intelligence Structure, 2000.

Aing (Yai Kyi Aung) camp north of Rangoon, and over a dozen other military intelligence centres located around the country.[85] There are probably others which have not yet come to the notice of international observers. According to AI, political prisoners have been ill-treated not only by the DDSI and its MIS units, but also by the SID, CID and BSI.[86] Sometimes people have been taken in and mistreated by military intelligence officers before being handed over to the Police, and formally arrested.[87]

The Ne Win regime's preoccupation with its own survival has long consumed precious resources and distracted the DDSI/MIS from pursuing its purely military intelligence functions. This situation remains under the SPDC, but some effort has been made in recent years to rectify the situation. The regime seems to have accepted, for example, that unless the *Tatmadaw* can command better strategic and operational intelligence capabilities, then it will remain vulnerable to both external and internal military threats. Perhaps more importantly, unless the *Tatmadaw*'s operational intelligence capabilities are improved, all the new arms and equipment it has acquired since 1988 will lack proper direction and coordination, and thus fail to realise their full potential.

Burma's SIGINT effort is still managed by the Directorate of Signals. International intercepts are reportedly the responsibility of specialist units based in the Defence Ministry compound in Rangoon, and are derived from the larger *Tatmadaw* communications facilities at Mingaladon and Hmawbi, and possibly the large military communications station in Taunggyi.[88] Since 1988, the Rangoon regime has clearly retained a capability to monitor, record and transcribe open source short-wave radio transmissions to Burma. The SLORC's interest in these broadcasts was graphically demonstrated in 1990, when the regime published *Skyful of Lies: B.B.C., V.O.A.: Their Broadcasts and Rebuttals to Disinformation*.[89]

There is also evidence to suggest that the scope of Burma's strategic SIGINT operations may have considerably widened in recent years. In addition to foreign radio traffic, Burma now seems able more easily to monitor radar and other electronic emissions (ELINT) emanating from outside the country. There have been persistent reports, for example, that China has provided Burma with a range of sophisticated equipment as part of a broader plan to upgrade its own SIGINT capabilities in the region.[90] Most attention has focussed on China's apparent role in establishing or upgrading a signals intercept station on Great Coco Island in the Andaman Sea. There have been several reports that, since 1992, this base has boasted a 50-metre high antenna and sensitive equipment capable of picking up not only radio and radar transmissions from ships in the vicinity, but also ELINT from ballistic missile tests at the Indian Defence Research and Development Laboratory in Hyderabad.[91] Some sources have even claimed that the Burmese are monitoring submarine activity around the Indian Navy's base at Vizag in eastern India, and listening in to the tri-service garrison at Port Blair on the Andaman islands.[92]

A number of other sites for new SIGINT stations have been suggested. For example, there have been numerous reports over the past few years that Burma has been approached by China to install (or at least upgrade) signals intelligence equipment at several places around the Burmese coast.[93] Once operational, this equipment could provide China (and presumably Burma as well) with a comprehensive electronic surveillance coverage of the Andaman Sea and Bay of Bengal.[94] One well-informed Burma-watcher has stated that the Burmese have come under pressure from the Chinese to permit the PRC's intelligence services access not only to Hainggyi and Great Coco islands (the places most often mentioned), but also to Ramree Island in the north and Zadetkyi Island along the Tenasserim coast. The latter is considered particularly sensitive as it is located off Kawthaung, Burma's southern-most point, and therefore close to the strategically important Malacca Straits.[95] Other possible sites of interest to the Chinese include Kadan Island, off the Burmese coast near Mergui (Myeik), and Heinze Island north of Tavoy (Dawei). It has been suggested that China wishes to build new facilities or improve old Burmese facilities on all these islands, with a view to conducting SIGINT operations against other regional countries.[96]

To support these claims, observers have cited reports of bilateral military agreements between the two countries. The most recent appears to have been negotiated in October 1996, and finalised in early 1997. According to the *Far Eastern Economic Review*, it specifically covers the exchange of intelligence on 'threats to their respective countries' and Chinese training for Burmese personnel in 'signals intelligence in coastal areas'.[97]

The full extent of China's involvement in Burma's intelligence improvement program, however, is very difficult to determine. Even greater uncertainty surrounds China's efforts to establish or use signals intelligence facilities around Burma's coastline to spy on other regional countries. While some of the reports on this subject are quite convincing, others are much less so, and most have yet to be confirmed by independent sources. There would be clear benefits to Burma in permitting China at least some of the access it desires, particularly if both countries share the product from SIGINT operations conducted from Burmese territory. Yet caution needs to be exercised over the extent to which Burma can be seen as an agent of the Chinese in this field. Given Burma's fierce independence and lingering suspicions of China's longer term strategic intentions, it is unlikely that the Rangoon regime would permit China all the access that it wants. Nor can any Chinese military presence be considered permanent, whatever the benefits of current intelligence sharing arrangements.

In addition to possible Chinese assistance, there have been reports of the Rangoon regime purchasing considerable quantities of electronic and communications equipment from several other suppliers, including Singapore, Russia and possibly Israel. It would be remarkable if none of it was related to intelligence collection, encryption or dissemination in some way. More importantly, the *Tatmadaw* has recently developed a sophisticated capability to intercept satellite transmissions to and from Burma. This became apparent in June 1997 when LTGEN Khin Nyunt revealed that the regime had been able to monitor and record portable satellite-phone conversations between Burmese dissidents in Rangoon and Bangkok.[98]

In addition to these activities at the strategic level, there has also been an effort to improve the *Tatmadaw*'s SIGINT capabilities in the field.[99] It appears that the equipment and technical advice available to signals personnel at the RMC, LID and battalion level has been significantly upgraded. In April 1997, for example, one regional journal reported the presence of 'a six-wheeled truck with wireless antennae, evidently a mobile signals intelligence facility' at Loi Htwe, near the Thai border. The truck was apparently monitoring radio traffic between UWSA units.[100] The report went on to say that 'the intelligence it picks up is shared with the Chinese' and speculated that Chinese experts were present at the site to train the Burmese operators.[101] Rangoon's ability to intercept and record insurgent radio traffic was graphically revealed in 1995. In a 28-part story entitled 'Whither KNU', published in the state-controlled newspaper *The New Light of Myanmar*, the regime quoted numerous radio conversations between insurgents, many of them verbatim. Some details of these conversations could have been fabricated, but the series gave several other important clues to the *Tatmadaw*'s substantial SIGINT capabilities.[102]

It would be expected that, if the Burma Army was making such an effort to improve its SIGINT capabilities, in order to intercept insurgent radio traffic, then it would also try harder to protect its own tactical communications. Indeed, this has occurred, probably with the help of China or another friendly country like Singapore. In early 1995, for example, the Karens around Manerplaw found it impossible to eavesdrop on attacking *Tatmadaw* units, which were using 'a special kind of wireless set' which defied interception. This was probably a frequency hopping radio provided by China.[103] It would appear, however, that Burmese COMSEC is still poor. Certain military codes and ciphers seem to have remained unchanged for long periods, and others can clearly still be broken. Reporting on a visit to the Karen front line in 1990, for example, the journalist Peter Mitchell stated that 'Radio intercepts were a valuable source of intelligence to the Karen, as they had broken the Burmese code some years earlier.'[104] Other observers too have remarked on the continuing capacity of various insurgent groups to intercept and read Burma Army communications, including those transmitted in code.[105]

Burma has long possessed a modest capability to produce and interpret overhead imagery intelligence (IMINT). After Independence, for example, the Burma Air Force could take aerial photographs from cameras fixed under its converted fighter and transport aircraft, and later the BAF acquired more stable platforms like the Beechcraft Model 65 Queen Air. The Cessna 550 Citation purchased by Ne Win as a VIP transport in 1982 has also been used for aerial survey work and could be used for military purposes if required. There is some evidence too that the BAF has employed its Fairchild Hiller FH-227 and Fokker F-27 Friendships for surveillance, and it is likely that these aircraft have been used to collect imagery of insurgent held areas. The SLORC seems to have used overhead imagery to monitor the activities of Thai logging firms granted concessions in 1989 to exploit Burmese teak reserves.[106] While no information on the subject is publicly available, the regime has probably taken steps in recent years to improve this capability, possibly with the assistance of friendly and technologically more advanced countries like China and Singapore. There has been speculation that the regime's intelligence sharing arrangements with the Chinese may include the provision of satellite imagery, but this cannot be confirmed.[107] For counter-insurgent operations in jungle or heavily wooded areas, the imagery provided by aircraft may be more suitable. In any case, high quality satellite imagery is now available from commercial sources, and it would appear that the *Tatmadaw* has already taken advantage of this development to build up its photographic coverage of the country.[108]

5.3 Intelligence and Security

Lacking any popular mandate, facing direct challenges from numerous insurgent groups and fearful of foreign espionage, the military regime in Rangoon soon came to rely heavily on its intelligence agencies for guidance and protection. The military intelligence apparatus, in particular, has developed enormous power and influence. Yet for all its strength and ability to delve into the heart of Burmese society, it has been guilty of a number of serious intelligence failures. In the mid-1960s, for example, the MIS failed to prevent the formation within the armed forces of allegedly communist anti-Ne Win cells.[109] In 1974 the DDSI failed to predict the upsurge of popular unrest which followed the return of Thant's remains from New York.[110] In 1983, the intelligence services failed to detect the entry into Burma of the three DPRK agents who planted a bomb at the Martyrs' Mausoleum in Rangoon. Even though Burma's military intelligence apparatus was considerably strengthened after the latter two incidents, it still badly misread the mood of the Burmese population in 1988, before large-scale protests against continued military rule erupted in the capital and other major population centres.

Following the massive internal unrest that year, surveillance of both the armed forces and civil population greatly increased. The regime was badly shaken by the size and extent of the pro-democracy demonstrations, and was particularly concerned that some members of all three armed Services marched with the demonstrators.[111] Even a few BSI officers reportedly joined the protests.[112] This concern grew even further after the 1990 general elections. The poll demonstrated that a large proportion of Burma's population, including many in the *Tatmadaw* itself, supported a return to democratic rule.[113] The fact that the regime permitted free and fair elections to be held at all, suggests that it had intelligence advice predicting a different outcome. More recently, considerable criticism has been levelled at Burma's intelligence agencies over their failure to prevent a campaign of terrorist bombings in Rangoon. Following a number of explosions in public places, like central Rangoon in December 1996, a parcel bomb was delivered to the home of Army Chief of Staff LTGEN Tin Oo. The parcel, which reportedly carried Japanese stamps, was opened by Tin Oo's daughter, who was killed in the resulting explosion.[114] The fact that a device of this kind could reach the home of a senior official, particularly in such a closely guarded community, clearly worried the regime and prompted a reassessment of its security measures.

One of the reasons why the DDSI/MIS and other Burmese intelligence agencies failed to predict or prevent events before 1988, was that they were subject to repeated purges of key personnel. Their considerable power and influence not only protected the Ne Win regime, but also constituted a potential threat to its existence. In particular, the Director of the MIS, and later the Director of Defence Services Intelligence, commanded considerable personal power, something that was always viewed with suspicion in Burma's highly charged political environment. As Robert Taylor has written, 'The head of military intelligence was always close to General Ne Win but often became so powerful as to be seen as a threat to his position'.[115] At different times in the 1960s, 1970s and again in the 1980s, internal crises within the regime resulted in the dismissal from office of the heads of military intelligence and their closest supporters. On each occasion, this effectively decapitated the country's intelligence apparatus and undermined its operational capabilities. It also encouraged a reluctance on the part of any one agency or agency head to be too bold, or to predict developments which might not be popular with the ruling hierarchy.

For example, during the 1960s there was a major shakeup of the MIS, after Ne Win accused it of disloyalty. Its Deputy Director, an Anglo-Burman named Kyaw Zwa Myint, apparently questioned the *Tatmadaw*'s new political role and tried to kill Ne Win.[116] After the 1974 worker and student riots, the popular Defence Minister and Armed Forces Chief of Staff, General Tin Oo, was forced to resign from his posts. In 1976 another purge was conducted, after 14 young military officers were arrested. They were tried for plotting to assassinate Ne Win and other senior military figures, including the Director General of the NIB, a Colonel also named Tin Oo.[117] Colonel (later Brigadier) Tin Oo (also known as 'MI' Tin Oo) had helped establish the MIS and reputedly 'served as Ne Win's "eyes and ears" in the military and the party'.[118] Defence Minister Tin Oo was charged with foreknowledge of the assassination plot and sent to prison. This was followed in 1977 by the dismissal or transfer of another group of senior officials, including a number of military intelligence officers known to be loyal to the ousted General.

In 1983 it was the turn of 'MI' Tin Oo, by then Joint General Secretary of the BSPP, to be dismissed from office, along with the Home and Religious Affairs Minister, Colonel Bo Ni. (Bo Ni was a protege of Tin Oo's and another former Chief of Intelligence.)[119] At the same time, a wholesale purge of the MIS took place, resulting in the removal of most officers appointed by 'MI' Tin Oo during his time as Director General of the NIB. Several former senior intelligence officers were also dismissed from their official positions. While Tin Oo was tried and convicted on charges of misappropriating government funds, and Bo Ni was convicted of corruption, most observers inside and outside Burma saw other reasons for their dismissal. According to Bertil Lintner,

> It was suggested at the time that the urbane MIS people had become too powerful for comfort and almost managed to establish a state within the state —

which threatened Ne Win's inner circle of hand-picked, less-than-intelligent yes-men.[120]

It is widely believed that Burma's failure to prevent the DPRK terrorist bombing in Rangoon later that year stemmed directly from these purges, and the 'entire collapse' of the country's key intelligence agency.[121]

These disruptions have clearly undermined the efficiency of Burma's intelligence apparatus, but other factors have contributed to its failures. For example, although the DDSI/MIS has been described as 'one of Asia's most efficient secret police forces', and has clearly amassed enormous amounts of information on particular Burmese organisations and personalities, its coverage seems to be much wider than it is deep.[122] Even with all the personnel it has at its command (including those of its sister agencies), it clearly cannot cover everything it would like. It has in effect set itself the target of monitoring the entire Burmese population, as well as everyone outside the country who may conceivably constitute a threat to the regime. This is an enormous task which would tax agencies much larger and better equipped than DDSI.

Also, the ability of the DDSI and MIS staff accurately to analyse all the information they obtain, is unclear. Over the years, the military regime has repeatedly demonstrated its deep-seated insecurity and its inability to manage criticism (both from within Burma and overseas) in a considered and rational fashion. Sometimes, the regime's fears seem to border on paranoia, as occurred in 1988 when the SLORC imagined that it was about to be invaded by the US. In such a climate, balanced and self-critical assessments are likely to be difficult. The intelligence agencies have been able to choose the best recruits, but political reliability has often been judged more important than intellectual qualities or a knowledge of the world outside Burma.[123] There will also be the problem, in such a closed society, of intelligence officers being reluctant to give their honest views, for fear of themselves falling under suspicion. In addition, the power and privileges enjoyed by the *Tatmadaw*, and the members of the country's intelligence agencies in particular, set them apart from the rest of the population. They clearly do not share the hardships, fears and aspirations of most Burmese. Even with their vast networks of informers, it seems difficult for the intelligence agencies accurately to gauge the popular mood and predict the behaviour of the average Burmese citizen.

The costs to Burma of this massive intelligence effort are impossible to calculate, but they must be considerable. Every country has legitimate intelligence requirements, but the regime's allocation of scarce resources (including precious foreign exchange) to the blanket surveillance of the entire population inevitably means that other critical areas of Burmese society, like education and health services, suffer the consequences. Leaving aside important human rights issues, serious questions must also be raised about the stability and ultimate survival of a system which depends to such an extent on its security apparatus. This is particularly the case, given the regime's obvious intelligence failures since the massive popular unrest in 1988, and the extent to which it feels obliged to monitor dissent within the armed forces themselves.

Notes

1. An earlier version of this chapter appeared as Andrew Selth, 'Burma's Intelligence Apparatus', *Intelligence and National Security*, Vol. 13, No. 4, Winter 1998, pp. 33-70. That article was drawn in turn from Andrew Selth, *Burma's Intelligence Apparatus*, Working Paper No. 308 (Strategic and Defence Studies Centre, Australian National University, Canberra, 1997).
2. Roberts, *Area Handbook for Burma*, p. 323.
3. The Special Investigation Department has sometimes been called the Special Intelligence Department.
4. Callahan, 'The Origins of Military Rule in Burma', p. 368.
5. Callahan, 'The Origins of Military Rule in Burma', pp. 387ff.
6. Interview, Canberra, May 1997.
7. Confidential cable dated 31 December 1978 from the US Embassy, Rangoon, to the Department of the Army, Washington DC, released to the author under the Freedom of Information (FOI) Act, case 594F-00, 28 February 2000.
8. *Burma and the Insurrections* and *Kuomintang Aggression Against Burma*, both released around this time, give an indication of both the nature and extent of the *Tatmadaw*'s intelligence activities.
9. This process began in 1949. Callahan, 'The Origins of Military Rule in Burma', pp. 409ff.
10. Harriet O'Brien, *Forgotten Land: A Rediscovery of Burma* (Michael Joseph, London, 1991), pp. 107-8.
11. *Ibid.*
12. *Ibid.* O'Brien states that this task was assigned to 'MI' Tin Oo, but he was only a junior officer at the time and did not become head of the MIS until 1972. A better candidate is COL Maung Lwin, the Director of the MIS when Ne Win seized power in 1962. See also Kin Oung, *Who Killed Aung San?*, pp. 81-2.
13. Kin Oung, *Who Killed Aung San?*, p. 81.
14. Tinker, *The Union of Burma*, p. 83 and p. 87. See also Mya Maung, *Totalitarianism in Burma: Prospects for Economic Development* (Paragon House, New York, 1992), p. 36.
15. Roberts, *Area Handbook for Burma*, p. 319.
16. Interview, Canberra, May 1997.
17. Kin Oung, *Who Killed Aung San?*, p. 81.
18. Lintner, *Outrage*, p. 63; and interview, Washington, February 2000. See also material provided under FOI request, case 594F-00, 28 February 2000.
19. See Mya Maung, *The Burma Road to Poverty* (Praeger, New York, 1991), p. 199; Mya Maung, *Totalitarianism in Burma*, p. 36; and Zaw Win, 'Heads roll as Burma purge nears end', *Sydney Morning Herald*, 19 June 1983.
20. Some scholars have called the NIB at this stage the National Intelligence Bureau. This is incorrect. See, for example, Bunge, *Burma*, p. 258.
21. Bunge, *Burma*, p. 258. See also Min Thu, 'Burmese intelligence revamped', *Bangkok Post*, 13 November 1983.
22. Tin Maung Maung Than, 'Burma in 1983: From Recovery to Growth?', *Southeast Asian Affairs 1984* (Institute of Southeast Asian Studies, Singapore, 1984), p. 118.
23. R.H. Taylor, 'The Military in Myanmar (Burma): What Scope for a New Role?', in Viberto Selochan (ed), *The Military, the State, and Development in Asia and the Pacific* (Westview Press, Boulder, 1991), p. 151, note 16.

24. Tin Maung Maung Than, 'Burma in 1983', p. 118.
25. *Ibid.*
26. Tin Maung Maung Than, 'Burma in 1983', pp. 118-19.
27. *Ibid.* See also Min Thu, 'Burmese intelligence revamped'.
28. Min Thu, 'Burmese intelligence revamped'. Details of these smaller agencies are given in Selth, *Burma's Intelligence Apparatus*, pp. 9-10.
29. John McBeth and M.C. Tun, 'Goodbye to the good life', *FEER*, 2 June 1983, p. 15.
30. Interviews, Bangkok, April 1995, and Canberra, October 1999.
31. For example, according to Bunge, the MIS also provided 'an information network devoted to such matters as taxes, customs duties and criminal investigation'. These particular functions were in fact exercised by other intelligence agencies. Their attribution to the MIS probably stems from the popular belief in Burma that all intelligence activities were carried out by the omnipresent 'MI'. Bunge, *Burma*, p. 259.
32. Min Thu, 'Burmese intelligence revamped'.
33. These names tend to be used inter-changeably, but cited more carefully can indicate the size and importance of particular units. Also, many reports in English simply cite MI units by number, without specifying their level of responsibility. The distinction between various levels in the DDSI/MIS structure, and the designation of particular units at each level, is more apparent to Burmese language speakers. Interviews, Sydney, October 1996; and Washington, February 2001. See also Bertil Lintner and Robert Karniol, 'Unrest swells the Burmese ranks', *JDW*, 13 June 1992, p. 1020; and Bunge, *Burma*, p. 258.
34. Amnesty International, *Myanmar: 'In The National Interest', Prisoners of conscience, torture, summary trials under martial law*, (Amnesty International, London, 1990), p. 28.
35. See, for example, *The Bomb Attack at the Martyrs' Mausoleum in Rangoon: Report on the findings by the Enquiry Committee and the measures taken by the Burmese Government* (Typescript in author's possession); and *Rangoon Justice: North Korean Terrorists on Trial* (Korean Overseas Information Service, Seoul, 1984).
36. Bertil Lintner, 'Myanmar's military intelligence', *International Defense Review*, Vol. 24, No. 1, 1991, p. 39. See also Lintner, *Outrage*, p. 66.
37. Personal communication, Bertil Lintner to the author, 7 November 1995. See also Tin Maung Maung Than, 'Burma in 1983', pp. 116-18.
38. Personal communication, Bertil Lintner to the author, 7 November 1995.
39. Material released to the author under FOI request, case 594F-00, 28 February 2000.
40. Min Thu, 'Burmese intelligence revamped'.
41. Interview, Sydney, October 1996. Amnesty International has claimed that the RMCs ran their own networks of informers, but this was more likely to have been the responsibility of MIS companies working within the Commands. See AI, *Myanmar: 'In The National Interest'*, p. 28.
42. Interview, Sydney, October 1996.
43. Interview, Canberra, May 1997.
44. AI, *Myanmar: 'In The National Interest'*, p. 28.
45. Aye Saung has described the atmosphere of fear and suspicion which prevailed on the Rangoon and Mandalay University campuses during the 1960s. Aye Saung, *Burman in the back row* (White Lotus, Bangkok, 1989), pp. 31-56.
46. Interview, Canberra, June 1997. See also Selth, *Death of a Hero*, p. 24.
47. See, for example, Lintner, *Burma in Revolt*, pp. 99ff; and John Prados, *Presidents' Secret Wars: CIA and Pentagon Covert Operations Since World War II* (William Morrow, New York, 1986), pp. 73ff. Also useful is David Wise and Thomas B. Ross, *The Invisible Government* (Jonathan Cape, London, 1964), pp. 129-35.
48. Kaznacheev, *Inside a Soviet Embassy*, pp. 179-202.

49. See, for example, Lintner, *The Rise and Fall of the Communist Party of Burma*, passim; and Nicholas Eftimiades, *Chinese Intelligence Operations* (Naval Institute Press, Annapolis, 1994), p. 76 and p. 99.

50. This capability existed at least as early as 1963. See Smith, *Burma: Insurgency and the Politics of Ethnicity*, p. 210.

51. During the 1970s, the author was told numerous stories by other diplomats in Rangoon about the rather amateurish efforts of the Burmese intelligence services to tap their telephones.

52. Interview, Sydney, October 1996. See also Selth, *Burma's Arms Procurement Programme*, p. 28.

53. Sometimes these antennae were used for other purposes. During the late 1960s, for example, the Soviet embassy in Rangoon was a key military intelligence listening post, collecting SIGINT about the Chinese and Vietnamese armed forces. See James Adams, *Sellout: Aldrich Ames, the Spy Who Broke the CIA* (Michael Joseph, London, 1995), p. 95.

54. Interview, Sydney, October 1996. The resources of the Burma Broadcasting Service were also used whenever necessary.

55. Evidence of the value of monitoring VOPB transmissions can be found in the *Yearbook on International Communist Affairs* (Hoover Institution Press, Stanford, annual). See also C.B. Smith, *The Burmese Communist Party in the 1980s* (Institute of Southeast Asian Studies, Singapore, 1984), pp. 100-11.

56. Interview, Sydney, October 1996.

57. Two years after his release from prison in 1966, Nu slipped out of Burma and began his own armed insurrection. See 'Nu said to set up base in Thailand', *New York Times*, 3 January 1971.

58. This equipment is on display at the Defence Services Museum in Rangoon. Personal observation, Rangoon, November 1996.

59. This practice seems to have been common among Burma's various insurgent groups. See, for example, Jake Border, 'Battle at Three Pagoda Pass: Burmese Attack Mon Army', *Soldier of Fortune*, August 1987, p. 77; Jonathan Falla, *True Love and Bartholomew: Rebels on the Burmese Border* (Cambridge University Press, Cambridge, 1991), p. 365; Lintner, *Land of Jade*, p. 199 and pp. 201-202; Mirante, *Burmese Looking Glass*, p. 268; and R.F. Staar (ed), *Yearbook on International Communist Affairs 1989: Parties and Revolutionary Movements* (Hoover Institution Press, Stanford, 1989), p. 172.

60. Personal communication, Martin Smith to the author, 9 November 1995.

61. The *Tatmadaw* was using coded Burmese language transmissions by 1951, but the Karens seem to have developed this capability even earlier. See Silverstein, *Burmese Politics*, p. 221; Smith, *Burma: Insurgency and the Politics of Ethnicity*, p. 86; and Falla, *True Love and Bartholomew*, p. 223.

62. See, for example, Border, 'Battle at Three Pagoda Pass', p. 77; and Andre and Louis Boucaud, *Burma's Golden Triangle: On the Trail of the Opium Warlords* (Asia 2000, Hong Kong, 1992), p. 74.

63. Personal communication, Martin Smith to the author, 9 November 1995. See also Falla, *True Love and Bartholomew*, p. 203.

64. Smith, *Burma: Insurgency and the Politics of Ethnicity*, p. 250.

65. Interview, Sydney, October 1996.

66. In this sense, the OSS duplicates the role of the Foreign Ministry's Myanmar Institute of Strategic and International Studies (MISIS), which was formed in 1992. MISIS has not been very active however and, while it draws on the resources of several official agencies, including the Ministry of Defence, it is essentially a Foreign Ministry creation. Interview, Rangoon, April 1995.

67. Interview, Sydney, October 1996. The DDSI position was elevated to full Colonel rank in 1988, and to Brigadier level a few years later.
68. Interview, Rangoon, December 1999.
69. Interview, Canberra, June 1997.
70. The MIS headquarters in Kone Myint Thaya, Mayagon Township, identified by AI in *Myanmar: 'In The National Interest'* (p. 29), was the former office of the President's Military Assistant. This position was abolished in 1983.
71. Interview, Canberra, October 1998.
72. Personal communication from Bangkok, 2 January 1996.
73. Lintner, 'Myanmar's military intelligence', p. 39. Also, personal communication, Lintner to the author, 7 November 1995.
74. See Amnesty International, *'No Law At All': Human rights violations under military rule* (Amnesty International, London, 1992), p. 13; Amnesty International, *Myanmar: Renewed repression* (Amnesty International, London, 1996), p. 11; AI, *Myanmar: 'In The National Interest'*, pp. 28ff; and interview, Canberra, May 1997.
75. Lintner and Karniol, 'Unrest swells the Burmese ranks', p. 1020. See also AI, *'No Law At All'*, p. 13.
76. Interview, Chiang Mai, November 1999. See also Maung Aung Myoe, *The Tatmadaw in Myanmar Since 1988*, p. 15.
77. AI, *Myanmar: Renewed repression*, p. 4. See also Lintner, 'Myanmar's military intelligence', p. 39.
78. See Selth, *Burma's Secret Military Partners*, for details of Burma's intelligence relationships with Singapore, Israel and Pakistan.
79. *Burma Communist Party's Conspiracy to take over State Power* (SLORC, Rangoon, 1989). See also *The Conspiracy of Treasonous Minions*.
80. For example, Order 1/90, promulgated in 1990, required that all households in the 42 townships of Rangoon Division register any visitors with the authorities. AI, *Myanmar: Renewed repression*, p. 4.
81. See, for example, 'Suu Kyi interview pulled from air', *Bangkok Post*, 30 May 1996; 'Slorc adamant it will never give up power', *The Nation*, 30 May 1996; and US State Department, *Burma: Country Report*.
82. See, for example, 'Report notes Burmese intelligence operations', *Naeo Na* (in Thai), 21 July 1994, FBIS-EAS-94-141, 22 July 1994, pp. 49-50.
83. Lintner, *Outrage*, p. 63.
84. See, for example, US State Department, *Burma: Country Report*; AI, *Myanmar: 'In The National Interest'*, p. 28; and Amnesty International, *Myanmar: The Institution of Torture* (Amnesty International, London, 2000). The latter report lists prisons and detention centres in Burma, including a large number of MIS units.
85. AI, *Myanmar: 'No law at all'*, p. 13; AI, *Myanmar: 'In The National Interest'*, p. 29; and AI, *Myanmar: The Institution of Torture*, p. 2.
86. See, for example, AI, *Myanmar: 'In The National Interest'*, p. 28.
87. AI, *Myanmar: 'In The National Interest'*, p. 19.
88. Interview, Sydney, October 1996.
89. This 285-page book reproduced the texts of almost all the news broadcasts made by the BBC and VOA in August 1988 about the political unrest then sweeping Burma. *Skyful of Lies: B.B.C., V.O.A.: Their Broadcasts and Rebuttals to Disinformation* (SLORC, Rangoon, 1988).
90. See, for example, Desmond Ball, 'Signals Intelligence in China', *Jane's Intelligence Review*, Vol. 7, No. 8, August 1995, p. 367.
91. Robert Karniol, 'Chinese puzzle over Burma's SIGINT base', *JDW*, 29 January 1994, p. 14.

92. Edmond Dantes, 'An In-depth look at the Asia-Pacific Air Forces and Future Procurement', *Asian Defence Journal*, January 1993, p. 28.
93. See Lintner, 'Enter the Dragon', p. 23; and Lintner, 'Arms for Eyes', p. 26.
94. Robert Karniol, 'Myanmar boosts naval power with frigates', *JDW*, 20 August 1993, p. 1.
95. Lintner, 'Enter the Dragon', p. 23; and 'Snooping Around', *FEER*, 4 August 1994, p. 2.
96. Lintner, 'Myanmar's Chinese connection', p. 24; Lintner, 'Enter the Dragon', p. 23; and Linter, 'Arms for Eyes', p. 26. One defence journal has stated that Chinese naval advisers have already been seen on Kadan (or King) Island, but this has not been confirmed. See 'Air Forces Survey - Myanmar', p. 34; and 'Rangoon stalls PRC on request to lease island for port', *Nihon Keizai Shimbun* (in Japanese), 20 January 1995.
97. 'Sino-Burmese Pact', *FEER*, 30 January 1997, p. 12. See also Rowan Callick, 'China and Burma strengthen ties with military agreement', *Australian Financial Review*, 24 January 1997.
98. See, for example, Khin Nyunt, 'How Some Western Powers Have Been Aiding and Abetting Terrorism'.
99. The best source on this subject is Ball, *Burma's Military Secrets*.
100. 'Looking Hard', *FEER*, 24 April 1997, p. 12.
101. *Ibid*.
102. *New Light of Myanmar*, 29 January-5 March 1995. The series was purportedly written by 'A Resident of Kayin State'. These (and some additional) articles were subsequently edited and published as *Whither KNU?* (News and Periodicals Enterprise, Rangoon, 1995). See also Ball, *Signals Intelligence in the Post-Cold War Era*, p. 88; and Kurt Hanson, 'Calamity at Kawmura', *Soldier of Fortune*, Vol. 20, No. 9, September 1995, p. 72.
103. *Whither KNU?*, p. 41.
104. Peter Mitchell, 'Karens fight to survive', *Asia-Pacific Defence Reporter*, Vol. 17, No. 4, October 1990, p. 15.
105. Personal communication, Martin Smith to author, 9 November 1995. See also Gehan Wijeyewardene, 'Burma Update', *ANU Reporter*, 10 June 1992, p. 6; Border, 'Battle at Three Pagodas Pass', p. 77; and Mirante, *Burmese Looking Glass*, p. 238.
106. See, for example, Falla, *True Love and Bartholomew*, p. 357.
107. 'Sino-Burmese Pact', p. 12.
108. Personal observation, Rangoon, December 1999. See also, for example, 'Spy satellites: the next leap forward: Exploiting commercial satellite technology', *International Defence Review*, January 1997, pp. 26-32.
109. Taylor, *The State in Burma*, p. 369.
110. Selth, *Death of a Hero*, p. 24.
111. Lintner, 'Backdown or bloodbath', p. 14; and William Stewart, 'Now a Coup', *Time*, 26 September 1988, p. 14.
112. Personal communication, Bertil Lintner to the author, 7 November 1995.
113. Lintner, 'Myanmar's military intelligence', p. 39.
114. See, for example, Stephen Brookes, 'Burma Parcel Bomb Plot', *Asia Times*, 9 April 1997. Details of the incident were published in 'Is It a Non-Violent Method', *Kyemon* (in Burmese), 6 May 1997.
115. Taylor, 'The Military in Myanmar (Burma)', p. 145.
116. Interview, Canberra, March 1997. See also Taylor, *The State in Burma*, p. 369.
117. 'Burma Reports an Officer Plot To Kill Ne Win and Seize Rule', *New York Times*, 21 July 1976.
118. Josef Silverstein, 'Burma in 1981: The Changing of the Guardians Begins', *Asian Survey*, Vol. 22, No. 2, February 1982, p. 182.

119. Tin Maung Maung Than, 'Burma in 1983', pp. 116-7. See also Lintner, *Outrage*, pp. 65-6.
120. Lintner, *Outrage*, p. 65. See also Rodney Tasker, 'The Power Game', *FEER*, 7 July 1983, p. 31.
121. The description is Dr. Maung Maung's, *The 1988 Uprising in Burma*, p. 183. Also, interview, Seoul, April 2001.
122. Lintner, *Outrage*, p. 63. See also Lintner, 'Myanmar's military intelligence', p. 39; and O'Brien, *Forgotten Land*, pp. 107-8.
123. See, for example, the material provided under FOI request 594F-00, 28 February 2000.

6

The Economic Dimension

The adage that armies travel on their bellies means in practice that military forces somehow reflect the economy which sustains them. The problem is to know the economy and, more important, to know the specifics of the 'somehow.' — Angelo Codevilla, *Informing Statecraft* (1972)

Burma's armed forces have always claimed a large share of the country's national budget, but the creation of the SLORC marked a significant turning point.[1]

Before 1988, the civil war, an invasion by Nationalist Chinese forces, and challenges to internal stability from ethnic, ideological and 'economic' insurgents, all helped justify sizeable annual funding allocations. The defence budget, however, was always limited by Burma's weak economy and the government's determination to resist offers of foreign assistance. Similarly, Burma's attempts during this early period to develop a domestic defence industry were subject to severe economic constraints, in particular a shortage of foreign exchange. Partly for these reasons, the *Tatmadaw* sought to create a separate network of private commercial enterprises that would ensure a regular supply of basic commodities at reduced prices, and free the armed forces from the demands and strictures of the annual budgetary process. It was only the advent of the socialist system in 1962 which prevented this from occurring.

Since 1988, purely economic factors appear to have played much less part in the regime's military expansion and modernisation program. Despite continuing budgetary problems and pressing demands for government assistance from other sectors of Burmese society, annual defence expenditure has grown dramatically, arms imports have significantly increased and a much greater effort has been made to develop indigenous arms industries. At the same time, the *Tatmadaw* has consolidated and expanded its independent economic base, to the extent that it is now the most important element of the national economy.

6.1 Burma's Defence Expenditure

Any estimation of the actual level of Burma's annual defence expenditure is a very risky exercise.[2] The term 'defence spending', for example, is nowhere clearly defined by the military regime and funds for defence-related activities are scattered throughout the budget under several different headings. Some defence disbursements have been deliberately hidden in the national accounts, while others have simply not been declared.[3] Nor is it always clear what methods of calculation or which exchange rates have been used by the regime in arriving at certain official figures. It is unlikely, for example, that full account is taken of the ubiquitous black market, and the budget fails fully to reflect such transactions as 'gifts' from other countries, barter deals and sales at special 'friendship prices'. In addition, Burma's declared annual estimates for defence (including supplementary budget allocations announced during the course of the financial year) do not necessarily reflect the final level of admitted expenditure. The picture is further confused by the *Tatmadaw*'s privileged position within the national economy, and its control of a wide range of industrial, commercial and financial enterprises (most quite unrelated to defence matters) which are used to support off-budget expenditures.[4]

As a result of difficulties like these, and the different accounting methods used by outside agencies for calculating their own statistics, published estimates of Burma's annual defence expenditure vary significantly between sources. Using figures provided by the Stockholm International Peace Research Institute (SIPRI) as a guide, however, it would appear that, before 1988, Burma's defence spending faltered a number of times, but overall grew steadily. It rose rapidly during the civil war in the 1950s, slowed down during the 1960s and early 1970s, then picked up, only to slow down again in the mid-1980s. According to SIPRI, defence expenditure (in current price terms) declined in only ten of the 40 years between Independence in 1948 and the creation of the SLORC — 1955, 1961, 1965, 1966, 1967, 1972, 1974, 1983, 1986 and 1987. While these broad trends are confirmed by the US Arms Control and Disarmament Agency (ACDA), the latter's figures sometimes contradict those given by SIPRI. For example, ACDA cites a decline in Burma's defence spending in 1982. It also registers an increase in 1987, and a decrease in 1988. SIPRI claims the opposite. Official Burmese government figures provided by the International Monetary Fund (IMF) and estimates made by the IISS differ yet again.[5]

As Robert Taylor has noted, the increases in the Burmese defence budget after the civil war were probably consistent with inflation and the general rise in central government expenditure (CGE), but the declines are more difficult to explain. The reduction in defence spending in 1955 may have been a reflection of the collapse in international rice prices after the boom of the Korean War years. The decline in 1961 was probably a result of the return to power of Nu's civilian administration after 14 months of military 'caretaker' government. The falls in defence expenditure in the mid-1960s and early 1970s probably stemmed from Burma's lack of economic growth at those times.[6] Similarly, the decline in defence expenditures during the mid-1980s seems to have been a direct result of the economic crisis which gripped Burma during that period, which in turn contributed to the domestic turmoil of 1988.[7]

Figure 10: Burma's Defence Expenditure, 1978-1987. By Year (Current US$ million).[8]

	1978	1979	1980	1981
US$m	157	184	211	253
% of GNP	3.5	3.6	3.5	3.6
% of CGE	23.1	24.4	21.9	22.3
	1982	1983	1984	1985
US$m	256	266	277	304
% of GNP	3.2	3.1	3.0	3.1
% of CGE	19.3	19.9	19.1	19.6
	1986	1987		
US$m	320	334		
% of GNP	3.0	3.1		
% of CGE	18.6	22.3		

In the ten years before the SLORC's takeover, Burma devoted the largest proportion of its CGE to the armed forces, of all the non-communist Asian countries.[9] In absolute terms, however, Burma's defence budget was quite low, amounting to less than US$3 billion for the period. It was also low compared with most other regional countries. Between 1977 and 1987, for example, 'Indonesia devoted to its military more than six times the financial resources committed to the military in Burma during the same period'.[10] Even the Philippines, with one of lowest defence expenditures of any Southeast Asian country, committed more than twice the financial resources to its armed forces than did Burma.[11] At least in the beginning, countries like Indonesia and the Philippines also had a much higher debt burden to carry than Burma, which shunned commitments to international financial institutions for fear of compromising its neutrality and losing its independence of action. The price of this policy, however, was a heavy burden on the domestic economy. Burma's self-reliant posture also placed severe constraints on the *Tatmadaw*'s ability to acquire modern arms and equipment.

Before 1988, Burma's arms imports were very modest. It received some material assistance from the UK, under the 1947 Let Ya-Freeman Agreement. Indeed, the UK initially attempted to establish itself virtually as Burma's sole supplier of arms and military equipment.[12] If this was ever a serious aim, it was never likely to be realised as Burma soon sought additional arms from the US and India. The Nu Government, however, was determined to adopt a neutral foreign policy. It declined further US military aid in 1951, largely because of the Mutual Defence Assistance Plan's (MDAP) changed eligibility requirements, and terminated its defence agreement with the UK in 1954.[13] In the years that followed, Burma remained reluctant to accept military assistance for fear of offending China, or of being drawn into the strategic competition between the superpowers. While sometimes prepared to accept very favourable concessionary terms, it insisted on paying for all its imports of arms and military equipment (mainly from the UK and US) until 1968, when deteriorating relations with China (including increased Chinese aid to the CPB) prompted the Ne Win regime to accept renewed offers of US aid.[14] Burma also sought to diversify the sources of its foreign weapons and military equipment, turning to 'non-aligned' countries like Israel, Yugoslavia and Sweden, while balancing its purchases from the US and UK with Soviet, German, French, Italian, Swiss, Australian and Canadian arms.

Figure 11: Arms Transfers to Burma, 1973-1987. By Major Supplier (Current US$ million).[15]

West Germany	100
United States	20
United Kingdom	10
France	5
Italy	5
Others	100
TOTAL	240

From 1950 until 1969 Burma's major arms imports averaged less than US$4 million a year.[16] These were mainly transfers of counterinsurgency equipment and ammunition, although in the mid-1950s Burma received a substantial 'gift' of artillery and infantry weapons from Yugoslavia. Between 1970 and 1988 the average expenditure on foreign arms rose to about US$18 million a year, but economic problems (and the consequent shortage of foreign exchange) continued to restrict the *Tatmadaw*'s purchases from abroad.[17] Higher levels of rice exports in the early 1970s (assisted by the introduction of new high yield varieties and double-cropping) brought some economic relief to the Burmese government, but the demands on the current account during the same period were increased by several large scale military operations against communist and other insurgent groups. Little foreign exchange was left over for capital equipment purchases. Increases in the size of the army, particularly during the late 1970s and early 1980s, also helped to ensure that the bulk of Burma's annual defence allocation was spent on manpower and operations, rather than on imported weapons and new equipment.[18]

Figure 12: Burma's Arms Imports, 1973-1987. By Year (Current US$ million).[19]

	1973	1974	1975	1976	1977
US$m	5	5	5	0	0
	1978	1979	1980	1981	1982
US$m	5	30	20	20	60
	1983	1984	1985	1986	1987
US$m	30	30	50	20	20

The effect of the regime's military expansion and modernisation program on Burma's national accounts after 1988 is very difficult to estimate with any accuracy. It is clear, however, that the SLORC and SPDC have devoted enormous resources to increasing the country's order of battle and creating more self-sufficient defence industries. As the US Embassy in Rangoon noted in 1996, 'Defense appears to be one of Burma's fastest growing sectors of Burma's economy' (sic).[20]

The ACDA calculated that Burma's defence expenditure in 1988 was about 3% of gross national product (GNP) or just under 24% of CGE.[21] Within a year, however, many Burma scholars were stating that the real level of defence spending was at least double that figure. Josef Silverstein, for example, estimated in 1989 that 50% of the official Burmese budget was devoted to purely military expenditures.[22] By 1993 Burma's estimated annual defence expenditure had risen to US$1520 million. According to the ACDA, this constituted an increase to 4.0% of GNP or 39.1% of CGE.[23] Even allowing for the pitfalls inherent in making such estimates, it is likely that these figures were still well below the actual level of Burma's defence expenditure. The SLORC itself admitted to spending 30% of Burma's 1991-92 annual budget on 'defence'. At the same time, it announced that such spending would rise to 35% during the 1992-93 financial year.[24] Some well informed observers have put the real level of the SLORC's purely military spending that year as high as 60% of the national budget.[25] The ACDA has estimated that, by 1995, Burma was spending 37.5% of its CGE on defence.

Figure 13: Burma's Defence Expenditure, 1988-1995.
By Year (Current US$ million).[26]

	1988	1989	1990	1991
US$m	779	993	1093	1357
% of GNP	2.9	3.5	3.6	4.3
% of CGE	23.7	24.7	22.3	29.4
	1992	1993	1994	1995
US$m	1650	1520	1698	1833
% of GNP	3.7	4.0	4.1	3.9
% of CGE	32.9	39.1	36.7	37.5

Burma's defence spending between 1995 and 2000 is equally difficult to determine. During this period the ACDA was integrated into the State Department to create the Bureau of Verification and Compliance (BVC), and a new method of calculating economic statistics seems to have been adopted. This resulted in some remarkable new figures which claim that between 1991 and 1996 Burma was consistently spending more than 75%, and sometimes up to 88%, of CGE on defence.[27] The discrepancy with figures published earlier by the ACDA was not explained. BVC figures for the 1996-2000 period have not yet been published.

Other available statistics confirm that, over the past five years, Burma's defence spending has remained very high. Similar confusion exists, however, over the actual levels of expenditure and even some of the broad trends. While their figures differ, both the Australian Defence Intelligence Organisation (DIO) and SIPRI have published tables showing a steady upward trend in local currency disbursements to defence since 1995, with a major increase occurring in 1999.[28] At the time, the Burmese leadership justified this increase by arguing that 'the equipment left after its long civil war is too old for the maintenance of its national security'.[29] Both DIO and SIPRI have pointed out, however, that in real terms Burma's annual defence expenditure fluctuated considerably during this period. According to DIO, real spending actually declined every year since 1990, except in 1994 and 1995. SIPRI agrees that real spending on defence declined in 1996, 1997 and 1998, but claims that it increased by 11% in real terms in 1999.[30]

There are also differences between the two agencies over the level of defence spending as a proportion of CGE and GDP. DIO has stated that defence expenditure has steadily declined as a percentage of Burma's GDP (to 1.3%) but, despite some fluctuations, has grown significantly as a percentage of CGE, to a level of almost 45% in 1999.[31] For its part, the latest SIPRI Yearbook has stated that

> While military spending in Myanmar constitutes a fairly typical share of GDP (about 3 per cent), its share in government expenditure is high (about 30 per cent), in particular in comparison with expenditure on education and health, which were allocated 10 and 2.5 per cent, respectively, for FY 1998/99.[32]

The latest issue of *The Military Balance* uses the same official Burmese figures as DIO. Using slightly different dollar values, it too shows a slight drop in defence spending from 1998 to 1999.[33]

All these figures, however, must be considered indicative only. Among other things, they do not take into account what the US Embassy in Rangoon has called 'hidden subsidies to the Ministry of Defence from other parts of the public sector, in the form of costless or below-cost provision of goods and services'.[34] For example, the *Tatmadaw* receives but does not pay for about one sixth of Burma's centrally generated electricity. The Ministry of Defence also purchases large amounts of fuels from the state petrochemical monopoly, the Myanmar Petroleum Products Enterprise (MPPE), at official prices. These are well below the market level.[35] In 1994/95, these privileges alone were reportedly equivalent to at least four billion kyats, or approximately 28% of the SLORC's declared unadjusted defence disbursements for that financial year.[36] There are other hidden subsidies enjoyed by the armed forces. An increasing share of the government's diminishing health budget, for example, seems to be devoted to the provision of health services to military personnel and their families. The state rice procurement agency, Myanmar Agricultural Produce Trading (MAPT) has increased the quota of paddy which must be sold to the government, for resale at cost price to the *Tatmadaw*. This extra paddy is then sold by regional military commanders at market prices to supplement their own incomes and the salaries of their troops.[37] None of these transactions appear in official budget figures.

In addition, since 1997 the regime, 'intent upon continuing its military buildup despite mounting financial problems', ordered the 12 Regional Commanders to meet their basic logistical needs locally, rather than rely on the central supply system.[38] This has caused considerable hardship for service personnel and local villagers alike. For example, many Burmese servicemen are now obliged to grow most of their own food. Under the 'five kinds, five plants' program, soldiers have to grow five plants each of five vegetables, as a way of supplementing other rations.[39] This practice is sometimes not possible, or the crops are insufficient to meet the basic needs of the troops. In these circumstances, there is an increased likelihood of the armed forces being forced to live off the land, appropriating food and other supplies from the local population as required.[40] Such practices are usually invisible to the government's accountants.

Similarly, there is no way of calculating the unofficial receipts which flow from the armed forces' positions of power, or their privileged access to goods and services throughout the country. As the US Embassy has stated,

> The visible consumption and investments of many officers and their immediate relatives suggest personal incomes greatly in excess of official wages and benefits, and some private rent-seeking by military personnel appears to be institutionalized and openly tolerated. For example, much of the gasoline openly sold at the market price...throughout Burma is widely and credibly alleged to be supplied by military officers, who obtain it from MPPE at a much lower official price.[41]

There have also been suggestions that some senior members of the *Tatmadaw* routinely sell promotions to the highest bidders among their subordinates.[42] The income from these and other such practices effectively supplements formal on-budget military personnel expenditures, but are never likely to be accounted for in published statistics.

Another area where Burma's official budget figures are misleading is that covering capital expenditure. In particular, there is considerable confusion surrounding the amount of defence expenditures which are hard currency denominated. As Robert Taylor has pointed out, by rejecting external military aid before 1988 the Rangoon regime placed itself at the mercy of internal economic conditions.[43] Since then, however, the regime has been much less reluctant to accept foreign assistance or to draw on Burma's own hard currency earnings to obtain modern weapons. In 1992-93, for example, the UNDP estimated that arms and military equipment accounted for more than one fifth of Burma's total imports.[44] In more recent years, the Ministry of Defence has clearly accounted for a large proportion of the central government's consumption of imported goods and services, not only in the form of arms, but also as technical advice, and equipment and raw materials for its arms factories.[45] Unfortunately, the level of this spending may never become known. For example, in 1997 Bertil Lintner estimated that 'Burma spends $200 million annually on foreign-currency-denominated defence expenditure —

mainly imports of military hardware from China — which is not recorded in official reports.'[46] As the US Embassy's 1996 Report dryly states, figures for defence expenditure 'cannot be inferred with confidence from the [Government of Burma's balance of payment] accounts, in which military imports and related financial inflows are either omitted or not explicitly identified as such'.[47]

Many of the actual imports, however, have been identified.[48] The regime has significantly compromised the country's professed neutrality in international affairs and actively encouraged special defence relationships with a number of regional countries. In particular, Burma has negotiated several major arms deals with China, which has assumed a place as its closest and most generous ally. In October 1989, for example, a delegation of 24 *Tatmadaw* officials, led by the then Army Commander-in-Chief LTGEN Than Shwe, travelled to China.[49] An arms deal valued at about US$1.4 billion was subsequently arranged.[50] Signed in mid-1990, it covered the delivery to Burma of fighter aircraft and naval patrol boats, tanks and armoured personnel carriers, field and anti-aircraft artillery, small arms and ammunition.[51] Other orders followed. In November 1994, after the visit to China of a delegation led by Burma Army Chief of Staff LTGEN Tin Oo, another package was negotiated which reportedly included an estimated US$400 million worth of helicopters, artillery pieces, armoured vehicles, naval gunboats, military parachutes and small arms.[52] In October 1996, during a visit to China by Army Commander GEN Maung Aye, a wide-ranging military cooperation agreement was negotiated. This agreement reportedly included 'fiscal assistance' to the Rangoon regime, probably in the form of more soft loans and relaxed terms for the payment of earlier arms shipments. It may have also included new orders of arms and equipment at friendship prices.[53] There are likely to have been other agreements between Rangoon and Beijing which have yet to become public knowledge.

Figure 14: Arms Transfers to Burma, 1987-1997.
By Major Supplier (current US$ million).[54]

United States	5
China	1160
Germany	25
Other Western Europe	55
Eastern Europe	60
Other East Asia	35
Others	40
TOTAL	1380

Over the past 12 years, the *Tatmadaw*'s Directorate of Procurement has placed orders for arms and military equipment with a number of other countries. It has purchased ground attack aircraft and patrol boats from Yugoslavia; assault and transport helicopters from Poland; combat helicopters from Russia; mortars and ammunition from Portugal; air defence weapons, small arms and ammunition from Pakistan and Singapore; artillery and small arms from Israel and the DPRK, and ammunition from Vietnam. There have also been reports that other arms deals have been concluded, or at the least were seriously considered, with agencies in Czechoslovakia, Bulgaria, South Africa, the ROK, Belgium and Chile.[55] The Rangoon regime has been anxious for the US to lift its arms embargo against Burma, presumably to obtain ammunition and spare parts for the *Tatmadaw*'s American arms and equipment. So far, these attempts have been unsuccessful, but the regime seems to have obtained US materiel from other suppliers, like Singapore and Vietnam.[56]

Claims of arms deals and other kinds of military assistance to the *Tatmadaw*, however, are difficult to verify. Few can be confirmed from independent sources. Most have been denied by both the Rangoon regime and spokesmen for the countries concerned. Singapore, Pakistan and Israel, for example, have all taken pains to conceal their substantial defence ties with the SLORC and SPDC.[57] While most reports are plausible, some (like claims of Soviet assistance to Burma in 1988) are much less so.[58] The arms deals with China, Russia and Pakistan were negotiated directly between the SLORC and relevant government agencies. Most of the other sales seem to have been arranged through private arms brokers in countries like Singapore, Thailand, Israel, Belgium, Sweden and the UK, with the munitions usually trans-shipped to Burma through entrepot ports like Singapore.[59] The North Korean artillery and ammunition deals were probably struck with the help of Thai, Singaporean or even Chinese intermediaries. It is possible that some of the countries providing these weapons and ammunition supplies did not even know that their final destination was to be Burma. Portugal's government seemed to be genuinely embarrassed by the disclosure in 1992 that a Portuguese company had sold arms to the SLORC in violation of a European Union (EU) embargo.[60] Similar claims have been made with regard to a large shipment of mortar ammunition from Vietnam in early 2001.[61]

Figure 15: Burma's Arms Imports, 1988-1997.
By Year (current US$ million).[62]

	1988	1989	1990	1991	1992
US$m	20	20	110	400	150
	1993	1994	1995	1996	1997
US$m	130	100	140	80	280

Published figures for conventional arms transfers to Burma usually reflect a substantial increase in imports in the first few years after the SLORC took over government, but suggest a decline in the early to mid-1990s before sales returned to higher levels. Once again, however, caution needs to be exercised in interpreting such statistics. While the regime's immediate needs would have been satisfied by its earlier orders, less emphasis is now being given to the purchase of finished military goods, in favour of dual-use capital goods, raw materials and intermediate goods used in the domestic manufacture of weapons and military equipment. It is unlikely that all imports such as these are detected and recorded by agencies like the ACDA - hence the apparent drop in defence-related imports in recent years.[63] The Rangoon regime has also been able to obtain or convert some items of non-military equipment for military use. Poland and Japan, for example, have provided Burma with a large number of four-wheel drive and heavy duty vehicles which seem to have found their way into the *Tatmadaw*'s motor pools.[64]

As noted above, the sources of funds for these transactions are very difficult to identify. In 1988, after Burma suffered the withdrawal of most development assistance and international finance, the SLORC faced a serious shortage of foreign exchange. By overturning the socialist economic policies of decades, however, the regime was able to draw on pre-contract bonuses and signature fees paid by foreign companies allowed unprecedented access to Burma's rich, and largely untapped, natural resources. These payments often amounted to over US$5 million each.[65] The regime also took full advantage of a range of grants, soft loans, special 'friendship' deals, barter arrangements and profits from the sale of overseas property.[66] The costs of two early arms consignments from Singapore, for example, appear to have been covered by the sale of logging and fishing concessions, and there have been reports that Burma paid for at least one third of its first Chinese arms deal with rice and timber.[67] The sale of the Burmese embassy property in Tokyo in 1989 netted the SLORC a windfall that financial year of more than US$300 million. In 1999 the SPDC used rice to pay for artillery from the DPRK.[68]

There have also been repeated accusations that the Rangoon regime has drawn heavily on funds generated from the illicit production and sale of narcotics. In early 1991, for example, Burma made a US$400 million cash down payment for Chinese arms through a Singapore bank. Yet no change was registered in Burma's known foreign exchange reserves, either before or after the sale.[69] In more recent years, recognised narcotics traffickers like Lo Hsing-han, Khun Sa and Lin Ming-xian (also known as Sai Lin) have openly formed alliances with senior regime figures and invested heavily in legitimate businesses in Burma, like hotels and bus lines. Bertil Lintner believes that 'this has resulted in a massive influx of drug money into the mainstream economy'.[70] The US government agrees. According to the State Department's International Narcotics Control Strategy Report for 1997, 'There is reason to believe that money laundering in Burma and the return of narcotics profits laundered elsewhere is a significant factor in the overall Burmese economy.'[71] The US government later estimated that Burma receives between US$700 million and $1 billion in foreign currency from heroin exports annually, or about the same as the total of all other exports.[72] It can be assumed that these funds have been drawn upon heavily by the regime to help pay for imports. Desmond Ball has gone further and stated that 'as much as US$1 billion worth of Chinese weapons, vehicles and other pieces of defence equipment has probably been acquired in direct drugs-for-arms deals with PLA officers in Yunnan'.[73]

Thus, statistics published by bodies like SIPRI, the ACDA, the IMF, DIO and the IISS are useful in indicating broad trends and orders of magnitude, but the actual cost to Burma of all its new arms, equipment and other military related imports is almost impossible to determine. Some published figures are clearly too low, while other estimates seem to be greatly exaggerated. Attempts to resolve this issue are further complicated by the Rangoon regime's program to expand the size and scope of the country's domestic defence industries.

6.2 Burma's Defence Industries

Burma's attempts to develop its own arms industries began in the early 1950s, when a factory was built to produce small arms ammunition and copies of the Italian 9mm TZ45 submachine gun (known in Burma as the BA52 or 'Ne Win Sten'). First produced in late 1944, production of the gun in Italy ceased at the end of the Second World War. When the design was offered for sale on the world market soon afterwards, the Nu Government purchased the machinery to manufacture a slightly modified version of the weapon at the Burma Army Ordnance Workshop near Inya Lake in Rangoon. At the same time, one of the Italian designers of the TZ45 went to Burma to oversee the construction of the factory and installation of the machinery. Production began as soon as the plant was completed, and by 1953 the BA52 was the standard submachine gun of the Burmese armed forces.[74]

The Burmese arms industry was given a major boost in 1956, when the state-owned West German company Fritz Werner GmbH agreed to build a factory in Rangoon with Heckler and Koch to produce *Gewehr* 3 (G3) automatic rifles and related 7.62mm ammunition.[75] Finance for the Burmese factory was provided on favourable terms by the FRG government. Reflecting a decision by the Ne Win regime to move Burma's defence industries to more secure sites, a second factory was later built in the 1960s near Prome (Pye) in Lower Burma to manufacture 7.62mm and 9mm small arms ammunition. A third was built to make explosives for both military and civilian use. More arms manufacturing facilities were built in the 1970s, including a plant to produce mortars and grenade launchers. All appear to have been constructed by Fritz Werner, some with the help of engineers from the *Gesellschaft fuer Technische Zusammenarbeit* (GTZ), the FRG's official Agency for Technical Cooperation.[76] In the early 1980s Fritz Werner also built the Burmese a trinitrotoluene (TNT) high explosives filling plant.[77] A number of German experts were based at Padaung to provide technical advice and help maintain these facilities.

In 1985, Myanma Fritz Werner Industries Co. Ltd. became the first foreign company legally to invest in Burma since the 1962 coup, when it entered into a joint venture arrangement with Burma's state-owned Heavy Industries Corporation (*Akyisar Sethmu Loat Ngun*, known by its Burmese initials as *Ka Sa La*).[78] The announced aim of this joint venture was to 'undertake development, production and assembly of machinery, equipment and accessories for industrial plants in Burma'.[79] As Martin Smith has noted, however, 'machinery' is 'a recurring euphemism in Burma for military equipment' and there have been several suggestions over the past 15 years that this joint venture was directly related to Burma's defence industrial program.[80]

For example, Mya Maung has stated that

> This venture was supposedly formed to develop heavy industries under the civilian Heavy Industries Corporation, *Ka Sa La*, but the Burmese people and foreign diplomats knew that the real effort was to construct army supply and weapon factories.[81]

This claim has been vigorously denied by Fritz Werner Industries, which has stressed that the (then) German government-owned company was founded 'to do business in the non-military field'.[82]

Known as *Ka Pa Sa* factories (after the initials of *Karkweye Pyitsu Setyoun*, the Burmese name for the Directorate of Defence Industries), Burma's arms factories are under the direct control of the Ministry of Defence, and are funded as part of the central government budget. There are twelve distinct 'industries', that make a wide range of military and consumer products. By far the largest of these 'industries' are those which make weapons, transport and tools for the armed forces.[83] In addition to *Ka Pa Sa* No. 1 near Inya Lake, there are now three other major *Ka Pa Sa* weapons and ammunition factories in the Rangoon-Mingaladon area. The largest weapons factory in Burma is reportedly at Sindell (Sinde, or Sintai), just south of Prome. There are also ammunition factories at Htonebo (Tonbo), Padaung and Nyaung Chidauk (Nyaung chi-dauk), all of which come within the broad confines of a large and well-guarded defence industrial complex situated on the western bank of the Irrawaddy River near Prome. Another complex of defence factories is located at Malun, west of the Irrawaddy River near Magwe. There are also ammunition and weapons factories at Inndaing (Intaing) in the Pegu District, and at Chauk. There may be others near Mandalay and Meiktila.[84]

Before 1988 these factories could produce automatic rifles and light machine guns, grenade launchers, light mortars, rifle and hand grenades, landmines, mortar bombs and ammunition for various kinds of small arms. Many of their products, however, depended on imported raw materials. Also, the *Tatmadaw* still relied on foreign firms for much of its heavy arms ammunition, support equipment and machine spare parts. The BAF and BN in particular were heavily dependent on logistics and technical support from overseas. Yet in September that year the SLORC suddenly faced a serious disruption to its military supplies, as influential members of the international community, including Burma's traditional arms suppliers, imposed sanctions against the Rangoon regime. For example, the US reportedly stopped a scheduled delivery of ammunition for the *Tatmadaw*'s old .30 calibre M1 and M2 carbines, and its 40mm M79 grenade launchers.[85] Even assistance from the FRG was suspended, after pointed questions were asked in the *Bundestag* about Fritz Werner's long involvement with Burma's arms industries, and the government of Helmut Kohl acceded to public pressure to suspend bilateral aid.[86] In July 1991 an embargo was imposed by the EU.[87] This was followed by a resolution in the European Parliament in April 1992 that all member states who were also members of the UNSC should propose a mandatory embargo against Burma's new military government. Without China's support any such resolution was bound to fail, and was never put forward. Since then, however, further sanctions have been imposed by individual countries and international organisations.

Determined to overcome these problems once and for all, the military government in Rangoon has made a major effort to find new sources of arms, military equipment and defence technology. Burma has also launched a major defence import substitution program. It has expanded and modernised its defence industries, importing substantial amounts of capital equipment for this purpose.[88] New machine tools and industrial plants seem to have come mainly from China, Singapore and Germany. The regime has also modernised two iron and steel mills, with a view to producing the high grade metals needed for arms production. One is at Ywama, outside Rangoon, and the other is at Maymyo, near a large state-owned iron ore mine. According to the US Embassy in Rangoon, 'These [iron and steel] mills, especially the one at Maymyo, may play a key role in the SLORC's ongoing defense import substitution effort'.[89] Maymyo is also the site of the *Tatmadaw*'s new Institute of Technology where, according to one source, 'the Government intends to train technicians and designers for its weapons manufacturing industry'.[90] It is likely that the regime's efforts to insulate itself from international pressures have included attempts to build up the country's stocks of strategic raw materials not available locally, including those required for the manufacture of weapons and ammunition.

The current extent of foreign involvement in Burma's arms industry is not clear. The new Berlin government is still one of Rangoon's largest bilateral debtors, but since 1988 Germany's business relationship with Burma has been quite modest. After a downturn in 1989, merchandise exports to Burma have remained reasonably steady at around US$35 million per year, or about 3% of Burma's total imports.[91] Fritz Werner GmbH has maintained commercial links with Burma but, despite repeated accusations from some activists, journalists and academics, it is adamant that it no longer sells arms or arms-related products to the military regime.[92] This claim is borne out by the US government. According to ACDA figures, Germany's recorded arms transfers to Burma since 1988 have dropped significantly. Between 1987 and 1991 they amounted to US$20 million, but by 1992 this had declined further to US$5 million.[93] There have been no recorded arms transfers to Burma from Germany after that time. Indeed, Germany's place as the prime source of Burma's military technology has been taken over by China and Singapore.

According to the *Far Eastern Economic Review*, Chinese engineers inspected a site near Magwe in 1991, with a view to building a factory complex which could produce M21 semi-automatic carbines, M22 assault rifles and M23 light machine guns, as well as 7.62mm ammunition for these weapons. All three are export versions of weapons currently in service with the PLA. Production was initially due to begin in early 1994.[94] The *FEER* story was followed by another report in January 1995, to the effect that 'Burma wants to enter into a joint venture with China to set up arsenals in Burma to produce weapons for defence and for export. The Burmese government is planning to build two arsenals, one in Rangoon.'[95] According to a

Chinese-language newspaper published in Thailand, Burmese officials repeatedly raised the question of such military assistance when they visited Beijing in 1994, and again during Chinese Premier Li Peng's visit to Rangoon in late December that year. China was said to have 'agreed in principle to consider the request', but no further action seems to have been taken.[96]

While China did not agree to build a small arms factory, a few years later it was apparently willing to help the *Tatmadaw* manufacture landmines.[97] While the output from Burma's own arms factories was probably able to satisfy the BA's demand for these weapons before 1988, it does not appear to have been enough for the campaigns waged against insurgents since then. Some time around 1998, a secret agreement between Rangoon and Beijing saw the construction of a factory near Meiktila solely to produce landmines.[98] Although sources disagree on the progress made since then, it is clear that serial production is already underway. From the limited information available, the new factory produces at least two types of anti-personnel (AP) landmines, designated the MM-1 and MM-2 ('MM' probably standing for 'Myanmar mine').[99] The MM-1 is a simple stake-mounted fragmentation AP mine, similar to the old Soviet POMZ or Chinese Type 59 mine. The MM-2 is a blast fragmentation AP mine, similar to the old Soviet PMN mine (copied in turn by the Chinese as the Type 58). Some reports list as many as five types of landmines now in production at the Meiktila factory, possibly including a directional fragmentation mine and an anti-vehicle mine. As landmines have become more plentiful, so their use by the BA against insurgents has escalated.[100]

Singapore too has stepped in to help modernise and expand Burma's indigenous defence industries, drawing on its well-developed expertise in this field. By the early 1990s, for example, Singaporean technicians had replaced the West German technicians based at Padaung, suggesting that a Singaporean company, or group of companies, had taken over Fritz Werner's advisory role at the regime's defence industrial complex nearby.[101] More significantly, in February 1998 Singapore provided Burma with a state-of-the-art facility to manufacture small arms and ammunition.[102] The modular, prefabricated factory was designed and built in Singapore in 1997 by state-owned Chartered Industries of Singapore, with help from Israeli consultants. The factory, which is reportedly capable of producing weapons and ammunition up to 37mm in calibre, was first tested in Singapore and then shipped to Burma early the following year. Its modular construction permits easy expansion of the plant in the future. Predictably, the Singapore government has denied that Singaporean companies have exported any arms to Burma or are in any way engaged in arms production in that country.[103] However, the new plant is currently being used to produce Burma's indigenously designed family of 'MA' automatic rifles, assault rifles and light machine guns.

After 1988 the Rangoon regime placed a high priority on the development and production of a replacement for the G3 automatic rifle. Not only was it considered too heavy and clumsy for the average Burmese footsoldier, but it was prone to jam.[104] Also, the suspension of German assistance in 1989 in protest over the regime's human rights abuses reminded the SLORC of its vulnerability to pressure from the Western democracies. Burmese army engineers soon began work on an indigenously produced 5.56mm assault rifle. One radical new design, known as the EMER K1, followed the shortened 'bullpup' configuration. It had a stamped, all-metal body, and a 30-round magazine taking 5.56mm M16 ammunition.[105] Several prototypes of this and other weapons were produced, including automatic rifle, assault rifle and light machine gun versions. The basic design which was finally chosen, however, seems to be based on the Chinese Type 56 and the Israeli Galil assault rifles. With the designations MA1, MA2, MA3 and MA4 for different versions ('MA' presumably standing for 'Myanmar Army'), full scale production of these weapons began in 1999.[106]

In 1991 an Israeli team visited Rangoon to discuss the sale to Burma of Uzi 9mm submachine guns. There were later unconfirmed reports that the Burma Army might try to develop a local version of this weapon, to be known as the BA94.[107] No signs of such a weapon have yet appeared, however, and the plan appears to have been dropped.

In addition to developing new infantry weapons, the Rangoon regime has improved Burma's capability to produce its own ammunition. It has long had the capacity to manufacture small calibre ammunition (such as 0.303 British, 7.62/51mm NATO and 9/19mm Parabellum bullets), and it would be logical to extend this to include 5.56mm ammunition for its new MA family of weapons.[108] Also, locally produced 51mm (BA78) and 81mm mortar bombs now permit the *Tatmadaw* to use these more modern weapons instead of its old British (and Burmese-made) 2-inch ML and 3-inch ML mortars.[109] Burma manufactures its own 60mm and 120mm mortar bombs, 41mm (BA92) and 51mm (BA80) rifle grenades, and has probably imported machinery to manufacture grenades for its 40mm launchers. The old (UK-made) Type 36 and (Burmese) BA77 anti-personnel hand grenades used by the army throughout the 1960s and 1970s have now been replaced by locally made BA88 (offensive), BA91 (defensive) and BA109 (general purpose) hand grenades. Burma's Defence Products Industries also manufactures its own mobile 81mm single tube artillery rocket system, known as the BA84.[110]

Steps have also been taken by the regime to manufacture its own light armoured personnel carriers, reconnaissance vehicles and scout cars. Since the early 1980s the *Tatmadaw* has built about 45 such vehicles, under the generic designation of BAAC (Burma Army Armoured Cars). BAAC-83 armoured personnel carriers (APC), BAAC-84 scout cars (SC), BAAC-85 SCs, BAAC-86 SCs, BAAC-87 APCs and BAAC-87 command and control carriers have all been added to the army's pool of combat motor vehicles over the past 20 years.[111] Most seem to be based on Mazda and Hino technology and parts, but for the later models Burma Army engineers appear to have used Nissan and Toyota components.[112] They are usually armed with 0.50 calibre heavy machine guns (HMG) or locally-made 7.62mm MG3 medium machine guns (MMG). One experimental armoured vehicle displayed in the Defence Services Museum in Rangoon has a mounted Chinese 12.7mm Type 85 HMG and a MG3 MMG. The Burma Army also boasts an indigenous 'Special Combat Vehicle'. This is essentially a long wheel base jeep armed with 7.62mm MG3 and 0.50 calibre Browning machine guns, a 60mm or 81mm mortar mounted in the back, and carrying a 84mm Carl Gustav recoilless gun with high explosive anti-tank (HEAT) rounds.[113]

During the 1950s, with advice and equipment supplied mainly by Yugoslavia, Burma developed a modest capacity to produce its own small naval vessels. By the 1960s, it was building ships up to the light corvette class (400 tons standard). After the 1962 military coup, however, and the subsequent decline of the Burmese economy, the navy was accorded a lower priority in the defence budget and work at Rangoon's shipyards slowed down as imported components (like marine engines and electronic systems) became harder to obtain. There was also a shortage of skilled manpower, particularly tradesmen and engineers familiar with modern equipment. While a number of small patrol craft were built in the years that followed, most effort was put into the repair and maintenance of the Burma Navy's existing fleet. This situation changed after 1988, however, as Chinese loans, materials and technical assistance facilitated a number of new ship building projects.[114] Two coastal patrol craft and four river patrol craft have already been built by the Naval Engineering Depot and the Myanma Shipyard in Rangoon. Work has nearly been completed on two newly-designed fast attack gunboats, and is proceeding on three new corvettes. The latter are based on Chinese hulls, Italian guns and Israeli electronics.

Burma has never been able to produce its own aircraft or major aircraft components. Although it has displayed considerable ingenuity in its workshops, and manufactured a range of spare parts, the BAF has always been heavily dependent on foreign suppliers and foreign expertise to keep its machines operational. This situation has remained under the SLORC and SPDC.

6.3 The Tatmadaw and the Economy

After Independence, and during the early stages of the civil war, private contractors and individual unit commanders were given responsibility for providing basic services and amenities for the troops. For a variety of reasons, however, they were unsuccessful. In response, the Ministry of Defence established a commercial venture modelled on the British Navy, Army and Air Force Institute, which had run canteens in Burma for Allied troops during the Second World War. Known as the Defence Services Institute (DSI), the Burmese venture was originally designed to 'cater for the welfare and needs of the troops and for the maintenance of morale', particularly in remote areas.[115] It began operations in 1951 with a loan from the Ministry of Defence. Military officers occupied all key managerial positions. Although later officially registered as a business, the DSI was not originally intended to be a profit-making concern. Its privileged access to goods and services, however, and its exemption from sales taxes, customs duties and port fees, soon resulted in large profits and it expanded rapidly.

When the military caretaker government was in power between 1958-1960, the DSI was able to operate completely free from civilian constraints and, in the words of one contemporary, enjoyed 'a bonanza'.[116] Not only was its expansion designed to benefit the armed forces, but it was also seen by the caretaker government as a means through which to bring some order to domestic trade.[117] By 1960 the DSI was running a huge economic complex which included banks, shipping lines and the largest import-export operation in the country. It also held Burma's sole coal import license, and controlled a hotel company, fisheries and poultry distribution businesses, a construction firm, a bookshop, a bus line and the largest department store chain in Burma.[118] With control of over 38 different firms and five holding companies, the DSI had become 'the largest and most powerful business organisation in the nation'.[119] As the DSI was also the country's largest importer, the armed forces gained considerable influence over trade dealing with foreign exchange, then as now a major factor in the Burmese economy. The DSI had also become a critical part of the *Tatmadaw*'s logistical base, providing basic necessities such as food and clothing to the troops.

Immediately after Ne Win's coup, plans were laid for an even more ambitious penetration of the civilian economy by the *Tatmadaw*. Ironically, the RC's adoption of doctrinaire socialist policies meant that all private businesses were taken over by the regime, and the economy was organised into 23 state corporations controlled by the armed forces. The DSI, and a sister organisation known as the Burma Economic Development Corporation (established in 1961), were themselves nationalised. As one commentator put it, 'The military government had beheaded its own stepson'.[120] Yet the nationalisation of the country's agriculture, industry and trade, in effect delivered Burma's entire national wealth into the hands of the armed forces. Through the central government apparatus, which the regime seeded with thousands of retired and serving military officers, the *Tatmadaw* controlled all state-operated economic enterprises, and used them either directly or indirectly to support its military activities.[121] No other legal sources of economic power were permitted to develop, although a separate unofficial economy (popularly known as State Corporation Number 24) quickly grew up to help overcome the problems posed by the failure of the official one.

Under the SLORC and SPDC a number of significant changes have been made to this system. The regime has recognised the shortcomings of the old socialist practices and made certain adjustments, but it is still determined to remain firmly in control of Burma's economy. Also, since 1988 a number of new organisations have been created to facilitate the *Tatmadaw*'s purely commercial operations under the regime's new 'open door' policies.

In 1990 the SLORC established the *Pyidaungsu Myanmar Naingngan Si Pwa Yae U Pai Ahpwe* (Union of Myanmar Economic Holdings Limited, or UMEH), 'with the object of carrying on business internally and abroad and making investment, etc, in the interest of the State and the citizens'.[122] Forty per cent of the capital shares were subscribed by the Ministry of Defence and the remainder by serving and retired members of the armed forces, or regimental organisations. The Directorate of Procurement, which is responsible for the regime's arms imports, initially held the Ministry's 40% equity in UMEH, which 'controls the lion's share of investment entering the country'.[123] The UMEH also managed the *Tatmadaw*'s pension funds, giving it a ready source of financing, and owned a controlling interest in the powerful Myawaddy Enterprises Group.[124] By 1999 the UMEH had established nearly 50 joint ventures with foreign firms. These covered fields as diverse as gem production, garment manufacture, food and beverage trading companies, timber-based industries, supermarkets, a bank, hotels, tourism, telecommunications equipment, steel production, concrete factories, automobiles and cosmetics. The UMEH is now under the control of the Adjutant General's Office.[125]

In addition, the *Tatmadaw* benefits directly from the *Pyidaungsu Myanmar Naingngan Si Pwa Yae Corporation* (Myanmar Economic Corporation, or MEC). Specifically exempted from the State-Owned Economic Enterprise Law of 1989, which reserves the right for the government to control 12 key areas of economic enterprise, the MEC was established

> in order to contribute towards the development of the State economy, to decrease defence expenditure by fulfilling the needs of the Tatmadaw, to carry out the welfare of the Tatmadaw service personnel and to implement other necessary matters for the Tatmadaw.[126]

The MEC is thus authorised to conduct business in almost any field of commerce and industry, completely unfettered by the laws which control other economic activities in Burma. Already the MEC has taken full advantage of this freedom and is rapidly developing the kind of status that was enjoyed by the DSI before the 1962 coup. The MEC is involved in such core areas as agricultural and commodity trading, banking and finance, natural gas and petroleum exploration, telecommunications and transport services. As one insider has put it, through the UMEH and MEC 'the Tatmadaw will be able to maintain its hold on various sectors of the economy'.[127]

As well as the UMEH (which is also designated State/Private Joint Venture (JVC) No.9), there are eight other state-operated joint venture corporations, dealing with agriculture, fisheries, trade, construction, hotels and medicines. All these joint ventures are reportedly under the direct control of the *Tatmadaw*'s Directorate of Procurement and are operated by serving or retired military officers.[128] With this being the case, then it must be assumed that a high percentage of the profits of the joint venture deals embarked upon to date must eventually return in one form or another to the armed forces. There is also considerable private participation in the economy by senior military officers. As Robert Taylor has written,

> The model of Thai and Indonesian officers, with their private sector business interests and their links with foreign capital, as well as the significant military perquisites which can be derived from foreign investment leading to more economic growth and an expanded resource base for the state, has not been lost upon the armed forces of Myanmar. What is the sense of having a politically dominant military which presides over a poverty stricken government which cannot provide sufficient resources to fund a modern, well equipped

and well paid army, is a question many officers have been asking themselves.[129]

It is now very difficult to establish any major business in Burma without the support of senior military officers, many of whom have their own interests in private companies throughout the country.

Another way in which the *Tatmadaw* has important economic interests stems from the days of the old BSPP government. Since 1989 the Directorate of Ordnance has taken over the management of a number of SOEs which had earlier been the responsibility of the Ministry of Industry. Some, relating for example to shoe, garment and textile manufacture, were purely for military supply. Other factories, however, including canning, pharmaceutical, leather and dairy produce factories, produced goods for public consumption. According to Maung Aung Myoe, 'these industries generate some income for the *Tatmadaw*, and also provide jobs for many families of the *Tatmadaw* rank-and-file'.[130] However, these old SOEs still suffer from many of the inefficiencies of the old socialist system, and are not likely to make the transition to profitable businesses for some time, if at all.

Although it has remained institutionally discrete, the *Tatmadaw* has effectively dominated all levels of government, civil administration and commerce in Burma since the 1962 military coup. Under the SLORC and SPDC this situation has remained, although changes to Burma's economic policies and foreign trade laws have encouraged the *Tatmadaw* to develop a number of new vehicles to pursue its commercial interests. As Bertil Lintner as written, 'at no time in Burmese history has the army been so powerful in politics and business'.[131] In these circumstances, it is virtually impossible for any outside agency to calculate with any confidence the real level of Burma's defence expenditure. Given its many and varied sources of income, official and unofficial, direct and indirect, it is unlikely that even the regime itself can fully account for all avenues of support now enjoyed by the armed forces, or determine exactly how all its funds are spent. The entire country has become a massive resource base on which the *Tatmadaw* can draw as it chooses, not only to sustain itself and conduct military operations, but also to perpetuate military rule.

Notes

1. An earlier version of this chapter appeared as Andrew Selth, 'Burma's Defence Expenditure and Arms Industries', *Contemporary Security Policy*, Vol. 19, No. 2, August 1998.

2. See R.H. Taylor, 'Burma: Defence Expenditure and Threat Perceptions', in Chin Kin Wah (ed), *Defence Spending in Southeast Asia* (Institute of South East Asian Studies, Singapore, 1987), pp. 252-80.

3. See, for example, *Foreign Economic Trends Report: Burma*, (US Embassy, Rangoon, 1996), pp. 9-10.

4. Mya Maung, *The Burma Road to Poverty*, pp. 92-5; and Thaung, 'Army's Accumulation of Economic Power in Burma, 1940-1990', *Burma Review*, No. 20, October 1990, pp. 17-22.

5. This paragraph draws on Taylor, 'Burma: Defence Expenditure and Threat Perceptions', p. 254; *SIPRI Yearbook 1992*, p. 256; *SIPRI Yearbook 1996: Armaments, Disarmament and International Security* (Oxford University Press, Oxford, 1996), p. 362; *World Military Expenditures and Arms Transfers 1988* (US Arms Control and Disarmament Agency, Washington, 1989), p. 36; *World Military Expenditures and Arms Transfers 1996* (US Arms Control and Disarmament Agency, Washington, 1997), p. 63; and International Monetary Fund, *Government Finance Statistics Yearbook 1995* (IMF, Washington, 1996), p. 435.

6. Taylor, 'Burma: Defence Expenditure and Threat Perceptions', p. 255.

7. Burma's gross domestic product (GDP) declined in both 1986 (-1.1%) and 1987 (-4.2%). See R.H. Taylor, 'The Military in Myanmar (Burma)', p. 142.

8. *World Military Expenditures and Arms Transfers, 1989* (US Arms Control and Disarmament Agency, Washington, 1990), p. 40.

9. Taylor, 'The Military in Myanmar (Burma)', p. 247.

10. A.L. Ross, 'Growth, Debt, and Military Spending in Southeast Asia', *Contemporary Southeast Asia*, Vol. 11, No. 4, March 1990, p. 245.

11. *Ibid.*

12. The Let Ya-Freeman Agreement stated that Burma was only to receive British Commonwealth military missions, and that the UK would give Burma all support for the purchase of war materiel. See also Stockholm International Peace Research Institute, *The Arms Trade with the Third World* (Paul Elek, London, 1971), p. 451.

13. Opinions differ over the degree to which Burma's refusal of US military aid in 1951 was prompted by a desire to keep out of the Cold War, or the difficulty of accepting American aid while criticising covert US support for the KMT in northern Burma. Clearly, both factors played a role. See Cady, *A History of Modern Burma*, pp. 619ff.

14. In 1958 Burma signed a bilateral agreement with the US ultimately worth US$85.5 million. It was phased out in 1970. During this period US arms were sold on concessionary terms which, in effect, allowed Burma to pay in its own soft currency. Being a sales agreement, however, it satisfied Burma's neutrality requirements. SIPRI, *The Arms Trade with the Third World*, p. 452. See also Taylor, 'Burma: Defence Expenditure and Threat Perceptions', p. 264.

15. *World Military Expenditures and Arms Transfers 1968-1977*, (US Arms Control and Disarmament Agency, Washington, 1979), p. 156; *World Military Expenditures and Arms Transfers 1972-82* (US Arms Control and Disarmament Agency, Washington, 1984), p. 96; and *World Military Expenditures and Arms Transfers 1988*, p. 112.

16. SIPRI, *The Arms Trade with the Third World*, p. 450. This figure, however, probably does not include the importation of raw materials and intermediate goods for Burma's own arms factories, most of which came from the FRG.

17. *World Military Expenditures and Arms Transfers 1968-1977*, p. 122; and *World Military Expenditures and Arms Transfers 1989*, p. 82.

18. During this period the size of the *Tatmadaw* rose from 153,000 to 186,000. See Taylor, 'The Military in Myanmar (Burma)', p. 142. See also Wiant and Steinberg, 'Burma: The Military and National Development', pp. 308-9.

19. *World Military Expenditures and Arms Transfers 1968-1977*, p. 122; and *World Military Expenditures and Arms Transfers 1989*, p. 82.

20. *Foreign Economic Trends Report: Burma*, p. 21.

21. *World Military Expenditures and Arms Transfers 1991-1992* (US Arms Control and Disarmament Agency, Washington, 1994), p. 56.

22. See 'US Senator calls for new sanctions against Burma', *The Nation*, 20 April 1989.

23. *World Military Expenditures and Arms Transfers 1996*, (US Arms Control and Disarmament Agency, Washington, 1997), p. 63. One research centre put Burma's defence

spending for 1990-91 at 6% of GDP. R.L. Sivard, *World Military and Social Expenditures 1996* (World Priorities, Washington, 1996), p. 171.

24. This accords with estimates published by the Economist Intelligence Unit in its *Country Profile: Thailand, Myanmar 1992-93*, (Economist, London, 1993), p. 43; and the United Nations Development Programme, *Human Development Report 1994* (Oxford University Press, Oxford, 1994), p. 42. See also 'Myanmar junta to increase defence spending', Reuters, 23 April 1992; and Ron Corben, 'Lawyers condemn Burmese regime', *The Australian*, 24 April 1992.

25. Martin Smith, 'The Burmese way to rack and ruin', in Article 19, *Index on Censorship*, No. 10, 1991, p. 45. See also David Leser, 'Guns, Money and Murder', *The Bulletin*, 28 April 1992, p. 20.

26. *World Military Expenditures and Arms Transfers 1996*, p. 63.

27. *World Military Expenditures and Arms Transfers 1998* (US Department of State, Bureau of Verification and Compliance, Washington, 2000), p. 75. See also Appendix 2.

28. *Defence Economic Trends in the Asia-Pacific Region, 1999* (Defence Intelligence Organisation, Canberra, 1999), p. 23; and *SIPRI Yearbook 2000: Armaments, Disarmament and International Security* (Oxford University Press, Oxford, 2000), p. 264.

29. *SIPRI Yearbook 2000*, pp. 247-8. See also 'Official: Burma completes military buildup', AFP, 19 May 1999.

30. *Defence Economic Trends*, p. 23; and *SIPRI Yearbook 2000*, p. 247.

31. *Defence Economic Trends*, p. 23.

32. *SIPRI Yearbook 2000*, p. 248.

33. International Institute for Strategic Studies, *The Military Balance 2000/2001* (Oxford University Press, London, 2000), p. 208.

34. This paragraph draws heavily on *Foreign Economic Trends Report: Burma*, p. 23.

35. For example, in the 1994/95 financial year Defence Ministry purchases from the MPPE were usually made at about 20 kyat per gallon for diesel fuel, and 25 kyat for petrol. The free market prices were about 150 kyat and 200 kyat respectively. *Ibid.*

36. *Foreign Economic Trends Report: Burma*, p. 23.

37. *Ibid.*

38. US State Department, *Burma: Country Report.*

39. Maung Aung Myoe, *The Tatmadaw in Myanmar Since 1988*, p. 25, note 31.

40. Interview, Mandalay, November 1996.

41. *Foreign Economic Trends Report: Burma*, p. 25.

42. *Foreign Economic Trends Report: Burma*, p. 23.

43. Taylor, 'Burma: Defence Expenditure and Threat Perceptions', p. 255.

44. UNDP, *Human Development Report 1994*, p. 42.

45. See Taylor, 'The Military in Myanmar (Burma)', pp. 139-52; and *Foreign Economic Trends Report: Burma*, p. 24.

46. Bertil Lintner, 'Safe at Home', *FEER*, 14 August 1997, p. 19.

47. *Foreign Economic Trends Report: Burma*, p. 24.

48. Selth, *Burma's Arms Procurement Programme.*

49. Lintner, 'Lock and load', p. 28. See also Bertil Lintner, 'Tugging the tiger's tail', *FEER*, 18 November 1989, pp. 19-20.

50. Published estimates of the value of this particular deal have ranged from US$400 million to US$1.4 billion. Subsequent deliveries to Burma suggest that the latter figure is closer to the mark. See Lintner, 'Myanmar's Chinese Connection', p. 23.

51. Yindee Lertcharoenchok, 'Beijing, Rangoon ink $1.2 billion arms deal', *The Nation*, 27 November 1990.

52. Bertil Lintner, '$400m deal signed by China and Myanmar', *JDW*, 3 December 1994, p. 1. See also P. Stobdan, 'Options for India', *Indian Express*, 4 January 1995.

53. Rowan Callick, 'China and Burma strengthen ties with military agreement', *Australian Financial Review*, 24 January 1997; and 'Sino-Burmese Pact', *FEER*, 30 January 1997, p. 12.

54. *World Military Expenditures and Arms Transfers 1991-1992*, p. 132; *World Military Expenditures and Arms Transfers 1995* (US Arms Control and Disarmament Agency, Washington, 1996), p. 155; and *World Military Expenditures and Arms Transfers 1998*, p. 168. The US sales occurred before September 1988. After 1995 the only major source of arms listed was China.

55. See, for example, Boyd, 'Burma arms itself against rebels in secret'; Lintner, 'Myanmar's Chinese Connection', p. 26; 'Junta takes delivery of Polish choppers', *Asian Defence Journal*, September 1992, p. 108; and 'But will the flag follow trade?', *Economist*, 8 October 1994, pp. 31-2.

56. No commercial exports to Burma have been licensed under the US Arms Export Control Act since 1989. At one stage the regime unsuccessfully tried to renew ties by trading on US concerns about the export of narcotics from the Golden Triangle. See 'Air Forces Survey: Myanmar', p. 36; and 'Burma offers drug king in return for US arms', *The Age*, 16 July 1994.

57. Selth, *Burma's Secret Military Partners*.

58. Bertil Lintner, 'Using the aid weapon', *FEER*, 17 November 1988, p. 34.

59. Rodney Tasker and Bertil Lintner, 'Difficult guests', *FEER*, 4 March 1993, p. 11.

60. Lintner, 'Myanmar's Chinese connection', p. 26.

61. This order, of 50-100,000 rounds of 82mm mortar ammunition valued at about US$2 million, was tran-shipped in Thailand. Robert Karniol, 'Myanmar stocks up on ammunition', *JDW*, 21 March 2001, p. 14.

62. *World Military Expenditures and Arms Transfers 1998*, p. 127.

63. *Foreign Economic Trends Report: Burma*, p. 22.

64. Personal observation, Rangoon, Taunggyi and Kalaw, April 1995.

65. Lintner, 'Oiling the iron fist', p. 29.

66. Bertil Lintner, 'Hidden reserves', *FEER*, 6 June 1991, pp. 12-13.

67. One third was paid for in kind, one third in cash and the other third under a very soft loan provided by China. Interview, Rangoon, April 1995. See also 'Burma', *Asia 1990 Yearbook*, (*FEER*, Hong Kong, 1991), p. 97; Jeremy Wagstaff, 'Burma buys arms from China', *The Nation*, 11 February 1991; and 'Myanmar in large arms barter deal with China', *Asian Aviation*, Vol. 11, No. 2, February 1991, pp. 88-9.

68. Interview, Rangoon, November 1999.

69. Bertil Lintner, *The Politics of the Drug Trade in Burma*, Occasional Paper No. 33 (Indian Ocean Centre for Peace Studies, University of Western Australia, Nedlands, 1993), pp. 41-8. See also 'The Golden Triangle's new king', *Economist*, 4 February 1995, pp. 25-6; and 'Heroin warlords cultivate Burmese leadership', *The Australian*, 6 February 1995.

70. Lintner, 'Safe at Home', pp. 18-20.

71. Cited in Barry Wain, 'Myanmar defends efforts to combat drug trade', *Asian Wall Street Journal*, 24 December 1998. See also Cathy Scott-Clark and Adrian Levy, 'Paddies lost to poppy program', *The Australian*, 11 May 1998.

72. Lintner, 'Safe at home', p. 19.

73. Desmond Ball, *Burma and Drugs: The Regime's Complicity in the Global Drug Trade*, Working Paper No. 336 (Strategic and Defence Studies Centre, Australian National University, Canberra, 1999), p. 7.

74. T.B. Nelson, *The World's Submachine Guns*, (Arms and Armour Press, London, 1977), Vol. 1, pp. 383-4 and pp. 636-7.

75. See Selth, *Burma's Secret Military Partners*, pp. 7-26; Smith, 'The Burmese way to rack and ruin', pp. 43-5; and Bruce Hawke, 'Exposed: Burma's weapons industry', *Jane's Pointer*, December 1998, pp. 34-5.

76. Mya Maung, *Totalitarianism in Burma*, p. 235.
77. Personal communication, Manager, Fritz Werner GmbH, to the author, 20 April 2000.
78. Mya Maung, *Totalitarianism in Burma*, p. 235. All industries in Burma employing more than 20 people had been nationalised by 1964.
79. Chit Tun, 'Burmese joint venture', *Financial Times*, 26 November 1984.
80. Smith, 'The Burmese way to rack and ruin', p. 43. See also Andrew Selth, 'Burma develops its ability to build arms', *Jane's Intelligence Review*, Vol. 8, No. 5, May 1996, pp. 233-5.
81. Mya Maung, *The Burma Road to Poverty*, pp. 200-1.
82. 'Correspondence', *Jane's Intelligence Review*, Vol. 8, No. 9, September 1996, p. 430. See also Personal communication, Manager, Fritz Werner GmbH, to the author, 20 April 2000; and Selth, *Burma's Secret Military Partners*, p. 13.
83. In addition to arms, ammunition and military vehicles, *Ka Pa Sa* factories also produce a wide range of military uniforms, boots, web equipment, sporting goods and eating utensils. Personal observations, Rangoon, April 1995 and December 1999.
84. This paragraph is largely taken from Mya Maung, *The Burma Road to Poverty*, pp. 200-01. See also *Foreign Economic Trends Report: Burma*, p. 21.
85. Bertil Lintner, 'Passing in the dark', *FEER*, 3 November 1988, p. 17.
86. Smith, 'The Burmese way to rack and ruin', p. 43.
87. See also 'European Union not to lift sanctions against Burma', *The Nation*, 27 July 2000.
88. *Foreign Economic Trends Report: Burma*, p. 21.
89. *Ibid.*
90. Hawke, 'Exposed: Burma's weapons industry', p. 8.
91. *Foreign Economic Trends Report: Burma*, pp. 121-2.
92. Personal communication, Manager, Fritz Werner GmbH, to the author, 20 April 2000. See also Selth, *Burma's Secret Military Partners*, pp. 23-6.
93. *World Military Expenditures and Arms Transfers 1991-1992*, p. 132; and *World Military Expenditures and Arms Transfers 1993-1994*, p. 141.
94. See Bertil Lintner, 'Rangoon's Rubicon', *FEER*, 11 February 1993, p. 28; and P. Stobdan, 'The dragon's arm across the bamboo curtain', *Pioneer*, 11 November 1993. The M21 is the export version of the Chinese Type 56 carbine (itself a copy of the Soviet SKS45 semi-automatic carbine). The M22 is the export version of the Type 56 assault rifle (the Chinese copy of the Soviet AK47) and the M23 is the export version of the Chinese Type 56 machine gun (essentially the same as the Soviet RPD light machine gun).
95. BBC *Summary of World Broadcasts*, FE/2200/B/5, 13 January 1995.
96. *Ibid.*
97. Interviews, Rangoon, November and December 1999.
98. One source has suggested that this factory was built near Prome. Interview, Rangoon, December 1999.
99. See, for example, Supradit Kanwanich, 'Caught in the crossfire', *Bangkok Post*, 30 August 1998; and Karen Human Rights Group (KHRG), 'Photo Set 2000-A: Landmines', found on the internet at http://metalab.unc.edu/freeburma/humanrights/khrg/archive/ph.../Landmines.htm (September 2000).
100. For details, see Andrew Selth, *Landmines in Burma: The Military Dimension*, Working Paper No. 352 (Strategic and Defence Studies Centre, Australian National University, Canberra, 2000). See also *Burma: Landmine Monitor Report 2000* (International Campaign to Ban Landmines, Bangkok, 2000); and Yeshua Moser-Puangsuwan and Andrew Selth, 'Myanmar's forgotten minefields', *Jane's Intelligence Review*, Vol. 12, No. 10, October 2000, pp. 38-42.

101. Lintner, 'Myanmar's Chinese connection', p. 26.
102. Bruce Hawke, 'Myanmar making small arms in imported factory', *JDW*, 22 July 1998, p. 14.
103. Selth, *Burma's Secret Military Partners*, pp. 27-43; and interviews, Singapore, May 1995 and November 1999. See also Lintner, 'Myanmar's Chinese Connection', p. 26.
105. This problem became worse as the moulds used to manufacture the G3 parts in Burma wore out, but could not be replaced.
106. 'Bullpup' weapons have the magazine in the butt, behind the pistol grip. Personal observation, Rangoon, April 1995. See also Selth, 'Burma's Defence Expenditure and Arms Industries', p. 37.
106. Interview, Rangoon, November 2000. These weapons have already been used on ceremonial occasions like the 1999 and 2000 Armed Forces Day parades, but have yet to be widely fielded.
107. Interview, Canberra, June 1995. This report may simply reflect confusion with the regime's plan to develop a weapon based on the Type 56 and Galil assault rifles.
108. *Jane's Infantry Weapons 1995-96* (Jane's Information Group, Coulsdon, 1997), p. 448, and earlier editions.
109. Burma probably also makes its own copy of the Chinese 60mm Type 63 mortar. See *The Military Powers Encyclopedia*, p. 46.
110. Interviews and personal observations, Rangoon, April 1995 and November 1996. See also *Jane's Armour and Artillery 1996-97* (Jane's Information Group, Coulsdon, 1996), p. 728.
111. Maung Aung Myoe, *The Tatmadaw in Myanmar Since 1988*, p. 26, note 38.
112. Personal observation, Rangoon, April 1995. See also *Jane's Armour and Artillery 1996-97*, p. 389. Japan has turned a blind eye to the conversion of Hino and Mazda assembly plants in Burma to military use, despite a prior pledge from the Burmese government that no economic assistance from Japan would be used by the armed forces. See Smith, 'The Burmese way to rack and ruin', p. 44.
113. Personal observation, Rangoon, April 1995 and November 1996.
114. China initially provided Burma with steel and credit for other stores, and in 1999 agreed to expand the dry dock facilities at Sinmalaik Shipyard. Interviews, Rangoon, November 1996 and November 1999.
115. Callahan, 'The Origins of Military Rule in Burma', pp. 439ff.
116. Thaung, 'Army's Accumulation of Economic Power', p. 18. See also Mya Maung, *The Burma Road to Poverty*, pp. 92-4.
117. Wiant and Steinberg, 'Burma: The Military and National Development', p. 310.
118. Wiant and Steinberg, 'Burma: The Military and National Development', pp. 482-3. See also Callahan, 'The Origins of Military Rule in Burma', p. 440.
119. Lissak, *Military Roles in Modernization*, p. 162. See also Thaung, 'Army's Accumulation of Economic Power', p. 18.
120. Thaung, 'Army's Accumulation of Economic Power', p. 20.
121. According to Thaung, between 1962 and 1973 the number of Burma's civil servants rose by nearly 70%. The vacancies created by a purge of nearly 2000 civil servants after 1962, however, and the thousands of new positions created by the Revolutionary Council, were largely filled by serving and former members of the armed forces, few of whom had any relevant qualifications or experience. Thaung, 'Army's Accumulation of Economic Power', p. 21. See also D.I. Steinberg, *Burma's Road Toward Development: Growth and Ideology Under Military Rule* (Westview, Boulder, 1981), p. 164.
122. Government of the Union of Myanmar, Ministry of Trade, Notification No. 7/90, Rangoon, 19 February 1990, quoted in Thaung, 'Army's Accumulation of Economic Power', p. 22.

123. Bertil Lintner, 'Absolute Power', *FEER*, 18 January 1996, p. 25.
124. *Foreign Economic Trends Report: Burma*, p. 21; and Lintner, 'Absolute Power', p. 25.
125. Maung Aung Myoe, *The Tatmadaw in Myanmar Since 1988*, p. 12.
126. Maung Aung Myoe, *The Tatmadaw in Myanmar Since 1988*, p. 13.
127. *Ibid*.
128. Mya Maung, *Totalitarianism in Burma*, p. 225.
129. Taylor, 'The Military in Myanmar (Burma)', pp. 141-2.
130. *Foreign Economic Trends Report: Burma*, p. 21.
131. Lintner, 'Absolute Power', p. 25.

7

The Burma Army

The military tradition is strong in Burma. The British chose to believe that the Burmese did not make good soldiers, but the basis of the State which they overthrew in the nineteenth century was in fact military. — John Keegan, *World Armies* (1983)

Whenever the Burmese armed forces are mentioned, it is usually the Burma Army (*Tatmadaw Kyi*) which springs to mind.[1] The army has always been by far the largest Service and has always received the lion's share of Burma's defence budget. It has played the most prominent part in Rangoon's military struggle against the 40 or more insurgent groups which have challenged central rule since 1948. After the 1962 coup, the army effectively dominated all political processes in the country and even branched out into commerce and industry. Its leading political role was reinforced in 1988 by the creation of the SLORC which, despite a number of personnel changes, consisted almost entirely of senior army officers. After 1997 the army's domination of the country's government continued under the SPDC.

Despite its preoccupation with retaining political power, the Burma Army has never lost sight of its defence role, and over the past 12 years it has implemented a wide range of measures which has significantly enhanced its military capabilities.

7.1 The Burma Army Before 1988

The Burma Army traces its origins to those nationalist military forces which were formed during the Second World War. These included the Burma Independence Army, the Burma Defence Army and the Burma National Army. Thanks to its switch in allegiance late in the war, this last force survived as the Patriotic Burmese Forces (PBF), and became the nucleus of the new Burma Army when the colonial administration left in 1948. As Hugh Tinker has noted, however, 'any hope of steady development of the new army was overturned by the onset of civil war'.[2] Almost immediately after the birth of the Union, three former battalions of the PBF mutinied, as did a number of the BA's new ethnic battalions. These mutinies, together with the outbreak of insurgencies with two communist parties and a number of other groups, soon threatened the survival of the central government in Rangoon. To protect the new Union and restore unity to the country, a rapid expansion of the army was authorised.

At Independence, the Burma Army consisted of 15 regular infantry battalions under two regional commands, assisted by 15 battalions of military police.[3] After the 1948 and 1949 mutinies, the army was reduced to a mere six front line battalions, or less than 3000 men.[4] A vigorous recruitment program was introduced, however, and by 1952 it had grown to 30 battalions. The following year it jumped in size to 41 battalions, mainly through the incorporation into the BA of the remaining *sit-wundan tats*, which had been raised in 1948 to help fight the insurgents.[5] These troops were supported by small armoured and artillery regiments, engineering units, a medical corps, and supply and signals elements. Some arms and military equipment were provided by the UK, US and India. With additional foreign assistance, this steady increase in strength continued until 1961, by which time the army had grown to some 85,000 men, including 57 infantry battalions. These forces were organised under five Regional Military Commands, with two independent infantry brigades based at Myitkyina and Pa-an.[6]

After the 1962 coup, there was a major diversion of army resources into political and administrative roles, but efforts were soon made to replace these losses. In October that year, for example, 27 new infantry battalions were created from the paramilitary Union Military Police, which was then formally disbanded. Under the Ne Win regime, the army grew steadily, but remained an overwhelmingly infantry force. By the time the 'civilian' BSPP government was formed in 1974, the BA had 114 infantry battalions, or about 145,000 men and women in uniform. By the beginning of 1988 it had grown even further, to about 184,000 officers and other ranks.[7] At that time there were 168 regular infantry battalions, two armoured battalions, four artillery battalions, and one light anti-aircraft artillery battalion.[8]

During this period the Burma Army was formally organised on the regimental system, but the basic manoeuvre and fighting unit was always the battalion. This comprised a headquarters unit, four rifle companies (usually of three platoons each), an administration company (with medical, transport, logistics and signals functions), and a heavy weapons company. The latter included mortar, machine gun and recoilless rifle platoons. The establishment strength of the battalion was formally set at 27 officers and 723 other ranks, but in fact rarely exceeded 500 and was sometimes much lower.[9] Before 1988, the Burma Regiment numbered more than 100 battalions and the Light Infantry Regiment some 40 battalions. Other regiments, with traditional ethnic-based names like the Burma Rifles, Kachin Rifles, Shan Rifles, Chin Rifles and Kayah Rifles, were much smaller, accounting for only about 20 more infantry battalions.[10] Of these units, 85 regular infantry battalions did not fall under any formal divisional structure but were independently assigned to garrison duties in Burma's (then) nine Regional Commands. The remaining 80 were light infantry battalions organised into eight specialised Light Infantry Divisions.[11]

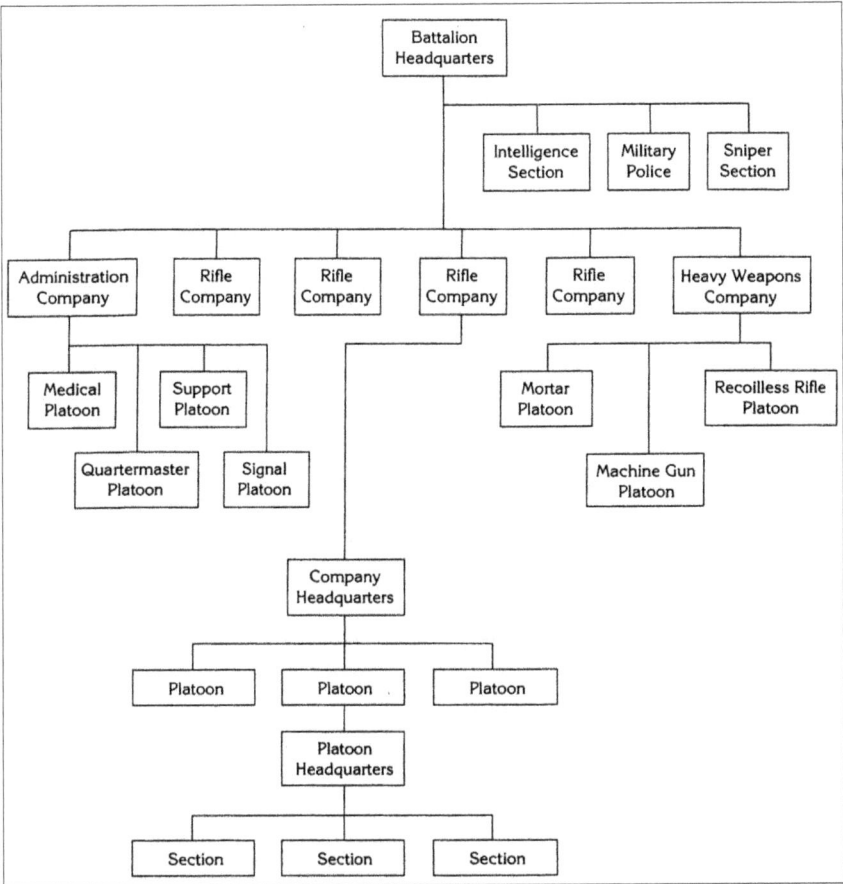

Figure 16: Burma Army Infantry Battalion Structure.

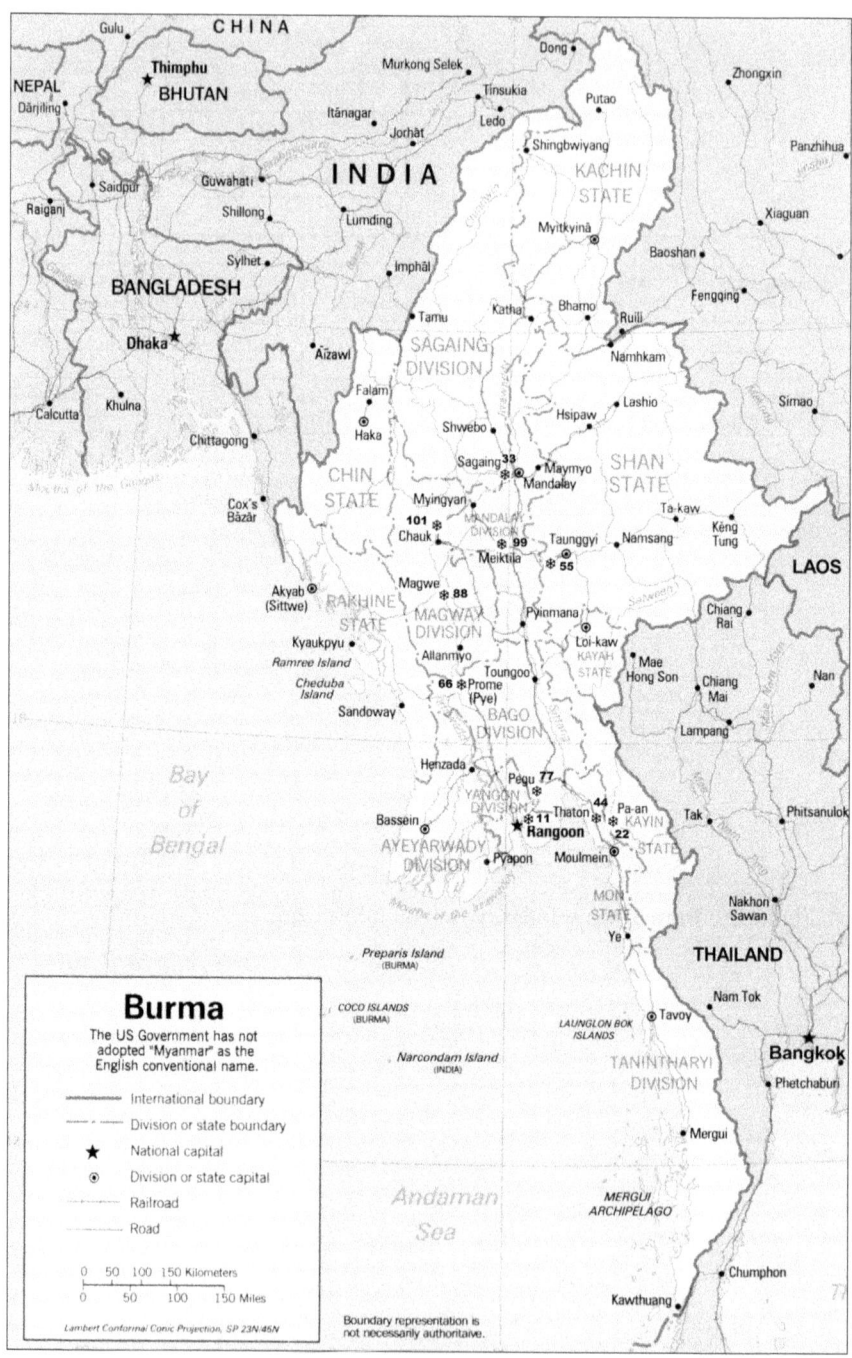

Figure 17: Light Infantry Division Headquarters

The first LID, the 77th, was formed in mid-1966 as a mobile strike force. It was largely responsible for the defeat of the CPB forces based in the forested hills of the central Pegu Yoma in the mid-1970s. Its headquarters is now at Pegu. In 1967 and 1968 two more LIDs were formed, the 88th and 99th, based at Magwe and Meiktila respectively. In the latter half of the 1970s, three more LIDs were raised (the 66th, 55th and 44th, in that order), with their headquarters at Prome, Aungban and Thaton. They were followed by another two LIDs created in the period leading up to the SLORC's takeover (the 33rd based at Sagaing, and the 22nd based at Pa-an).[12] In 1988 each LID consisted of 10 light infantry battalions specially trained in counter-insurgency warfare, under three Tactical Operational Commands. These TOCs were commanded by Brigadier or Colonel level officers and were in many respects similar to Brigades in Western armies. Each was made up of three or more combat battalions, with small command and support elements. One battalion was held in reserve.

The LIDs were considered 'the backbone of Ne Win's support'.[13] The soldiers received better pay and benefits than their counterparts in the regional commands, and were stationed on main lines of communication where families were not unduly affected by local economic conditions. While some LIDs were used to occupy territory and deny it to anti-government forces, they generally constituted the regime's elite shock troops dedicated to 'search and destroy' operations against insurgents and narcotics-based armies. With Israeli help, one LID battalion was given parachute training, but airborne operations were rare.[14] From time to time, these battle-hardened forces were called upon to quell civil disturbances in the major population centres. The 77th LID performed such a role in Rangoon during the 1974 U Thant disturbances, as did the 22nd and 33rd LIDs during the pro-democracy demonstrations of August and September 1988.

Artillery and armoured units were not used in an independent role, but were deployed in support of the infantry by the Defence Ministry as required.

In addition to manpower problems, the BA also faced severe shortages of arms and equipment. As already noted, the Nu Government was reluctant to accept foreign military aid, but the serious insurgent threat faced by Rangoon soon forced it to turn to other countries for help. Under their 1947 bilateral defence agreement, the UK provided Burma with technical advice, loans and shipments of surplus military equipment. To a limited extent, this assistance continued even after the withdrawal of the BMM in 1954. India provided one shipment of small arms and ammunition as a gesture of support. The US was initially slow to assist the BA but eventually provided a considerable amount of ammunition, war materiel and training, first under the MDAP and later under the Military Assistance Program (MAP).[15] During the 1950s weapons and training were also provided by Yugoslavia and Israel, both of which were seen to share Burma's non-aligned credentials. After 1958 further arms and equipment were purchased from the US under a special sales arrangement, which permitted the Burmese to pay in local currency, but this program was suspended for political reasons between 1971 and 1981.[16]

As a result of this rather haphazard procurement pattern, the Burma Army came to possess a wide variety of equipment from many different sources. Much of it was old and of limited utility. Without substantial military aid, however, or a greatly increased flow of foreign currency, the BA could not carry out any comprehensive modernisation program. This encouraged the army to retain and maintain almost all the equipment that it ever acquired. As one observer noted in 1983, the fact that so much of it was kept in functioning order 'was a testament to the skill and inventiveness of the army's maintenance personnel, who have long had the task of making do with what little was available'.[17] It was also a reflection of the nature of the security threats the Rangoon government faced at that time, and the relatively limited military ambitions which the regime had set for itself before the SLORC took over.[18]

Before 1988 the standard Burmese infantry weapon was the 7.62mm BA63 automatic rifle, a locally-produced version of the Heckler and Koch G3. The Burma Army also used a shorter, lighter assault version, known as the BA72 (or G2). There was a third version of the G3, known as the BA100, which was more accurate and reliable, but it was used primarily as a sniper's weapon. The BA also had US-made Colt 5.56mm M16A1 automatic rifles (about 500 of which were fitted with 40mm M203 grenade launchers) and German-made 7.62mm FN FAL automatic rifles. The M16s effectively replaced the BA's old 7.62mm Armalite AR10s, a small order for which was filled before production of this weapon ceased in 1961.[19] The FN FALs were surplus West German weapons, provided to Burma in the early 1960s.[20] Many soldiers, however, still carried 0.30 calibre M1 and M2 carbines provided by the US in the 1950s under the MAP, and a few may have even had old 0.303 inch Lee Enfield rifles. The locally-produced BA52 submachine gun was superceded by the British 9mm Sterling L2, some of which were probably acquired during the late 1950s. The British Sten guns seen in Burma around this time were left over from the Second World War, when this weapon was issued in large numbers to Allied guerrilla forces fighting the Japanese. As a side-arm, officers used a 9mm Browning High Power/FN 35 semi-automatic pistol, but for a while many carried old Smith and Wesson or Enfield 0.38 calibre service revolvers. By 1988, however, most of the more obsolete weapons in the BA's armouries had been passed on to Police and People's Militia units.

The typical Section support weapon was the locally-manufactured 7.62mm BA64 light machine gun (LMG), also known as the G4. This was essentially the G3 automatic rifle fitted with a heavy barrel and bipod. The G4 replaced the British 0.303 calibre Bren general purpose machine gun (GPMG), although there is evidence that the Burmese continued to use the Bren for some time, after modifying it to take the 7.62mm NATO standard ammunition produced in their own arms factories.[21] Company fire support generally consisted of German-designed 7.62mm MG3 medium machine guns (made in Burma's own factories) and Belgian 7.62mm FN MAG GPMGs. Also, during the 1950s, when the US was providing Burma with military assistance, the *Tatmadaw* received a quantity of Browning 0.30 inch M1919 A4 MMGs. Although a little heavy and cumbersome for the infantry, these were employed as support weapons until the 1970s. Browning 0.50 calibre (12.7mm) M2HB heavy machine guns were also widely used.[22] There have been a few reports that the BA sometimes employed Oerlikon 20mm cannons against insurgent defensive positions.[23] While the Burma Navy mounts these weapons on its gunboats, their use by the army in this fashion has not been confirmed. It is more likely that the weapons in question were Hispano-Suiza 20mm cannons (closely related to the Oerlikon), which were mounted on some of the BA's armoured vehicles.[24]

The Burma Army also possessed a number of direct fire infantry support weapons. These included some 3000 US-made 40mm M79 grenade launchers, which were delivered to Burma in 1985. The BA also had a collection of 57mm M18, 75mm M20 and 106mm M40 recoilless rifles, all from the US. The M18s and M20s were at least of Korean War vintage, and were probably provided to the BA under the MAP. There have also been reports of Burmese soldiers using old US-made 3.5 inch (88.9mm) M20 shoulder-fired rocket launchers (or 'super bazookas') against insurgent groups, but this has not been confirmed.[25] After 1982 the army took delivery of around 1200 Swedish 84mm M2 Carl Gustaf free-flight rocket launchers.[26] None of the insurgent forces facing the BA had armoured vehicles, but these anti-tank rocket launchers were highly versatile, and were used against bunkers and other fortified positions with devastating effect. Around this time the BA preferred to use Western equipment, but it is likely also to have obtained (perhaps from Yugoslavia) some lightweight 40mm RPG-2 and RPG-7 rocket propelled grenade launchers.

The BA used a variety of mortars for fire support. Most were imported but some were made in Burma. For example, the BA had a large number of old British Ordnance (as well as locally-produced) ML 2-inch (50mm) and ML 3-inch (76mm) weapons.[27] It also had 60mm light mortars (probably US M-19s but also BA100s made in Burma), 81mm medium mortars (probably including some old US M29s and Tampella medium mortars), ex-Soviet bloc 82mm M43 mortars, and a range of 120mm heavy mortars.[28] The latter seems to have been a diverse collection of Yugoslavian (UBM 52), Israeli (Soltam M-65 and K6), French (Hotchkiss-Brandt MO-120-60) and Finnish (Tampella) weapons. While some of these 120mm weapons were true heavy mortars, it is likely that, where possible, lighter versions were chosen for greater mobility.

The army's field and anti-aircraft artillery suffered from the problems of age, shortages of spare parts and ammunition, and a lack of suitable transport. The BA inventory in 1988 probably included about 50 old British 25-pounder (88mm) field guns and some 5.5-inch (140mm) medium guns. For howitzers, the BA relied on about 100 Yugoslavian 76mm M48 B1 mountain guns provided by Marshal Tito in the 1950s, and a similar number of US-made 105mm M101 howitzers delivered under the MAP. The army maintained about 60 anti-tank guns of different types and vintages (mainly old British 57mm 6-pounders and 76.2mm 17-pounders). There has been one report that in 1987 the army took delivery of a number of ex-Soviet 122mm BM-21 multiple rocket launchers (MRL) from Vietnam, but this has yet to be confirmed.[29] Burma's air defence artillery consisted of about

10 Bofors 40mm L60 Mk.1 anti-aircraft guns and a number of veteran 3.7-inch (94mm) Mk.3A towed anti-aircraft guns provided by the UK in the 1950s from Second World War surplus stocks.[30] A number of old Yugoslavian 20mm M38 anti-aircraft guns were also still in service.

All these weapons were kept in good condition, considering the circumstances, but the lack of all-weather roads made their deployment difficult and ammunition shortages prevented sustained fire for any period.

Before 1988 the Burma Army's heavy equipment was also obsolete. There were about 22 Second World War vintage British Comet medium tanks (acquired from the UK in 1954), 40 Humber one-ton APCs which were bought in 1950, 6 Ferret scout cars (acquired in 1956) and 51 Daimler SCs (purchased by Rangoon in 1961). Of the latter, Burma possessed two variants, one fitted with a machine gun turret and one without.[31] The BA also maintained a fleet of about 80 old Universal T-16 tracked Bren gun carriers, some with mounted 20mm Hispano-Suiza Mk.5 cannon. This was all that was left of a shipment of 380 Bren carriers made to Burma from the UK between 1950 and 1959.[32] From the early 1980s BA engineers began building locally designed BAAC APCs and SCs. While the wheeled armoured vehicles saw plenty of service, the operational value of the Comet tanks was limited. Even if they were still serviceable, the *Tatmadaw* lacked sufficient heavy road transporters and had difficulty taking them to areas of operation far from their bases at Hmawbi and Meiktila. The utility of these vehicles was also greatly limited by their age and the nature of the terrain over which they would have to operate. Many bridges in the rural districts could not take the weight of a tank transporter, or even a tank. Armoured vehicles of all kinds were deployed around major population centres during civil disturbances, however, to give the infantry greater firepower and to intimidate protesters.[33]

The army's road transport was provided by an assorted collection of old and new motor vehicles, including Land Rovers, Bedfords and Austin trucks from the UK, Willy's jeeps and Dodge weapons carriers from the US, German Unimog lorries, Toyota DA-80 and FA-60 trucks, and Mitsubishi and Toyota four-wheel drive general purpose vehicles from Japan, and locally-made 3.5-ton Hino diesel trucks. The army's motor pool also included a range of smaller vehicles, mainly Japanese Mazdas (many of which were assembled in Burma).[34] The demands made on these vehicles were immense, and they were further tested by the shortage of sealed all-weather roads. In many border areas there were no roads at all. Rail and riverine transport was used to carry military supplies whenever possible, but they could usually only service bases in rear areas. Supplies were dropped to troops in the field by parachute, but this option was restricted by the BAF's limited resources.[35] In the hills, pack mules were often used to carry heavy equipment, weapons and rations, and troops on operations usually moved on foot. It was common Burma Army practice to force convicts and local civilians to act as porters, carrying ammunition and other supplies from forward bases to the front line.[36] As one observer has noted, it was 'an exceedingly antiquated way of fighting a well-trained and armed enemy in a terrain ideally suited for guerrilla warfare'.[37]

The Burma Army's training structure at this time was multi-layered, and geographically dispersed. Recruits were given basic training in depots like those at Pawngyi, Meiktila and Maymyo. Additional training and refresher courses were conducted by individual units, under the broad direction of Regional Commanders. Specialised and more advanced training, however, was conducted at specific BA instruction centres. For example, courses for NCOs were conducted at a dedicated Non-Commissioned Officers' School. Infantry officers attended courses for platoon, company and battalion commanders at either the Burma Army Central School (opened in 1952) or the Burma Army Combat Forces School (opened in 1955 at Bahtoo). These courses lasted between three to five months.[38] Armour and artillery officers also attended the latter school. More specialised training was conducted at schools operated by individual corps, such as the Administrative Support Training School (opened in Maymyo in 1964), and the Land/Air Warfare School and Paratroops' School, both opened at Hmawbi in 1958. (These two schools were merged in 1963). The Medical and Engineering Corps also had their own technical training centres.[39]

When the SLORC took power, the BA had been fighting insurgent groups and narcotics-based armies for 40 years. During this time it had acquired a reputation as a tough and resourceful military force. In 1981, for example, it was described as 'probably the best in Southeast Asia, apart from Vietnam's'.[40] This judgement was echoed in 1983, when another observer noted that 'Burma's infantry is generally rated as one of the toughest, most combat seasoned in Southeast Asia'.[41] In 1985, a foreign journalist with the rare experience of seeing Burmese soldiers in action against ethnic insurgents was 'thoroughly impressed by their fighting skills, endurance and discipline'.[42] Other commentators at the time characterised the BA as 'the toughest, most effective light infantry jungle force now operating in Southeast Asia'.[43] Even the Thais, not known to praise the Burmese lightly, have described the BA as 'skilled in the art of jungle warfare' and (albeit privately) Thai soldiers readily acknowledge the toughness and determination of their Burmese counterparts.[44] Yet despite its military reputation, the army was unable to achieve its core aims.

The much-vaunted 'Four Cuts' strategy introduced in the mid-1960s had initially succeeded in cutting off many insurgent groups from their sources of food, funds, intelligence and recruits.[45] It had the additional effect, however, of driving them further into the rugged frontier areas of Burma where they were much harder to dislodge. The forced resettlement of villagers and scorched earth policies associated with the Four Cuts program continued, but were much less effective, and added to the alienation of the local population.[46] After the mid-1970s, the army was strong enough to dominate the southern and central lowlands, and put down occasional protests in the urban centres. Yet it did not possess the manpower, firepower, mobility or logistical support necessary to occupy all disputed territories or to achieve decisive results against any of the major insurgent groups. Most military analysts calculate that to achieve victory against well-established guerrillas, the government forces need to outnumber them by at least ten to one. Yet before 1988 the BA was faced with a combined opposition of at least 25,000-35,000 armed insurgents.[47] The ratio was barely five to one.

As a consequence, the Rangoon government reverted to a policy of isolation and attrition, hoping to cut off the insurgents' supplies and wear away their strength until the army could either defeat them on the battlefield or force them to negotiate.[48] Hamstrung by all its deficiencies, however, (and other problems like the annual monsoon), the army soon found that its own strength and staying power was being tested. It was difficult for the BA to mount more than one or two major operations each year, or to sustain them for any extended period. Also, lacking the numbers and logistical resources, the army was forced to tackle insurgent groups individually, hoping not to be faced with more than one major campaign in different parts of the country at the same time. The regime did not have the airlift capacity needed to move troops long distances quickly and, without either an adequate road network or suitable cross-country vehicles, found it difficult to bring its heavier equipment to bear on the insurgents' well defended bases. Insurgent groups were thus given periodic respites from the fighting and opportunities to recover their strength. In the vicious skirmishes and assaults which came to characterise counter-insurgent operations in Burma before 1988, the army was frequently out-gunned and out-manoeuvred by its opponents, who often enjoyed better sources of supply, shorter lines of communication and greater support from the local population.[49]

The months leading up to the military takeover in 1988 were particularly difficult for the army. A series of campaigns against the main insurgent groups around Burma's northern and eastern borders had seriously depleted the government's stocks of essential materiel.[50] Burma's chronic foreign exchange problems had made it difficult to purchase fresh military supplies.[51] Nor could the country's own arms factories meet the demand. These problems were heightened for the regime by the massive pro-democracy demonstrations in the main population centres that August and September. Towards the end of the year, the CPB attempted to take advantage of the regime's weaknesses by launching a new military offensive in northeastern Shan State.[52] At the same time the Kachin Independence Army (KIA) increased its operations in the country's rugged far north and the KNLA began a new campaign along the Burma-Thai border. On all three fronts the fighting was fierce and casualties were high.[53] Some groups even began to infiltrate back into 'white' areas of central Burma which had long been considered secure from the insurgent problem.[54] There was a fear that some of these anti-government groups would join forces in an attempt to overthrow the military regime. To make matters worse for the SLORC, it feared an invasion by the Western democracies, aimed at ending the *Tatmadaw*'s human rights abuses and sending it back to the barracks.

As 1988 drew to a close, the prospect for the military regime was one of continued bitter fighting, possibly against larger and better armed opponents, with few resources and no likelihood of a concrete result. It was a situation which the new military leadership was determined to change.

7.2 The Burma Army After 1988

Almost as soon as the SLORC took power, the Burma Army began an extraordinary period of growth. Within a year it had grown from about 184,000 to 200,000 officers and men. The number of infantry battalions rose by ten to 178.[55] Drawing on a 'comprehensive order of battle' it had obtained, *Jane's Defence Weekly* reported in 1992 that the BA then consisted of 109 garrison battalions and 76 mobile battalions, plus various support elements.[56] 'Intelligence sources' were quoted the same year to the effect that China had 'promised to help equip an entire new Burmese division, and sell equipment for more than 70 new infantry battalions to be raised over the next five years'.[57] Judging by later events, this report was probably accurate. By 2000 the BA had reached some 370,000 all ranks. There were 437 infantry battalions, including 266 light infantry battalions. About 337 were in garrison with the RMCs, while the remainder were shared between the LIDs, which had been increased to ten.[58] LID 11 was formed in December 1988 to bolster security in and around Rangoon. Its HQ is at Htaukkyan, near Mingaladon. LID 101 was added in 1991, with its HQ at Pakkoku.[59]

Those infantry battalions which had formerly carried ethnic designations, such as the Chin Rifles and Kachin Rifles, were given purely numeric titles and turned into light infantry battalions. This step, which had in fact begun as early as 1983 when these regiments lost their exclusive ethnic character, was to emphasise the country's need for unity, despite its diverse ethnic composition.

The BA's other combat and support arms have also undergone a dramatic transformation. There are now ten armoured battalions (five equipped with tanks and five with APCs), 43 artillery battalions and 37 independent artillery companies attached to RMCs. The number of anti-aircraft artillery battalions has risen to seven. There are also at least 11 independent engineer battalions and 16 signal battalions.[60] The BA's six medical battalions have grown to 14 battalions. A number of existing military hospitals have been upgraded and enlarged, and 12 new hospitals have been constructed, including a new 500-bed orthopedic hospital and a new 700-bed general hospital.[61] In addition, the number of military intelligence companies has increased to 40, from about 12 before 1988. These new intelligence units have been assigned not only to potential centres of civil unrest like the major towns and cities, but also to posts along the China, India and Bangladesh borders.[62] Other army units have also been assigned to these areas. As *Jane's Defence Weekly* reported in 1992,

> Before 1988...Burma's borders with Bangladesh and India were covered by five battalions of regular infantry. Today the same zones are covered by more than 32 battalions. Shan State in Burma's north-east has also seen a build-up of government strength, with about 20 of the newly formed battalions stationed there.[63]

This trend continued throughout the 1990s. For example, by late 1999 there were ten battalions of light infantry along the Bangladesh border alone.[64]

It is always difficult to arrive at an accurate Burmese order of battle but, by any estimate, it was a remarkable expansion in a relatively short period.

At the same time, a number of changes were made to the army's command structure, including the creation of several new subordinate headquarters. The number and location of these HQs tend to change, as circumstances demand and resources permit, but in late 2000 there were four Regional Operations Commands, 14 Military Operations Commands, and a much larger number of Tactical Operations Commands.

The first ROCs were opened in 1992 in Mergui and Loikaw. There are now four, at Loikaw, Bhamo, Kalay and Mongsat, and at least one more is under consideration.[65] These HQs were created by the BA to improve command and control, and to more closely manage particularly complex areas of insurgent activity. While technically subordinate to the local Regional Commander, they enjoy considerable autonomy, with their own budget and independent status. First created in 1995, the MOCs are in some ways similar to LIDs (or infantry divisions in Western armies). They consist of a small headquarters, commanding about 10 infantry battalions and organic support units, for use at the Regional Commander's discretion. MOCs are currently based at Kyaukmai, Loilin, Mogaung, Hmawbi, Kyauktaw, Pyinmana, Phaign, Tavoy (2), Kalay, Kyaukpadaung, Kawkareik, Bokepyin and Theinni.[66] There are also 34 TOCs, three each in 10 of the RMCs, while two (Western and South Western Commands) only have two.[67] TOCs generally serve as operational headquarters, similar to Western-style brigades, but they have also been used to give the *Tatmadaw* a presence in more remote areas of the country. As a special case, Rangoon Command is divided into four sub-regions, probably to cope with outbreaks of internal unrest, but also to divide any forces that might be used to move against the government.[68]

These structural changes seem to have been prompted by a combination of factors, including the much larger number of troops in the field, the need to coordinate a greater number of support units, and the demands of more complex military operations. Some measures may have been introduced to help the 12 Regional Commanders cope with their combined political and military workloads.

The BA has also been experimenting with new and larger military formations. For example, two LIDs have already been converted to what the BA calls 'infantry brigades', roughly equivalent to a mechanised division in Western armies. These 'brigades' each consist of about nine infantry 'regiments' (battalions, in Western parlance) under three TOCs, with affiliated artillery, armoured reconnaissance, and tank 'regiments'. There are also a number of supporting units, including communications, medical and logistics 'regiments', two companies of engineers, a provost company and an ordnance unit.[69] The Brigade headquarters are reportedly known as *Na Ba Ha*. The BA has also put considerable effort into increasing its mobility. For example, towards the end of the 1990s an attempt was made to create an air-mobile infantry division, using the *Tatmadaw*'s new Polish and Russian helicopters. It was hoped that such units could act in a similar fashion to US troops during the Vietnam War, flying into war zones at short notice, taking insurgent forces by surprise, and then returning to secure bases.[70] While sound in theory, this initiative was unsuccessful, largely because Burma lacked the resources required to conduct this style of warfare over extended periods. Other initiatives have included the purchase of 3000 2.5 ton trucks from China to create motorised infantry units.[71] There is a much larger number of light infantry battalions, and they are more evenly distributed between commands. Most LIDs now include a mix of light and regular infantry battalions.[72] Efforts have also been made to improve the army's logistics system.

Changes in size and structure are not the only modifications which have been made to the BA under the SLORC and SPDC. Faced with a range of immediate threats, and the longer term need to equip Burma's much larger and more diverse armed forces, the regime embarked on a massive arms procurement program.

The regime's first priority in 1988 was to replenish the *Tatmadaw*'s supply of basic munitions. While its traditional sources were no longer available, other countries were quick to come to the SLORC's rescue. The first was Singapore. In early October 1988 hundreds of boxes marked 'Allied Ordnance, Singapore', were unloaded from two vessels of Burma's Five Star Shipping Line in Rangoon's port.[73] These shipments included mortars, ammunition and raw materials for Burma's arms factories. The consignment also contained 84mm rockets for the *Tatmadaw*'s Carl Gustav recoilless guns, which had been made by Chartered Industries of Singapore under licence from Forenade Fabriksverken in Sweden. The shipment thus violated an agreement under which the original export licence had been granted, requiring that any re-exports only be made with the permission of the Swedish Government. No such clearance was granted.[74] In August 1989 Singapore was again accused of providing arms to the SLORC when weapons and ammunition originating in Belgium and Israel were trans-shipped to Burma, apparently with the assistance of SKS Marketing, a newly-formed Singapore-based joint venture with the Burmese military government.[75] These latter shipments reportedly included second-hand 40mm RPG-2 grenade launchers and 57mm anti-tank guns of Eastern bloc origin. Bertil Lintner has suggested that these weapons may have come from Palestinian stocks captured in southern Lebanon by Israel in 1982, and re-sold to Burma.[76]

In an obvious attempt to outflank India, Pakistan was also quick to take advantage of the army's need to re-stock its armoury. In January 1989 a senior official from Pakistan's arms industry visited Burma to offer the SLORC weapons and ammunition.[77] Two months later, a delegation of senior *Tatmadaw* officers led by Air Force Commander-in-Chief MAJGEN Tin Tun made an unpublicised visit to Islamabad. Also in the delegation was Burma's Director of Ordnance and Director of Defence Industries. An agreement was apparently reached for Pakistan to sell the SLORC 150 machine guns, 50,000 rounds of ammunition and 5,000 120mm mortar bombs.[78] Not long after the first deliveries were made, unexploded mortar bombs bearing the marks of the government-owned Pakistan Ordnance Factories

(POF) were recovered by Karen insurgents from the battlefields along Burma's eastern border.[79] In August 1989 Burmese officials met again with POF representatives, this time in Bangkok, to arrange further arms sales.[80] Pakistan subsequently sent Burma mortars, rocket launchers, assault rifles and ammunition valued at about US$20 million. Until the practice was stopped by the US, many of these weapons were siphoned off foreign arms shipments sent to Pakistan for use by the anti-Soviet *mujahideen* in Afghanistan.[81] Pakistan may have also provided Burma with 106mm M40 A2 recoilless rifles, which the BA now has mounted on some of its jeeps.[82] These arms sales were reportedly halted by Benazir Bhutto in 1991, but later resumed under her successor as Prime Minister, Nawaz Sharif.

The weapons and ammunition which were obtained from these countries met the SLORC's immediate needs. Other shipments followed, however, under a much more comprehensive procurement program. Most came from China. For the infantry, the PRC reportedly provided 10,000 7.62mm Type 56 assault rifles, 40mm RPG-7 rocket-propelled grenade launchers, 82mm and 122mm mortars (probably Type 67 and Type 55), as well as 57mm and 75mm recoilless guns (probably including Type 52 and Type 56).[83] Ammunition was supplied for all these weapons, together with 62mm and 66mm HEAT projectiles.[84] Burma produced its own anti-personnel landmines, but BA stocks were boosted by additional Chinese weapons, including Type 58 stake fragmentation mines, Type 58 blast mines and Type 69 bounding fragmentation mines.[85] There have also been reliable reports that China has provided Burma's infantry with night vision devices, communications equipment and military parachutes.[86]

Following their earlier shipments, Singapore and Pakistan have both supplied Burma with additional infantry weapons and equipment. Direct shipments to Burma from Singapore have reportedly included M16 automatic rifles and 5.56mm ammunition (apparently in defiance of an export agreement attached to their licensed production in Singapore), 7.62mm assault rifles and ammunition, night vision goggles and a wide range of communications equipment.[87] In addition, since 1988 'Singapore has become the entrepot for a gray market in arms for Burma'.[88] Singaporean brokers have facilitated the sale of munitions from several other sources. Singapore has also been the main trans-shipment point for arms delivered to Burma from countries such as Israel, Belgium, Portugal, Sweden and the UK.[89] The details of these transactions are unclear, but they have amounted to 'tens of millions of dollars' worth of weapons and military equipment over the past 12 years.[90] For its part, in 1999 Pakistan supplied Burma with two shiploads of ammunition, valued at US$3.2 million. They included 0.38 calibre revolver ammunition, 7.62mm machine gun ammunition (and spare barrels for the BA's MG3 machine guns), 77mm rifle-launched grenades, 76mm, 82mm and 106mm recoilless rifle rounds, 120mm mortar bombs, 37mm anti-aircraft gun ammunition, and shells for both 105mm and 155mm artillery pieces. There were even rounds for the Burma Army's vintage 25-pounder field guns. In addition, the POF has provided Burma's arms factories with components for ammunition manufacture such as primers, fuses and metallic links for machine gun belts.[91]

The Rangoon regime has also turned to other suppliers to arm and equip its new infantry battalions. In late 1992, for example, it was discovered that a Portuguese arms manufacturer had sold the SLORC about US$1.5 million worth of arms and ammunition, in direct violation of the EU arms embargo. Included in the shipment were 120mm heavy mortars, 81mm medium mortars, and possibly some 60mm light mortars. There were also said to be at least 20,000 mortar bombs and artillery shells in the order.[92] For its part, Israel has contributed at least one consignment of Uzi 9mm submachine guns to the Burma Army's armouries.[93] In late 1990 the DPRK sold Burma 20 million rounds of 7.62mm rifle ammunition.[94] In early 2001 it was reported that the SPDC had purchased 50-100,000 82mm mortar bombs from Vietnam.[95] While specific orders have not been identified, the army's munitions holdings suggest that in recent years France may have sold Burma some mortar bombs, while Belgium, Bulgaria, Czechoslovakia, South Africa and the ROK may have provided additional small arms or ammunition to the Rangoon regime.

Since 1988, the BA has obtained a wide range of heavier equipment, most of it from China.[96] To modernise and strengthen its armoured warfare capabilities, the regime has purchased about 100 Norinco Type 69II main battle tanks (MBT), and about 105 Type 63 light tanks. The BA also has a small number of Type 59D MBTs and possibly some Type 80 MBTs.[97] One regional defence journal has suggested that the regime has purchased a number of Type 85IIM main battle tanks from China, but this has not yet been confirmed.[98] Rangoon appears to have acquired more than 300 Norinco tracked APCs, mainly Type 85 models, but also about 55 Type 90 variants.[99] These vehicles began arriving in the early 1990s.[100] The tanks and APCs acquired by the BA have been distributed among five armoured battalions and five tank battalions based in central Burma, under No.71 Armoured Operations Command HQ at Pyawbwe.[101] These units also manage the 44 BAAC APCs and SCs produced by the *Tatmadaw* in its own workshops between 1983 and 1991.

The Chinese are also reported to have sold Burma more than 100 towed artillery pieces over the past 12 years. These weapons include Norinco WP52 155mm towed howitzers (probably acquired in 1997), some 122mm Type 54 howitzers, possibly some 106mm weapons and a number of anti-tank guns.[102] The BA has taken delivery of at least 30 Norinco 107mm Type 63 multiple rocket launchers.[103] This is a 12-round MRL normally mounted on the Type 81 four-by-four truck. It is possible that several 19-round 130mm Type 63 MRLs were also supplied.[104] For ground-based air defence, the regime has purchased at least 24 Chinese 37mm Type 74 twin barrel towed anti-aircraft guns, with their associated mobile generators, radars and directors. Chinese arms salesmen advertise the Type 702 fire control radar with this system, but some sources have identified the units sold to Burma as having the Type 311.[105] It has also been reported that the BA has obtained some Norinco twin 57mm Type 80 self-propelled anti-aircraft gun systems. There are indications, however, to suggest that this may not be correct, and that the order was in fact for about 12 Norinco single barrel 57mm towed anti-aircraft gun systems, complete with generators, fire control radars and directors. Then again, both systems may have been supplied.[106]

Some artillery pieces have come from other countries. For example, in the late 1990s the BA acquired about 16 Soltam 155mm long range guns from Israel, and about 12 130mm Type 59 field guns from the DPRK. The latter sale followed a visit to Pyongyang by the BA Director of Procurement in June 1999.[107]

As strategic assets, the longer-range guns have probably been placed under the control of the Directorate of Armour and Artillery in the Defence Ministry. Other weapons have been allocated to the two Artillery Operation Command HQs in Kyaukpadaung and Oaktwin (near Toungoo). A few may be stationed at the new Armour and Artillery School at Bahtoo. In a break with the past, independent artillery companies have been assigned to some of the RMCs, LIDs, ROCs and MOCs. For example, artillery units can now be found in places like Lashio, Bhamo, Meiktila, Namsang, Monywa, Tavoy and Aungban.[108] It is not known, however, if these companies consist of soldiers equipped with recoilless rifles and heavy mortars (customarily described as 'artillery' by the BA), or units equipped with field pieces.

With the possibility of a foreign invasion in mind, the regime has made a considerable effort since 1988 to improve Burma's ground-based air defences. According to the journal *Asian Aviation*, around 1991,

> Myanmar acquired a surplus BAe Dynamics Bloodhound Mk II surface-to-air missile [SAM] system withdrawn from service by the Rep. of Singapore AF. The package is understood to have also included missiles and three Scorpion target illuminating radars.[109]

An investigative reporter for the Australian Special Broadcasting System television network is convinced that more than one Bloodhound system was sold to Burma by Singapore.[110] If these reports are true, then the Bloodhound would be the first guided missile system to be introduced into the *Tatmadaw*'s arsenal. However, while some of the evidence is compelling, the *Asian Aviation* and SBS reports have yet to be confirmed.[111] Included in an arms deal with China in 1994 was a shipment (possibly of 200 units or more) of Hongying HN-5A man-portable, shoulder-launched SAMs.[112] This weapon has a heat-seeking guidance system, like the old Soviet SA-7 'Grail' on which it is based. The BA also has some SA-7 missiles, which it inherited when drug lord Khun Sa's Mong Tai Army (MTA) surrendered to the SLORC in 1996. More recent acquisitions by the army have included at least 100 SA-16 'Gimlet' SAMs manufactured in Bulgaria, and some US 'Stinger' SAMs from Pakistan.[113] It is not known whether the latter were taken from stocks originally intended for the Afghan resistance, or are weapons supplied by the US to the Pakistan armed forces. There has been one unconfirmed report that Burma has arranged to buy additional Gimlet SAMs from Singapore, where they are soon to be manufactured under licence.[114]

Since 1988 the BA has acquired a range of new road transport and heavy duty vehicles. China alone has provided more than 5000 vehicles since 1988, including

6.5-tonne Aeolus trucks, five-tonne Jiefang trucks, two-tonne Lan Jian trucks, two-tonne Kungi trucks, and about 300 other heavy duty machines.[115] The latter appear to have included some tank recovery vehicles, armoured bridge layers and a number of wheeled tank transporters.[116] In addition, the SLORC has purchased a number of Star 266 road cranes and Star 12.5-ton trucks from Poland. Other purchases since 1988 include Nissan Container Carriers, Nissan five-ton diesel trucks and Nissan Patrol four wheel drive general purpose vehicles, all from Japan, and possibly a number of AR-51 Zastava light all terrain vehicles from Yugoslavia.[117] Hino 3.5 and 6.5 ton trucks are being produced in Burma and, despite promises to Japan, many find their way to the BA's vehicle parks. The army also uses MAN tactical bridges from Germany, but it is not known when they were added to the BA's inventory.[118]

Deliveries of the new Chinese equipment began almost as soon as the first deal was signed, with the arrival in Rangoon in August 1990 of a Chinese freighter carrying small arms and ammunition, radar equipment and anti-aircraft weapons.[119] For most of this materiel, however, the BA was forced to wait until the completion in October 1992 of a large new bridge over the Shweli River, which runs along the Burma-China border between Namkhan and Muse. An extensive program of road and bridge building on both sides of the border has also been undertaken, with a view in part to expediting further arms deliveries.[120] By the end of 1993 arms were said to be flowing into Burma 'at a faster pace than at any time since the first deliveries [from China] took place in August 1990'.[121] Since the mid-1990s, the pace of Chinese acquisitions seems to have slowed, partly for economic reasons, and partly because the Rangoon regime has tried to diversify its sources of arms. Yet the Burma Army's armouries, artillery parks and vehicle depots are apparently still not full. Whether they come from China, Pakistan, Singapore, Israel or somewhere else, shipments of arms and equipment continue to arrive, by land, air and sea.

The rapid expansion of the army, and its acquisition of a wide range of new weapons and equipment, made it imperative for the BA to increase the size and scope of its training facilities. As part of this effort, a new Armour and Artillery School was opened at Bahtoo in 1990, and by the end of the decade 750 artillery officers and 315 armour officers had graduated. Also in 1990 a Mechanical and Electrical Engineering School was opened in Maymyo, replacing the old Corps Centre there. In 1997 the Burma Army Engineering Corps Centre was transformed into the Defence Services Engineering Training School. It offers a wide range of instruction for officers and other ranks in both field and civil engineering. A second Combat Forces School was established at Thandaung in 2000, to help ease the burden on the Bahtoo school.[122] The Signals, Medical and Intelligence Corps have also benefited from expanded training programs and facilities. While all these schools will profit from the experience of BA officers posted overseas, they are unlikely to have any foreign personnel on their directing staffs. The Burma Army is intensely proud of its own military traditions and it can be expected that, as far as possible, it will devise its own doctrine and teaching methods.

7.3 The New Burma Army

With its greatly increased numbers, new weapons, greater mobility, and improved support systems, the Burma Army in 2000 must be considered a formidable force. Arguments over the exact numbers aside, it is now one of the largest ground forces in Southeast Asia.[123] While its new arms and equipment may not be state-of-the-art, it is better equipped than at any time in its history, and compares favourably with the armies of its regional neighbours. As a result of its 50 years of continuous active service, the BA has more direct experience of combat in the field than many comparable forces. While this experience has mainly been in counter-insurgent warfare, its development over the past 12 years should now permit it to perform a much wider range of both unconventional and conventional defence roles.

At first sight, these assumptions would appear to be well justified. During the 1991-92 dry season, for example, the *Tatmadaw* was able to conduct concurrent campaigns against ethnic and religious minorities along the borders with Thailand, Bangladesh and India. From the scope and nature of these operations it was clear that the Burma Army had benefited considerably from its expansion and modernisation programs.[124] Its newfound strength was confirmed during later campaigns, including the 1994-95 dry season offensive against the Karen insurgent strongholds of Manerplaw and Kawmura.[125] There were several reasons for the army's victories in 1995, when so many earlier campaigns against the Karens had failed, and some were clearly unrelated to improvements in the armed forces.[126] Yet this latter campaign still demonstrated that by then the BA was in a position to concentrate its strength more quickly, bring much greater force to bear on its enemies, and sustain its operations longer, than had been the case in the past. The size of the campaign, the rapid reinforcement of the units deployed, and the sustained fire from recoilless guns, mortars and artillery against the Karen camps, for example, all suggested much better logistics structures, improved road transport, more modern weapons and increased ammunition stocks.[127]

On paper at least, the army's conventional defence capabilities should also have improved. Not only is the BA now much larger, but it is more mobile and has greatly improved armour, artillery and air defence inventories. Its command, control, communications, computer and intelligence systems have been expanded and refined. It is developing larger and more integrated formations which should lend themselves to better coordinated action by different combat arms. Burma may still have relatively modest weapon systems compared to its larger neighbours, but it is now in a much better position to deter external aggression and to respond to such a threat should it ever arise. That said, doubts must still be held about the BA's ability fully to capitalise on its new structure and materiel acquisitions. This applies as much to the conduct of counter-insurgent operations as to the performance of larger-scale, conventional defence roles.

The rapid expansion of the army since 1988 has placed it under considerable strain. Many units are well under strength and training has suffered. There is a shortage of qualified and experienced officers and NCOs, who have been spread thinly among the new infantry battalions. This problem is compounded by the regime's preference for the army's higher ranks to be filled by ethnic Burmans.[128] The 1991-92, 1992-93 and 1994-95 dry season offensives against various ethnic insurgent groups (notably the Kachins and Karens) may have demonstrated some of the army's new material strengths, but they also highlighted a number of major shortcomings in its doctrine, tactics and leadership. There were persistent reports, for example, of large-scale assaults being launched with insufficient combat intelligence, inadequate planning and poor coordination of all the units involved.[129] It is also clear that during the dry season campaigns against the Karens between 1990 and 1995, and the 1993-94 offensives against Khun Sa's MTA, 'human wave' tactics were used, with Burmese officers forcing large numbers of young, inexperienced and poorly trained soldiers to mount mass assaults against heavily fortified defensive positions manned by tough and resourceful guerrillas. BA casualties from all these campaigns were reported to be very high.[130] Since then there have been fewer campaigns of this magnitude, but nor have there been any signs of these tactics being reviewed.

In these circumstances, it is hardly surprising that there have been persistent reports of low morale and a lack of commitment in the army's ranks, particularly in the field. During operations against Karen insurgents in the Irrawaddy River delta in 1991, for example, local commanders were apparently ordered to 'shoot deserters on the spot'.[131] A BA operational order captured by the KNU in 1992 ordered officers not to lead their men from the front, but to 'use stick to force them forward'.[132] Young Burmese soldiers captured by Karens during dry season offensives along the Thai border over the past decade have consistently complained of poor living conditions, inadequate rations and low morale. It is also common for BA prisoners and deserters to complain of brutal treatment from their officers, both in the barracks and on operations.[133] Some 15-year old recruits interviewed by Western journalists have claimed that they were given whisky by their officers because they were 'scared to go to the front', and Karen insurgents have often claimed that Burmese soldiers are drugged before being sent into battle.[134] Corruption has always existed in the Burma Army, but since 1988 it has reached unprecedented levels, and the lowest ranking soldiers are the first to suffer. As the 1990s drew to a close, the rate of desertions from the army was increasing sharply.[135]

Even allowing for a certain amount of exaggeration on the part of those giving these reports, and those receiving them, they all point to serious deficiencies in training, leadership and morale.

Some of these problems seem to have arisen because the Burma Army has largely rejected its British traditions and relies instead on the styles of command and instruction which it learnt from the Japanese during the Second World War. This approach emphasises highly centralised control, a sharp distinction between ranks, rigid discipline and unquestioning obedience to orders, rather than the encouragement of innovation and initiative, or attention to matters of personnel welfare.[136] At times, concerns about the political reliability of soldiers called upon to shoot unarmed demonstrators, or to destroy rural villages, seem to take priority over attention to purely military skills. The very strict mental and physical regime normally enforced within the ranks, however, is matched by an extraordinary degree of license in the field. In another echo of past Japanese military practice, there have been persistent reports over the past 12 years of BA officers permitting their men to loot, rape, torture and even murder civilian villagers and porters, while on active duty.[137] This behaviour may reflect a general lowering of standards in the officer corps, but it also appears to be part of a deliberate strategy by the army to terrorise the local population and ensure its submission to Rangoon.

Quite apart from the obvious (and very serious) human rights issues raised by these reports, to most professional observers this kind of leadership undermines the soldiers' discipline and morale, and ultimately detracts from their military efficiency.

Nor can the Burma Army's new weapons and equipment be counted upon to tip the scales entirely in the regime's favour. Despite the training provided overseas, and by foreign experts in Burma, many soldiers still seem to find much of their new equipment unfamiliar and, in some cases, difficult to handle. For example, there have already been numerous complaints, particularly about those items provided by China:

> The artillery pieces were clumsy and heavy and misfired frequently. The armoured vehicles broke down often and were in any case useless against the rebels who operate in Myanmar's mountainous frontier areas. Chinese army trucks were not nearly as good as the Japanese-supplied Hino and Nissan vehicles which the Burmese army also uses.[138]

According to another source, 'when 155mm computer-guided artilleries were transferred, the Chinese removed hard discs from some of the computers'.[139] There have also been problems with maintenance and the supply of spare parts. Shortages still occur, even on operations. In fighting against Khun Sa in mid-1993, for example, Burmese troops were said to be badly out-gunned by members of the insurgent SSA and MTA.[140] Despite the BA's massive arms purchases in recent years, observers said that the Burmese soldiers appeared to lack small arms and combat radios, and were 'being attacked with the more sophisticated weapons of the guerrillas'.[141] Fighting was fierce, but Burmese troops could not make much headway. Even now, after all the improvements made to the BA logistics system, there are persistent reports of troops in the field going hungry, lacking adequate medical supplies, and wanting other basic necessities.[142]

Some of the Burma Army's problems lie in the nature of Burma itself — its large size, its varied physical geography, extreme tropical climate and complex racial composition. As was demonstrated during the Second World War, these features can pose formidable challenges to armies far better equipped and supported than the current Burmese force. Burma's international isolation since 1948, and the manifest failure of Ne Win's 'Burmese Way to Socialism' between 1962 and 1988, deprived the government of the funds it needed to build a comprehensive and strategically beneficial network of all-weather roads, railways, bridges and airfields.[143] This will inevitably limit the value of some of the army's heavier equipment, particularly in counter-insurgency campaigns. Also, the steadfast refusal of the military hierarchy in Rangoon to contemplate any meaningful political settlement with Burma's ethnic minorities, particularly after 1962, helped to encourage separatist tendencies and exacerbated long-standing internal security problems. Insurgent groups have been greatly strengthened by the harsh treatment meted out to the minority peoples by the armed forces during its annual counter-insurgency campaigns.

Some of these problems might be overcome, or at the least made more manageable, during a protracted guerrilla war in which the central government enjoyed certain military advantages, could isolate its enemies (both physically and politically) and could ignore international opinion. Even if this could be achieved (and experience has shown the difficulties of doing so), such circumstances would not apply in a war against an external aggressor. The Burma Army lacks experience in extended, large-scale conventional operations. There were a number of major campaigns against the KMT remnants during the 1950s and early 1960s, and some later engagements against insurgent groups had the flavour of set-piece battles.[144] Yet, for most of the time the army has been preoccupied with defeating tough, well-armed but relatively small bands of guerrillas concentrated in remote rural areas. Until the SLORC took power, these operations were usually carried out at battalion level. The regime benefited too from the fact that, despite occasional 'alliances', few insurgent groups successfully coordinated their campaigns against the central government. The KNDO and CPB were the only groups which professed to have any intention of actually marching on Rangoon.

In theory at least, the BA's new and more elaborate command structure gives it the ability to concentrate and apply force more quickly, more flexibly and more strongly, in response to changing requirements. Yet it is still based on geographically defined Regional Military Commands and mobile infantry divisions. While both answer to a single BSO in the Defence Ministry, this division of assets and responsibilities will make larger, more complex operations difficult. The larger formations being created are largely untested. There still seems to be a tendency only to plan operations for limited periods. For example, the BA has long mapped out its future activities on the basis of two defined operational periods divided by a rest period. These are from 1 January until 30 April (the end of the dry season), 1 May until 31 August (the monsoon period, to rest and refit) and 1 September until 31 December (the beginning of the next dry season). Also, while there are now many more infantry battalions based around Burma's borders and in insurgent-affected areas, it would appear that each major military operation is planned as an individual task, with the required forces being brought together from different commands solely for the purpose of that campaign. This permits the flexible use of troops and equipment, but seems a very inefficient use of resources.[145] Larger-scale conventional operations would put such a staff system under considerable strain.

There are other deficiencies. Burmese soldiers have a commitment to remain in 'inactive reserve status' for a period after the termination of their period of enlistment. These veterans currently receive refresher training but, aside from them, the army has no real strategic reserve. Despite the regime's hopes, the millions of barely-trained and often resentful civilians in the USDA, civil service, Auxiliary Fire Brigade, Myanmar Red Cross and other such organisations, hardly constitute a reliable reserve force. Nor, it appears, does Burma have any tested national mobilisation plan. Joint operations have always been difficult, as demonstrated by the lack of coordination between the army and air force during successive dry season offensives against ethnic insurgents.[146] More recent large-scale joint exercises may have helped in this regard but it would be remarkable if there were not still major problems of conception, coordination and execution to be ironed out. Even greater difficulties would be experienced in the unlikely event that the Burma Army was obliged to conduct combined operations with the armed forces of another country. Indeed, there is only one case in which this is known to have occurred since Independence in 1948, and that can hardly count as a precedent.[147]

If Burma was ever attacked, the Burma Army would fight hard and well with the resources it had. Defending a country the size of Burma, however, against co-ordinated assaults by a well-prepared force armed with modern weapons, would be a completely new experience for the BA which would test it severely. In these circumstances, much would depend on the combat capabilities of the other two Services.

Notes

1. An earlier version of this chapter was published as Andrew Selth, 'The Myanmar Army Since 1988: Acquisitions and Adjustments', *Contemporary Southeast Asia*, Vol. 17, No. 3, December 1995.
2. Tinker, *The Union of Burma*, p. 323.
3. Published figures for Burma's order of battle are notoriously unreliable, but they can be useful for conveying orders of magnitude, if not actual force levels. The following paragraphs draw on the official figures cited by Maung Aung Myoe in *Building the Tatmadaw* (p. 24), and the IISS's *Military Balance* for the years in question. See also Selth, *Burma's Order of Battle*, and Appendix 1.
4. Tinker, *The Union of Burma*, p. 326; Dr Maung Maung puts the 1949 figure at 'a few thousand men' in *Burma's Constitution* (Martinus Nijhoff, The Hague, 1959), p. 143.
5. Tinker, *The Union of Burma*, p. 326.
6. Maung Aung Myoe, *Building the Tatmadaw*, p. 25.
7. Maung Aung Myoe, *Military Doctrine and Strategy in Myanmar*, p. 13.
8. *The Military Balance 1988-1989*, p. 159. See also Tin Maung Maung Than, 'Burma's National Security and Defence Posture', p. 48.
9. Bunge, *Burma*, pp. 253-4.
10. *Ibid. The Military Powers Encyclopedia* (p. 38) states that the ethnic regiments accounted for less than 5% of the Burma Army's active battalions. See also John Keegan, *World Armies* (Macmillan, London, 1983), p. 88.
11. *The Military Balance 1988-1989*, p. 159.
12. A Correspondent, 'Reining in the Majors', *FEER*, 17 September 1987, p. 14; and Lintner and Karniol, 'Unrest swells the Burmese ranks', p. 1020.

13. 'Reining in the majors', p. 14.

14. The only known airborne operation was in 1959, against the Burma Communist Party (Red Flags) near Magwe.

15. Between 1950 and 1984 the US provided US$72.1 million in grants under the MAP. Between 1950 and 1994, it also gave about US$5.8 million under the International Military Education and Training (IMET) program. Burma also received aircraft and other military equipment under the International Narcotics Control Program (INCP). See *Foreign Military Sales, Foreign Military Construction Sales and Military Assistance Facts, as of September 30, 1994* (US Department of Defence, Washington, 1995), p. 70 and p. 95.

16. Burma's refusal to renew its military aid program with the US in 1971 was directly related to Rangoon's resumption of normal ties with Beijing after a diplomatic breach in mid-1967. Chi-shad Liang, *Burma's Foreign Relations: Neutralism in Theory and Practice* (Praeger, New York, 1990), p. 168.

17. Bunge, *Burma*, p. 254.

18. The following paragraphs draw on several sources, in particular *The Military Balance 1988-1989*, pp. 156-7; *The Military Balance 1995/96*, pp. 161-2; *Jane's Infantry Weapons 1987-88* (Jane's Information Group, Coulsdon, 1987), p. 945; *Jane's Infantry Weapons 1994-95* (Jane's Information Group, Coulsdon, 1994), p. 686; *Jane's Armour and Artillery 1987-88* (Jane's Information Group, Coulsdon, 1987), p. 866; and *Jane's Armour and Artillery 1994-95* (Jane's Information Group, Coulsdon, 1994), p. 677.

19. E.C. Ezell, *Small Arms of the World: A Basic Manual of Small Arms* (Stackpole, Harrisburg, 1983), p. 30.

20. The Germans dubbed the FN FAL the G1, a practice which the Burmese also followed.

21. Personal observation, Rangoon, April 1995.

22. The MG3 is sometimes listed (incorrectly) as the MG42.

23. Tom Peterson, 'Karen Kill Zone', *Soldier of Fortune*, Vol. 15, No. 3, March, 1990, p. 31. See also Tom Peterson, 'Bad Day at Thingannyinaung', *Soldier of Fortune*, Vol. 15, No. 2, February 1990, p. 31; and Mike Williams, 'Gutsy Karens Continue to Bloody Burmese Butchers', *Soldier of Fortune*, Vol. 15, No. 2, February 1990, p. 35.

24. Personal observation, Rangoon, April 1995.

25. Selth, *Burma's Order of Battle*, pp. 14-16.

26. *Jane's Infantry Weapons 1996-97* (Jane's Information Group, Coulsdon, 1996), p. 233. See also Bertil Lintner, 'An export backfires', *FEER*, 8 September 1983, pp. 26-7. These recoilless guns were presumably the 'Swedish field artillery' to which Jon Anderson referred in *Guerrillas* (Harper Collins, London, 1994), p. 74.

27. The Burma Army was reportedly still using British 2-inch mortars against insurgents as late as 1990, although the ammunition was 30-40 years old and often failed to explode. Peterson, 'Karen Kill Zone', p. 31.

28. *Jane's Infantry Weapons 1995-96* (Jane's Information Group, Coulsdon, 1995), p. 678.

29. *The Military Powers Encyclopedia*, p. 37.

30. *Jane's Armour and Artillery 1981-82* (Jane's, London, 1981), p. 579. As no weapon in the BA's armoury ever seems to be discarded, it seems a safe assumption that they were still in use, or at least in store, in 1988.

31. Personal observation, Rangoon, April 1995. See also James Smith, 'Myanmar's Armed Forces - Retaining Power', *Jane's Intelligence Review*, Vol. 3, No. 9, September 1991, pp. 188-9.

32. Maung Aung Myoe, *The Tatmadaw in Myanmar Since 1988*, p. 26, note 38. These Bren gun carriers appeared on the streets of Rangoon in 1988 when the army deployed to crush the pro-democracy movement. Lintner, *Outrage*, pp. 131ff.

33. Personal observation, Rangoon, December 1974. See also Lintner, *Outrage*, p. 131; and Selth, *Death of a Hero*, p. 18.
34. Personal observation, Rangoon and Taunggyi, April 1995.
35. Personal observation, Rangoon, April 1995.
36. The harsh treatment received by these porters has been described on many occasions, most recently in the ILO *Report of the Commission of Enquiry*, 1998. See also Kerry Brewster, 'Dateline', Australian Special Broadcasting Service (SBS) television network, 25 March 1995; and Amnesty International, *The Kayin State in the Union of Myanmar: Allegations of Ill-treatment and Unlawful Killings of Suspected Political Opponents and Porters Seized Since 18 September 1988* (Amnesty International, London, 1989).
37. Smith, *Burma: Insurgency and the Politics of Ethnicity*, p. 100.
38. Interview, Sydney, October 1996. See also Maung Aung Myoe, *Officer Education and Leadership Training*, pp. 8-9.
39. Maung Aung Myoe, *Officer Education and Leadership Training*, pp. 8-10.
40. John McBeth, 'Rangoon wears them down', *FEER*, 29 May 1981, p. 20.
41. Rodney Tasker, 'A rag-tag armed force which gets the job done', *FEER*, 7 July 1983, pp. 32-3.
42. Lintner, *Land of Jade*, p. viii.
43. 'Terror on the border', *Asiaweek*, 21 February 1992, p. 25.
44. *The Defence of Thailand 1994* (Government of Thailand, Bangkok, 1994), p. 15; and interviews, Bangkok, April 1995.
45. Smith, *Burma: Insurgency and the Politics of Ethnicity*, pp. 258ff.
46. See, for example, Rodney Tasker and Bertil Lintner, 'Second Coming', *FEER*, 15 July 1993, p. 24.
47. Smith, *Burma: Insurgency and the Politics of Ethnicity*, p. 90. See also Lintner, *The Rise and Fall of the Communist Party of Burma*, pp. 105-8; Smith, *Ethnic Groups in Burma*, p. 34; and Bill Barnes, 'Burma's democrats fight on in the face of fear', *The Australian*, 12 January 1993.
48. O'Ballance, 'Burma', pp. 28-35.
49. Insurgent groups were able to purchase modern weapons on the blackmarket, drawing on funds generated by 'taxes' imposed on cross-border smuggling operations. Other groups had access to funds generated from the sale of narcotics. A few, like the CPB, were supported by foreign governments. Smith, *Burma: Insurgency and the Politics of Ethnicity*, p. 100. See also Anderson, p. 73.
50. *Asia 1988 Yearbook* (*FEER*, Hong Kong, 1988), pp. 106-7.
51. Before the political crisis in late 1988, Burma's foreign exchange reserves were barely sufficient to cover the cost of two weeks' imports. The Economist Intelligence Unit, *Thailand, Burma: Country Profiles, 1989-1990* (Economist, London, 1990).
52. Despite accusations by the SLORC that the CPB helped engineer the 1988 demonstrations, and later manipulated pro-democracy figures like Aung San Suu Kyi, the CPB was just as surprised by the events of 1988 as the regime itself. The CPB only staged one major military offensive after September 1988, and by April 1989 it had collapsed. See *Burma Communist Party's Conspiracy to take over State Power*; and Lintner, *The Rise and Fall of the Communist Party of Burma*, pp. 44-6.
53. Lintner, *Outrage*, pp. 151-4.
54. Lintner, *Outrage*, pp. 151ff. See also 'Troops tend cities, rebels infiltrate central Burma', AFP, 24 October 1988.
55. Maung Aung Myoe, *Building the Tatmadaw*, p. 24; and *The Military Balance 1988-1989*, p. 159.
56. Lintner and Karniol, 'Unrest swells the Burmese ranks', p. 1020.
57. Lintner, 'Centrifugal forces', p. 16.

58. Interview, Chiang Mai, November 1999. See also Selth, *Burma's Order of Battle*, pp. 10-11; and Maung Aung Myoe, *The Tatmadaw in Myanmar Since 1988*, pp. 13-16.

59. Lintner and Karniol, 'Unrest swells the Burmese ranks', p. 1020. In 1993 Tin Maung Maung Than suggested that there were 11 LIDs, but this additional formation cannot be identified. See 'Neither Inheritance nor Legacy', p. 60, note 126.

60. Selth, *Burma's Order of Battle*, pp. 11-12. See also Maung Aung Myoe, *The Tatmadaw in Myanmar Since 1988*, p. 15.

61. Maung Aung Myoe, *The Tatmadaw in Myanmar Since 1988*, p. 15.

62. Lintner and Karniol, 'Unrest swells the Burmese ranks', p. 1020.

63. *Ibid.*

64. Interview, Rangoon, December 2000.

65. Maung Aung Myoe, *The Tatmadaw in Myanmar Since 1988*, p. 14. The ROCs are sometimes referred to as Regional Control Commands.

66. Selth, *Burma's Order of Battle*, pp. 10-11. The MOCs are sometimes called Operational Control Commands or Mobile Operations Commands.

67. Interview, Canberra, October 1997.

68. Interview, Rangoon, November 1999.

69. Interview, Rangoon, November 1999. See also 'Organisation of a brigade and the special characteristics of a brigade', typescript in the author's possession.

70. Interview, Rangoon, November 1999.

71. *Ibid.*

72. For example, 33 LID and 44 LID each have three regular infantry battalions and seven light infantry battalions. In 88 LID there are five light infantry battalions and five regular infantry battalions, while 101 LID consists entirely of regular infantry battalions. Interview, Chiang Mai, November 1999; and Selth, *Burma's Order of Battle*, pp. 10-11.

73. Lintner, *Outrage*, p. 140. See also 'Singapore-made arms for Rangoon', AFP, 26 October 1988; and Bertil Lintner, 'Consolidating Power', *FEER*, 5 October 1989, p. 23.

74. Lintner, *Outrage*, p. 140. See also Smith, 'The Burmese way to rack and ruin', p. 45; and Lintner, 'An export backfires', pp. 26-7.

75. Smith, 'The Burmese way to rack and ruin', pp. 43-5. See also Lintner, 'Consolidating power', p. 23.

76. Lintner, 'Myanmar's Chinese connection', p. 26. See also Ron Corben, 'Arms deals tighten Burma junta's grip', *Herald*, 9 December 1990; and Lintner, 'Using the aid weapon', p. 34.

77. Interview, Rangoon, April 1995.

78. Daljit Singh, 'The Eastern Neighbour: Myanmar', *Indian Defence Review*, October 1992, p. 33. The Institute for Asian Democracy has claimed that Pakistan sold Burma 150,000 rounds of ammunition, but this seems too high. Alan Boyd has stated that the deal also included 76mm and 130mm mortar bombs, but Burma is not known to possess weapons of either calibre. See *Towards Democracy in Burma*, p. 58; and Alan Boyd, 'Burma arms itself against rebels in secret', *The Australian*, 18 May 1990.

79. Bertil Lintner, 'The Islamabad Link', *India Today*, 10 September 1989, pp. 60-1.

80. Lintner, 'Consolidating power', p. 23.

81. Lintner, 'Hidden reserves', p. 12.

82. Personal observation, Rangoon, April 1995.

83. The rifles and ammunition alone were reported to be worth US$290 million. See Lintner, 'Rangoon's Rubicon', p. 28. See also Bertil Lintner, 'Hardware for hardliners', *FEER*, 1 December 1994, p. 12; Bertil Lintner, 'Collective insecurity', *FEER*, 3 December 1992, p. 22; Bertil Lintner, 'Chinese arms bolster Burmese forces', *JDW*, 27 November 1993, p. 11; and Lintner, 'Myanmar's Chinese connection', p. 26.

84. Personal observation, Rangoon, April 1995.

85. See Selth, *Landmines in Burma*.
86. Lintner, 'Arms for Eyes', p. 26; and interview, Rangoon, November 1999.
87. Lintner, 'Myanmar's Chinese connection', p. 26. See also Selth, *Burma's Secret Military Partners*, pp. 33-4.
88. Marvin C. Ott, 'From Isolation to Relevance: Policy Considerations', in *Burma: Prospects for a Democratic Future*, p. 78. See also William Ashton, 'Burma receives advances from its silent suitors in Singapore', pp. 32-4.
89. Tasker and Lintner, 'Difficult guests', p. 11. Burmese insurgents have also bought weapons through middlemen in Singapore. See Bertil Lintner, 'Drugs and Economic Growth: Ethnicity and Exports', in Rotberg, *Burma*, p. 177.
90. Trevor Watson, 'Report from Asia', ABC FM radio, 17 July 1994.
91. Interview, Rangoon, December 1999. See also Selth, *Burma's Secret Military Partners*, pp. 61-3; and William Ashton, 'Myanmar's military links with Pakistan', *Jane's Intelligence Review*, Vol. 12, No. 6, June 2000, pp. 27-9.
92. According to Bertil Lintner, the deal was arranged through a Portuguese company, dealing with Singaporean brokers who did not divulge the final destination of the arms. See 'Portuguese Men-of-War', *FEER*, 12 November 1992, p. 8.
93. William Ashton, 'Myanmar and Israel develop military pact', *Jane's Intelligence Review*, Vol. 12, No. 3, March 2000, pp. 35-8. Uzi submachine guns only seem to have been distributed to special army units. The bodyguards of senior regime figures, for example, carry them, as do soldiers assigned to protect foreign visitors. See, for example, Angus McDonald, *The Five Foot Road: In Search of a Vanished China* (Angus and Robertson, Sydney, 1995), p. 177.
94. 'Burma buys AK-47 rounds', *JDW*, 2 February 1991, p. 139. Several observers have suggested that the ammunition was destined for the United Wa State Army, which had signed a cease-fire agreement with the SLORC. Given the UWSA's continuing involvement in the narcotics trade, which China officially condemned, it would have been too embarrassing for the SLORC to ask China for the ammunition. See, for example, interview, Canberra, October 1995; and Smith, 'The Burmese way to rack and ruin', p. 45.
95. Karniol, 'Myanmar stocks up on ammunition'.
96. The following paragraphs have been drawn largely from the reporting of Bertil Lintner, in particular 'Oiling the iron fist', p. 28; 'Lock and load, p. 28; 'Hidden reserves', p. 12; 'Rangoon's Rubicon', p. 28; and 'Myanmar's Chinese connection', p. 26. See also Yindee Lertcharoenchok, 'Beijing, Rangoon ink $1.2 billion arms deal'; Lintner, '$400m deal signed by China and Myanmar', *JDW*, 3 December 1994, p. 1; and Lague, 'Evans seeks support for ban on Burma'.
97. Interviews, Rangoon, November and December 1999.
98. Micool Brooke, 'The Armed Forces of Myanmar', *Asian Defence Journal*, January 1998, p. 13. Another source has suggested that the BA has about 50 of these tanks. Interview, Rangoon, December 1999.
99. Some sources have referred to the purchase of infantry fighting vehicles (IFV), but this appears to reflect confusion between APCs and IFVs of this type. Also, some reports speak of Type 92 APCs. See Lintner, 'Myanmar's Chinese connection', p. 23; *Jane's Armour and Artillery 1994-95*, pp. 272ff; Bates Gill and J.N. Mak, *Arms Transparency and Security in South-East Asia* (Oxford University Press, Oxford, 1997), p. 121; and Brooke, 'The Armed Forces of Myanmar', p. 11.
100. Lintner, 'Chinese arms bolster Burmese forces', p. 11. See also Lintner, 'Hardwear for hardliners', p. 12; and Lintner, 'Arms for Eyes', p. 26.
101. For example, armoured units can be found at Hmawbi, Magwe and Meiktila. Interview, Chiang Mai, November 1999. See also Maung Aung Myoe, *The Tatmadaw in Myanmar Since 1988*, p. 14.

102. Lintner, 'Arms for Eyes', p. 26; Brooke, 'The Armed Forces of Myanmar', p. 11 and p. 13; and Maung Aung Myoe, *The Tatmadaw in Myanmar Since 1988*, p. 14.
103. Lintner, 'Arms for Eyes', p. 26.
104. *Ibid.* See also Lintner, 'Rangoon's Rubicon', p. 28; and Lintner, '$400m deal signed by China and Myanmar', p. 1.
105. See Gill and Mak, *Arms Transparency and Security in South-East Asia*, p. 122.
106. Personal observation, Rangoon, April 1995. See also *Jane's Land Based Air Defence 1996-97* (Jane's Information Group, Coulsdon, 1996), p. 170. As with the Type 74 guns, there is some confusion whether the fire control radars provided were Type 311 or 702.
107. Interviews, Chiang Mai and Rangoon, November 1999.
108. Interview, Chiang Mai, November 1999. See also Maung Aung Myoe, *The Tatmadaw in Myanmar Since 1988*, p. 15.
109. 'Air Forces Survey: Myanmar', p. 36.
110. Interview, Sydney, May 1995. See also Kerry Brewster, 'Dateline', SBS Television, 25 March 1995.
111. William Ashton, 'Myanmar: Invasion fears prompt search for air defences', *Asia-Pacific Defence Reporter*, Vol. 27, No. 2, March 2001, pp. 32-4.
112. *Jane's Land-Based Air Defence 1996-97*, p. 323. The Institute for Asian Democracy's figure of 55,000 HN-5A missiles seems too high. *Towards Democracy in Burma*, p. 58; See also Gill and Mak, *Arms Transparency and Security in South-East Asia*, p. 121; and *Jane's Electro-Optical Systems 1995-96* (Jane's Information Systems, Coulsdon, 1995), p. 114.
113. Interview, Canberra, November 2000; and Robert Karniol, 'Myanmar boosts defence with Igla surface-to-air missiles', *JDW*, 17 January 2001, p. 17. See also 'Myanmar delegation visits Pakistan Ordnance Factories', *The Nation*, 11 July 2000; and 'Myanmar', Military Procurement International, Vol. 11, No. 4, 15 February 2001, p. 13. 'Gimlet' is the NATO name for the Russian 'Igla' SAM.
114. Micool Brooke, 'South-East Asian targets for Russia's Igla and Kilo', *Asia-Pacific Defence Reporter*, Vol. 26, No. 4, June/July 2000, p. 34.
115. Interviews and personal observation, Rangoon, November and December 1999.
116. Personal observation, Rangoon, April 1995. There has been speculation that some of this equipment, such as the (possibly Type 72) tank recovery vehicles and armoured bridge layers, are in fact of Eastern bloc origin and were provided by Yugoslavia or Poland.
117. Personal observation, Rangoon, April 1995. See also *Jane's Military Vehicles and Logistics, 1995-96* (Jane's Information Group, Coulsdon, 1995), p. 770.
118. *Jane's Military Vehicles and Logistics, 1996-97* (Jane's Information Group, Coulsdon, 1996), p. 155.
119. Lintner, 'Myanmar's Chinese connection', p. 12. See also Lintner, 'The Volatile Yunnan Frontier', p. 86.
120. The infrastructure development along the China-Burma border has also been undertaken to facilitate cross-border trade, estimated in 1995 to be about US$1.5 billion per year, and increasing rapidly. See Lintner, 'Rangoon's Rubicon', p. 28; and Lintner, 'Arms for Eyes', p. 26.
121. Lintner, 'Arms for Eyes', p. 26.
122. Maung Aung Myoe, *Officer Education and Leadership Training in the Tatmadaw*, pp. 9-12.
123. According to the IISS, Vietnam is the only Southeast Asian country which currently has a larger standing army. See *The Military Balance 2000/2001*, p. 217. See also Udai Bhanu Singh, 'Growth of Military Power in South-east Asia', *Asian Strategic Review 1994-95* (Institute for Defence Studies and Analysis, New Delhi, 1995), pp. 312ff.

124. This has been suggested by several observers. See, for example, James Walsh, 'The Dogs of War', *Time*, 17 February 1992, pp. 18-19; Teresa Poole, 'Refugees flee Burma to escape army offensive', *Independent*, 28 January 1992; Nick Cuming-Bruce, 'Burma batters separatist stronghold', *Guardian*, 11 February 1992; and Lintner, 'Centrifugal forces', p. 16.

125. Bertil Lintner, 'Loss and exile', *FEER*, 16 February 1995, p. 23; and 'The Fall of Manerplaw', *Asiaweek*, 17 February 1995, pp. 31-2. See also Patrick Lescot, 'Burma launches assaults on rebel base', *The Australian*, 10 February 1995.

126. Of critical importance was a major split in the Karen insurgent forces, and the defection to Rangoon of hundreds of Buddhist Karen guerrillas. See, for example, William Ashton, 'Karen down but not out', *Asia-Pacific Defence Reporter*, Vol. 21, No. 8/9, May/June 1994, p. 18. It is also significant that by this time the SLORC had reached cease-fire agreements with most other major insurgent groups, thus freeing army resources for redeployment from other areas of the country.

127. Interviews, Bangkok, April 1995. See also Yindee Lertcharoenchok, 'Kawmura falls to Rangoon forces', *The Nation*, 22 February 1995.

128. *Review* Correspondents, 'Masses in revolt against stifling authoritarian grip', *FEER*, 25 August 1988, p. 12.

129. See, for example, 'Burmese Rebels Await A Foe's Lucky Number'; and Falla, *True Love and Bartholomew*, p. 219.

130. On all these matters see, for example, Mitchell, 'Karens fight to survive', pp. 15-19; Edith Mirante, 'Up Into Kachin Country', *Asiaweek*, 22 November 1991, p. 22; Peterson, 'Karen Kill Zone', pp. 26ff; Williams, 'Gutsy Karens Continue to Bloody Burmese Butchers', p. 35; David Watts and Erskine McCullough, 'Burmese troops bombard rebel HQ', *The Australian*, 25 February 1992; and Kurt Hanson, 'Calamity at Kawmura', *Soldier of Fortune*, Vol. 20, No. 9, September 1995, pp. 36-7 and pp. 70-3.

131. Bertil Lintner, 'Return to the delta', *FEER*, 14 November 1991, p. 26. See also Alan Clements, 'Dragon King's Fire', *Newsweek*, 7 April 1992, p. 72.

132. Karen National Union Department of Foreign Affairs Media Release, Manerplaw, 18 March 1992. See also 'Blood on the Ridge', *Asiaweek*, 13 March 1992, p. 30; and Bertil Lintner, 'Military guns silent', *FEER*, 28 May 1992, p. 26.

133. See, for example, the interviews in the NCGUB's annual *Human Rights Yearbook*; *No Childhood At All*, pp. 38-55; Betsy Apple, *School for Rape* (Earthrights International, Bangkok, 1998), pp. 51-77; and 'Junta army officers' cruel treatment compel soldiers to retaliate', *Burma News Update*, February 1999, p. 2.

134. See 'Burmese Rebels Await A Foe's Lucky Number'; Lindsay Murdoch, 'Rangoon tightens the noose around defiant Karen guerrillas', *The Age*, 30 January 1995; and '40 die as Burmese hit KNU base', *Bangkok Post*, 9 February 1995. Claims of BA soldiers being intoxicated in battle may be based on the fact that the most common anti-malaria medicine distributed to BA troops is quinine mixed with rum, which has often been found in their water bottles. Personal communication, Bertil Lintner to the author, 17 October 1995; See also Rodney Tasker, 'Slow death of a dream', *FEER*, 13 June 1985, p. 44.

135. Interview, Rangoon, November 1999. See also 'Supplies shortage, malaria causing death and desertion among soldiers', DVB, 27 July 2000. Another cause for low morale is the amount of time soldiers now spend on infrastructure-building projects.

136. The Burma Army still uses some of the insignia and rank titles of the old Imperial Japanese Army. It even marches to old Japanese military tunes. Interview, Rangoon, December 1999; and Keegan, *World Armies*, p. 89.

137. There is now an extensive literature on this subject. See, for example, *Myanmar* (Amnesty International, London, 1990); *Burma: Entrenchment or Reform? Human Rights Developments and the Need for Continued Pressure* (Human Rights Watch/Asia, New

York, 1995), pp. 19-23; *Human Rights and Progress towards Democracy in Burma*, Report of the Joint Standing Committee on Foreign Affairs, Defence and Trade, Parliament of the Commonwealth of Australia (Australian Government Publishing Service, Canberra, 1995); US State Department, *Burma: Country Report*; and the NCGUB's annual *Human Rights Yearbooks*.

138. Lintner, 'Myanmar's Chinese connection', p. 26. See also 'Myanmar and China: But will the flag follow trade?', pp. 31-2.

139. Maung Aung Myoe, *The Tatmadaw in Myanmar Since 1988*, p. 26, note 40.

140. See, for example, 'The King of the Shan', *Asiaweek*, 15 June 1994, p. 26. The large numbers and wide range of weapons available to the MTA can be seen in Maung Pho Shoke, *Why Did U Khun Sa's MTA Exchange Arms for Peace* (Meik Kaung Press, Rangoon, 1999), pp. 94-8.

141. 'Heavy toll in Burmese fighting', *Sydney Morning Herald*, 17 July 1993. See also Bertil Lintner, 'Fighting Weather', *FEER*, 30 June 1994, p. 24; and 'Burma', *JDW*, 30 July 1994, p. 19.

142. Interview, Mandalay, November 1996. Also see, for example, 'Chin people have to supply army rations', *Burma News Update*, 9 February 1999, p. 2.

143. There have been suggestions that the failure to develop an adequate communications network in Burma's border areas was a deliberate strategy by the Ne Win regime to deter military incursions by neighbouring countries. (Smith, *Burma: Insurgency and the Politics of Ethnicity*, p. 257). While this is partly true, other factors have contributed to the lack of development along the frontier, such as Burma's economic problems and Rangoon's inability to exercise control over the areas in question.

144. See, for example, Lintner, *Burma in Revolt*, pp. 101ff; and Tin Maung Maung Than, 'Burma's National Security and Defence Posture', pp. 40-4.

145. Interview, Rangoon, November 1999.

146. Interview, Rangoon, April 1995. See also 'Karens fight off massive Myanmar army assault', *Bangkok Post*, 14 March 1992; and 'Blood on the Ridge', p. 30.

147. In 1961 about 5,000 BA soldiers and 20,000 PLA soldiers combined to attack the KMT remnants in northern Burma. Yet the two forces did not operate closely together, simply coordinating their deployments to trap the KMT forces in what later became known as 'the Mekong River Operation'. See Lintner, *Burma in Revolt*, p. 165.

8

The Burma Navy

...the Burmese had never possessed sea-going ships of their own and although the local populations of Arakan and Tenasserim had many small coastal craft the only effective sea links between these two regions and the delta were maintained by larger vessels belonging to either British or Indian concerns. — C.A. Fisher, *South-east Asia: A Social, Economic and Political Geography* (1964)

Of all the Burmese armed forces, the Burma Navy (*Tatmadaw Yay*) is the most often overlooked and the least understood.[1] Burma has never had a sea-faring tradition, and in contemporary studies of the country, or surveys of sea power in the Asia-Pacific region, it is usually assumed that Burma's security concerns remain purely land-based. If this was ever the case, it is no longer so.

Before 1988 the BN was small and, inevitably, its role in the many counter-insurgency campaigns waged by the central government was much less conspicuous than those of the other two Services. Also, since the 1962 coup, the navy has held only a token position in the military regime which, under various guises, has run the country. Yet the navy has always been, and remains, an important factor in Burma's security. The dramatic expansion of the Burma Navy under the SLORC and SPDC suggests that the new generation of military leaders in Rangoon not only shares this view, but envisages a greatly expanded external defence role for this arm of the *Tatmadaw*.

8.1 The Burma Navy Before 1988

The Burma Navy had its beginnings in the Burma Royal Navy Volunteer Reserve. This force was formed in 1940 and, although very small, played an active part in Allied operations against the Japanese during the Second World War.[2] In December 1947 the Union of Burma Navy was formed with 700 men. The fleet initially consisted of a small but diverse collection of ships transferred from the UK under the arrangements made for Burma's independence in January 1948. It included an ex-Royal Navy *River* class frigate and four Landing Craft Gun (Medium) (LCG(M)).

Armed with two 25-pounder (88mm) guns and two 2-pounder (44mm) guns, these LCG(M)s were used primarily as support gunboats.[3] A number of additional motor gunboats soon joined the fleet, some on loan or charter from the RN.[4] In 1950 and 1951, the US provided 10 coastguard cutters (*CGC*) under the Mutual Defence Assistance Program, 'to deter insurgents from attacks against river craft and towns in the Irrawaddy delta'.[5] These vessels were 25 metres long and displaced 49 tons.

Together with a flotilla of small motor launches and converted civilian craft, these vessels played an important part in Rangoon's fight against the ethnic and ideological insurgent groups which threatened the Union government in its early days.[6] The navy performed both defensive and offensive roles, protecting convoys, carrying supplies, ferrying troops and giving much needed fire support. While it was instrumental in relieving the port city of Moulmein (captured by Karen insurgents in 1948), and later the Irrawaddy delta town of Bassein, the navy's effort was directed almost entirely towards riverine operations. The lack of good roads in Burma, and the threat of insurgent ambushes, meant that water transport took on particular importance.[7] One armed river patrol boat defected to the Karens, but throughout this early period the navy was largely unopposed and managed to maintain control over Burma's crucial inland waterways.[8]

In the years that followed the navy acquired a number of additional vessels, mostly from the UK and US. In 1956 and 1957, for example, the UK sold Burma five 50-ton Saunders-Roe *Dark* class convertible motor torpedo/motor gunboats. In 1958 it added an *Algerine* class escort minesweeper (1040 tons standard) fitted for mine-laying.[9] In the late 1950s and early 1960s the US sold Burma six *PGM* type coastal patrol craft. A few years later, the US provided seven more *CGC* type patrol boats.[10] In the mid-1960s the Burma Navy also took delivery of two former US Navy corvettes. They were a *PCE-827* class ship displacing 640 tons, and an *Admirable* class vessel of 650 tons.[11] Both were originally commissioned in the mid-1940s. In 1978 the US also provided the Burma Navy with six small river patrol craft.[12] Burma's close relations with Yugoslavia during this period, and Rangoon's wish to diversify the sources of its military supplies, was reflected in the acquisition of 35 Yugoslavian-built patrol craft. In 1958 the navy took delivery of 10 *Y-301* class river gunboats.[13] This was followed in 1965 by 25 smaller *Michao* class river patrol launches, which were mainly used to ferry troops during counter-insurgency operations.

With further assistance from Yugoslavia, Burma also produced a number of its own naval vessels. In 1960, for example, the BN commissioned two 400-ton *Nawarat* class river gunboats (later designated corvettes) which had been built in Burma's own Government Dockyard at Dawbon near Rangoon.[14] Their armaments included one ex-army 25-pounder field gun and a Bofors 40mm gun purchased from Sweden. In spite of their size, both were used primarily for river patrols and rarely ventured out to sea. Burmese shipyards also built the navy a number of smaller patrol craft. In 1969, for example, two improved versions of the Yugoslavian *Y-301* class river patrol boat were built at Sinmalaik, up-river from Rangoon.[15] In addition, local shipyards built a number of landing craft (based largely on US designs) and utility motor launches. They also adapted a number of civilian craft for military use. During this period the navy operated up to nine converted river transports leased from the Inland Water Transportation Board. At around 100-tons displacement each, these two-decked, shallow draft vessels were used primarily for riverine patrols, escort duties and to provide logistics support to the army.[16]

This rather mixed fleet was supported by a number of auxiliaries. In 1962 the BN acquired a converted 2217-ton passenger ship for use as a coastal transport vessel.[17] A light forces support ship, displacing 520 tons, was bought from Japan in 1967.[18] In addition, during the 1960s the navy purchased a number of second-hand Landing Craft Medium (LCM) and Landing Craft Utility (LCU) type vessels from the US, mainly to support riverine operations. Four *Abamin* class LCUs (each displacing 250 tons) were provided by Japan in the early 1970s.[19] Nor were survey tasks ignored. In 1958 a small 108-ton vessel was purchased by the BN to conduct river surveys. This was followed in 1965 by an ocean survey ship from Yugoslavia. Displacing 1059 tons, it carried two surveying motor boats and had the option of embarking a helicopter. A Singaporean fishery research ship, arrested in Burmese waters in 1974, was taken into navy service as a survey vessel around 1981.[20] The auxiliaries were usually unarmed, although most of the landing craft carried a 20mm cannon or heavy machine gun. The ocean survey ship was armed with two Bofors 40mm guns and two Oerlikon 20mm cannons. The other survey ships were either armed with 20mm Oerlikon cannons or 0.5 inch heavy machine guns.[21]

Most of these vessels were acquired in the 1960s when, largely with US assistance, the Burma Navy expanded rapidly. By the beginning of the 1970s, however, the BN had fallen on harder times. The addition of a few small US patrol craft barely managed to keep pace with the loss or deterioration of older vessels. Towards the end of the decade, however, the Ne Win Government took a renewed interest in offshore patrolling and the protection of Burma's maritime resources. This prompted a long overdue naval replacement program. In 1979 and 1980 the BN acquired six *Carpentaria* class inshore patrol boats from Australia. The same year the navy took delivery of three 128-ton *Swift* type coastal patrol boats from Singapore. These purchases were followed in 1980, 1981 and 1982 by the delivery of three 385-ton offshore patrol vessels of the *Osprey* class, built in Denmark.[22] The *Osprey* and *Swift* class vessels were armed with Bofors 40mm guns and Oerlikon 20mm cannons. Their ranges were 4,500 and 1,800 miles respectively. The smaller (26-ton) *Carpentaria* class patrol boats had a range of 950 miles at 18 knots, and carried one Oerlikon 20mm cannon.[23] All these new patrol boats were formally operated by the People's Pearl and Fishery Corporation (PPFC), but effectively acted as extensions of the navy.

Also during the early 1980s, Burma's shipyards built three 128-ton *PGM*- type patrol boats. Their design was heavily influenced by the *PGM*-class vessels provided by the US 20 years before, but the Burmese versions were three metres longer and 28 tons heavier. They were armed with two 40mm Bofors guns and two 12.7mm heavy machine guns. A fourth unit was planned, but never built.[24]

By 1988 the Burma Navy's strength was about 100 vessels, ranging in displacement from about 8 tons to 650 tons. Their age varied from 5 to 50 years old. *Jane's Fighting Ships* has noted that 'the unique characteristic of this Navy is that no ship ever seems to be scrapped'.[25] This overstates the case, but it is true that considerable efforts were made by the BN to keep its vessels operational for as long as possible. Under normal conditions, the older hulls might have been expected to deteriorate badly, but operating mainly in fresh water kept corrosion to within containable limits. Also, a number of smaller craft, such as the former US coastguard cutters provided in 1960, were given new hulls by Burmese dockyards to prolong their service life.[26]

Figure 18: Burma Navy Strength, 1988

Corvettes	4
Offshore Patrol Vessels	3
Coastal Patrol Craft	12
Inshore Patrol Vessels	6
River Patrol Craft	36
Gunboats	21
Survey Vessels	2
Support Ships	2
Transports	14

As the navy took on more vessels, so it also recruited more men. This was a gradual process, however, reflecting both the government's financial problems and the low priority accorded to the navy by the army-dominated military hierarchy. In 1951 the BN's strength was 135 officers and 1599 ratings.[27] By the time of the 1962 coup, the navy had grown to around 3000 officers and ratings.[28] Over the next ten years it doubled in size to 6200.[29] By the early 1980s, the navy had reached a level of 9,000 men. Between 1980 and 1988, however, the size of the navy seems to have fallen to about 7000 (not counting 250 men provided by the PPFC to operate its patrol boats). This reduction in personnel was probably due in part to Burma's worsening economic problems, but could also reflect the demise of the navy's larger vessels. A frigate or ocean minesweeper, for example, required a crew of 140 men, and a corvette about 50. Yet an *Osprey* class offshore patrol vessel only needed a crew of 20, and a *Carpentaria* class patrol boat only 10 crewmen. Even so, manpower shortages meant that few BN vessels carried a full complement at all times.

A naval infantry battalion (of 800 men) was formed in 1964, followed by a second battalion in 1967. They were deployed mainly to the Arakan and Tenasserim areas, and to the Irrawaddy delta, to assist in counter-insurgency operations, but also performed other security duties. For reasons which are unclear, both battalions were dissolved in 1968.[30]

Most of the vessels operated by the navy and PPFC during this period were relatively small, thinly armoured and carried light armament. As their nature suggested, the primary task of the BN was patrolling the country's rivers and inshore waters in support of the army's counter-insurgency operations. Typically, about one-third of the fleet was dedicated to this 'Strategic Naval Flotilla' (*Sit Byu Ha Yay Yin Su*) at any time. The navy was used for reconnaissance, to provide fire support, put soldiers ashore and to help maintain static defences around strategic towns. Most major population centres in the Irrawaddy River delta, for example, had at least one armed landing craft assigned to them, with a dedicated force of about 10 men to manage the 20mm cannon or 0.50 inch HMG which was usually mounted on board. The BN also helped supplement the army's logistics supply system during counter-insurgency campaigns. Even after the insurgent threat had diminished, moving stores by sea and river was often more cost-effective than by road or air.[31]

The navy's secondary role was coastal surveillance and fisheries protection. As far as the navy's slim resources allowed, it patrolled Burma's 148,000 square kilometre maritime claim against fish poaching, smuggling, insurgent movements and pirate activity. Coastal operations in the Tenasserim Division were particularly intensive, as these groups tried to take advantage of the Mergui Archipelago's proximity to Thailand and Malaysia, and the area's many islands and inlets, to conduct their activities.[32] Operations in the Andaman Sea and Bay of Bengal were less common, due largely to logistics problems and the poor sea-keeping qualities of the navy's smaller vessels. Fisheries protection, however, required surveillance in the open seas. Accordingly, some long-range patrols were conducted by the BN's larger warships and, after 1982, the three *Osprey* class patrol boats.[33] Operations further afield were rare. As the Burma Navy's flagship, however, the frigate *UBS Mayu* made several longer voyages before it was decommissioned, including a number of diplomatic visits to regional countries.[34]

There was no separate fleet air arm but, when needed, the navy drew on the resources of the Burma Air Force for maritime surveillance and other forms of air support. The BAF's smaller helicopters, like the KB-47G Siouxs, Kaman Huskies and Aerospatiale Alouettes, for example, assisted the navy at different times and were occasionally embarked on larger vessels like the *Osprey* class patrol craft and Burma's ocean survey ship.[35] These aircraft performed support duties and carried out short-range patrols, but none carried any sensors or weapons. The BN also used the BAF's land-based Fokker F-27 and Fairchild-Hiller FH-227B aircraft to conduct patrols of Burma's long coastline and extensive maritime claims. A number of sources have stated that three Fokker F-27M Maritime Enforcer surveillance aircraft were added to the BAF's inventory in the early 1980s, specifically to perform this role. This claim cannot be confirmed, however, and clashes with other reports that such aircraft are still on order.[36] Whatever type was used for these tasks before 1988, it appears that they were unarmed, and only carried weather radars and wingtip searchlights.[37]

The Burma Navy maintained a modest underwater repair and combat capability. Both SCUBA and 'hard hat' surface-fed diving apparatus was used.[38] The navy's main diving vessel was a 520-ton former torpedo tender obtained from Japan in 1967, which was used as a combined diving base and floating workshop.[39] Sometimes the navy called upon a larger (706 tons) buoy tender, operated by the Rangoon Port Authority, to assist in diving operations. The BN also kept a number of inflatable dinghies equipped with outboard motors. Divers were trained at a special diving school at Kyaukpyu, on Burma's Arakan coast. While few details are available, it appears that their primary role was underwater clearance and ship repair, although it seems likely that some capability existed for special operations.

Little is known about the BN's operational art and doctrine during this period but, reflecting its British origins, it seems to have been based largely on Royal Navy practice. Over the years, however, the BN incorporated lessons learned from other countries. At the same time, operational procedures were constantly being adapted to suit local circumstances.[40]

By 1988 the organisation of the BN had undergone several changes, but still reflected its British origins. When they were operational, the frigate, escort minesweeper and four corvettes all fell under the control of the Strategic Naval Command (*Sit Byu Ha Yay Hta Na*), based at the Defence Ministry in Rangoon.[41] The remainder of the fleet was normally assigned by the Naval Vice Chief of Staff through three regional naval commands (*Tatmadaw Yay Tat Hta Na Choke*), each managed by a naval Captain.[42] The largest was Irrawaddy Naval Region Command, which had its headquarters at Monkey Point in Rangoon. Arakan Naval Region Command was based at Sittwe and covered the coast from Bangladesh to the Irrawaddy delta. Tenasserim Naval Region Command had its headquarters at Moulmein. There were functionally separate naval bases, each under a Commander, at Yadanabon (in Rangoon), Bassein, Sittwe and Moulmein. While not listed as bases, smaller naval facilities were maintained on Great Coco Island and among the islands of the Mergui Archipelago. The latter could be found in places like Mali (Malei) Island and Zadetkyi Island. Some were probably little more than sheltered anchorages.[43]

While all these commands were answerable to the navy, their assets were sometimes put under the operational control of the Commanders of their respective Military Regions (all of whom were army officers).

Burma's main naval dockyard was located at Rangoon, where facilities existed to handle most kinds of ship repair. It was also where virtually all naval supplies were stored and issued.[44] There were also maintenance and repair facilities at Seikkyi near the mouth of the Rangoon River and Sinmalaik, upstream from Monkey Point. Burma's main Naval Training Centre was at Syriam. This had a limited curriculum, however, and many Burmese navy officers were sent overseas for advanced training. Such postings included the UK, US, Japan, Denmark, Sweden and Yugoslavia.

The BN's Hydrographical Department was based at Monkey Point. It produced its own charts, although old British Admiralty charts were often used, with directions and amendments overprinted in the Burmese language.[45] The navy's ex-Yugoslavian ocean survey ship seems to have been kept busy, and periodic surveys were conducted of inland waterways using smaller vessels. This was made neces-

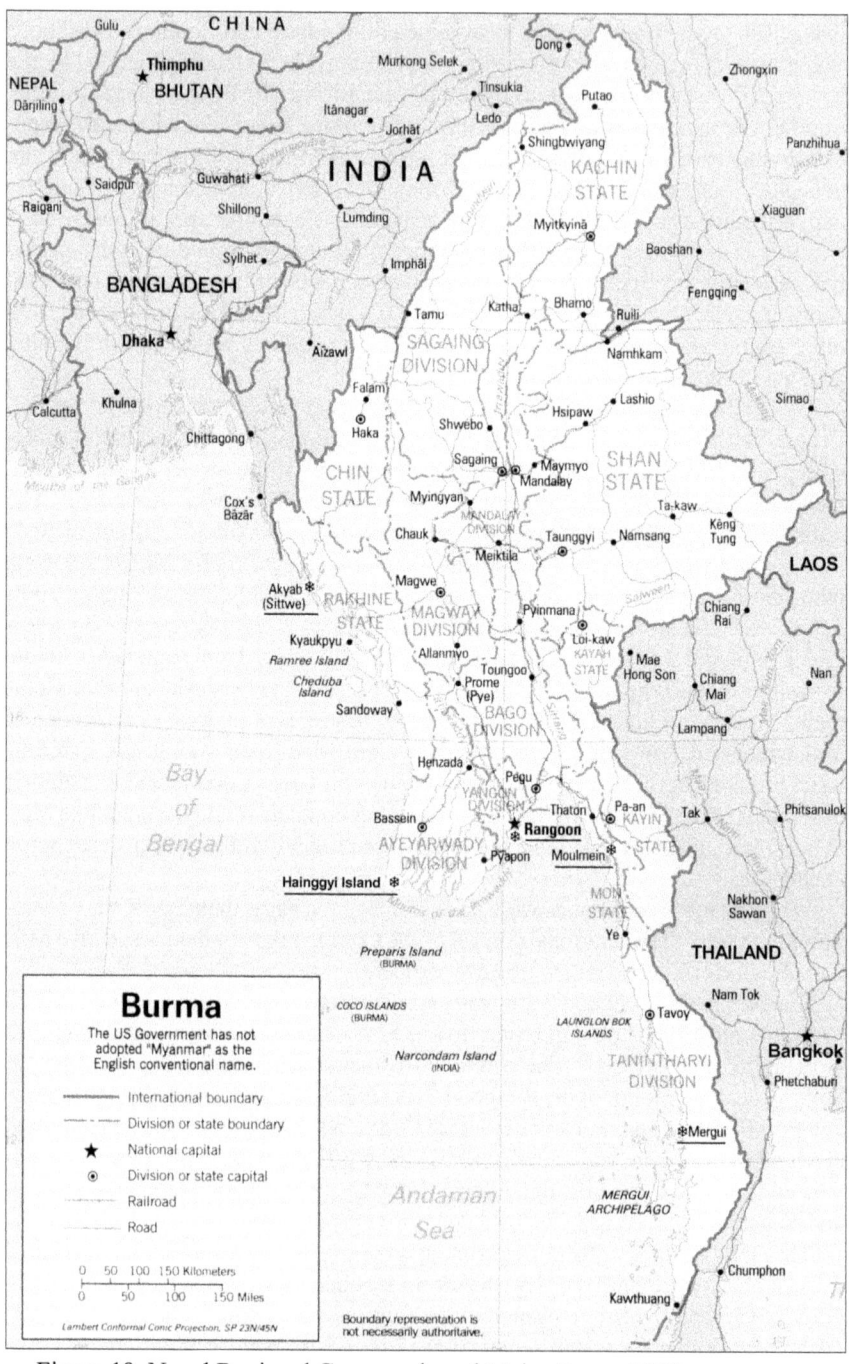

Figure 19: Naval Regional Commands and Major Bases, 2000.

sary by the shifting river channels, caused by silting and flooding during the monsoons.

Considered overall, the navy's role before 1988 was quite modest. It was small, ill-equipped and starved of funds. It was also crippled by its almost total dependence on foreign logistics. Many vessels were inadequately crewed. As a consequence, the navy was little more than an internal security and coastal protection force. It had no blue water capability.[46] The five *Dark* class motor torpedo boats had given the navy a potential offensive capability against major surface vessels, but they were decommissioned in 1975. The Burma Navy had also lost its one frigate (which was decommissioned in 1979) and its escort minesweeper (which was taken out of service in 1982). Thus, when the SLORC took power in 1988 the *Tatmadaw*'s largest ships were the four ageing corvettes, and they were of limited utility. The navy had no effective defence against air or sub-surface attack. Nor did it have any real capacity to defend itself against major surface vessels. It had no underway replenishment capability and little endurance.

Fortunately for the Ne Win Government, during this period Burma faced no serious maritime threat. The regime's most pressing security problems were land-based, from an alienated civil population and the insurgent groups scattered around the country's periphery. Hence, first priority for the country's scarce resources was always given to the army and then to the air force. Even though an effort was made to police Burma's territorial waters, particularly after 1980, the navy did not have the capacity seriously to tackle the enormous problems of smuggling and the poaching of Burma's marine resources. This situation may have changed if large deposits of hydrocarbons had been found offshore but, despite the efforts of several foreign oil companies during the preceding 15 years, by 1988 that had not occurred. Before the advent of the SLORC, it seemed that the navy would be left forever to make do as best it could, ineffectually trying to patrol Burma's long coastline and navigable rivers in its vintage craft.

8.2 The Burma Navy After 1988

That situation changed dramatically after 1988. Over the past 12 years the Burma Navy has been restructured and its capabilities significantly upgraded. The BN now has its own Commander-in-Chief at three-star level, and the ranks for other senior officers have risen accordingly. Naval manpower has nearly doubled, to about 16,000 officers and ratings.[47] The number of naval regional commands has been increased to five, to manage a greatly increased range and level of operations. Headquarters have been identified at Rangoon (Irrawaddy Naval Region Command), Sittwe (Danyawaddy Naval Region Command), Hainggyi Island (Panmawaddy Naval Region Command), Moulmein (Mawyawaddy Naval Region Command) and Mergui (Thanintharyi Naval Region Command).[48] Each are commanded by a BN Commodore. In addition, a Naval Training Command has been created at Seikkyi, and a Naval Shipyard HQ formed (also at Commodore level).

Under the SLORC and SPDC, the navy has acquired a large number of new and more capable vessels. As part of a major arms deal negotiated with China in 1989, Burma purchased 10 *Hainan* class (Type 37) coastal patrol boats. These 375-ton vessels are 59 metres long and capable of 30 knots. They have an effective range of 1300 miles at 15 knots. This class is usually armed with twin 57mm and 25mm guns both fore and aft. They also carry anti-submarine mortars, depth charges and are fitted with rails for mine laying. Six of these patrol boats were delivered to Burma in January 1991 and another four arrived in mid-1993. All 10 were later variants of the *Hainan* class which had already seen service with the PLA Navy.[49] There were a number of reports that, in November 1994, an order was placed with the Chinese for an additional six vessels of the same class. However, it appears that this order was for another type of patrol boat, and the reports of additional *Hainan* class vessels being purchased were incorrect.[50]

In December 1990 the SLORC purchased three *PB-90* class coastal patrol boats from Yugoslavia. They were originally built by Brodotechnika for an African country and were completed in 1986 and 1987. When this sale fell through they were laid up until the SLORC purchased them at a much reduced price. They arrived in Burma in October 1990.[51] It has been suggested that these three vessels are powered by Rolls Royce Proteus gas turbine engines, and were originally armed with Swedish 40mm Bofors guns. If this was the case, the sale to Burma would have broken agreements which Yugoslavia had signed with both the UK and Sweden. These accusations appear to be based on the mistaken belief that the *PB-90* vessels are the same as *Koncar* class missile patrol boats.[52] According to *Jane's Fighting Ships*, however, the 80-ton, 28-metre *PB-90* boats are powered by diesel engines. They have a maximum speed of 32 knots and an effective range (at 25 knots) of 400 nautical miles. Under Burmese command, they have been fitted with eight 20mm M-75 cannons, one quad mount on the forecastle and one aft. They also carry two 128mm launchers for illuminants.[53]

Burma's new military leaders were keen to acquire some frigates to replace the country's obsolete *PCE-827*, *Admirable* and *Nawarat* class corvettes.[54] As bilateral defence ties with China rapidly grew during the 1990s, the SLORC set its sights on two or three *Jiangnan* or *Jianghu* class frigates, to help the Burma Navy patrol the country's territorial seas and to protect its maritime resources from unauthorised exploitation. Vessels from a number of countries, notably Thailand, Malaysia and Singapore, were taking increasing advantage of Burma's low naval capabilities illegally to exploit its rich fishing grounds. The DDSI estimated in 1995 that there were about 1,000 fishing vessels illegally in Burma's EEZ at any one time.[55] The Rangoon regime, however, could not afford even the special 'friendship' prices for the frigates being asked by Beijing. Other potential suppliers, such as Russia and the Ukraine, insisted on hard currency payments, which the *Tatmadaw* could also ill afford.[56] As a compromise, the SPDC has purchased three Chinese hulls, and is currently fitting them out as corvettes in Sinmalaik dockyard. The first of these new warships was commissioned and commenced sea trials in 2000.[57]

According to reliable reports, these new vessels will each be about 75 metres long and displace about 1200 tonnes. Their electronics suites are to be fitted by an Israeli firm. Despite the EU embargo against arms sales to Burma, the ships' main armament is likely to be a 76mm OTO Melara Compact gun imported (apparently through a third party) from Italy. The three corvettes will probably also be fitted with anti-submarine warfare (ASW) systems, but it is not known what, if any, surface-to-surface missiles (SSM) and surface-to-air missiles the ships will carry. Given Burma's very close relationship with China, however, the arms embargo imposed against Burma by the Western democracies and the SPDC's continuing shortage of foreign exchange, it would not be surprising if the three corvettes were also fitted with Chinese SSM and air defence systems.[58] These vessels are expected to be based in Rangoon as part of the Strategic Naval Command.

In addition, since 1988 China has undertaken to provide Burma with a number of smaller vessels for coastal and offshore patrols.[59] In December 1995 the BN took delivery of two *Houxin* class guided missile patrol boats from China. Two more arrived the next year and another two followed in late 1997. These 430-ton fast attack craft have a range of 750 miles at 18 knots, and are heavily armed. They carry four C-801 ('Eagle Strike') SSMs, capable of active radar homing to 40 kilometres at a speed of 0.9 mach.[60] By late 1996, 24 of these missiles had already been shipped to Rangoon.[61] *Houxin* class patrol boats also have two twin 37mm guns and two twin 14.5mm guns. The six Burmese vessels seem to be based at Monkey Point. They may eventually be reassigned to other commands, but it is unlikely that the BN will be able to duplicate the missile maintenance and loading facilities currently being established in the capital. The acquisition of these *Houxin* class attack craft significantly increases the navy's offensive striking power, and gives it an anti-ship cruise missile capability for the first time. It is possible that more such vessels are on order, and have still to be delivered.[62]

In its early days, the Burma Navy was familiar with both magnetic and acoustic mines, and related mine sweeping systems.[63] Since the loss of its escort minesweeper in 1982, Burma did not have a credible mine-warfare capability. The *Hainan* class patrol boats carry rails for 12 mines, however, and the Rangoon regime is reported to have ordered one or possibly two Chinese-built ocean minesweepers, probably of the *T-43* class.[64] This particular minesweeper is 60 metres long and displaces 520 tons (standard). It is normally fitted with two BMB-2 anti-submarine mortars, and carries 12 to 16 mines. It also has 37mm, 25mm and 14.5mm guns.[65] These vessels were expected to arrive in Rangoon in 1995, but this order too seems to have been delayed because of Burma's financial difficulties. However, a new defence agreement with China, signed in 1996, may allow for their delivery under extended credit arrangements.[66] Even if the *T-43* minesweeper deal falls through, there is still a chance that the BN will acquire some sea mines from China. For example, the PLA has been developing a number of modern systems, like the EM-52 rocket-propelled mine, which it has been actively promoting through international arms exhibitions.[67] Should Burma acquire such weapons, or even less sophisticated naval mines, then its ability to protect its ocean approaches and inland waterways would be much improved.[68]

Two other foreign additions to the BN since 1988 have been a tanker and a transport auxiliary. Formerly registered in Singapore, the 55-metre-long tanker was arrested in Burmese territorial waters in 1991 and subsequently taken into the navy. With its bunkers full it displaces 4000 tons and can travel at 15 knots.[69] This is the first major replenishment vessel to be operated by the BN and, despite the serendipitous nature of the tanker's acquisition, gives a clear illustration of the *Tatmadaw*'s determination to extend the scope and duration of its naval operations. The transport vessel was also acquired in 1991, but details of the sale are unknown. One source has described it as a former Norwegian coastal cargo ship of about 700 tons displacement, acquired by the BN as transport for stores and personnel. Another source has suggested that it may be used for survey work, but this seems unlikely.[70]

Not all the BN's new ships have been imported. Since 1988 the navy has ordered or taken delivery of a number of other vessels built in Burma's own shipyards, which have been receiving assistance from China. These acquisitions include three *Myanmar* class coastal patrol boats. Construction was begun in 1991 at the Central Naval Engineering Depot in Rangoon. After a long delay, one of these vessels was commissioned in 1996, another followed in 1998 and a third was in service by 2000. A fourth is currently under construction. They are 45 metres long and have a full load displacement of about 213 tons. They may be fitted for C-801 SSMs.[71] Also, the Myanma Shipyard has produced two Burma *PGM* type coastal patrol craft, which were delivered to the Customs Service in 1993. Both vessels were subsequently taken over by the navy.[72] In addition, four river patrol craft have been built at the Naval Engineering Depot in Rangoon. With some modifications, their design was taken from similar craft built in Burma for the navy in the mid-1980s. These new patrol craft were completed in 1990 and 1991. Each carry one Oerlikon 20mm cannon and one or two 0.50 inch heavy machine guns.[73] The Burma Navy plans eventually to build up to 12 of these vessels, funds permitting.

To make way for all these new vessels, and perhaps yield experienced crews, some of the older units in the Burma Navy are being taken out of service. The two former US corvettes, for example, were decommissioned in 1994, after all their ASW and mine-sweeping equipment was removed.[74] While still on the Fleet List in 1999, they are expected to be laid up when the three new corvettes become fully operational. The two old *Nawarat* class corvettes are also being downgraded, and in 1989 lost some of their already modest armament.[75] It is possible that they too will be decommissioned in a few years time, or used only for training purposes.

At some time during this period the *Swift* and *Carpentaria* class patrol boats operated by the People's Pearl and Fishery Corporation (now known as the People's Pearl and Fishery Board, or PPFB) appear to have been absorbed by the navy. Burma's three *Osprey* class patrol boats are still run by the PPFB, but to all intents and purposes function as naval vessels. The navy can also call upon Burma's state-owned merchant fleet for logistics support if required. Lloyds registers 127 vessels of 540,232 tons gross.[76]

Figure 20: Burma Navy Strength, 2000

Corvettes	7 (including 2 decommissioned, and 3 under construction)
Guided Missile Patrol Boats	6
Mine Warfare Vessels	1 or 2 on order
Coastal Patrol Boats	30
River Gunboatst	18
River Patrol Craft	46
Amphibious Vessels	18
Survey Vessels	3
Auxiliaries	17

Prior to 1988, the Burma Navy had little need for (or capacity to operate) sophisticated electronic warfare (EW) systems. The ex-US corvettes carried Raytheon SPS-5 surface search radars and hull-mounted RCA QCU-2 sonars, but most BN vessels were only fitted with Raytheon or Decca single band navigation or surtface search radars.[77] Yet the *Hainan* class patrol boats provided by China carry a number of more modern systems. They include the BM/HZ8610, a sensitive and accurate electronic warfare support measures (ESM) system which possesses a sophisticated radar signal processing capability and 'provides direction finding and analysis of threat radar equipment'.[78] They are fitted with the 'Pot Head' naval radar, the main function of which is surface target detection, with supplementary air warning capabilities. The *Hainan* vessels also carry 'High Pole' IFF radars, Raytheon Pathfinder navigational radars, and hull mounted 'Stag Ear' sonars.[79] The *Houxin* class patrol boats carry 'Square Tie' surface and air search radars, as well as intercept and jamming ESM/ECM capabilities. Together, these systems constitute a major advance in the BN's electronic order of battle.

It is not known what electronic systems Israel is fitting to Burma's three new corvettes, but at the very least they are likely to carry a fire control radar, surface and air search radars, navigational and weather radars, and hull-mounted sonars. Electronic counter measures (ECM) systems installed could include radar warning receivers, noise jammers and decoy launchers. This is the customary fit for this class of naval vessel and the minimum necessary for the corvettes to be fully operational in the role envisaged for them in the seas around Burma.[80]

Given the unfamiliar nature and relative sophistication of the BN's new vessels, it was inevitable that their purchase would be accompanied by an extensive program of training overseas. In 1989, for example, the Burma Navy sent crews to China to train on the *Hainan* patrol boats, and another group went to Yugoslavia after the *PB-90* vessels were ordered in 1990. Lengthy training in China was required for the crews of the *Houxin* class guided missile patrol boats.[81] Burma Navy personnel have also been sent to Pakistan for training (including in 'submarine warfare'), and it is possible that some other countries have secretly assisted the BN in this manner.[82] In addition, there have been reports that around 100 Chinese naval personnel were sent to Burma in the early 1990s to assist the BN in operating its new vessels, training local crews and maintaining new electronic equipment.[83] Some well-informed observers believe that PLA Navy technicians are still in Burma, working on BN bases, while others visit from time to time to help with repairs and maintenance.[84] Whether or not this is true, it is likely that further Chinese assistance will be required in due course, particularly as the Burma Navy has no prior experience in using or maintaining more sophisticated weapon systems such as SSMs.

As well as increasing the size of its fleet and the technical capabilities of individual units, the BN has embarked on a major program to upgrade Burma's naval infrastructure. This appears to include the development of existing bases at Sittwe near the Bangladesh border, and at Mergui near the southern Thai border. A new naval facility has been constructed on Hainggyi Island (mainly because of silting problems at Bassein) and activity has been reported on Great Coco Island, in the Andaman Sea.[85] A number of other river and coastal ports also appear to be marked for improvement, including Kyaukpyu on Ramree Island off the Arakan coast, and Sandoway about 125 kilometres further south.[86] There has also been construction work at Seikkyi near the mouth of the Rangoon River. Opposition groups have reported the construction (or planned construction) of other naval facilities at Heinze (Hayn-ze), Maungmakan (Maungmagan) and Launglon Bok islands (all off Tavoy), Kadan Island, Pyinzabu Island and Letsutaw (Letsok-aw) Island, all in the Mergui Archipelago, and at Kawthaung (Kawthoung) on the Kra Isthmus.[87] There have also been suggestions that a major new naval base is to be built with Chinese help at Heinle, near Tavoy, to permit the transfer of Mawyawaddy Naval Region Command from Moulmein.[88] These reports, however, have yet to be confirmed. The nature of this construction activity is not always clear. At different bases, however, access channels are being deepened, dockside and navigation facilities improved and accommodation upgraded. At some, the fuel storage capacity is being increased.[89]

Improved maritime surveillance capabilities seem to have been a high priority for the Rangoon regime since it was surprised by a US fleet in Burmese waters in 1988. There have since been reports that Burma's coastal surveillance and signals intelligence capabilities are being improved. For example, some analysts believe that the Chinese have helped Burma to instal radar equipment with a range of 150 nautical miles on Ramree Island, Great Coco Island and Zadetkyi Island.[90] Hainggyi Island and Zadetkale Island may have also received new radar equipment, installed with Chinese help.[91] In addition, there have been repeated claims that the Chinese have reached an agreement with the SLORC, and later the SPDC, to instal or upgrade SIGINT equipment at strategic locations around the Burmese coast, to provide both countries with a better coverage of the Andaman Sea and Bay of Bengal.[92] If these reports are true, then Burma will have a comprehensive surveillance picture of its EEZ and ocean approaches for the first time. One source has even claimed that Burma plans to instal a number of Chinese Silkworm SSMs around its coast to help deter a sea-borne attack.[93]

8.3 The New Burma Navy

All this activity has been followed keenly by other countries in the region. Some Royal Thai Navy (RTN) officials, for example, have expressed reservations about Burma's dramatic naval expansion and modernisation program. Thailand is also concerned about increasingly aggressive BN patrols against Thai fishing vessels in Burma's EEZ, but public comments by RTN officers about the increased naval threat from Burma seem to be aimed mainly at increasing Thailand's own naval budget.[94]

More has been heard from India, which is concerned not so much by the improvements to Burma's navy and its naval facilities, but by the involvement of China in the Burmese modernisation program.[95] As one Indian strategic analyst has observed,

> These developments [in Burma's navy] in themselves are not of major worry to Burma's neighbours. Regional navies are indeed much more formidable. It is the Chinese connection and the improvements carried out by it recently of Burma's maritime facilities which raise doubts.[96]

It has been suggested that the Chinese are assisting Burma to develop its naval infrastructure so that these new and improved facilities can be used to support Chinese warships and submarines on extended voyages to the Indian Ocean. As noted earlier, some observers have suggested that these deployments will be aimed at protecting China's sea lines of communication to the Middle East oil fields, a strategy that will require the PLA Navy to dominate the Malacca Straits.[97] Some Indian defence writers have even claimed that the new naval facilities, such as those on Hainggyi Island, will be used as a base for China's future nuclear submarine fleet, the main target of which will be the Indian Navy.[98]

The full extent of China's involvement in Burma's naval infrastructure improvement program, however, is very difficult to determine. While some reports on this subject are quite convincing, others are less so, and most have yet to be confirmed by independent sources. China has consistently denied that it is involved in the construction of any naval facilities, although a number of 'civilian' contracts for the upgrading of Burmese ports and the installation of new naval radars may have been undertaken by PLA personnel, or with the PLA's help.[99] There are clear benefits to Burma in taking advantage of China's expertise and permitting it at least some of the access it desires. Yet caution needs to be exercised over the question of PLA Navy deployments to the Indian Ocean (at least in the near term) and the extent to which Burma can be seen as an agent of the Chinese in this field. With its current naval order of battle, and limited blue water capabilities, regular PLA naval deployments to the Indian Ocean are still a distant prospect. Also, given Burma's fierce independence and continuing suspicions of China's longer-term strategic intentions, it is unlikely that the Rangoon regime would permit China all the access that it wants. Nor can any Chinese presence in Burma be considered permanent, whatever the apparent benefits of current arrangements.

Despite occasional comments to the contrary, all regional countries seem to accept that Burma's naval expansion program since 1988 is essentially defensive, rather than offensive, in nature.[100] The BN still has no real power projection capability. While it is now capable of a greater degree of sea denial, it cannot achieve sea control. Yet Burma's new warships and upgraded maritime facilities significantly increase its naval strength. Its *Hainan* class coastal patrol boats and *Houxin* guided missile attack craft give the BN the potential for significant improvements in the areas of anti-submarine and anti-surface warfare, and to a lesser extent air defence. Its more modern patrol vessels boost the BN's capabilities closer inshore. Taken together with its improved naval infrastructure, Burma is now in a better position than at any time in its history to patrol its inland waterways, police its territorial waters and enforce its extensive maritime claims. With the commissioning of its three new corvettes, and the acquisition of one or two *T-43* ocean minesweepers from China, Burma will have an (albeit limited) blue water capability for the first time since the retirement of its one Second World War vintage frigate in 1979.

These developments have contributed to a major change in the pattern of BN deployments. The acquisition of larger, more capable vessels has permitted a much greater emphasis on external defence and surveillance of Burma's maritime claims. Longer-range and more extended patrols are now easier to manage. The navy has also taken on some new roles. For example, soon after taking over government, the SLORC authorised extensive offshore oil and gas exploration by about a dozen foreign companies. While initial results were disappointing, large natural gas deposits were found at two sites in the Andaman Sea and already arrangements have been made to sell the gas to Thailand. While the most vulnerable part of the project is the overland pipeline, the navy will have an important role in protecting the offshore extraction facilities.[101] In addition, since 1988 the poaching of marine resources and overfishing by licenced foreign vessels have attracted increased attention.[102] Rangoon has been anxious to assert its control over Burma's rich fishing grounds, and to prevent the loss of its natural resources to the fishing fleets of other countries. Despite repeated Thai offers of joint naval patrols, the Rangoon regime has preferred to act independently.[103] To do this, however, a larger and more capable navy was clearly needed.

The navy also retains an important counter-insurgency role. The number of active insurgencies in Burma has declined significantly as a result of the ceasefire agreements reached with the SLORC and SPDC, but demands are still made on the navy by the other arms of the *Tatmadaw*. For example, naval patrols along the Arakan coast and rivers were traditionally of minor importance, but since 1991 they have been significantly increased to support Burma Army operations against the local Muslim population. Rohingya insurgent groups formed at that time are still active. The outbreak of renewed Karen insurgent activity in the Irrawaddy River delta later the same year caused the military government serious concern, and once again the navy was called upon to support the army's counter-insurgency operations. It is likely that these internal security problems contributed to the decision to construct the new naval facility at Hainggyi Island, signalling a continuing counter-insurgency role for the navy. The navy still patrols southern waters to prevent insurgent resupply from Thailand.

For all its obvious benefits, however, the rapid expansion of the Burma Navy has brought its own problems. There have been major difficulties in absorbing all the new vessels into the fleet, and keeping them operating at full capacity.[104] The more sophisticated equipment purchased since 1988, such as the C-801 SSMs and new EW systems, is technically more demanding, and skilled manpower is still in short supply. The range of spare parts required in stock has greatly increased, and much of it needs to be imported. Also, some of the new vessels have not lived up to their expectations. The three *PB-90* coastal patrol craft purchased from Yugoslavia, for example, initially proved 'unsatisfactory in service', because of propulsion problems.[105] The naval equipment provided by China is said to be below standard and, according to the *International Defense Review*, 'complaints have been voiced also over the poor performance of the *Hainan* class patrol boats'.[106] According to one dissident source,

> Another matter of concern for the naval officers was that machinery bought for the navy were all second-hand. The 10 naval vessels purchased from China a few years ago are now unserviceable and only two are useable from another purchase of six vessels.[107]

The precise nature of the problems being experienced with these vessels is not known, but they are clearly causing the *Tatmadaw* some concern. For all the benefits they are expected to bestow, the commissioning of the new corvettes and eventual arrival of the Chinese minesweepers will add considerably to the navy's financial, manpower and maintenance burdens.

The navy also suffers from another problem. Ever since the 1962 military coup all political processes in Burma have been dominated by the army. Ne Win's original 17-man Revolutionary Council included only one naval officer. Members of the BN later held senior positions in the regime's tame Burma Socialist Programme Party, and in the parliament which was created in 1974. Their membership gave the navy a voice in national affairs and promoted the image of armed forces unity. After 1988 there were a few naval officers in the SLORC, and the Commander-in-Chief of the Navy is a member of the SPDC. A senior naval officer is one of Burma's Deputy Prime Ministers, and a few BN officers have been included in the Cabinet, but these are largely token appointments. The political positions granted to the navy over the years have always been overshadowed by those held by army officers. In practical terms, this means that the navy's interests will never be considered before those of the army, nor will its needs be met until those of the army have been satisfied.

Given the overwhelming size of the Burma Army, and the nature of the country's perceived internal security problems, this situation is not surprising. Yet the navy has always had to endure a measure of distrust. Throughout its early years, many in the army were suspicious of the navy.[108] They distrusted the navy's British roots, the large proportion of Anglo-Burmans and ethnic minorities in its ranks, and the fact that a large proportion of navy officers were trained overseas. Of necessity, training at foreign institutions continued for the navy even after the 1962 coup, when most military links with the outside world were severed.[109] Also, the navy has tended to recruit better educated men from urban areas, rather than the less educated rural recruits which have traditionally formed the bulk of the army. Both this overseas experience and the higher educational levels of naval personnel have given rise to suspicions on the part of the military regime that these factors have 'contaminated' the personnel concerned, and made them politically unreliable. Such concerns were compounded in 1988 when a number of naval officers and men joined in the pro-democracy demonstrations that year.[110]

An insight was given into these inter-Service rivalries in August 2000, when the Burma Navy's Commander-in-Chief was summarily dismissed from his post. It has been suggested that his sudden 'retirement' was because the navy's Chinese warships performed poorly in an exercise held in the Andaman Sea that July, at which PLA Navy observers were present.[111] Whatever the real reason, the navy chief's abrupt dismissal sparked a strong protest from other naval officers, nearly 20 of whom were also dismissed. A number of others tendered their resignations. As the dispute unfolded, several related issues emerged, such as the resentment felt by the BN over the army's domination of the *Tatmadaw*, and concern over the way the Burma Army has attempted to exert its authority over the navy in Burmese waters. There have been suggestions that corrupt army officers have colluded with smugglers and 'bandits' against naval units, even to the extent that shots have been fired.[112] These reports have yet to be confirmed, but clearly there are strong underlying tensions between naval personnel and others in the armed forces.

Despite any misgivings the army hierarchy may have, however, the Rangoon regime clearly sees an important and continuing role for the navy. In barely 12 years the fleet has almost doubled and further major additions are expected. An ambitious program has been implemented to improve the navy's infrastructure and ocean surveillance capabilities. This is a significant investment by the military government in an area which has long been neglected. First the SLORC, and now the SPDC, seem determined that in the future Burma will exercise much greater control over its territorial waters than was possible in the past. It also signals a readiness to act more aggressively to protect Burma from any maritime threat that may emerge in the future.

Notes

1. An earlier version of this chapter appeared as Andrew Selth, 'The Burma Navy Under the SLORC', *Journal of Contemporary Asia*, Vol. 29, No. 2, 1999.

2. Tinker, *The Union of Burma*, p. 321 and p. 325. See also S. Woodburn Kirby *et al*, *The War Against Japan* (Her Majesty's Stationery Office, London, 1958), Vol. 2, pp. 10-11, p. 26 and p. 89.

3. *Jane's Fighting Ships 1963-64* (Jane's, London, 1963), p. 28.

4. For example, the RN lent the BN two small minesweepers. This was followed by five motor launches, converted to small gunboats. Until 1959 the Rangoon Port Authority operated a 750-ton *Bar* class boom defence vessel, also on loan from the Royal Navy. *Jane's Fighting Ships 1951-52* (Jane's, London, 1951), p. 159; *Jane's Fighting Ships 1953-54* (Jane's, London, 1953), p. 28; and *Jane's Fighting Ships 1963-64*, p. 28.

5. From the *Third Report on MDAP*, cited in SIPRI, *The Arms Trade with the Third World*, p. 451.

6. Tinker, *The Union of Burma*, pp. 287-8. The RN provided 11 harbour defence motor launches, for use as motor gunboats. *Jane's Fighting Ships 1953-54*, p. 28.

7. Between 1949 and 1951 the ships of the Inland Water Transportation Board carried more freight than the railways. These vessels were often armoured, and were escorted where possible by Burma Navy vessels. Tinker, p. 288.

8. Tinker, *The Union of Burma*, p. 325.

9. *Jane's Fighting Ships 1963-64*, p. 28.

10. *Jane's Fighting Ships 1982-83* (Jane's, London, 1982), p. 60.

11. The *PCE-827* type was transferred to the BN in June 1965, the *Admirable* type in March 1967.

12. *Jane's Fighting Ships 1997-98*, (Jane's Information Systems, Coulsdon, 1997), p. 79.

13. *Jane's Fighting Ships 1997-98*, p. 81.

14. *Jane's Fighting Ships 1997-98*, p. 79.

15. Bernard Prezelin (ed), *Naval Institute Guide to Combat Fleets of the World 1995* (Naval Institute Press, Annapolis, 1995), p. 431.

16. *Jane's Fighting Ships 1997-98*, p. 81.

17. *Jane's Fighting Ships 1973-74* (Jane's, London, 1973), p. 56.

18. *Ibid.* See also *Jane's Fighting Ships 1996-97* (Jane's Information Systems, Coulsdon, 1996), p. 81.

19. *Jane's Fighting Ships 1997-98*, pp. 81-2. The army also operated a number of small landing craft. The Burma Navy could call upon the country's small merchant fleet to assist with logistics. The size of these ships, however, limited their use to the main coastal ports.

20. *Jane's Fighting Ships 1997-98*, p. 82.

21. *Ibid.*

22. *Jane's Fighting Ships 1997-98*, pp. 80-2.

23. *Ibid.*

24. Prezelin, *Naval Institute Guide*, p. 431.

25. *Jane's Fighting Ships 1997-98*, p. 79.

26. *Jane's Fighting Ships 1997-98*, p. 81.

27. Callahan, 'The Origins of Military Rule in Burma', p. 429.

28. *Jane's Fighting Ships 1963-64*, p. 28.

29. *Jane's Fighting Ships 1973-74*, p. 254. According to the *Tatmadaw*'s own records, in 1964 the BN had 306 officers and 7595 ratings. It is not clear, however, whether there was a dramatic rise in numbers under the RC, or if Jane's figures are too low. See Maung Aung Myoe, *Building the Tatmadaw*, p. 27.

30. There are, however, still references in *Jane's Fighting Ships* and other sources to 'naval infantry' or 'marines'. Maung Aung Myoe, *Building the Tatmadaw*, p. 27.

31. Personal observation, Rangoon, April 1995.

32. See, for example, Mirante, *Burmese Looking Glass*, pp. 255ff.

33. Tin Maung Maung Than, 'Burma's National Security and Defence Posture', p. 51.

34. See, for example, Selth, 'Australian Defence Contacts with Burma', p. 464.

35. *Jane's Fighting Ships 1996-97* stated that the BN still used eight KB-47G Sioux and 10 SA-316B Allouette III helicopters for maritime work (p. 80). However, by 1988 all the

KB-47Gs had been taken out of service and barely six Allouettes were still airworthy. In any case, neither aircraft was used exclusively by the navy. See also 'Myanmar (Union of)', *Military Technology*, January 1995, p. 292.

36. See, for example, G. Jacobs, 'South Asian Naval Forces', *Asian Defence Journal*, December 1984, p. 54; *Jane's Fighting Ships 1996-97*, p. 80; and Prezelin, *Naval Institute Guide*, p. 430.

37. *Jane's Fighting Ships 1996-97*, p. 80. Details of land-based and sea-borne aircraft have not been included in later editions of this work.

38. Personal observation, Rangoon, April 1995.

39. *Jane's Fighting Ships, 1997-98*, p. 83.

40. See 'Myanmar', *Jane's Sentinel Security Assessment: Southeast Asia*, pp. 333-54.

41. Literally translated as the Tactical Naval Flotilla Operation Command, it has also been called the Major War Vessels Command.

42. See Randal Gray (ed), *Conway's All The World's Fighting Ships, 1947-1982* (Naval Institute Press, Annapolis, 1983), p. 324.

43. Some of the older English names for these islands have now been replaced by Burmese names. Mali Island, for example, was called Tavoy Island on UK Admiralty charts, while Zadetkyi Island (or Zadetkyi Kyun) was named St. Matthew's Island. See *Bay of Bengal Pilot* (Royal Navy Hydrographer, Taunton, 1978), Vol. NP. 21, pp. 118ff; and Nelles Maps, *Burma (Myanmar)* (Nelles Verlag, Munich, 199?).

44. Bunge, *Burma*, p. 255.

45. Personal observation, Rangoon, April 1995 and November 1999.

46. Tin Maung Maung Than, 'Burma's National Security and Defence Posture', p. 50.

47. *Jane's Fighting Ships 1997-98*, p. 79. Some observers have suggested that the BN's manning levels have already reached 20,000. Interview, Rangoon, April 1995.

48. Interviews, Rangoon, April 1995 and November 1999. See also Selth, *Burma's Order of Battle*, pp. 19-22; and D. Banerjee, 'Burma's naval activity raises doubts', *Bangkok Post*, 18 July 1994.

49. *Jane's Fighting Ships 1997-98*, p. 126. See also Lintner, 'Arms for Eyes', p. 26; and Prezelin, *Naval Institute Guide*, p. 430.

50. Larry Jagen, 'Defence Links between Rangoon, Beijing viewed', BBC, 19 August 1994; See also Lintner, 'Myanmar's Chinese connection', p. 24. and *Jane's Fighting Ships 1997-98*, p. 80.

51. Robert Karniol, 'Yugoslav patrol boats for Burma', *JDW*, 5 January 1991, p. 14.

52. *Jane's Fighting Ships 1997-98*, p. 880. See also *Towards Democracy in Burma*, p. 58; and Lintner, 'Oiling the iron fist', p. 30.

53. *Jane's Fighting Ships 1997-98*, p. 80.

54. *Jane's Fighting Ships 1997-98*, p. 79; and *Jane's Fighting Ships 1994-95* (Jane's Information Systems, Coulsdon, 1994), p. 124.

55. Interview, Rangoon, April 1995. See also Andrew Selth, 'The Myanmar Navy: From Brown Water to Blue Water', *Naval Forces*, Vol. 19, No. 6, 1998, pp. 30-3.

56. Interview, Rangoon, April 1995. See also Robert Karniol, 'Myanmar boosts naval power with frigates', *JDW*, 20 August 1993, p. 1; Aung Zaw, 'Burmese island focus of strategy moves by China', *The Nation*, 2 September 1994; and Lintner, 'Hardware for Hardliners', p. 12.

57. William Ashton, 'Myanmar Navy boosts sea power with corvettes', *Jane's Navy International*, Vol. 105, No. 8, October 2000, p. 39.

58. *Ibid.*

59. See, for example, Lintner, '$400m deal signed by China and Myanmar', p. 1; and 'Myanmar in large arms barter deal with China', *Asian Aviation*, February 1991, p. 88.

60. *Jane's Fighting Ships 1997-98*, p. 125.

61. Interview, Rangoon, November 1996.
62. 'Burma builds helicopter fleet with Mi-171B buy', *JDW*, 4 September 1996, p. 19.
63. Personal observation, Rangoon, April 1995. See also A.W. Grazebrook, 'The Navies of Southeast Asia', *Naval Forces*, Vol. 17, No. 2, 1996, p. 88.
64. There have been claims that the BN is acquiring up to six of these vessels, but this is unlikely. See 'Myanmar', *Asian Defence Yearbook 1998-1999* (Syed Hussain Pub Sdn Bhd, Kuala Lumpur, 1999), p. 106.
65. *Jane's Fighting Ships 1997-98*, p. 128.
66. Merrill, 'A closer look at Sino-Burmese military links', p. 323. See also Merrill, 'Myanmar's China connection: A cause for alarm?', pp. 20-1.
67. Interview, Canberra, October 1997. See also *Jane's Underwater Warfare Systems 1997-98* (Jane's Information Systems, Coulsdon, 1997), pp. 226-8.
68. In late 2000 a Burma Navy patrol boat exploded and sank near Mergui. It was speculated that it may have hit a sea mine, but it is more likely to have suffered from a mechanical failure. 'Naval vessel exploded near southern Burma's Daung Kyun: 8 killed, 3 missing', DVB (in Burmese), 22 November 2000.
69. *Jane's Fighting Ships 1997-98*, p. 83.
70. Prezelin, *Naval Institute Guide*, p. 432. See also *Jane's Fighting Ships 1997-98*, p. 83.
71. *Jane's Fighting Ships 1999-2000* (Jane's Information Systems, Coulsdon, 2000), p. 80; and *Special Report 1995: World Warship Construction*, (Jane's Information Group, Coulsdon, 1995), p. 8. Slightly different specifications for the gunboats are given in Prezelin, *Naval Institute Guide*, p. 430.
72. *Jane's Fighting Ships 1997-98*, p. 80.
73. *Jane's Fighting Ships 1997-98*, p. 81. See also J.V.P. Goldrick and P. D. Jones, 'Regional Naval Reviews: Far East', *US Naval Institute Proceedings* 117/3/1057, March 1991, p. 143.
74. *Jane's Fighting Ships 1997-98*, p. 79.
75. *Ibid.*
76. *Jane's Fighting Ships 1999-2000*, p. 80.
77. Units included Raytheon 1500 and 1900 sets, and Decca 110 and 1226 sets. *Jane's Fighting Ships, 1997-98*, pp. 77ff. See also Jacobs, 'South Asian Naval Forces', p. 54.
78. *Jane's Radar and Electronic Warfare Systems 1996-97* (Jane's Information Systems, Coulsdon, 1996), p. 447. See also Norman Friedman, *The Naval Institute Guide to World Naval Weapons Systems, 1994 Update* (Naval Institute Press, Annapolis, 1994), p. 53.
79. *Jane's Fighting Ships, 1997-98*, p. 80 and p. 126.
80. Ashton, 'Myanmar Navy boosts sea power with corvettes', p. 39.
81. Interview, Rangoon, November 1996.
82. See Selth, *Burma's Secret Military Partners*.
83. Lintner, 'Myanmar's Chinese connection', p. 24. See also 'Chinese Premier dismisses reports of Indian Ocean bases', AAP, 29 December 1994.
84. Interviews, Rangoon, November 1996 and November 1999.
85. Robert Karniol, 'New base is boost to naval power', *JDW*, 12 September 1992, p. 31; and Karniol, 'Myanmar boosts naval power with frigates', p. 1.
86. 'But will the flag follow trade', pp. 31-2. See also Lintner, 'Enter the Dragon', p. 23; and *Jane's Fighting Ships, 1997-98*, p. 79.
87. NCGUB, *Human Rights Yearbook 1994*, p. 76. Kadan Island was formerly known as King Island, and Pyinzabu Island was named Bentinck Island. On some older maps, Letsutaw (or Letsok-aw) Island is called Letsutan Island. Kawthaung used to be known as Victoria Point. See also *Bay of Bengal Pilot*, Vol. NP. 21, pp. 118ff.
88. 'PRC To Provide Assistance to Burma for Transfer of Mawyawadi Naval base', DVB (in Burmese), 11 June 2000.

89. Interview, Rangoon, November 1996.
90. Interview, Rangoon, November 1996.
91. 'Air Forces Survey - Part 10: Myanmar', *Asian Aviation*, Vol. 14, No. 6, June 1994, p. 34; and Bruce Hawke, 'Myanmar installs new naval radar' *JDW*, 21 February 2001, p. 14.
92. Ball, *Burma's Military Secrets*. See also Selth, 'Burma's Intelligence Apparatus', pp. 33-70.
93. Interview, Rangoon, December 1999.
94. Interview, Bangkok, November 1996. See also M.G. Rolls, 'Thailand's Post-Cold War Security Policy and Defence Programme', in Colin McInnes and M.G.Rolls (eds), *Post-Cold War Security Issues in the Asia-Pacific Region* (Frank Cass, Ilford, 1994), pp. 101-3.
95. See, for example, Lintner, 'Enter the Dragon', p. 23: and 'Jitters over naval buildup', *Asian Defence Journal*, January 1993, p. 165.
96. Banerjee, 'Burma's naval activity raises doubts'.
97. See, for example, Malik, 'Burma slides under China's shadow', pp. 319-22; and Rahul Roy-Chaudhury, 'Strategic Trends in the Indian Ocean', *Strategic Analysis*, Vol. 19, No. 6, September 1996, pp. 885-900. For a more cautious appraisal, see Merrill, 'A closer look at Sino-Burmese military links', p. 323.
98. Baranwal, *SP's Military Yearbook 1992-93*, pp. 371-377. For a more sober view, see Ashton, 'Chinese Bases in Burma - Fact or Fiction?', pp. 84-87.
99. Interview, Rangoon, November 1996. See also Banerjee, 'Burma's naval activity raises doubts'.
100. The Rangoon regime's claims in this regard seem to have been accepted by the US Director of Naval Intelligence. See *DNI Posture Statement* (Office of Naval Intelligence, Washington, DC, 1994), p. 22.
101. 'Regional Reviews: Far Eastern Navies', *US Naval Institute Proceedings* 113/3/1009, 057, March 1987, p. 68. See also 'War and Money', *Asiaweek*, 10 March 1995.
102. Interview, Rangoon, November 1996. See also Gordon Fairclough, 'Floating Flashpoint', *FEER*, 13 March 1997, pp. 53-54.
103. Interview, Rangoon, April 1995 and November 1999. See also 'Thailand, Indonesia navies to discuss joint patrols to curb illegal fishing', *The Nation*, 26 August 2000.
104. Interview, Rangoon, April 1995.
105. *Jane's Fighting Ships 1997-98*, p. 80.
106. Lintner, 'Myanmar's Chinese connection', p. 26. See also Jagen, BBC broadcast, 19 August 1994.
107. This statement seems to be referring to the *Hainan* and *Houxin* class patrol boats, but may only be referring to the former. 'Burmese naval officers dissatisfied with sacking of navy chief', DVB (in Burmese), 12 September 2000.
108. Selth, *Transforming the Tatmadaw*, pp. 161-2. See also Callahan, 'The Origins of Military Rule in Burma', pp. 428-30.
109. These included postings to the UK and US. See also *Jane's Sentinel Security Assessment: Southeast Asia*, pp. 333-54.
110. Lintner, 'Backdown or bloodbath', p. 14; and William Stewart, 'Now A Coup', *Time*, 26 September 1988, p. 14.
111. 'Burmese Leader Fails Chinese Test', *FEER*, 31 August 2000, p. 10.
112. 'Burmese naval officers dissatisfied with sacking of navy chief'.

9

The Burma Air Force

With its handful of obsolete [aircraft], ... the Burma air force ranked as the least impressive in Asia. But that would be no consolation to those beneath the bombs it did manage to deliver. — Bertil Lintner, *Land of Jade* (1990)

The army has always dominated the Burmese armed forces and will continue to do so.[1] Since the creation of the SLORC in 1988, however, the Burma Air Force (*Tatmadaw Lei*) has increasingly claimed a share of international attention. This has been due mainly to its rapid expansion, and its acquisition of several new and more modern types of aircraft. These additions to the BAF's inventory give it the potential for significantly increased operational capabilities. For long a mere adjunct to the ground forces in their internal security role, the BAF is now emerging as a significant force in its own right with a much greater capacity for conventional air defence.

9.1 The Burma Air Force Before 1988

The BAF traces its origins back to the UK's Burma Act of 24 December 1947, which set the stage for the country's independence.[2] In many respects, its early history is the story of its aircraft acquisitions. Yet, from the very beginning, Burma's serious economic problems and neutral foreign policy placed severe limits on the development of the BAF's operational capabilities.

In the years immediately following Independence, the BAF benefited from British assistance, and the US provided some equipment and training during the 1960s and early 1970s. As military aid was resisted by both the Nu and Ne Win Governments, however, the BAF was forced to rely on comparatively obsolete aircraft, often purchased second-hand. In 1948 the UK transferred four Supermarine Spitfire F.18 fighters to the BAF, and three more were later acquired from Singapore.[3] Fifteen Airspeed AS.10 Oxfords, five Airspeed AS.65 Consuls and four Beagle Auster D.5 aircraft were later provided to give light transport lift.[4] Six de Havilland DH.82 Tigermoths followed to assist with training. In 1950 the BAF also acquired nine Douglas C-47 Skytrain transport aircraft, including one presented as a gift from Indonesia.[5] Twenty old Supermarine Seafire Mk.15s were 'de-navalised' and added to the BAF's inventory in 1953. The following year the BAF purchased 30 Supermarine Spitfire F.9s from Israel. These aircraft, while cheap, had already seen service with the British, Israeli, Czechoslovakian and Italian air forces.[6] Over the next five years Burma acquired 10 de Havilland Chipmunk DH C-1 trainers and 38 Hunting Provost T-53 trainers from the UK.[7] While unsuited to a ground attack role, the BAF fitted the latter four aircraft types with machine guns, bomb racks and rocket launchers for counter-insurgency operations.[8]

During the mid-1950s an effort was made to upgrade the BAF's offensive capabilities. In 1954 and 1955 Burma acquired eight de Havilland Vampire T-55 trainers from the RAF for its Advanced Flying Unit. These aircraft gave the BAF its first experience of jet aircraft and, despite some initial problems, it appears to have been a happy one. Modified by the BAF to carry bombs and Hispano 20mm cannon, the Vampires performed surprisingly well in counter-insurgency operations.[9] The last one fell to insurgent ground fire in 1978. Their more complex engineering stretched the BAF's resources, however, and it later returned to propellor-driven aircraft. In 1957 Burma purchased 18 reconditioned Hawker Sea Fury FB.11s from the Royal Navy Fleet Air Arm, to act as Burma's front line fighters. This delivery was followed a year later by three two-seater Sea Fury T.20 trainers.[10]

After the 1962 coup, the Ne Win regime added a number of new and more modern aircraft types to the BAF order of battle. Details of specific orders and dates of delivery are not always clear, but it seems that in 1963 eight Lockheed T-33A Shooting Star jets were purchased from the US to upgrade the BAF's combat capabilities. Over the next four years another 14 T-33s were delivered to Burma, prompting the claim that 'the procurement of T-33s made the BAF the strongest air force in the South East Asian region then'.[11] These aircraft were not taken out of service until 1984. In 1968 there were several reports that the US had sold Burma some North American F-86F Sabre fighters, but none were in fact delivered.[12] From 1956 the US provided Burma with 10 Cessna T-37C Dragonfly basic jet trainers under the MAP, for use in counter-insurgency operations. From 1976, however, most training and combat needs were met by 20 SIAI-Marchetti SF-260W Warrior piston-engined aircraft which the BAF purchased from Italy. Ten arrived that year, and the remainder followed later.[13] These aircraft were augmented in the late 1970s with two Pilatus PC-6A Porters and five Pilatus PC-6B Turbo-Porters from Switzerland.[14] In 1979 the BAF took delivery of eight Pilatus PC-7 Turbo-Trainers, with another eight following by 1980. Burma was given an option to buy additional PC-7 aircraft, but instead ordered four of the more powerful PC-9 version, the first country to do so. These aircraft arrived in Burma in 1986. An additional three PC-7s and three more PC-9s were delivered to Rangoon in the early 1990s.[15]

These purchases of armed training and liaison aircraft by the BAF were made in the face of repeated offers from the UK and US of more specialised combat aircraft. Burmese policy at the time seems to have been to reduce the costs of both the initial purchase and subsequent operations by buying smaller, cheaper aircraft which could be used for both training and (after modification) internal security roles. Thus, the designation of Burmese aircraft as trainers or combat machines has always been a rather academic one. For example, as their designation suggests, the T-33s were two-seat jet trainers, but were armed and used for ground strikes against insurgents. The SF-260s were supplied with hard points on their wings for the same purpose. They were subsequently armed and used to supplement the modified Pilatus PC-7 and PC-9 trainers in counter-insurgency operations.[16] Both Pilatus types were armed with French Matra rocket packs, (fitting 68mm Brandt rockets), bomb racks and podded 7.62mm machine guns.[17] It was apparently confusion over the combat role of these aircraft which led an Australian company to export repaired Pilatus engine parts to Burma in 1991, despite the Hawke Government's ban on arms sales to Burma.[18]

For many years Douglas C-47 Skytrains, Beechcraft D-18S Expeditors and Bristol Mk.21 Freighters were the mainstay of the BAF's transport arm.[19] During the late 1970s and early 1980s, however, Burma acquired five second-hand Fokker F-27 and Fairchild-Hiller FH-227 turboprop aircraft. One Fokker F-27 arrived in 1976, two FH-227s arrived in 1978, an F-27 MK 500 was delivered in 1981 and a FH-227 J followed in 1982.[20] These were used for VIP transport, surveillance and general transport duties.[21] Some were adapted to military needs by the addition of a side cargo-door and replaced the BAF's few remaining Douglas C-47s. At one stage, the BAF had plans to acquire a number of Lockheed C-130 Hercules transport aircraft but they were abandoned around 1982, probably due to the cost. The BAF also showed some interest in the Australian GAF Nomad short take-off and landing (STOL) aircraft before production lines closed down in 1984, but no firm orders were ever lodged.

There has never been any clear distinction between civilian and military aircraft in Burma and, during major counter-insurgency campaigns, all state-owned aircraft were considered available for troop transport and medical evacuation, as required. The civil airline, Union of Burma Airways (UBA), began operations in 1948 with a fleet of six de Havilland DH-104 Dove light passenger and transport aircraft. In 1950 nine Douglas DC-3 Dakotas were introduced to service routes to Bangkok and destinations in India and Pakistan. In the years that followed, Vickers VC-2 Viscounts, Fokker F-27 Friendships and a Boeing 727 were added to the fleet.[22] By the late 1980s, UBA operated five Fokker F-27 and three Fokker F-28 Fellowship passenger planes which could be used to supplement military airlift capabilities in an emergency.[23] For example, in 1977, during the battle of Chinshwe against the CPB, a number of UBA aircraft were taken over to evacuate wounded soldiers to Rangoon from northern Shan State.[24]

A range of other aircraft provided the BAF with liaison and light transport capabilities. Nine single-engined de Havilland DHC-3 Otters were acquired from Canada in 1957 and 1958. These reliable utility aircraft were not phased out until 1985, but their role was gradually taken over by the Pilatus PC-6s. From 1957 the BAF also operated 10 US-made Cessna 180s.[25] In August 1982 the Burmese government purchased a Cessna 550 Citation II business jet, which was maintained and flown by the BAF. It was mainly a VIP transport but, together with a small number of Beechcraft Model 65 Queen Air twin engine executive aircraft, it was also used for aerial survey and surveillance work.[26] In 1975 the US donated five Ayres S-2R Turbo Thrush crop-dusting aircraft to Burma under the INCP, for spraying opium poppy fields with chemical defoliants. Despite some claims, it is most unlikely that these small and highly vulnerable aircraft were used for low level reconnaissance flights over insurgent areas.[27]

The BAF has long maintained a helicopter fleet for transport and observation duties. Between 1956 and 1958, Japan provided Burma with 12 Kawasaki-Bell KB-47G Sioux light trainer and reconnaissance helicopters as part of war reparations.[28] Reports that this package also included some Kawasaki-Vertol KV-107 II twin-rotor transport helicopters are incorrect.[29] From 1958 until 1978, however, the BAF operated a small fleet of US-built Vertol H-21 Shawnee medium transport helicopters, assisted during the early 1960s by one Mil Mi-4 'Hound' utility helicopter presented to Ne Win as a gift from the USSR. Between 1961 and 1965 the BAF took delivery of 13 jet-powered Aerospatiale SA-316B Alouette IIIs from France, but by 1988 a bare half dozen of them were still airworthy. One was usually embarked on the Burma Navy's hydrographic survey ship.[30] In 1962 the US provided Burma with seven Kaman HH-43B Huskie light transport helicopters, mainly for search and rescue duties. It added another nine Huskies in 1968, but by 1979 none were still flying. According to SIPRI, between 1982 and 1984 France sold Burma four Aerospatiale SA-342L Gazelle light utility helicopters, but this has not been confirmed.[31] References in some sources to Aerospatiale SA-330J Puma medium lift helicopters in the BAF fleet are incorrect, but these aircraft are operated by the country's civil airline and are probably used by the air force.[32]

The BAF received a major boost after 1975 when the US donated 18 Bell 205A Iroquois and seven Bell 206B Jet Ranger helicopters to Burma under the INCP. Replacement parts, training, maintenance support and telecommunications equipment were all included in the aid package.[33] The Iroquois were intended exclusively for anti-narcotics patrols, but the US restrictions were never likely to be observed and by the early 1980s all these helicopters had been fully integrated into the BAF for military operations. They were used for resupply, casualty evacuation and liaison purposes. Around the same time, the BAF also acquired a twin-engined Bell 212 helicopter for VIP transport. By 1988, accidents and ground fire had reduced the number of Iroquois still serviceable to about 12, and the number of airworthy Jet Rangers to about six.[34]

The BAF's armoury included a wide range of gravity bombs and air-to-ground rockets. The former included 250lb, 80lb, 28lb and 20lb bombs. The latter ranged from 128mm rockets supplied by Yugoslavia, 68mm rockets from France and 57mm rockets from Poland, to smaller 37mm weapons. A variety of US-manufactured bombs and rockets were also held in Burmese stores, including different sized cluster bombs, 250lb napalm bombs, and 500lb and 250lb opalm canisters (an incendiary weapon akin to napalm). There were 3.25 inch rockets, 3-inch rockets armed with either a 60lb or 25lb warhead, and 2.75 inch rockets. The BAF also stocked a variety of munitions for producing white phosphorous smoke.[35] In addition to bombs and rockets, BAF aircraft were armed with 30mm, 23mm and 20mm cannon, 0.5 inch (12.7mm) heavy machine guns, and 0.303 inch (7.7mm) light machine guns.

Figure 21: Burma Air Force Strength, 1988

Counter-insurgency:	
Pilatus PC-7	14 (also training)
Pilatus PC-9	4
Lockheed T-33A	5
Transport:	
Fokker F-27F	1
Fairchild-Hiller FH-227	6
Pilatus PC-6A/B	7
Beechcraft D-18S	3
Liaison:	
Cessna 180	6
Cessna 550	1
Beechcraft 65	?
Helicopters:	
Bell 205	12
Bell 206	6
Aerospatiale SA-316B	6
Training:	
SIAI-Marchetti SF-260W/M	13 (also counter-insurgency)
Cessna T-37C	9
Other:	
Ayres S-2R	5

The same economic problems that hindered the modernisation of the BAF's inventory also contributed to serious maintenance problems. The lack of spare parts, in particular, led to a high ratio of unserviceable aircraft. Like other parts of the *Tatmadaw*, however, the BAF became expert at improvisation and adaption, as seen in the remarkably long life of its aircraft and the transformation of its trainers into reasonably effective light ground attack planes. Still, the BAF suffered badly from a lack of skilled manpower and, foreign exchange permitting, was often forced to hire foreign experts to maintain its aircraft. Between 1975 and the mid-1980s, for example, Italian engineers were contracted to service and repair the air force's SIAI Marchetti SF-260s in Burma. Also, the shortage of aviation grade fuel (which Burma had to import specially in drums) forced the sale in 1990 of the

BAF's entire fleet of SF-260s.[36] This problem had prompted the BAF to consider converting to turboprop power as early as 1982, but any steps in that direction were prohibited by the cost.

At its inception, the BAF's primary mission was to provide transport, logistic and close combat support for the Burma Army in its counter-insurgency operations. Although small and poorly equipped, the BAF played an important role in the years immediately following Independence, as the *Tatmadaw* fought to keep the central government from being overrun by ethnic, communist and other insurgent groups. Despite the capture of a few aircraft by Karen insurgents, the BAF's command of the air was unchallenged.[37] It repeatedly enabled Rangoon to break up insurgent concentrations and resupply its own forces, which at one stage were confined to the country's main population centres. During the late 1950s and early 1960s the BAF was also called upon to defend Burmese air space against incursions by foreign aircraft, as Communist and Nationalist Chinese forces carried their struggle into northern Burma, and both the US and Taiwan provided the *Kuomintang* remnants with covert support. In the 1960s and 1970s the BAF's resources were devoted to counter-insurgency operations, but its role later expanded to include the monitoring of opium poppy production in the Golden Triangle and the spraying of poppy fields with chemical defoliants.[38]

Throughout this period the BAF's manpower levels remained low. At first, the force was extremely small, consisting of only eight officers and 20 airmen.[39] Six of the officers were veterans of the Burma Air Force Volunteer Reserve, which had been formed by the British colonial administration in 1940. Some had also served with the Royal Air Force during the Second World War. The other two officers had been trained by the Imperial Japanese Army Air Service during Japan's four-year occupation of Burma.[40] From this number in 1948, the BAF had grown to some hundreds by 1953, but attrition rates were high.[41] Within two years of Ne Win's coup, however, the BAF's numbers had risen to 323 officers and 5877 other ranks.[42] Over the next 15 years it gradually grew to around 9,000 officers and airmen, at which level it remained until the SLORC's appearance in 1988.[43] In some areas, however, the formal manning structure existed only on paper and many BAF units were badly under strength. An Air Force Regiment (of 800 men) was formed in 1966 to provide security for the BAF's bases, but it was also required to perform combat duties.[44]

Reflecting its origins, the BAF's organisation, rank structure and operational procedures were patterned along British lines. BAF headquarters was located in the Ministry of Defence. There was a small number of regional air bases, each broadly responsible for particular areas of operation. There were designated combat (both air defence and counter-insurgency), training, transport and liaison squadrons (*Tatmadaw Lei Ou*). Radar and other signals units were organised into electronic warfare squadrons. While the BAF was responsible for its own administration and training, it was closely integrated with the army for operations. Generally speaking, BAF aircraft were considered strategic assets and remained under the command of the BAF Chief of Staff in Rangoon. Operational control was sometimes passed to Regional Commanders, however, during counter-insurgency campaigns. There was no separate army aviation unit nor, despite reports to the contrary, did the Burma Navy have its own fleet air arm. BAF F-27 and F-227 aircraft were used for long-range maritime and coastal patrols, and the BAF's smaller helicopters were sometimes embarked on BN vessels, but all military aircraft in Burma formally remained under the command of the air force.[45]

By 1988 the BAF's main operational base was at Mingaladon, which was then Burma's only international civil airport. It was also the site of the BAF's principal supply, armament, maintenance and repair facilities. A number of Military Police and Intelligence units were also stationed there. The second largest air base was at Meiktila, south of Mandalay and closer to the BAF's main areas of operation. It was also home to the BAF's specialist training facilities, including its Administrative Training School, Technical Training School, Electronic Training School and Central Inspection Unit. BAF Intelligence personnel were also based there. The main flight training base was at Shante, near Meiktila. Other BAF units were based at Hmawbi and Myitkyina.[46] Occasionally, airfield detachments were based at places like Lashio and Kentung, to help support operations against the CPB. The EW squadrons were usually co-located with air crew at the larger airfields. However, a number were posted to smaller sites around the country, like Loi Mwe, Kutkai and Namsang.[47]

Depending on the kind of aircraft operating, and the state of the facilities at each location, the BAF could also use the many civil airfields scattered around the country. Navigation aids were often old or unserviceable, however, and many runways were unsuitable for jet fighters and larger transport aircraft.[48] Only 24 airfields had permanent-surface, all-weather runways, like those at Moulmein and Mergui in the south, Sittwe and Sandoway in the west, and Heho (near Taunggyi) in the east. Only 10 had runways over 1800 metres and only three - Mingaladon, Mandalay and Myitkyina - had runways over 2,400 metres.[49]

The BAF has always been heavily dependent on other countries for training. Initially, it was assisted by the RAF component of the BMM.[50] Also, foreign pilots and technicians usually accompanied aircraft deliveries to train local ground and air crew. Occasionally, BAF pilots were sent overseas to learn how to fly new aircraft and, until 1962, both BAF pilots and ground crew received training in places like the UK, US and Australia.[51] The BAF's own flight training program seems to have been based on a graduated progression from gliders to light trainers, and then to more advanced aircraft. For this purpose, the BAF purchased 10 Slingsby B-31 gliders in 1955. These were followed by a succession of other gliders, including Zadar, Jetstruck, Olympic, Dart 50, Capstan T-49 and Swallow aircraft.[52] The Tigermoths were withdrawn from service in 1956, but by then the BAF had a large number of Hunting Provosts, which was a two-seat basic trainer before it was armed and used for ground attack.[53] Sometimes, purchases of new combat aircraft included a number of two-seat training versions, such as the Sea Fury T.20s. By the early 1980s the BAF was using Pilatus PC-7s and SF-260s as both combat and basic training aircraft.[54]

By the time the SLORC took over government, the Burma Air Force had established its credentials as an important arm of the *Tatmadaw*, but faced a number of major problems. It was too small and ill equipped to perform its primary missions and was hard pressed to keep its machines flying. Burma had no credible air defence and its counter-insurgency squadrons consisted largely of training aircraft modified to perform in a ground attack role. BAF aircrews often showed considerable courage but lacked the necessary skills and equipment to perform at the highest level. Ground to air coordination was poor. The BAF had not received any machines specifically designed for combat operations since the arrival of the SF-260s nearly ten years before. Logistics and maintenance difficulties (due mainly to a lack of spare parts) kept serviceability rates low. Without a major re-evaluation of the BAF's role and capabilities, it seemed destined to remain a largely ineffective force constantly struggling to survive in the face of competing resource pressures from the army and other sectors of the Burmese economy.

9.2 The Burma Air Force After 1988

Since 1988 this picture has changed significantly. Details of specific orders and actual deliveries are difficult to obtain but, from the information available, it is clear that the BAF has benefited greatly from the Rangoon regime's arms buying efforts. There has also been a number of major changes to the BAF's organisation and structure.

In 1989 the BAF Chief of Staff accompanied the then army commander, LTGEN Than Shwe, on his arms-buying trip to China, and in 1990 the BAF's Commander-in-Chief, LTGEN Tin Tun, also paid a visit there. As a result of these and other contacts the BAF has received a major injection of Chinese aircraft and equipment. For example, in May 1991 it took delivery of 10 Chengdu F-7M 'Airguard' fighters and two GAIC FT-7 twin-seat trainer aircraft. In May 1993 another squadron of 10 F-7 and two FT-7 aircraft was delivered. The US$130-160 million price tag was reportedly paid for in part by shipments of Burmese rice and hardwood.[55] According to reliable reports, a third squadron of these aircraft types was delivered in 1996 and a fourth followed in late 1997.[56] Six additional F-7s are thought to have been delivered in 1998, possibly to replace aircraft lost through accidents or on operations.[57] As a derivative of the Mikoyan MiG-21 'Fishbed' interceptor, the F-7 is based on fighter designs but it can be fitted with rocket pods and converted into a serviceable ground attack aircraft. The FT-7 is the export version of the GAIC JJ-7, itself a copy of the MiG-21 'Mongol-B' trainer. The new F-7 fighters were initially based at Hmawbi but were later dispersed to other airfields.[58]

China has also provided Burma with about four squadrons (12 aircraft each) of second-hand NAMC A-5C close air support and ground attack aircraft. An upgraded, export version of the NAMC Q-5 'Fantan', the A-5C is a simple but rugged fighter-bomber well suited to counter-insurgency operations. The first squadron was flown to Burma by Chinese pilots in September 1994 and the second probably arrived in early 1996.[59] It is believed that one more squadron arrived soon after and a fourth was delivered in early 1998.[60] At least one squadron of A-5s was based at Meiktila. Another was originally due to be stationed at a large new air base at Namsang, in the southern Shan States, but was held back in central Burma, apparently because of the threat from insurgent SAMs. Khun Sa's MTA, for example, held a number of SAM-7s and possibly even 'Stinger' SAMs.[61] Kayah insurgents were also believed to have some SAMs. A third A-5 squadron is currently based at Myitkyina, in Burma's far north, but may eventually transfer to Namsang or Toungoo.[62]

There were several reports in 1990 that the SLORC had ordered at least one squadron of Shenyang F-6 fighters (a Chinese copy of the Mikoyan MiG-19 'Farmer'), to be delivered later that year or in 1991.[63] While a small number of FT-6 two-seat trainers are now in service with the BAF, it seems the main F-6 order was abandoned, either in favour of additional F-7s or perhaps even the A-5s (which is also a MiG-19 variant).[64] There have also been rumours that the SLORC was interested in the SAC F-8 II 'Finback' multi-role fighter.[65] This is an export version of the J-8 II twin-engine air superiority fighter with a secondary capacity for ground attack. No firm orders appear to have been placed with the Chinese, probably because the F-8 II upgrade program was thrown into doubt after the Tienanmen Square massacre in 1989, and the withdrawal of promised US technical assistance. Burma had no pressing strategic imperative for an air superiority fighter, but the regime's interest in purchasing such an aircraft remain high.

In addition to the FT-7s and FT-6s, the regime has looked to China for other jet training aircraft. After considerable speculation, it was revealed in June 1998 that Beijing would finance a US$20 million sale of seven NAMC/PAC Karakorum K-8 trainers to the BAF.[66] An order for additional K-8 aircraft soon followed. Twelve, or possibly 16, of the two-seat jet trainers have already been delivered to Shante air training base.[67] Burma is the first customer outside China and Pakistan to receive this aircraft. Its acquisition considerably increases the BAF's ability to train pilots for its expanding fleet of Chinese interceptors and ground attack aircraft. Also, if necessary, the K-8 can be configured for ground attack, with a 23mm gun pod under the fuselage and external storage points. It can carry PL-7 air-to-air missiles (AAM), a 12-round pod of 57mm rockets, or bombs weighing up to 250kg.[68]

The Chinese have not forgotten the BAF's transport arm. In late 1991 it was reported by *Flight International* that a senior delegation led by Burma's Air Force Chief of Staff had again visited Beijing, this time to discuss the possible purchase of three new aircraft types. These were the SAC Y-8 general purpose medium range transport, the 17-seat Harbin Y-12 STOL utility aircraft and the Changhe Z-8 heavy lift helicopter.[69] Two SAC Y-8D aeroplanes (China's export version of the Soviet Antonov An-12 'Cub') were delivered to Burma in September 1993, two more had arrived by late 1994, and another two arrived in mid-1997.[70] No other firm orders for transport aircraft have yet been revealed, although in 1993 a regional defence journal speculated that China may supply the *Tatmadaw* with up to six Harbin Y-12s and the same number of another turboprop aircraft, the Xian Y-14.[71]

The Changhe Z-8 helicopter referred to by *Flight International* is the unauthorised Chinese version of the Aerospatiale SA-321 Super Frelon. Since the journal's 1991 report, the Rangoon regime's possible interest in this aircraft has not reappeared. There have been rumours of other helicopter deals, however, and according to *Jane's Defence Weekly* another arms package negotiated by the SLORC with China in 1994 included some 20 helicopters.[72] The specific type being purchased was not revealed, but they were unlikely to be heavy lift models. A number of other reports referred to them as 'assault' helicopters, but it is not known what this description might mean in the Chinese context.[73] It was suggested that these helicopters were being purchased for an assault against Khun Sa's headquarters at Ho Mong, but no sales eventuated before the drug lord surrendered in 1996.[74]

China is clearly keen to sell the BAF more aircraft, partly for economic reasons but also to draw Burma more deeply into a mutually beneficial strategic relationship. To do this, China will continue to offer the Rangoon regime significant financial inducements, as seems to have occurred in a new bilateral defence cooperation agreement signed in late 1996.[75] The agreement reportedly covered the training of BAF pilots and ground crew in the operation and maintenance of Chinese fighter aircraft. The agreement also stated that China would offer Burma 'fiscal assistance'. According to Kay Merrill, this term 'probably covers the provision of soft loans to help Burma escape its current financial woes and the offer of special friendship prices on current and future arms buys'.[76] These developments suggest that the regime is considering the purchase of even more Chinese aircraft in the future.

While Rangoon has looked first to China to meet the BAF's needs, it has not ignored other suppliers. In 1990, for example, the SLORC ordered 20 SOKO G-4 Super Galebs (Seagulls) from Yugoslavia, under a barter deal involving the supply of Burmese timber.[77] These aircraft were designed to operate both as jet trainers and light ground attack aircraft.[78] They usually carry a 23mm cannon in a removeable ventral pod and have four underwing stores points for rockets and bombs. Six G-4s were delivered to Burma in early 1991 and were based at Meiktila. They were intended partly for training but soon after arrival saw action against Karen insurgents and narcotics traffickers along the Burma-Thai border.[79] A second batch of six G-4s arrived in 1992 and, for a period, were stationed at Mingaladon.[80] It has been suggested that these G-4 deliveries were in violation of an agreement between the UK and Yugoslavia covering the re-export of the Galebs' Rolls Royce Viper turbojet engines, but the status of the Burmese sale is unclear.[81] In any case, the balance of the Burmese order is unlikely to be filled. Despite the civil war in the former Republic of Yugoslavia, the SOKO factory at Mostar continued production for a period, but was abandoned in 1992 with a number of airframes left unfinished.[82] The BAF has since been unable to get spare parts for its G-4s, all 12 of which have been grounded indefinitely.

Despite reports in the news media that President Lech Walesa attempted to halt arms sales to Burma because of concerns over its poor human rights record, the BAF has managed to obtain two squadrons (or about 18 aircraft) of PZL Swidnik

Mil Mi-2 'Hoplite' helicopters from Poland, at the cost of about US$50 million.[83] While a relatively old design, one version of this aircraft still makes an effective gunship. The sale was finalised in 1990 and 12 of the aircraft arrived in Rangoon in July 1992 with 100 tonnes of ammunition and other equipment. The remainder of the order arrived later. There are reliable reports that most, if not all, of the Burmese Mi-2s have been fitted with a range of weapons to perform in a ground attack role, or to act as troop transports. A number armed with 12.7mm machine guns and air-to-ground rockets, for example, saw service against Karen and Kachin insurgents soon after their arrival in 1992.[84] One year later, the BAF took delivery of 12 PZL Swidnik W-3 Sokol (Falcon) multi-purpose helicopters, which are believed to have been part of a larger order cancelled by the former USSR Air Force.[85] In one configuration, these helicopters carry 12 passengers, but they too can be armed and operated as gunships. The Burmese hoped to receive armed versions, but diplomatic pressures prevailed. It is believed that the Burmese W-3s are currently being used for transport, search and rescue, and medical evacuation purposes.[86]

Even before 1988, the USSR had been trying to sell military aircraft to Burma, but without any success. When it became apparent that the SLORC was looking to upgrade the air force, Moscow quickly took steps to try and cash in on this sales bonanza. In mid-1991, for example, the Soviet Embassy in Rangoon approached the military regime with an offer to provide long-term credits to enable Burma to buy a range of aircraft.[87] These reportedly included Mil Mi-8 'Hip' and Mi-17 'Hip-H' helicopters. Both the Mi-8 and Mi-17 are essentially medium lift transport helicopters, but they can also be used for medical evacuation and (fitted with external stores) employed in an assault role. In addition, in May 1991 a Soviet delegation visiting from Aviaeksport apparently offered the Burmese some Tupolev Tu-154 'Careless' medium-range transports, and during a later approach the Soviet embassy offered to sell the regime several rear-loading Antonov An-32 'Cline' short-to-medium range utility transports. The latter aircraft were portrayed as replacements for (the renamed) Myanmar Airways' ageing fleet of Fokker F-27s.[88]

The SLORC also seems to have been offered a number of Soviet and Russian combat aircraft. For example, in his testimony before a subcommittee of the US House of Representatives Armed Services Committee in March 1991, the US Director of Naval Intelligence (DNI) stated that a number of Sukhoi Su-7/17 'Fitter' aircraft had been exported to Burma the previous year.[89] If the US report was accurate, then this multi-role fighter-bomber would have given a major boost to the BAF's intercept and ground attack capabilities. Unfortunately, no details of the sale were given to Congress, and to date there have been no confirmed sightings of this aircraft in Burma. A regional defence journal has suggested that a Burmese delegation visiting Moscow in 1995 expressed an interest in purchasing some 'Fitter' aircraft, but this cannot be confirmed.[90] On balance, it seems unlikely that any Su-17s have yet been acquired by the BAF. One newspaper has reported a Soviet offer of the Sukhoi Su-26, but this seems to be an error. If any such approach was made, it is more likely that the offer was of the Sukhoi Su-25 'Frogfoot' ground attack jet, which performed well in Afghanistan.[91]

While details are not available, at least some of the efforts made by Soviet and Russian arms salesmen over the years have borne fruit. In late 1995 it was reported that Burma Army Chief of Staff LTGEN Tin Oo had led a delegation to Moscow that year, to negotiate a major arms deal. The following month, two Mil Mi-17 1B helicopters were delivered to Rangoon in a Russian transport plane. Five more Mi-17s followed shortly afterwards.[92] In 1996 it was revealed that the regime had ordered an additional five helicopters of the same type. The contract reportedly included unspecified 'surface equipment' and spares.[93] A third delivery of about five aircraft may have followed.[94] As has long been Burmese practice, the helicopter sales included a training package for the air and ground crew due to operate and maintain these aircraft. According to the *Far Eastern Economic Review*, a group of Russian technicians arrived in Rangoon in late January 1996 to discuss maintenance of these helicopters with the BAF.[95] While technically described as transports, some of the Mi-17s have been armed and are being used as gunships.[96] The BAF is reportedly 'extremely satisfied' with their performance.[97]

The number of officers attached to the Burmese Defence Attaché's office in Moscow was increased to oversee this and other unspecified arms sales with the Russians. These other projects included the proposed purchase of two kinds of Russian combat aircraft. The regime has reportedly expressed interest in obtaining a number of specialised combat helicopters like the Mil Mi-34, the export version of the Mi-24 'Hind' assault helicopter which was widely used in Afghanistan.[98] No details are available, but such an acquisition would clearly be aimed at helping the *Tatmadaw* in its campaigns against those ethnic insurgent groups and narcotics-based armies that have refused to sign ceasefire agreements.[99]

Also, after the collapse of the BAF's plans to purchase the Chinese F-8 'Finback', the purchase of a multi-role fighter from Russia became a more attractive option, and was also discussed during LTGEN Tin Oo's visit to Moscow. There were several reports during the late 1990s that the regime was trying to purchase about one squadron of Mikoyan MiG-29 'Fulcrum' air superiority fighters, similar to those operated by Malaysia, India and Bangladesh.[100] According to one senior Russian official in 1996, the deal repeatedly struck problems because of Burma's economic difficulties. The military regime had offered a barter deal involving Burmese primary products as a partial offset, but the Russians were anxious to receive a greater proportion of the payment in hard currency.[101] These problems were eventually overcome, however, and in July 2001 it was revealed that Burma had signed a contract with the Russian Aircraft Building Corporation for eight surplus MiG-29 fighters and two MiG-29UB dual-seat trainers. According to *Jane's Intelligence Weekly*, the aircraft were acquired for US$130 million. About 30% of this sum was to be paid immediately, while the rest was to be paid over the next decade.[102] The Fulcrums give the BAF the opportunity to take an ambitious leap forward in technology and operational capability.

Since 1988 the BAF has also purchased a wide range of air-delivered munitions, mostly from China. These include about 360 PL-2A air-to-air missiles, a Chinese copy of the Soviet 'Atoll' short range infra-red (IR) seeking AAM.[103] The

BAF has also taken delivery of at least one shipment of PL-5 AAMs, another short-range missile with an IR seeker, but with a greater off-boresight capability than the PL-2.[104] F-7 aircraft can carry PL-2 AAMs, while the PL-5 can be carried by both the F-7 and the A-5.[105] There has been a report that Israel plans to sell Burma Rafael Python 3 IR dogfight missiles and Litening laser designator pods, for laser-guided bombs, but no deliveries have yet been noted.[106] Nor is it known what weapons might be included in the Russian MiG-29 deal. For air-to-surface rockets, the BAF now relies on 57mm Types 1 and 2, 90mm Type 1, HF-16B 57mm pod, HF-7 90mm pod, S-8 80mm and 12 Tube 80mm pod weapons.[107] Most are Chinese. There have been reports that the BAF has acquired AT-2 'Sagger' and AT-6 'Spiral' air-to-surface missiles from Russia (and possibly other former Eastern bloc countries) for its helicopter gunships.

Figure 22: Burma Air Force Strength, 2000

Interceptors	50 (plus 8 on order)
Fighter/Ground Attack	48
Counter-insurgency	33
Transport	14
Training	31 (plus 2 on order)
Liaison	10
Helicopters	66
Others	9

The BAF also has a range of gravity bombs, once again mostly obtained from China. These include 100 kilogram (kg) Type 1 and Type 2 general purpose (GP) bombs, 250kg Type 2 GP, Type 1 incendiary and Type 1 high explosive incendiary bombs. It may have some low drag GP bombs in its inventory. Some sources also list BL7 115kg GP, BL9 120kg fragmentation and SEI 227kg bombs.[108] The BAF's new aircraft are armed with a variety of guns, most of which are of 20mm, 23mm and 30mm calibre.[109]

Since 1988 the BAF has taken delivery of a range of new electronic equipment, both airborne and ground-based systems. The F-7 aircraft purchased from China, for example, carry a comprehensive avionics suite installed by GEC-Marconi. However, they do not have tactical radar systems, which make them vulnerable to missile attack. To help overcome this problem, at least three squadrons may be fitted with Israeli Elta EL/M-2032 air-to-air radars.[110] Also, some of the BAF's Y-8 aircraft (which can stay in the air for about 11 hours) have been 'equipped with mobile tactical radars and other electronic equipment to provide air-to-air and ground-to-air communications links'.[111] The A-5s have benefited from Italian technology. When Burma takes delivery of its MiG-29s an entirely new range of Russian avionics will be acquired. In addition, it has been reported that the BAF ordered three maritime surveillance aircraft in 1990, but could not pursue the deal because of the arms embargo against Burma.[112] If the BAF should ever acquire specialised aircraft like the F-27 Maritime Enforcer, then they would probably

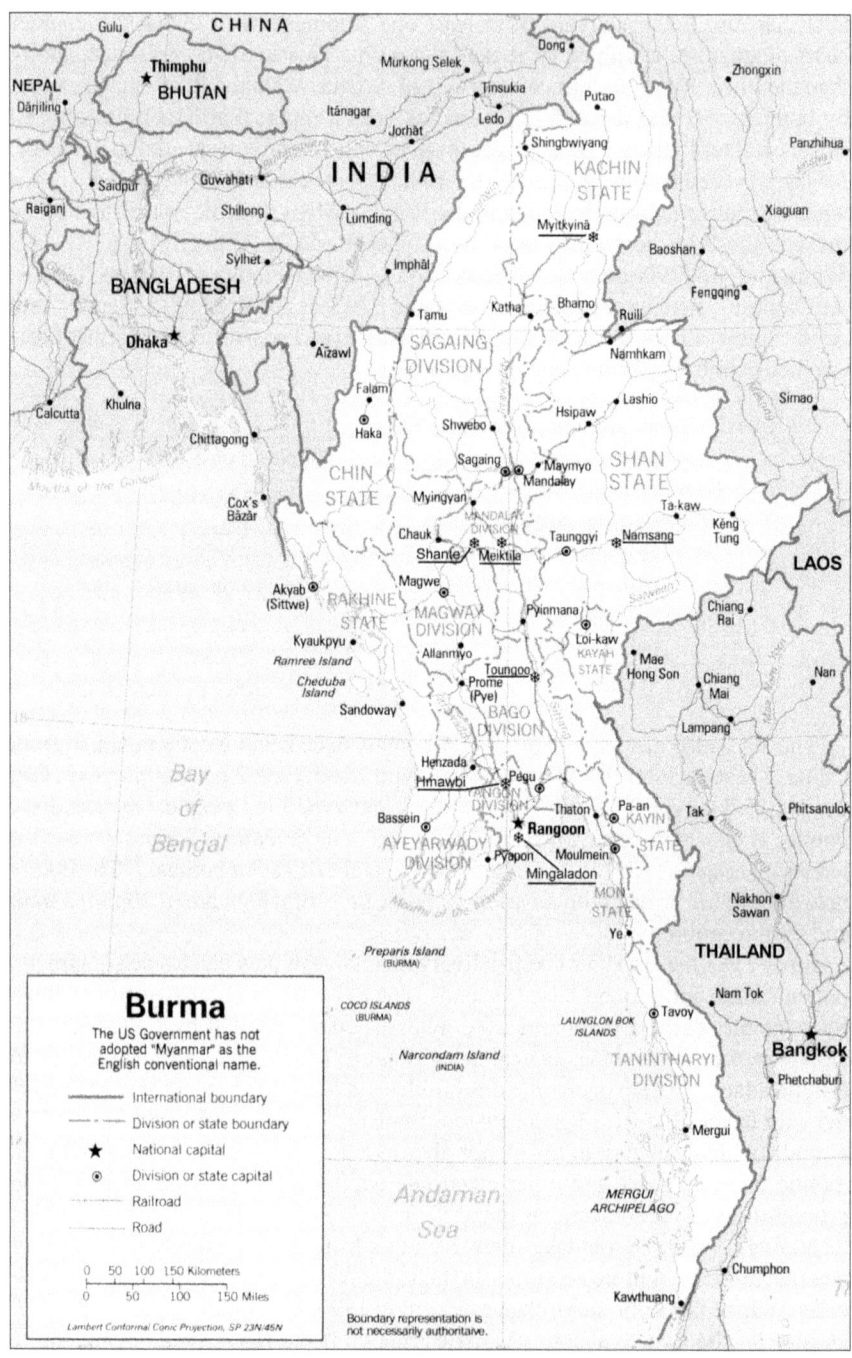

Figure 23: Burma: Major Air Force Bases, 2000.

carry a range of sophisticated sensors like pulse-compression search radars, passive and active acoustic systems, and electronic surveillance and monitoring systems. While already familiar to other regional air forces, these systems would be new to Burma's electronic order of battle.

Before 1988, Burma's radar equipment was obsolete and believed to be of poor resolution. Much had been provided by the US under the MAP. During the mid-1960s, for example, the BAF installed US-made TPS-ID search radars (which had a range of 160 miles) and AN/TPN-12A ground control approach radars.[113] The air force had operated a network of early warning and ground control intercept radars for some time but, even if coupled with the more modern civil equipment installed with foreign assistance (mainly to improve the safety of international airliners flying over Burma), the coverage was still very limited.[114] New ground-based systems reportedly provided by China since 1988 include JLP-40 tactical air defence and surveillance radars, and JLG-43 height-finding radars, which can operate together. The JLP-40 is similar to the Russian 'Bar Lock' radar, from which it has probably been derived. The JLG-43 follows the pattern of the Russian 'Cake' series radars.[115] New radar information processing systems have also been installed. While not the latest technology, this new equipment marks another major advance in the BAF's potential capabilities.

The adoption of new roles, such as conventional air defence, has necessitated other changes. In addition to upgrading its navigational aids and airfield radar facilities, for example, it is believed that the BAF has expanded its electronic warfare capability, with a much larger number of EW units dispersed to locations around the country's periphery. It is difficult to identify the new early warning stations, but the BAF has reportedly established or upgraded stations at Tachilek, Kutkai, Loi Mwe, Namsang and Wan Mai, all in the east.[116] There may also be an EW unit on Hainggyi Island, at the mouth of the Bassein River. (There has long been a small EW station on Great Coco Island in the Andaman Sea, but it is probably operated by the navy.) Although few details are available, other EW units are likely to have been posted to Burma's northern, western and southern approaches as well. The Chinese appear to be assisting in the expansion of Burma's capabilities in this regard.[117]

Inevitably, the acquisition of all these new aircraft types and more advanced C^3I equipment has necessitated the training of BAF personnel overseas. Both pilots and ground staff were posted to China before the delivery of the first F-7s, for example, and another group was sent during 1992-93 to train on the A-5s. In mid-1994 about 30 Burmese engineers and technicians were sent to Shaanxi for instruction in the maintenance and repair of the new Y-8 transports.[118] In early 1995 a number of Burmese pilots was reportedly sent to China to undergo a conversion course on the new type of helicopter being purchased, but this deal seems to have fallen through.[119] More training is being offered by the Chinese under the defence agreement signed in 1996. In addition, and in a major departure from past Burmese policy, a number of PLA air force instructors appear to have been posted to Burma from time to time, to assist with the introduction of the new Chinese machines.[120] For example, it was reported in April 1997 that 12 Chinese instructors were based at Namsang air base to teach BAF pilots 'to fly, shoot and drop bombs from Chinese made fighter bomber planes'.[121] Another 20 Chinese instructors on the base were believed to be training Burmese ground crew and communications technicians on new Chinese equipment.

China has not been alone in offering this kind of assistance. As part of its Mi-2 and W-3 sales, Poland gave in-country training to about 30 Burmese helicopter pilots and ground crew. Yugoslavia provided a similar service, by training BAF pilots at the Yugoslav Air Force Academy in Zadar before the delivery of the G-4s in 1991 and 1992.[122] Russia sent a team of technicians and instructors to Burma after the BAF acquired its Mi-17 helicopters, and can be expected to provide training to the BAF's MiG-29 pilots and ground crew.[123]

To manage the transformation of the BAF in recent years, the regime has developed a new command and control structure. The BAF's Commander in Chief and Chief Engineer still work from the Defence Ministry in Rangoon, but the number of regional bases (designated Air Base Headquarters) has increased to cope with the larger number and wider distribution of BAF assets. These now include Mingaladon, Myitkyina, Hmawbi, Toungoo and Namsang. There is also a Maintenance Air Base at Mingaladon, Ground Training Base at Meiktila and the Flying Training Base at Shante.[124] It is also likely that certain key functions, relating to maintenance and armament (formerly based at Mingaladon), have been decentralised and can now be performed at other major bases. This would not only be more efficient, but would also help manage the much larger number of aircraft in the BAF's inventory.

In addition to the massive injection of resources into the BAF's operational squadrons, the regime has undertaken a major program to expand and upgrade Burma's aviation infrastructure. Large new BAF bases are being constructed at Toungoo and Namsang, and improvements made to the base at Myitkyina. It has been suggested that Moulmein and Bassein airfields are also being substantially upgraded, to permit more military aircraft to use the civil facilities there.[125] There have been reports of a major new air base being constructed near Mergui.[126] When completed, these projects will provide much better support for the fighters and helicopters in the fleet.[127] The BAF will also be much closer to the main areas of insurgent operations, and within a short flight of Burma's borders. Smaller airfields and helicopter landing pads have been established or improved in areas like northern Arakan State, where operations against Rohingya refugees and insurgents in recent years have increased the demand for air support.[128] Opposition groups have also identified small air bases at places like Kutkai, Loi Mwe, Lashio and Bahtoo, all in the Shan State, but the status of these facilities is unclear. Most are probably only landing fields, or radar and early warning stations.[129]

The projected improvements to Burma's network of civil airfields will also benefit the BAF. With Chinese and Singaporean assistance, two new international airports are being constructed, one at Hanthawaddy, near Pegu, (to replace Mingaladon International Airport) and the other at Tada-U near Mandalay. Facilities at a number of other airfields, such as Mingaladon, Bassein, Heho, Moulmein and Mergui, are being improved, and runways are being substantially lengthened and strengthened. It is expected that most of Burma's main civil airfields will gradually be upgraded, to cater for the influx of foreign tourists being sought by the regime. It is uncertain when all these construction projects will be completed, as problems have arisen over funding. When fully functional, however, they will be better able to support the BAF's new jet aircraft, as part of an extensive program to provide the BAF with greater range and flexibility. It is also relevant that, between them, Myanma Airways and Air Mandalay now operate eight Fokker F-27s, three Fokker F-28s, three ATR 72-210 Quick Change turboprop aircraft and two Puma helicopters. Also, Myanma Airways International runs three Boeing 737-400 jets. These airlines are served by about 50 pilots.[130] The aircraft of Myanma Airways at least would be available for military use, if required.

Since 1988 most published estimates of the BAF establishment have remained steady at about 9,000 officers and airmen, but this is too low. A figure of 15,000 is more accurate.[131] The number of personnel may increase further over the next few years as the air force seeks to manage the much larger number of aircraft, and aircraft types, which are now being introduced into service.

9.3 The New Burma Air Force

Before the SLORC's takeover, the Burma Air Force was a small, under-strength counter-insurgency force flying obsolete fighters and modified training aircraft. It was struggling to keep its machines in the air. In early 1985, for example, it was claimed that barely half the BAF's aircraft could fly.[132] Despite some notable successes, such as in the battle for Myawaddy in 1974, when air power proved decisive, the air force was held in contempt by most insurgent groups.[133] By 2000, however, the BAF could boast about five squadrons of F-7 fighters, four squadrons of A-5 fighter/ground attack aircraft, a squadron of G-4 ground attack planes and two squadrons of armed Mi-2 helicopters. It also had a squadron of K-8 jet training aircraft, as well as some FT-7 and FT-6 trainers. The BAF's transport arm had been swollen by two squadrons of W-3 helicopters, two of Mil-17 helicopters and six Y-8 transports. Other aircraft were on order or being evaluated. The air force's new communications equipment could give a rudimentary picture of the air situation around the country for the very first time, and help direct aircraft during operations. It was a major transformation.[134]

Some news reports have stated that the BAF's new acquisitions have taken Burma 'into the space age', but none of the aircraft types ordered or received by the regime so far are state-of-the-art.[135] Nor do they compare very favourably with the air forces of Burma's larger neighbours. They have the benefit, however, of being tested models with proven records, and are at a level of technical sophistication appropriate to Burma's developing capacities for operation, maintenance and repair. On paper at least, they significantly enhance the BAF's combat capabilities for both air defence and ground strike. They are more powerful, more versatile, and able to operate more effectively and for longer periods than any aircraft in

Burma's inventory before 1988. There has been a significant reduction in insurgent activity since 1989, but counter-insurgency will remain the BAF's primary mission for the foreseeable future. Despite the regime's fears, and occasional tensions with Thailand, India and Bangladesh in recent years, there is little likelihood that the BAF's new acquisitions will be challenged by aircraft from a foreign power.

There are still some serious problems for the BAF to overcome, however, and it remains to be seen how effectively its new arms and equipment will be absorbed and operated. Despite the rather exaggerated claims made by some observers, the purchase of these new and technically more advanced weapon systems does not immediately translate into improved military capabilities.[136] There will be problems integrating the new aircraft and their associated equipment into existing inventories and learning how to operate them together. New doctrines and operating procedures will need to be developed, particularly for joint operations with the army and navy. Even with Chinese help, these difficulties will not be overcome quickly. In particular, much will depend on greatly improved intelligence, training, logistics and maintenance procedures. The purchase of such a diverse range of aircraft from so many different suppliers may offer certain political and strategic advantages, but it is bound to cause problems. There will be a continuing requirement for a wide range of training, both for pilots and ground crew, in Burma and possibly overseas.

The BAF will have to maintain an extensive range of maintenance skills and spare parts. Given its poor record to date, this will pose a real challenge, even if the necessary foreign exchange can be found. Already problems have been experienced in keeping the new Chinese and Yugoslav aircraft fully operational.[137] For example, there have been complaints that the new Chinese aircraft 'are of poor quality and performance'.[138] The F-7s were not even fitted with the electronics required to fire AAMs, something which the Burmese had to devise for themselves.[139] In addition, the regime will have to contend with the continuing ban on arms sales to Burma from some important suppliers. Spare parts for the old US helicopters will become more difficult to obtain, although a number of arms dealers seem prepared to overlook the regime's unsavoury reputation. Burma's pariah status will pose other problems. For example, plans by an Australian company to establish Pilatus aircraft engine overhaul facilities in Burma in 1991 foundered on the problem of the international arms embargo.[140] The BAF has been unable to keep its G-4s flying, after they suffered UK sanctions and the closure of the SOKO plant in the former Republic of Yugoslavia.[141]

Major repairs and regular overhauls are likely to remain a problem for other reasons. For example, it is understood that any major overhauls of the BAF's F-7s and A-5s can only be carried out in China, a source of some concern to Burma's military hierarchy. The six Y-8 transports were grounded for a year while the BAF waited for China to send a technical team to conduct repairs.[142] Even for some work on its older aircraft the BAF is still obliged to seek overseas assistance. In 1991, for example, the BAF sent its Pratt and Whitney PT6A turboprop engines from its PC-7 and PC-9 aircraft to Australia for overhaul. (Pilatus now has no commercial links with Burma.) After that avenue was closed off by the Australian government the BAF contracted a Malaysian firm, Airod Sdn Bhd, to maintain its Pilatus engines (which in some cases are now nearly 20 years old).[143] According to *Jane's Defence Weekly*, 'technicians from Myanmar are also being trained by Airod Sdn Bhd under the agreement', the full terms of which are not known.[144]

This is quite apart from the need to develop greater combat skills. The BAF does not have a very good reputation for its flying abilities or the accuracy of its bombing and air-to-ground rocket attacks. Indeed, according to one thoughtful and well-informed observer, its pilots 'had a splendid reputation for incompetence'.[145] For example, during the 1989-90, 1992-93 and 1994-95 dry season offensives against ethnic insurgents, there were persistent reports of aircraft flying too high for accurate bombing, and poorly executed strafing runs against insurgent positions by both old Pilatus propellor-driven aircraft and new Chinese jets.[146] Several reasons have been offered for this situation, including inappropriate aircraft, poor training, inadequate intelligence, insufficient liaison with the ground forces, and the timidity of the BAF pilots. All are probably valid to a greater or lesser degree. For example, according to one knowledgeable source, even in mid-1994 few BAF pilots were confident about flying the F-7 solo. Other factors are also important, such as the BAF's need to conserve its scarce resources. Even now, Burma's fighter pilots are lucky to get more than 10 hours flying time each month.[147]

Given the nature of the aircraft and munitions purchased from China, it is relevant that, apart from a few isolated contacts with US and Taiwanese aircraft over 25 years ago, the Burma Air Force has had little direct experience of air-to-air combat. In 1960, for example, a BAF aircraft was shot down by a Nationalist Chinese fighter. In 1961 a PB4Y-2 Privateer from Taiwan, secretly delivering supplies to KMT remnants in northern Burma, was shot down by a flight of Burmese Hawker Sea Fury fighters.[148] Since then, however, the BAF has faced no such threats. It is possible that the BAF's lack of expertise in this area is being rectified by the Chinese during their training courses (perhaps using the air-to-air missiles they have sold to Burma), but this seems unlikely. Although China has sold Burma aircraft capable of supersonic speeds, it did not even provide training for supersonic flight.[149] It cannot be expected that Burma's pilots will be able to develop real confidence in aerial combat without a great deal more training and experience. Given the difficulty of obtaining this expertise, it is fortunate for the BAF that it is unlikely to be called upon to protect Burma against an air attack in the foreseeable future.

Before 1988 the greatest threat to BAF aircraft was from equipment failure (usually due to age or poor maintenance), or pilot error. In mid-1974, for example, five T-33 jets took off from Mingaladon and inexplicably flew into a mountain, effectively halving the air force's combat capabilities at one stroke.[150] The risk of pilot error remains, and there have already been credible reports that several of the BAF's new aircraft (both jets and helicopters) have been lost through accidents.[151] Over the past few decades several BAF aircraft of different types have been shot down by ground fire (usually from 0.50 calibre or 12.7mm HMG). If one insurgent claim is correct, even the new Chinese fighter-bombers are not safe from such attacks.[152] Indeed, with the acquisition of man-portable SAMs by some insurgent groups, this threat has grown significantly.[153] Slow and low-flying helicopters and light aircraft are particularly vulnerable. The presence of these weapons probably helps account for the circumspection of BAF pilots attacking insurgent strongholds, and the SLORC's reluctance to use its new Chinese aircraft against Khun Sa before 1996.

The BAF presents the Rangoon regime with other challenges. Although the air force has played a relatively minor role in Burma's internal political upheavals over the past 40 years, it has not escaped public criticism. As a part of the *Tatmadaw*, it has been closely associated with Ne Win's Revolutionary Council, the BSPP government, the SLORC and now the SPDC. Also, BAF personnel have been used to support the army and police during times of serious civil unrest (as in the case of the 1974 U Thant disturbances in Rangoon).[154] Although it has not been directly involved in the periodic killings of protesters by the security forces in Burma's population centres, the BAF's role in bombing rural settlements and insurgent camps during the *Tatmadaw*'s long-running counter-insurgency campaigns has drawn bitter denunciations from combatants and non-combatants alike. The BAF has also borne the brunt of international criticism over the spraying of ethnic minority villages with toxic defoliants in the mid-1980s.

These criticisms are not new, but they can have real, practical effects. The BAF has traditionally attracted many of the *Tatmadaw*'s better educated recruits. The technical complexity of both flying and maintaining the BAF's aircraft require skills which have always been in very short supply in Burma. (For many years Burma Airways Corporation was forced to employ expatriate pilots, a practice reluctantly copied since 1992 by Air Mandalay.) After the 1988 pro-democracy demonstrations were crushed, however, there was a marked increase in the flow out of the country of its intelligentsia, including many tertiary level and technical students who might have otherwise joined the air force.[155] Of those who remained, many were reluctant to contemplate a military career. As a consequence, the regime has had to make a special effort to attract recruits for the BAF, for example by arranging a special intake of cadets into the DSA in 1996. It has also tried to capitalise on the glamour attached to flying the BAF's new fighter aircraft. This may solve the regime's immediate problems, but doubts remain whether or not the *Tatmadaw* can continue to attract sufficient qualified recruits to keep all its new aircraft flying.

Over the past 12 years the Rangoon regime has made a concerted effort to upgrade the BAF from a small, poorly equipped and relatively ineffectual Service plagued by accidents and unserviceable aircraft, into a much more powerful force. In this short period, it has acquired more than 150 new combat aircraft, including fighters, ground attack aircraft, transports and helicopters. Other orders are being considered. Burma's new and upgraded airfields should add flexibility and reach to BAF operations. These developments, however, will not translate into improved military capabilities unless the regime also underpins its ambitious acquisition program with a major effort to improve the direction, operation and maintenance of its new aircraft. A greater priority will also need to be given to recruitment, training and the development of better ground facilities. Failure to do this will mean that the BAF's impressive new assets will simply become expensive new liabilities.

Notes

1. An earlier version of this chapter was published as Andrew Selth, 'The Myanmar Air Force Since 1988: Expansion and Modernisation', *Contemporary Southeast Asia*, Vol. 19, No. 4, March 1998.

2. Tinker, *The Union of Burma*, p. 321. Some sources incorrectly state that the BAF was created in the early or mid-1950s. See, for example, M.J.H. Taylor, *Encyclopedia of the World's Air Forces* (Patrick Stephens, Wellingsborough, 1988), p. 29; Victor Flintham, *Air Wars and Aircraft: A Detailed Record of Air Combat, 1945 to the Present* (Arms and Armour Press, London, 1989), p. 218; and Peter Arnold, 'Burmese Treasures', *Fly Past*, November 1996, p. 26.

3. Reports that the Burmese received 'a flight' of de Havilland DH.98 Mosquito fighter-bombers around this time are incorrect. See *Myanmar Air Force*, p. 60; and Flintham, *Air Wars and Aircraft*, p. 218.

4. SIPRI, *The Arms Trade with the Third World*, p. 451; and *Air Britain Archive*, Vol. 2, 1988, p. 34. Reports that the BAF acquired 40 Oxfords are incorrect. See Maung Aung Myoe, *Building the Tatmadaw*, p. 28; and *Myanmar Air Force*, p. 60. The Consuls were basically the same aircraft as the Oxfords, but configured for civilian use.

5. Personal observation, Rangoon, April 1995. The Douglas aircraft provided were probably C-47A or C-47D variants, both of which have been in the BAF's inventory at different times.

6. B. Cull, D. Nicolle and S. Aloni, *Wings Over Suez* (Grub Street, London, 1996), pp. 57-9. See also Peter Arnold, 'Burma Stars', *Aeroplane Monthly*, January 1996, pp. 24-30; and P. R. Arnold and Ken Ellis, 'Burmese Lions: British Fighter Exports to Burma', *Air Enthusiast*, Vol. 71, September/October 1997, pp. 48-52.

7. The Spitfires were taken out of operational service in 1957, and the Seafires followed in 1958. The Provosts were still being used by the BAF as late as 1983.

8. In late 1960 and early 1961, for example, BAF Spitfires and Sea Furies took part in the combined BA-PLA operation to attack KMT strongholds in northern Burma. Flintham, *Air Wars and Aircraft*, p. 218.

9. *Myanmar Air Force*, p. 45.

10. Ron Mackay, *Hawker Sea Fury In Action* (Squadron/Signal Publications, Carrollton, 1991), p. 38.

11. *Myanmar Air Force*, p. 64.

12. Interview, Washington, October 1995. Sabre 'fighter-bombers' were listed in Burma's order of battle in *The Military Balance 1970-71* (Institute for Strategic Studies, London, 1970), p. 61. The (renamed) International Institute for Strategic Studies (IISS) removed the reference the following year. See also Stockholm International Peace Research Institute, *Arms Trade Registers: The Arms Trade with the Third World* (MIT Press, Cambridge, 1975), p. 4; and SIPRI, *The Arms Trade with the Third World*, p. 454.

13. The last of the type ceased operational service with the BAF in 1989.

14. The declared value of this deal was US$13.5 million. Smith, 'The Burmese way to rack and ruin', p. 44. See also *Myanmar Air Force*, p. 66.

15. *Myanmar Air Force*, p. 68. See also Gill and Mak, *Arms, Transparency and Security in Southeast Asia*, p. 121; *Towards Democracy in Burma*, p. 58; and 'Far East Air Arms: Southern Region - Burma (Myanmar)', *World Airpower Journal*, Vol. 8, Spring 1992, pp. 140-2.

16. 'Air Forces Survey: Myanmar', *Asian Aviation*, Vol. 14, No. 6, June 1994, p. 36.

17. 'Air Forces Survey: Myanmar', p. 35; and 'Far East Air Arms: Southern Region - Burma (Myanmar)', p. 142. See also *The Military Powers Encyclopedia*, p. 39.

18. Roy Eccleston, 'Export to Burma approved despite Evans call for ban', *The Australian*, 3-4 August 1991; and Roy Eccleston, 'Row over sale of plane parts to Burma', *The Australian*, 13 August 1991.

19. The military variant of the Beechcraft D-18S is the Beechcraft C-45, which sometimes appears in the BAF's published order of battle.

20. *Myanmar Air Force*, p. 66.

21. 'Far East Air Arms: Southern Region - Burma (Myanmar)', p. 142.

22. R.E.G. Davies, *Airlines of Asia Since 1920* (Paladwr, Mclean, 1997), pp. 120-6. See also R.G.G. Paran, 'Myanma Airways Set to Grow', *Asian Airlines and Aerospace*, March 1996, pp. 30-2.

23. *Asian Aviation*, Vol. 11, No. 2, February 1991, p. 58.

24. In 1975 the author flew in a UBA F-27 from Heho to Rangoon, which was also being used for medical evacuation. Several rows of passenger seats had been removed so that stretchers occupied by wounded soldiers could be laid out on the aircraft floor.

25. Instead of the Cessna 180, some sources cite the U-17, the military variant of the Cessna 185 Skywagon. This appears to be incorrect. See, for example, T.N. Dupuy *et al*, *The Almanac of World Power* (Presidio, San Rafael, 1980), p. 86. See also *Jane's Aircraft Upgrades 1995-96* (Jane's Information Systems, Coulsdon, 1995), p. 322.

26. Personal observation, Rangoon, April 1995. The Citation has sometimes been grounded due to a lack of funds for its regular overhauls. See 'Air Forces Survey: Myanmar', p. 36.

27. Mirante, *Burmese Looking Glass*, p. 217.

28. An additional KB-47G was provided by the Kayah State Government. All these aircraft had been taken out of service by 1973. Reports in Jane's publications that some KB-47G helicopters are still operational, and attached to the Burma Navy, are incorrect. See, for example, *Jane's Fighting Ships 1996-97* (Jane's Information Group, Coulsdon, 1996), p. 80.

29. *The Military Balance* listed 10 KV-107s in 1975-1976, but only two in 1978-1979. SIPRI listed only three (reportedly acquired in 1968) in *Arms Trade Registers*, p. 4. These aircraft have been confused with Burma's Vertol H-21 Shawnee helicopters (which are often omitted from published BAF orders of battle). See also 'The Burmese Air Force', *Military Technology*, p. 9; Taylor, *Encyclopedia of the World's Air Forces*, p. 29; and *Myanmar Air Force*, p. 62.

30. 'Air Forces Survey: Myanmar', p. 36.

31. Gill and Mak, *Arms, Transparency and Security in Southeast Asia*, p. 121.

32. *Jane's World Airlines* (Jane's Information Group, Coulsdon, 1997), Part 2, A12/01. See also *World Aviation Directory* (McGraw-Hill, Washington, 1997), p. 69.

33. Mya Maung, *The Burma Road to Poverty*, p. 198.

34. 'Far East Air Arms: Southern Region - Burma (Myanmar)', p. 142.

35. Personal observation, Rangoon, April 1995; and Interview, Bangkok, November 1996.

36. *Ibid*. See also 'World's Air Forces - Burma (Myanma)', *Flight International*, 27 November-3 December 1991, p. 38; and 'Air Forces Survey: Myanmar', p. 36.

37. Tinker, *The Union of Burma*, p. 324. In 1949 Karen insurgents hijacked a Cathay Pacific passenger aircraft at Meiktila and forced the two civilian pilots to fly them to Maymyo,

which was taken unawares. An Oxford transport and a Spitfire landed and were captured, before it was realised that the airfield was in Karen hands. See C.E. Eather, *We Flew in Burma* (Chingchic Publishers, Surfers Paradise, 1993), pp. 92-4.

38. Smith, 'The Burmese way to rack and ruin', p. 44.

39. Callahan, 'The Origins of Military Rule in Burma', p. 430.

40. In 1944 the Japanese sent 10 graduates of Burma's Officer Training School to Japan, where they graduated from the Army Air Force Academy. *Ibid*. See also *Myanmar Air Force*, pp. 4-21.

41. Callahan states that by 1953 the BAF had two operational squadrons, but does not give the number of personnel or aircraft. ('The Origins of Military Rule in Burma', p. 430).

42. Maung Aung Myoe, *Building the Tatmadaw*, p. 29.

43. International Institute for Strategic Studies, *The Military Balance, 1988-89* (IISS, London, 1988), p. 160. See also *The Military Balance 1987-1988* (IISS, London, 1987), p. 155; and *The Military Balance 1995/96* (IISS, London, 1995), p. 162. Some sources claim that by 1988 the strength of the BAF was only 8,000. See 'The Burmese Air Force', *Military Technology*, Vol. 12, No. 2, 1988, p. 9.

44. *Myanmar Air Force*, pp. 68-9.

45. See, for example, *Jane's Fighting Ships 1996-97*, p. 80.

46. Bunge, *Burma*, p. 255. See also 'Air Forces Survey: Myanmar', pp. 34-5.

47. Maung Aung Myoe, *Building the Tatmadaw*, p. 29.

48. *Country Economic Brief: Burma (Myanmar)*, (Department of Foreign Affairs and Trade, Canberra, 1996), p. 35.

49. *The Military Powers Encyclopedia*, p. 27.

50. Tinker, *Burma: The Struggle for Independence*, Vol. 2, pp. 734-6. During the crisis of 1949, members of this British unit even helped the BAF manufacture crude bombs to drop on insurgent forces. Tinker, *The Union of Burma*, p. 42.

51. Tinker, *The Union of Burma*, pp. 324-5 and p. 332; and Selth, 'Australian Defence Contacts with Burma', pp. 451-68.

52. Personal observation, Rangoon, April 1995; *Myanmar Air Force*, p. 68; and Arnold and Ellis, p. 50.

53. *Jane's All The World's Aircraft 1958-59* (Jane's, London, 1959), pp. 90-1.

54. See, for example, 'The Burmese Air Force', *Military Technology*, p. 9.

55. 'Myanmar's air power boosted', *JDW*, 11 December 1993, p. 13; and 'Myanmar in large arms barter deal with China', *Asian Aviation*, Vol. 11, No. 2, February 1991, pp. 88-9. See also 'Air Forces Survey: Myanmar', pp. 34-5; and Lintner, 'Arms for Eyes', p. 26.

56. Interview, Rangoon, November 1999. See also IISS, *The Military Balance, 2000/2001*, p. 189. One journal has suggested that the third squadron arrived in early 1994. See 'More F-7s For Myanmar AF', *Vayu Aerospace Review*, Vol. 5, 1994, p. 14. China only declared the sale of 12 'combat aircraft' to Burma in 1993. See *United Nations Register of Conventional Arms: Report to the Secretary General*, UNGA A/49/352, 1 September 1994, p. 16.

57. Interview, Rangoon, November 1999.

58. See, for example, 'Myanmar', *Jane's World Air Forces: Order of Battle and Inventories*, (Jane's Information Systems, Coulsdon, 1996), Issue 1.

59. Although most reports refer to the A-5M, the A-5C version may have also been supplied. 'Myanmar: New Chinese arms package', *World Airpower Journal*, Vol. 22, Autumn 1995, p. 11. See also R.J. Francillon (ed), *The Naval Institute Guide to World Military Aviation, 1995* (Naval Institute Press, Annapolis, 1995), p. 605; 'Myanmar's air power boosted', p. 13; and Lintner, 'Arms for Eyes', p. 26. The report 'Chinese Takeaway', *FEER*, 22 September 1994, p. 12, was premature. The aircraft in question were A-5s being ferried to Meiktila by Chinese pilots. Personal communication, Bertil Lintner to the author, 5 October 1994.

60. Interview, Rangoon, November 1999.

61. Personal communication, Bertil Lintner to the author, 5 October 1994. *The Nation* reported on 18 December 1993 that Khun Sa had received at least 12 SAM-7s from an arms stockpile in Thailand in return for a consignment of heroin. See also Bertil Lintner, 'Slow Strangle', *FEER*, 14 April 1994, p. 19; 'Air Forces Survey: Myanmar', p. 35; and 'Myanmar's air power boosted'.

62. *Jane's World Air Forces*, Issue 1.

63. SIPRI has stated that 12 F-6s were due to be delivered, and had probably arrived, in 1990. Stockholm International Peace Research Institute, *SIPRI Yearbook 1991: World Armaments and Disarmament* (Oxford University Press, Oxford, 1991), p. 252. See also Yindee Lertcharoenchok, 'Beijing, Rangoon ink $1.2 billion arms deal'; 'Myanmar in large arms barter deal with China', p. 88; and 'Burma (Myanmar)', *World Airpower Journal*, Vol. 8, Spring 1992, p. 142.

64. The author was told by BAF personnel in 1995 that 'a small number' of FT-6 trainers had arrived from China and were already in service. Interview, Rangoon, April 1995.

65. 'Air Forces Survey: Myanmar', p. 36.

66. Bruce Hawke, 'Myanmar is first export customer for K-8 trainer', *JDW*, 24 June 1998, p. 14. See also 'Military Might', *Air Force Monthly*, March 1998, pp. 19-20; Dantes, 'An In-depth Look at the Asia-Pacific Air Forces and Future Procurement', p. 28; and Prasun Sengupta, 'Force Modernisation Continues for Asia-Pacific Air Forces', in *Asia-Pacific Military Balance 1994/95* (ADPR Consult, Kuala Lumpur, 1994/95), p. 89.

67. 'Myanmar', *Air International*, January 2000, p. 4; and interview, Rangoon, November 1999.

68. *Jane's All the World's Aircraft, 1997-98* (Jane's Information Group, Coulsdon, 1998), p. 65.

69. John Bailey, 'Myanmar and China in Z-8 helicopter talks', *Flight International*, 30 October-5 November 1991, p. 18. See also 'Air Forces Survey: Myanmar', p. 36.

70. Interview, Rangoon, November 1999; and 'Myanmar: New Chinese arms package', p. 11. See also 'More F-7s For Myanmar AF', p. 14.

71. Dantes, 'An In-depth Look at the Asia-Pacific Air Forces and Future Procurement', p. 28. This latter aircraft type cannot be identified. See also 'Air Forces Survey: Myanmar', p. 36.

72. Bertil Lintner, '$400m deal signed by China and Myanmar', p. 1. In February 1991 *Asian Aviation* also referred to the purchase of Chinese helicopters by Burma, but no details were given. See 'Myanmar in large arms barter deal with China', p. 88; and 'Myanmar: New Chinese arms package', p. 11.

73. Lintner, 'Hardware for hardliners', p. 12. See also 'Myanmar', *Air International*, Vol. 48, No. 1, January 1995, p. 4; and 'Burma (Myanmar)', *JDW*, 7 January 1995, p. 19.

74. Lintner, '$400m deal signed by China and Myanmar', p. 1.

75. 'Sino-Burmese Pact', *FEER*, 30 January 1997, p. 12. See also 'Sino-Myanmar Pact Inked', *Asian Defence and Diplomacy*, Vol. 3, No. 3, March 1997, p. 16.

76. Merrill, 'A closer look at Sino-Burmese military links', p. 323.

77. 'Super Galebs for Myanmar', *JDW*, 29 June 1991, p. 1172. Some sources have stated that as many as 30 G-4s were ordered. See, for example, 'Burma: Equipment updated', *World Airpower Journal*, Vol. 4, Winter 1990/91, p. 8; Smith, 'Myanmar's Armed Forces - Retaining Power', p. 388; and Lintner, 'Oiling the iron fist', pp. 29-30.

78. The G-4s may have been intended by the BAF to be replacements for its T-33A trainers, which were grounded in 1992 and taken out of service in 1994. The G-4 is not, however, a modified version of the older US aircraft, as reported in 'Burmese Air Support', *FEER*, 25 October 1990, p. 9. See also 'Burma: Equipment updated', p. 8; and 'Burma (Myanmar)', *World Airpower Journal*, Vol. 8, Spring 1992, p. 142.

79. *Jane's World Air Forces*, Issue 1.

80. Personal observation, Mingaladon, November 1996. See also 'Super Galebs total 12', *JDW*, 18 April 1992, p. 646; 'Air Forces Survey: Myanmar', p. 35; and 'SOKO G-4 Super Galeb', *World Airpower Journal*, Vol. 20, Spring 1995, p. 18.

81. Lintner, 'Oiling the iron fist', p. 30. *The Military Powers Encyclopedia* (p. 39) has suggested that the Anglo-Yugoslavian agreement did not initially cover the re-export of the Rolls Royce engines.

82. Tooling was reportedly moved to the Utva factory at Pancevo, but production was not resumed. See *Jane's All The World's Aircraft 1994-95*, p. 658; and 'SOKO G-4 Super Galeb', p. 18. A number of sources has incorrectly stated that 20 G-4s were delivered to Burma by mid-1991. See, for example, 'World's Air Forces: Burma (Myanma)', *Flight International*, 27 November-3 December 1991, p. 38; and *Jane's Aircraft Upgrades 1995-96* (Jane's Information Systems, Coulsdon, 1995), p. 464.

83. Charles Wallace, 'Burmese junta buys arms for big push', *Sydney Morning Herald*, 6 October 1992. See also 'Air Forces Survey: Myanmar', p. 36; and 'Myanmar: More Polish helicopters', *World Airpower Journal*, Vol. 12, Spring 1993, p. 10.

84. 'Against the wind', *FEER*, 23 July 1992, p. 6. See also 'Junta takes delivery of Polish choppers', *Asian Defence Journal*, September 1992, p. 108; and Bertil Lintner, 'One More to Go', *FEER*, 21 October 1993, p. 32. One W-3 helicopter may have been delivered at the same time. 'Polish arms for Burma', *FEER*, 13 August 1992, p. 6.

85. It was initially reported that 20-30 W-3s were ordered, but this seems incorrect. 'Against the Wind', p. 6; and 'Polish arms for Burma', p. 6. See also 'Southeast Asian Aircraft Inventories', *Asian Defence Journal*, February 1996, pp. 37-8. The *World Airpower Journal* confuses this order with the earlier delivery of 20 Mi-2s. See 'More Polish helicopters', *World Airpower Journal*, Vol. 12, Spring 1993, p. 10. See also 'Military Might', p. 19.

86. Personal observation and interviews, Rangoon, April 1995. Also, 'Military Might', p. 19; 'Air Forces Survey: Myanmar', p. 36.

87. 'Soviets may sell Myanmar jets, helicopters', *Straits Times*, 3 August 1991; Also, 'Soviets offer planes and helicopters to Burma', *Bangkok Post*, 3 August 1991; and 'Air Forces Survey: Myanmar', p. 35.

88. 'Soviets may sell Myanmar jets, helicopters'; 'Soviets offer planes and helicopters to Burma'; and 'Moscow proposes aircraft sales to Myanmar', Radio Rangoon (in English), 2 May 1991.

89. Statement of Rear Admiral Thomas A. Brooks USN, Director of Naval Intelligence, before the Seapower, Strategic, and Critical Materials Subcommittee of the House Armed Services Committee on Intelligence Issues, 7 March 1991.

90. Brooke, 'The Armed Forces of Myanmar', p. 14.

91. 'Soviets offer planes and helicopters to Burma'.

92. 'From Russia, With Choppers', *FEER*, 21 December 1995, p. 14. 'Myanmar military buys gunships from Russia', *Asian Aviation*, Vol. 16, No. 1, December 1995/January 1996, p. 51. Brooke has suggested that the earlier Mi-8 versions were also looked at ('The Armed Forces of Myanmar', p. 14).

93. Robert Karniol, 'Burma builds helicopter fleet with Mi-17 1B buy', *JDW*, 4 September 1996, p. 19. See also 'Helicopters', *Asian Aviation*, November 1996, p. 49; and 'Military Might', p. 19.

94. Interview, Rangoon, November 1999.

95. 'Chopper Deal', *FEER*, 14 March 1996, p. 12. This report states that eight Mi-17s had arrived in Rangoon by this time, but this seems to be an error.

96. Ibid.

97. Brooke, 'The Armed Forces of Myanmar', p. 14.

98. Anton Zhigulsky, 'Russia Courts Myanmar in E.Asian Sales Push', *Defense News*, 4-10 March 1996, p. 16.

99. William Ashton, 'Myanmar turns to Russia for arms', *Asia-Pacific Defence Reporter*, Vol. 22, No. 7/8, July-August 1996, p. 13. See also Andrew Selth, 'Burma Adds Russian Aircraft to its Inventory', *Jane's Intelligence Review*, Vol. 8, No. 5, May 1996, p. 235.

100. Anatoly Yurkin, 'Malaysia to Receive New Batch of MiG-29s', Itar-Tass, 3 January 1996. See also Zhigulsky, 'Russia Courts Myanmar'; and 'Myanma', *Air International*, Vol. 50, No. 2, February 1996, p. 68.

101. Interview, Rangoon, November 1996.

102. Nikolai Novichkov, 'Myanmar signs for surplus MiG-29s', *JDW*, 11 July 2001, p. 15. See also Bertil Lintner, 'MiGs Spell Trouble', *FEER*, 2 August 2001, p. 23.

103. Gill and Mak, *Arms, Transparency and Security in Southeast Asia*, pp. 121-3. See also 'China helping Myanmar build defence base', *Hindustan Times*, 1 May 1993; R.B. Gill, 'Curbing Beijing's arms sales', *Orbis*, Vol. 36, No. 3, Summer 1992, p. 385; *SIPRI Yearbook 1991*, p. 252; and *Jane's Air-Launched Weapons*, Issue 27. (Jane's Information Group, Coulsdon, 1997).

104. *Jane's Air-Launched Weapons*, Issue 27.

105. *Ibid.*

106. 'Myanmar', *Military Procurement International*, Vol. 7, No. 15, 1 August 1997, p. 3.

107. *Jane's Air-Launched Weapons*, Issue 27. See also Alan Boyd, 'Burma arms itself against rebels in secret', *The Australian*, 18 May 1990.

108. *Jane's Air-Launched Weapons*, Issue 27. See also Gill and Mak, *Arms, Transparency and Security in Southeast Asia*, pp. 121-3. See also 'China helping Myanmar build defence base'; Gill, 'Curbing Beijing's arms sales', p. 385; and *SIPRI Yearbook 1991*, p. 252.

109. *Jane's Air-Launched Weapons*, Issue 27.

110. 'Myanmar', *Military Procurement International*, Vol. 7, No. 15, 1 August 1997, p. 3.

111. Maung Aung Myoe, *The Tatmadaw in Myanmar Since 1988*, p. 27, note 41.

112. Prezelin, *Naval Institute Guide to Combat Fleets of the World 1995*, p. 430.

113. Personal observation, Rangoon, April 1995.

114. Some of the BAF's radar equipment is so old that in 1999 the BAF was obliged to hire technicians from India to conduct repairs. Interview, Rangoon, December 1999.

115. 'Air Forces Survey: Myanmar', p. 36; and 'Myanmar's air power boosted', p. 13. See also *Jane's Radar and Electronic Warfare Systems, 1995-96*, (Jane's Information Group, Coulsdon, 1995), p. 11.

116. Interview, Rangoon, November 1996.

117. *Jane's Radar and Electronic Warfare Systems, 1995-96*, p. 11. See also William Ashton, 'The Burmese Air Force', *Jane's Intelligence Review*, Vol. 6, No. 10, October 1994, p. 465; and Ashton, 'Chinese Bases in Burma - Fact or Fiction?', pp. 84-7.

118. 'Air Forces Survey: Myanmar', p. 36.

119. 'Burma (Myanmar)', *JDW*, 7 January 1995, p. 19.

120. Lintner, 'Hidden reserves', p. 13. See also Bertil Lintner, 'Regional rivals leading Burma astray', *JDW*, 15 June 1991, pp. 1053-4; and Pushpindar Singh, 'Chinese Fighters for Myanmar', *Asian Defence Journal*, September 1991, p. 95.

121. Shan Human Rights Foundation, 'SLORC Troops Taught to Fly Chinese Fighter Planes', *Burmanet News*, 24 April 1997.

122. Radoljub Matovic, 'G-4 in the Union of Myanmar', unidentified article in author's possession. This article, published in 1991, includes an interview with *Thura* Khin Maung Win, who led the BAF team which trained on the G-4s in Yugoslavia. See also 'Super Galebs for Myanmar' p. 1172.

123. 'Chopper Deal', p. 12.

124. Interviews, Rangoon, November and December 1999.

125. *Jane's World Air Forces* states that a squadron of F-7 fighters is based at Moulmein, but this has not been confirmed.

126. 'Rangoon junta building new air base in Southern Burmese town', DVB (in Burmese), 28 September 2000.
127. See, for example, R.J. Francillion (ed), *The Naval Institute Guide to World Military Aviation 1995* (Naval Institute Press, Annapolis, 1995), p. 148; and 'Air Forces Survey: Myanmar', p. 35.
128. See, for example, 'Terror on the Border', *Asiaweek*, 21 February 1992, p. 23.
129. Interview, Rangoon, November 1996; NCGUB, *Human Rights Yearbook 1994: Burma*, p. 76; and 'Air Forces Survey: Myanmar', p. 34.
130. 'Myanma Airways Set to Grow', pp. 30-2; *Asian Aviation*, Vol. 15, No. 8, August 1995, p. 38; and *Jane's World Airlines*, pp. A12/01 and A32/32. Air Mandalay is a joint venture between Myanma Airways and a Singaporean partner. It was established in 1994. See also 'Go Slow For Air Mandalay', *Vayu Aerospace Review*, Vol. 4, 1994, p. 13.
131. Interviews, Rangoon, November and December 1999.
132. Clare Hollingworth, 'Burma's uncertain future', *Pacific Defence Reporter*, Vol. 11, No. 8, February 1985, p. 18.
133. Falla, *True Love and Bartholomew*, p. 28 and p. 363.
134. Selth, *Burma's Order of Battle*, pp. 17-19.
135. See, for example, Jeremy Wagstaff, 'Burma buys arms from China', *The Nation*, 11 February 1991.
136. See, for example, Smith, 'Myanmar's Armed Forces - Retaining Power', p. 389.
137. See, for example, 'From Russia, With Choppers'.
138. Maung Aung Myoe, *The Tatmadaw in Myanmar Since 1988*, p. 26, note 4.
139. Interview, Canberra, September 1997.
140. An 'application in principle' from Australia's Hawker de Havilland Ltd to set up such a facility was prevented by the Australian government. See David Lague, 'Evans seeks support for ban on Burma', *Australian Financial Review*, 27 May 1991.
141. 'Far East Air Arms: Southern Region - Burma', p. 142.
142. Maung Aung Myoe, *The Tatmadaw in Myanmar Since 1988*, p. 26, note 4.
143. Eccleston, 'Export to Burma approved despite Evans call for ban'; and Eccleston, 'Row over sale of plane parts to Burma'.
144. 'Myanmar, Malaysia sign overhaul deal', *JDW*, 17 September 1997, p. 15. See also 'Myanmar', *Military Procurement International*, Vol. 7, No. 9, 1 October 1997, pp. 10-11.
145. Falla, *True Love and Bartholomew*, p. 367.
146. See, for example, 'Blood on the Ridge', *Asiaweek*, 13 March 1992, p. 30; 'Karens fight off massive Myanmar army assault', *Bangkok Post*, 14 March 1992; Tom Peterson, 'Bad Day at Thingannyinaung', *Soldier of Fortune*, Vol. 15, No. 2, February 1990, p. 28; Adam Kelliher, 'Under fire - Karen rebels take junta's bombing raids', *The Australian*, 7 March 1992; and Adam Kelliher, 'Burmese Battlegound', *US News and World Report*, 16 March 1992, pp. 16-17.
147. Interview, Rangoon, November 1999.
148. From personal observation in Rangoon during April 1995, the latter incident has assumed considerable importance in BAF folklore. See also Smith, *Burma: Insurgency and the Politics of Ethnicity*, p. 188; and 'The Burmese Air Force', *Military Technology*, p. 9.
149. Interview, Canberra, October 1997. See also Maung Aung Myoe, *The Tatmadaw in Myanmar Since 1988*, p. 26, note 4.
150. Flintham, *Air Wars and Aircraft*, p. 218.
151. See, for example, Yindee Lertchareonchok, 'Seven die when Burma 'copter and jets collide', *The Nation*, 10 March 1992; and 'Air Force Chinese-made F-7 fighter crashes in Tada-U, pilot killed', DVB (in Burmese), 29 October 2000.
152. For example, insurgent ground fire brought down a SF-260 and a Vampire in 1978, two helicopters in June 1982, a Bell 205 in February 1984, and a PC-7 in 1986. Flintham,

Air Wars and Aircraft, p. 218. See also 'Burmese jets bomb rebel base', Reuters, 2 March 1992.

153. The UWSA purchased some HN-5 SAMs from China in early 2000. See Anthony Davis, 'Myanmar heat turned up with SAMs from China, *JDW*, 28 March 2001, p. 14.

154. Selth, *Death of a Hero*, p. 23.

155. Nyan Htut, 'Sackings, exodus of government workers bodes ill for Burma', *Canberra Times*, 20 December 1991; and Myint Thein, 'Burma's well-educated are leaving', *Bangkok Post*, 19 March 1995.

10

Burma and Exotic Weapons

> The annals of history show that down through the ages man has sought to enlist the aid of chemistry and disease in his conduct of warfare, but it was not until the 20th century that science made it possible. — US Army Chemical Corps handbook, cited in Seymour M. Hersh, *Chemical and Biological Warfare: The Hidden Arsenal* (1970)

For nearly two decades, Burma has stood accused of 'probably having' an offensive chemical weapons (CW) capability.[1] Despite repeated denials by the military regime in Rangoon, accusations of CW use by the Burmese armed forces against ethnic insurgents and narcotics-based armies continue to appear. More recently, there have been claims that biological warfare (BW) agents have also been used against ethnic insurgent groups and their supporters. In 1998, for example, the prestigious Jane's defence publishing house stated that 'A biological warfare capability appears to exist, a fact supported by various well-documented reports, including photographs of air-dropped weapons. It is likely that a chemical warfare capability also exists.'[2] None of these claims has ever been verified by independent observers, but doubts remain. Since 1988 they have been given added focus by suggestions that the SLORC and SPDC have received specialist technical assistance from China, as a way of assisting the regime to force the last few ethnic insurgent groups to give up their struggle against the central government in Rangoon. A few observers have even canvassed the possibility that Burma may one day wish to acquire nuclear weapons.

10.1 Chemical Weapons

Over the past decade, Burmese officials have repeatedly denied that Burma has a CW capability. In 1988, for example, Burma's representative to the United Nations Conference on Disarmament stated categorically that Burma did not possess, nor had developed, produced, stockpiled or used chemical weapons. He added: 'Nor will she do so in future'.[3] Formal protests have been lodged by the regime against news media organisations which have claimed otherwise.[4] Yet, despite these denials, Burma is still accused of having produced and used CW.

One of the first public references to this issue was in 1982, when the *International Defense Review* reported that 'in recent years, chemical agents have been used in...Burma'.[5] The same author published another article three years later in which he repeated this claim, referring to the 'use of combined agents as well as of newly developed CW agents in...the Burma triangle'.[6] In 1984, newspapers in the United States and Australia, citing what was claimed to be a leaked US Special National Intelligence Estimate (SNIE), stated that Burma had been making efforts to acquire a domestic capability to produce mustard gas since early 1981.[7] The SNIE reportedly went on to say that the Burmese were buying chemical production plant and protective gear from the FRG.[8] Apart from sulphur, which the Burmese were said to be importing from Italy, the raw materials for the production of the gas were obtained locally. According to these news reports, the SNIE estimated that Burma would be self-sufficient in the operation of the CW plant by the end of 1984. It identified local insurgents as the most likely target for future Burmese CW attacks.[9]

These claims were repeated by academic researchers and the international news media in 1985, and were made again by SIPRI in 1987.[10] That year, the Institute reported in its annual *Yearbook* that Burma was 'said to be producing mustard gas using plant and chemicals imported from Italy and the Federal Republic of Germany'.[11] More importantly, in March the following year the US Director of Naval Intelligence, Rear Admiral William Studeman, speaking in Washington before a sub-committee of the House of Representatives Armed Services Committee, stated categorically that Burma was one of a number of countries 'developing' a chemical warfare capability.[12] This claim was strengthened in 1991, when Rear Admiral Thomas Brooks, the new DNI, told the Seapower, Strategic and Critical Materials Sub-Committee of the House Armed Services Committee that Burma 'probably possessed' an offensive chemical weapons capability.[13] One member of the US Senate Armed Services Committee later went so far as to state categorically that Burma possessed chemical weapon stocks, although he was careful to note that this was not the official view of the US government.[14] Increasingly, Burma began to be listed in the academic and defence literature as a probable CW proliferant.[15]

Shortly after Rear Admiral Studeman's testimony to the US Congress, the Boston-based *Christian Science Monitor* published a story by one of its staff writers suggesting that Fritz Werner GmbH, long known for its close links with the Ne Win regime's military supply program, had 'played an important role in building Burma's chemical weapons capability'.[16] Citing US intelligence sources, the American journalist E.A. Wayne suggested that 'German companies sold equipment, supplies, and possibly know-how under the guise of standard commercial sales'.[17] The article also stated that the US government had privately raised its concerns over this matter with the FRG government, but could not be certain that all sales to Burma had stopped. More cautiously, but clearly conscious of chemical weapons scandals involving German companies in places like Libya and Iraq, some German MPs also expressed their concerns over Fritz Werner's activities in Burma.[18] Suspicions of Burma's interest in CW, and Germany's possible role, were strengthened in September 1991. Under public pressure, the German government revealed that, between 1978 and 1989, a total of 15 Burma Army officers had received 'ABC Protection' training (i.e., training in protective measures against atomic, bacteriological and chemical warfare) from the *Bundeswehr* at Sonthofen Military Academy in the FRG.[19]

Soon after public reports about a possible Burmese CW program began to appear, a number of claims were made that chemical weapons were being used by the Burmese armed forces against their domestic opponents. Karen insurgents based along the Thai-Burmese border, for example, told Thai news reporters in 1984 that the Burma Army had used 'toxic gas', which had been fired into insurgent camps in artillery shells and mortar bombs. This attack was apparently so intense that the Karens were forced to abandon their positions.[20] In early 1992 the Karens claimed that several of their soldiers had suffered burns, rashes and partial paralysis as a result of CW attacks by the Burma Air Force.[21]

The Karens were not the only insurgents to make such claims. In July 1992 a Thai newspaper cited KIA insurgents in Burma's far north, who claimed to have in their possession an air-delivered 'gas weapon' which had been dropped on them by the BAF. Through their political arm, the Kachin Independence Organisation (KIO), the insurgents said that they had intercepted Burma Army radio broadcasts ordering soldiers to withdraw 300 metres from the front line before the air strikes were made. Burmese soldiers later captured by the KIA reportedly confirmed the order.[22] The inference drawn by the Kachins from the order was that precautions of this kind were necessitated by the use of a special weapon. According to another news report of the incident, a Kachin spokesman said that 'the SLORC had threatened to use weapons of mass destruction for some time, but this was the first documented case involving chemical warheads.'[23] The report also stated that the KIA had obtained 'several' unexploded shells containing chemical warheads.[24] Later the same year, there were reports that the BA had fired CW artillery rounds, in another operation against the KIA in Burma's far northeast.[25]

In a 1991 study sponsored by the Federation of American Scientists (FAS) it was suggested that in the opium-producing Golden Triangle area of north-eastern Burma, the SLORC had 'contaminated the drug-smuggling trails with a persistent agent, presumably mustard'. The information was provided by 'a knowledgeable press source'. No other details were given, but the authors of the FAS study gave the report some weight. Indeed, they stated that this story was at the time 'the only specific report that gives credence to the claim that Burma possessed even experimental amounts of lethal CW agents'.[26] No further reports of such CW use, however, have ever been published.

Further claims of Burmese CW use were made by Karen insurgents in early 1995. Members of the KNLA told news reporters and human rights groups that the Burmese armed forces had used chemical weapons in their large scale dry season offensive against the Karen strongholds at Manerplaw and Kawmura. At Manerplaw the Burmese reportedly used 'chemical shells fired by heavy artillery' which 'disperse smaller cluster-like bombs filled with chemicals that explode about 20m above the ground with the force sufficient to "shear a coconut tree trunk"'.[27] After the fall of Kawmura a month later, the Karens spoke of 'chemical gas' being employed against them before they were forced to retreat into Thailand.[28] Other insurgents at Kawmura referred to 'a number of tear-gas like rockets' which caused chest pains, breathing difficulties, nausea and stinging eyes.[29] Later that year, there were reports of 'mysterious ailments' and 'ugly seeping wounds', allegedly as a result of these CW attacks. One report in a Thai newspaper suggested that the decision to use chemical weapons at Kawmura followed a visit to the area by DDSI chief LTGEN Khin Nyunt. Another senior Burmese army officer was quoted as saying (of CW) that 'We use it because it is necessary to use it'.[30] It was claimed that a later artillery bombardment of the Karen base at Kawmura by the Burma Army was designed to destroy all traces of CW use.

The latest claims of CW use by the *Tatmadaw* were made in April 2001, when Shan State Army (South) troops encountered 'gas weapons' during the battle of Pakhee. According to the insurgent commander, during this clash shells were fired by the BA: 'They exploded in mid-air, emitting a black smoke that changed into white. Many of our men went dizzy and some of them unconscious....At first we thought they were dead, but after some time they regained their consciousness'.[31]

The difficulty with evaluating all these claims, however, and in making any firm judgements about Burma's past or current CW status, is that no reports of CW attacks by the Burmese armed forces have ever been verified by independent sources. Indeed, the Thai authorities have issued a number of specific denials that CW has been used. In 1995, for example, the Chairman of the Thai-Burmese Border Coordinating Committee stated that 'Burmese government soldiers did not use chemical weapons in suppressing minority groups. Examinations of those who have come to a hospital for treatment do not provide any evidence that they were subjected to chemicals'.[32]

Inevitably, this has led to a certain amount of official scepticism that the Burmese have CW. Questioned about the issue in 1988, for example, the Staff Director of the Arms Control Subcommittee of the US House of Representatives Committee on Foreign Affairs stated that he doubted Admiral Studeman's report that chemical weapons were being developed in Asia. In particular, he felt that the DNI's case against Burma was based only on circumstantial evidence.[33] The Australian government responded to the 1992 news reports by saying that 'it had no knowledge of chemical weapons being used in the conflict' between the SLORC and Karen separatists.[34]

The truth is hard to discern. In 1984 the Karens would have been aware of news reports about a possible Burmese CW plant, and may have seized the opportunity to publicise the ruthless nature of the Ne Win regime's counter-insurgency campaigns. On close examination, a photograph of the 'CW' weapon retrieved by the KIA in 1992 revealed it to be a HEAT rocket projectile, probably fired from a BAF aircraft to destroy Kachin defensive positions. The KIA may have genuinely been under the impression that they had obtained proof of Burmese CW use but, at the same time, they would have been quick to recognise the opportunity to use the international news media for propaganda purposes. The CW artillery shells reportedly captured by the Kachins around the same time were never produced for examination by independent experts. This is not to say, however, that the insurgents have simply been engaged in a campaign to capitalise on the widespread opposition to chemical weapons. There are a number of other possible explanations for the phenomena cited. Over the years, it has been suggested that toxic defoliants, white phosphorous (WP) rounds, fumes from artillery shells or even tear gas may have been mistaken for more lethal chemical agents.

With US assistance, the Burmese armed forces used dangerous herbicides like 2,4-D (an ingredient in Agent Orange) in Upper Burma throughout the mid-1980s, in an effort to destroy opium poppy crops taxed by insurgent groups or marketed by local drug lords. In 1985, for example, a Royal Thai Army (RTA) team investigated the reported use of chemicals being dropped by the BAF on insurgent areas along the Thai-Burma border. The team's conclusion was that the chemicals were defoliants being used to destroy opium plantations.[35] Insurgents and refugees trying to escape the aerial spraying have claimed, however, that the defoliants were being dropped purely as a counter-insurgency weapon, without any regard for human life. As Stan Sesser has written,

> supporters of the [ethnic] minority groups charged that Rangoon was unwilling to risk flying those [crop-dusting] planes to the major opium-growing areas and instead used the herbicides to poison vegetable crops in the villages of the ethnic minorities fighting the government.[36]

Others have claimed that the US-supplied aircraft and herbicides were used 'primarily as weapons in an extensive war against tribal groups'.[37] Whether or not this was the case, aerial spraying of 2,4-D (and possibly other kinds of herbicides) by the BAF was so intense and so indiscriminate during the mid-1980s that it provoked widespread criticism from the international community. There were numerous claims, for example, that 2,4-D was being ingested by local villagers causing 'extensive human toxicity' and occasionally even death.[38] These claims ceased after 1988, however, when the withdrawal of US aid prevented the continuation of the spraying program.[39]

White phosphorous is commonly used by the armed forces of many countries as an incendiary, to create a smoke screen and for marking targets. It can be fired in aircraft rockets, artillery rounds and mortar bombs, all of which are in the *Tatmadaw*'s armoury. WP is not normally used as an anti-personnel weapon but, if employed in this way, can inflict serious burns. Even if only used as an incendiary or target marker, it is possible that people near the point of explosive impact will be burned.[40] Chemical burns from WP can take longer to heal than thermal burns and in this regard are similar to mustard gas.[41] Also, if a sufficient amount of WP is absorbed through the skin or inhaled, it can cause serious internal injuries and even be fatal. While it is difficult to be certain without specialist medical advice, some of the injuries and symptoms described by Burmese insurgents claiming to be the victims of CW seem to be consistent with WP burns or WP poisoning.[42] When questioned directly about the alleged use of CW by the Burmese armed forces, spokesmen for the military regime have denied its use, but conceded that some of the insurgent claims could refer to the effects of WP.[43]

In at least one case, the reported use of CW seems to have sprung from the inevitable side-effects of intense and prolonged barrages from field artillery, mortars and recoilless guns. In early 1995, for example, a Western observer in the Karen stronghold at Kawmura noted that 'the smoke was so thick that many soldiers began to vomit and collapse, giving rise to the Karen claim that chemical weapons were being used'.[44] One 'informed Western diplomatic source' was later quoted as saying that an investigation had been conducted into the Karen claims of CW use, but the results had been inconclusive. This observer felt that the Karens were more likely to have suffered the effects of cordite poisoning and battle fatigue. This problem was apparently exacerbated by the claustrophobic atmosphere and poor ventilation of the bunkers in which the Karen insurgents sheltered from the *Tatmadaw*'s repeated artillery bombardments.[45]

Tear gas is less likely to be a factor. By 1996, the SLORC appears to have purchased modern riot control equipment from Western suppliers, and trained men in their use. Before then, however, the military regime in Rangoon consistently bypassed the use of 'benign' chemical agents in favour of more direct methods of crowd control, namely mass arrests and shooting at people with live ammunition.[46] Indeed, after the 1988 massacres in Rangoon SLORC Chairman SENGEN Saw Maung told a group of news reporters that the army was forced to open fire on the crowds of pro-democracy demonstrators because the regime did not possess any tear gas.[47] While they have not endorsed the regime's logic, the factual basis for this explanation has been accepted by a number of well-informed Burma-watchers.[48] In any case, tear gas fired at insurgents in the Burmese jungle would probably be of limited utility, and its use in this manner by the Burma Army has rarely been publicly reported.[49] In April 2001, however, the Shan State Army (South) concluded that they had been attacked with 'tear gas bombs'.[50]

Another area of uncertainty is the possible location of Burma's CW production plant and CW testing facilities. The site of the factory has been the subject of speculation, both inside and outside Burma, for many years. The exiled National Coalition Government of the Union of Burma, for example, has given broad hints that 'Fritz Werner has also built "fertiliser" and "bottling" factories in Burma for the SLORC, all of which are highly secure locations'.[51] One insurgent group has alleged that chemical weapons have been produced at Warzi (Wasi), at the country's mint, 'which has been run by German technicians'.[52] Another site often identified by local sources as Burma's secret CW facility is a heavily guarded fertiliser plant across the Irrawaddy River from the ancient capital of Pagan, in central Burma.[53] Other sites have also been mooted, including a number in the military regime's extensive defence-industrial complex near Prome, but no evidence has ever been put forward to confirm any of these claims. Nor have any possible CW test sites been publicly identified, although some of the uninhabited islands off Burma's coast could lend themselves to such a purpose.

In these circumstances, a number of important questions are left unanswered. Assuming that the original reports were correct, and it was built in the first place, the fate of Burma's CW production plant is unknown. Some well-informed observers suspect that it was quietly closed down in the mid-1980s, after the US government made 'private' representations to the Ne Win regime and the existence of a secret CW program was revealed in the international news media.[54] Nor is it known what CW stocks might have been produced during the plant's period of operation, and whether or not they were weaponised. Whatever the answers to these questions may be, since 1988 the SLORC and SPDC seem to have given the development of CW a much lower priority than the acquisition of more modern conventional weapons. These are less controversial and better suited to the suppression of internal dissent, particularly in urban centres. Economic factors would also be influential. The regime needs to restore relations with — and thus the flow of aid and finance from — Japan and the West, and could feel that the continued pursuit of an indigenous CW program was counter-productive at present. Consideration also needs to be given to the original purpose behind any earlier Burmese CW program.

Most analyses of Burma's possible CW program have concluded that it was aimed at the country's many insurgent groups, and perhaps even the narcotics-based armies which had large fixed camps in the Shan States.[55] Given the difficulties being experienced by the *Tatmadaw* operating in the mountains from the late 1970s onwards, it is possible that the Ne Win regime saw chemical weapons as a means of attacking insurgent concentrations, and heavily defended bases that could not be taken by other means. Despite the rugged terrain, thick vegetation and often humid climate of Burma's border regions, chemical weapons could be highly effective against insurgent camps. Casualties were also bound to occur among the local population, but this was not likely to have concerned the Burman-dominated military hierarchy in Rangoon.

This explanation seems logical enough, but the insurgent threat in the late 1970s and early 1980s, when the CW plant is believed to have been planned and built, was no worse than it had been for many years. Indeed, following the defeat of ethnic separatists and communist guerrillas in lower and central Burma in the mid-1970s, it could be argued that the Ne Win regime was stronger than ever. There was certainly no prospect that the central government would fall as a result of insurgent action. Also, given the location of the surviving insurgent camps close to Burma's borders, and the support provided to some of the major groups by neighbouring countries, any use of CW against these insurgents would pose the risk of causing a major international incident. It would also be very difficult to keep such attacks secret from the international community. On balance, it is more likely that the primary impetus behind any clandestine Burmese CW program was strategic developments in the wider Asia-Pacific region.

Towards the end of the 1970s, when serious consideration of a Burmese CW program probably began, a number of important shifts had occurred in the regional strategic balance.[56] The communist victories in Vietnam and Cambodia in 1975 had raised Burmese fears about the security of Laos and even Thailand. There was a strong feeling in Rangoon at the time that, should Thailand become unstable or, worse still, fall to the communists, then Burma would be gravely threatened. This fear was heightened by the Vietnamese invasion of Cambodia in December 1978, and barely diminished when China invaded Vietnam the following year. While very experienced in counter-insurgency operations, Burma's small and poorly equipped armed forces, consisting almost entirely of light infantry, would have found it very difficult to resist a conventional attack from a more modern, better-equipped force. To a nervous Burmese leadership, chemical weapons probably appealed as a force multiplier which could quickly and relatively cheaply redress the military imbalance.

It is perhaps also relevant that around this time there was increased international attention being given to the global proliferation of chemical weapons. Since 1963, when five countries admitted to having a CW capability, the number known or suspected of such a capability had grown to at least 13.[57] During the 1979 conflict between China and Vietnam, both sides accused the other of using chemical weapons. Also, in September 1981 the Reagan Administration in the US drew attention to this problem by charging the Soviet Union with the use of 'mycotoxins' — popularly known as Yellow Rain — in Southeast Asia.[58] Although these accusations were later proven to be unfounded, the publicity given to the use of CW in Southeast Asia seems to have had an impact on the thinking of a number of regional governments, including the military regime in Rangoon. If such broad strategic factors led to the initiation of a Burmese CW program in the late 1970s or early 1980s, however, the question arises whether they might do so again. It must also be asked whether Burma's accession to the new Chemical Weapons Convention (CWC) reflects any significant change in Rangoon's thinking.

Burma's formal position with regard to international instruments governing chemical weapons is unclear. According to one source, upon regaining its independence from the UK in 1948, Burma automatically became a State Party to the 1925 Geneva Protocol for the Prohibition of the Use in War of Asphyxiating, Poisonous or Other Gases, and of Bacteriological Methods of Warfare. In accordance with reservations registered earlier by the UK, this did not prohibit the possession or development of CW, and the Burmese government retained the right of retaliation in kind if ever attacked with CW.[59] Few authoritative sources share this view, however, and Burma is rarely listed as either a signatory or a State Party to the 1925 Geneva Protocol.[60] Burma's approach to the CWC is also open to question, although in January 1993 the Burmese Foreign Minister, Ohn Gyaw, signed the Convention at a ceremony in Paris. This followed considerable efforts on the part of several countries to persuade the SLORC to join in regional consultations on the issue of chemical weapons proliferation, and to become a party to the CWC.

The CWC entered into force, and thus became international law, on 28 April 1997. Should the SPDC ratify the Convention, then Burma would be obliged to observe a number of restrictions on its use of CW. Except in certain specified circumstances (such as legitimate research), Burma would be forbidden to develop, produce or otherwise acquire, stockpile or retain chemical weapons. It would have formally undertaken not to use chemical weapons or engage in any military preparations to use them. Also, within ten years, Burma would be required to destroy any chemical weapons it owned, or that were located in any place under its jurisdiction or control. In addition, Burma would be obliged under the CWC to destroy any CW production facilities it possessed, or which were located on its soil.[61]

Despite the SLORC's apparent readiness to accede to these requirements, doubts persist about Burma's CW status. Given its extremely poor international record, particularly since the SLORC took power in 1988, and repeated accusations of CW use in recent years, there is little confidence in the military regime's continuing denials that Burma ever established a CW production facility in the early 1980s, or has used CW since then. Also, ever since Ne Win's seizure of power in 1962, the leadership in Rangoon has been extremely sensitive about Burma's sovereignty, and reluctant to accept any foreign judgements about its security policies. Even if Burma no longer has a CW program, it is unlikely to accept any intrusive challenge inspections — a fundamental aspect of the CWC — to confirm this. Such inspections would also be necessary to verify that Burma no longer held any stocks of chemical weapons which were produced under a discontinued program. In these circumstances, it is not surprising that questions have been raised about Burma's willingness to abide by all the undertakings contained in the Convention.

Since 1993, questions have also been asked about Burma's adherence to similar conventions prohibiting the manufacture and use of biological weapons.

10.2 Biological Weapons

Whether or not Burma has accepted the 1925 Geneva Protocol, which bans not only CW but also BW, Burma is a signatory to the 1972 Bacteriological (Biological) and Toxin Weapons Convention.[62] This instrument went further than the Geneva Protocol, in that it banned the development, production, stockpiling and acquisition of such weapons. The Convention entered into force in 1975. It did not include any provision for verification or international monitoring, although this issue is currently being addressed. Burma has not yet ratified the 1972 Convention, but acknowledges these international legal obligations, and has even attended meetings in Geneva to discuss a strengthening of the BW Convention — to date the only non-State Party to do so. Yet, at the same time, Burma has been accused of possessing and even using BW against minority peoples along its eastern frontier.

Reports of possible BW use by the *Tatmadaw* along the Thai-Burmese border have varied. In early 1993, for example, there were references to BAF aircraft spraying a yellow powder over rural villages. There have also been reports of aircraft dropping small balloons filled with 'a foul-smelling "black-yellow-green" liquid'.[63] Most often, however, opposition groups have pointed to the mysterious and reportedly lethal 'radiosondes', or 'white boxes,' which have been found. In early 1994 the Karen Human Rights Group compiled a comprehensive report in which it stated:

> On August 12, 1993...SLORC planes dropped dozens, maybe scores...of strange devices consisting of a 2-meter parachute with a "white box" and one or two balloons hanging underneath....Between 3 days and 2 weeks later, villagers in the drop area and some areas downriver started getting sick with a disease resembling cholera or shigella.[64]

The symptoms of this disease were severe diarrhoea, in some cases combined with vomiting. Death usually followed within a few days, mainly from dehydration. The disease was highly contagious and quickly spread to other villages in the Thaton and Papun districts, north of Moulmein.

In late 1994 these claims were investigated by an international human rights group led by Baroness Cox, the Deputy Speaker of the UK House of Lords. The team from Christian Solidarity International (CSI), which included an expert on tropical diseases, added weight to earlier claims by stating that it had 'very strong circumstantial evidence' that the SLORC had used germ warfare against Karen villages in eastern Burma. Baroness Cox and other members of CSI reported that over 300 Karens had died from epidemics, which appeared to have resulted from air drops of 'parachutes with balloons' and 'white boxes' by the BAF as far back as April 1993.[65] An Australian member of the CSI team also claimed that Burmese military personnel had visited Germany in 1993 for training in 'germ warfare'.[66]

According to the *Bangkok Post*, scientists have examined some of the 'white boxes' in question, which were recovered by Karen villagers. They were subsequently identified as harmless 'radiosondes', or pressure-measuring devices made in the United States and routinely used in meteorological surveys.[67] There have also been suggestions that they were in some way related to Thai rain-making experiments. Yet these explanations have been rejected by members of CSI. They have claimed that such pressure-measuring devices are normally carried by large hydrogen balloons at great heights, not scattered at lower altitudes from aircraft or suspended from small parachutes. It has been suggested by members of CSI that the white boxes contained dangerous bacteria which could be released by a controlled explosion over villages sympathetic to insurgent groups. CSI has also claimed that, immediately after the boxes were dropped, Burmese troops stopped going into the affected areas and even local traders were barred from entering. This imposition of an apparent 'quarantine area', and the fact that the *Tatmadaw* had earlier sent officers to Germany for training in biological warfare defence, have also been cited as evidence of the SLORC's complicity in the deliberate spread of disease.[68]

The public case against Burma was taken further in mid-1995 when the influential UK newspaper *The Times* published a report stating that 'Germ warfare is being used by the Burmese military Government to eliminate the last remnants of resistance among the Karen guerrillas fighting for autonomy, British chemical and biological warfare experts believe'.[69] The article referred to 'more than 300 deaths' from cholera, dysentery and other diseases after 'a series of mysterious objects' were dropped by aeroplanes over insurgent-held areas. It also stated that experts at the UK's Porton Down Defence Research Establishment had carried out tests on such objects, which had been brought back from Burma by two British film-makers.[70] The results of these tests were described as 'inconclusive', but the British experts were later quoted as saying that the objects were 'consistent with the covert use of germ warfare'.[71] Around the same time, allegations that Burma was using BW to attack the Karens were repeated on British television, in the Channel Four program *Secret Asia*.[72]

The truth of all these claims is very hard to determine. The fact that independent scientists in Thailand and Canada have reportedly examined the 'white boxes' dropped by the BAF and found them to be harmless pressure-measuring devices, and the UK tests were inconclusive, suggests that other explanations may be necessary for the outbreaks of disease in eastern Burma over the past few years. It is possible, for example, that they have been caused by the spread to Burma of a new strain of cholera, known as *Vibrio cholerae* 0139 or 'Bengal' cholera.

Scarcely known before 1992, *v.cholerae* 0139 caused a major epidemic in India that year, which later spread to Bangladesh.[73] Medical investigators reported that 'the strain seems to have pandemic potential. It is important that other countries in southeast Asia are aware of the strain's potential to cause severe morbidity and mortality'.[74] By early 1993 there were reports of the disease occurring in Thailand, prompting the warning that 'the risk of *v.cholerae* 0139 spreading throughout Thailand and neighbouring countries is genuine'.[75] A particularly virulent strain of cholera, it has displaced other bacteria as the main cause of diarrhoeal disease in South Asia. As no natural immunity has been developed against it, and it is resistant to many of the drugs normally used to combat cholera, the Bengal strain has resulted in many deaths.[76] It is possible that the outbreaks of cholera-like diseases reported in eastern Burma in early and late 1993 simply reflect the spread of this particular strain. In such circumstances, the imposition of a quarantine zone around the affected areas by the Burma Army would not be unusual. This explanation has apparently been accepted by Canadian officials, among others.[77]

More recently, there have been suggestions by some anti-regime groups that the SPDC is allowing HIV/AIDS to spread throughout the frontier areas, as a form of 'germ warfare'. In claims reminiscent of stories which have circulated in Africa and the Caribbean, it is said that the SPDC is using the virus not only as a means of weakening military resistance to rule by Rangoon, but also as a way of physically eliminating minority racial and cultural groups.[78] Such claims, however, appear to be completely without foundation. As Chris Beyrer has pointed out, the extraordinarily rapid growth of HIV/AIDS in Burma is related largely to intravenous drug use and unprotected sex. Corrupt practices on the part of individual military officers may encourage the growth of the pandemic, but it is 'a health and human disaster' completely beyond the SPDC's control.[79] Allowed to go unchecked, it has the potential to devastate the entire Burmese population, a fact that seems slowly to be dawning on the military regime.[80]

In examining the question of BW in Burma, a large number of questions remain unanswered, and a number of others still need to be asked. For example, the possible motives of the SLORC in developing or using such weapons in the early 1990s are not clear. The regime was firmly in power and faced no real military threats. Indeed, almost all the major insurgent groups in Burma had reached cease-fire agreements with the SLORC while others, like the Karens, were gravely weakened by repeated offensives. From the evidence available, there seems to have been little or no strategic gain from the reported use of BW in eastern Burma. Most of the regime's resources have been put into developing the armed forces' conventional capabilities. Nor is it known why the SLORC might drop BW over isolated rural villages instead of known insurgent bases, like Manerplaw. The attacks may have been simply to test BW agents and their means of distribution but, if so, the risk of an introduced disease spreading to other parts of Burma would have been high. Given the very poor state of Burma's medical services, any large outbreak would be impossible to contain. Should it spread across the nearby border to Thailand, the international repercussions would be extremely damaging to the Rangoon regime.

Taken as a whole, the case for Burmese possession and use of BW is not persuasive. The SLORC's brusque denials of opposition claims, however, have tended to arouse suspicions, rather than dispel them. For example, the SLORC has dismissed Karen attempts to interest 'spying correspondents' in the KNU's claims of CW use. The CSI team which investigated the claims of BW use was dismissed as 'a mere half-baked motley trying to mix religion with politics' (*sic*).[81] This attitude, combined with the regime's known readiness to use any means available to suppress domestic dissent, can only fuel speculation that it has biological weapons, is prepared to use them if the need was felt to be great enough, and indeed may have already done so.

10.3 Nuclear Weapons

Despite a few rather odd suggestions to the contrary, there has never been any sign that Burma has even considered the acquisition or use of nuclear weapons.[82] Nor is it likely to do so. Not only has Burma lacked the technical expertise and industrial capacity to make nuclear weapons, but it has no pressing strategic imperative to take such a step. Despite occasional perceptions of threats from some of the nuclear powers, including the US, China and India, the Rangoon government has never seen these apparent dangers in terms of nuclear strikes and, for its part, Burma has shown no inclination to develop a retaliatory nuclear capability. On the contrary, ever since Independence successive Burmese governments have consistently sought to counter nuclear threats and enhance the country's security by opposing the manufacture, deployment and use of nuclear weapons by anyone, anywhere in the world.

Burma has an impressive record of supporting international legal instruments designed to limit nuclear weapons proliferation and use. Burma was among the first countries to become a State Party to the 1963 Partial Test Ban Treaty, banning nuclear weapons tests in the atmosphere, in outer space and under water. It has signed and ratified the 1967 Outer Space Treaty, which prohibits the placing into orbit around the earth of any objects carrying nuclear weapons, the installation of such weapons on celestial bodies, or any other manner of stationing weapons of mass destruction in outer space. Burma is also a State Party to the 1968 Nuclear Non-Proliferation Treaty (NPT) which, *inter alia*, prohibits the transfer by nuclear weapons states, to any recipients whatsoever, of nuclear weapons or of control over them. Similarly, Burma has signed (but not yet ratified) the 1972 Seabed Treaty, prohibiting the emplacement of nuclear weapons, other weapons of mass destruction or related structures, on the ocean floor beyond the limits of a 12-mile seabed zone.[83]

Since 1988, this policy stance has been confirmed by the SLORC and SPDC. In 1995, for example, Burma entered into a safeguards agreement with the International Atomic Energy Agency, as required under the NPT. Burma has always supported the concept of nuclear free zones, and in December 1995 signed the Treaty on the Southeast Asia Nuclear Weapon-Free Zone (the Bangkok Treaty). This agreement includes a reaffirmation by the ten signatory states of the obligations assumed under the NPT, and contains a ban on the development, manufacture, possession, control, stationing or transport, testing or use of nuclear weapons.[84] In the United Nations General Assembly the regime has also confirmed Burma's longstanding opposition to nuclear weapons and pressed for their complete abolition. In September 1996, for example, the Burmese Foreign Minister told the UNGA:

> The proliferation of arms, particularly weapons of mass destruction, remains the greatest potential threat to mankind's survival. All states, large and small, nuclear and non-nuclear, have a vital interest in ensuring the success of negotiations on disarmament....It is essential that nuclear weapon states show the political will to accommodate the concerns of non-nuclear weapon states to achieve a mutually acceptable basis for universal disarmament.[85]

Ohn Gyaw also noted that Burma regarded the Comprehensive Test Ban Treaty as 'an essential step towards nuclear disarmament', and welcomed its adoption by the General Assembly earlier that month.[86]

Burma is also an active member of the UN Conference on Disarmament, which in recent years has focussed its attention on an item entitled 'Process of nuclear disarmament in the framework of international peace and security, with the objective of the elimination of nuclear weapons'.[87]

Notwithstanding Burma's clear policy position on nuclear weapons, there has been some disquiet expressed over Burma's increasing interest in acquiring nuclear technology. There have been reports, for example, that the SPDC plans to build a nuclear power plant in Burma with the help of Russia.[88] However, the impetus behind such an initiative seems to be prestige, and possibly Burma's chronic shortage of electric power generating capacity, rather than any wish to develop nuclear weapons. The concerns most commonly expressed relate more to the wisdom of such a project, given Burma's parlous economic position, Russia's poor reputation in the nuclear field, the low level of technological expertise in Burma and the danger of any nuclear accident affecting neighbouring countries. It is also relevant that Burma has vast reserves of natural gas which, given other cheap supplies in the region, it is unlikely to be able to sell once the current contract with Thailand runs out. Natural gas and hydro-electric power generating plants of the kind currently being considered by the regime make infinitely more sense than a costly and potentially dangerous nuclear facility.[89]

In this context, it is worth noting that Burma has never possessed ballistic missiles. Nor has it expressed any serious interest in acquiring them, despite rumours in 1999 that the SPDC had asked China for some M-11 short-range ballistic missiles, of the kind reportedly held by Pakistan.[90] Burma does not have the technical expertise or industrial capacity to develop an indigenous ballistic missile capability.

10.4 Rangoon and Exotic Weapons

Before 1988, claims of Burmese CW use seemed designed largely to discredit the Ne Win regime and draw attention to the harsh nature of its counter-insurgency campaigns. The inference of some of the more recent reports about Burma's possible development and use of exotic weapons, however, is that Burma has benefited in this area from its close military relationship with China. In 1990, for example, the KNU claimed that the Chinese had sold tonnes of chemical weapons to the SLORC for use against insurgent groups, and in 1995 similar accusations were made after the fall of Kawmura.[91] Should it be discovered that China was in any way assisting the military regime in Rangoon with an exotic weapons program, there would be serious repercussions for Burma's (and China's) relations with both regional countries and members of the wider international community.

China has taken Germany's place as the prime source of Burma's military technology, and it is conceivable that Beijing is secretly providing Rangoon with the specialised equipment and expertise necessary to manufacture chemical and biological weapons. Despite repeated denials, China has long been suspected of having active CW and BW development programs of its own, and in 1979 was even accused of using CW against Vietnam.[92] China has also demonstrated a readiness to share some of its most sensitive technology with its closest friends and allies, as seen in the apparent transfer of ballistic missile and nuclear weapon expertise to Pakistan. Given the rapid development of its military and other ties with China since 1988, it is possible that Burma is now viewed in the same privileged category. Even if China was not actively participating in a clandestine Burmese exotic weapons program, it is possible that it has provided training for Burmese scientists and technicians. It could even be the case that the possible CW and BW attacks reported in Burma since 1988 have been secret field tests of Chinese weapons, conducted with active Burmese cooperation.

However, there is no evidence of any kind to confirm claims of such close collaboration, and on balance it is most unlikely. The first reports of Burma's indigenous CW program appeared during the early 1980s, almost six years before the SLORC's takeover of power and some seven years before its close strategic relationship with China began to develop. At that time the Chinese were still actively assisting the CPB in its military campaign against the Rangoon government. Burma's strictly neutral foreign policy and historical suspicions of China aside, bilateral relations were simply not close enough for the Chinese to be invited to participate in such a program. Nor would the Chinese be likely to assist the Ne Win regime develop a weapon that could be used against its own allies, or indeed against China itself. Even if Rangoon sought to develop such ties with Beijing after 1989, perhaps faced with the FRG's reluctance to be associated with an international pariah like Burma, the chances of China wishing to be associated with such a controversial and potentially counter-productive scheme seem remote. Rather, China has preferred to sell the SLORC large quantities of conventional weapons, usually at a lower level of technological sophistication and much less danger to itself.

The available evidence of Burma's possible development, or use, of exotic weapons is still too thin to permit any confident judgements. Anecdotal advice and the US SNIE appear to provide firm evidence of Burma's intention at least to manufacture CW in the late 1970s and early 1980s, and the case against Germany's involvement in secret CW production elsewhere in the world is overwhelming.[93] Yet, as a leaked national intelligence document, the SNIE cannot be properly verified and no independent confirmation of a CW production plant has ever been produced. Evidence of BW manufacture and use in Burma is even more unreliable. No specific samples of harmful bacteria dropped from aircraft have ever been isolated or identified. On close reading, the support reportedly given by the Porton Down laboratories in the UK, to claims of Burmese BW attacks during 1993, does not specifically confirm actual BW use, simply the possibility that such kinds of attack are possible.[94] Despite the many claims that have been made over the past 15 years, no independent verification has been possible in any of the cases of CW or BW use which have been reported. A number of alternative explanations are possible for all the incidents cited to date. Nuclear weapons have never figured in Burmese government thinking.

None of this is to say that Burma would not be prepared to develop or even use particular exotic weapons in the future. Despite frictions with Thailand and uncomfortable relations with India and Bangladesh, Burma faces no appreciable external threat at present. Burma's relationship with China, its main traditional enemy, is now closer than it has ever been. Yet over the years Ne Win, and his military governments, have shown a capacity for muddled thinking, if not paranoia. The same sense of insecurity has been evident in the SLORC and SPDC. The regime continues to fear that Burma might become the target of external powers looking to support the democratic movement. Under the impression that it was faced with such a threat, chemical or biological weapons might start looking attractive to an isolated and fearful regime in Rangoon. The DPRK, for example, already offers an example of how a small, poor and friendless state can win major concessions from the international community by threatening to develop or use weapons of mass destruction.

Also, should it become known that any of Burma's neighbours were developing CW or BW capabilities of their own, Burma could be prompted to follow suit. Indeed, the original US SNIE reportedly stated that one reason behind Burma's initial CW program was because it had been 'sensitised by its neighbours' possession of chemical weapons'.[95] Given the close relationship which currently exists between Burma and China, the latter's secret CW and BW capabilities are not likely to encourage a new Burmese program. More worrying would be the prospect of India developing a significant CW arsenal, as insurance against a possible CW threat from Pakistan. Although bilateral relations with India are gradually improving after a low point in the late 1980s, Burma would not like to feel vulnerable to any Indian threat. Thailand has also been suspected of considering an exotic weapons production program at different times, and in some sources it is even cited as a possible CW proliferant.[96] In these circumstances, there is a danger that CW might once again be seen by the military regime in Rangoon as a cost-effective way of defending itself.

Notes

1. An earlier version of this chapter appeared as Andrew Selth, *Burma and Weapons of Mass Destruction*, Working Paper No. 334 (Strategic and Defence Studies Centre, Australian National University, Canberra, 1999).

2. NBC Inventories: Burma (Myanmar)', *Jane's NBC Protection Equipment, 1997-98* (Jane's Information Group, Coulsdon, 1998).

3. See, for example, Conference on Disarmament document CD/PV.452, 29 March 1988. See also Stockholm International Peace Research Institute, *SIPRI Yearbook 1990: World Armaments and Disarmament* (Oxford University Press, Oxford, 1990), p. 134.

4. M. Burck and C.C. Flowerree, *International Handbook on Chemical Weapons Proliferation* (Greenwood Press, New York, 1991), p. 437.

5. Stelzmuller, 'NBC Defence: a German viewpoint', *International Defense Review*, Vol. 15, November 1982, p. 1571.

6. H. Stelzmuller, 'The NBC Threat - Effective Protection and Countermeasures', *Armada International*, Vol. 8, December 1985, p. 208. The 'Burma triangle' mentioned here is clearly the 'Golden Triangle', encompassing north-eastern Burma, northern Thailand and western Laos, which produces a large proportion of the world's opium (and heroin).

7. Dale Van Atta, 'The Chemical Club Grows', *National Times*, 21-27 December 1984.

8. See Selth, *Burma's Secret Military Partners*, pp. 14-19.

9. Van Atta, 'The Chemical Club Grows'.

10. See, for example, L.R. Ember, 'Worldwide Spread of Chemical Arms Receiving Increased Attention', *Chemical and Engineering News*, Vol. 64, No. 15, 14 April 1986, pp. 8-16; and Don Oberdorfer, 'Chemical arms curbs are sought', *Washington Post*, 9 September 1985.

11. Stockholm International Peace Research Institute, *SIPRI Yearbook 1987: World Armaments and Disarmament* (Oxford University Press, Oxford, 1987), p. 110.

12. Statement of Rear Admiral William O. Studeman, USN, Director of Naval Intelligence, before the Seapower, Strategic and Critical Materials Subcommittee of the House Armed Services Committee on Intelligence Issues, Washington, 1 March 1988.
13. Statement of Rear Admiral Thomas A. Brooks USN, 7 March 1991.
14. J.S. McCain, 'Proliferation in the 1990s: Implications for US Policy and Force Planning', *Strategic Review*, Vol. 17, No. 3, Summer 1989, p. 11. This article was later reprinted in *Military Technology*, Vol. 1/90, 1990, pp. 262-7.
15. See, for example, E.D. Harris, 'Chemical Weapons Proliferation in the Developing World', in *RUSI and Brassey's Defence Yearbook 1989* (Brassey's, London, 1989), pp. 67-88. Several other references are listed in *Proliferation of Weapons of Mass Destruction: Assessing the Risks* (US Congress, Office of Technology Assessment, Washington, 1993), pp. 80-1.
16. E.A. Wayne, 'Tracking chemical weapons in the Gulf war', *Christian Science Monitor*, 13 April 1988.
17. *Ibid*. According to Burmese opposition groups, in 1984 the FRG exported DM16.1 million worth of chemical pre-products to Burma, and DM7.5 million worth of chemical end products. NCGUB, *Human Rights Yearbook 1994*, p. 244.
18. Smith, 'The Burmese way to rack and ruin', pp. 43-4.
19. *Is the SLORC Using Bacteriological Warfare?*, Preliminary Report based on information independently gathered by the Karen Human Rights Group, 15 March 1994 (Typescript, Bangkok, 1994). See also NCGUB, *Human Rights Yearbook 1994*, pp. 243-4. ABC Warfare is still included on the curriculum of the *Tatmadaw*'s Command and General Staff College.
20. 'Burmese accused of toxic gas warfare', *Bangkok Post*, 1 February 1984.
21. KHRG, *Is the SLORC Using Bacteriological Warfare?*
22. 'Kachin rebels claim government using chemical weapons' *The Nation*, 24 July 1992.
23. Ian McPhedran, 'Chemical weapons enter Burma civil war: report', *Canberra Times*, 7 August 1992.
24. *Ibid*.
25. KHRG, *Is the SLORC Using Bacteriological Warfare?*
26. Burck and Flowerree, *International Handbook on Chemical Weapons Proliferation*, p. 428.
27. Ron Corben, 'Attack ends hopes of Burmese rebels', *The Australian*, 28-29 January 1995. See also 'Manerplaw falls to Burmese', *Bangkok Post*, 28 January 1995.
28. Sutin Wannabovorn, 'Chemical shells used, say Karen', *Canberra Times*, 22 February 1995; and Sutin Wannabovorn, 'Karens retreating, say Burma using chemical weapons', *Asian Age*, 22 February 1995.
29. 'Karen guerrillas pull out of last major stronghold', *Bangkok Post*, 22 February 1995; and Yindee Lertcharoenchok, 'Kawmoora falls to Rangoon forces', *The Nation*, 22 February 1995.
30. 'Evidence of Slorc gas attack mounts', *The Nation*, 12 May 1995.
31. '"Chemical weapons" were tear gas bombs, said Yawdserk', *BurmaNet News*, 26 June 2001.
32. 'No Evidence of Chemical Weapon Use by Burma', Broadcast on Thai radio (in Thai), 25 February 1995. Foreign Broadcast Information Service, FBIS-EAS-95-079, 25 April 1995, p. 68.
33. Michael Richardson, 'Australia Holding Chemical Arms Talks', *International Herald Tribune*, 13-14 August 1988.
34. A spokesman for the Australian Foreign Minister added that his government would be happy to study any evidence of the use of such weapons. McPhedran, 'Chemical weapons enter Burma civil war: report'.

35. 'Military to probe Burmese chemicals', *Bangkok Post*, 24 August 1985.
36. Stan Sesser, *The Lands of Charm and Cruelty: Travels in Southeast Asia* (Alfred Knopf, New York, 1993), p. 200. See also Smith, 'The Burmese way to rack and ruin', p. 44.
37. W.H. Overholt, 'Dateline Drug Wars: Burma, The Wrong Enemy', *Foreign Policy*, Vol. 77, Winter 1989-90, pp. 177-8.
38. 'Rebels in Burma Say Rangoon Uses Herbicide Against Them', *New York Times*, 30 November 1986. See also Smith, 'The Burmese way to rack and ruin', pp. 43-5; Mirante, *Burmese Looking Glass*, pp. 146ff, pp. 174ff and pp. 222ff; and Falla, *True Love and Bartholomew*, p. 357 and p. 364.
39. The SLORC could not afford to maintain the Ayres S-2R Turbo-Thrush crop-spraying aircraft provided by the US, or purchase adequate supplies of defoliants.
40. Stockholm International Peace Research Institute, *Incendiary Weapons* (MIT Press, Cambridge, 1975), pp. 155-60, pp. 198-201 and pp. 209-23.
41. SIPRI, *Incendiary Weapons*, p. 200.
42. *Ibid.* See also *Chemical Shells at Kaw Moo Rah*, A Special Independent Report by the Karen Human Rights Group, KHRG 95-08, 24 February 1995.
43. Interviews, Rangoon, April 1995.
44. Kurt Hanson, 'Calamity at Kawmura', *Soldier of Fortune*, Vol. 20, No. 9, September 1995, p. 72.
45. *Ibid.* Also, personal communication, Bertil Lintner to the author, 17 October 1995.
46. SENGEN Saw Maung stated in 1989 that before the army was ordered to shoot at pro-democracy demonstrators in 1988, four rubber bullets were fired, then 12 guage shotguns were used. 'Saw Maung: "I Saved Burma" ', *Asiaweek*, 27 January 1989, p. 24.
47. *Ibid.*
48. See, for example, Sesser, *The Lands of Charm and Cruelty*, p. 221. Given earlier reports of Burmese mustard gas production, the question arises whether the army also lacked gas masks.
49. Two exceptions to this rule are Ron Corben, 'Karen rebels to fight on despite stronghold's fall', *The Australian*, 22 February 1995; and 'Chemical Shells at Kaw Moo Rah'.
50. '"Chemical weapons" were tear gas bombs, said Yawdserk', *BurmaNet News*, 26 June 2001.
51. NCGUB, *Human Rights Yearbook 1994: Burma*, p. 244.
52. McPhedran, 'Chemical weapons enter Burma civil war: report'. The Burmese mint was initially equipped with the help of the GDR, but control was transferred to FRG technicians in the early 1970s. The suggestion that the mint facilities hide Burma's secret CW plant stems from the fact that the German firm now providing technical support at Wasi is Fritz Werner GmbH.
53. Smith, 'The Burmese way to rack and ruin', p. 44.
54. Interview, Rangoon, November 1999.
55. Van Atta, 'The Chemical Club Grows'; See also Ember, 'Worldwide Spread of Chemical Arms Receiving Increased Attention', p. 13; and Harris, 'Chemical Weapons Proliferation in the Developing World', p. 75.
56. A former senior member of the *Tatmadaw* has told the author that a 'small' chemical weapons program was under consideration by the Ne Win regime in the late 1970s. This officer believed that a pilot CW plant was subsequently built. Interview, Rangoon, November 1996.
57. Oberdorfer, 'Chemical Arms Curbs Are Sought'.
58. *Ibid.* For a more detailed treatment of this issue, see Sterling Seagrave, *Yellow Rain* (Abacus, London, 1982).
59. Burck and Flowerree, *International Handbook on Chemical Weapons Proliferation*, p. 428. The 1947 agreement recognising Burma's independence included an article which

bound the new Burmese government to accept 'All obligations and responsibilities heretofore devolving on the Government of the United Kingdom which arise from any valid international instrument'. The UK had ratified the 1925 Geneva Protocol (with reservations) in 1930. See Tinker, *Burma: The Struggle for Independence*, Vol. 2, p. 794.

60. See, for example, *1995 United Nations Disarmament Yearbook*, (Centre for Disarmament Affairs, New York, 1996), pp. 264-5; Stockholm International Peace Research Institute, *SIPRI Yearbook 1996: Armaments, Disarmament and International Security* (Oxford University Press, Oxford, 1996), p. 770; and Trevor Findlay, 'The Strategic Benefits for Southeast Asia and the South Pacific of a Chemical Weapons Convention', in Trevor Findlay (ed), *Chemical Weapons and Missile Proliferation, With Implications for the Asia/Pacific Region* (Lynne Rienner Publishers, Boulder, 1991), p. 82.

61. See Conference on Disarmament document CD/1173, 3 September 1992, Appendix.

62. Burma has yet to ratify this convention. *The United Nations Disarmament Yearbook: 1995*, pp. 264-5; *SIPRI Yearbook 1996*, p. 778-9; and Findlay, *Chemical Weapons and Missile Proliferation*, p. 83.

63. NCGUB, *Human Rights Yearbook 1994: Burma*, pp. 235-243.

64. KHRG, *Is the SLORC Using Bacteriological Warfare?*.

65. '"Strong evidence" over Burma's germ warfare', *Bangkok Post*, 17 November 1994. See also NCGUB, *Human Rights Yearbook 1994: Burma*, pp. 235-236; and 'Myanmar: Germ warfare against rebels', *Asian Recorder*, 10-16 December 1994, p. 24439.

66. NCGUB, *Human Rights Yearbook 1994: Burma*, p. 236.

67. '"Strong evidence" over Burma's germ warfare'.

68. *Ibid.* See also KHRG, *Is the SLORC Using Bacteriological Warfare?*

69. Reprinted as 'Burma junta accused of germ war', *The Australian*, 11 July 1995.

70. The Porton Down Defence Research Establishment is now the Protection and Life Sciences Division of the UK Defence Evaluation Research Agency.

71. 'Burma junta accused of germ war'.

72. *Chemical Weapons Convention Bulletin* No. 29 (September 1995), p. 26.

73. M.J. Albert *et al*, 'Large outbreak of clinical cholera due to *vibrio cholerae* non-01 in Bangladesh', *Lancet*, Vol. 341, No. 8846, 13 March 1993, p. 704.

74. M.J. Albert *et al*, 'Large epidemic of cholera-like disease in Bangladesh caused by *Vibrio cholerae* 0139 synonym Bengal', *Lancet*, Vol. 342, No. 8868, 14 August 1993, pp. 387-90 and p. 430.

75. Manas Chongsa-nguan *et al*, 'Vibrio cholerae 0139 Bengal in Bangkok', *Lancet*, Vol. 342, No. 8868, 14 August 1993, pp. 430-1.

76. F.G. Morris, *et al*, 'Vibrio cholerae non-01 - the eighth pandemic?', *Lancet*, Vol. 342, No. 8868, 14 August 1993, pp. 382-3; and Tapas Ray, 'Another pandemic', *Frontline*, 11 March 1994, pp. 78-9.

77. NCGUB, *Human Rights Yearbook 1994: Burma*, p. 236. See also pp. 242-3 for a survey of other possible explanations for the outbreaks of disease in eastern Burma.

78. Interview, Washington, May 1998.

79. Beyrer, *War in the Blood*, pp. 36-52. See also p. 145.

80. Already the HIV rate among heroin addicts in Burma is the highest in the world. Beyrer, *War in the Blood*, p. 44. See also Ma Thanegi's interview with SPDC Secretary 1, LTGEN Khin Nyunt, *Myanmar Times*, 15-21 January 2001; and Sarah Stewart, 'Myanmar facing AIDS catastrophe', AAP, 27 November 2000.

81. 'Whither KNU - 14', *New Light of Myanmar*, 11 February 1995. See also Baranwal, *SP's Military Yearbook 1993-94*, p. 91.

82. See, for example, Max Singer and Aaron Wildarsky, *The Real World Order: Zones of Peace / Zones of Turmoil* (Chatham House, Chatham, 1993), p. 67.

83. *SIPRI Yearbook 1996*, pp. 773ff.

84. *1995 United Nations Disarmament Yearbook*, p. 254.
85. 'Statement by U Ohn Gyaw, Minister for Foreign Affairs and Chairman of the Delegation of Myanmar in the General Debate of the Fifty-First Session of the United Nations General Assembly, New York, 27 September 1996', Embassy of the Union of Myanmar, Canberra, *Newsletter* 12/96 (18 October 1996).
86. *Ibid.*
87. NCGUB, *1995 United Nations Disarmament Yearbook*, p. 98.
88. See, for example, 'Official: Pakistan ready to export peaceful nuclear capability', *Khabrain* (in Hindu), 15 July 2000; and Veronika Voskoboinikova, 'Myanmar shows interest in Russian research reactor', Tass, 22 December 2000.
89. See, for example, 'Burma receives $120 million loan from China to build hydroelectric power plant', Radio Myanmar (in Burmese), 15 September 2000; and 'Burma-China sign MOU for construction of two small moveable LNG refineries', Radio Myanmar (in Burmese), 6 October 2000.
90. Interview, Rangoon, December 1999.
91. Alan Boyd, 'Burmese junta calls in troops', *The Australian*, 31 October 1990; and 'Karen guerrillas pull out of last major stronghold'.
92. See *Proliferation of Weapons of Mass Destruction: Assessing the Risks*, p. 65 and pp. 80-2.
93. See for example K.R. Timmerman, *The Death Lobby: How the West Armed Iraq* (Fourth Estate, London, 1992), pp. 105ff; and Christopher Andrew, *For the President's Eyes Only: Secret Intelligence and the American Presidency from Washington to Bush* (Harper Collins, New York, 1995), pp. 501-2.
94. 'Burma junta accused of germ war'.
95. Van Atta, 'The Chemical Club Grows'.
96. See, for example, Ember, 'Worldwide Spread of Chemical Arms', p. 9.

11

The Tatmadaw Today

> The key to a contemporary understanding of the future of Myanmar's politics is an understanding of the army, just as it was in 1948, 1958, 1962 and 1988. If one is to understand the army, one has to comprehend the interests and attitudes of the current military regime. — R.H. Taylor, 'Myanmar: Military Politics and the Prospects for Democratization', *Asian Affairs* (February 1998)

Over the past decade, Burma has been the only country in the entire Asia-Pacific region in which the armed forces have steadily continued to expand. Also, it has consistently spent a greater proportion of its central government outlays on defence than any other regional country.[1] As a consequence, the *Tatmadaw* is now the largest and best equipped military force that Burma has ever mustered. It is the second largest in Southeast Asia and, given Vietnam's plans for future troop reductions, could become the largest before too long. According to the US State Department's conservative estimate, the *Tatmadaw* is already the 18th largest armed force in the world. By using other figures, it could in fact be the 15th largest.[2] Compared to those of its fellow ASEAN members, Burma's order of battle is now very comprehensive, and likely to become more so. Its armed forces today thus constitute a very large and well-equipped organisation capable of exercising considerable power at home, and increasing influence abroad.

The *Tatmadaw*'s extraordinary growth since 1988 has attracted widespread criticism. The Western democracies and their allies have been the most outspoken. Their criticisms have tended to focus on three main issues: the military regime's continued abuses of human rights, particularly its treatment of NLD General Secretary Aung San Suu Kyi and the ethnic minorities; the refusal of the armed forces to hand over authority to the civilian government elected in 1990; and the allocation of scarce national resources to the defence sector, when other areas of Burmese society are clearly desperate for government support. Also, while Burma still tends to be overlooked in studies of regional security, concern has been expressed by a number of its neighbours over Rangoon's close strategic relationship with Beijing, and the dependence which is expected to result from the *Tatmadaw*'s large-scale purchases of Chinese arms and equipment.

These are all important issues which deserve close attention. Despite support for Burma by some regional countries, continuing international concern will place considerable diplomatic pressure on the Rangoon regime. It will add to its sense of insecurity and restrict its economic development plans. These criticisms will also affect the *Tatmadaw*'s professional standing, limit its options for future arms purchases, and influence its strategic perceptions. There is, however, another way of looking at the development of the Burmese armed forces since 1988. While significant in the terms cited by the regime's critics, it is important also to examine the *Tatmadaw* purely as a military institution, and to look at its development from a more technical, defence-related standpoint. Not only can this contribute to a more comprehensive and balanced understanding of events since 1988, but such an examination can also assist in the consideration of several other critical questions. These include the *Tatmadaw*'s future defence role, the possibility of a split within its ranks and the attitude of the armed forces towards an eventual transition to a democratically elected civilian government.

11.1 The Tatmadaw Transformed

Despite all the criticisms which the *Tatmadaw*'s expansion and modernisation program has attracted over the past 12 years, some improvement of Burma's military capabilities was not without justification. Judged against objective criteria, and compared with military developments in other regional countries, a number of the measures taken by the SLORC and SPDC do not seem unusual. Indeed, it could even be argued that some were long overdue.

In considering the *Tatmadaw*'s growth since 1988, and the upgrading of its equipment inventory, it needs to be borne in mind that both started from a low base. The Rangoon government has always been forced to rely on manpower rather than machinery to fight its wars. Yet, given the size of Burma's population, and the range of security problems which it has faced since Independence, the armed forces have been relatively small. This was still the case in 1988, when the proportion of Burmese men and women in uniform was at least comparable to Thailand and Singapore, which faced far fewer security problems.[3] This situation has now changed, but in terms of soldiers per head of population, Burma still ranks well behind Brunei, Singapore and Cambodia.[4] Also, there is evidence to suggest that, in some respects, the *Tatmadaw*'s rapid expansion since 1988 has occurred more on paper than in reality. While the number of combat units has undoubtedly increased, the actual fighting strength of the armed forces may not be as great as appearances first suggest. In particular, the demands of government and administration have absorbed a large proportion of the *Tatmadaw*'s resources.[5] This burden will increase as Burma adopts a comprehensive socio-political system based on the armed forces, similar to the Indonesian *dwi fungsi* model.

In addition, the Burmese armed forces have always operated very frugally. For example, before the SLORC took over government, Burma's public expenditures per soldier were estimated by one researcher to be the lowest of any country in the

Asia-Pacific region.[6] Military pay and privileges tended to be better than those enjoyed by most other sectors of Burmese society, but for many personnel in the lower ranks conditions were still very difficult. Those benefits they did receive were balanced by the high risk of death or injury while on operations against the country's numerous insurgent groups and narcotics-based armies. While some other armed forces might have envied Burma's high 'tooth to tail' ratio, the average Burmese soldier usually went into battle on foot, armed with weapons that were often inferior to those of his opponents. He could have no confidence in the availability of ammunition resupply, regular rations or medical evacuation if wounded. Heavy weapons support was frequently absent and air cover was unreliable.[7] Given the examples provided by campaigns conducted over the past 12 years, and anecdotal evidence from deserters and captured BA personnel, this situation has not significantly altered in some ways, despite all the improvements made under the SLORC and SPDC. As noted above, there continue to be problems with inadequate logistics, low morale, poor leadership and outmoded doctrine. All have been aggravated by the rapid expansion of the armed forces and seem likely to remain unresolved for some time.

Personnel management was not the only area where the *Tatmadaw* was deficient. Before 1988 its inventories of weapons and military equipment simply did not stand comparison with those of most other regional countries. Burma's policies of neutrality in foreign affairs and economic self-sufficiency were given a higher priority than the benefits of military assistance of the kind provided — often quite lavishly — to some of its neighbours. While the *Tatmadaw* has always taken a large share of the annual budget, Burma's perennial economic problems meant that arms imports remained very low. Most of the weapons and weapons platforms acquired before 1988 were secondhand, and many had to be modified in-country to meet specific operational requirements. The difficulty of obtaining spare parts from abroad also meant that, at any one time, a large proportion of the *Tatmadaw*'s military vehicles, combat aircraft and naval vessels was unserviceable. Burmese C^3I systems were weak and unreliable. During the 1970s and 1980s, the Ne Win regime could only look on with envy as countries like Thailand, Malaysia and Singapore, drawing on foreign aid or their superior economic resources, began to upgrade their armed forces with better arms and equipment.[8] Not only could they afford more sophisticated weapon systems but, to an increasing extent, they could support them with a more developed scientific and industrial base. Even lowly Bangladesh managed to acquire more modern arms (from China) than the Burmese could field. In this sense, it could be claimed that the development of more capable armed forces in Burma after 1988 was quite justified.[9]

Burma may not have faced any major external threats since 1988, but there was some basis for the regime's claim to have a strong strategic rationale for improvements to the *Tatmadaw*'s capabilities. In the aftermath of the Cold War, the strategic environment was changing. Most regional countries were concerned about the uncertain outlook and, until the Asian financial crisis struck, many were quietly taking military precautions against eventualities. In considering these issues,

Burma was acutely conscious of its delicate position between China and India. Burma also shared long and porous borders with five different countries. In the 40 years since Independence, all five had a record of difficult relations with Burma, and in the years leading up to the SLORC's takeover at least three had in different ways assisted armed forces hostile to the central government. China had provided substantial material and diplomatic support to the CPB. India had supported anti-regime ethnic groups in Burma's northwest and immediately after the 1988 demonstrations provided funds and refuge to pro-democracy activists.[10] As a way of creating a buffer between itself and socialist Burma, Thailand had long given at least passive support to Rangoon's political opponents, ethnic insurgent groups, black marketeers and narcotics traffickers based along its border. Also, Burma had a long and broken coastline, surrounded by extensive maritime claims, and its airspace covered several major east-west air routes. Yet Burma had never been in a position to defend its territory from external attack, guard its natural resources against unauthorised exploitation, or prevent intruders from crossing its borders.[11] In these circumstances, some measures to improve the capability of the *Tatmadaw* were only to be expected, regardless of who exercised power in Rangoon.

When questioned about Burma's arms procurement program, spokesmen for both the military regime and the various arms suppliers have been quick to point out that the new weapon systems were for defensive purposes only.[12] As far as a distinction can be made between defensive and offensive weapons, this is correct. For all its acquisitions (or orders) of armoured vehicles, long-range artillery, interceptor aircraft and blue-water naval vessels, Burma still does not possess any real power projection capability. Nor is one in prospect. There are no signs, for example, of Burma acquiring (or being able to afford) long range bombers, air-to-air refuelling aircraft, submarines or ballistic missiles. Accusations of exotic weapons development and use, and therefore the potential for a proliferation of these weapons in the region, are still unproven. The growth and modernisation of the *Tatmadaw* does not in itself significantly change the regional strategic balance, nor pose a serious threat to any other country. Although reservations have been expressed by Burma's immediate neighbours, notably Thailand and India, these have usually been related to a potential, rather than a current, threat.[13] Also, few of the arms and equipments purchased by the Rangoon regime can be considered state-of-the-art. While a marked improvement on Burma's older inventory, they still cannot match the best weapon systems of its larger neighbours, or of more advanced regional countries like Singapore. Indeed, given the complaints heard about some of the *Tatmadaw*'s latest acquisitions, questions can even be raised about their combat effectiveness.

Even if these and other problems were overcome, additions to an order of battle do not automatically translate into real improvements in military capabilities. The acquisition of new arms and equipment needs to be based on a balanced and coherent strategic plan, something for which the Burmese leadership has not been noted in the past. While attempts are apparently being made in this regard, current thinking should not give any grounds for concern. The joint exercise scenarios tested to date are essentially defensive. It will also take some time before all these new weapon systems can be fully absorbed into the *Tatmadaw*'s order of battle. Most of the new additions will depend for their full operational effectiveness on further improvements to Burma's C^4I resources. There will be a greatly increased requirement for specialised training, and the development of new doctrines and operating procedures, particularly for more complex conventional operations. Major new weapon systems also require new facilities for storage, transport, maintenance and repair. Unlike some other Southeast Asian countries, Burma's indigenous scientific and industrial base is not sufficiently developed to support more sophisticated weapons platforms and military equipment, meaning a greater dependence on foreign expertise and imported spare parts. Given all these factors, it is likely to be some time before the *Tatmadaw*'s real operational capabilities match its new material strength.

Despite all these arguments in support of a larger, more balanced and better equipped *Tatmadaw*, however, it is still difficult to escape the conclusion that the military regime has devoted so much of Burma's resources to the armed forces largely for domestic political reasons. All the regime's rhetoric aside, the rapid expansion and modernisation of the armed forces after 1988 seems to have been based in one way or another on a fear that the *Tatmadaw* might lose its monopoly of political power. The increased recruitment campaign and arms procurement program seem aimed above all else at preventing, or if necessary quelling, renewed civil unrest in the main population centres. Efforts to defeat or neutralise ethnic insurgent groups in the countryside can also be seen as part of the regime's continuing determination to impose its own peculiar vision of the modern Burmese (here read Burman) state upon the entire country.[14] It has also felt the need to guard against an international coalition aiming to end human rights abuses and restore democratic rule. In pursuing all these aims, the SLORC and SPDC can claim some successes over the past 12 years.

While Burma's economy remains very weak, and a potential source of unrest, the regime has significantly strengthened its domestic political position. As one international study has remarked,

> The military government in Burma/Myanmar does presently appear to be as strong as at any time in the country's history. It controls all public aspects of the country's political life and important parts of the private sector economy. It has put in place all of the institutional means, including a robust and well-organised domestic intelligence apparatus, needed to ensure the continuity of military rule. It is showing no weakening in its determination to hold on to power.[15]

The likelihood of another serious challenge from urban dissidents has receded. In the countryside, well over half of the major ethnic insurgent groups have entered into cease-fire arrangements with Rangoon, while others (including the once-powerful Karens) have been gravely weakened by internal divisions and military offensives. Exiled Burmese and pro-democracy activists abroad are still deeply committed to political change, and in some cases are supported by governments and philanthropic organisations, but they are becoming increasingly marginalised in the determination of Burma's future.[16] The plans of radical groups to mount terrorist campaigns in Burma's cities are doomed to failure.[17] In terms of international relations, the regime has won back some of the diplomatic ground which it lost after 1988. Burma's strategic position has also improved through its improved military capabilities, close relationship with China and membership of ASEAN.[18] As the International Crisis Group has noted, the regime 'is presently very comfortable in its resistance to internal and external pressures for change'.[19]

There are a number of developments, however, which could disrupt the steady consolidation of military rule.[20] One would be a resumption of open anti-regime activity by Aung San Suu Kyi who, after six years detention without trial, was released from house arrest in 1995. Despite considerable impediments she has managed to play a continuing role in her country's political affairs. Her popular following in Burma is such that, under certain circumstances, she could reawaken public demands for a return to democratic rule.[21] Already, she and her party have been able to draw attention to popular grievances, question the validity of the national constitutional convention process, and underline the illegitimacy of the military government.[22] While some in the armed forces are bitterly opposed to granting Aung San Suu Kyi any political role, the SPDC has reluctantly recognised that, if only because of her international standing, it needs to take her into account in plotting the country's future. However, the regime's hold on Burmese society is currently very strong. If the military leadership was concerned about its ability to manage a resurgence of popular protest it is unlikely to have authorised Aung San Suu Kyi's release, let alone grant her the (albeit negative) publicity she still receives in the local news media. If it was felt necessary, there is little doubt that the army would once again be called in to restore what the regime calls 'law and order', just as it did in 1988.

The regime would also be concerned at any prospect of an early resumption of hostilities with the major insurgent groups and narcotics-based armies in Burma's north and east. The drain on the country's resources, and the increased demands on the armed forces, would be a severe setback to the regime's plans. It would mean that less attention could be paid to the consolidation of military rule, the management of civil administration, the improvement of the economy and the campaign to win greater international acceptance. Trade with China, Thailand and India would be sorely affected, tourism and investment would be harder to attract, and there would be a risk of another foreign exchange crisis. The considerable latitude that has already been accorded to some of the major cease-fire groups suggests that the regime is prepared to give ground in the short term, rather than risk the collapse of the delicate truce arrangements currently in place. For example, the UWSA is not only growing larger and more powerful, but it is expanding its territorial base and increasing its manufacture of narcotics for export. All these factors are adding to the frictions between Thailand and Burma.

A recurrence of the 1988 uprising or a return to the fighting of the past would cause the SPDC major problems, but it could survive. A much more worrying prospect for the regime would be a loss of loyalty and cohesion in the armed forces, its sole power base.

11.2 Challenges to Tatmadaw Unity

Historically, the Burmese armed forces have been remarkably unified by Asian standards. As Mary Callahan has pointed out,

> Over the last five decades, while the officer corps in Thailand, Indonesia, and the Philippines periodically have been torn apart by politicially mobilized factionalism, Burma's military leadership has faced no serious challenges from within the ranks.[23]

It could be claimed that this relative stability has stemmed in large part from the presence and influence of Ne Win throughout this entire period. Even now he probably serves as a brake on disruptive behaviour by key members of the armed forces. Yet the possibility of a split in the *Tatmadaw* is still a highly sensitive issue in Burma. Perhaps more than anything else, it arouses deep concerns on the part of the armed forces hierarchy. Since the 1948 mutinies, but more so since the 1962 coup, considerable efforts have been made to prevent such a problem from arising.[24]

The most potent and pervasive weapon in the regime's arsenal has been the intelligence apparatus. Through the MIS and an extensive network of uniformed officers and paid informers, the DDSI has kept a close watch not only on the civilian population but also on the members of the *Tatmadaw* itself. Senior officers have been moved around the country frequently to prevent them from building up personal followings, or individual power bases in particular geographical areas.[25] Some have been co-opted into the regime's formal political structure where they can more easily be controlled, while others have been kept away from power centres altogether, for example through diplomatic postings overseas.[26] Severe punishments have been meted out to any officers considered 'disloyal' to the regime, or who overstep the bounds of 'permissable' behaviour. For example, in 1987 over 200 young army officers were arrested for criticising the regime's handling of the economy. A large number of others were transferred.[27] In such cases, seniority does not count. In August 2000 the Deputy Minister for National Planning and Economic Development (a Brigadier with excellent prospects) was arrested when he embarrassed the regime by speaking too frankly about its economic mismanagement.[28]

On the other hand, a wide range of rewards have been bestowed on 'loyal' officers, in the way of promotions, comfortable postings, special privileges, business opportunities and other perquisites. The *Tatmadaw*'s complete domination of Burma's society and economy has permitted it to look after its own, and to encourage continued support for the military government. It is relevant that many in the armed forces leadership are connected by family, financial and other personal ties.

Since 1988, members of the regime and its supporters have constantly asserted that the *Tatmadaw* is a united and cohesive organisation free from any threat of internal fracture. For example, referring to some of the problems encountered in the past, Maung Aung Myoe has stated:

> Splits along the lines of racial background, organisational origins and political affiliations have been resolved. The gap between staff officers and field commanders has been settled. There is no discrimination against one school of graduates over another in promotion. The only problem remaining at present is succession to the top jobs.[29]

Yet this claim is worth examining closely. For, despite all the measures taken by the regime to prevent tensions from arising, credible reports of dissatisfaction and even active dissent within the armed forces continue to surface.[30] Just as in Burmese society as a whole, so in the *Tatmadaw,* any signs of pluralism or non-conformity seem to provoke a deep sense of insecurity on the part of the regime. In Burma's closed society accurate details are very difficult to obtain, but a number of broad themes keep recurring.

Ever since the 1962 coup, differences have arisen in the *Tatmadaw* over the place of the armed forces in Burmese society, and the degree to which they should exercise a political role.[31] Support for the military leadership was strong but there were frequent purges of malcontents, with particular senior officers posted abroad or forced into early retirement. Such measures were not always successful. In 1976, for example, the regime uncovered a plot by a number of disillusioned young officers to overthrow President Ne Win and take the army back to the barracks. In 1988 about 1000 relatively junior members of the armed forces, from all three Services, joined the pro-democracy demonstrations in Rangoon, calling for a return to civilian rule. At the time, one former senior *Tatmadaw* officer told the BBC that the pro-democracy movement had the support of 60 per cent of the army.[32] There was also considerable disquiet reported on the part of many soldiers who were later ordered to shoot down unarmed demonstrators, including women and children.[33] Two years later, the NLD's landslide victory in the general elections was a severe shock to the regime, not least because the overwhelming vote for the opposition forces (including in some military cantonment districts) suggested a considerable sympathy for the NLD among the armed forces, and thus the potential for a serious difference of view over the *Tatmadaw*'s future role in Burma. Despite attempts to win back the loyalties of such people, occasional rumblings of discontent can still be heard among some of the younger officers, and in the ranks.[34]

In this regard, Aung San Suu Kyi poses a particular problem for the regime. Aung San, Burma's much revered independence leader who was assassinated in 1947, was her father. He was also the founder of the Burmese armed forces who, significantly, resigned his military position in order to pursue a political career. While some in the armed forces bitterly resent her involvement in national politics, his daughter is accorded considerable respect by many in the *Tatmadaw*, and she speaks about Aung San with some authority. Ne Win has consistently (and rather obviously) tried to share Aung San's mantle as a 'co-father' of the armed forces. Yet he was in a different faction of the nationalist movement and was never nominated by Aung San to be his military successor. In July 1989 Aung San Suu Kyi referred publicly to serious differences between Ne Win and her father, a forbidden subject since the 1962 coup. She also declared that Ne Win had taken the *Tatmadaw* down a different path from that mapped out by her father. Aung San Suu Kyi appealed over the heads of the military leadership to more moderate elements in the armed forces, asking them to honour her father's memory and support her demand for a return to democratic civilian government. This implicit call for members of the *Tatmadaw* to question their own leaders seems to have been a trigger which prompted her arrest. Another senior NLD figure imprisoned at the same time was Tin Oo, a former Army Chief of Staff and Defence Minister who retained a considerable following in the armed forces.[35] The SLORC was determined to prevent any faction developing in the *Tatmadaw* which might heed the call from these two respected figures, to eschew politics and return to the barracks.[36]

There has also been considerable speculation over the internal dynamics of the ruling military hierarchy. Individual members of the SLORC and SPDC have been characterised by observers as either 'moderates' or 'hard liners', and have been held accountable for perceived shifts in the regime's policies. For example, there have been strong rumours of disagreements within the regime over the best approach to be taken towards Aung San Suu Kyi, and how to respond to the pressures being applied against the regime by members of the international community.[37] The so-called 'moderates', reportedly led by DDSI chief LTGEN Khin Nyunt, were initially believed to have lost out to the 'hardliners' (led by Army Commander-in-Chief GEN Maung Aye) in their wish to soften Burma's image abroad. After Aung San Suu Kyi's unexpected release from house arrest and Burma's application to join ASEAN, the 'moderates' were felt to be in the ascendant. Incidents like the attack on Aung San Suu Kyi's motorcade by a violent mob in late 1996 were interpreted as attempts by the hardliners to reassert their control over the policy debate.[38] The regime's heightened campaign since mid-1999 to destroy the NLD's national infrastructure and reduce its membership prompted speculation of a reversion to hardline tactics. The secret discussions held between the SPDC and Aung San Suu Kyi which began in late 1999, however, have suggested to many a return to the approach favoured by the 'moderates'.

The apparent manoeuvering of these factions within the military hierarchy has also been connected with the postings of particular senior officers to positions either of influence or obscurity. The diplomatic community in Rangoon, for example, thrives on theories about what such changes might mean in terms of support for individual members of the ruling Council. Speculation of this kind is commonplace in Burma's closed society, however, and rumours of factionalism are very difficult to confirm. In any case, the purported distinction between 'moderates' and 'hardliners' should not be overrated, nor obscure the fact that all members of Burma's military hierarchy share a number of core beliefs. Policy disagreements and personal differences clearly exist in the highest circles of the *Tatmadaw*, and favours are doubtless dispensed with some return in mind, but it is unlikely that any major decision would be taken, or taken in such a manner, which would seriously threaten armed forces unity. This would apply not only to questions of broad government policy, but more so to central issues like who should succeed the ailing SENGEN Than Shwe. Much has been made of the apparent rivalry between Khin Nyunt and Maung Aye, but neither are likely to risk — or be permitted to risk — a serious fracture in the armed forces simply to gain the top position.[39]

Over the years, other issues have arisen with the potential to cause internal problems for the *Tatmadaw*. One persistent theme has been that of centre-periphery tensions. Both before and after 1988 there were reports of resentment and antagonism between the (often younger and more junior) officers on active service in the field and those officers assigned to more comfortable administrative or political duties in rear areas. This problem has persisted, despite the practice of rotating field officers through staff positions in places like the Defence Ministry.[40] While these tensions may not be unusual in themselves, since 1988 the much greater difference between the hardships experienced by front line troops in Burma and the opportunities for corruption and personal profits in the rear, have given this issue added significance.[41] These tensions have a parallel in the difficult relationship which developed in the mid-1990s between members of the SLORC and the Regional Commanders. After 1988 the demise of the BSPP and the lapse of earlier posting policies permitted the Regional Commanders virtually to become semi-independent warlords, wielding considerable political and economic power in their respective fiefdoms.[42] The purge of corrupt Ministers from the SLORC in 1997, its reorganisation as the SPDC, and the related rotation of Regional Commander positions, was clearly an attempt by the *Tatmadaw* leadership to re-assert firm central control.[43] Whether or not this move is successful remains to be seen, but the decision not to divide the much larger *Tatmadaw* into two separate armies (designated Irrawaddy East and Irrawaddy West) suggests that there are still fears of serious rivalries emerging.[44]

There have also been persistent reports of suspicion and rivalry between the graduates of Burma's Defence Services Academy and the Officer Training School.[45] These differences were made worse by the 1976 plot against Ne Win, which was felt to have sprung from members of a particular DSA class. For a long time this led to a reluctance by the *Tatmadaw* leadership to appoint DSA graduates to senior positions. As Bertil Lintner has pointed out, this discrimination was something which in itself led to further tensions within the Burma Army officer corps.[46] For a while the heat seemed to go out of this issue, as the rapid expansion of the BA after 1988 created a greater demand for experienced officers and opened up promotion opportunities. However, there are now increasing reports of senior figures in the regime attempting to strengthen their personal power bases by appointing DSA or OTS alumni to positions of influence. For example, after 1995 the number of DSA graduates in key positions has risen markedly. In 1999, 45 of the *Tatmadaw*'s 88 most senior commanders were from the Academy. It has been suggested that this is part of a deliberate strategy by GEN Maung Aye (a member of the DSA's first intake) to outflank his rival, LTGEN Khin Nyunt (a graduate of OTS class 25), before the regime's most senior position is filled again.[47]

In addition, tensions appear to have arisen between those officers who owe their promotions primarily to their ties with Ne Win, and those who have followed a more professional career path. To a large extent, control over the government and armed forces is no longer exercised by the ageing Ne Win, and his standing among the younger generation in the *Tatmadaw* is not as great as it once may have been.[48] There are now many in the ranks who do not consider the armed forces a professional career. As an historical figure prominent in Burma's early struggles against ethnic and ideological insurgents, however, and later Chief of the country's armed forces, the 'Old Man', or 'Number One', still commands a degree of respect and loyalty in military circles. More importantly, he has for many years seeded the army with like-minded protégés, many of whom, like LTGEN Khin Nyunt, now hold powerful positions. It has been suggested that many senior *Tatmadaw* officers, including some at the highest levels, resent the power currently held by Khin Nyunt, because of his political connections and lack of combat experience.[49] Ne Win is now old and infirm, and his power is on the wane. Until his death, however, he will continue to exercise influence over the regime's policies and act, even if only passively, to protect his favourites.

The antagonism felt towards Khin Nyunt is exacerbated by the suspicion which has customarily been directed towards all professional intelligence officers in the *Tatmadaw*. They have often been credited with more influence than they have in fact held, but there has long been a feeling in the armed forces that members of the DDSI and MIS enjoy too much independence and wield too much power. The periodic purges of the Intelligence Corps under Ne Win were apparently prompted by the fear that this power might be directed against his own position. Since 1988 parallels have been drawn between Khin Nyunt and ambitious CNIs in the past. There have even been suggestions that GEN Maung Aye is trying to develop his own independent intelligence capabilities, so that he is not dependent for information and gossip on an apparatus that owes its first loyalty to his rival.[50] At a more prosaic level, Regional Commanders have resented the fact that MIS units report direct to Rangoon without going through the normal chain of command. Intelligence officers also suffer from the fact that they are charged with monitoring the political reliability of the armed forces themselves, a role that is hardly likely to endear them to their colleagues. Awareness of these tensions probably underlies some of the differences perceived to exist between the 'moderate' 'intelligence faction' (led by LTGEN Khin Nyunt), and the 'hard line' 'army faction' (led by GEN Maung Aye).

Maung Aung Myoe has stated that 'Rivalry between the three Services of the *Tatmadaw* has been eliminated'. Yet, in this area too, tensions are still apparent.[51]

The Burma Army has always been accepted as the senior Service but there were, and still are, real antagonisms between the army and the other two Services. Some of this ill-feeling stems from their different historical traditions. During the early days of the nationalist struggle, the navy and air force were seen to be on the wrong side. The two 'technical' Services tended to rely on the Anglo-Burmese community and ethnic minorities (notably the Karens) for their recruits. During the Second World War most Burmese members of the air force and navy supported the Allies, in direct contrast to the army which was dominated by Burma's anti-colonial, and for a period pro-Japanese, nationalist movement.[52] Despite the manifest efforts of the BAF and BN to support the Union government after 1948, they retained many British characteristics which were viewed with suspicion by Ne Win and the other Japanese-trained army officers around him. It is relevant too that the navy and air force tended to recruit better educated men from urban areas, and send them overseas for training, whereas the army has traditionally relied on poorly educated rural youths trained mainly in Burma. The fact that the army has always been accorded priority in the distribution of resources has also caused resentment.

Since 1988 an effort has been made to redress some of these problems, for example through shared officer training programs and the greater resources now available to the navy and air force. The differences which remain, however, seem to go well beyond the inter-Service rivalries which are traditional in the armed forces of other countries. These feelings can only be exacerbated by incidents like the dismissal of the BN Commander-in-Chief and 17 other senior naval officers in August 2000.[53]

Aggravating the ethnic tensions apparent in the *Tatmadaw* is the regime's long-held vision of the future state of Burma, which is overwhelmingly Burman and Buddhist. Soon after Independence, the Commander-in-Chief of the *Tatmadaw* and Burma Police Force, an experienced and highly professional Karen soldier named Smith Dun, was removed by Prime Minister Nu out of a misplaced concern over his loyalty to the Union.[54] He was replaced by his deputy, Ne Win. Ever since then, members of the minority ethnic peoples have found it very difficult to rise to senior positions in the armed forces. As David Steinberg has noted, 'there is now no senior member of the Burmese military ruling elite who comes from a minority. This "Burmanization" has been one of the major social changes under the military'.[55] A few Sino-Burmese (including Ne Win himself) and Anglo-Burmese in the officer corps have constituted the exceptions which prove the rule. As with being Burman, the regime also equates loyalty with being Buddhist. Muslims and Christians are actively discouraged from joining the *Tatmadaw*. Those that do so suffer discrimination in the ranks, and any who wish to rise above the middle ranks are strongly encouraged to convert to Buddhism. During the 1990s there was only one non-Buddhist at the ministerial level, and that person was the only non-Buddhist flag officer.[56]

After 1988 some new tensions have arisen. One obvious source is the regime's more relaxed recruitment policies and the loosening of controls on the behaviour of senior officers. The lowering of age, health and other standards, for example, has been resented by the more committed and professional members of the *Tatmadaw*. There is also a strong perception that, of those now volunteering for military service, fewer are joining out of a genuine sense of patriotism. Rather, they seem to be signing up purely to gain access to the power and privileges attached to *Tatmadaw* membership. It has been widely claimed that there has been a significant increase in the proportion of poorly educated, self-interested and unscrupulous men in both the officer corps and the ranks.[57] A very high proportion of officer candidates now come from military families, leading to accusations of preferment and favouritism.[58] Also, the greatly increased civil and administrative powers of army officers over local communities has expanded the scope for corruption and selective patronage. The occasional practice of selling promotions has caused considerable resentment. In conditions of service, the gap between the higher ranks and the lower ranks of the *Tatmadaw* are now greater than ever.[59] All these problems have eroded discipline, weakened personal commitment and further undermined the *Tatmadaw*'s professionalism. This trend is of particular concern to those in the armed forces with higher ethical standards, many of whom have reportedly resigned rather than serve in an institution where such practices are openly tolerated.[60]

In addition, there seems to be considerable unease in the *Tatmadaw* over the degree of Chinese influence which has been allowed to develop in the country. The SLORC's decision to turn to China for diplomatic, military and economic support after 1988 was probably unanimous. Indeed, given the widespread international condemnation of the regime, the imposition of arms embargoes and the withdrawal of aid and international finance, it was felt that there were few other options. As one leading SLORC figure put it,

> What military supplies that are necessary must be provided. When you need them, you have to buy at the right price. Previously we bought from all over the world but now some Western countries don't want to sell to us, so we have to go to those who will....[61]

It was also an arrangement that China welcomed and facilitated. Yet most in the *Tatmadaw* are intensely nationalistic, and there are reportedly strong differences over the degree to which Burma has come to rely on China, the country which only a few years before was aiding the CPB. Such concerns have been exacerbated by the negative social impact of the regime's 'open door' economic policies, which have led to a flood of Chinese settlers and businessmen establishing themselves in northern Burma.[62] While disagreements on this issue within the regime appear to be contained, there have been reports of continuing suspicion in the leadership over China's long-term motives, as well as dissatisfaction at lower levels. On occasion, this may have gone beyond the usual grumbling about the indifferent quality of Chinese arms and equipment. In 1992, for example, an assassination plot was hatched against LTGEN Khin Nyunt, apparently on the grounds that he was the prime architect of Burma's pro-China policy.[63]

These reports of tensions in the *Tatmadaw* constitute a potentially explosive problem in a country where the unity and loyalty of the armed forces is deemed essential for political power and continued control over all the disparate elements of the Union. The air force and navy could do little on their own to shake the foundations of the state, but a major split in the ranks of the army, for any of the reasons cited above, would lead to very serious problems for the military regime. There are a number of compelling reasons, however, why a major split of this kind is unlikely to occur.[64]

Of central importance is the fact that there are many in the armed forces, at all levels, who sincerely believe the regime's oft-repeated claim that the *Tatmadaw* alone has been responsible for maintaining Burma's independence and unity since 1948. The danger of a breakaway by some of the ethnic minorities, for example, was held up as the main reason for the military overthrow of Nu's government in 1962.[65] The same fears remain. In the minds of many officers and their men, the loss of control caused by a serious split in the armed forces would be disastrous for Burma. The possible consequences range from a resurgence of popular unrest in the main population centres to increased ethnic insurgent activity in the countryside. In extreme circumstances, a mutiny by a large part of the army (as occurred in 1948) could lead to another civil war, or even the fragmentation of the country. This message has been reinforced by the regime since 1988, with repeated appeals to nationalist sentiment and military tradition. It has been underlined by constant reminders of all those members of the *Tatmadaw* who have fallen in battle fighting for the Union.[66] At the same time, the regime has claimed that the NLD, supported as it is by ethnic parties and purportedly left wing groups, would squander the country's hard-won independence and be unable to control the diverse political forces that would be let loose under a civilian government. In addition, it is claimed, the NLD would hand Burma over to foreign political and economic interests. Acceptance of such claims may not in itself prevent differences from arising within the *Tatmadaw*, but it would be a strong factor militating against a major breakdown in discipline.

In addition, many members of the armed forces appear to be afraid that, should they lose control of their own fate, they will be forced to face the consequences of their harsh rule over the past 38 years.[67] Since Ne Win seized power, the military regime has been repeatedly condemned for its gross violations of human rights, with many neutral observers describing it as one of the most brutal in the world.[68] During the 1988 demonstrations, and again after the 1990 elections, there were numerous calls by students and pro-democracy figures (including NLD Chairman Kyi Maung) for members of the regime to be brought before tribunals of the kind convened to judge war criminals after the Second World War.[69] There have even been demands for members of the SLORC and SPDC to be tried by the international community *in absentia*, as has occurred with respect to crimes against humanity in the former Republic of Yugoslavia. More recently, the trial of former ROK President Chun Doo-hwan, and the attempts to bring Chile's General Augusto Pinochet to trial, have reminded senior Burmese military figures that, even years after the event, they can still be called to account for past misdeeds. Given the inevitable outcome of such trials, there is little likelihood that any members of the current armed forces hierarchy would willingly permit anything to occur which might put them in such a vulnerable position.

It is relevant too that many members of the Burmese armed forces (in particular its most senior officers) have long enjoyed considerable social and financial privileges, as the regime has tried to retain their loyalty and protect them from the results of its own economic mismanagement. Pay scales have been less of an incentive, although in August 1988, in an obvious attempt to purchase the support of the rank and file of the armed forces in the face of rising popular unrest, President Sein Lwin awarded the *Tatmadaw* a 45% pay rise.[70] In April 2000 a pay increase of up to 600% was approved, for many of the same reasons.[71] In addition, a large number of military officers have profited directly from the regime's 'open door' economic policies. Many have acquired strong financial interests in the commercial ventures which the regime has negotiated with companies from Thailand, Singapore, the ROK and elsewhere, and have used their positions to invest in businesses of their own.[72] Corruption existed in the *Tatmadaw* before 1988, but over the past decade it has reached unprecedented levels. A major split in the armed forces, particularly one which might lead to a civilian government, would not only risk the loss of many customary privileges and benefits, but in many cases would occasion considerable personal costs as well.

It has sometimes been suggested that the greatest threat to the regime will be from a revolt of 'young Turks' within the *Tatmadaw*'s officer corps. Observers cite the hardships endured by these officers, their resentment at the disparities between ranks, and their frustration at the failure of the military hierarchy to solve the country's many ills. Not all would wish to replace the current system, but many would like to make it work better. Yet, if such a movement exists, the obstacles to these officers achieving their aims are considerable. Burma's government and armed forces are very hierarchical. Most decisions are made at the very highest level, in Rangoon. Regional Commanders occupy the lowest level at which independent decisions of any importance can be made outside the capital. Military discipline is strong, and rigorously enforced. This leaves little scope for relatively junior officers (who command companies or battalions at most) to gather support across the country, and coordinate their actions, let alone mobilise any military units. Besides, communications links are monitored carefully, and the MIS is always on the alert for signs of organised discontent.[73]

Despite some appearances (and the regime's persistent claims), Burma's armed forces are not monolithic. Rather, they are a collection of finely balanced institutional and personal loyalties. Over the past 38 years considerable pains have been taken to manage these often conflicting pressures, to ensure that major ructions do not occur. Under the SPDC, rivalries may exist, policy differences within the leadership may become highly charged, and Ne Win's death could even lead to a spill of positions, but for a number of reasons a major split in the armed forces is still unlikely. The bonds that tie the members of the regime together are currently stronger than the issues which divide them. In particular, the potential consequences of such a split would be well known and would help inhibit any moves which might cause such a development to occur.

11.3 Burma and Military Rule

Given what appears to be the rather ad hoc nature of policy making in Rangoon, and the country's unpredictable economic fortunes, the regime's plans have doubtless been revised and amended many times over the past 12 years. As far as the military hierarchy is concerned, however, the future of the *Tatmadaw* is not in doubt. It may be facing problems which threaten to slow down or possibly even derail the continued expansion and modernisation of the armed forces, but the SPDC has given a number of clear signs that it is still determined to continue along its current broad direction.

In his keynote speech at successive Armed Forces Day celebrations, SPDC Chairman Senior General Than Shwe has emphasised the continued development of the armed forces. For example, he has stated:

> We must build our *Tatmadaw* to be a strong, capable and modern one to be able to discharge these [political, economic and social] duties successfully and defend the nation to ensure its existence till eternity. In other words, to be strong, capable and modern is the goal of our *Tatmadaw*.[74]

> In terms of strength, [the *Tatmadaw*] should have adequate manpower and materials.[75]

> To be a *Tatmadaw* which is capable of defending a peaceful, modern and prosperous nation, it is essential to be modern, strong and highly capable.... History has taught us a great lesson that our nation was subjugated because we lacked a modern *Tatmadaw*.[76]

There is a firm belief that 'only if the Armed Force is strong, will the Nation be strong'.[77] From these and other statements along the same lines, it is clear that the armed forces will continue to get the lion's share of the country's resources. This will permit not only further improvements in the *Tatmadaw*'s order of battle and fighting capabilities, but also the consolidation of its political power and the militarisation of Burmese society.

Despite claims by one of the SPDC's official spokesmen that 'Myanmar's arms purchases have slowed to a trickle', there is little evidence that the regime has abandoned its ambitious arms acquisition program.[78] To the contrary, in a speech at the Defence Services Academy in Maymyo on 8 April 1999, SENGEN Than Shwe declared that Burma would continue to acquire 'high technology or state-of-the-art weaponry and other modernisation' to ensure that the *Tatmadaw* could 'measure up to armies around the world'.[79] For example, the navy still hopes to acquire a number of ocean minesweepers and possibly another 10 patrol boats, all from China, and plans are in place to produce more locally-built vessels.[80] The air force is still actively pursuing orders for additional fighter-interceptors and tactical strike fighters, assault helicopters, transports and training aircraft, mainly from China and Russia. Also being sought are dual-use air traffic control systems and ground-to-air communication systems.[81] The army has plans to buy light anti-tank weapons and medium range anti-armour missiles, 3-D air-space surveillance radars and radio trunk communications.[82] The Defence Ministry is pursuing the installation of a sophisticated military satellite communications network to cover the entire country. As far as personnel is concerned, the regime may be struggling to reach its earlier target of 500,000 but, as one source has put it, 'Downsizing the *Tatmadaw* is not an option for the foreseeable future'.[83] Burma's defence industries are to be expanded to produce 'high-tech weapons for use in electronic warfare'.[84]

Whether all these plans will eventually go ahead, and when, remains to be seen. After some modest growth in the mid-1990s, Burma once again faces serious economic problems. Despite the reassurances of senior regime figures, these problems look set to continue for some time. The early rush of foreign investment in tourism and light manufacturing industries generated by the SLORC's market-oriented reforms has practically dried up, partly as a result of poor economic management by the regime and partly as a result of the Asian financial crisis.[85] Although Burma remains heavily dependent on its agricultural exports, these have been badly hit by a succession of natural disasters. Also, as long as it refuses to improve its human rights record, Burma will continue to face a suspension of foreign aid (from most major donors, at least) and an effective ban on international financial flows from organisations like the World Bank and Asian Development Bank. Yet, the SPDC is still devoting a large proportion of the national budget to Defence — officially 34 per cent of CGE in the 1999/2000 financial year, but more like 44 per cent in reality.[86] The SPDC may be trying to resist the temptation of further Chinese assistance, but this would only constitute a problem if the regime intends to repay its debts, or if it cannot persuade Beijing eventually to renounce them.[87]

Broadly speaking, the quality of the Burmese armed forces is likely to continue to grow. Progress may be slow in some particular areas, and it may take time for the three Services to learn how to use their new weapon systems to the greatest effect, but technical problems can be overcome and new operating procedures can be learnt. In some areas, the *Tatmadaw* has a well-deserved reputation for adaptability and improvisation. Measures are also being taken to 'nurture highly proficient human resources' and to 'give personnel of the Armed Forces comprehensive training in the strategy and tactics of conventional warfare and from there to proceed to advanced methods of modern warfare'.[88] Academic standards at the *Tatmadaw*'s higher level training institutions are to be upgraded.[89] Despite continuing problems, the quality of core personnel can be expected gradually to improve. Already the closure of other avenues of education and social advancement has forced many young Burmese to consider a military career. There is likely to be a restructuring of the armed forces to provide better support to the fighting units, on which the regime depends for its survival. A number of foreign governments seem prepared — albeit covertly — to assist in this process. Unless the government changes, the outlook is for the *Tatmadaw* slowly to become a bigger, more modern and more capable defence force. The overall trend is thus for the more proficient use of military force, against a wider range of potential adversaries.

There is also the critical political dimension to consider. For a much stronger, better equipped and more efficiently managed *Tatmadaw* gives the SPDC greater means to consolidate its political power, exercise continued control over the economy and, even more than at present, to shape and manipulate Burmese society.

The armed forces' increased strength will permit the regime to enforce its will over the country in a way never before possible. Indeed, the *Tatmadaw*'s greater size and military capabilities, combined with the shrewd management of various ethnic and narcotics-based insurgent groups, already means that (formally at least) the central government's writ runs over more of Burma than at any time since it regained its independence in 1948.[90] Having achieved this aim, it is unlikely that the SPDC or any successor military regime would willingly allow large tracts of the country once again to be removed completely from its control. However, any lasting solution to Burma's complex ethnic problems will depend to a large degree on the willingness and ability of the *Tatmadaw* to countenance some sort of political compromise. A continuing insistence by the regime on a strong central government in Rangoon dominated by ethnic Burmans, at the expense of any power-sharing arrangements with minority racial groups, will inevitably see a return to the bitter and costly fighting of the past.

The nature of Burmese society too is changing. The regime has sought to neutralise concerns within its ranks and encourage a commitment to military rule by effectively isolating the armed forces from the rest of the population and insulating them against the kinds of pressures which most of their civilian compatriots feel. The net effect of this policy has been to create a virtual state within a state, with the members of the *Tatmadaw*, their relatives and supporters constituting a privileged caste within Burmese society. Even more than was the case under the BSPP, the armed forces now have their own exclusive social order, their own well-funded educational institutions, their own modern health facilities, their own cultural organisations, their own internal support mechanisms and retirement funds, all of which tend to be spared the restrictions and closures suffered by their civilian equivalents.[91] Outside this charmed circle the rest of the population is alienated and disenfranchised, their lives controlled by a plethora of laws and regulations which restrict almost every aspect of their behaviour. They suffer a lack of fundamental human rights, economic hardship and deteriorating communal services. The development of an autonomous civil society (as it is known in the West) seems remote, and the election of a more representative government an unlikely prospect.[92]

The creation of a privileged caste of military personnel seems designed to ensure the loyalty of those on whom the regime currently depends for its position, while creating a new generation of military leaders prepared to carry the process forward. Yet, by relying on the armed forces to guarantee the country's unity and stability, the regime has mortgaged Burma's vast and diverse political, economic and social resources to continued dependence on military strength. The future stability and prosperity of the country will depend not so much on the capacity of the armed forces to crush dissent and physically eliminate its opponents, but rather on its willingness to contemplate a future for the country in which the *Tatmadaw* does not have first call on its resources and is not the sole source of political power.

Notes

1. Its nearest rival, Singapore, only spent about half as much, in proportional terms. DIO, *Defence Economic Trends in the Asia-Pacific Region*, 1999, p. 47.
2. *World Military Expenditures and Arms Transfers 1998*, p. 3.
3. Burma had a ratio of 1 serviceman/woman to every 200 people. The equivalent Thai ratio was 1:210 and the Australian ratio was 1:236. *The Military Balance 1988-1989*, pp. 159-60. See also Khin Nyunt, 'The Tatmadaw as Preserver of the Union'; and interview, Rangoon, April, 1995.
4. See *The Military Balance 2000/2001* for comparisons; and Singh, 'Growth of Military Power in South-East Asia', p. 313.
5. Wain, 'Myanmar Military Growth Worries The Neighbours'.
6. Sivard, *World Military and Social Expenditures, 1987-88*, p. 48.
7. See, for example, William Dowell, 'Allies but not Friends', *Time*, 29 May 1995, p. 32. The 'tooth to tail' ratio is the proportion of men and women in front line combat units compared with those in rear-echelon support roles. It is thus one measure of the fighting efficiency of a country's armed forces.
8. See, for example, Graeme Cheeseman and Richard Leaver, *Trends in Arms Spending and Conventional Arms Trade in the Asia-Pacific Region*, Working Paper No. 32 (Australian Defence Studies Centre, Australian Defence Force Academy, Canberra, 1995).
9. Tin Maung Maung Than, 'Neither Inheritance nor Legacy', p. 60, note 127.
10. For example, until 1991, the daughter of former Prime Minister Nu was permitted to make broadcasts critical of the SLORC over All India Radio. Interview, New Delhi, May 1995. See also 'The Indian Connection', *Asiaweek*, 6 April 1990, p. 23.
11. Wain, 'Myanmar Military Growth Worries The Neighbours'.
12. Interviews, Rangoon, April 1995, and Washington, February 2001.
13. See, for example, Rolls, 'Thailand's Post Cold-War Security Policy and Defence Programme', *Contemporary Security Policy*, pp. 101-3; and 'Thai General warns of Burma Army expansion', *Bangkok Post*, 7 January 2000.
14. For an earlier discussion of this issue, see Taylor, *The State in Burma*.
15. *Burma/Myanmar: How Strong is the Military Regime?*, International Crisis Group (ICG), Asia Report No. 11, 21 December 2000, p. ii.
16. See, for example, Bertil Linter, 'Arrested Development', *FEER*, 2 March 1995, pp. 28-9.
17. Interviews, Bangkok, April 1995. See also Anderson, *Guerrillas*, pp. 159-62.
18. See, for example, William Ashton, ' "Charm offensive" working', *Asia-Pacific Defence Reporter*, Vol. 21, No. 6/7, December 1994/January 1995, pp. 41-3.
19. *Burma/Myanmar: How Strong is the Military Regime?*, p. ii.
20. The ICG has listed a number of 'actual and potential sources of vulnerability' which it believes the regime suffers. Most of these conditions have existed since 1988, however, and while some could cause the regime serious problems none are likely in themselves to bring about its collapse. *Burma/Myanmar: How Strong is the Military Regime?*, pp. 20-40.

21. See, for example, Bertil Lintner, *Aung San Suu Kyi and Burma's Unfinished Renaissance* (Peacock Press, Bangkok, 1990); and Josef Silverstein, 'Aung San Suu Kyi: Is She Burma's Woman of Destiny?', *Asian Survey*, Vol. 30, No. 10, October 1990, pp. 1007-19. Aung San Suu Kyi's own philosophy can be found in *Freedom From Fear and other writings*, ed. Michael Aris (Penguin, London, 1991), *Letters from Burma* (Penguin, London, 1997), and *The Voice of Hope* (Penguin, London, 1997).

22. 'Suu Kyi pledges to fight', *Canberra Times*, 4 December 1995; and 'Myanmar: No Talking Here', *Asiaweek*, 8 December 1995, p. 40.

23. Callahan notes, however, that serious intra-army tensions arose in 1958 and 1976. Mary P. Callahan, 'Cracks in the Edifice? Military-Society Relations in Burma Since 1988', in Pedersen, Rudland and May, *Burma/Myanmar: Strong Regime, Weak State?*, p. 47.

24. See, for example, Bertil Lintner, 'Purges and spies make army Ne Win's hardest asset', *FEER*, 22 September 1988, p. 16. See also 'Masses in revolt against stifling authoritarian grip', pp. 12-13.

25. See, for example, Callahan, 'Cracks in the Edifice?', pp. 39-40.

26. After 1988, for example, the number of *Tatmadaw* officers appointed to the most senior government positions expanded from 21 to 64. This number was reduced by the SPDC, but all Regional Military Commanders are now full members of the ruling Council.

27. 'Reining in the majors', p. 14.

28. Bertil Lintner, 'Burmese Rifts', *FEER*, 5 October 2000, p. 15.

29. Maung Aung Myoe, *Building the Tatmadaw*, p. 31.

30. Interviews, Rangoon, November and December 2000.

31. For a discussion of the growth of professionalism in the *Tatmadaw*, see Lissak, *Military Roles in Modernisation*, pp. 155ff and Callahan, 'The Origins of Military Rule in Burma', *passim*.

32. Admittedly, this was General Tin Oo, by that time a senior figure in the opposition NLD. See Lintner, 'Backdown or bloodbath', p. 14; Stewart, 'Now a Coup', p. 14; and Smith, *Burma: Insurgency and the Politics of Ethnicity*, p. 10.

33. Bertil Lintner, 'Dissent in the Ranks', *FEER*, 17 August 1989, p. 22.

34. See, for example, 'Junior officers in Burma to face military tribunal for supporting NLD', DVB (in Burmese), 1 September 2000.

35. Bertil Lintner, 'Sowing the wind', *FEER*, 3 August 1989, pp. 11-12; and Rodney Tasker, 'Haunting Memories', *FEER*, 13 July 1989, p. 30.

36. The senior NLD leadership consists of a number of retired senior army officers. They are now dismissed by the regime as a 'disgruntled faction' which was 'pushed out' of the *Tatmadaw*. Interview, Rangoon, December 1999.

37. See, for example, 'Statement by Dr Josef Silverstein', 7 September 1995.

38. See, for example, 'Suu Kyi's convoy attacked', *Canberra Times*, 11 November 1996; and 'Myanmar faces new criticism over Aung San Suu Kyi attack', *Asian Defence Journal*, December 1996, p. 64.

39. See, for example, Robert Horn, 'Two to Tangle', *Time*, 18 December 2000.

40. LTGEN Khin Nyunt is an exception to this rule.

41. See, for example, 'Reining in the Majors', p. 14; and V.G. Kulkarni, 'Straining at the seams', *FEER*, 7 July 1988, pp. 16-18.

42. M.P. Callahan, 'Junta Dreams or Nightmares? Observations of Burma's Military Since 1988', *Bulletin of Concerned Asian Scholars*, Vol. 31, No. 3, 1999, pp. 52-8. See also Maung Aung Myoe, *The Tatmadaw in Myanmar*, p. 17.

43. Callahan, 'Cracks in the Edifice?', p. 39.

44. Steinberg, *Burma: The State of Myanmar*, p. 66, note 28.

45. See Bunge, *Burma*, pp. 252-3; Lintner, 'Burma - Struggle for Power', pp. 466-71; and Bertil Lintner, 'Simple Soldiers', *FEER*, 1 July 1993, p. 24.

46. Ironically, the plot was led by an OTS graduate. See Lintner, 'Burma - Struggle for Power', pp. 466-71; and Bertil Lintner, 'Myanmar's influential chief may be losing power', *JDW*, 12 June 1993, p. 29.

47. Maung Aung Myoe, *The Tatmadaw in Myanmar Since 1988*, p. 18.

48. One *Tatmadaw* source is reported to have stated that less than 25% of the armed forces feel any personal loyalty to Ne Win. See Lintner, 'Dissent in the ranks', p. 22.

49. See, for example, Bertil Lintner, 'Cracks in the rock', *FEER*, 24 October 1991, p. 11-12; and Lintner, 'Dissent in the ranks', p. 22.

50. 'Power play', *FEER*, 12 June 1997, p. 12.

51. Maung Aung Myoe, *Building the Tatmadaw*, pp. 21-2 and pp. 30-1; See also Maung Aung Myoe, *The Tatmadaw in Myanmar Since 1988*, pp. 18-19.

52. Personal communication, Mary Callahan to the author, 10 November 1995.

53. Lintner, 'Burmese Rifts', p. 15.

54. See Smith Dun, *Memoirs of the Four-Foot Colonel*, Data Paper No. 113, Southeast Asia Program (Cornell University, Ithaca, 1980).

55. Steinberg, *Burma: The State of Myanmar*, p. 73.

56. Steinberg, *Burma: The State of Myanmar*, p. 94.

57. Interviews, Mandalay, November 1996, and Washington, February 2000. See also Callahan, 'Cracks in the Edifice', p. 32.

58. Steinberg has pointed out that about 80% of DSA students are the children of present or retired military officers, or their influential friends. Steinberg, *Burma: The State of Myanmar*, p. 92.

59. See, for example, 'Defence Services concerned about unrest, issue free army rations', *Burma News Update*, September 1999, pp. 9-10. Also, interview, Mandalay, November 1996.

60. Interviews, Rangoon, April 1995; Mandalay, November 1996; and Rangoon, November and December 1999. See also Fink, *Living Silence*, pp. 143-58.

61. Khin Nyunt, 'The Tatmadaw as Preserver of the Union'.

62. These immigrants enter the country both legally and illegally. Interview and personal observation, Maymyo, November 1996. See also Mya Maung, 'On the Road to Mandalay', pp. 447-59.

63. 'Killers cooled?', *Asiaweek*, 27 November 1992, p. 43; and Bertil Lintner, 'Murmur in the ranks', *FEER*, 18 February 1993, p. 20. See also Lintner, 'Myanmar's Chinese connection', p. 23.

64. William Ashton, 'Fearful army blocks transfer of power', *Asia-Pacific Defence Reporter*, Vol. 17, No. 6/7, December 1990/January 1991, pp. 52-4.

65. Dr Maung Maung, *Burma and General Ne Win* (Asia Publishing House, Bombay, 1969), p. 291.

66. While some observers have put the total number of casualties from armed conflict in Burma between 1948-1995 at about 21,000, the number is clearly much larger. After the 1988 takeover, SLORC Chairman SENGEN Saw Maung put the figure at around one million. This is much closer to the real figure, which will probably never be known. R.L. Sivard, *World Military and Social Expenditures 1996*, p. 19; and interview, Washington, February 2000.

67. See, for example, Alan Boyd, 'Burma junta fears probe of massacre', *The Australian*, 30 May 1990.

68. See, for example, 'The World's Most Repressive Regimes', report by Freedom House to the 57th Session of the UN High Commission on Human Rights, Geneva, March 2001, extract in *BurmaNet News*, 5 April 2001.

69. 'We'll play fair', *Asiaweek*, 13 July 1990, p. 28; and 'Staying Cool', *Asiaweek*, 22 June 1990, p. 21.

70. Daniel Benjamin et al, 'Out...In 17 Days', *Time*, 22 August 1988, p. 21.
71. 'Myanmar forces get pay hike', AFP, 2 April 2000: and 'Pay increase for the Myanmar forces', *JDW*, 26 April 2000.
72. See, for example, John Badgley, 'The Burmese Way to Capitalism', in *Southeast Asian Affairs 1990* (Institute for Southeast Asian Studies, Singapore, 1990), pp. 229-39; and Callahan, 'Cracks in the Edifice', pp. 47-8.
73. Interviews, Singapore and Rangoon, November 1999.
74. Senior General Than Shwe, Address on the 51st Anniversary of Armed Forces Day, Rangoon, 27 March 1996. Embassy of the Union of Myanmar, Canberra, *Newsletter* No. Sp. A/96, 4 April 1996, p. 1.
75. Senior General Than Shwe, Speech given on Armed Forces Day (27 March 1997?), cited in Brooke, 'The Armed Forces of Myanmar', p. 13.
76. Senior General Than Shwe, Address on the 54th Anniversary of Armed Forces Day, Rangoon, 27 March 1999. Embassy of the Union of Myanmar, Canberra, *Newsletter* 6/99, 9 April 1999, p. 1.
77. Thein Swe, 'Human Resource Development in Nation Building', p. 155.
78. 'Official: Burma Completes Military Buildup'.
79. 'Junta to buy hi-tech arms', *Bangkok Post*, 9 April 1999. See also Thein Swe, 'Human Resource Development in Nation Building', p. 160.
80. Selth, 'The Burma Navy Under the SLORC', pp. 227-47.
81. 'Myanmar', *Asian Defence Journal*, Asian Defence Yearbook 1998-1999, p. 106.
82. *Ibid*.
83. Maung Aung Myoe, *Building the Tatmadaw*, p. 30.
84. 'Defence Industries to Produce High-Tech Weapons', *BurmaNet News*, 16 April 2001.
85. Barry Wain, 'Yangon's Socialism Leads to Village Misery', *Asian Wall Street Journal*, 16 April 1999. See also Roger Mitton, 'Hard Times in Yangon', *Asiaweek*, 3 April 1998, pp. 26-8.
86. 'Junta Chief Promises New High-Tech Weaponry', *Burma News Update*, April 1999, p. 4; and DIO, *Defence Economic Trends in the Asia-Pacific Region*, 1999, p. 47.
87. The SPDC reportedly turned down an offered credit of US$100 million for additional arms purchases. Anthony Davis, 'Burma casts wary eye on China', *Jane's Intelligence Review*, Vol. 11, No. 6, June 1999, p. 41. Also, interview, Rangoon, November 1999.
88. 'Junta to buy hi-tech arms'; and Thein Swe, 'Human Resource Development in Nation Building', p. 160.
89. 'Junta Chief Promises New High-Tech Weaponry'.
90. See, for example, Merrill, 'Burma looks set to reject the lessons of history'.
91. Without continuing official patronage, forced membership and the lure of special privileges, the USDA would quickly disappear. See Steinberg, 'Mobilizing the Masses', and Steinberg, *Burma: The State of Myanmar*, pp. 98-115.
92. See, for example, David I. Steinberg, 'A Void in Myanmar: Civil Society in Burma', in Burma Netherlands and Transnational Institute (eds), *Strengthening Civil Society in Burma: Possibilities and Dilemmas for International NGOs* (Silkworm Books, Chiang Mai, 1999), pp. 1-14.

12

The Tatmadaw in a Democracy

> It is important that in the building up of the Defence Forces of Burma, Burmese opinion should be fully consulted in order that these Forces may be established and expanded on lines acceptable to the Burmese people. — Aung San, *Memorandum on the Proposed Reorganisation of Burma Patriotic Forces* (1945)

The final outcome of Burma's military expansion and modernisation program will depend on a number of factors, not the least of which is the future of military rule in Burma.[1] Should a democratically elected civilian government come to power, as might have occurred after the National League for Democracy's landslide election victory in May 1990, then the Burmese armed forces could become a completely different kind of national institution. Given Burma's important geostrategic position and enduring security concerns, the NLD's vision for the *Tatmadaw* is bound to have a number of characteristics in common with that favoured by the current regime. Yet, given the profound differences between the two sides in their approach to governing and defending Burma, there is also likely to be a considerable divergence of views. The future of the Burmese armed forces will be critically dependent, therefore, on the outcome of the power struggle currently being conducted between the country's military leadership and the pro-democracy forces symbolised by Aung San Suu Kyi.

12.1 Burma's Uncertain Future

Because it deals mainly with the future, any examination of this subject must necessarily be speculative. No one can confidently predict what Burma might look like in five years time, let alone by the end of the next decade. The problems that will need to be resolved before a democratic government of some kind can come to power, and after it does so, are enormously difficult and complex[2]. Political, economic, social, strategic and other factors are all inextricably intertwined, and cannot easily be separated — either by the Rangoon government for policy implementation, or by foreign researchers for academic analysis. In addition, the security environment, both within Burma and in the wider region, is not static, and the way in which the Burmese armed forces might evolve is subject to many diverse influences. These range from changes in China's external policies, to the attitudes of the ethnic minorities, to the fortunes of individual army officers in Rangoon. As for the ideal size and shape of the *Tatmadaw*, that too is subject to considerable debate. Different observers of the Burmese scene, including those with specialised military qualifications, reach different conclusions.[3]

Until late 1999, Burma's main opposition parties had said and published little about the country's defence, including their vision for the future of the armed forces. There were several reasons for this. Firstly, in Burma the idea of detailed and formally endorsed policy platforms has traditionally carried much less weight than in Western democratic countries.[4] Secondly, since its formation in 1989, the NLD has been engaged in a desperate struggle to survive in the face of persistent efforts by the military regime to destroy it. It has been difficult even to arrange party meetings to discuss specific policies. Thirdly, the NLD has focussed its attention on issues which have more immediate relevance to, and impact upon, its constituents, in particular those matters relating to democratic freedoms and human rights. Fourthly, the extreme sensitivity of defence issues in Burma, and the harsh reaction of the regime to any perceived challenges to the current role of the armed forces, has made it difficult for anyone in Burma to formulate or articulate their views on this subject without incurring the wrath of the authorities. The regime has long claimed the right to exercise a monopoly over all aspects of Burma's national security debate.

Indeed, the development and publication of a detailed policy on defence matters by the NLD could have simply provided the regime with an easy target for attack, and another excuse for punitive action against Aung San Suu Kyi and her supporters. One reason for this is the extreme sensitivity of the current military hierarchy to any suggestion that the *Tatmadaw* has abandoned the ideals and vision of its founder (and Aung San Suu Kyi's father), independence hero Aung San, who is still revered on all sides of Burmese politics. For example, Aung San Suu Kyi's arrest in 1989 (and subsequent incarceration without trial for six years) seems to have been triggered not just by her direct appeals for support from more moderate elements of the armed forces, but also by her public criticisms of Ne Win's leadership of the *Tatmadaw* since her father's assassination in 1947. The regime was particularly incensed by the suggestion that the modern *Tatmadaw* was the *Tatmadaw* of Ne Win, not Aung San. Speaking with the authority of her father, Aung San Suu Kyi had directly attacked one of the most important myths nurtured by the regime since Ne Win's coup d'etat in 1962.

It is possible, however, to reach some broad conclusions about the likely future shape, size and role of the country's armed forces under a civilian democratic government. Aung San Suu Kyi and other senior NLD figures have made numerous public statements relating to, if not specifically about, this subject. More importantly, in late 1999 the party released a formal defence platform, which examined the issue in more detail. A number of other opposition groups have commented on the expected nature of the *Tatmadaw* under democratic rule. In addition, enough is known about Burma's geostrategic position, its enduring defence requirements and the security challenges it currently faces, to venture an opinion on the kind of armed forces which would be logical, if not necessary, under a democratic government. This framework can then be measured against what might be possible in the circumstances in which a new democratic government in Burma is likely to find itself.

In conducting such an exercise, however, a clear distinction needs to be drawn between the theory and the practice.

2.2 The Theory

As General Secretary of the NLD, Aung San Suu Kyi's personal views on Burma's defence and armed forces are informed by her deep commitment to a democratic government and improved human rights in Burma. Her guiding principles, however, clearly derive from Aung San.[5] As might be expected, given this provenance, she has made it clear on numerous occasions since 1988 that she fully accepts the legitimacy of the armed forces as an institution of the state, and personally holds it in high regard. For example, only days after the massacre of unarmed pro-democracy demonstrators in August that year she said: 'The present armed forces of Burma were created and nurtured by my father....Let me speak frankly. I feel strong attachment for the armed forces. Not only were they built up by my father, as a child I was cared for by his soldiers'.[6] Ten years later, her views remained the same: 'The army is held in high esteem by our National League for Democracy. Because my father founded the army I have a special attachment and regard for it'.[7]

Aung San Suu Kyi envisages an important role for the armed forces in the future, provided that they fully respect the rights of the Burmese people, and are subject to their direction — as exercised through a democratically elected civilian Parliament. In this respect, Aung San Suu Kyi and her party are unequivocal. For example, at the first of her massed rallies in August 1988, she quoted her father:

> The armed forces are meant for this nation and this people, and it should be such a force having the honour and respect of the people. If instead the armed forces should come to be hated by the people, then the aims with which this army has been built up would have been in vain.[8]

Again in 1989 she stated:

> My father didn't build up the Burmese Army in order to oppress the people.... He made many speeches where he specifically said, don't start oppressing the people just because you have weapons. You are to serve the country. You are for the country, the country is not for you.[9]

In numerous other speeches by Aung San Suu Kyi the same theme has emerged:

> An effective army works and specialises in matters relating to defence of the country and its people. Then only will they earn the love and respect of the people. The National League for Democracy cannot accept interference in political affairs by the army.[10]

The distinction being made between the *Tatmadaw* of Aung San and the *Tatmadaw* of Ne Win is not as explicit as it was made in 1989, just before Aung San Suu Kyi's arrest, but it is still clear.

On numerous occasions over the past 12 years, Aung San Suu Kyi has directly appealed for the sympathy and support of the members of the armed forces. For example, in her speech at the Shwedagon Pagoda on 26 August 1988, she said:

> May I also from this platform ask the personnel of the armed forces to reciprocate this kind of understanding and sympathy? May I appeal to the armed forces to become a force in which the people can place their trust and reliance. May the armed forces become one which will uphold the honour and dignity of our country.[11]

Aung San Suu Kyi has consistently called upon the armed forces to abjure politics. Yet, at the same time, she has asked them to support the opposition's continuing demands for the military regime to convene the parliament promised before the NLD's landslide victory. After the 1990 general elections, for example, she said:

> When my father founded the army, it was not for the purpose of interfering in politics. Rather, it was for the purpose of supporting the people in their political struggle. I address all the people in the Army and say that because of your love of your country it is your duty and responsibility to provide back up support to fulfill the wishes and desires of the people.[12]

This theme has continued to feature in Aung San Suu Kyi's public speeches. In August 1999, for example, she called upon the armed forces 'to work hand in hand to achieve democracy, where the people govern the country'.[13] She added:

> There is no question that the people's government will honour the role of the *Tatmadaw*....We also want the Tatmadaw to know what we are trying to do for our country. To achieve this understanding we need to have the freedom to communicate and discuss.[14]

In the same statement, Aung San Suu Kyi declared that the armed forces need not fear retribution from a civilian government.

Despite these explicit calls for support, Aung San Suu Kyi has consistently stated that, contrary to the repeated accusations of the regime, neither she nor the NLD have any desire to split the armed forces or to 'incite discord and disintegration', of the kind which crippled Burma after the country regained its independence.[15] As early as August 1988 she stated:

> What I wish to say is that at this time there is a certain amount of dissension between the people and the army. This rift can lead to future dangers....I would therefore not wish to see any splits and struggles between the army which my father built up and the people who love my father so much.[16]

Again in 1990 she said: 'I know a split army is against the interests of the nation ... We just want what my father wanted; a professional army that understands that a really honourable army doesn't engage in politics'.[17]

Time after time, she has repeated that it was not the NLD's intention to divide the *Tatmadaw*, as 'dissension within the army means trouble for the country'.[18] In 1995, for example, she said:

> The people and the military personnel cannot be separated. We have been accused of working to split the army, to drive a wedge between them and the people. This is absolutely false. We have no desire for the army to split. That is why we always claim that the people include the army....It is necessary that the people love and trust the defence forces. The people and the defence forces must work together to form a modern and effective army.[19]

Given the implacable opposition of many senior members of the *Tatmadaw* to Aung San Suu Kyi and the NLD, however, it is not clear how the armed forces can support the cause of democracy in Burma without there being in some way 'discord and dissension' in the ranks.

Over the past 12 years statements by other senior members of the NLD also refer back to Aung San, whose broad vision for the armed forces of Burma is still seen as a viable model for the modern *Tatmadaw*. His statements about the armed forces are also seen as directly relevant to the more immediate problems faced by the democratic movement. For example, on 27 March 1999, NLD Deputy Chairman Tin Oo gave a speech on defence issues in which he quoted extensively from the speeches of Aung San.[20] The excerpts chosen by the former Defence Minister and Army Chief highlighted a number of key principles which clearly illustrate the NLD's current policy position:

> This armed forces should be something that the people of this country will revere, adore and depend on. But, if in the hearts of the people there is resentment against this armed forces then the establishment of this armed forces will be futile.
> This armed forces has not been established for any one individual. It has been established for the entire country — for all the people. This army has not been established for one group, one party, or one set of people. It has been es-

tablished for the entire country — for all its citizens.

The armed forces has not been created for the purpose of persecuting the people, nor for the purpose of exercising power with weapons. The army is the servant of the country. The country is never the servant of the army.[21]

The NLD statement emphasised that these precepts should still be followed. Again drawing a clear distinction between the *Tatmadaw* envisaged by Aung San and that developed by Ne Win and his protégés, the statement concluded:

> When such a genuine democratic government is born it will be possible to revive and establish an armed forces envisaged by our martyred leader General Aung San, father of the army and architect of our independence; an armed forces that appreciates his spirit and will abide by his instructions; an armed forces that will be loved and revered as in the days when resistance was launched against the colonial and fascist systems.[22]

In a personal statement to the members of the armed forces, former General Tin Oo joined Aung San Suu Kyi in calling for the armed forces to work towards a democratic government in Burma, as envisaged by Aung San. After outlining his own long career in the Burma Army, Tin Oo stated that 'Achieving democracy will not hurt the Defence Services personnel, it will benefit them instead'.[23] On the nature of the *Tatmadaw* under a democratic government, he was not specific, but said:

> It is also not true that the military should be made up of many personnel. We need to strive for quality and excellence, individually and as a group. I want the Defence Services to be modernised and developed; the Defence Services that will safeguard democracy; and the Defence Services which respects the people as their mothers and fathers and is loved by the people in return.[24]

This statement directly challenges the comment made by former SLORC Chairman SENGEN Saw Maung, who told the armed forces in 1990 that 'only the *Tatmadaw* is our mother and father'.[25]

Since 1989, the views of Aung San Suu Kyi, Tin Oo and other senior NLD figures like Kyi Maung have all stemmed from, and contributed to, a number of formal NLD statements which broadly touched on this subject.[26] For example, in the NLD's manifesto, which was produced before the 1990 general elections, the party outlined a number of broad principles on defence, as follows:

> 11.A. The military is born out of the people, and it must be for the people, loved by the people, free from politics, and one that the people can rely upon.
>
> B. It must be a modern military practising strategies in accordance with the geography and environment of the country.

C. There must be plans for looking after the welfare of the families of those who fell in battle, and also of veterans.[27]

Understandably, given the extraordinary circumstances leading up to the elections, little thought seems to have been given at the time to how these broad statements of principle might later be translated into specific policies, or how they might be used to set guidelines for the future development of the armed forces.

Since its overwhelming victory in the 1990 elections, the NLD has progressively developed and refined its policy position. For example, at the party's celebration of the sixth anniversary of the elections, a 'firm guideline for action' was promulgated, as follows: 'The *Tatmadaw* is an essential and necessary organization for the country. We have decided to endorse the NLD's position which says that the *Tatmadaw* should be a dignified force that protects and fulfills the democratic practices'.[28]

This was followed by a more elaborate policy statement in a document entitled 'Political Goals and Intent of the NLD', which read in part:

> As in the practice of democracy the Power of State will lie in the three pillars such as the Judiciary, the Executive and the Legislature. The *Tatmadaw* and the whole mechanism for defence will fall under the Executive. It will have to abide by the Constitution, and be a *Tatmadaw* for the people and loved by the people. Only in specific and necessary times will the military stand as a separate pillar owing to the importance of the task....The country's defence will be undertaken according to Burma's geopolitics, the military will be equipped with a qualitative and effective strategy, and built to a modern and high standard.[29]

The statement added that Burma's national defence would depend on the participation of all citizens, for example through people's militias and compulsory military service. This would transform the *Tatmadaw* into 'a People's *Tatmadaw*'.[30] It would be separated from party politics. A law would be passed to provide benefits for the families of those who fell in battle.[31]

This policy was taken further in 1998. In September that year the Committee Representing the Peoples' Parliament (CRPP) — the NLD's answer to the regime's consistent refusal to call the elected parliament — created 10 smaller committees, each charged with certain policy studies. As part of this effort, the Defence Affairs Committee of the CRPP was asked to prepare a report on 'the establishment of a modern army in a democracy'.[32] This committee was placed under the leadership of NLD Deputy Chairman Tin Oo. By November 1999 the Defence Committee had produced a *Report on the Formation of a Modern Tatmadaw in the Democratic Era*.[33] This document rehearsed earlier statements by the party on defence issues, and set out a number of key policy principles. The first stressed that the speeches, teachings and policies of Aung San were to be taken as a guide for the implementation of the party's defence policy.

Other key findings included:

- The Ministry of Defence should no longer be under military control, but be answerable to a Minister of Defence, who would report to the elected Parliament.
- The Commander-in-Chief of the armed forces should be considered a political post and have a fixed term of appointment.
- Military intelligence should be confined to operational issues. Broader defence and national security matters should be the responsibility of a body reporting directly to the head of state.
- The *Tatmadaw* should be a modern force, emphasising quality before quantity. Its size should be reconsidered, 'taking into account the country's economic development, its scientific and technological development, its economic status and its human resources'.[34]
- Defence personnel should share the wealth and poverty of the people. Defence expenditure should be decided by the People's Parliament according to available resources.
- There should only be one national *Tatmadaw*. All other armed groups in Burma, including those with official or semi-official status, should be disbanded.
- The recruitment and training of military officers and other ranks needs to be reviewed. Greater attention needs to be given to the role of women in the armed forces. The current ideological indoctrination of military personnel would be replaced by teachings on democracy and related issues.
- The *Tatmadaw* should be armed with modern and standard equipment and ammunition. Rather than obtain arms from 'any or every country and with all sorts', advantage should be taken of Burma's expected close ties with other democracies, when seeking new equipment. Local factories should also provide arms and ammunition.
- Burma's defence policies should reflect its delicate geostrategic position, and be fashioned accordingly, emphasising cordial and peaceful relations with all its neighbours.
- Burma's strategy should be 'defence in depth', which requires the full commitment of the entire country. A national service law should be passed to facilitate this.
- Military personnel will be confined to military functions and, except in emergencies, should not be used to fill civil service positions. Their conditions of service and benefits would be regularly reviewed in light of the dangers of their profession.

The CRPP Defence Affairs Committee's statement finished by saying that a more comprehensive report on 'the formation of a democratic and modern *Tatmadaw*' would be presented after the People's Parliament had been convened. In the meantime, the committee encouraged discussion and debate on the key issues which it had raised.[35]

No other Burmese opposition groups have formulated a position on defence in this sort of detail. However, the NLD's broad vision of the armed forces under a democratic government is shared by the exiled National Coalition Government of the Union of Burma. Since its formation in 1990 the NCGUB has consistently agitated for fundamental political change in Burma, based on a *Principles and Policy Statement* which was published in 1991. The section on Defence reads:

1. We will reorganise an army; that identifies itself with the people, is loyal to the people, is subservient to and respects the constitution of the country, and one that the people love.
2. As a defence service of the country, the military personnel must conduct their duties in accordance with the law of the country.
3. Based on the actual needs of the country, a modern army will be established.
4. The army shall under no circumstances, be influenced by a single individual, or a single party.[36]

Similar views have been expressed by the Federation of Trade Unions — Burma (FTUB). For example, in 1999 a senior FTUB official stated:

The Burmese army must be for the people, by the people, of the people. The ordinary Burmese people provide tax for allowances, uniforms, food, arms, equipment and every other type of supplies for the army. A real democratic Burmese army would think that whatever the army wants to do, it must first see whether the people agree with that action or not.[37]

Like the NLD, the NCGUB and FTUB appear to draw heavily on Aung San's speeches, and wider democratic practices, for their own guiding principles on the future of the Burmese armed forces.

Extrapolating from these and other statements of opposition policy, wider reference to Aung San's writings, and interviews with key NLD figures, some picture can be gleaned of the ideal *Tatmadaw*, as envisaged by the members of Burma's democratic movement.[38] Firstly, the *Tatmadaw* would not only survive a change of government in Rangoon but would remain a key institution of the state. Secondly, it would be responsible (through a Defence Minister and Cabinet) to an elected civilian parliament.[39] It would be a single, unified force under a prescribed organisational structure.[40] Thirdly, the *Tatmadaw* would be a smaller and much more professional organisation than at present. It would also be more representative in terms of its ethnic composition, gender balance and, if possible, the socio-economic background of its members. Fourthly, the *Tatmadaw*'s political, economic and social roles would be severely curtailed, although it would retain a heavy responsibility to assist the new government with the tasks of reconstruction and nation building. In particular, the *Tatmadaw*'s intelligence arm would be required to eschew the dominant political role it has adopted since 1962, and concentrate on purely strategic and operational matters. Finally, while involuntary recruitment would be abolished, a form of selective national service would be introduced.

In purely military terms, the *Tatmadaw* under a democratic government would be organised primarily for the defence of the country against external threats.[41] It would also have the capability to respond to serious internal security challenges, such as those posed by the narcotics-based armies in Burma's northeast, but it would not normally be used to quell domestic political dissent. If such measures were considered necessary, they would be left to a better led and better trained Police Force. The *Tatmadaw* would most likely be organised along conventional lines, with a Ministry of Defence, three discrete Services and subordinate commands and bases around the country, much as occurs at present. The army would remain the largest Service, but greater attention would be given to the navy and air force. There would be no pressing reasons to change the current two tier structure, with the army divided into mobile formations and garrison troops, but there would be fewer of the latter and a greater distribution of 'strategic' assets like armoured and artillery battalions. Individual units of all three Services would be composed of members of all ethnic groups. Despite the NLD's proposed introduction of a federal political structure giving greater autonomy to the ethnic minorities, there would not be a return to the ethnically based regiments which were created by the British colonial regime. Members of the ethnic minorities, including non-Buddhists, would be free to rise through the ranks to the highest levels.

To be truly 'modern and effective', the *Tatmadaw* would be well armed with contemporary weapons and equipment, drawn from a wide range of countries, as appropriate.[42] These countries would include Burma's traditional arms suppliers, like the Western democracies. Burma's military training programs would also reflect a wider range of international contacts.

In some respects, it would not be too difficult for an elected democratic government in Rangoon to give form to this vision of a new *Tatmadaw*. Many elements would remain much the same as before. In other ways, there would probably be strong support for change from within the armed forces themselves. In a number of key areas, however, it would prove much more difficult to translate this theory into practice.

12.3 The Practice

Should a civilian government be elected in Burma, the expected adoption of broad democratic principles and practices would inevitably dictate that the way in which military force was officially viewed and used would be quite different than it is now. There would also be some obvious adjustments made to government priorities for policy attention and funding. Yet, initially, and on the surface at least, it is unlikely that there would be many immediate or dramatic changes in the *Tatmadaw* itself.

Under current circumstances, the installation of a genuinely democratic government in Rangoon could not occur without at least the passive support of the armed forces. The *Tatmadaw* constitutes such a powerful and all-pervasive influence in the country at present that some compromise or agreement would have had to be reached with the democratic movement simply for another relatively free and fair election to have been held, and for a new government to be permitted to take office.[43] Any such deal would almost certainly include, as one of its core conditions, an undertaking by the democratic movement not to attack the institution of the armed forces nor to deprive it of its historically important place in Burmese society. The new Defence Minister would have to be someone trusted by the military hierarchy, and the armed forces would probably demand to be included in discussions on certain key issues, including those relating to external relations and internal security. Nor could a democratic government expect to engage in a campaign of reprisals against serving and retired members of the *Tatmadaw* for their past actions, or to indulge in wholesale dismissals of the officer corps. The armed forces would also insist on retaining control over all senior *Tatmadaw* appointments. While some key figures would doubtless be asked to resign or retire, this would have to be with the agreement of the military leadership.

In return for such concessions, the armed forces would presumably undertake to return to their barracks. This would take time, however, as it would clearly be unwise for the *Tatmadaw* simply to walk away from all its old administrative positions until a new government structure and expanded civilian bureaucracy was in place. To do so could risk even greater economic and social problems than occur at present. Indeed, with its enormous resources, modern equipment, technical expertise, tested command structure and internal communications networks, the *Tatmadaw*'s role in national reconstruction and development would be crucial.[44] The armed forces would also have to permit the new government sufficient freedom to exercise its popular mandate. For these arrangements to work, the military leadership would have to be prepared to give up certain critical areas of decision making, including economic and social policy. Some issues would probably be quarantined, however, and even if it was never explicitly stated, the armed forces would always retain an effective power of veto. For example, any suggestion that the Union would be seriously weakened or even dismembered by the new government under its proposed power-sharing arrangements with the ethnic minorities, would see severe pressure brought to bear. As a last resort, the *Tatmadaw* could even stage another coup, a threat which would be well understood by the democratic leadership.

There would be other reasons why a new democratic government would not want seriously to weaken the armed forces or precipitously overturn current policies. For example, the new government would still be a very fragile body, highly vulnerable to pressures from both outside and inside the country. Knowing this, it would almost certainly share the *Tatmadaw*'s current wish to have a strong, capable defence force able to preserve Burma's sovereignty, defend its territorial integrity, and protect its natural resources from unauthorised exploitation. It would take a while to replace military men in the administration with trained civil servants. A new democratic government would probably also support, in principle at least, the current regime's arguments in favour of achieving greater balance in the *Tatmadaw*, improving its supporting infrastructure and modernising its weapons inventory. The idea of raising the level of Burma's research and industrial base, and being more self-sufficient in arms production, has appeal on both sides of the political divide. Similarly, a new democratic government, anxious to win the support of the armed forces rank and file, and to prevent a continuation of the abuses which are now commonplace, would recognise the need to improve the lot of the average serviceman and woman, and would support any programs aimed at doing so.

Perhaps the most obvious changes to the armed forces, should a democratically elected civilian government of some kind come to power in Rangoon, would be a reduction in the *Tatmadaw*'s overall size, a decline in defence expenditure, and a change in the focus and activities of the country's military intelligence apparatus.

As early as the 1990 election campaign there were a number of indications that, under a NLD government, the *Tatmadaw* would be drastically reduced in size. Much greater emphasis would be placed on peaceful negotiations with ethnic insurgent groups and the development of a realistic and enduring federal style of political system which gave the ethnic minorities much greater autonomy. It was suggested at the time that, by abandoning the military regime's policy of crushing the ethnic insurgencies and imposing a highly centralised, Burman-dominated political system on the country, the then 200,000-strong armed forces could be reduced to a border protection force as small as 20,000-30,000 men.[45] Since then, the regime has itself negotiated cease-fire agreements with most major ethnic insurgent groups and narcotics-based armies. The Karens are holding out but have suffered a disastrous internal rupture and several major defeats in the field. The military challenges posed by other small insurgent groups are relatively slight. As noted above, however, this much improved (albeit still very fragile) internal security situation has not prompted any reduction in the size of the *Tatmadaw*. To the contrary, it has helped fuel its growth and permitted a greater diversion of resources to the control of the country's government and administration.

Should the NLD achieve government in the near future, it is most unlikely that any serious attempt would be made to reduce the size of the *Tatmadaw* to the very low levels mooted before the 1990 elections. For the reasons given above, large and immediate reductions would be strongly resisted by the armed forces hierarchy. Once in power, a democratic government would probably recognise that Burma would still need a strong, well-equipped and balanced defence force for both external defence and internal security. As a result of negotiations between the new government and the military leadership, however, the size of the armed forces could probably be halved to around 200,000 without weakening Burma's security. Such a reduction would need to be carried out gradually. A weak and vulnerable new administration would not want to be faced with the sudden problem of large numbers of resentful and military-trained ex-servicemen wandering around the countryside making trouble, as occurred after the Second World War and again just after Independence. In any case, the abolition of forced recruitment, voluntary resignations, retirements and other natural wastage would help the numbers drop markedly. The expected growth of the domestic economy under a democratic government would offer a major attraction for military personnel with technical and entrepreneurial skills. The more efficient administration of the three Services, stronger measures against corruption and reduced opportunities for abuses of power would further reduce the numbers in the ranks, without recourse to large scale dismissals.

Cuts to manpower would help reduce the financial burden currently imposed by the *Tatmadaw*, but in Burma personnel costs have always been low. Other measures would be required to help fund the comprehensive economic rehabilitation of the country and greatly improved social services which have long been demanded by the civilian population. Fortunately for a new democratic government, efforts to renew the country's infrastructure and improve living conditions would inevitably attract significant support from the Western democracies and other aid donors, like Japan. International financial flows to Burma would quickly be restored. With such help, and under more professional management, it could be expected that the domestic economy would improve. Still, Defence would be bound to suffer a major reduction in its share of the national budget. Sectors like health and education, starved of funds since 1988, would get a much higher priority, and development projects ignored or bypassed by the military regime would have a greater chance to win state funding.[46] All this would inevitably be at the expense of new arms, military equipment and upgraded defence facilities. Yet it could be strongly argued that Burma's essential defence needs have already been more than met by the massive expansion and modernisation program of the past 12 years, and all that would be required in the foreseeable future would be funds for salaries, equipment repairs and base maintenance.

In any case, not all the aid provided by other countries needs to be in the form of loans, capital and technical expertise. If the *Tatmadaw* genuinely stepped back from domestic politics, became more professional and stopped its human rights abuses, significant defence assistance would soon be forthcoming. Some countries, like the US and UK, both of which have championed the cause of democracy in Burma since 1988, would be prepared to assist with the reform of the armed forces, through training courses, equipment and possibly even arms. Anti-narcotics campaigns would almost certainly attract generous US assistance, as occurred in the 1970s and 1980s. Other countries, like Australia, would be prepared to re-open military training courses to Burmese officers, and ASEAN countries like Singapore would feel able publicly to acknowledge and further develop their close security ties. In these circumstances, it might be expected that the current close military relationship between Burma and China would suffer. No Burmese government could afford to ignore China's overwhelming strategic weight, and for some years the *Tatmadaw* would still be heavily dependent on China for spare parts for all its arms and equipment. However, a new and democratically elected government in Rangoon would be much more willing and able to cultivate strategic relationships with a wider range of countries, adding to Burma's security through both military and non-military means. This would be welcomed and supported by most of Burma's regional neighbours, as well as many other countries further afield.

Perhaps one of the most difficult challenges which would face a democratic government seeking to change the *Tatmadaw*, would be the reform of Burma's powerful military intelligence apparatus. The immediate aim would be to redefine its role, and turn its focus away from surveillance of the civil population to more legitimate military duties. As was the case before Ne Win's coup, responsibility for this aspect of internal security would probably be given to the Police Force and the country's other (ostensibly civilian) specialised security services and intelligence agencies.[47] Yet, ever since 1962, the DDSI and MIS have become so much a part of the military regime's power base, and such a strong arm of government, that this reform process would be bound to prove very difficult. The armed forces hierarchy would be reluctant to lose such a powerful weapon in its arsenal, at least until it was completely satisfied that a new civilian government could be trusted not to threaten the *Tatmadaw* and its core interests. Even then, there would doubtless be some in the officer corps who would be unwilling to let go of such a useful political tool. Still, the reform of the country's intelligence services must be given a high priority. For, if such a system remained in place, a democratic government would not be able to function freely or effectively. In addition, the new government's credibility with the civilian population would be undermined by its inability to dismantle the repressive machinery of the old regime, as exemplified by the military intelligence apparatus.

Looking ahead, the kind of *Tatmadaw* which might emerge from all these changes would be smaller and leaner. It would also be better suited to both the country's unique geography and the kinds of threats which a new democratic government was likely to face. Given the harsh nature of the terrain around Burma's borders, and the need to conserve resources, there may even be a trend back to the *Tatmadaw* of earlier years. For example, assuming a greatly reduced threat from ethnic insurgents as a result of agreed power-sharing arrangements, there could be less emphasis on maintaining static garrisons. Instead, there could be much more reliance on well-armed rapid reaction forces which could be moved around the country quickly to meet specific contingencies. In contrast to the regime's approach to warfare since 1988, which has been characterised by long campaigns of attrition relying on sheer weight of numbers, massive firepower and frontal assaults, the army would in the future rely much more on mobility, versatility and a concentrated application of force. Modern, light, and man-portable weapons would be given a higher priority than main battle tanks and heavy artillery, neither of which are well suited to campaigns in difficult terrain and tropical climates. A much greater reliance would be placed on the air force, not just for air defence, but for surveillance, ground and sea strike, transport, resupply, and medical evacuation. In this regard, many of the military regime's aircraft acquisitions since 1988 (in particular the purchase of about 45 helicopters) have been quite useful. The navy too could remain much the same shape as it is now, but there would probably be an increased priority given in the future to anti-ship and air defence missile systems. Steps would have to be taken by all three Services to resolve deep-rooted logistical problems.

Questions relating to the *Tatmadaw*'s size, structure, weapons inventory and war-fighting methods, however, are not the only issues that a new government would need to consider. There are other changes that would be critical if the proper groundwork was to be laid for the *Tatmadaw* of the future. For example, there would need to be a considerable improvement in the standards of personnel management and conditions of service, to attract and retain the best recruits. Even more importantly, a major effort would need to be put into the recruitment, education and training of a new kind of Burmese officer, one that was prepared to give his or her allegiance to a national ideal much closer to Aung San's original vision for the government and the armed forces, than to the kind of philosophical underpinnings for military rule which have been put forward by the regime since it first seized power. Many of the broad principles expounded by the armed forces hierarchy since 1962 may have been valid in themselves, but they have been corrupted and distorted through years of propaganda to serve much narrower and far less legitimate ends. An effort to restore and revive the original ideals of Burma's officer corps would be necessary not only to ensure the immediate survival of a new democratic government in Rangoon but also the long-term development and consolidation of a more professional and apolitical *Tatmadaw*. For, unless this fundamental shift occurred, and initial grudging acceptance of an elected government became genuine support, then democracy in Burma would always be under threat.

Such changes will also be needed to sustain these young officers and their men when they were called upon to protect Burma from external pressures and to carry the government's fight to the narcotics-based armies in the northeast. For eventually Burma will need to confront large, well-armed and independent organisations like the United Wa State Army and the Myanmar National Democratic Alliance Army, and halt their narcotics production. Ultimately, this can only be done by physically wresting back control of their territory and disarming them. Such campaigns will not be easy, and casualties would be high, but ironically conflicts of this kind could help the rebirth of the Burmese armed forces. Conducted professionally, and for clearly defined reasons against an easily identifiable and well-recognised threat, they would help nourish a sense of national purpose, a greater degree of personal commitment, and the development of an *esprit de corps* among Burma's next generation of fighting forces. Wider nation-building efforts, such as infrastructure development, aid to the civil population and disaster relief, would also be important in helping to restore the *Tatmadaw*'s pride and self-respect. Its standing in the community, eroded by Ne Win's 1962 *coup d'etat*, and irreparably harmed by the army's massacre of thousands of unarmed demonstrators in 1988, would be greatly improved. Should that occur, then the armed forces would come much closer to Aung San's ideal of being revered, adored and depended upon by the people of Burma.

12.4 Conclusion

For all their criticisms of the military regime and the role of the armed forces in the past, Aung San Suu Kyi and other senior pro-democracy leaders realised at an early stage of their campaign to win office that they needed to overcome the *Tatmadaw*'s fears if they were ever to loosen its grip on power and form a viable civilian government.[48] Hence Aung San Suu Kyi's appeals to the more moderate and professional elements of the armed forces before she was placed under house arrest in July 1989. Since her release in July 1995, she and her colleagues have continued to seek a dialogue with the military regime, recognising that under current circumstances a peaceful transition to democratic rule can only occur with its concurrence, if not active support.[49] Although Aung San Suu Kyi's position hardened as the SLORC and later the SPDC continued to ignore her, and attack her party, she continued to state her wish to work with the armed forces, not against them. While actively seeking the *Tatmadaw*'s support, she has specifically ruled out encouraging a mutiny. To make any real progress, other assurances may need to be given, as has already occurred for example in places like the ROK, South Africa and Chile. An accommodation with the armed forces, including an amnesty for its past actions, may not be popular with some of the more radical elements in the democracy movement, both within Burma and abroad. Without it, however, little progress can be made towards the kind of society that the majority of the Burmese population so clearly wants.

Such a compromise would not only be to the manifest benefit of the Burmese people, but it would also be in the long-term interests of the armed forces themselves. For unless they are prepared to retreat from their current hard-line position, and allow a much greater measure of popular participation in government, they will always be weakened by their alienation from the civil population and face the potential threat of armed opposition. The *Tatmadaw*'s historical reputation as the guardian of the Burmese people and protector of the Union has now been severely damaged. It is finding it difficult to attract the kind of recruits that it will increasingly need to serve in a more complex and technically demanding strategic environment. Also, the *Tatmadaw*'s rigid centralist policies and the predominance of ethnic Burmans in its higher ranks will further encourage the country's minority peoples to see the armed forces simply as an instrument of 'big race' domination and oppression. The *Tatmadaw* may continue to increase in size and acquire more modern weapons systems but, as long as these critical issues are left unresolved, its real military capabilities will remain limited and its professionalism suspect.

Notes

1. This chapter draws in part on Andrew Selth, *The Burmese Armed Forces Next Century: Continuity or Change?*, Working Paper No. 338 (Strategic and Defence Studies Centre, Australian National University, Canberra, 1999).

2. See, for example, M.P. Callahan, 'Democracy in Burma: The Lessons of History', National Bureau of Asian Research, *Analysis*, Vol. 9, No. 3, May 1998, pp. 5-26. Of course, concepts of democracy differ greatly between countries, and groups within countries, even among those peoples which support and have already adopted 'democratic' systems of government.

3. There is apparently a lively debate on the optimum size and structure of Burma's armed forces in specialised Burmese language journals published by the Ministry of Defence in Rangoon. These journals, however, are not available to the wider public.

4. Power in Burma has traditionally been highly personalised and, even during the 'democratic era', political parties played a secondary role to their leaders. Similarly, policy platforms have tended to be more a reflection of the leaders' views, rather than the result of widespread debate and compromise. Some have argued that the NLD under Aung San Suu Kyi also fits this pattern. See, for example, Roger Mitton, 'How Things Look Inside the NLD', *Asiaweek*, 16 July 1999, pp. 28-9.

5. Interview, Rangoon, November 1996.

6. Aung San Suu Kyi, Speech at the Shwedagon Pagoda, 26 August 1988, reproduced in *Freedom from Fear*, pp. 193-4. References to the 'army' in this and subsequent statements by Aung San Suu Kyi and the NLD are shorthand for the entire armed forces.

7. 'The General Secretary's, Daw Aung San Suu Kyi's Request', (undated) statement by Aung San Suu Kyi provided to the author by the NCGUB, 20 April 1999.

8. Cited in *Freedom from Fear*, p. 195.

9. Cited in Silverstein, 'Aung San Suu Kyi: Is She Burma's Woman of Destiny?', p. 1013.

10. 'The General Secretary's, Daw Aung San Suu Kyi's Request'.

11. *Freedom from Fear*, p. 195.

12. 'The General Secretary's, Daw Aung San Suu Kyi's Request'.

13. Dan Eaton, 'Army has nothing to fear from civilian rule', AAP, 7 August 1999.

14. *Ibid.*

15. 'The General Secretary's, Daw Aung San Suu Kyi's Request'.

16. *Freedom from Fear*, pp. 194-5.

17. Cited in Silverstein, 'Aung San Suu Kyi: Is She Burma's Woman of Destiny?', p. 1013.

18. Aung San Suu Kyi, speaking at a NLD press conference in Rangoon on 29 November 1995. See also Bertil Lintner, 'A Turn for the Worse', *FEER*, 23 November 1995, p. 38; and 'Lost illusions', *Economist*, 2 December 1995, p. 24.

19. Aung San Suu Kyi press conference, 29 November 1995.

20. The date of 27 March 1945 (when Aung San and the BNA changed sides) was commemorated as 'Resistance Day', until changed by Ne Win to 'Armed Forces Day'. The NLD is now arguing that the original name should be restored.

21. This speech was later issued by the NLD's Central Executive Committee as 'A Discourse on the Fifty Fourth Anniversary of Resistance Day', Statement No. 50 (3/99), Rangoon, 27 March 1999.

22. *Ibid.*

23. 'NLD's Tin Oo Urges Soldiers to Work Towards Democracy', *BurmaNet News*, 9 August 1999.

24. *Ibid.*

25. Address delivered by Senior General Saw Maung, Commander-in-Chief of The Defence Services at the 45th Anniversary of the Armed Forces Day (Resistance Day), 27 March 1990, p. 36.

26. NLD Party Chairman Kyi Maung also made at least one major speech on defence issues before his retirement. No English translation of his comments is available. According to Aung San Suu Kyi, however, he too drew heavily on her father's speeches for inspiration. Interview, Rangoon, November 1996.

27. Translated typescript of mimeographed original in the author's possession.

28. *Report of the Defence Committee of the Committee Representing the People's Parliament: Report on the Formation of a Modern Tatmadaw in the Democratic Era*, 1999. Unofficial translation, as a typescript in the author's possession.

29. *Ibid.*

30. It is not clear what form the proposed national service scheme would take. One senior NLD figure has suggested that it would be similar to that which operated before 1988, under which people with specialist skills (like doctors and engineers) could be called up. Other NLD officials, however, envisage the conscription of all healthy Burmese men and women of a certain age for set periods. Interviews, Rangoon, November 1999.

31. *Report of the Defence Committee of the Committee Representing the People's Parliament.*

32. 'Resolutions Taken on the 27th May 1999 by the Committee Representing the Peoples' Parliament', *BurmaNet News*, 30 May 1999.

33. *Report of the Defence Committee of the Committee Representing the People's Parliament.*

34. *Ibid.*

35. *Ibid.*

36. *Principles and Policy Statement of the National Coalition Government of the Union of Burma*, (NCGUB Ministry of Information, n.p. , 1991).

37. 'Military can't hold out for ever in Burma', *The Nation*, 17 July 1999.

38. Interviews, Rangoon, November 1996.

39. For Aung San's views on Burma's government and social organisation see Silverstein, *The Political Legacy of Aung San*.

40. Suggestions by some members of the SLORC that, under the NLD, the leadership of the armed forces would be rotated among the military leaders of Burma's main ethnic groups, is a distortion of comments made some time ago, and seem designed largely to undermine public confidence in the NLD's ability to manage the country's vital security interests. Interview, Rangoon, November 1996.

41. This would mark a major departure for the *Tatmadaw*, which at present sees Burma's main security threats as deriving from internal factors. See Tin Maung Maung Than, 'Myanmar: Preoccupation with Regime Survival, National Unity and Stability', pp. 390-416.

42. Interview, Rangoon, November 1996.

43. This begs the question, of course, of what the constitution might be, under which such steps could take place.

44. Ironically, the same point was made in 1961. See T.N. Dupuy, 'Burma and Its Army', *The Antioch Review*, Vol. 20, No. 4, Winter 1960-61, pp. 428-40.

45. Rodney Tasker and Bertil Lintner, 'The plot thickens', *FEER*, 21 June 1990, pp. 21-2.

46. The World Bank report on Burma prepared in 1999 estimated that military spending accounted for 32% of the 1998 budget. On a per capita basis, this was nine times that spent on health and two times that spent on education. 'Burma's debt is pushing economy to the brink', *International Herald Tribune*, 15 November 1999.

47. The other specialised security and intelligence agencies in Burma would need to be included in these reforms. While theoretically civilian, they have long been led by former or

serving military personnel, and been effectively subordinate to DDSI. See Selth, *Burma's Intelligence Apparatus*.

48. Louise Williams, 'Revenge is not our priority, says Opposition', *Sydney Morning Herald*, 4 July 1990.

49. See, for example, 'A Careful Hero', *Asiaweek*, 4 August 1995, pp. 16-17; and Gordon Fairclough, 'Winds of Change', *FEER*, 31 August 1995, pp. 24-6.

Appendix 1

Burma's Order of Battle

Despite all the difficulties of obtaining reliable information about Burma's armed forces, a serious researcher is not without some sources to turn to for information on its order of battle. Of particular value are interviews with current and former members of the *Tatmadaw* who, often at some risk to themselves, are prepared to share their first-hand knowledge. The many groups (both inside Burma and abroad) opposed to the country's military government are also fertile ground for research. For example, some insurgent groups have compiled detailed assessments of the *Tatmadaw*, drawing on information obtained from their own experiences, Burma Army deserters, prisoners of war, tactical radio intercepts and sundry other sources. From time to time useful (if rather fragmentary) information appears in the Burmese news media, and the displays in the Defence Services Museum in Rangoon give a number of important clues to the *Tatmadaw*'s past and present capabilities. There are also occasional reports of arms sales to Burma and other military developments in foreign newspapers, defence journals and current affairs magazines. Clearly, some caution needs to be exercised but, carefully collated and analysed, the information derived from these sources can be very useful.

Some published secondary sources are also helpful. A Burmese order of battle can be found in *The Military Balance*, published each year by the International Institute for Strategic Studies in London. This is one of the better known and more accessible public guides but, as noted earlier, the details provided are often contradicted by other sources and cannot be considered definitive. The relevant chapter of *Jane's Sentinel Security Assessment* for Southeast Asia draws on the expertise of a number of Burma specialists, and provides a much more detailed description of Burma's armed forces. This information is also used in other Jane's publications, like *Jane's World Air Forces* and *Jane's World Armies*, but it is not always kept up-to-date. *Jane's Fighting Ships* remains the most authoritative source on the development of the Burmese navy, but can still contain errors. Basic data about Burma's armed forces can also be found in annual surveys like the *World Defence Almanac*, *Military Powers Encyclopedia* and *SP's Military Yearbook*. These and other such publications are highly derivative, however, and none can claim to be either accurate or comprehensive. Given all these difficulties, certain allowances must be made for the following tables.

While every care has been taken to ensure the accuracy and completeness of the order of battle given below, some units, weapons platforms (or even whole weapon systems) may have been omitted. The secrecy surrounding Burma's armed forces and arms procurement programs has sometimes meant that news of certain developments and acquisitions has taken some time to leak out. Also, the tables may include some arms which have been used in the past, but are no longer in the *Tatmadaw*'s current inventory. For example, while some of the Burma Army's older weapons have been replaced, the Burmese security forces have a long history of never discarding any arms which might fall into the wrong hands, or which could conceivably be of use in a future emergency. It is likely that at least a proportion has been stored in its armouries. Alternatively, some of the more obsolete weapons may have been passed down to the Police Force or (before they were disbanded) to local militia units. Such weapons are thus still considered available for use in certain circumstances, either by the Burma Army itself or by paramilitary forces acting in its support.

Under current circumstances, it is impossible to estimate with any confidence the numbers of certain weapons or weapons platforms in use. Most figures given below are estimates, or are based on unconfirmed reports in the open literature. While particular arms deliveries may become known, it is very difficult to account for any losses, whether on operations, through accidents, or simply because of a lack of spare parts. It is known, for example, that since 1988 a number of the Burma Air Force's new aircraft have crashed through pilot error or mechanical failure. Some have been lost to insurgent ground fire. Also, some aircraft (like the G-4s) have been grounded for lengthy periods due to a lack of spare parts or the requisite technical skills. Details of the types and numbers of weapons platforms in these categories, however, are very difficult to obtain. Also, no attempt has been made to estimate the numbers of small arms held. Burma has been awash with infantry weapons since the end of the Second World War and, as Martin Smith has noted, for many people insurgency has become a way of life. It is unlikely that even the *Tatmadaw*, with all its intelligence sources, could provide accurate figures of all the weapons held by some insurgent groups.

In the following tables, question marks against particular entries indicate uncertainty about certain aspects of the entry, or even the entry itself. The notation 'NA' means that no estimates are available. Where local names have been given to certain weapons, usually deriving from their production in Burma, or the weapons used are produced by more than one country, they have either been listed separately (where different versions of these weapons are believed to be held), or the alternative names are given in brackets. This practice has also been followed where particular weapons have been given different designations by the manufacturer or are commonly known by different names. Specific designators or mark numbers have been given when known, but some may be incorrect. For consistency, the alphabetical and numerical designations of the various arms listed have all been given hyphens, for example M-16 (automatic rifle) or F-7 (fighter-interceptor). The name of the country which originally designed and/or manufactured these arms has been given in brackets at the end of each entry. Unless otherwise specified, 'USSR' or 'Russia' has been used to represent all former Eastern bloc countries.

For all these reasons, the order of battle given below can only be considered an interim assessment, pending the availability of more complete and more accurate information. Yet it does convey the much greater strength and diversity of the *Tatmadaw*, as it has developed since 1988.

PART I: THE TATMADAW

TOTAL PERSONNEL:

Formal war establishment: 500,000
Tatmadaw personnel in uniform: 400,000
Total armed forces (including Police Force): 472,000

COMMAND STRUCTURE

Commander-in-Chief, Defence Services
Deputy Commander-in-Chief, Defence Services

ARMY

Commander-in Chief, Army

General Staff

Chief of Staff
    Military Training General
    Directorate of Signals
    Directorate of Defence Industries
    Directorate of Security Printing
    Directorate of People's Militias and Psychological Warfare
    Directorate of Military Engineers (Field)
    Directorate of Armour and Artillery
    Colonel, General Staff
    Defence Services Museum and Historical Research Institute
    Directorate of Public Relations and Border Troops
    Department of Defence Services Computers
Chief of the Office of Strategic Studies
    Directorate of Defence Services Intelligence
Chief of the Bureau of Special Operations

Regional Military Commands
Light Infantry Divisions
Regional Operation Commands
Military Operation Commands
Tactical Operation Commands

Adjutant-General's Office

Adjutant-General
    Vice Adjutant-General
    Directorate of Medical Services
    Directorate of Resettlement
    Provost-Marshal Office

Quartermaster-General's Office

Quartermaster-General
    Vice Quartermaster-General
    Directorate of Military Engineers (Civil)
    Directorate of Supply and Transport
    Directorate of Ordnance Services
    Directorate of Electrical and Mechanical Engineers

NAVY

Commander-in Chief, Navy
    Vice Chief, Navy
    Naval Regional Commands
    Captain, General Staff

AIR FORCE

Commander-in Chief, Air Force
    Vice Chief, Air Force
    Air Base Headquarters
    Colonel, General Staff

INDEPENDENT DEPARTMENT

Judge Advocate General
Inspector General
Military Appointments-General
Directorate of Procurement
Records Office

Central Military Accounts
Camp Commandants

THE BURMA ARMY

PERSONNEL: 370,000 all ranks

REGIONAL MILITARY COMMANDS (RMC): 12

Northern Command (covering Kachin State, Headquarters (HQ) at Myitkyina,
   33 battalions under command)
North Eastern Command (northern Shan State, HQ at Lashio,
   30 battalions under command)
Eastern Command (southern Shan State, HQ at Taunggyi,
      42 battalions under command, including 16 battalions
      under a Regional Command HQ at Loikaw)
Triangle Region Command (eastern Shan State, HQ at Kengtung,
   28 battalions under command)
Central Command (Mandalay Division, HQ at Mandalay,
   17 battalions under command)
South Eastern Command (Mon and Karen States, HQ at Moulmein,
   36 battalions under command)
Coastal Region Command (Tenasserim Division, HQ at Mergui,
      43 battalions under command, including 8 battalions
      under two MOCs at Tavoy)
Southern Command (Pegu and Magwe Divisions, HQ at Toungoo,
   27 battalions under command)
South Western Command (Irrawaddy Division, HQ at Bassein,
   11 battalions under command)
Western Command (Arakan and Chin States, HQ at Akyab,
   33 battalions under command)
North Western Command (Sagaing Division, HQ at Monywa,
   25 battalions under command)
Rangoon Command (Rangoon Division, HQ at Mingaladon,
   12 battalions under command)

These RMC control 337 regular infantry and light infantry battalions, as shown above.

There are four Regional Operations Commands, at Loikaw, Bhamo, Kalay and Mongsat.

There are 14 Military Operations Commands, at Kyaukmai, Loilin, Mogaung, Hmawbi, Kyauktaw, Pyinmana, Phaign, Tavoy (2), Kalay, Kyaukpadaung, Kawkareik, Bokepyin and Theinni. Two more MOC are currently under consideration.

There are also 34 Tactical Operations Commands.

LIGHT INFANTRY DIVISIONS (LID): 10

77 LID (established in 1966, HQ at Pegu)
88 LID (1967, Magwe)
99 LID (1968, Meiktila)
66 LID (mid-1970s, Prome)
55 LID (late 1970s, Aungban)
44 LID (late 1970s, Thaton)
33 LID (mid-1980s, Sagaing)
22 LID (1987, Pa-an)
11 LID (1988, Htaukkyan)
101 LID (1991, Pakokku)

Each LID consists of 10 battalions, based at and around the Division Headquarters. These are usually light infantry battalions, but a number of LIDs also command regular infantry battalions. For example, 33 LID and 44 LID each have three infantry battalions, 88 LID has five infantry battalions, and 101 LID consists entirely of regular infantry battalions.

SUMMARY OF COMBAT UNITS:

437 infantry battalions, consisting of 171 infantry battalions and 266 light infantry
     battalions. (This reportedly includes 1 airborne battalion)
10 armoured battalions (5 tank, 5 APC) in one armour division
43 artillery battalions (plus 37 independent artillery companies attached
     to regional commands) in three artillery divisions.
7 anti-aircraft artillery battalions

Other units:

40 military intelligence units
16 signals battalions
11 electrical and mechanical engineer battalions
14 medical battalions

ARMOURED VEHICLES:

Tanks:

NA	Type 85 MBT (PRC)?
NA	Type 80 MBT (PRC)?
100	Type 69II MBT (PRC)
8	Type 59D MBT (PRC)

22   Comet medium tanks (UK)
105   Type 63 light tanks (PRC)

Other Tracked Armoured Vehicles:

250   Type 85 APC (PRC)
55   Type 90 APC (PRC)
80   Universal T-16 Bren gun carriers (UK)

Wheeled Armoured Vehicles:

40   Humber APC (UK)
6   Ferret SC (UK)
50   Daimler SC (UK)
44   locally-built armoured vehicles, as follows:
        BAAC-83 APC (Burma)
        BAAC-84 SC (Burma)
        BAAC-85 SC (Burma)
        BAAC-86 SC (Burma)
        BAAC-87 APC (Burma)
        BAAC-87 Command and Control Carrier (Burma)

ARTILLERY:

Towed Artillery:

57mm	NA	6-pounder (UK)
76.2mm	NA	17-pounder (UK)
	100	M-48 B1 mountain guns (Yugoslavia)
88mm	50	25-pounder field guns (UK)
105mm	96	M-101 howitzers (US)
	NA	M-56 howitzers (Yugoslavia)?
122mm	NA	Type 54 howitzers (PRC)
130mm	12	M-46/Type 59 field guns (DPRK)
140mm	NA	5.5-inch medium guns (UK)
155mm	16	Soltam (Israel)
	NA	WP-52 howitzers (PRC)

Rocket Launchers:

81mm	NA	BA-84 (Burma)
107mm	30	Type 63 MRL (PRC)
122mm	NA	BM-21 MRL (USSR/Vietnam)?
130mm	NA	Type 63 MRL (PRC)

Air Defence Systems:

20mm	NA	M-38 AAG (Yugoslavia)
37mm	24	Type 74 AAG (PRC)
40mm	10	Bofors L/60 Mk.1 AAG (UK/US?)
57mm	12	Type 80 Twin AAG (PRC)
	NA	Type 59 Twin AAG (PRC)?
94mm	NA	3.7-inch Mk.3A AAG (UK)
SAMs	NA	BAe Dynamics Bloodhound Mk.II SAM (UK/Singapore)

Man-Portable Air Defence Weapons:

	NA	SA-7 SAM (Russia)
	NA	Hongying HN-5A SAM (PRC)
	NA	SA-16 SAM (Bulgaria/Singapore)
	NA	Stinger FIM-92A(?) SAM (US/Pakistan)

OTHER CREWED WEAPONS:

Light and Medium Mortars:

2 inch	NA	Ordnance ML (UK, Burma)
3 inch	NA	Ordnance ML (UK, Burma)
60mm	NA	*Ka Pa Sa* BA-100 (Burma)
	NA	Type 63 (PRC)
	NA	M-19 (US)
81mm	NA	M-29 (US)
	NA	*Ka Pa Sa* BA-90 (Burma)
82mm	NA	M-43 (Russia)
	NA	Type 53 (PRC)
	NA	Type 67 (PRC)
	NA	Type 76 (PRC)

Heavy Mortars:

120mm	NA	*Ka Pa Sa* BA-97 (Burma)
	NA	Hotchkiss-Brandt MO-120-60 (France)
	NA	MA-6 ?
	80	Soltam M-65 (Tampella M-65) (Israel, Finland)
	NA	Soltam K-6 (Israel)
	NA	Tampella Mk.2 (Israel, Finland)
	NA	Type 53 (PRC)
	NA	UBM-52 (Yugoslavia)

122mm	NA	Type 55 (PRC)
	NA	Type 56 (PRC)

Rocket Launchers and Recoilless Rifles:

57mm	NA	M-18 (US)
	NA	Type 36 (PRC)
75mm	200	M-20 RCL (US)
	NA	Type 52 RCL (PRC)
	NA	Type 56 RCL (PRC)
82mm	NA	Type 65 (PRC)
	NA	Type 78 (PRC)
84mm	1200	FFV Carl Gustaf M-2 (Sweden, Singapore)
3.5in	NA	M-20 rocket launcher (US)
106mm	NA	M-40A1 (US)
	NA	M-40A2 (US, Pakistan)

Light and General Purpose Machine Guns:

0.30in	Browning M-1919A4 MMG (US)
0.303in	Bren LMG (UK)
7.62mm	Bren L-4A4 LMG (UK)
	Ka Pa Sa BA-64 LMG (Heckler and Koch G4) (Burma, FRG)
	Ka Pa Sa MA-3 LMG (Burma)
	MG-3 GPMG (FRG, Burma, Pakistan)
	FN MAG GPMG (Belgium)

Heavy Machine Guns and Cannon:

0.50in	Browning M-2HB HMG (US, Belgium)
12.7mm	Type 85 HMG (PRC)
20mm	Hispano Mk.5 automatic cannon (UK)

INDIVIDUAL WEAPONS:

Pistols:

9mm:	Browning HP (FN-35) semi-automatic (US, Belgium)
0.38in	Smith and Wesson revolver (US, UK)
0.38in	Enfield revolver (UK)

Repeating Rifles:

0.303in	SMLE Mk.V (UK)
	Lee Enfield No.4 (UK)

Self-Loading and Assault Rifles:

5.56mm	Colt M-16A1 (US, Singapore)
	Ka Pa Sa MA-1 (Burma)
	Ka Pa Sa MA-2 AR (Burma)
0.30in	Winchester M-1 carbine (US)
	Winchester M-2 carbine (US)
7.62mm	Armalite AR-10 (US)
	FN FAL (G1) (Belgium, FRG)
	Ka Pa Sa BA-63 (Heckler and Koch G-3A2) (G3) (Burma, FRG)
	Ka Pa Sa BA-100 (Heckler and Koch G-3A3ZF) (Burma, FRG)
	Ka Pa Sa BA-72 AR (Heckler and Koch G-3K) (G2) (Burma, FRG)
	Kalashnikov AK-47 AR (Russia)
	Type 56 AR (PRC)
12 Gauge	Remington shotgun (US)
	other (US?)

Submachine Guns:

9mm	IMI Uzi (Israel)
	IMI Mini-Uzi (Israel)
	Sterling L2-A3 (UK)
	Ka Pa Sa BA-52 (TZ-45) (Burma, Italy)

Grenade Launchers:

40mm	RPG-2 (Type 56 ATGL, B40) (Russia, PRC)
	RPG-7 (Type 69 ATGL) (Russia, PRC)
	M-79 (US)
	M-203 (US)

Rifle and Hand Grenades:

41mm	BA-92 RG (Burma)
51mm	BA-80 RG (Burma)
	Type 36 HG (UK)
	BA-77 anti-personnel HG (Burma)
	BA-88 offensive HG (Burma)
	BA-91 defensive HG (Burma)
	BA-101 general purpose HG (Burma)
	BA-109 HG (Burma)

Anti-Personnel Land Mines:

    MM-1 SFM (Burma)
    POMZ-2 SFM (USSR, Burma)
    POMZ-2M SFM (USSR, Burma)
    Type 58 SFM (PRC)
    Type 59 SFM (PRC)
    LTM-76 SFM (India)
    LTM-73 SFM (India)

    M-18 DFM (US)
    Type 69 DFM (PRC)
    ? DFM (Burma)

    M-16 A1 BFM (US)
    Type 69 BFM (PRC)
    V-69 BFM (Singapore)?

    MM-2 BM (Burma)
    Type 58 BM (PRC)
    PMN BM (USSR)
    Type 72 BM (PRC)
    M-14 BM (US)

    Type 59 box blast mine (PRC)
    PMD box blast mine (Russia)?

Anti-Vehicle Mines:

    M-7 A2 (US)
    Type 59 (PRC)?

THE BURMA NAVY

PERSONNEL: 16,000

PRINCIPAL BASES AND UNITS:

Headquarters: Ministry of Defence, Rangoon
Strategic Naval Command (HQ Rangoon)
Naval Training Command (Seikkyi)
Naval Shipyard Headquarters (Rangoon)
Central Naval Hydrographic Depot (Rangoon)
Central Naval Diving and Salvage Depot (Rangoon)
Central Naval Engineering Depot (Rangoon)

Central Naval Stores Depot (Rangoon)
Central Naval Communications Depot (Rangoon)
Central Naval Armaments Depot (Seikkyi)

Naval Regional Commands, Bases and 'Frontline Camps':

Irrawaddy Regional Command (HQ Rangoon)
        Thanhlyet Soon (Rangoon)
        Bassein
        Coco Island (Naval Radar Unit)
Danyawaddy Regional Command (HQ Sittwe)
        Kyaukpyu
        Sandoway
Panmawaddy Regional Command (HQ Hainggyi Island)
Mawyawaddy Regional Command (HQ Moulmein)
Tanintharyi Regional Command (HQ Mergui)
        Zadetkyi (St Matthew's) Island
        Mali (Tavoy or Dawei) Island
        Palai Island
        Kadan (King) Island
        Sakanthit (Sellore) Island
        Lambi (Sullivan) Island
        Pearl (Sir J.Malcolm) Island
        Zadetkale (St Luke's) Island (Naval Radar Unit)

MAJOR SURFACE COMBATANTS: 4

Corvettes (FS): 4 (plus 3 under construction)

1	*Admirable* class (US) (decommissioned in 1994 but still on fleet list)
1	PCE 827 class (US) (decommissioned in 1994 but still on fleet list)
2	*Nawarat* class (Burma) (being phased out)
3	class unknown, currently under construction at Sinmalaik shipyard

PATROL FORCES: 118

Guided Missile Patrol Boats (PGG): 6

6   *Houxin* class (PRC) (probably armed with 4 C-801 SSM each)

Coastal Patrol Boats (PC): 30

10	*Hainan* class (PRC)
2	*Myanmar* class (Burma)
3	PB 90 class (Yugoslavia)

6   PGM type (US)
6   Burma PGM type (Burma)
3   *Swift* class (US/Singapore)

River Gunboats (PGR): 16

2   Improved Y 301 class (Burma)
10 Y 301 class (Yugoslavia)
4   river gunboats (Burma)

River Gunboats (PCR): 2

2   CGC type (US/Burma)

River Patrol Craft (PBR): 46

9   river patrol craft (Burma)
6   river patrol craft (US)
6   *Carpentaria* class (Australia)
25 *Michao* class (Yugoslavia)

MINE WARFARE FORCES: 2?

2   T-43 class ocean minesweepers (PRC) (on order?)

AMPHIBIOUS FORCES: 18

4   *Abamin* class LCU (Japan)
1   LCU (Burma)
10 LCM 3 type (US)
3   LCU (Burma?) (operated by the Burma Army)

SURVEY VESSELS: 3
1   ocean survey ship (Yugoslavia)
1   survey vessel (Singapore)
1   river survey vessel (Netherlands)

AUXILIARIES: 17

1   coastal transport (AK) (Norway)
1   tanker (AOT) (Thailand)
1   diving support vessel (YDT) (Japan)
1   ocean transport vessel (AKL) (Burma?)
4   river transport vessels (AKL) (Burma?)
1   buoy tender (ABU) (Thailand)

7   MFV (Burma?)
1   Presidential Yacht

MERCANTILE MARINE:

Lloyds registers 127 vessels of 540,232 tons gross. As all are owned and operated by the state, they are considered available for military service in times of emergency.

THE BURMA AIR FORCE

PERSONNEL AND EQUIPMENT:

15,000 all ranks
185 combat aircraft (including about 45 armed helicopters)

PRINCIPAL BASES AND UNITS:

Headquarters: Ministry of Defence, Rangoon
Maintenance Air Base (Mingaladon)
Ground Training Base (Meiktila)
Flying Training Base (Shante)

Air Base Headquarters:

Mingaladon
Myitkyina
Hmawbi
Toungoo
Namsang

The Air Force also uses Burma's civilian airfields and numerous smaller airstrips around the country. Radar units are based at Lashio, Hmawbi, Namsang, Loimwe and Kutkhai.

FIGHTERS:

Interceptors:

50   Chengdu F-7E/K/M (PRC)
8   MiG-29 (Russia) (on order)

Fighter/Ground Attack:

48   NAMC A-5C/M (PRC)

COUNTERINSURGENCY AIRCRAFT:

12 SOKO G-4 (Yugoslavia)
7   Pilatus PC-9 (Switzerland)
14 Pilatus PC-7 (Switzerland)

TRANSPORT AIRCRAFT:

6   SAC Y-8D2 (PRC)
2   Fokker F-27 (Netherlands)
3   Fairchild-Hiller FH-227B (US)
3   Beechcraft D-18S (US)

TRAINING AIRCRAFT:

2   MiG-29UB (Russia) (on order)
10 GAIC FT-7 (PRC)
4   Shenyang FT-6 (PRC)
12 NAMC/Karakorum K-8 (PRC/Pakistan)
5   Pilatus PC-7 (Switzerland)

LIAISON AIRCRAFT:

4   Cessna 180 (US)
1   Cessna 550 (US)
5   Pilatus PC-6A/B (Switzerland)

HELICOPTERS:

12 Bell 205 (US)
6   Bell 206 (US)
6   SA-316B Alouette III (France)
12 PZL W-3 (Poland)
18 Mil Mi-2 (Poland)
12 Mil Mi-17 (Russia)

OTHER AIRCRAFT:

4   Ayres S-2R (US)
2   Beechcraft 16 (US)

PART II: PARAMILITARY FORCES

FRONTIER FORCES

The Frontier Forces (*Na Sa Kha*) are now found on all five of Burma's international borders. They appear to consist primarily of Burma Army personnel (including intelligence officers), assisted by members of the police, immigration and customs services. Its total strength is unknown.

THE BURMA POLICE FORCE

The People's Police Force (formally established in 1964) was reorganised as the Myanmar (Burma) Police Force on 1 October 1995, under the control of the Ministry of Home Affairs.

TOTAL PERSONNEL: 72,000

Including 4500 Combat Police.

HEADQUARTERS: (Rangoon)

Director-General of Police
Deputy Director General
General Staff Department
        Security and Crime Division
        Drugs Elimination Division
        Planning and Training Division
        Chemical Examination Department
Personnel Department
Logistics Department

STATE AND DIVISION POLICE FORCES: 17

The Police command structure is based on established civil jurisdictions. Each of Burma's seven States and seven Divisions has a MPF Commanding Officer, based at headquarters in the respective capital city.

Karen State (capital at Pa-an)
Kachin State (Myitkyina)
Chin State (Hakha)
Mon State (Moulmein)
Arakan State (Akyab)
Shan State (Taunggyi)
Kayah State (Loikaw)

Rangoon Division (Rangoon)
Sagaing Division (Sagaing)
Mandalay Division (Mandalay)
Magwe Division (Magwe)
Pegu Division (Pegu)
Tenasserim Division (Tavoy)
Irrawaddy Division (Bassein)

There are also three additional State Police Forces, with headquarters at Lashio (Shan North) and Kengtung (Shan East) in the Shan State, and Prome (Pegu West) in Pegu Division.

Members of all these forces are assigned to positions at District, Township or Police Station level.

SPECIAL DEPARTMENTS: 4

Special Intelligence Department (Special Branch)
Criminal Investigation Department
Railways Police Department
City Development Police Department

TRAINING CENTRES: 3

Central Institute of Police Training: Maymyo
No.1 Police Training Depot
No.2 Police Training Depot

RESERVE UNITS: 2

Highway Patrol
Oil Field Security

These units have reportedly absorbed some personnel formerly in the People's Militia.

COMBAT BATTALIONS: 9

Bn.1: (HQ at Hlawga)
Bn.2: Maungtaw
Bn.3: Shwemyayar
Bn.4: Patheingyi
Bn.5: Hmawbi
Bn.6: Shwepyitha
Bn.7: Kyauktan

Bn.8: Mingaladon/Padamyo Myo Thit
Bn.9: Hlaingthaya

These specially-trained combat battalions (of about 500 men each) have reportedly absorbed the former *lon htein* security control police. They are assisted by two support battalions (including signals units).

ANTI-NARCOTICS TASK FORCES:
Nineteen special Anti-Narcotic Task Forces have been established under the direction of the Central Committee for Drug Abuse Control.

THE PEOPLE'S PEARL AND FISHERY BOARD

The People's Pearl and Fishery Board (formerly the People's Pearl and Fishery Department, now possibly renamed again) has three fishery protection vessels. They are operated by the Burma Navy, however, and to all intents and purposes function as naval vessels.

OFFSHORE PATROL BOATS (OPV):

3   *Osprey* class (Denmark)

In some sources, Burma's six *Carpentaria* class river patrol craft and three *Swift* type coastal patrol boats are also listed as fishery protection vessels. The strength of the PPFB (when operating 12 patrol boats) was given as 250 men. While this may have been the case some years ago, it appears that these nine other vessels have now been completely absorbed by the navy, and only the *Osprey* class vessels remain under formal control of the PPFB (or its successor).

MILITIA FORCES

Although some references still list the People's Militia as another of Burma's paramilitary organisations, and give it a strength of about 35,000, the PM (as it existed before 1988) has been formally disbanded. However, basic military training has been given to many rural villagers, who are expected to contribute military service to the state when required.

In addition, many of the insurgent groups which have negotiated cease-fire agreements with Rangoon have been given 'militia' status and sometimes act as surrogates for the *Tatmadaw*.

OTHER PARAMILITARY FORCES

Basic military training has also been given to members of a number of other official organisations, including:

The Auxiliary Fire Brigades (104,000 members, with a target of 300,000)
The Myanmar Red Cross Society (250,000, including
        160,000 'Red Cross Brigade' members)
Union Solidarity and Development Association (14 million)
The Civil Service
War Veterans Organisation

Organisations 'under the influence' of the *Tatmadaw* include:

The Myanmar Maternal and Child Welfare Association
        (340,000 permanent members and 1.1 million ordinary members)
The Myanmar Women's Entrepreneurial Association.

Appendix 2

Burma's Defence Expenditure

The most reliable and comprehensive statistics published on Burma's defence expenditure have been compiled by the Stockholm International Peace Research Institute, the US Arms Control and Disarmament Agency, the International Monetary Fund and the International Institute for Strategic Studies. Over the past five years the Australian Defence Intelligence Organisation has also published useful statistics on defence economic trends in the Asia-Pacific region. Yet these five institutions differ markedly in the figures they produce. The differences stem in part from varying definitions of military expenditure. Although some conventions exist for the reporting of defence spending, the Burmese government does not follow them. It is therefore difficult to be certain what military activities are subsumed under the budgetary heading of Defence. It is also apparent that Burma does not include all current and capital expenditures, including arms purchases, in its declared budget. In addition, in compiling their figures the five institutions listed use different accounting methods.

The available figures from the IMF, SIPRI, ACDA, IISS and DIO are given below for comparison. They must be considered indicative only, however, and while helpful in assessing trends and orders of magnitude, considerable caution must be exercised in their use. Given all the problems outlined in Chapter Six, the inescapable conclusion is that no single government or private research institution is in a position to produce completely accurate and comprehensive figures for Burma's defence expenditure. This probably includes the Burmese government itself.

International Monetary Fund

Information used by the IMF is derived from voluntary returns made by national governments, based on data provided by government or central bank respondents. The IMF does not include in its figures the cost of pensions for military personnel, police, border and coast guards, receipts of military aid grants-in-kind, interest on military debt or intra-governmental transfers. It does, however, include civil defence spending and military expenditure financed by cash grants. The figures below are for the Burmese financial years beginning 1 April, and are given in millions of kyats.

	1988	1989	1990	1991	1992
Kyats m.	1763	4331	5436	6086	9126
	1993	1994	1995	1996	1997
Kyats m.	13,884	17,694	23,813	28,952	30,135

Source: International Monetary Fund, *Government Finance Statistics Yearbook 1999* (IMF, Washington, DC, 1999), p. 518.

Stockholm International Peace Research Institute

SIPRI generally uses the standard NATO definition of military expenditure, which includes all current and capital expenditure on the armed forces, the cost of defence departments (ministries) and other government agencies engaged in defence projects, as well as intra-governmental financial transfers. The figures given below for annual military expenditures are given in billions of kyats, at current prices, and US$ million at constant 1995 prices (CPI deflated), using official Burmese exchange rates. The 1999 figure is an estimate only.

	1990	1991	1992	1993	1994
Kyats bn.	5.2	5.9	8.4	12.7	16.7
US$ m.	3007	2610	3023	3480	3699
% of GDP	4.1	3.9	4.5	5.1	4.6
	1995	1996	1997	1998	1999
Kyats bn.	22.3	24.3	28.8	34.6	44.3
US$ m.	3932	3681	3364	2668	2969
% of GDP	4.7	4.0	3.6	3.1	NA

Source: Stockholm International Peace Research Institute, *SIPRI Yearbook 2000: Armaments, Disarmament and International Security* (Oxford University Press, Oxford, 2000), p. 273.

US Arms Control and Disarmament Agency

The ACDA drew its data from a number of sources, including the IMF, the CIA's *World Factbook*, the SIPRI *Yearbook* and the IISS's *Military Balance*. The ACDA did not publish any national currency data, but converted its estimates to constant US dollars, using a base-year exchange rate. The figures below are given in current US$ million and US$ million at constant 1995 prices. The figure for 1995 was an estimate.

Appendix: Burma's Defence Expenditure 315

	1989	1990	1991	1992	1993
US$m (current)	993	1093	1357	1650	1520
US$m ('95 prices)	1190	1256	1500	1775	1594
% of GNP	3.5	3.6	4.3	3.7	4.0
% of CGE	24.7	22.3	29.4	32.9	39.1
	1994	1995	1996	1997	1998
US$m (current)	1698	1833	NA	NA	NA
US$m ('95 prices)	1741	1833	NA	NA	NA
% of GNP	4.1	3.9	NA	NA	NA
% of CGE	36.7	37.5	NA	NA	NA

Source: *World Military Expenditures and Arms Transfers, 1996* (US Arms Control and Disarmament Agency, Washington, DC, 1997), p. 63.

Since the ACDA's absorption into the State Department in the late 1990s, and the creation of the Bureau of Verification and Compliance, different methods of calculating these statistics appear to have been used, with some startling results. While the BVC's figures do not go past 1996, they are radically different from those compiled earlier by the ACDA, and are given below for comparison.

	1989	1990	1991	1992	1993
US$m (current)	NA	NA	2330	3030	3490
US$m ('97 prices)	NA	NA	2640	3360	3770
% of GNP	NA	NA	7.2	8.3	8.8
% of CGE	NA	NA	49.4	74.3	88.6
	1994	1995	1996	1997	1998
US$m (current)	3330	4340	3960	NA	NA
US$m ('97 prices)	3520	4490	4030	NA	NA
% of GNP	7.6	9.1	7.6	NA	NA
% of CGE	74.5	84.0	75.5	NA	NA

Source: *World Military Expenditures and Arms Transfers 1998* (Bureau of Verification and Compliance, State Department, Washington, DC, 2000), p. 75.

International Institute for Strategic Studies

In compiling its statistics on non-NATO countries, the IISS takes official defence budgets and adjusts the figures to include all other known military-related expenditures. Particular estimates may vary from year to year, as updated data becomes available from governments, or revisions are made by the IISS itself in the light of new information. Where this occurs, the later figure has been given below. Allowances have also been made for the fact that, during the period under review, the IISS appears to have changed its method of listing defence budgets. Defence expenditure as a percentage of GDP is only given for a few years. The figures given below are in current US$ million and (where indicated) US$ billion.

	1990	1991	1992	1993	1994
US$m/bn	858	971	1.2bn	1.4bn	1.8bn
% of GDP	NA	NA	NA	NA	6.1
	1995	1996	1997	1998	1999
US$m/bn	1.9bn	1.6bn	2.2bn	2.1bn	2.0
% GDP	6.2	NA	NA	NA	NA

Sources: Annual entries for Burma/Myanmar in *The Military Balance 1989-1990* (International Institute for Strategic Studies, London, 1989) through to *The Military Balance 2000-2001* (Oxford University Press, London, 2000).

Australian Defence Intelligence Organisation

For the past five years DIO has released to the public its annual publication entitled *Defence Economic Trends in the Asia-Pacific*, which provides comprehensive unclassified data on defence spending trends in the region and the defence budgets of individual countries. There is also a very useful discussion of the difficulties in compiling accurate statistics of this kind. Its main sources include official figures provided by national governments, IMF publications and the *United Nations Monthly Bulletin of Statistics*. DIO also draws on other data where necessary, including the IISS *Military Balance*. The figures given below are in constant 1995 US dollars. The 1998 and 1999 figures are estimates only.

	1990	1991	1992	1993	1994
US$bn	2.9	2.9	2.6	2.2	2.4
% of GDP	3.6	3.6	2.9	2.4	2.4
% of CGE	22.3	24.3	26.3	24.1	23.6
	1995	1996	1997	1998	1999
US$bn	2.7	2.5	2.2	1.8	1.6
% GDP	2.6	2.2	1.8	1.5	1.3
% of CGE	23.8	27.3	29.3	36.4	44.8

Source: *Defence Economic Trends in the Asia-Pacific 1999* (Defence Intelligence Organisation, Canberra, 1999), p. 23.

Select Bibliography

OFFICIAL PUBLICATIONS

Burma

The Bomb Attack at the Martyrs' Mausoleum in Rangoon: Report on the findings by the Enquiry Committee and the measures taken by the Burmese Government (typescript, Rangoon, 1983).
Brief History of the Myanmar Army (Defence Services Museum and Historical Research Institute, Rangoon, 1999).
Burma and the Insurrections (Government of the Union of Burma, Rangoon, 1949).
Burma Communist Party's Conspiracy to Take Over State Power (SLORC, Rangoon, 1989).
A Concise History of Myanmar and the Tatmadaw's Role, 1948-1988, 2 vols. (Ministry of Education, Rangoon, 1989 and 1991).
The Conspiracy of Treasonous Minions Within the Myanmar Naing-ngan and Traitorous Cohorts Abroad (Ministry of Information, Rangoon, 1989).
The Correlation of Man and His Environment: The Philosophy of the Burma Socialist Programme Party (Burma Socialist Programme Party, Rangoon, 1963).
Endeavours of the Myanmar Armed Forces Government for National Reconsolidation (State Peace and Development Council, Rangoon, 2000).
Foreign Policy of the Revolutionary Government of the Union of Burma (Burma Socialist Programme Party, Rangoon, 1968).
History of the Myanmar Air Force (Committee for Compilation of the History of the Tatmadaw (Air), Rangoon, 1997).
History of the Tatmadaw (5 vols) (News and Periodicals Corporation, Ministry of Information, Rangoon, 1994-97) (in Burmese).
Hla Min, *Political Situation of Myanmar And Its Role In The Region* (Office of Strategic Studies, Rangoon, 1999).
Human Resource Development and Nation Building in Myanmar (Office of Strategic Studies, Rangoon, 1998).
Is Trust Vindicated? A chronicle of the various accomplishments of the Government headed by General Ne Win during the period of tenure from November, 1958 to February 6, 1960 (Director of Information, Rangoon, 1960).
Kuomintang Aggression Against Burma (Ministry of Information, Rangoon, 1953).
Measures Taken for Border Areas and National Races Development, 2 vols (Central Committee for Border Areas and National Races Development, Rangoon, 1991?).
The Myanmar Police Force (Ministry of Home Affairs, Government of the Union of Myanmar, Rangoon, 2000).

Skyful of Lies: BBC, VOA: Their Broadcasts and Rebuttals to Disinformation (News and Periodicals Enterprise, Ministry of Information, Rangoon, 1990).
Whither KNU? (by 'a resident of Kayin State') (News and Periodicals Enterprise, Ministry of Information, Rangoon, 1995).

United States

Country Reports on Human Rights Practices: Reports submitted to the Committee on Foreign Relations, US Senate, and Committee on International Relations, US House of Representatives (Bureau of Democracy, Human Rights and Labor, US Department of State, Washington, DC, annual).
Foreign Economic Trends Report: Burma (US Embassy, Rangoon, 1996).
Foreign Military Sales, Foreign Military Construction Sales and Military Assistance Facts, as of September 30, 1995 (US Department of Defence, Washington, DC, 1996).
Limits in the Seas, No. 36, National Claims to Maritime Jurisdictions, US Department of State, Bureau of Oceans and International Environmental and Scientific Affairs, Washington, DC, 1995.
Proliferation of Weapons of Mass Destruction: Assessing the Risks (Office of Technology Assessment, US Congress, Washington, DC, 1993).
The World Factbook (Central Intelligence Agency, Washington, DC, annual).
Union of Burma: Background Notes (US Department of State, Washington, DC, 1971).
World Military Expenditures and Arms Transfers, (US Arms Control and Disarmament Agency, Washington, DC, annual to 1996).
World Military Expenditures and Arms Transfers, (Bureau of Verification and Compliance, US State Department, Washington, DC, 2000).

Other

Burma: The Struggle for Independence, 1944-1948, 2 vols, ed. Hugh Tinker (Her Majesty's Stationery Office, London, 1984).
Country Economic Brief: Myanmar (Department of Foreign Affairs and Trade, Canberra, periodical).
Defence Economic Trends in the Asia-Pacific Region (Defence Intelligence Organisation, Canberra, annual).
Human Rights and Progress Towards Democracy in Burma, Report of the Joint Standing Committee on Foreign Affairs, Defence and Trade, Parliament of the Commonwealth of Australia (Australian Government Publishing Service, Canberra, 1995).
Rangoon Justice: North Korean Terrorists on Trial (Korean Overseas Information Service, Seoul, 1984).
Report of the Commission of Inquiry appointed under Article 26 of the Constitution of the International Labour Organisation to examine the observance by Myanmar of the Forced Labour Convention, 1930 (No. 29), Official Bulletin, Vol. 81, Series B, Geneva, 2 July 1998, available on the internet at http://www.ilko.org/public/english/standards/relm/gb/docs/gb273/myanmar.htm.

The Blue Helmets: A Review of United Nations Peace-Keeping (United Nations Department of Public Information, New York, 1996).
The Defence of Thailand (Ministry of Defence, Bangkok, annual).
United Nations Development Programme, *Human Development Report 1994* (Oxford University Press, Oxford, 1994).
United Nations Disarmament Yearbook (Centre for Disarmament Affairs, New York, annual).

MAJOR WORKS ON BURMA BY THE AUTHOR

Articles and Chapters

Ashton, William (pseud), 'Burma receives advances from its silent suitors in Singapore', *Jane's Intelligence Review*, Vol. 10, No. 3, March 1998.

——, 'Burma's armed forces: preparing for the 21st century', *Jane's Intelligence Review*, Vol. 10, No. 11, November 1998.

——, 'Burma's Chemical Weapons Status', *Jane's Intelligence Review*, Vol. 7, No. 6, June 1995.

——, 'The Burmese Air Force', *Jane's Intelligence Review*, Vol. 6, No. 10, October 1994.

——, 'The Burmese Navy', *Jane's Intelligence Review*, Vol. 6, No. 1, January 1994.

——, 'Chinese Bases in Burma — Fact or Fiction?', *Jane's Intelligence Review*, Vol. 7, No. 2, February 1995.

——, 'Israel sets sights on Myanmar', *Asia-Pacific Defence Reporter*, Vol. 25, No. 1, December 1999/January 2000.

——, 'Karens down but not out', *Asia-Pacific Defence Reporter*, Vol. 21, No. 8/9, May/June 1995.

——, 'Myanmar: Air Force gets arms boost', *Asia-Pacific Defence Reporter*, Vol. 18, No. 5, November 1991.

——, 'Myanmar: Chinese naval base: many rumours, few facts', *Asia-Pacific Defence Reporter*, Vol. 19/20, No. 12/1, June/July 1993.

——, 'Myanmar: Fearful army blocks transfer of power', *Asia-Pacific Defence Reporter*, Vol. 17, No. 6/7, December 1990/January 1991.

——, 'Myanmar: Foreign military training a mixed blessing', *Asia-Pacific Defence Reporter*, Vol. 24, No. 2, February/March 1998.

——, 'Myanmar: Invasion fears prompt search for air defences', *Asia-Pacific Defence Reporter*, Vol. 27, No. 2, March 2001.

——, 'Myanmar: The armed forces expand', *Asia-Pacific Defence Reporter*, Vol. 23, No. 1, January 1997.

——, 'Myanmar and Israel develop military pact', *Jane's Intelligence Review*, Vol. 12, No. 3, March 2000.

——, 'Myanmar junta forges secret defence ties', *Asia-Pacific Defence Reporter*, Vol. 26, No. 4, June/July 2000.

——, 'Myanmar Navy acquires SSM Capability', *Asia-Pacific Defence Reporter*, Vol. 25, No. 1, December 1999/January 2000.

——, 'Myanmar Navy boosts sea power with corvettes', *Jane's Navy International*, Vol. 105, No. 8, October 2000.
——, 'Myanmar revamps its military intelligence apparatus', *Asia-Pacific Defence Reporter*, Vol. 24, No. 2, June/July 1998.
——, 'Myanmar turns to Russia for arms', *Asia-Pacific Defence Reporter*, Vol. 22, No. 7/8, July/August 1996.
——, 'Myanmar's military links with Pakistan', *Jane's Intelligence Review*, Vol. 12, No. 6, June 2000.
——, 'What's in a Name: Burma', *Quadrant*, Vol. 316/39, No. 5, May 1995.
Selth, Andrew, 'The Armed Forces and Military Rule in Burma', in Robert I. Rotberg (ed), *Burma: Prospects for a Democratic Future* (Brookings Institution, Washington, 1998).
——, 'Australian Defence Contacts With Burma, 1948-1987', *Modern Asian Studies*, Vol. 26, No. 3, July 1992.
——, 'Burma and Biological Weapons', *Jane's Intelligence Review*, Vol. 7, No. 11, November 1995.
——, 'Burma and Exotic Weapons', *Strategic Analysis*, Vol. 19, No. 3, June 1996.
——, 'Burma and the Strategic Competition Between China and India', *Journal of Strategic Studies*, Vol. 19, No. 2, June 1996.
——, 'Burma develops its ability to build arms', *Jane's Intelligence Review*, Vol. 8, No. 5, May 1996.
——, 'The Burma Navy Under the SLORC', *Journal of Contemporary Asia*, Vol. 29, No. 2, 1999.
——, 'Burma: "Hidden Paradise" or Paradise Lost?', *Current Affairs Bulletin*, Vol. 68, No. 6, November 1991.
——, 'Burma's Defence Expenditure and Arms Industries', *Contemporary Security Policy*, Vol. 19, No. 2, August 1998.
——, 'Burma's Expanding Armed Forces: National Defence or National Disgrace?', *Current Affairs Bulletin*, Vol. 73, No. 3, October/November 1996.
——, 'Burma's Intelligence Apparatus', *Intelligence and National Security*, Vol. 13, No. 4, Winter 1998.
——, 'Burma's Military Expansion Program: Plans and Perceptions', *Journal of Contemporary Asia*, Vol. 26, No. 4, 1996.
——, 'The Burmese Army', *Jane's Intelligence Review*, Vol. 7, No. 11, November 1995.
——, 'Can Burma's Military Regime Survive?', *Australian Quarterly*, Vol. 68, No. 3, Spring 1996.
——, 'The Future of the Burmese Armed Forces', in Morten B. Pedersen, Emily Rudland and R.J. May (eds), *Burma-Myanmar: Strong Regime, Weak State?* (Crawford House, Adelaide, 2000).
——, 'Landmines in Burma: Forgotten Weapons in a Forgotten War', *Small Wars and Insurgencies*, Vol. 12, No. 2, Summer 2001.
——, 'Myanmar', in *Jane's Sentinel Security Assessment: Southeast Asia* (Jane's Information Systems, Coulsdon, 1997 and 2000) (with Bertil Lintner and John B. Haseman).

——, 'The Myanmar Air Force Since 1988: Expansion and Modernisation', *Contemporary Southeast Asia*, Vol. 19, No. 4, March 1998.
——, 'The Myanmar Army Since 1988: Acquisitions and Adjustments', *Contemporary Southeast Asia*, Vol. 17, No. 3, December 1995.
——, 'The Myanmar Navy: From Brown Water to Blue Water', *Naval Forces*, Vol. 19, No. 6, 1998.
——, 'Myanmar's forgotten minefields', *Jane's Intelligence Review*, Vol. 12, No. 10, October 2000 (with Yeshua Moser-Puangsuwan).
——, 'Race and Resistance in Burma, 1942-1945', *Modern Asian Studies*, Vol. 20, No. 3, July 1986.
——, 'Strategic Change in the Asia-Pacific Region', *The RUSI Journal*, Vol. 139, No. 5, October 1994.

Books, Monographs and Research Papers

Selth, Andrew, *'Assisting the Defence of Australia': Australian Defence Contacts With Burma, 1945-1987*, Working Paper No. 218 (Strategic and Defence Studies Centre, Australian National University, Canberra, 1990).
——, *Burma: A Strategic Perspective*, The Asia Foundation, Working Paper No. 13 (San Francisco, 2001).
——, *Burma and Weapons of Mass Destruction*, Working Paper No. 334 (Strategic and Defence Studies Centre, Australian National University, Canberra, 1999).
——, *Burma's Armed Forces Under Civilian Rule: A Return to the Past?*, Working Paper No. 02/01 (Technical Advisory Network of Burma, Washington, 2001)
——, *Burma's Arms Procurement Programme*, Working Paper No. 289 (Strategic and Defence Studies Centre, Australian National University, Canberra, 1995).
——, *Burma's Defence Expenditure and Arms Industries*, Working Paper No. 309 (Strategic and Defence Studies Centre, Australian National University, Canberra, 1997).
——, *Burma's Intelligence Apparatus*, Working Paper No. 308 (Strategic and Defence Studies Centre, Australian National University, Canberra, 1997).
——, *Burma's Order of Battle: An Interim Assessment*, Working Paper No. 351 (Strategic and Defence Studies Centre, Australian National University, Canberra, 2000).
——, *Burma's Secret Military Partners*, Canberra Papers on Strategy and Defence No. 136 (Strategic and Defence Studies Centre, Australian National University, Canberra, 2000).
——, *Death of a Hero: The U Thant Disturbances in Burma, December 1974*, Australia-Asia Paper No. 49 (Centre for the Study of Australia-Asia Relations, Griffith University, Brisbane, 1993).
——, *Landmines in Burma: The Military Dimension*, Working Paper No. 352 (Strategic and Defence Studies Centre, Australian National University, Canberra, 2000).
——, *The Burma Air Force*, Working Paper No. 315 (Strategic and Defence Studies Centre, Australian National University, Canberra, 1997).
——, *The Burma Navy*, Working Paper No. 313 (Strategic and Defence Studies Centre, Australian National University, Canberra, 1997).

——, *The Burmese Armed Forces Next Century: Continuity or Change?*, Working Paper No. 338 (Strategic and Defence Studies Centre, Australian National University, Canberra, 1999).
——, *Transforming the Tatmadaw: The Burmese Armed Forces Since 1988*, Canberra Papers on Strategy and Defence No. 113 (Strategic and Defence Studies Centre, Australian National University, Canberra, 1996).

MAJOR ARTICLES AND CHAPTERS

Badgley, John, 'The Burmese Way to Capitalism', in *Southeast Asian Affairs 1990* (Institute for Southeast Asian Studies, Singapore, 1990).
Ball, Desmond, 'Signals Intelligence in China', *Jane's Intelligence Review*, Vol. 7, No. 8, August 1995.
——, 'Signals Intelligence in India', *Intelligence and National Security*, Vol. 10, No. 3, July 1995.
Bray, John, 'Ethnic minorities and the future of Burma', *The World Today*, August/September 1992.
Callahan, M.P., 'Burma in 1995', *Asian Survey*, Vol. 36, No. 2, February 1996.
——, 'Democracy in Burma: The Lessons of History', National Bureau of Asian Research, *Analysis*, Vol. 9, No. 3, May 1998.
——, 'Junta Dreams or Nightmares? Observations of Burma's Military Since 1988', *Bulletin of Concerned Asian Scholars*, Vol. 31, No. 3, 1999.
Chao-Tzang Yawnghwe, 'Burma: The Depoliticization of the Political', in Muthiah Alagappa (ed), *Political Legitimacy in Southeast Asia: The Quest for Moral Authority* (Stanford University Press, Stanford, 1995).
Cribb, Robert, 'Burma's Entry Into ASEAN: Background and Implications', *Asian Perspective*, Vol. 22, No. 3, 1998.
Davis, Anthony, 'Burma casts wary eye on China', *Jane's Intelligence Review*, Vol. 11, No. 6, June 1999.
Ember, L.R., 'Worldwide Spread of Chemical Arms Receiving Increased Attention', *Chemical and Engineering News*, Vol. 64, No. 15, 14 April 1986.
Harris, E.D., 'Chemical Weapons Proliferation in the Developing World', in *RUSI and Brassey's Defence Yearbook 1989* (Brassey's, London, 1989).
Lintner, Bertil, 'Burma — Struggle for Power', *Jane's Intelligence Review*, Vol. 5, No. 10, October 1993.
——, 'Global Reach: Drug Money in the Asia Pacific', *Current History*, April 1988.
——, 'Myanmar's Chinese connection', *International Defence Review*, Vol. 27, No. 11, November 1994.
——, 'Myanmar's military intelligence' *International Defence Review*, Vol. 24, No. 1, January 1991.
——, 'The Indo-Burmese Frontier - A Legacy of Violence', *Jane's Intelligence Review*, Vol. 6, No. 1, January 1994.
——, 'The Volatile Yunnan Frontier', *Jane's Intelligence Review*, Vol. 6, No. 2, February 1994.
Malik, Mohan, 'Myanmar's Role in Regional Security: Pawn or Pivot?', *Contemporary Southeast Asia*, Vol. 19, No. 1, June 1997.

——, 'Sino-Indian Rivalry in Myanmar: Implications for Regional Security', *Contemporary Southeast Asia*, Vol. 16, No. 2, September 1994.
——, 'Burma slides under China's shadow', *Jane's Intelligence Review*, Vol. 9, No. 7, July 1997.
McCain, J.S., 'Proliferation in the 1990s: Implications for US Policy and Force Planning', *Strategic Review*, Vol. 17, No. 3, Summer 1989.
Merrill, Kay, 'A closer look at Sino-Burmese military links', *Jane's Intelligence Review*, Vol. 9, No. 7, July 1997.
——, 'Burma looks set to reject the lessons of history', *Jane's Intelligence Review*, Vol. 11, No. 8, August 1999.
——, 'Myanmar's China connection: a cause for alarm?', *Asia-Pacific Defence Reporter*, Vol. 24, No. 1, January 1998.
Misra, K.P., 'Burma's Farewell to the Nonaligned Movement', *Asian Affairs*, Vol. 12, No. 1, February 1981.
Mya Maung, 'On the Road to Mandalay: A Case Study of the Sinonization of Upper Burma', *Asian Survey*, Vol. 34, No. 5, May 1994.
Overholt, W.H., 'Dateline Drug Wars: Burma: The Wrong Enemy', *Foreign Policy*, No. 77, Winter, 1989-90.
Pan Qi, 'Opening the Southwest: An Expert Opinion', *Beijing Review*, Vol. 28, No. 35, 2 September 1985.
Rolls, M.G., 'Thailand's Post-Cold War Security Policy and Defence Programme', in Colin McInnes and M.G. Rolls (eds), *Post-Cold War Security Issues in the Asia-Pacific Region* (Frank Cass, Ilford, 1994).
Ross, A.L., 'Growth, Debt and Military Spending in Southeast Asia', *Contemporary Southeast Asia*, Vol. 11, No. 4, March 1990.
Roy-Chaudhury, R., 'Strategic Trends in the Indian Ocean', *Strategic Analysis*, Vol. 19, No. 6, September 1996.
——, 'Trends in the Delimitation of India's Maritime Boundaries', *Strategic Analysis*, Vol. 22, No. 10, January 1999.
Silverstein, Josef, 'Aung San Suu Kyi: Is She Burma's Woman of Destiny?', *Asian Survey*, Vol. 30, No. 10, October 1990.
——, 'Burma in 1981: The Changing of the Guardians Begins', *Asian Survey*, Vol. 22, No. 2, February 1982.
Singh, Bilveer, 'ASEAN's Arms Procurements: Challenge of the Security Dilemma in the Post Cold War Era', *Comparative Strategy*, Vol. 12, No. 2, April-June 1993.
Singh, Swaran, 'Myanmar: China's Gateway to the Indian Ocean', *Journal of Indian Ocean Studies*, Vol. 3, No. 1, November 1995.
Singh, U.B., 'Growth of Military Power in South-East Asia', in *Asian Strategic Review 1994-95* (Institute for Defence and Strategic Analysis, New Delhi, 1995).
——, 'Recent Trends in Relations Between Myanmar and China', *Strategic Analysis*, Vol. 18, No. 1, April 1995.
Smith, James, 'Myanmar's Armed Forces — Retaining Power', *Jane's Intelligence Review*, Vol. 3, No. 9, September 1991.
Smith, Martin, 'The Burmese way to rack and ruin', Article 19, *Index on Censorship*, No. 10, 1991.

——, 'A State of Strife: The Indigenous Peoples of Burma', in R.H. Barnes, Andrew Gray and Benedict Kingsbury (eds), *Indigenous Peoples of Asia* (Association for Asian Studies, Ann Arbor, 1995).

Steinberg, D.I., 'A Void in Myanmar: Civil Society in Burma', in Burma Netherlands and Transnational Institute (eds), *Strengthening Civil Society in Burma: Possibilities and Dilemmas for International NGOs* (Silkworm Books, Chiang Mai, 1999).

——, 'Myanmar as Nexus: Sino-Indian Rivalries on the Frontier', *Studies in Conflict and Terrorism*, Vol. 16, No. 1, 1993.

——, 'The Union Solidarity Development Association: Mobilization and Orthodoxy', *Burma Debate*, Vol. 4, No. 1, January-February 1997.

Stelzmuller, F.H., 'NBC Defence: a German viewpoint', *International Defence Review*, No. 15, November 1982.

——, 'The NBC Threat — Effective Protection and Countermeasures', *Armada International*, No. 8, December 1985.

Stobdan, P., 'China's Forays into Burma — Implication for India', *Strategic Analysis*, Vol. 16, No. 1, April 1993.

Sundhaussen, Ulf, 'Indonesia's New Order: A Model for Myanmar', *Asian Survey*, Vol. 35, No. 8, August 1995.

Taylor, R.H., 'Burma', in Zakaria Haji Ahmad and Harold Crouch (eds), *Military-Civilian Relations in South-East Asia* (Oxford University Press, Singapore, 1985).

——, 'Burma: Defence Expenditure and Threat Perceptions', in Chin Kin Wah (ed), *Defence Spending in Southeast Asia* (Institute of South East Asian Studies, Singapore, 1987).

——, 'Burma: Political Leadership, Security Perceptions and Policies', in Mohammed Ayoob and Chai-Anan Samudavanija (eds), *Leadership Perceptions and National Security: The Southeast Asian Experience* (Institute of Southeast Asian Studies, Singapore, 1989).

——, 'Perceptions of Ethnicity in the Politics of Burma', *Southeast Asian Journal of Social Science*, Vol. 10, No. 1, 1982.

——, 'The Military in Myanmar (Burma): What Scope for a New Role?', in Viberto Selochan (ed), *The Military, the State, and Development in Asia and the Pacific* (Westview, Boulder, 1991).

Thaung, 'Army's Accumulation of Economic Power in Burma, 1940-1990', *Burma Review*, No. 20, October 1990.

Tin Maung Maung Than, 'Burma in 1983: From Recovery to Growth?', *Southeast Asian Affairs 1984* (Institute of Southeast Asian Studies, Singapore, 1984).

——, 'Burma in 1987: Twenty-Five Years After the Revolution', *Southeast Asian Affairs 1988* (Institute of Southeast Asian Studies, Singapore, 1988).

——, 'Burma's National Security and Defence Posture', *Contemporary Southeast Asia*, Vol. 11, No. 1, June 1989.

——, 'Myanmar: Myanmar-ness and Realism in Historical Perspective', in Ken Booth and Russell Trood (eds), *Strategic Cultures in the Asia-Pacific Region* (St Martin's Press, New York, 1999).

——, 'Myanmar: Preoccupation with Regime Survival, National Unity, and Stability', in Muthiah Alagappa (ed), *Asian Security Practice: Material and Ideational Influences* (Stanford University Press, Stanford, 1998).

——, 'Myanmar Democratization: Punctuated Equilibrium or Retrograde Motion?', in Anek Laothamatas (ed), *Democratization in Southeast and East Asia* (Institute of Southeast Asian Studies, Singapore, 1997).
——, 'Neither Inheritance nor Legacy: Leading the Myanmar State since Independence', *Contemporary Southeast Asia*, Vol. 15, No. 1, June 1993.
Wiant, J.A. and D.I. Steinberg, 'Burma: The Military and National Development', in J.S. Djiwandono and Yong Mun Cheong (eds), *Soldiers and Stability in Southeast Asia* (Institute of Southeast Asian Studies, Singapore, 1988).

BOOKS, MONOGRAPHS AND RESEARCH PAPERS

Allen, Louis, *Burma: The Longest War, 1941-1945* (Dent and Sons, London, 1984).
Amnesty International, *Human rights violations against Muslims in the Rhakine (Arakan) State* (Amnesty International, London, 1992).
——, *Myanmar* (Amnesty International, London, 1990).
——, *Myanmar: Human rights after seven years of military rule* (Amnesty International, London, 1995).
——, *Myanmar: 'In the National Interest': Prisoners of conscience, torture, summary trials under martial law* (Amnesty International, London, 1990).
——, *Myanmar: 'No Law at All': Human rights violations under military rule* (Amnesty International, London, 1992).
——, *Myanmar: Renewed repression* (Amnesty International, London, 1996).
——, *Myanmar: The Institution of Torture* (Amnesty International, London, 2000).
——, *The Kayin State in the Union of Myanmar: Allegations of Ill-treatment and Unlawful Killings of Suspected Political Opponents and Porters Siezed Since 18 September 1988* (Amnesty International, London, 1989).
Apple, Betsy, *School for Rape* (Earthrights International, Bangkok, 1998).
The APT Yearbook 1999 (Asia-Pacific Telecommunity, Bangkok, 1999).
Asia Report: Myanmar, Coalition to Stop the Use of Child Soldiers, London, 2000, found at http://www.childsoldiers.ord/reports_asia/myanmar.html.
Asia Yearbook (Far Eastern Economic Review, Hong Kong, annual).
Asia Watch, *Human Rights in Burma (Myanmar)* (Asia Watch, New York, 1990).
Aung San Suu Kyi, *Freedom From Fear and other writings*, ed. Michael Aris (Penguin, London, 1991).
——, *Letters From Burma* (Penguin, London, 1997).
——, *The Voice of Hope: Conversations with Alan Clements with contributions by U Kyi Maung and U Tin U* (Penguin, London, 1997).
Aye Saung, *Burman in the Back Row* (White Lotus, Bangkok, 1989).
Ba Than, *The Roots of the Revolution: A brief history of the Defence Services of the Union of Burma and the Ideals for which they stand* (Guardian, Rangoon, 1962).
Ball, Desmond, *Burma and Drugs: The Regime's Complicity in the Global Drug Trade*, Working Paper No. 336 (Strategic and Defence Studies Centre, Australian National University, Canberra, 1999).
——, *Burma's Military Secrets: Signals Intelligence (SIGINT) from the Second World War to Civil War and Cyber Warfare* (White Lotus, Bangkok, 1998).

——, *Signals Intelligence in the Post-Cold War Era: Developments in the Asia-Pacific Region* (Institute of Southeast Asian Studies, Singapore, 1993).
Baranwal, Jayant, (ed), *SP's Military Yearbook* (Guide Publications, New Delhi, annual).
Bay of Bengal Pilot (Royal Navy Hydrographer, Taunton, 1978).
Beyrer, Chris, *War in the Blood: Sex, Politics and AIDS in Southeast Asia* (Zed Books, London, 1998).
Boucard, Andre and Louis, *Burma's Golden Triangle: On the Trail of the Opium Warlords* (Asia 2000, Hong Kong, 1992).
Bunge, F.M. (ed), *Burma: a country study* (American University, Washington, 1983).
Burck, G.M. and Flowerree, C.C., *International Handbook on Chemical Weapons Proliferation* (Greenwood Press, New York, 1991).
Burma: Landmine Monitor Report 2000 (International Campaign to Ban Landmines, Bangkok, 2000).
Burma/Myanmar: How Strong is the Military Regime?, International Crisis Group, Asia Report No. 11, Brussels, 21 December 2000.
Cady, J.F., *A History of Modern Burma* (Cornell University Press, Ithaca, 1978).
Carey, Peter (ed), *Burma: The Challenge of Change in a Divided Society* (Macmillan, London, 1997).
Cheeseman, Graeme, and Leaver, Richard, *Trends in Arms Spending and Conventional Arms Trade in the Asia-Pacific Region*, Working Paper No. 32 (Australian Defence Studies Centre, Australian Defence Force Academy, Canberra, 1995).
Danitz, Tiffany and Strobel, W.P., *Networking Dissent: Cyber-Activists Use the Internet to promote Democracy in Burma*, United States Institute of Peace, Virtual Diplomacy Report, 8 November 1999, on the internet at http://www.usip.org/oc/vd/vdr/vburma/vburma_intro.html.
Donnison, F.S.V., *Public Administration in Burma: A Study of Development During the British Connexion* (Royal Institute of International Affairs, London, 1953).
Dupuy, T.N. (ed), *The Almanac of World Military Power* (Bowker, New York, annual).
Economist Intelligence Unit, *Country Profile: Cambodia, Laos, Myanmar* (The Economist, London, 1995).
——, *Country Profile: Myanmar (Burma)* (The Economist, London, annual from 1996).
——, *Country Profile: Thailand, Myanmar* (The Economist, London, annual to 1994).
Ezell, E.C., *Small Arms Of The World* (Stackpole, Harrisburg, 1990).
Falla, Jonathan, *True Love and Bartholomew: Rebels on the Burmese Border* (Cambridge University Press, Cambridge, 1991).
Fink, Christina, *Living Silence: Burma Under Military Rule* (Zed, London, 2001).
Fisher, C.A., *South-east Asia: A Social, Economic and Political Geography* (Methuen, London, 1964).
Flintham, Victor, *Air Wars and Aircraft: A Detailed Record of Air Combat, 1945 to the Present* (Arms and Armour Press, London, 1989).
Francillon, R.J. (ed), *The Naval Institute Guide to World Military Aviation 1995* (Naval Institute Press, Annapolis, 1995).
Gill, Bates and Mak, J.N. (eds), *Arms, Transparency and Security in Southeast Asia* (Oxford University Press, Oxford, 1997).

Haseman, J.B., *Burma's Myriad National Security Challenges: The Historical Background and Contemporary Events*, Working Paper No. 50 (Australian Defence Studies Centre, Australian Defence Force Academy, Canberra, 1997).
Henderson, J.W. et al., *Area Handbook for Burma* (American University, Washington, 1971).
Human Rights Watch/Asia, *Burma: Entrenchment or Reform? Human Rights Developments and the Need for Continued Pressure* (Human Rights Watch/Asia, New York, 1995).
——, *Rohingya Refugees in Bangladesh: The Search for a Lasting Solution*, Human Rights Watch/Asia, Vol. 9, No. 7, August 1997.
International Institute for Strategic Studies, *The Military Balance* (IISS and Oxford University Press, London, annual).
International Monetary Fund, *Government Financial Statistics Yearbook* (IMF, Washington, annual).
Jane's All the World's Aircraft (Jane's Information Group, Coulsdon, annual).
Jane's Aircraft Upgrades (Jane's Information Group, Coulsdon, annual).
Jane's Air-Launched Weapons (Jane's Information Group, Coulsdon, periodic).
Jane's Armour and Artillery (Jane's Information Group, Coulsdon, annual).
Jane's Fighting Ships (Jane's Information Group, Coulsdon, annual).
Jane's Infantry Weapons (Jane's Information Group, Coulsdon, annual).
Jane's Land-Based Air Defence (Jane's Information Group, Coulsdon, annual).
Jane's Military Communications (Jane's Information Group, Coulsdon, annual).
Jane's Military Vehicles and Logistics (Jane's Information Group, Coulsdon, annual).
Jane's Mines and Mine Clearance (Jane's Information Group, Coulsdon, annual from 1996).
Jane's Nuclear, Biological and Chemical Weapons (Jane's Information Group, Coulsdon, annual).
Jane's Radar and Electronic Warfare Systems (Jane's Information Group, Coulsdon, annual).
Jane's Sentinel Security Assessment: Southeast Asia (Jane's Information Group, Coulsdon, periodic).
Jane's Space Directory (Jane's Information Group, Coulsdon, annual).
Jane's World Air Forces: Order of Battle and Inventories (Jane's Information Group, Coulsdon, periodic).
Jane's World Airlines (Jane's Information Group, Coulsdon, 1997).
Kaznacheev, Aleksandr, *Inside a Soviet Embassy: Experiences of a Russian Diplomat in Burma* (Lippincott, Philadelphia, 1962).
Kent, George, and Valencia, M.J., *Marine Policy in Southeast Asia* (University of California Press, Berkeley, 1985).
Kin Oung, *Who Killed Aung San?* (White Lotus, Bangkok, 1996).
Kunstadter, Peter (ed), *Southeast Asian Tribes, Minorities, and Nations*, 2 vols, (Princeton University Press, Princeton, 1967).
Lang, Hazel, *Fear and Sanctuary: Burmese Refugees in Thailand* (Cornell Southeast Asia Program, Ithaca, 2001).
Lebra, J.C., *Japanese-Trained Armies in Southeast Asia: Independence and Volunteer Forces in World War II* (Heinemann, Hong Kong, 1977).

Liang, Chi-shad, *Burma's Foreign Relations: Neutralism in Theory and Practice* (Praeger, New York, 1990).
Lintner, Bertil, *Aung San Suu Kyi and Burma's Unfinished Renaissance* (Peacock Press, Bangkok, 1990).
——, *Burma in Revolt: Opium and Insurgency Since 1948* (Silkworm Books, Chiang Mai, 1999).
——, *Land of Jade: A Journey Through Insurgent Burma* (Kiscadale, Edinburgh, 1990).
——, *Outrage: Burma's Struggle for Democracy* (White Lotus, Bangkok, 1990).
——, *The Drug Trade in Southeast Asia*, Special Report No. 5, *Jane's Intelligence Review*, April 1994.
——, *The Politics of the Drug Trade in Burma*, Occasional Paper No. 33 (Indian Ocean Centre for Peace Studies, University of Western Australia, Nedlands, 1993).
——, *The Rise and Fall of the Communist Party of Burma (CPB)* (Cornell University, Ithaca, 1990).
Lissak, Moshe, *Military Roles in Modernization: Civil-Military Relations in Thailand and Burma* (Sage, Beverly Hills, 1976).
Maung Htin Aung, *A History of Burma* (Columbia University Press, New York, 1967).
Maung Aung Myoe, *Building the Tatmadaw: The Organisational Development of the Armed Forces in Myanmar, 1948-98*, Working Paper No. 327 (Strategic and Defence Studies Centre, Australian National University, Canberra, 1998).
——, *Military Doctrine and Strategy in Myanmar: A Historical Perspective*, Working Paper No. 339 (Strategic and Defence Studies Centre, Australian National University, Canberra, 1999).
——, *Officer Education and Leadership Training in the Tatmadaw: A Survey*, Working Paper No. 346 (Strategic and Defence Studies Centre, Australian National University, Canberra, 2000).
——, *The Tatmadaw in Myanmar Since 1988: An Interim Assessment*, Working Paper No. 342 (Strategic and Defence Studies Centre, Australian National University, Canberra, 1999).
Maung Maung, *Burmese Nationalist Movements 1940-1948* (Kiscadale, Edinburgh, 1989).
——, *From Sangha to Laity: Nationalist Movements of Burma, 1920-1940*, Australian National University Monographs on South Asia No. 4 (Manohar, Delhi, 1980).
Maung Maung, Dr, *Burma and General Ne Win* (Asia Publishing House, Bombay, 1969).
——, *Burma in the Family of Nations* (Djambatan, Amsterdam, 1956).
——, *The 1988 Uprising in Burma*, Monograph No. 49 (Yale University Southeast Asia Studies, New Haven, 1999).
——, *To a Soldier Son* (Sarpay Beikman, Rangoon, 1974).
——, (ed), *Aung San of Burma* (Martinus Nijhoff, The Hague, 1962).
Military Bureaucracy of the SLORC, All Burma Students Democratic Front, Documentation and Research Centre, Mae Hong Son, 4 September 1995.
The Military Powers Encyclopedia: Southeast Asia (Societe I^{3}C, Paris, 1991).
Min Maung Maung, *The Tatmadaw and its leadership role in national politics* (Ministry of Information, Rangoon, 1993).

Mirante, Edith, *Burmese Looking Glass: A Human Rights Adventure and A Jungle Revolution* (Grove Press, New York, 1993).
Moscotti, A.D., *British Policy and the Nationalist Movement in Burma, 1917-1937* (University Press of Hawaii, Honolulu, 1974).
——, *Burma's Constitution and Elections of 1974* (Institute of Southeast Asian Studies, Singapore, 1977).
Mya Maung, *The Burma Road to Capitalism: Economic Growth versus Democracy* (Praeger, Westport, 1998).
——, *The Burma Road to Poverty* (Praeger, New York, 1991).
——, *Totalitarianism in Burma: Prospects for Economic Development* (Paragon House, New York, 1992).
Mya Win, *Tatmadaw's Traditional Role in National Politics* (Ministry of Information, Rangoon, 1992).
National Coalition Government of the Union of Burma, *Human Rights Yearbook: Burma* (NCGUB Human Rights Documentation Unit, Bangkok, annual from 1995).
Nelson, T.B., *The World's Submachine Guns* (Arms and Armour Press, London, 1977).
No Childhood At All: A Report About Child Soldiers in Burma (Images Asia, Chiang Mai, 1997).
O'Brien, Harriet, *Forgotten Land: A Rediscovery of Burma* (Michael Joseph, London, 1991).
Pedersen, Morten B., Rudland, Emily and May, R.J. (eds), *Burma-Myanmar: Strong Regime, Weak State?* (Crawford House, Adelaide, 2000).
The Pentagon Papers (Bantam Books, Toronto, 1971).
Pettman, Ralph, *China in Burma's Foreign Policy*, Contemporary China Papers No. 7 (Contemporary China Centre, Australian National University, Canberra, 1973).
Prezelin, Bernard (ed), *Naval Institute Guide to Combat Fleets of the World 1995* (Naval Institute Press, Annapolis, 1995).
Roberts, T.D. et al., *Area Handbook for Burma* (American University, Washington, 1968).
Rotberg, R.I. (ed), *Burma: Prospects for a Democratic Future* (Brookings Institution, Washington, 1998).
Sesser, Stan, *The Lands of Charm and Cruelty: Travels in Southeast Asia* (Alfred Knopf, New York, 1993).
Silverstein, Josef, *Burmese Politics: The Dilemma of National Unity* (Rutgers University Press, New Brunswick, 1980).
——, (ed), *The Political Legacy of Aung San*, Southeast Asia Program Series No. 11 (Cornell University, Ithaca, 1993).
Sivard, R.L., *World Military Expenditures and Arms Transfers* (World Priorities, Washington, annual).
Slim, William, *Defeat Into Victory* (Cassell, London, 1956).
Smith, C.B., *The Burmese Communist Party in the 1980s* (Institute of Southeast Asian Studies, Singapore, 1984).
Smith, Graham, *Military Small Arms* (Salamander, London, 1994).
Smith, Martin, *Burma: Insurgency and the Politics of Ethnicity* (Zed Books, London, 1999).

———, (with Annie Allsebrook), *Ethnic Groups in Burma: Development, Democracy and Human Rights* (Anti-Slavery International, London, 1994).
Smith, W.H.B., *Small Arms of the World* (Stackpole, Harrisburg, 1983).
Soley, L.C. and J.S. Nicholls, *Clandestine Radio Broadcasting: A Study of Revolutionary and Counter-revolutionary Electronic Communication* (Praeger, New York, 1987).
Steinberg, D.I., *Burma: A Socialist Nation of Southeast Asia* (Westview, Boulder, 1982).
———, *Burma: Prospects for Political and Economic Reconstruction*, World Peace Foundation Reports, No. 15 (World Peace Foundation, Cambridge, 1997).
———, *Burma: The State of Myanmar* (Georgetown University Press, Washington, 2001).
———, *Burma's Road Toward Development: Growth and Ideology Under Military Rule* (Westview, Boulder, 1981).
———, *The Future of Burma: Crisis and Choice in Myanmar*, Asian Agenda Report No. 14 (The Asia Society and University Press of America, Lanham, 1990).
Stockholm International Peace Research Institute, *Arms Trade Registers: The Arms Trade with the Third World* (MIT Press, Cambridge, 1975).
———, *Incendiary Weapons* (MIT Press, Cambridge, 1975).
———, *The Arms Trade with the Third World* (Paul Elek, London, 1971).
———, *Yearbook: World Armaments and Disarmament* (Oxford University Press, Oxford, annual).
Taylor, R.H., *Foreign and Domestic Consequences of the KMT Intervention in Burma*, Department of Asian Studies Data Paper No. 93 (Cornell University, Ithaca, 1973).
———, *The State in Burma* (Hurst and Co., London, 1987).
Tilman, R.O., *The Enemy Beyond: External Threat Perceptions in the ASEAN Region* (Institute for Southeast Asian Studies, Singapore, 1984).
Tinker, Hugh, *The Union of Burma: A Study of the First Years of Independence* (Oxford University Press, London, 1957).
Towards Democracy in Burma (Institute for Asian Democracy, Washington, 1992).
Trager, F.N., *Burma: From Kingdom to Independence: A Historical and Political Analysis* (Pall Mall, London, 1966).
Woodman, Dorothy, *The Making of Burma* (Cresset, London, 1962).
World Radio TV Handbook: The Directory of International Broadcasting (WRTH Publishing, Milton Keynes, 2000).

PERIODICALS

Magazines and Journals

Aeroplane Monthly
Air Enthusiast
Air International
ANU Reporter
Armada International

Asia-Pacific Defence Reporter
Asian Airlines and Aerospace
Asian Aviation
Asian Communications
Asian Defence and Diplomacy
Asian Defence Journal
Asian Recorder
Asiaweek
Burma Debate
Burma News Update
Burma Review
Bulletin
Defense and Foreign Affairs
Diplomacy
Economist
Far Eastern Economic Review
Flight International
Fly Past
Frontline
India Today
Indian Defence Review
International Defence Review
Jane's Defence Weekly
Jane's Intelligence Review
Jane's International Defence Review
Jane's Pointer
Lancet
Military Technology
Newsweek
Pacific Defence Reporter
Popular Communications
Quadrant
Soldier of Fortune
Thai-Yunnan Newsletter
Time
US Naval Institute Proceedings
US News and World Report
Vayu Aerospace Review
World Airpower Journal

Newspapers

The Age (Melbourne)
Asian Age (New Delhi)
Asia Times (Bangkok)
Asian Wall Street Journal (Hong Kong)

The Australian (Sydney)
Australian Financial Review (Sydney)
Bangkok Daily News (Bangkok)
Bangkok Post (Bangkok)
Business Times (Kuala Lumpur)
Canberra Times (Canberra)
Christian Science Monitor (Boston)
Defense News (Washington)
Financial Times (London)
Guardian (London)
Herald (Melbourne)
Hindustan Times (Delhi)
Independent (London)
Indian Express (Delhi)
International Herald Tribune (Paris)
Kyemon (Rangoon)
Myanmar Times (Rangoon)
The Nation (Bangkok)
National Times (Sydney)
New Light of Myanmar (Rangoon)
New York Times (New York)
Pioneer (New Delhi)
South China Morning Post (Hong Kong)
Straits Times (Singapore)
Sydney Morning Herald (Sydney)
Thailand Times (Bangkok)
The Times (London)
Times of India (New Delhi)
Washington Post (Washington)
Working People's Daily (Rangoon)

UNPUBLISHED WORKS

Aung Than, 'Rural Telecommunications in Myanmar', paper presented to the Asia-Pacific Telecommunity Seminar on Rural Telecommunications, 6-12 February 1991, Brisbane, Australia.
Callahan, M.P., 'The Origins of Military Rule in Burma', unpublished PhD thesis, Cornell University, 1996.
Karen Human Rights Group, 'Chemical Shells at Kaw Moo Rah', A Special Independent Report by the Karen Human Rights Group, (Typescript, Bangkok, 24 February 1995).
——, 'Is The SLORC Using Bacteriological Warfare?', Preliminary Report based on information independently gathered by the Karen Human Rights Group (Typescript, Bangkok, 1994).

Maung Aung Myoe, 'The Counterinsurgency in Myanmar: The Government's Response to the Burma Communist Party' unpublished PhD thesis, Australian National University, 1999.
Principles and Policy Statement of the National Coalition Government of the Union of Burma (NCGUB Ministry of Information, n.p., 1991).
Report of the Defence Committee of the Committee Representing the People's Parliament: Report on the Formation of a Modern Tatmadaw in the Democratic Era, 1999. Unofficial translation, typescript in the author's possession.
Yoon Won-zoon, 'Japan's Occupation of Burma, 1941-1945', unpublished PhD thesis, New York University, 1971.

OTHER SOURCES

Agence France Presse
Associated Press
Australian Associated Press
BBC Summary of World Broadcasts
BurmaNet News
Foreign Broadcast Information Service
Reuters
Special Broadcasting Service Television (Australia)

Index

A

A Concise History of Myanmar and the Tatmadaw's Role, xxvi
Administrative Support Training School, 163
Afghanistan, 215
  defence policy, 41
  strategic environment (post-1988), 20
AIDS. *See* HIV/AIDS
Air Mandalay, 221, 231n.130
Akha, 34
All India Radio, 109
Amnesty International, 115
Apprentice Officer scheme, 84
Arakan State
  annexation, 8, 13, 22n.29
  defence policy, 41
  demographics, 5, 7
Armour and Artillery School, 171
Arms Control and Disarmament Agency (United States), 131, 134-35, 138-40, 313, 314-15
Arms embargo
  Australia, 207, 222, 231n.140
  Burma Air Force, 207, 222, 231n.140
  Burma Navy, 193
  defence industry, 141-42
  European Union, 138, 193
  Russia, 217
  United States, 138
Arms procurement
  contemporary government
    Burma Air Force, 222, 223, 224-25
    expansion rationale, 256-57
    policy agenda, 268-69
  defence expenditure
    arms imports (1973-1987), 133*f*
    arms transfers (1973-1987), 133*f*
    military expansion, 133, 149n.18
    post-1988, 137-40
    pre-1988, 132-33

democratic future, 284
See also specific countries
Asia Handbook (Tinker), 3
Asian Affairs, 253
Asian Aviation, 170
Asiasat, 65, 66
Assam, 14
Association of Southeast Asian Nations
  Burmese membership, xxvii, 17
  contemporary government, 253, 261
  democratic future, 287
  strategic environment (post-1988), 17, 19, 20
Attlee, Clement, 8
Aung San, General, xxx, xxxii
  assassination, 8
  Aung San Suu Kyi (daughter), 276-80
  Burma Independence Army, 10
  Burma National Army, 10
  civilian status, 11
  founder of Burmese armed forces, 260-61
  Japanese military control, 10
  military concessions, 11, 24n.51
  Minister for Defence (1943), 10
  nationalist coalition (1941), 8, 10
  Thirty Comrades, 10, 23n.41
  vision of government, 283, 289
Aung San Suu Kyi, xxviii, xxx, 114, 178, 272, 275*f*
  Aung San (father), 276-80
  contemporary government, 253, 258, 260-61
  defence policy, 38-39, 40, 41
  East Timor relations, 42
  publications, 275
  research source, xxviii
  speculative analysis, 276
  theoretical analysis, 277-82
Australia
  arms procurement, 133, 186
  Burma Air Force (contemporary)

334

Index   335

arms embargo, 222, 231n.140
military assistance, 222-23
Burma Air Force (pre-1988)
aircraft procurement, 207
arms embargo, 207
training, 211
Burma Navy (pre-1988), 186
chemical weapons, 236, 250n.34
communications installation, 65, 66
military assistance, 65, 66, 82, 90, 222-23, 287
training, 82, 83, 86, 90, 97n.52, 211
Australian National University, xxvi
Australian Special Broadcasting System, 170
Auxiliary Fire Brigades, 81, 97n.42

B

Bacteriological and Toxin Weapons Convention, 241, 251n.62
Ba Maw, 8, 10
Bangkok Post, 242
Bangladesh
borders
geographically, 4
land disputes, 4
strategic environment (post-1988), 17-18, 20
chemical weapons, 247
defence policy
democratic movement, 40-41, 46n.57
Rohingya refugees, 41-42
Ba Than, xxvi
Bay of Bengal
geostrategic position, 4, 13, 19
international rivalry (pre-1988), 13
strategic environment (post-1988), 19
Belgium, arms procurement, 138, 167, 168
Bhutto, Benazir, 168
Biological weapons
Bacteriological and Toxin Weapons Convention, 241, 251n.62
Burma Air Force, 241-43
counter-insurgency, 241-43, 244
foreign training, 242, 246-47
Geneva Protocol (1925), 241
germ warfare, 242-43
HIV/AIDS, 243-44, 251n.80
human rights, 242
Karen, 242-43, 244

Karen Human Rights Group, 242
Karen National Union, 244
overview, 233
Porton Down Defence Research Establishment (United Kingdom), 243, 247
State Law and Order Restoration Council, 242, 244
State Peace and Development Council, 243-44
utilization debate, 241-44
Christian Solidarity International, 242, 244
government denial, 244
government motives, 244
international response, 242-43
Karen Human Rights Group, 242
media reports, 242-43
Vibrio cholerae 0139, 243
white boxes, 241-43
See also Chemical weapons
Bo Ni, 122
Brief History of the Myanmar Army, 31-32
British Broadcasting Corporation, 65
British Military Mission, 159
communications, 61, 62-63
training, 211
Brooks, Thomas, 234
Brunei, 41
Buddhism, 3
Bulgaria, arms procurement, 138, 169, 170
Bureau of Special Investigations
post-1988
command structure, 113
functions, 113
human rights, 118
pre-1988
command structure, 101, 104-5
formation, 102
functions, 102-3, 105
Bureau of Verification and Compliance, 134-35
Burma Act, 205
Burma Air Force
base locations
air base headquarters, 307
pre-1988, 210, 211
2000, 218*f*
biological weapons, 241-43
chemical weapons, 235, 236-37
command structure
Commander-in-Chief, 59, 297

control, 50, 59
post-1988, 55, 59, 279
pre-1988, 50
rank structure, 55
communications, 61, 62, 64
contemporary
  air-to-air missiles, 222
  arms embargo, 222, 231n.140
  arms procurement, 222, 223, 224-25
  counter-insurgency, 221, 222, 223-24, 232n.152
  ethnic insurgency, 223
  foreign assistance, 222-23
  inter-Service rivalry, 263-64, 267-68
  joint military operations, 222
  maintenance, 222-23, 224-25
  modernisation, 221-22
  operations, 221-22
  State Law and Order Restoration Council, 224
  surface-to-air missiles, 223-24, 232n.152
  training, 222, 223, 224-25
counter-insurgency aircraft, 308
defence industry, 145
fighters
  fighter/ground attack, 307
  interceptors, 307
helicopters, 308
indoctrination, 92-94, 99n.111
intelligence
  post-1988, 120-21
  pre-1988, 101, 106, 108
liaison aircraft, 308
other aircraft, 308
post-1988
  aircraft procurement, 212-17, 219
  Air Force strength (2000), 217*f*
  Air Mandalay, 221, 231n.130
  air-to-air missiles, 216-17
  Australian arms embargo, 207
  base location (2000), 218*f*
  Chinese People's Liberation Army, 219-20
  civilian airfields, 220-21
  command structure, 55, 59, 220, 279
  Director of Naval Intelligence (United States), 215
  electronic warfare, 219
  ethnic insurgency, 214, 215, 216
  expansion, 220-21

  foreign assistance, 214, 219
  foreign training, 214, 219-20
  human rights, 214-15
  intelligence, 120-21
  Kachin, 215
  Karen, 214, 215
  Military Assistance Program, 219
  modernisation, 220-21
  Myanmar Airways, 221
  Myanmar Airways International, 221
  narcotics control, 214, 216
  overview, 205
  radar equipment, 217, 219
  State Law and Order Restoration Council, 213, 214, 215
  surface-to-air missiles, 213, 228n.61
pre-1988
  Administrative Training School, 211
  aircraft procurement, 205-10, 211
  Air Force strength (1988), 209*f*
  armoury, 208-9
  base locations, 210, 211
  Burma Act, 205
  Burma Air Force Volunteer Reserve, 210
  Central Inspection Unit, 211
  civilian aircraft, 207
  civilian airfields, 211
  command structure, 50, 210-11
  Communist Party of Burma, 207, 225n.24
  counter-insurgency, 206, 210, 225n.8
  Electronic Training School, 211
  ethnic insurgency, 210
  expansion, 210, 227n.41
  foreign assistance, 205, 209
  foreign training, 210, 211
  helicopters, 208
  ineffectiveness, 212
  intelligence, 101, 106, 108
  International Narcotics Control Program, 208
  Karen, 210, 227n.37
  Kuomintang, 210
  maintenance, 209
  narcotics control, 208, 210
  origins, 205
  overview, 205
  State Law and Order Restoration Council, 210, 212
  Technical Training School, 211

Index   337

training, 211
Union of Burma Airways, 207
publications, xxvi
recruitment
  expansion, 78, 79, 96n.29
  retention, 80
total personnel/equipment, 307
training
  Apprentice Officer scheme, 84
  Command and General Staff College, 85
  contemporary, 222, 223, 224-25
  Defence Services Academy, 84
  expansion, 85
  foreign assistance, 87
  foreign institutions, 86
  pre-1988, 211
training aircraft, 308
transport aircraft, 308
Burma Air Force Volunteer Reserve, 210
Burma Army
  chemical weapons, 235, 236, 238
  communications, 61-64, 65, 68, 74n.90
  contemporary
    Burma Navy domination, 199-200
    Communist Party of Burma, 175
    desertion, 173, 183n.135
    equipment inadequacy, 174, 183n.143
    ethnic groups, 172, 173
    ethnic insurgency, 172, 173, 175
    expansion, 172, 182n.123
    experience, 172
    financial constraints, 174
    geographical constraints, 174
    human rights, 173-74
    human wave tactic, 173
    ideological constraints, 174
    inter-Service rivalry, 199-200, 263-64, 267-68
    Japanese style command, 173-74, 183n.136
    joint military operations, 176, 183n.147
    Kachin, 173
    Karen, 172, 173, 182n.126
    Karen National Defence Organisation, 175
    Karen National Union, 173
    Kuomintang, 175
    modernisation, 172
    morale, 173-74
    operations, 175
    reserves, 176
    State Law and Order Restoration Council, 175
    training inadequacy, 172-73
  defence industry, 141-42, 144-45
    Burma Army Armoured Cars, 144, 153n.112
    Special Combat Vehicle, 144-45
  defence policy, 41
  indoctrination, 92-94, 99n.111
  intelligence, 101, 106, 108, 112
    post-1988, 165, 171
  organisation
    combat unit summary, 299
    Light Infantry Division, 299
    Regional Military Command, 298-99
    total personnel, 298
  post-1988
    Armour and Artillery School, 171
    armoured personnel carriers, 169, 180n.99
    arms procurement, 166-71
    Bloodhound system, 170
    Chin, 159
    Combat Forces School, 171
    command structure, 166
    Defence Services Engineering Training School, 171
    ethnic groups, 165
    expansion, 165-66
    heavy equipment, 169-70
    infantry battalions, 165-66, 169
    infantry weapons, 168
    intelligence, 165, 171
    Kachin, 159
    Karen, 168
    Light Infantry Division, 165-66, 167, 170, 179n.72
    main battle tanks, 169
    Mechanical and Electrical Engineering School (1990), 171
    military formations, 166-67
    Military Operations Commands (MOCs), 166, 170
    multiple rocket launchers (MRLs), 169
    overview, 155
    Regional Military Command, 170
    Regional Operations Commands, 166, 170

road transport, 170-71
scout cars, 169
Signals, Medical and Intelligence Corps, 171
State Law and Order Restoration Council, 165, 167-68, 169, 170, 171
State Peace and Development Council, 167, 169
surface-to-air missiles, 170
Tactical Operations Commands, 166
training, 171
Uzi submachine guns, 169, 180n.93
pre-1988
   Administrative Support Training School, 163
   anti-aircraft artillery, 161-62
   arms procurement, 159-62
   battalions, 156, 157*f*
   British Military Mission, 159
   Burma Army Central School, 163
   Burma Army Combat Forces School, 163
   Burma Defence Army, 155
   Burma Independence Army, 155
   Burma National Army, 155
   Burma Socialist Programme Party, 156
   command structure, 156
   Communist Party of Burma, 164, 178n.52
   counter-insurgency, 163-64, 178n.49
   expansion, 155-56
   field artillery, 161-62
   financial constraints, 156, 176n.3
   four cuts strategy, 163-64
   heavy equipment, 162, 178n.32
   human rights, 164
   infantry weapons, 160, 161
   isolation/attrition strategy, 164
   Kachin Independence Army, 164
   Karen National Liberation Army, 164
   Land/Air Warfare School (1958), 163
   Light Infantry Division, 156, 158*f*, 159
   Military Assistance Program, 159, 161, 177n.15
   mortars, 161
   mutinies (1948/1949), 155-56
   Mutual Defence Assistance Plan, 159
   Non-Commissioned Officer School, 163
   overview, 155
   Paratroops' School, 163
   Patriotic Burmese Forces, 155-56
   road transport, 162, 178n.36
   State Law and Order Restoration Council, 160, 163, 164, 178n.52
   support weapons, 160-61, 177n.22
   Tactical Operations Commands, 159
   training, 163
   Union Military Police, 156
publications, xxvi
recruitment
   expansion, 78, 79, 96n.29
   retention, 80
training
   Apprentice Officer scheme, 84
   Command and General Staff College, 85
   contemporary, 172-73
   Defence Services Academy, 84
   expansion, 85
   foreign institutions, 86
   institutions, 82, 83
   Officer Training School, 83, 97n.55, 262-63
   post-1988, 171
   pre-1988, 163
Burma Army, armaments
   armoured vehicles
      other tracked vehicles, 300
      tanks, 299-300
      wheeled, 300
   artillery
      air defence systems, 301
      air defence weapons, man-portable, 301
      rocket launchers, 300
      towed, 300
   individual weapons
      anti-personnel land mines, 304
      anti-vehicle mines, 304
      grenade launchers, 303
      pistols, 302
      repeating rifles, 302-3
      rifle/hand grenades, 303
      self-loading/assault rifles, 303
      submachine guns, 303
   other crewed weapons
      heavy machine guns/cannon, 302

heavy mortars, 301-2
light/general purpose machine guns, 302
light/medium mortars, 301
rocket launchers/recoilless rifles, 302
Burma Army, command structure
  Adjutant-General's Office, 297
    Adjutant-General, 297
  Commander-in-Chief, 49-50, 59, 296
  General Staff
    Chief, Special Operations Bureau, 296-97
    Chief, Office of Strategic Studies, 296
    Chief of Staff, 296
  Quartermaster-General's Office, 297
    Quartermaster-General, 297
  reorganisation
    Adjutant-General's Office, 50
    Bureaus of Special Operations, 50, 55, 71n.7
    Burma Socialist Programme Party, 51, 55
    control, 50, 51, 55, 59
    Defence Services Museum and Historical Research Institute, 55
    departments, 50, 55, 71n.5
    Directorate of Defence Services Computers, 55
    Directorate of Public Relations and Border Troops, 55
    engineers, 50, 55, 71n.8
    General Staff, 50, 55
    headquarters, 51, 71n.9
    Light Infantry Division, 50, 51, 55, 59
    Office of Strategic Studies, 55
    post-1988, 51, 55, 59-60, 296-97
    pre-1988, 49-50, 51
    Quartermaster-General's Office, 50
    rank structure, 50, 51, 55, 71n.14
    Regional Military Command additions, 55, 59
    Regional Military Command, 50, 51, 54*f*, 55, 58*f*, 59, 71n.9
    Tactical Operations Command, 51
Burma Army Central School, 163
Burma Army Combat Forces School, 163
Burma Defence Army, 155
  formation, 10
Burma Economic Development Corporation, 146
Burma Independence Army, 155

formation, 10
Japanese threat, 10, 23n.42
Thirty Comrades, 10, 23n.41
Burma National Army, 155
  formation, 10, 23n.43
  indoctrination, 89
Burma Navy
  amphibious forces, 306
  auxiliaries, 306-7
  base locations
    post-1988, 191
    pre-1988, 189-91, 202n.43
    regional commands/bases, 190*f*
  base organisation, 304-5
  command structure
    Air Base Headquarters, 297
    Colonel, General Staff, 297
    Commander-in-Chief, 59, 297
    contemporary, 199-200
    control, 50, 59
    post-1988, 55, 59, 191, 297
    pre-1988, 50, 189, 190*f*
    rank structure, 55
    Vice Chief, 297
  communications, 61, 62
  contemporary
    Burma Army domination, 199-200
    Burma Socialist Programme Party, 199
    Chinese People's Liberation Army, 197-98
    command structure, 199-200
    counter-insurgency, 198-99
    electronic warfare, 199
    ethnic insurgency, 198-99
    exclusive economic zone, 197
    expansion, 197-99, 200
    expansion response, 197-98
    fisheries protection, 197
    foreign assistance, 197-98, 199
    inter-Service rivalry, 199-200, 263-64, 267-68
    Karen, 198
    Malacca Straits, 197
    minesweepers, 199
    Muslim population, 198
    operations, 198-99
    State Law and Order Restoration Council, 198, 199, 200
    State Peace and Development Council, 198, 199, 200

surface-to-surface missiles, 199
vessel procurement, 199
defence industry, 141-42, 145
defence policy, 33-37
indoctrination, 92-94, 99n.111
intelligence, 101, 106, 108
major surface combatants, 305
Corvettes, 305
mercantile marine, 307
mine warfare forces, 306
organisation
  bases/units, 304-5
  naval regional commands/bases/frontline camps, 305
  total personnel, 304
patrol forces
  Coastal Patrol Boats, 305-6
  Guided Missile Patrol Boats, 305
  River Gunboats, 306
  River Patrol Craft, 306
post-1988
  arms procurement, 193-94, 196
  base locations, 191
  Chinese People's Liberation Army, 196
  coastal surveillance, 196
  command structure, 191
  decommissioned vessels, 194
  Directorate of Defence Services Intelligence, 192
  electronic counter measures, 195
  electronic support measures, 195
  electronic warfare, 195, 203n.77
  European Union embargo, 193
  exclusive economic zone, 192, 196
  expansion, 191
  foreign assistance, 195-96
  foreign training, 195-96
  infrastructure modernisation, 196, 203n.87
  minesweepers, 193-94, 203n.68
  modernisation, 191, 196
  Navy strength (2000), 195f
  overview, 184
  radar equipment, 195, 196, 203n.77
  shipyard production, 194
  signals intelligence, 196
  State Law and Order Restoration Council, 192, 196
  State Peace and Development Council, 192, 196

surface-to-surface missiles, 196
training, 195-96
vessel procurement, 192-94, 196
pre-1988
  auxiliary vessels, 186
  base locations, 189-91, 202n.43
  Burma Royal Navy Volunteer Reserve, 184
  coastal surveillance, 188
  command structure, 50, 189, 190f
  counter-insurgency, 187, 188, 191
  decommissioned vessels, 188
  ethnic insurgency, 185
  expansion, 187
  fisheries protection, 188
  Inland Water Transportation Board, 186, 201n.7
  joint military operations, 188, 202n.35
  Karen, 185
  Landing Craft Medium, 186
  Landing Craft Utility, 186
  Navy strength (1988), 187f
  operations, 187-89, 191
  origins, 184-85
  overview, 184
  People's Pearl and Fishery Corporation, 186, 187-88
  regional commands/bases, 190f
  shipyard production, 186, 189
  State Law and Order Restoration Council, 191
  Strategic Naval Flotilla, 188
  underwater operations, 188-89
  Union of Burma Navy, 184
  vessel procurement, 184-86
  water transport, 185, 186, 201n.7
recruitment
  expansion, 78, 79, 96n.29
  retention, 80
survey vessels, 306
training
  Apprentice Officer scheme, 84
  Command and General Staff College, 85
  Defence Services Academy, 84
  expansion, 85
  foreign institutions, 86
  foreign training, 195-96
  post-1988, 195-96
BurmaNet, 69-70
BurmaNet News, 69

Burmans
  demographics, 5
  recruitment, 9-10, 23n.40, 77
Burma Royal Navy Volunteer Reserve (1940), 184
Burma Signals Training Regiment (1951), 62
Burma Socialist Programme Party
  Burma Army, 156
  Burma Navy, 199
  contemporary government, 262, 270
  defence policy
    external threats, 39
    internal affairs, 35
  historical framework, 9, 12, 15
  indoctrination, 87-88, 91
  intelligence, 104, 105
  international rivalry (pre-1988), 15
  publications, 88
  recruitment, 76-77
  training, 78
Bush, George, 18

C

Cambodia
  chemical weapons, 240
  defence policy, 41
Canada
  aircraft procurement, 207
  arms procurement, 133
  biological weapons, 243
Central Intelligence Agency
  international rivalry (pre-1988), 14
  publications, 314
Chemical and Biological Warfare: The Hidden Arsenal (Hersh), 233
Chemical Weapons Convention, 240-41
Chemical weapons
  Asia-Pacific region, 239-40, 250n.56
  Burma Air Force, 235, 236-37
  Burma Army, 235, 236, 238
  capability debate
    academic research, 234, 235
    administrative denial, 233-34, 236, 241
    alternative explanations, 237
    Armed Services Committee, 234
    Directorate of Defence Services Intelligence, 236
  Director of Naval Intelligence (United States), 234, 236
  Federation of American Scientists, 235
  media reports, 233-34, 235, 236-37, 239
  resource reliability, 233, 235, 236
  Royal Thai Army, 237
  Special National Intelligence Estimate (United States), 234, 247
  Stockholm International Peace Research Institute, 234
  United Nations Conference on Disarmament (1988), 233-34
  Chemical Weapons Convention, 240-41
  Communist Party of Burma, 247
  counter-insurgency, 235-38, 239, 240
  ethnic insurgency, 235-38, 239
  foreign training, 235, 246-47
    ABC protection, 235
  Fritz Werner GmbH (West Germany), 234, 238
  gas weapons, 234, 235, 236
  Geneva Protocol (1925), 240
  Golden Triangle, 234, 235, 248n.6
  HEAT rocket, 236-37
  human rights, 235-36
  international relations, 240-41, 259n.59
  Kachin Independence Army, 235, 236-37
  Kachin Independence Organisation, 235
  Karen, 235-37, 238
  Karen National Liberation Army, 235-36
  material procurement, 234-35
  mustard gas, 234, 235
  mycotoxins, 240
  narcotics control, 234, 235, 237, 239
  overview, 233
  production plants, 238-39, 250n.52
  riot control, 238, 250n.46
  Shan, 236, 238, 239
  State Law and Order Restoration Council, 235, 236, 238, 239, 240-41
  State Peace and Development Council, 239, 241
  tear gas, 236, 238
  testing facilities, 238-39
  toxic defoliants, 237, 250n.39
  white phosphorous (WP), 237-38

Yellow Rain, 240
  See also Biological weapons
Chief of National Intelligence, 104, 263
child soldiers, 20, 78, 95-96, 182, 325, 329
Chile
  arms procurement, 138
  human rights, 266-67
Chin
  Burma Army, 159
  demographics, 7
  recruitment, 9-10, 23n.40, 77
China
  arms procurement
    Burma Air Force (post-1988), 212-14, 216-17, 219, 228n.64
    Burma Army (post-1988), 167, 168, 169, 170, 179n.83, 181n.112
    Burma Navy (contemporary), 199
    Burma Navy (post-1988), 192, 193-94, 196, 203n.64
    defence expenditure, 132-33, 137, 138, 139, 151n.67
    government agenda, 268-69, 274n.87
  biological weapons, 246-48
  borders
    geographically, 4
    international rivalry (pre-1988), 13, 14, 15
    land disputes, 4, 13
    strategic environment (post-1988), 16-20, 25n.77
  chemical weapons, 240, 246-48
  communications
    equipment procurement, 63-64
    satellite networks, 65, 66
  Cultural Revolution, 16
  defence industry, 141, 142-43, 152n.94, 153n.114
  defence policy
    external threat, 39, 41, 42, 46n.51
    trade, 36, 45n.39
  defence policy (contemporary)
    Burma Navy, 197-98, 199
    international criticism, 253, 265
    policy agenda, 268-69, 274n.87
  demographics, 7
  indoctrination, 89, 92, 98n.90
  intelligence
    assistance, 118-19, 120
    equipment, 115, 118-19, 128n.96
  threat, 101, 109
  training, 115
  Japan invasion (1937), 13
  military assistance, 93-94, 99n.112, 195-96, 220, 287-88
    intelligence, 118-19, 120
    non-military equipment, 170-71, 181n.116
  nuclear weapons, 246
  trade, 5, 22n.18
    defence policy, 36, 45n.39
  training, 86, 87, 115, 195-96, 219-20
  Vietnam invasion (1979), 16
Chinese People's Liberation Army
  Burma Air Force (post-1988), 219-20
  Burma Navy
    contemporary, 197-98
    post-1988, 196
  geostrategic position
    international rivalry (pre-1988), 14
    strategic environment (post-1988), 19
  insurgency groups, 11
Christian Science Monitor, 234
Christian Solidarity International, 242, 244
Chun Doo-hwan, 266-67
Civilian aircraft, 207, 221
Civilian airfields
  post-1988, 220-21
  pre-1988, 211
Civilian communications. *See* Communications
Civilian rule
  contemporary government, 260, 266, 267, 276
  pre-1988, 49
  speculative analysis, 276
  See also Democratic future; Democratic movement
Civilian surveillance, 121, 122-23
Clinton, Bill, 18
Codevilla, Angelo, 130
Cold War, 15-16
Colombo Plan, 15
Combat Forces School, 171
Command and General Staff College, 85
Command structure
  democratic future, 283, 284, 285, 292n.40
  government reorganisation
    Advisory Group, 60

Burma Socialist Programme Party, 51, 55
Law and Order Restoration Council, 51, 55
National Intelligence Bureau, 60
post-1988, 51, 55, 59-60
State Law and Order Restoration Council, 51, 55, 59-60
State Peace and Development Council, 59-60
independent department
  post-1988, 55, 297-98
  pre-1988, 50
joint staff, 50
overall command
  Commander-in-Chief, 49-50, 59, 296
  control, 49-50, 55, 59
  Defence Ministry (1988), 52-53*f*
  Defence Ministry (2000), 56-57*f*
  Deputy Commander-in-Chief, 50, 296
  headquarters, 50, 71n.3
  post-1988, 51, 55, 59-60, 71n.15, 296
  pre-1988, 49-50
  rank structure, 49*f*, 50, 51, 55, 71n.2
overview, 48
personnel
  formal war establishment, 296
  loyalty, 37
  total armed forces, 296
  in uniform, 296
post-1988
  Burma Air Force, 55, 59
  Burma Army, 51, 55, 59-60, 71n.14
  Burma Navy, 55, 59
  government, 51, 55, 59-60
  military, 51, 55, 59
  overall command, 51, 55, 59-60, 296
  rank structure, 51, 55
pre-1988
  Burma Air Force, 50
  Burma Army, 50, 51
  Burma Navy, 50
  civilian rule, 49
  1948, 48
  1962, 48-49
  1974, 49
  overall command, 49-50
  rank structure, 50
rank structure
  Burma Air Force, 55
  Burma Army, 50, 51, 55, 71n.14

Burma Navy, 55
  overall command, 49*f*, 50, 51, 55, 71n.2
  post-1988, 51, 55
  pre-1988, 50
reorganisation influences
  constitution, 49
  government, 48-49
  People's Assembly, 49
  Revolutionary Council, 48-49
  State Law and Order Restoration Council, 49, 51, 55, 71n.1
  See also Paramilitary forces; *specific branch*
Committee Representing the People's Parliament, 281-83
Communications
  Burma Air Force
    expansion, 62
    long distance networks, 64
    structure, 61
  Burma Army
    base distribution, 61-62
    control, 62
    difficulties, 61, 64, 65
    equipment distribution, 64
    equipment procurement, 62-64
    ethnic recruitment, 61
    headquarters, 61-62
    information technology, 68, 74n.90
    insurgency groups, 61
    long distance networks, 64
    Signal Corps, 61-62
    structure, 61-62
  Burma Navy
    expansion, 62
    structure, 61
  civil system
    cellular, 66-67, 74n.69
    government control, 65, 67, 74n.67
    government improvement, 65-67, 73n.62, 74n.80
    government utilization, 60-61
    long distance, 66-67
    satellite networks, 66-67
    telephones, 66, 74n.80
  Directorate of Defence Services Intelligence, 62, 68-70
  equipment installation
    Australia, 65, 66
    Japan, 65

344 Burma's Armed Forces

Myanmar Posts and Telecommunications, 65-67
Taiwan, 66
Thailand, 65, 66
United States, 65-66
equipment procurement
China, 63-64
India, 64
interception, 63-64
Japan, 62, 63, 73n.43
Myanmar Posts and Telecommunications, 67
radar equipment, 63-64
Singapore, 63
Soviet Union, 63
Thailand, 64
United Kingdom, 61, 62-63, 64, 73n.43
United States, 62, 63
West Germany, 63
Yugoslavia, 63
government control
British Broadcasting Corporation, 65
civil system, 65, 67, 74n.67
Communist Party of Burma, 65
Defence Forces Broadcasting Unit, 65
Democratic Voice of Burma, 65
information technology, 68-70
Myawaddy Radio Station, 65
Norway, 65
Patriotic Youth Front Radio, 65
Radio Free Asia, 65
United Kingdom, 65, 109
United States, 65
Voice of America, 65, 109
Voice of the People of Burma, 65, 74n.67, 109
information technology
BurmaNet, 69-70
BurmaNet News, 69
Computer Science Development Law, 68-69
Cyber Warfare Department, 67, 70
Defence Services Academy, 68
Directorate of Defence Services Computers, 67-69
Directorate of Defence Services Intelligence, 68-70
electronic monitoring, 68-70
government control, 68-70
government development, 68-70

Intergraph Image Station, 68, 74n.90
MyanmarNet, 70
National League for Democracy, 69
Singapore, 67, 68
State Law and Order Restoration Council, 67-70
terrorism, 70
training, 67-68, 86-87
Myanmar Posts and Telecommunications
equipment installation, 65-67
equipment procurement, 67
information technology, 68
national security, 60, 63-64
foreign investment, 60, 63-64
satellite networks, 64-65
Asiasat, 65, 66
China, 65, 66
Global System for Mobiles, 66
Standard-A earth station, 66
Standard-B earth station, 66
United States, 65
State Law and Order Restoration Council, 63-64, 67-70
training
Burma Signals Training Regiment (1951), 62
communications security, 61
Defence Services Signals and Electronic School, 62
elementary cryptography, 61
information technology, 67-68, 86-87
intelligence, 60
interception, 61
Let Ya-Freeman Agreement, 61
signals operations, 61
United Kingdom, 61, 62-63
Communications security, 61, 112, 120, 126n.61
Communism
geostrategic position, 13, 14, 16
international rivalry (pre-1988), 13, 14
strategic environment (post-1988), 16
Communist Party of Burma
Burma Army, 164, 175, 178n.52
chemical weapons, 247
communications control, 65, 109
contemporary government, 265
guerrilla warfare, 90
intelligence, 109, 115
international rivalry (pre-1988), 14

Computer Science Development Law, 68-69
Confucianism, 3
Constitution, 49, 76-77
Criminal Investigation Department
　post-1988
　　command structure, 113
　　functions, 113
　　human rights, 118
　pre-1988, 101
　　command structure, 104-5
　　functions, 105
Cyber Warfare Department, 67, 70
Czechoslovakia
　arms procurement, 138, 169
　training, 91

D

Defence Economic Trends in the Asia-Pacific, 316
Defence expenditure
　arms procurement
　　arms imports (1973-1987), 133*f*
　　arms transfers (1973-1987), 133*f*
　　military expansion, 133, 149n.18
　　post-1988, 137-40
　　pre-1988, 132-33
　contemporary government
　　expansion, 253, 271n.1
　　expansion rationale, 254-55
　　international criticism, 253
　　policy agenda, 268, 269
　democratic future, 286, 287, 292n.46
　post-1988
　　arms imports (1988-1997), 138*f*
　　arms procurement, 137-40
　　arms transfers (1987-1997), 137*f*
　　Bureau of Verification and Compliance, 134-35
　　central government expenditure, 134-35
　　European Union arms embargo, 138
　　five kinds/five plants program, 136
　　gross domestic product, 135
　　military logistics, 136
　　Myanmar Agricultural Product Trading, 135
　　Myanmar Petroleum Products Enterprise, 135, 150n.35
　　narcotics control, 139
　　1988-1995*f*, 134
　　overview, 130
　　resource reliability, 134-37, 139-40
　　State Law and Order Restoration Council, 134, 135, 138-39
　　State Peace and Development Council, 134, 138, 139
　　United States arms embargo, 138
　pre-1988
　　arms procurement, 132-33
　　central government expenditure, 131, 132
　　international contrast, 132
　　Let Ya-Freeman Agreement, 132, 149n.12
　　Mutual Defence Assistance Plan, 132
　　1978-1987, 132*f*
　　overview, 130
　　research sources, 131
　　resource reliability, 131
　　trends, 131-32
　See also Research literature
Defence Forces Broadcasting Unit, 65
Defence industry
　ammunition, 144
　assault rifles, 144, 153n.105
　automatic rifles, 143-44, 153n.104
　Burma Air Force, 145
　Burma Army, 141-42, 144-45
　　Burma Army Armoured Cars, 144, 153n.112
　　Special Combat Vehicle, 144-45
　Burma Navy, 141-42, 145
　Defence Products Industries, 144
　European Union embargo, 141-42
　foreign assistance, 141-45
　Fritz Werner GmbH (West Germany), 140, 141-42, 143
　Heavy Industries Corporation (*Ka Sa La*), 140-41
　human rights, 143-44
　Ka Pa Sa factories, 141, 152n.83
　landmines, 143, 152n.98
　Myanmar Fritz Werner Industries Co. Ltd., 140-41
　State Law and Order Restoration Council, 141-42, 143-44, 145
　State Peace and Development Council, 145
　submachine gun (BA52), 140
　trinitrotoluene explosives, 140

United Nations Security Council embargo, 141-42
Defence Intelligence Organisation (Australia), 135, 139-40, 313, 316
Defence policy
  Burma Socialist Programme Party
    external threats, 39
    internal affairs, 35
  democratic movement
    external threats, 40-41
    internal affairs, 33, 37, 44n.22, 45n.43
  economic interests
    exclusive economic zone, 36
    internal affairs, 36-37, 45n.41
    sanctions, 39-40
  external threats
    Burma Army, 41
    Burmese Muslims, 41-42
    democratic movement, 40-41
    economic sanctions, 39-40
    foreigner suspicion, 38-39
    human rights, 39-40, 41-42
    international developments, 42-43
    International Force East Timor, 42, 47n.69
    overview, 28
    policy adjustment, 39-40
    political sanctions, 39-40
    refugees, 41-42
    regional populations, 39, 46n.51
    vulnerability, 43
  goals
    controversy regarding, 29, 30-31, 32-33
    formalization reticence, 28-29, 32-33
    four people's desires, 30
    National Defence Mission, 31-32
    national solidarity, 29, 39
    non-alignment, 29, 32
    peaceful coexistence, 29, 32
    self-defence, 29
    Than Shwe speech, 30-32, 42-43
    three national causes, 30
    twelve national objectives, 30
  internal affairs
    Burma Navy, 33-37
    cease-fire arrangements, 34, 35, 38
    counter-insurgency failure, 34-35
    Democratic Karen Buddhist Army, 34
    democratic movement, 33, 37, 44n.22, 45n.43
    economic interests, 36-37, 45n.41
    elections, 33, 37-38, 41, 280, 281
    ethnic insurgency, 33, 34-36, 41-42, 43, 44n.27
    exclusive economic zone, 36
    government special zones, 34
    insurgency groups, 33-36, 44n.24, 45n.30
    Karen National Liberation Army, 34
    Karen National Union, 35
    Kar Kwe Ye, 34, 44n.26
    military expansion, 33-37, 42-43
    military loyalty, 37
    military modernisation, 33-34, 35, 36-37, 42-43
    military permanence, 35-36
    narcotics, 34, 35
    National Constitution Convention, 37-38
    National Unity Party, 37, 45n.45
    political structure, 33, 37-38
    power retainment, 33, 37-38
    Shan State Army, 34
    smuggling, 35, 36, 45n.40
    trade, 36, 45n.39
    United Wa State Army, 34
  National League for Democracy
    external threats, 38
    goals, 29
    internal affairs, 38
  political structure
    elections, 33, 37-38, 41, 280, 281
    internal affairs, 33, 37-38
    sanctions, 39-40
  State Law and Order Restoration Council
    external threats, 40, 41-42
    goals, 29, 30-32
    internal affairs, 33-35, 37
  State Peace and Development Council
    external threats, 40, 43
    goals, 29
    internal affairs, 35
  United Nations
    cooperative relations, 29
    elections (1990), 41
    Haiti, 41
    peace-keeping operations, 29, 42, 43n.7
    Rohingya refugees, 41-42

Index 347

United Nations Development Programme, 40, 46n.52
United Nations High Commissioner for Refugees, 41-42
United Nations Transitional Administration in East Timor, 42, 47n.69
Defence Products Industries, 144
Defence Services Academy
  Burma Air Force, 84
  Burma Army, 84
  Burma Navy, 84
  communications, 68
  contemporary rivalry, 262-63
  training, 84
Defence Services Engineering Training School, 171
Defence Services Institute, 145-46, 147
Defence Services Museum and Historical Research Institute
  A Brief History of the Myanmar Army, 31-32, 37
  formation, 55
  research source, xxviii
Defence Services Officer's Training School, 83
Defence Services Signals and Electronic School, 62
Democratic future
  arms procurement, 284
  Aung San Suu Kyi
    speculative analysis, 276
    theoretical analysis, 277-82
  command structure, 283, 284, 285, 292n.40
  Committee Representing the People's Parliament, 281-83
  defence expenditure, 286, 287, 292n.46
  economy, 287
  ethnic groups, 276, 284, 285, 286, 290
  external threats
    military ideal, 284, 292n.41
    practical analysis, 285
    speculative analysis, 276, 277
    theoretical analysis, 281
  Federation of Trade Unions - Burma, 283
  foreign training, 287-88
  human rights, 276
  intelligence, 284, 286, 288, 293n.47
  military compromise
    ethnic groups, 290
  international relations, 290
  State Law and Order Restoration Council, 290
  State Peace and Development Council, 290
  military ideal
    arms procurement, 284
    command structure, 283, 284, 292n.40
    ethnic groups, 284
    external threats, 284, 292n.41
    intelligence, 284
    military role, 283-84
    modernisation, 284
    National League for Democracy, 283-84
    organisation, 283
    personnel, 283
    recruitment, 284
  military ideology, 276
  military operations, 288-89
  modernisation, 284, 286
  narcotics control, 286, 289
  National Coalition Government of the Union of Burma, 283
  National League for Democracy
    defence principles, 280-81
    family benefits, 281, 292n.30
    goals publication, 281
    manifesto, 280-81
    military ideal, 283-84
    people's militias, 281
    policy position, 277, 279-81
    practical analysis, 286
    speculative analysis, 276-77
    theoretical analysis, 277-84
  Ne Win
    speculative analysis, 276
    theoretical analysis, 278, 280
  organisation, 283, 285
  overview, 275
  personnel, 283
  practical analysis, 284-90
    command structure, 285
    defence expenditure, 286, 287, 292n.46
    economy, 287
    ethnic groups, 285, 286
    external threats, 285, 289
    foreign assistance, 287-88
    foreign training, 287-88
    intelligence, 286, 288, 293n.47

military government, 285
military operations, 288-89
military policy, 285-86
military reduction, 286-87
military support, 285, 289-90
modernisation, 286, 288-89
narcotics control, 286, 289
organisation, 285
recruitment, 289
recruitment, 284, 289
speculative analysis
  academic research, 275-76
  Burmese sources, 275-76, 291n.3
  civilian rule, 276
  democracy concepts, 291n.2
  ethnic groups, 276
  external threats, 276, 277
  human rights, 276
  National League for Democracy, 276-77
  policy platforms, 276, 279-80, 291n.4
theoretical analysis
  Committee Representing the People's Parliament, 281-83
  defence principles, 280-81
  external threats, 281
  family benefits, 281, 292n.30
  Federation of Trade Unions - Burma, 283
  military support, 277-78
  military unity, 278-79
  National Coalition Government of the Union of Burma, 283
  National League for Democracy, 277-84
  people's militias, 281, 292n.30
Democratic Karen Buddhist Army, 34
Democratic movement
  contemporary government
    expansion rationale, 256, 258, 271n.20
    internal challenges, 256, 258, 260, 266, 271n.20
  defence policy
    external threats, 40-41
    internal affairs, 33, 37, 44n.22, 45n.43
  democratic regime, 8-9
  1988 events, xxv, 12-13
  strategic environment (post-1988), 15-16, 18, 19

See also Democratic future; National League for Democracy ; *specific groups*
Democratic People's Republic of Korea. *See* North Korea
Democratic Voice of Burma, 65
Denmark, arms procurement, 186
Directorate of Defence Services Computers, 55, 67-69
Directorate of Defence Services Intelligence
  Burma Navy (post-1988), 192
  chemical weapons, 236
  communications, 62, 68-70
  contemporary government, 259, 261, 263
  democratic future, 288
  human rights, 115, 118
  post-1988, 113, 114, 115, 118, 192
  pre-1988, 105-6, 108
  research source, xxviii
  security failures, 121-24
Directorate of Military Training
  foreign institutions, 86
  formation (1953), 83
Directorate of Peoples Militias and Public Relations, 88
Director of Naval Intelligence (United States), 215, 234, 236
Dun, Smith, 264

E

East Asia, 3
Eastern Europe, 16
East Germany
  intelligence, 103
  international rivalry (pre-1988), 15
  training, 83
East Timor
  defence policy, 42, 47n.69
  International Force East Timor, 42, 47n.69
  strategic environment (post-1988), 19
  United Nations Transitional Administration in East Timor, 42, 47n.69
Economy
  defence policy
    exclusive economic zone, 36
    internal affairs, 36-37, 45n.41
    sanctions, 39-40

democratic future, 287
geostrategic position
  agriculture, 7
  average annual per capita income, 7
  development, 7
  efficiency, 7
  least developed country, 7, 22n.25
  light industrial sector, 7
  military ideology, 7
  oil industry, 7, 18
  poverty, 7
  privatisation, 7
  rice production, 7
  state-owned enterprises, 7
  strategic environment (post-1988), 17, 18, 19
historically, 12
military control
  Burma Economic Development Corporation, 146, 153n.121
  Defence Services Institute, 145-46, 147
  Ministry of Defence, 145
  Myanmar Economic Corporation, 147
  Myawaddy Enterprises Group, 147
  senior military officers, 147-48
  State Corporation Number 24, 146
  State Law and Order Restoration Council, 146-47, 148
  State-Owned Economic Enterprise Law, 147
  state-owned enterprises, 148
  State Peace and Development Council, 146, 148
  State/Private Joint Venture No. 9, 147
  Union of Myanmar Economic Holdings Limited, 146-47
military ideology, 7
policy agenda, 269
strategic environment (post-1988), 17, 18, 19
See also Defence expenditure; Military financial restraints
Elections. *See* Politics
Electronic counter measures, 195
Electronic intelligence, 118
Electronic monitoring, 68-70
Electronic support measures, 195
Electronic Training School, 211
Electronic warfare (EW)
  Burma Air Force, 219

Burma Navy, 195, 199, 203n.77
Estimating Foreign Military Power (Towle), xxv
Ethnic groups
  Burma Army
    contemporary, 172, 173
    post-1988, 165
  contemporary government
    Burma Army, 172, 173
    expansion rationale, 256, 257-58, 259
    internal challenges, 264, 266, 273n.66
    international criticism, 253
  defence policy, 33, 34-36, 41-42, 43, 44n.27
  democratic future, 276, 284, 285, 286, 290
  demographics, 5, 7
  historical framework
    recruitment, 9-10, 23n.40, 77
    United Kingdom, 8
  recruitment, 77, 79
    communications, 61
    1925, 9-10, 23n.40
  research terminology, xxx
  See also specific group
Ethnic insurgency
  Burma Air Force
    contemporary, 223
    post-1988, 214, 215, 216
    pre-1988, 210
  Burma Army, 172, 173, 175
  Burma Navy
    contemporary, 198-99
    pre-1988, 185
  chemical weapons, 235-38, 239
  contemporary government
    Burma Air Force, 223
    Burma Army, 172, 173, 175
    Burma Navy, 198-99
    expansion rationale, 256, 257-58, 259
    defence policy, 33, 34-36, 41-42, 43, 44n.27
  See also specific group
European Union
  arms embargo, 138, 193
  defence industry embargo, 141-42
Exclusive economic zone
  Burma Navy
    contemporary, 197
    post-1988, 192, 196
  defence policy, 36

geostrategic position, 4

F

Far Eastern Economic Review, 216
Federal Republic of Germany. *See* West Germany
Federation of American Scientists, 235
Federation of Trade Unions - Burma, 283
Finland, arms procurement, 161
Fisher, C. A., 184
Five columns' coordination, 91
Five kinds/five plants program, 136
Flight International, 213, 214
forced labour, 20, 95, 96, 318
Four cuts strategy, 91-92, 99n.99, 163-64
Four people's desires, 30
Fourth Burma Rifles, 12
France
    aircraft procurement, 207, 208
    arms procurement, 133, 161, 169
    international rivalry (pre-1988), 7-8, 13
Fritz Werner GmbH (West Germany)
    chemical weapons, 235, 238
    defence industry, 140, 141-42, 143
Frontier Force, 81

G

Geneva Protocol, 240, 241
Geostrategic position
    administrative divisions, 6f
    Andaman Sea, 4, 17
    Asia-Pacific region defined, 3, 21n.2
    Bangladesh
      borders, 4
      land disputes, 4
      strategic environment (post-1988), 17-18, 20
    Bay of Bengal, 4
      international rivalry (pre-1988), 13
      strategic environment (post-1988), 19
    China
      borders, 4
      international rivalry (pre-1988), 13, 14, 15
      land disputes, 4, 13
      strategic environment (post-1988), 16-20, 25n.77
    Chinese People's Liberation Army
      international rivalry (pre-1988), 14
      strategic environment (post-1988), 19
    coastline
      accessibility, 4
      contiguous zone, 4
      continental shelf, 4
      disputes, 4
      exclusive economic zone, 4
      fishing rights, 4
      islands, 4
      sea lines of communication, 4
      security, 4
      size, 4
      territorial sea, 4
      trade, 4, 5
    communications, 5
    communism
      international rivalry (pre-1988), 13, 14
      strategic environment (post-1988), 16
    cultural competition
      Buddhism, 3
      Confucianism, 3
      Hinduism, 3
    demographics
      Arakanese, 5, 7
      birth rate, 5
      Burmans, 5
      Chin, 7
      Chinese, 7
      ethnic groups, 5, 7
      Indians, 7
      Kachin, 7
      Karen, 5, 7
      Kayah, 7
      Lahu, 7
      Mandalay, 7
      Mon, 5, 7
      Moulmein, 7
      Palaung, 7
      PaO, 7
      population, 5
      population density, 5, 22n.22
      Rangoon, 7
      Rohingya, 7
      rural population, 7
      Shan, 5, 7
      urban population, 7
      Wa, 7
    East Asia, 3
    economy
      agriculture, 7
      average annual per capita income, 7

development, 7
efficiency, 7
least developed country, 7, 22n.25
light industrial sector, 7
military ideology, 7
oil industry, 7, 18
poverty, 7
privatisation, 7
rice production, 7
state-owned enterprises, 7
strategic environment (post-1988), 17, 18, 19
India
  borders, 4
  international rivalry (pre-1988), 13, 14
  land disputes, 4, 13
  strategic environment (post-1988), 17-18, 20, 21
Indian Ocean
  international rivalry (pre-1988), 13
  strategic environment (post-1988), 17, 18, 19
international interest
  contemporary, 3-4, 15-21, 21n.5
  diminishment, 15-16
  historically, 3
international rivalry (pre-1988)
  Assam, 14
  Burma Socialist Programme Party, 15
  Central Intelligence Agency, 14
  Colombo Plan, 15
  communist insurgency, 13, 14
  Communist Party of Burma, 14
  East Germany, 15
  France, 7-8, 13
  Indochina, 14
  Israel, 15
  Korean War, 14
  Kuomintang, 14-15, 25n.71
  Non-Aligned Movement, 15
  North Korea, 15
  Southeast Asia Treaty Organisation, 14
  Taiwan, 14
  West Germany, 15
  World War II, 13
  Yugoslavia, 15
Japan, 18, 26n.88
land
  accessibility, 4, 5
  border disputes, 4, 13
  boundaries, 4
  self-containment, 5
  size, 4
  smuggling, 4, 5
  trade, 4, 5, 22n.18
Laos
  borders, 4
  strategic environment (post-1988), 16
Malacca Straits
  international rivalry (pre-1988), 14
  strategic environment (post-1988), 18, 19
Malaya, 13, 14
Malaysia, 18
Mergui Archipelago, 4, 18
Middle East, 18, 20
natural resources
  fishing grounds, 7
  teak reserves, 7
Pakistan, 17-18
physical geography, 6f
sea lines of communication
  coastline, 4
  strategic environment (post-1988), 18, 19
Singapore, 18, 20
South Asia, 3
Southeast Asia
  cultural competition, 3
  strategic environment (post-1988), 16-17, 18, 20
South Korea
  international rivalry (pre-1988), 15
  strategic environment (post-1988), 18
Soviet Union
  international rivalry (pre-1988), 14, 15
  strategic environment (post-1988), 16
strategic environment (post-1988), 15-21
  Afghanistan, 20
  arms procurement, 17, 19, 20-21
  Association of Southeast Asian Nations, 17, 19, 20
  Cold War, 15-16
  communism collapse, 16
  democracy, 15-16, 18, 19
  Eastern Europe, 16
  East Timor, 19
  economy, 17, 18, 19
  elections (1990), 15-16
  global power shift, 16

HIV/AIDS, 20
human rights, 15-16, 19
interest diminishment, 15-16
Irrawaddy River, 19
Japan, 18, 26n.88
Mergui Archipelago, 18
Middle East, 18, 20
narcotics, 20
Nepal, 17-18
Pakistan, 17-18
Rohingya, 20
Singapore, 18, 20
Sri Lanka, 17-18
State Law and Order Restoration Council, 16, 20
State Peace and Development Council, 20
Thailand
  borders, 4
  international rivalry (pre-1988), 14
  land disputes, 4
  strategic environment (post-1988), 16
transportation
  air transport, 5, 13
  bridges, 5
  Burma Road, 5, 13
  Chindwin River, 5
  Irrawaddy River, 5
  Ledo Road, 5
  railways, 5
  rivers, 5
  roads, 5
  Salween River, 5
  Sittang River, 5
  waterways, 5, 13
United Kingdom
  international rivalry (pre-1988), 7-8, 13
  strategic environment (post-1988), 15-16
United Nations
  international rivalry (pre-1988), 14, 15
  strategic environment (post-1988), 16
United Nations General Assembly, 15
United Nations Security Council, 19
United States
  international rivalry (pre-1988), 14-15
  strategic environment (post-1988), 15-16
Vietnam
  international rivalry (pre-1988), 14, 15

  strategic environment (post-1988), 16
Yunnan Province
  international rivalry (pre-1988), 14
  strategic environment (post-1988), 19
German Democratic Republic. *See* East Germany
Global System for Mobiles, 66
Golden Triangle, 234, 235, 248n.6
Gudgin, Peter, 100
Guerrilla warfare, 89, 90
Guerrilla Warfare (Guevara), 90
Guevara, Che, 90
Gusmao, Xanana, 42

H

Haiti, 41
Heavy Industries Corporation (*Ka Sa La*), 140-41
Hersh, Seymour M., 233
Hinduism, 3
Historical framework
  Aung San, General
    assassination, 8
    Burma Independence Army, 10
    Burma National Army, 10
    civilian status, 11
    Japanese military control, 10
    military concessions, 11, 23n.51
    Minister for Defence (1943), 10
    nationalist coalition, 8, 10
    Thirty Comrades, 10, 23n.41
  Ba Maw government, 8, 10
  France, 7-8, 13
  insurgency groups
    Chinese People's Liberation Army, 11
    Kuomintang, 10-11, 14
    military, 10
    military reorganisation, 10-11
    Muslim *Mujahids*, 10
    1949, 8-9
  Japan
    administration, 8, 10
    Ba Maw government, 8, 10
    bombing (1941), 8
    Burma independence, 10
    Burma Independence Army, 10, 23n.42
    Chinese invasion (1937), 13
    government installation (1942), 8

international rivalry (pre-1988), 13
military control, 10
military threat, 10
nationalist resistance, 8
training, 10
kingdoms
  Burman, 7
  Chinese invasions, 7
  King Alaungpaya, 7
  King Anawrahta (1044), 7
  King Thibaw, 13
  military role, 9
  Mongol invasion (1287), 7
  Mon kingdom, 7
  pre-11th century, 7
  18th century, 7
military government
  British concessions, 11, 24n.51
  caretaker government, 11-12
  control, 12-13
  democratic movement, 12-13
  economic status, 12
  Fourth Burma Rifles, 12
  ideology, 12
  leadership (1962-1988), 12-13
  State Law and Order Restoration Council, 13
military reorganisation
  Burma Defence Army, 10
  Burma Independence Army, 10, 23n.42
  Burma National Army, 10, 23n.43
  insurgency groups, 10-11
  Japanese independence, 10
  Japanese military control, 10
  Japanese threat, 10
  Territorial Forces, 11
  Thirty Comrades, 10, 23n.41
military role
  British rule, 9
  ethnic recruitment (1925), 9-10, 23n.40
  kingdoms, 9
  Members of Parliament, 9-10
Ne Win
  Burma Socialist Programme Party, 9, 12, 15
  caretaker government, 9, 11-12
  Deputy Prime Minister, 11
  elections (1960), 9
  Fourth Burma Rifles, 12

Japanese military control, 10
leadership (1949), 11
military control (1962), 9
Minister for Defence, 11
Minister for Home Affairs, 11
personal insecurity, 12
Revolutionary Council, 9
Nu
  civilian status, 11
  democratic regime, 8-9
  insurgency groups (1949), 8-9
  international rivalry (pre-1988), 14, 15, 25n.72
  party split (1958), 9
United Kingdom
  Arakan annexation, 8, 13, 22n.29
  colonialism (1886-1923), 8
  colonialism extension (1937), 8
  ethnic groups, 8
  independence (1948), 8
  international rivalry (pre-1988), 7-8, 13-14
  military concessions, 11, 24n.51
  nationalist rebellion (1930), 8
  Tenasserim annexation, 8, 13, 22n.29
  wars (1824-1885), 7-8, 22n.29
  World War I, 9
  World War II, 8, 10, 13
Histories, The (Polybius), 48
HIV/AIDS
  biological weapons, 243-44, 251n.80
  strategic environment (post-1988), 20
Holmes, Richard, 76
Human intelligence
  post-1988, 115, 196
  pre-1988, 108-9
Human rights
  biological weapons, 242
  Burma Air Force, 214-15
  Burma Army, 164, 173-74
  chemical weapons, 235-36
  contemporary government, 253, 257, 266-67
  defence industry, 143-44
  defence policy, 39-40, 41-42
  democratic future, 276
  intelligence violations, 115, 118
  Karen, 242
  strategic environment (post-1988), 15-16, 19
Human Rights Watch, 115

I

Imagery intelligence, 120-21
India
  arms procurement, 156, 159, 167
  borders
    international rivalry (pre-1988), 13, 14
    land disputes, 4, 13
    strategic environment (post-1988), 17-18, 20, 21
  Burma Navy (contemporary), 197
  chemical weapons, 247, 248
  communications equipment, 64
  defence policy
    external threat, 39, 46n.51
    trade, 36, 45n.39
  demographics, 7
  intelligence, 101, 109, 118
  trade, 36, 45n.39
  training, 82, 83, 86, 87
Indian Ocean
  international rivalry (pre-1988), 13
  strategic environment (post-1988), 17, 18, 19
Indochina
  indoctrination, 92, 99n.103
  international rivalry (pre-1988), 14
Indoctrination
  Burma Air Force, 92-94, 99n.111
  Burma Army, 92-94, 99n.111
  Burma National Army, 89
  Burma Navy, 92-94, 99n.111
  Burma Socialist Programme Party
    foreign institutions, 88
    four cuts strategy, 91
    ideology development, 88
    ideology incompatibility, 87-88
    training centres, 88
  counter-insurgency
    domestic training, 93, 94
    foreign assistance, 90, 93-94, 99n.112
    foreign training, 91, 93
    four cuts strategy, 91-92, 99n.99
    guerrilla warfare, 89, 90
    institution formation, 90
    joint military operations, 92-94, 99n.111
    low-intensity conflict, 92-93
    military limitations, 90-91
    people's war, 90-91, 94
    publications, 90
    total people's war, 94
  external threats
    China, 89, 92, 98n.90
    Indochina, 92, 99n.103
    Japan, 89
    Kuomintang, 89, 99n.91
    Thailand, 92
    total people's war, 92, 94
  financial constraints, 90-91, 93
  four cuts strategy, 91-92, 99n.99
  people's militias, 90-91, 94
  people's war
    five columns' coordination, 91
    village militias, 90-91, 94
  population mobilisation, 89, 92
    military loyalty, 94
    population alienation, 94-95
  State Law and Order Restoration Council, 92, 94-95
  State Peace and Development Council, 94-95
  strategy contradictions, 88-89
  total people's war, 92, 94
Indonesia
  aircraft procurement, 205-6, 225n.5
  defence expenditure, 132
  defence policy, 35, 36, 41, 42, 47n.69
  dwi fungsi model, 36, 254
  International Force East Timor, 42, 47n.69
Inland Water Transportation Board, 186, 201n.7
Intelligence
  contemporary government, 259, 261, 263
  democratic future, 284, 286, 288, 293n.47
  post-1988
    Burma Air Force, 120-21
    command structure, 112-13, 114
    communications security, 120
    electronic intelligence, 118
    equipment procurement, 115, 118-19
    expansion, 113-14, 118-21, 128n.96
    foreign assistance, 118-19, 120-21
    foreign training, 114-15
    functions, 113, 114
    human intelligence, 115, 196
    human rights, 115, 118
    imagery intelligence, 120-21
    intelligence structure (1988), 107*f*

intelligence structure (2000), 110-11f, 116-17f
Ministry of Foreign Affairs, 113
Ministry of Home Affairs, 113
Ministry of Immigration and National Registration, 113
Ministry of National Planning and Economic Development, 113
signals intelligence, 118-20, 196
State Law and Order Restoration Council, 112-13, 114-15, 118, 120-21
State Peace and Development Council, 112-13, 114-15, 118
pre-1988
 Burma Air Force, 101, 106, 108
 Burma Army, 101, 106, 108, 112
 Burma Navy, 101, 106, 108
 Burma Socialist Programme Party, 104, 105
 civil affairs, 102
 command structure, 101, 102, 103-5, 106, 108
 communications security, 112, 126n.61
 counter-insurgency, 100, 101, 106, 108, 109, 112, 126n.57
 development of, 101-4
 equipment procurement, 112, 115, 118-19, 126n.58
 external threats, 100, 101, 106, 108-9, 112
 financial constraints, 100
 foreign assistance, 101-2, 108-9, 112
 foreign training, 103
 functions, 102-3, 105-6, 108-9
 human intelligence, 108-9
 ineffectiveness, 100-102, 112
 interception capability, 109, 112, 126n.50
 Military Intelligence Training Centre, 103
 Ministry of Foreign Affairs, 101, 103, 105
 Morse Code, 112
 reorganisation, 104-6, 108
 Revolutionary Council, 103-4, 105
 signals intelligence, 60, 109, 126n.53
 student subversion, 108, 125n.45
 subversive activity, 108-9, 112
 training, 60, 103

security failures
 civilian surveillance, 121, 122-23
 coverage, 123
 financial constraints, 123
 military insecurity, 123
 officer suspicion, 123-24
 terrorism, 121
 See also specific bureaus/departments
Intergraph Image Station, 68, 74n.90
International Atomic Energy Agency, 245
International Defense Review, 199, 234
International Force East Timor, 42, 47n.69
International Institute for Strategic Studies
 defence expenditure, 131, 139-40, 313, 315-16
 publications, xxvii, 135, 294, 314, 316
International Monetary Fund, 131, 139-40, 313-14
International Narcotics Control Program, 208
International Security, 28
Iraq
 chemical weapons, 234-35
 defence policy, 41
Irrawaddy River
 strategic environment (post-1988), 19
 transportation, 5
Israel
 aircraft procurement, 206
 arms procurement, 133, 137, 138, 159, 161, 167, 168, 169, 170, 195, 217
 defence industry, 144, 145
 intelligence
  assistance, 103, 120
  equipment, 119
 international rivalry (pre-1988), 15
 training
  assistance, 82, 87
  institutions, 82, 83, 86
Italy
 aircraft procurement, 206, 225n.13
 arms procurement, 133, 193
 chemical weapons, 234
 defence industry, 145
 military assistance, 209

J

Jane's Defence Weekly, 214
Jane's Fighting Ships, 187, 192, 202n.35
Jane's Intelligence Weekly, 216

Jane's Sentinel Security Assessment, xxvii
Japan
    aircraft procurement, 208, 226n.28
    arms procurement, 160, 162, 186
    Burma Air Force, 208, 210, 226n.28, 227n.40
    Burma Army, 173-74, 183n.136
    Burma Navy, 186
    communications
        equipment installation, 65
        equipment procurement, 62, 63, 73n.43
    defence industry, 144, 153n.12
    historical framework
        administration, 8, 10
        Ba Maw Government, 8, 10
        bombing (1941), 8
        Burma independence, 10
        Burma Independence Army, 10, 23n.42
        Chinese invasion (1937), 13
        government installation, 8
        international rivalry (pre-1988), 13
        military control, 10
        military threat, 10
        nationalist resistance, 8
        training, 10
    indoctrination, 89
    intelligence equipment, 112
    non-military equipment, 139
    strategic environment (post-1988), 18, 26n.88
    training, 210, 227n.40
    institutions, 10, 82, 83
Jervis, Robert, 28
Joint military operations
    Burma Air Force, 222
    Burma Army, 176, 183n.147
    Burma Navy, 188, 202n.35
    democratic future, 288-89
    indoctrination, 92-94, 99n.111

K

Kachin
    Burma Air Force (post-1988), 215
    Burma Army
        contemporary, 173
        pre-1988, 159
    demographics, 7
    ethnic insurgency, 34
    recruitment, 9-10, 23n.40, 77
Kachin Independence Army
    Burma Army, 164
    chemical weapons, 235, 236-37
Kachin Independence Organisation, 235
Ka Pa Sa factories, 141, 152n.83
Karen
    biological weapons, 242-43, 244
    Burma Air Force (post-1988), 214, 215
    Burma Army
        contemporary, 168, 172, 173, 182n.126
        post-1988, 168
    Burma Navy, 185, 198
    chemical weapons, 235-37, 238
    demographics, 5, 7
    recruitment, 77
    communications, 61
    1925, 9-10, 23n.40
Karen Human Rights Group, 242
Karen National Defence Organisation, 61, 90, 175
Karen National Liberation Army, 34, 164
    chemical weapons, 235-36
Karen National Union, 35, 173, 244
Kar Kwe Ye, 34, 44n.26
Kayah
    demographics, 7
    ethnic insurgency, 34
    recruitment, 77
Keegan, John, 76, 155
Khin Nyunt
    chemical weapons, 236
    command structure, 55
    contemporary government, 261-63, 265
    defence policy, 39
    intelligence, 106, 113, 114, 119
Khun Sa, 139, 170, 173, 213, 214, 228n.61
Kim Dae Jung, 18
Kingdoms. *See* Historical framework
Kissinger, Henry, 18, 26n.88
Kohl, Helmut, 141
Korean War, 14
Kuomintang
    Burma Air Force (pre-1988), 210
    Burma Army (contemporary), 175
    indoctrination, 89, 99n.91
    insurgency groups, 10-11, 14
    intelligence threat, 101, 108
    international rivalry (pre-1988), 14-15, 25n.71

Kyaw Zwa Myint, 122
Kyi Maung, 266, 280, 292n.26

L

Lahu, 7
Land/Air Warfare School (1958), 163
landmines, 20, 71, 141, 143, 152, 168, 180, 320, 321, 326
Land of Jade (Lintner), 205
Laos
  borders, 4
  chemical weapons, 240
  strategic environment (post-1988), 16
Lebanon, arms procurement, 167
Let Ya-Freeman Agreement, 61, 132, 149n.12
Libya, chemical weapons, 234-35
Lin Ming-xian, 139
Lin Piao, 90
Lintner, Bertil, 205, 262
Li Peng, 143
Lo Hsing-han, 139

M

Malacca Straits
  Burma Navy (contemporary), 197
  geostrategic position
    international rivalry (pre-1988), 14
    strategic environment (post-1988), 18, 19
Malaya, 13, 14
Malaysia
  arms procurement, 192
  defence policy, 41, 42
  strategic environment (post-1988), 18
  training, 87
Mao Tse-tung, 90
Maung Aung Myoe
  defence policy
    external threats, 41
    goals, 30-31, 32
    internal affairs, 33, 38
    inter-Service rivalry, 263-64
    officer privilege, 260
    state-owned enterprises, 148
Maung Aye
  arms procurement, 137
  contemporary government, 261-63

Mechanical and Electrical Engineering School, 171
Media reports
  biological weapons, 242-43
  chemical weapons, 233-34, 235, 236-37, 239
  secondary sources, 294
Memorandum on the Proposed Reorganisation of Burma Patriotic Forces (Aung San), 275
Mergui Archipelago, 4, 18
Middle East
  Burma Navy (contemporary), 197
  defence policy, 41-42
  strategic environment (post-1988), 18, 20
Military Assistance Program
  Burma Air Force, 219
  Burma Army, 159, 161, 177n.15
Military Balance, The, xxvii, 135, 294, 314, 316
Military financial restraints
  Burma Army, 156, 176n.3
  expansion, 174, 254-55
  indoctrination, 90-91, 93
  intelligence, 100, 123
Military government, contemporary
  arms procurement
    Burma Air Force, 222, 223, 224-25
    expansion rationale, 256-57
    policy agenda, 268-69
  Association of Southeast Asian Nations, 253, 261
  Aung San Suu Kyi, 253, 258, 260-61
  Burma Socialist Programme Party
    internal challenges, 262
    policy agenda, 270
  defence expenditure
    expansion, 253, 271n.1
    expansion rationale, 254-55
    financial constraints, 254-55
    international criticism, 253
    policy agenda, 268, 269
  democratic movement
    expansion rationale, 256, 258, 271n.20
    internal challenges, 256, 258, 260, 266, 271n.20
  economy, 269
  ethnic groups
    Burma Army, 172, 173
    expansion rationale, 256, 257-58, 259

internal challenges, 264, 266, 273n.66
international criticism, 253
expansion
  defence expenditure, 253, 271n.1
  international criticism, 253-54, 257
  personnel, 254, 271n.3
  policy agenda, 268-69
  regional contrast, 253
expansion rationale
  arms procurement, 256-57
  defence expenditure, 254-55
  democratic movement, 256, 258, 271n.20
  equipment deficiency, 255
  ethnic insurgency, 256, 257-58, 259
  financial constraints, 254-55
  narcotics control, 258
  operations strategy, 255-56
  personnel management, 254-55, 271n.7
  politics, 257-59
human rights, 253, 257, 266-67
intelligence, 259, 261, 263
internal challenges
  Burma Air Force, 263-64, 267-68
  Burma Army, 262-64, 267-68
  Burma Navy, 263-64, 267-68
  Burma Socialist Programme Party, 262
  China policy, 253, 265
  civilian rule, 260, 266, 267
  Communist Party of Burma, 265
  Defence Services Academy, 262-63
  democratic movement, 256, 258, 260, 266, 271n.20
  Directorate of Defence Services Intelligence, 259, 261, 263
  ethnic groups, 264, 266, 273n.66
  hard-liners, 261-62, 263
  human rights, 253, 257, 266-67
  intelligence, 259, 261, 263
  international consequences, 266-67
  inter-Service rivalry, 263-64, 267-68
  junior officers, 122, 267
  military hierarchy, 260-62
  military insecurity, xxvii, 260
  Military Intelligence Service, 259, 263
  military role, 260
  military unity, 260, 266, 267-68
  moderates, 261-62, 263

National League for Democracy, 260, 261, 266
non-conformity, 260
officer careers, 263
officer ethics, 265
officer investments, 267
officer privilege, 259-60, 264-65, 267
officer rivalry, 262-65
Officer Training School, 262-63
pluralism, 260
recruitment policy, 264-65
Regional Military Commands, 262, 263
senior officer postings, 261-62
senior officers, 259, 272n.26
international criticism
  China policy, 253, 265
  defence expenditure, 253
  elections (1990), 253, 266
  ethnic groups, 253
  expansion, 253-54
  human rights, 253, 257, 266-67
Khin Nyunt, 261, 262, 263, 265
Maung Aye, 261, 262, 263
modernisation, 268-70
narcotics control, 258
Ne Win, 260-61, 263, 264, 266
officer privilege
  internal challenges, 259-60, 264-65, 267
  policy agenda, 270-71
officer rivalry, 262-65
personnel management
  expansion, 254, 271n.3
  expansion rationale, 254-55, 271n.7
policy agenda
  arms procurement, 268-69
  Burma Socialist Programme Party, 270
  China policy, 268-69, 274n.87
  defence expenditure, 268, 269
  economy, 269
  expansion, 268-69
  foreign aid, 269
  military unity, 270-71
  modernisation, 268-70
  officer privilege, 270-71
  politics, 270
  societal transformation, 270
  training, 269-70

politics
  expansion rationale, 257-59
  policy agenda, 270
  rivalries
    Defence Services Academy, 262-63
    inter-Service, 199-200, 263-64, 267-68
    officer, 262-65
    Officer Training School, 262-63
  State Law and Order Restoration Council
    expansion rationale, 254-55, 256, 257, 271n.10
    internal challenges, 261, 262, 265, 266
    policy agenda, 269
  State Peace and Development Council
    expansion rationale, 254, 255, 257, 258, 259
    internal challenges, 261, 262, 266, 267
    policy agenda, 268-69, 270
    training, 269-70
Military government, historically
  Aung San, General, 8, 10, 11, 23n.41, 23n.51
  Ba Maw Government (1943), 8, 10
  British concessions, 11
  caretaker government, 11-12
  control, 12-13
  democratic movement, 12-13
  economic status, 12
  Fourth Burma Rifles, 12
  ideology, 12
  insurgency groups, 10-11, 14
  leadership (1962-1988), 12-13
  military role, 9-10, 23n.40
  Ne Win, 9, 11-12
  Nu, 8-9, 11, 14, 15, 25n.72
  reorganisation, 10-11, 23n.42
  State Law and Order Restoration Council, 13
Military government ideology
  Burma Army (contemporary), 174
  Burma Socialist Programme Party, 87-88
  democratic future, 276
  economy, 7
  foreign training, 87-88
  historically, 12
  indoctrination, 87-88
Military government insecurity
  foreign training, 87-88
  intelligence, 123
  international criticism, 254

personnel non-conformity, 260
pluralism, 260
Military government reorganisation
  command structure
    Advisory Group, 60
    Burma Air Force, 55, 59, 279
    Burma Army, 49-50, 51, 54*f*, 55, 58*f*, 59-60, 296-97
    Burma Navy, 55, 59, 297
    Burma Socialist Programme Party, 51, 55
    independent department, 55, 297-98
    Law and Order Restoration Council, 51, 55
    National Intelligence Bureau, 60
    overall command, 51, 55, 59-60, 71n.15, 296
    post-1988, 51, 55, 59-60
    pre-1988, 49-51
    rank structure, 51, 55
    reorganisation influences, 48-49, 51, 55, 71n.1
    State Law and Order Restoration Council, 51, 55, 59-60
    State Peace and Development Council, 59-60
  historically
    Burma Defence Army, 10
    Burma Independence Army, 10, 23n.42
    Burma National Army, 10, 23n.43
    insurgency groups, 10-11
    Japanese 'independence' (1943), 10
    Japanese military control, 10
    Japanese threat, 10
    Territorial Forces, 11
    Thirty Comrades, 10, 23n.41
  intelligence, 104-6, 108
  Myanmar Police Force, 309
  People's Pearl and Fishery Board, 311
  People's Police Force, 81
  See also Burma Army, command structure
Military Intelligence (Gudgin), 100
Military Intelligence Service
  contemporary government, 259, 263
  democratic future, 288
  post-1988, 115, 118
  pre-1988
    command structure, 101, 104-6, 125n.33

expansion, 105-6, 125n.31
formation (1958), 102
functions, 102, 105-6, 124n.12
security failures, 121-24
Military loyalty, 37, 77, 78, 94
Military personnel
   command structure
      formal war establishment, 296
      loyalty, 37
      total armed forces, 296
      in uniform, 296
   democratic future, 283
   total personnel
      Burma Air Force, 307
      Burma Army, 298
      Burma Navy, 304
      Myanmar Police Force, 309
   See also specific branch
Ministry of Defence, 145
Ministry of Foreign Affairs, intelligence
   post-1988, 113
   pre-1988, 101, 103, 105
Ministry of Home Affairs, 113
Ministry of Immigration and National Registration, 113
Ministry of National Planning and Economic Development, 113
Mon
   demographics, 5, 7
   recruitment, 77
Mong Tai Army, 170, 213
Muslim population, 198
Mutual Defence Assistance Plan, 132, 159
Myanmar Agricultural Product Trading, 135
Myanmar Airways, 221
Myanmar Airways International, 221
Myanmar Economic Corporation, 147
Myanmar Fritz Werner Industries Co. Ltd., 140-41
Myanmar Maternal and Child Welfare Association, 81, 97n.44
Myanmar National Democratic Alliance Army, 289
MyanmarNet, 70
Myanmar Petroleum Products Enterprise, 135, 150n.35
Myanmar Police Force. *See* Paramilitary forces
Myanmar Posts and Telecommunications
   equipment installation, 65-67

procurement, 67
information technology, 68
Myanmar Red Cross Society, 81, 97n.42
Myanmar Women's Entrepreneurial Association, 81
Myawaddy Enterprises Group, 147
Myawaddy Radio Station, 65

N

Narcotics
   Burma Air Force
      post-1988, 214, 216
      pre-1988, 208, 210
   chemical weapons, 234, 235, 237, 239
   contemporary government, 258
   defence expenditure, 139
   defence policy, 34, 35
   democratic future, 286, 289
   International Narcotics Control Program, 208
   Myanmar Police Force, 311
   strategic environment (post-1988), 20
National Coalition Government of the Union of Burma, 283
National Constitution Convention, 37-38
National Defence College, 85
National Defence Mission, 31-32
National Intelligence Bureau
   post-1988, 112-13
   pre-1988
      Chief of National Intelligence, 104
      command structure, 104-5
      Control Board, 104
      formation, 103
      membership, 103
      Military Assistant to the President and Council of State, 104
      National Intelligence Bureau Law, 104-5
      reorganisation, 60, 103-5, 104-5
Nationalism
   defence policy, 29, 39
   historically, 8, 10
National League for Democracy
   contemporary government, 260-61, 266
   defence policy, 29, 38, 39
   formation, 276
   information technology, 69
   See also Democratic future

National Service Law and People's Militia Act, 76-77, 79, 96n.24
National Unity Party, 37, 45n.45
Natural resources
  energy, 246, 252n.89
  geostrategic position, 7
Nepal, 17-18
Ne Win
  contemporary government, 260-61, 263, 264, 266
  democratic future
    speculative analysis, 276
    theoretical analysis, 278, 280
  historical framework
    Burma Socialist Programme Party, 9, 12, 15
    caretaker government, 9, 11-12
    Deputy Prime Minister, 11
    elections (1960), 9
    Fourth Burma Rifles, 12
    Japanese military control, 10
    leadership, 11
    military control, 9
    Minister for Defence, 11
    Minister for Home Affairs, 11
    personal insecurity, 12
    Revolutionary Council, 9
    military coup (1962), xxv, 15
  military policy, xxvii-xxviii
New Light of Myanmar, 32, 70, 120
Non-Aligned Movement, 15
Non-alignment policy, 29, 32
Non-Commissioned Officer School, 163
North Korea
  arms procurement, 137, 138, 139, 169, 170, 180n.94
  chemical weapons, 247
  intelligence, 106, 121, 123
  international rivalry (pre-1988), 15
Norway
  arms procurement, 194
  communications, 65
Nu
  historical framework
    civilian status, 11
    democratic regime, 8-9
    insurgency groups (1949), 8-9
    international rivalry (pre-1988), 14, 15, 25n.72
    party split (1958), 9
    military coup (1962), xxv, 15

Nuclear energy alternatives
  hydro-electric power, 246, 252n.89
  natural gas, 246
Nuclear Non-Proliferation Treaty, 245
Nuclear weapons
  ballistic missiles, 246
  government opposition, 244-45
    Comprehensive Test Ban Treaty, 245
    International Atomic Energy Agency, 245
    nuclear free zones, 245
    Nuclear Non-Proliferation Treaty (1968), 245
    Outer Space Treaty (1967), 245
    Partial Test Ban Treaty (1963), 245
    Seabed Treaty (1972), 245
    Southeast Asia Nuclear Weapon-Free Zone Treaty (1995), 245
    United Nations Conference on Disarmament, 245
    United Nations General Assembly, 245
    State Law and Order Restoration Council, 245
    State Peace and Development Council, 245-46
    technology acquisition, 245-46

O

Office of Strategic Studies
  command structure, 113
  formation, 113
  functions, 113, 126n.66
  post-1988, 113, 126n.66
  research source, xxviii
Officer Training School
  Burma Army, 83, 97n.55, 262-63
  contemporary rivalry, 262-63
  formation, 83
  instruction, 83
  location, 83
  recruitment, 83, 97n.55
  renaming, 83
Ohn Gyaw, 240, 245
Outer Space Treaty, 245

P

Pakistan
  arms procurement, 137, 138, 167-68, 170, 179n.78

chemical weapons, 248
defence policy, 41
strategic environment (post-1988), 17-18
training, 82, 83, 86, 87, 195
Pakistan Ordnance Factories, 167-68
Palaung
  demographics, 7
  ethnic insurgency, 34
PaO
  demographics, 7
  ethnic insurgency, 34
Paramilitary forces
  Frontier Force, 309
  insurgency groups, 311
  Myanmar Police Force
    anti-narcotics task forces, 311
    combat battalions, 310-11
    command structure, 309-10
    formation, 309
    headquarters, 309
    reorganisation, 309
    reserve units, 310
    special departments, 310
    state/division police forces, 309-10
    total personnel, 309
    training centres, 310
  other forces, 311-12
  People's Pearl and Fishery Board
    Offshore Patrol Boats, 311
    reorganisation, 311
  See also People's Militia
Paratroops' School, 163
Partial Test Ban Treaty, 245
Patriotic Burmese Forces, 155-56
Patriotic Youth Front Radio, 65
People's Assembly, 49
People's Auxiliary Forces, 81
People's Militia
  democratic future, 281, 292n.30
  indoctrination, 90-91, 94
  paramilitary forces, 311
  recruitment
    current status, 81-82
    expansion, 78
    formation, 78
    National Service Law and People's Militia Act, 76-77, 79, 96n.24
People's Pearl and Fishery Board
  Offshore Patrol Boats, 311
  reorganisation, 311

People's Pearl and Fishery Corporation, 186, 187-88
People's Police Force
  base distribution, 81
  command structure, 81
  expansion, 78, 80-81
  organisation, 81
  reorganisation (1995), 81
People's Republic of China. *See* China
People's war, 90-91, 94
  total people's war, 92, 94
People's War (Lin Piao), 90
Philippines
  defence expenditure, 132
  training, 86, 87
Pinochet, Augusto, 266-67
Poland
  aircraft procurement, 208
  arms procurement, 137, 214-15
  non-military equipment, 139, 171
  training, 220
Politics
  contemporary government
    democratic future, 275
    elections (1990), 253, 266, 275, 280-81
    expansion rationale, 257-59
    policy agenda, 270
  defence policy
    elections, 33, 37-38, 41, 280, 281
    internal affairs, 33, 37-38
    sanctions, 39-40
  elections
    1960, 9
    1990, 15-16, 41, 253, 266, 275, 278, 280, 281
    contemporary government, 253, 266
    defence policy, 33, 37-38, 41, 280, 281
    strategic environment (post-1988), 15-16
  See also Democratic future; Democratic movement; *specific leadership*
Polybius, 48
Population mobilisation, 89, 92, 94-95
Porton Down Defence Research Establishment (United Kingdom), 243, 247
Portugal, arms procurement, 137, 168, 169, 180n.92
Principles and Policy Statement (NCGUB), 283

Index 363

R

Radio Free Asia, 65
Recruitment
  age requirements, 77, 78
  minors, 78-79, 95n.17
  benefits, 77, 78
  Burma Air Force
    expansion, 78, 79, 96n.29
    retention, 80
  Burma Army
    expansion, 78, 79, 96n.29
    retention, 80
  Burma Navy
    expansion, 78, 79, 96n.29
    retention, 80
  Burma Socialist Programme Party,
    76-77
  conscription
    constitution, 76-77
    expansion, 79-80
    National Service Law and People's
      Militia Act, 76-77, 79, 96n.24
    quotas, 79
  democratic future, 284, 289
  enlistment term, 77
  ethnic groups, 77, 79
    communications, 61
    1925, 9-10, 23n.40
  expansion, 77-78, 79-80
    resource reliability, 80, 96n.29
  females, 77, 78, 81
  Frontier Force
    base distribution, 81
    command structure, 81
    organisation, 81
  insurgency groups, 78, 79, 82
  loyalty, 77, 78
  overview, 76
  People's Militia
    current status, 81-82
    expansion, 78
    formation, 78
  People's Police Force
    base distribution, 81
    command structure, 81
    expansion, 78, 80-81
    organisation, 81
    reorganisation (1995), 81
  pre-1988, 76-77
  prestige, 77, 78

  qualifications, 77, 78
  retention, 80, 96n.33
  illness, 80, 96n.34
  State Law and Order Restoration
    Council
    conscription, 77, 79
    expansion, 78, 79-80
  State Peace and Development Council,
    79-80
  volunteers, 76, 77
  See also Indoctrination; Training
*Report on the Formation of a Modern
  Tatmadaw in the Democratic Era*,
  281-83
Republic of Korea. *See* South Korea
Research literature
  academic research
    Burmese sources, xxvi, 294-95
    chemical weapons, 234, 235
    democratic future, 275-76
  Burmese sources
    academic research, xxvi, 294-95
    annuals, xxvi-xxvii, 294-95, 314
    democratic future, 275-76, 291n.3
    language translations, xxvi
    military affairs, xxvi-xxvii,
      xxxiii(n.17)
    military propaganda, xxvi
    military publications, xxvi, 294-95
    reliability, xxvii, 294-95, 296, 313
  defence expenditure
    accounting methods, 313, 314, 315-16
    accuracy, 313
    Arms Control and Disarmament
      Agency (United States), 131,
      134-35, 138-40, 313, 314-15
    completeness, 313
    Defence Intelligence Organisation (Australia), 135, 139-40, 313, 316
    International Institute for Strategic
      Studies, 131, 139-40, 313, 315-16
    International Monetary Fund, 131,
      139-40, 313-14
    resource reliability, 313
    Stockholm International Peace Research Institute, 131, 135, 139-40,
      313, 314
  military focus, xxvii
  military policy influence, xxvii-xxviii
  order of battle
    accuracy, 294-95, 296

completeness, 294-95, 296
consistency, 295-96
omissions, 295
sources, xxvi-xxvii, 294-95
post-1988, xxvi
primary sources, xxviii
resource reliability
  chemical weapons, 233, 235, 236
  defence expenditure, 131, 134-37, 139-40, 313
  exotic weapons, 247
  recruitment, 80, 96n.29
scarcity of, xxv-xxvii
secondary sources
  Burmese exiles, xxviii-xxix
  Defence Services Museum, 294
  field trips, xxviii
  former military members, xxviii, 294
  insurgency groups, 294
  interviews, xxviii-xxix
  media reports, 294
  official literature, xxviii
  organisational representatives, xxviii
  personal observation, xxix, xxviii
  private citizens, xxviii
  value of, xxvii
Research terminology
  acceptance of, xxx, xxxiii(n.22)
  Burmese names
    formal titles, xxxi
    honorifics, xxxi
    surnames, xxxi
  country names
    Socialist Republic of the Union of Burma (1974), xxix
    Union of Burma (1948), xxix
    Union of Myanmar (1989), xxix
  ethnic groups, xxx
  opposition groups, xxx
  peoples, xxix
  rivers, xxix
  states/divisions/cities/towns, xxix
Reserve units
  Burma Air Force, 210
  Burma Army, 176
  Burma Navy, 184
  Myanmar Police Force, 310
Revolutionary Council
  command structure reorganisation, 48-49
  historical framework, 9
  intelligence, 103-4, 105
Rohingya
  defence policy, 41-42
  demographics, 7
  refugees, 41-42
  strategic environment (post-1988), 20
Roots of the Revolution, The (Ba Than), xxvi
Royal Thai Army, 237
Royal Thai Navy, 197
Russia
  arms procurement, 137, 138
  arms embargo, 217
  Burma Air Force (post-1988), 215-16, 217, 219
  Burma Navy (post-1988), 192
  nuclear weapons, 245-46
  training, 220

S

Saudi Arabia, 41
Seabed Treaty (1972), 245
Sea lines of communication, 4, 18, 19
Secret Asia, 243
Sein Lwin, 267
Shan
  chemical weapons, 236, 238, 239
  demographics, 5, 7
  ethnic insurgency, 34
Shan State Army, 34
Sharif, Nawaz, 168
Signals, Medical and Intelligence Corps, 171
Signals intelligence
  post-1988, 118-20, 196
  pre-1988, 60, 109, 126n.53
Singapore
  aircraft procurement, 205
  arms procurement, 137, 138, 139, 151n.56, 167, 168, 170, 186, 192, 194
  Burma Navy, 186, 192, 194
  Chartered Industries of Singapore, 143, 167
  communications
    equipment, 63
    information technology, 67, 68
  defence industry, 143
  defence policy, 42
  intelligence
    equipment, 119

training, 115
military assistance, 86-87, 220
strategic environment (post-1988), 18, 20
training, 86-87, 115
Singapore Armed Forces (SAF), 86-87
Skyful of Lies B.B.C., V.O.A.: Their Broadcasts and Rebuttals to Disinformation, 118, 127n.89
small arms, 20, 137, 140-43, 153, 159, 169, 171, 174, 177, 295, 326, 329, 330
Smuggling
defence policy, 35, 36, 45n.40
geostrategic position, 4, 5
Soldiers: A History of Men in Battle (Keegan/Holmes), 76
South Africa, arms procurement, 138, 169
South Asia, 3
Southeast Asia
chemical weapons, 239-40
defence policy, 41
geostrategic position
cultural competition, 3
strategic environment (post-1988), 16-17, 18, 20
See also specific countries
South-east Asia: A Social, Economic and Political Geography (Fisher), 184
Southeast Asia Nuclear Weapon-Free Zone Treaty, 245
Southeast Asia Treaty Organisation, 14
South Korea
arms procurement, 138, 169
defence policy, 42
geostrategic position
international rivalry (pre-1988), 15
strategic environment (post-1988), 18
human rights, 266-67
Soviet Union
aircraft procurement, 208, 226n.28
arms procurement, 133, 138, 161, 215-16, 229n.85
Burma Air Force
post-1988, 215-16, 229n.85
pre-1988, 208, 226n.28
chemical weapons, 240
communications equipment, 63
defence policy, 35
geostrategic position
international rivalry (pre-1988), 14, 15

strategic environment (post-1988), 16
intelligence
assistance, 103
equipment, 112, 119
threat, 108-9
training
assistance, 87
institutions, 83, 86
Special Investigation Department
post-1988
command structure, 113
functions, 113
human rights, 118
pre-1988, 101
command structure, 104-5
functions, 103, 105
Special National Intelligence Estimate (United States), 234, 247, 248
Sri Lanka, 17-18
State Corporation Number 24, 146
State Law and Order Restoration Council
Burma Air Force
contemporary, 224
post-1988, 213, 214, 215
pre-1988, 210
Burma Army
contemporary, 175
post-1988, 165, 167-68, 169, 170, 171
pre-1988, 160, 163, 164, 178n.52
Burma Navy
contemporary, 198, 199, 200
post-1988, 192, 196
pre-1988, 191
command structure
reorganisation, xxv, 51, 55, 59-60
reorganisation influence, 49, 51, 55, 71n.1
contemporary government
expansion rationale, 254-55, 256, 257, 271n.10
internal challenges, 261, 262, 265, 266
defence industry, 141-42, 143-44, 145
defence policy
external threats, 40, 41-42
goals, 29, 30-32
internal affairs, 33-35, 37
democratic future, 290
exotic weapons
biological weapons, 242, 244, 246-48
chemical weapons, 235, 236, 238,

239, 240-41, 246-48
  Communist Party of Burma, 247
  external threats, 247-48
  foreign training, 246-47
  Porton Down Defence Research Establishment (United Kingdom), 247
  resource reliability, 247
  Special National Intelligence Estimate (United States), 247, 248
formation (1988), xxv, 13, 16
indoctrination, 92, 94-95
information technology, 67-70
intelligence, 112-13, 114-15, 118, 120-21
military economic control, 146-47, 148
military policy
  China relations, xxviii
  economic influences, xxviii
  expansion, xxvii-xxviii
  funding, xxviii
  modernisation, xxvii-xxviii
  Socialism, xxviii
nuclear weapons, 245
publications, xxvi, 118, 127n.89
recruitment
  conscription, 77, 79
  expansion, 78, 79-80
strategic environment (post-1988), 16, 20
training
  foreign assistance, 86
  foreign institutions, 86, 87
  indoctrination, 88
  institution expansion, 84-85
State-Owned Economic Enterprise Law, 147
State-owned enterprises, 7, 148
State Peace and Development Council
  biological weapons, 243-44
  Burma Army, 167, 169
  Burma Navy
    contemporary, 198, 199, 200
    post-1988, 192, 196
  chemical weapons, 239, 241
  contemporary government
    expansion rationale, 254, 255, 257, 258, 259
    internal challenges, 261, 262, 266, 267
    policy agenda, 268-69, 270
  defence industry, 145

defence policy
  external threats, 40, 43
  goals, 29
  internal affairs, 35
democratic future, 290
formation, xxv, 59
indoctrination, 94-95
intelligence, 112-13, 114-15, 118
military economic control, 146, 148
nuclear weapons, 245-46
post-1988
  authoritative power, 60
  Burma Army, 167, 169
  Burma Navy, 192, 196
  command structure, 59-60
  control, 60
  office additions, 60
  office deletions, 60
  responsibilities, 60
  strategic environment, 20
publications, xxvi
recruitment, 79-80
training
  foreign assistance, 86
  indoctrination, 88
  institution expansion, 84-85
State/Private Joint Venture No. 9, 147
Stockholm International Peace Research Institute
  chemical weapons, 234
  defence expenditure, 131, 135, 139-40, 313, 314
  publications, 234, 314
Strategic Naval Flotilla, 188
Studeman, William, 234, 236
Surveillance
  civilian, 121, 122-23
  coastal, 188, 196
Sweden
  arms procurement, 133, 138, 167, 168, 185, 192
  Burma Navy
    post-1988, 192
    pre-1988, 185
Switzerland
  aircraft procurement, 206, 225n.14
  arms procurement, 133
  training, 91
System of Correlation of Man and His Environment, The, 88

T

Taiwan
  communications installation, 66
  international rivalry (pre-1988), 14
Taylor, R. H., 253
Technical Training School, 211
Thailand
  arms procurement, 138, 192
  biological weapons, 243, 247, 248
  borders
    international rivalry (pre-1988), 14
    land disputes, 4
    strategic environment (post-1988), 16
  Burma Navy
    contemporary, 197
    post-1988, 192
  chemical weapons, 235, 236, 237, 240
  communications
    equipment installation, 65, 66
    equipment procurement, 64
  defence policy, 36, 41, 42, 45n.39
  indoctrination, 92
  intelligence
    equipment, 112
    threat, 101, 109
  Royal Thai Army, 237
  Royal Thai Navy, 197
  trade, 36, 45n.39
Than Shwe, 30-32, 42-43, 137, 212, 262, 268
Thant, 15, 25n.75
Thirty Comrades, 10, 23n.41
Three national causes, 30
Times, The, 242-43
Tinker, Hugh, 3
Tin Oo, xxviii, 121, 122, 137, 216, 261, 279, 291n.20
Tin Tun, 167, 212
Total people's war, 92, 94
Towle, Philip, xxv
Trade
  China, 5, 22n.18
  coastline, 4, 5
  defence policy, 36, 45n.39
  India, 36, 45n.39
  land, 4, 5, 22n.18
  Thailand, 36, 45n.39
Training
  Apprentice Officer scheme
    formation, 84
    instruction, 84
    recruitment, 84
  Auxiliary Fire Brigades, 81, 97n.42
  Burma Air Force
    Apprentice Officer scheme, 84
    Command and General Staff College, 85
    contemporary, 222, 223, 224-25
    Defence Services Academy, 84
    expansion, 85
    foreign assistance, 87
    foreign institutions, 86
    pre-1988, 211
  Burma Army
    Apprentice Officer scheme, 84
    Command and General Staff College, 85
    contemporary, 172-73
    Defence Services Academy, 84
    expansion, 85
    institutions, 82, 83, 86
    Officer Training School, 83, 97n.55, 262-63
    post-1988, 171
    pre-1988, 163
    training institutions, 82, 83
  Burma Navy
    Apprentice Officer scheme, 84
    Command and General Staff College, 85
    Defence Services Academy, 84
    expansion, 85
    foreign institutions, 86
    post-1988, 195-96
  Burma Socialist Programme Party, 78, 88
  Command and General Staff College
    formation, 85
    instruction, 85
    location, 85
    post-commission training, 85
    recruitment, 85
  communications, 61, 62-63, 67-68, 86-87
  Defence Services Academy, 83
    formation, 84
    instruction, 84
    recruitment, 84
  Defence Services Officer's Training School, 83
  Directorate of Military Training
    foreign institutions, 86

formation, 83
Directorate of Peoples Militias and Public Relations, 88
foreign institutions
  Australia, 82, 83, 86, 97n.52
  China, 86, 87
  Czechoslovakia, 91
  East Germany, 83
  India, 82, 83, 86, 87
  indoctrination, 88
  intelligence, 103
  Israel, 82, 83, 86
  Japan, 10, 82, 83
  Malaysia, 87
  military ideology, 87-88
  military insecurity, 87-88
  Pakistan, 82, 83, 86, 87
  Philippines, 86, 87
  recruitment, 85-86
  Singapore, 87
  Soviet Union, 83, 86
  United Kingdom, 82, 83, 86
  United States, 82, 83, 86, 98n.69
  West Germany, 86, 91, 98n.69
  Yugoslavia, 83, 86, 91
government agenda, 269-70
institution expansion
  instruction, 84
  recruitment, 84
  skills specialization, 84, 85
insurgency groups, 87-88
intelligence, 60, 103
Myanmar Maternal and Child Welfare Association, 81, 97n.44
Myanmar Police Force, 310
Myanmar Red Cross Society, 81, 97n.42
Myanmar Women's Entrepreneurial Association, 81
National Defence College
  formation, 85
  instruction, 85
  location, 85
  post-commission training, 85
Officer Training School
  formation, 83
  instruction, 83
  location, 83
  recruitment, 83, 97n.55
  renaming, 83
People's Auxiliary Forces, 81
post-commission, 85

publications, 83, 97n.54
State Law and Order Restoration Council
  foreign assistance, 86
  foreign institutions, 86, 87
  indoctrination, 88
  institution expansion, 84-85
State Peace and Development Council
  foreign assistance, 86
  indoctrination, 88
  institution expansion, 84-85
Union Solidarity and Development Association, 81, 94, 95
War Veterans Association, 81, 97n.42
See also Indoctrination; Recruitment; specific countries
Transportation
  Burma Army, 162, 170-71, 178n.36
  Burma Navy, 185, 186, 201n.7
  geostrategic position, 5, 13
Truth, The, 69
Twelve national objectives, 30

U

Ukraine, arms procurement, 192
Union Military Police, 156
Union of Burma, xxix
Union of Burma Airways, 207
Union of Burma Navy (1947), 184
Union of Myanmar, xxix
Union of Myanmar Economic Holdings Limited, 146-47
Union Solidarity and Development Association, 81, 94, 95
United Kingdom
  arms procurement, 132, 133, 138, 156, 159, 160, 161, 162, 168, 177n.27, 184-85, 192, 201n.4
  biological weapons, 242-43, 247
  British Military Mission, 61, 62-63, 159, 211
  Burma Air Force (pre-1988)
    aircraft procurement, 205, 206-7, 225n.3
  Burma Act, 205
  military assistance, 205
  training, 210, 211
  Burma independence, xxv
  Burma Navy
    post-1988, 192

pre-1988, 184-85, 201n.4
chemical weapons, 240
communications
　British Broadcasting Corporation, 65
　British Military Mission, 61, 62-63
　control, 65
　equipment procurement, 61, 62-63, 64, 73n.43
　training, 61, 62-63
geostrategic position
　international rivalry (pre-1988), 7-8, 13
　strategic environment (post-1988), 15-16
historical framework
　Arakan annexation, 8, 13, 22n.29
　colonialism (1886-1923), 8
　colonialism extension (1937), 8
　ethnic groups, 8
　independence, 8
　international rivalry (pre-1988), 7-8, 13-14
　military concessions, 11, 24n.51
　nationalist rebellion (1930), 8
　Tenasserim annexation, 8, 13, 22n.29
　wars (1824-1885), 7-8, 22n.29
intelligence
　assistance, 101
　British Broadcasting Corporation, 109
　training, 101
military assistance, 83, 97n.54, 287
training, 82, 83, 86, 97n.54
　communications, 61, 62-63
　intelligence, 101
United Nations
　defence policy
　　cooperative relations, 29
　　elections (1990), 41
　　Haiti, 41
　　peace-keeping operations, 29, 42, 43n.7
　　Rohingya refugees, 41-42
　geostrategic position
　　international rivalry (pre-1988), 14, 15
　　strategic environment (post-1988), 16
United Nations Conference on Disarmament, 233-34, 245
United Nations Convention on the Law of the Sea, 4
United Nations Development Programme, 40, 46n.52

United Nations General Assembly
　international rivalry (pre-1988), 15
　nuclear weapons, 245
United Nations High Commissioner for Refugees, 41-42
United Nations Monthly Bulletin of Statistics, 316
United Nations Register of Conventional Arms, xxvi-xxvii
United Nations Secretary General, 15, 25n.75
United Nations Security Council
　defence industry embargo, 141-42
　strategic environment (post-1988), 19
United Nations Transitional Administration in East Timor, 42, 47n.69
United States
　arms procurement, 132, 137f, 149n.13, 156, 159, 160-61, 162, 170, 177n.15, 185-86, 187, 219
　arms embargo, 138
　concessionary terms, 133, 149n.14
　Burma Air Force (post-1988), 219
　Burma Air Force (pre-1988)
　　aircraft procurement, 206-9, 226n.25
　　military assistance, 205
　　training, 211
　Burma Navy (pre-1988), 185-86, 187
　chemical weapons, 234, 235, 236, 237, 239, 240
　communications
　　equipment installation, 65-66
　　equipment procurement, 62, 63
　　government control, 65
　　satellite networks, 65
　defence industry, 141
　defence policy
　　Bangladesh, 40-41, 46n.57
　　democratic movement, 40-41, 46n.55
　　Gulf War, 41
　geostrategic position
　　Central Intelligence Agency, 14
　　international rivalry (pre-1988), 14-15
　　strategic environment (post-1988), 15-16
　intelligence
　　assistance, 101, 103
　　training, 103
　training
　　Burma Air Force (pre-1988), 211
　　institutions, 82, 83, 86, 98n.69

intelligence, 103
United Wa State Army, 34, 258, 289

V

Vietnam
    arms procurement, 137-38, 151n.56, 161, 169
    chemical weapons, 240
    geostrategic position
        Chinese invasion (1979), 16
        international rivalry (pre-1988), 14, 15
        strategic environment (post-1988), 16
    training, 87
Voice of America, 65, 109
Voice of the People of Burma, 65, 74n.67, 109

W

Wa
    demographics, 7
    ethnic insurgency, 34
Walesa, Lech, 214-15
Wayne, E. A., 234
West Germany
    arms procurement, 133, 137*f*, 160, 162, 177n.20
    biological weapons, 242
    chemical weapons
        materials, 234-35
        production, 238, 247, 250n.52
        training, 235
    communications equipment, 63
    defence industry, 140, 141-42, 143-44
    intelligence assistance, 103
    international rivalry (pre-1988), 15
    non-military equipment, 171

training
    chemical weapons, 235
    institutions, 86, 91, 98n.69
World Armies (Keegan), 155
World Factbook, 314
World War I, 9
World War II, 8, 10, 13

Y

Yearbook, 234, 314
Yugoslavia
    aircraft procurement, 208
    arms procurement, 133, 159, 161, 162, 185, 186, 192, 199, 214, 228n.78, 229n.81
    SOKO factory, 214, 222, 229n.82
    Burma Air Force
        post-1988, 214, 228n.78, 229n.81
        pre-1988, 208
    Burma Navy
        contemporary, 199
        post-1988, 192
        pre-1988, 185, 186
    communications equipment, 63
    defence industry, 145
    defence policy, 35
    human rights, 266-67
    intelligence
        assistance, 103
        equipment, 112
    international rivalry (pre-1988), 15
    military assistance, 82
    non-military equipment, 171
    training, 83, 86, 91, 195, 220
Yunnan Province
    international rivalry (pre-1988), 14
    strategic environment (post-1988), 19

Milton Keynes UK
Ingram Content Group UK Ltd.
UKHW022323270224
438561UK00016B/1834